D1334710

INTERACTIVE COMPUTER GRAPHICS

A Top-Down Approach with WebGL **7**TH EDITION

GLOBAL EDITION

INTERACTIVE COMPUTER GRAPHICS

A Top-Down Approach with **WebGL** | **7**TH EDITION

GLOBAL EDITION

EDWARD ANGEL
University of New Mexico

•

DAVE SHREINER
ARM, Inc.

Global Edition contributions by

ARUP BHATTACHARYA
SOUMEN MUKHERJEE
RCC Institute of
Information Technology,
Kolkata

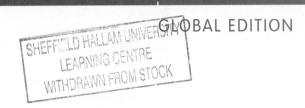

PEARSON

Boston   Columbus   Indianapolis   New York   San Francisco   Upper Saddle River
Amsterdam   Cape Town   Dubai   London   Madrid   Milan   Munich   Paris   Montreal   Toronto
Delhi   Mexico City   Sao Paulo   Sydney   Hong Kong   Seoul   Singapore   Taipei   Tokyo

Editorial Director, ECS Marcia Horton
Head of Learning Asset Acquisition, Global Edition Laura Dent
Acquisitions Editor Matt Goldstein
Assistant Acquisitions Editor, Global Edition Aditee Agarwal
Associate Project Editor, Global Edition Uttaran Das Gupta
Program Manager Kayla Smith-Tarbox
Director of Marketing Christy Lesko
Marketing Assistant Jon Bryant
Director of Production Erin Gregg
Senior Managing Editor Scott Disanno
Senior Project Manager Marilyn Lloyd
Manufacturing Buyer Linda Sager
Senior Manufacturing Controller, Production, Global Edition Trudy Kimber
Cover Designer Lumina Datamatics
Manager, Text Permissions Tim Nicholls
Text Permission Project Manager William Opaluch
Media Project Manager Renata Butera
Cover Image Abstract Studio/Shutterstock

Pearson Education Limited
Edinburgh Gate
Harlow
Essex CM20 2JE
England

and Associated Companies throughout the world

Visit us on the World Wide Web at: www.pearsonglobaleditions.com

© Pearson Education Limited 2015

ISBN 10: 1-292-01934-4
ISBN 13: 978-1-292-01934-5

British Library Cataloguing-in-Publication Data
A catalogue record for this book is available from the British Library

10 9 8 7 6 5 4 3 2 1
14

Typeset by Cypress Graphics in Minion and Avenir 10/12 pt.

Printed and bound by Courier Kendallville in The United States of America.

To Rose Mary   —E.A.

To Vicki, Bonnie, Bob, Cookie, and Goatee   —D.S.

CONTENTS

PREFACE

This book is an introduction to computer graphics with an emphasis on applications programming. The first edition, which was published in 1997, was somewhat revolutionary in using OpenGL and a top-down approach. Over the succeeding 16 years and 6 editions, this approach has been adopted by most introductory classes in computer graphics and by virtually all the competing textbooks.

The sixth edition reflected the recent major changes in graphics software due to major changes in graphics hardware. In particular, the sixth edition was fully shader-based, enabling readers to create applications that could fully exploit the capabilities of modern GPUs. We noted that these changes are also part of OpenGL ES 2.0, which is being used to develop applications for embedded systems and handheld devices, such as cell phones and tablets, and of WebGL, its JavaScript implementation. At the time, we did not anticipate the extraordinary interest in WebGL that began as soon as web browsers became available that support WebGL through HTML5.

As we continued to write our books, teach our SIGGRAPH courses, and pursue other graphics-related activities, we became aware of the growing excitement about WebGL. WebGL applications were running everywhere, including on some of the latest smart phones, and even though WebGL lacks some of the advanced features of the latest versions of OpenGL, the ability to integrate it with HTML5 opened up a wealth of new application areas. As an added benefit, we found it much better suited than desktop OpenGL for teaching computer graphics. Consequently, we decided to do a seventh edition that uses WebGL exclusively. We believe that this edition is every bit as revolutionary as any of the previous editions.

New to the Seventh Edition

- WebGL is used throughout.
- All code is written in JavaScript.
- All code runs in recent web browsers.
- A new chapter on interaction is included.
- Additional material on render-to-texture has been added.
- Additional material on displaying meshes has been added.
- An efficient matrix–vector package is included.
- An introduction to agent-based modeling has been added.

A Top-Down Approach

Recent advances and the success of the first six editions continue to reinforce our belief in a top-down, programming-oriented approach to introductory computer graphics. Although many computer science and engineering departments now support more than one course in computer graphics, most students will take only a single course. Such a course usually is placed in the curriculum after students have already studied programming, data structures, algorithms, software engineering, and basic mathematics. Consequently, a class in computer graphics allows the instructor to build on these topics in a way that can be both informative and fun. We want these students to be programming three-dimensional applications as soon as possible. Low-level algorithms, such as those that draw lines or fill polygons, can be dealt with later, after students are creating graphics.

When asked "why teach programming," John Kemeny, a pioneer in computer education, used a familiar automobile analogy: You don't have to know what's under the hood to be literate, but unless you know how to program, you'll be sitting in the back seat instead of driving. That same analogy applies to the way we teach computer graphics. One approach—the algorithmic approach—is to teach everything about what makes a car function: the engine, the transmission, the combustion process. A second approach—the survey approach—is to hire a chauffeur, sit back, and see the world as a spectator. The third approach—the programming approach that we have adopted here—is to teach you how to drive and how to take yourself wherever you want to go. As the old auto rental commercial used to say, "Let us put *you* in the driver's seat."

Programming with WebGL and JavaScript

When Ed began teaching computer graphics 30 years ago, the greatest impediment to implementing a programming-oriented course, and to writing a textbook for that course, was the lack of a widely accepted graphics library or application programming interface (API). Difficulties included high cost, limited availability, lack of generality, and high complexity. The development of OpenGL resolved most of the difficulties many of us had experienced with other APIs and with the alternative of using home-brewed software. OpenGL today is supported on all platforms and is widely accepted as a cross-platform standard.

A graphics class teaches far more than the use of a particular API, but a good API makes it easier to teach key graphics topics, including three-dimensional graphics, lighting and shading, client–server graphics, modeling, and implementation algorithms. We believe that OpenGL's extensive capabilities and well-defined architecture lead to a stronger foundation for teaching both theoretical and practical aspects of the field and for teaching advanced concepts, including texture mapping, compositing, and programmable shaders.

Ed switched his classes to OpenGL about 18 years ago and the results astounded him. By the middle of the semester, *every* student was able to write a moderately complex three-dimensional application that required understanding of three-dimensional viewing and event-driven input. In the previous years of teaching computer graphics, he had never come even close to this result. That class led to the first edition of this book.

This book is a textbook on computer graphics; it is not an OpenGL or WebGL manual. Consequently, it does not cover all aspects of the WebGL API but rather explains only what is necessary for mastering this book's contents. It presents WebGL at a level that should permit users of other APIs to have little difficulty with the material.

Unlike previous editions, this one uses WebGL and JavaScript for all the examples. WebGL is a JavaScript implementation of OpenGL ES 2.0 and runs in most recent browsers. Because it is supported by HTML5, not only does it provide compatibility with other applications but also there are no platform dependences; WebGL runs within the browser and makes use of the local graphics hardware. Although JavaScript is not the usual programming language with which we teach most programming courses, it is the language of the Web. Over the past few years, JavaScript has become increasingly more powerful and our experience is that students who are comfortable with Java, C, or C++ will have little trouble programming in JavaScript.

All the modern versions of OpenGL, including WebGL, require every application to provide two shaders written in the OpenGL Shading Language (GLSL). GLSL is similar to C but adds vectors and matrices as basic types, along with some C++ features such as operator overloading. We have added a JavaScript library **MV.js** that supports both our presentation of graphics functions and the types and operations in GLSL.

Intended Audience

This book is suitable for advanced undergraduates and first-year graduate students in computer science and engineering and for students in other disciplines who have good programming skills. The book also will be useful to many professionals. Between us, we have taught well over 100 short courses for professionals; our experiences with these nontraditional students have had a great influence on what we chose to include in the book.

Prerequisites for the book are good programming skills in JavaScript, C, C++, or Java; an understanding of basic data structures (linked lists, trees); and a rudimentary knowledge of linear algebra and trigonometry. We have found that the mathematical backgrounds of computer science students, whether undergraduates or graduates, vary considerably. Hence, we have chosen to integrate into the text much of the linear algebra and geometry that is required for fundamental computer graphics.

Organization of the Book

The book is organized as follows. Chapter 1 provides an overview of the field and introduces image formation by optical devices; thus, we start with three-dimensional concepts immediately. Chapter 2 introduces programming using WebGL. Although the first example program that we develop (each chapter has one or more complete programming examples) is two-dimensional, it is embedded in a three-dimensional setting and leads to a three-dimensional extension. We introduce interactive graphics in Chapter 3 and develop event-driven graphics within the browser environment. Chapters 4 and 5 concentrate on three-dimensional concepts. Chapter 4 is concerned with defining and manipulating three-dimensional objects, whereas Chapter 5 is concerned with viewing them. Chapter 6 introduces light–material interactions and shading. Chapter 7 introduces many of the new discrete capabilities that are now supported in graphics hardware and by WebGL. All these techniques involve working with various buffers. These chapters should be covered in order and can be taught in about 10 weeks of a 15-week semester.

The last five chapters can be read in almost any order. All five are somewhat open-ended and can be covered at a survey level, or individual topics can be pursued in depth. Chapter 8 surveys implementation. It gives one or two major algorithms for each of the basic steps, including clipping, line generation, and polygon fill. Chapter 9 includes a number of topics that fit loosely under the heading of hierarchical modeling. The topics range from building models that encapsulate the relationships between the parts of a model, to high-level approaches to graphics over the Internet. Chapter 9 also includes an introduction to scene graphs. Chapter 10 introduces a number of procedural methods, including particle systems, fractals, and procedural noise. Curves and surfaces, including subdivision surfaces, are discussed in Chapter 11. Chapter 12 surveys alternate approaches to rendering. It includes expanded discussions of ray tracing and radiosity, and an introduction to image-based rendering and parallel rendering.

Appendix A presents the details of the WebGL functions needed to read, compile, and link the application and shaders. Appendices B and C contain a review of the background mathematics. Appendix D discusses sampling and aliasing starting with Nyquist's theorem and applying these results to computer graphics.

Changes from the Sixth Edition

The reaction of readers to the first six editions of this book was overwhelmingly positive, especially to the use of OpenGL and the top-down approach. In the sixth edition, we abandoned the fixed-function pipeline and went to full shader-based OpenGL. In this edition, we move to WebGL, which is not only fully shader-based— each application must provide at least a vertex shader and a fragment shader–but also a version that works within the latest web browsers.

Applications are written in JavaScript. Although JavaScript has its own idiosyncrasies, we do not expect that students with experience in a high-level language, such as Java, C, or C++, will experience any serious problems with it.

As we pointed out earlier in this preface, every application must provide its own shaders. Consequently, programmable shaders and GLSL need to be introduced in Chapter 2. Many of the examples produce the same output as in previous editions, but the code is very different.

In the sixth edition, we eliminated a separate chapter on input and interaction, incorporating the material in other chapters. With this edition, we revert to a separate chapter. This decision is based on the ease and flexibility with which we can integrate event-driven input with WebGL through HTML5.

We have added additional material on off-screen rendering and render-to-texture. These techniques have become fundamental to using GPUs for a variety of compute-intensive applications such as image processing and simulation.

Given the positive feedback we've received on the core material from Chapters 1–6 in previous editions, we've tried to keep the changes to those chapters to a minimum. We see Chapters 1–7 as the core of any introductory course in computer graphics. Chapters 8–12 can be used in almost any order, either as a survey in a one-semester course or as the basis of a two-semester sequence.

Support Materials

The support for the book is at www.pearsonglobaleditions.com/Angel. Support material that is available to all readers of this book includes

- Sources of information on WebGL
- Program code
- Solutions to selected exercises
- PowerPoint lectures
- Figures from the book

Additional support materials, including solutions to all the nonprogramming exercises, are available only to instructors adopting this textbook for classroom use. Please contact your school's Pearson Education representative or visit www.pearsonglobaleditions.com/Angel for information on obtaining access to this material.

Acknowledgments

Ed has been fortunate over the past few years to have worked with wonderful students at the University of New Mexico. They were the first to get him interested in OpenGL, and he has learned much from them. They include Ye Cong, Pat Crossno, Tommie Daniel, Chris Davis, Lisa Desjarlais, Kim Edlund, Lee Ann Fisk, Maria Gallegos, Brian Jones, Christopher Jordan, Takeshi Hakamata, Max Hazelrigg, Sheryl Hurley, Thomas Keller, Ge Li, Pat McCormick, Al McPherson, Ken Moreland, Martin Muller, David Munich, Jim Pinkerton, Jim Prewett, Dave Rogers, Hal Smyer, Dave Vick, Hue (Bumgarner-Kirby) Walker, Brian Wylie, and Jin Xiong. Many of the examples in the color plates were created by these students.

The first edition of this book was written during Ed's sabbatical; various parts were written in five different countries. The task would not have been accomplished without the help of a number of people and institutions that made their facilities available to him. He is greatly indebted to Jonas Montilva and Chris Birkbeck of the Universidad de los Andes (Venezuela), to Rodrigo Gallegos and Aristides Novoa of the Universidad Tecnologica Equinoccial (Ecuador), to Long Wen Chang of the National Tsing Hua University (Taiwan), and to Kim Hong Wong and Pheng Ann Heng of the Chinese University of Hong Kong. Ramiro Jordan of ISTEC and the University of New Mexico made possible many of these visits. John Brayer and Jason

Stewart at the University of New Mexico and Helen Goldstein at Addison-Wesley somehow managed to get a variety of items to him wherever he happened to be. His website contains a description of his adventures writing the first edition.

David Kirk and Mark Kilgard at NVIDIA were kind enough to provide graphics cards for testing many of the algorithms. A number of other people provided significant help. Ed thanks Ben Bederson, Gonzalo Cartagenova, Tom Caudell, Kathi Collins, Kathleen Danielson, Roger Ehrich, Robert Geist, Chuck Hansen, Mark Henne, Bernard Moret, Dick Nordhaus, Helena Saona, Dave Shreiner, Vicki Shreiner, Gwen Sylvan, and Mason Woo. Mark Kilgard, Brian Paul, and Nate Robins are owed a great debt by the OpenGL community for creating software that enables OpenGL code to be developed over a variety of platforms.

At the University of New Mexico, the Art, Research, Technology, and Science Laboratory (ARTS Lab) and the Center for High Performance Computing have provided support for many of Ed's projects. The Computer Science Department, the Arts Technology Center in the College of Fine Arts, the National Science Foundation, Sandia National Laboratories, and Los Alamos National Laboratory have supported many of Ed's students and research projects that led to parts of this book. David Beining, formerly with the Lodestar Astronomy Center and now at the ARTS Lab, has provided tremendous support for the Fulldome Project. Sheryl Hurley, Christopher Jordan, Laurel Ladwig, Jon Strawn and Hue (Bumgarner-Kirby) Walker provided some of the images in the color plates through Fulldome projects. Hue Walker has done the wonderful covers for previous editions and some of the examples in the Color Plates.

Ed would also like to acknowledge the informal group that started at the Santa Fe Complex, including Jeff Bowles, Ruth Chabay, Stephen Guerin, Bruce Sherwood, Scott Wittenberg, and especially JavaScript evangelist Owen Densmore, who convinced him to teach a graphics course in Santa Fe in exchange for getting him involved with JavaScript. We've all gained by the experience.

Dave would like first to thank Ed for asking him to participate in this project. We've exchanged ideas on OpenGL and how to teach it for many years, and it's exciting to advance those concepts to new audiences. Dave would also like to thank those who created OpenGL, and who worked at Silicon Graphics Computer Systems, leading the way in their day. He would like to recognize the various Khronos working groups who continue to evolve the API and bring graphics to unexpected places. Finally, as Ed mentioned, SIGGRAPH has featured prominently in the development of these materials, and is definitely owed a debt of gratitude for providing access to enthusiastic test subjects for exploring our ideas.

Reviewers of the manuscript drafts provided a variety of viewpoints on what we should include and what level of presentation we should use. These reviewers for previous editions include Gur Saran Adhar (University of North Carolina at Wilmington), Mario Agrular (Jacksonville State University), Michael Anderson (University of Hartford), Norman I. Badler (University of Pennsylvania), Mike Bailey (Oregon State University), Marty Barrett (East Tennessee State University), C. S. Bauer (University of Central Florida), Bedrich Benes (Purdue University), Kabekode V. Bhat (The Pennsylvania State University), Isabelle Bichindaritz (University of Washington,

Tacoma), Cory D. Boatright (University of Pennsylvania), Eric Brown, Robert P. Burton (Brigham Young University), Sam Buss (University of California, San Diego), Kai H. Chang (Auburn University), James Cremer (University of Iowa), Ron DiNapoli (Cornell University), John David N. Dionisio (Loyola Marymount University), Eric Alan Durant (Milwaukee School of Engineering), David S. Ebert (Purdue University), Richard R. Eckert (Binghamton University), W. Randolph Franklin (Rensselaer Polytechnic Institute), Natacha Gueorguieva (City University of New York/College of Staten Island), Jianchao (Jack) Han (California State University, Dominguez Hills), Chenyi Hu (University of Central Arkansas), George Kamberov (Stevens Institute of Technology), Mark Kilgard (NVIDIA Corporation), Lisa B. Lancor (Southern Connecticut State University), Chung Lee (California State Polytechnic University, Pomona), John L. Lowther (Michigan Technological University), R. Marshall (Boston University and Bridgewater State College), Hugh C. Masterman (University of Massachusetts, Lowell), Bruce A. Maxwell (Swathmore College), Tim McGraw (West Virginia University), James R. Miller (University of Kansas), Rodrigo Obando (Columbus State University), Jon A. Preston (Southern Polytechnic State University), Andrea Salgian (The College of New Jersey), Lori L. Scarlatos (Brooklyn College, CUNY), Han-Wei Shen (The Ohio State University), Oliver Staadt (University of California, Davis), Stephen L. Stepoway (Southern Methodist University), Bill Toll (Taylor University), Michael Wainer (Southern Illinois University, Carbondale), Yang Wang (Southern Methodist State University), Steve Warren (Kansas State University), Mike Way (Florida Southern College), George Wolberg (City College of New York), Xiaoyu Zhang (California State University San Marcos), Ye Zhao (Kent State University). and Ying Zhu (Georgia State University). Although the final decisions may not reflect their views—which often differed considerably from one another—each reviewer forced us to reflect on every page of the manuscript.

The reviewers for this edition were particularly supportive. They include Mike Bailey (Oregon State University), Patrick Cozzi (University of Pennsylvania and Analytic Graphics, Inc) and Jeff Parker (Harvard University). All of them were familiar with previous editions and excited about the potential of moving their classes to WebGL.

We would also like to acknowledge the entire production team at Addison-Wesley. Ed's editors, Peter Gordon, Maite Suarez-Rivas, and Matt Goldstein, have been a pleasure to work with through seven editions of this book and the OpenGL primer. For this edition, Marilyn Lloyd and Kayla Smith-Tarbox at Pearson have provided considerable help. Through seven editions, Paul Anagnostopoulos at Windfall Software has always been more than helpful in assisting with TeX problems. Ed is especially grateful to Lyn Dupré. If the readers could see the original draft of the first edition, they would understand the wonders that Lyn does with a manuscript.

Ed wants to particularly recognize his wife, Rose Mary Molnar, who did the figures for his first graphics book, many of which form the basis for the figures in this book. Probably only other authors can fully appreciate the effort that goes into the book production process and the many contributions and sacrifices our partners make to that effort. The dedication to this book is a sincere but inadequate recognition of all of Rose Mary's contributions to Ed's work.

Dave would like to recognize the support and encouragement of Vicki, his wife, without whom creating works like this would never occur. Not only does she provide warmth and companionship but also provides invaluable feedback on our presentation and materials. She's been a valuable, unrecognized partner in all of Dave's OpenGL endeavors.

Ed Angel
Dave Shreiner

Pearson would like to thank the following persons for reviewing the Global Edition: Chitra Dhawale (PR Pote College of Engineering and Management, Amravati), Mohanesh Bevoor Mahalingappa (National Institute of Engineering, Mysore), and Pankaj K. Sa (National Institute of Technology, Rourkela).

INTERACTIVE COMPUTER GRAPHICS

A Top-Down Approach with **WebGL** | **7**TH EDITION

GLOBAL EDITION

CHAPTER 1

GRAPHICS SYSTEMS
AND MODELS

It would be difficult to overstate the importance of computer and communication technologies in our lives. Activities as wide-ranging as filmmaking, publishing, banking, and education have undergone revolutionary changes as these technologies alter the ways in which we conduct our daily activities. The combination of computers, networks, and the complex human visual system, through computer graphics, has been instrumental in these advances and has led to new ways of displaying information, seeing virtual worlds, and communicating with both other people and machines.

Computer graphics is concerned with all aspects of producing pictures or images using a computer. The field began humbly 50 years ago, with the display of a few lines on a cathode-ray tube (CRT); now, we can generate images by computer that are indistinguishable from photographs of real objects. We routinely train pilots with simulated airplanes, generating graphical displays of a virtual environment in real time. Feature-length movies made entirely by computer have been successful, both critically and financially.

In this chapter, we start our journey with a short discussion of applications of computer graphics. Then we overview graphics systems and imaging. Throughout this book, our approach stresses the relationships between computer graphics and image formation by familiar methods, such as drawing by hand and photography. We will see that these relationships can help us to design application programs, graphics libraries, and architectures for graphics systems.

In this book, we will use **WebGL,** a graphics software system supported by most modern web browsers. WebGL is a version of OpenGL, which is the widely accepted standard for developing graphics applications. WebGL is easy to learn, and it possesses most of the characteristics of the full (or desktop) OpenGL and of other important graphics systems. Our approach is top-down. We want you to start writing, as quickly as possible, application programs that will generate graphical output. After you begin writing simple programs, we shall discuss how the underlying graphics library and the hardware are implemented. This chapter should give a sufficient overview for you to proceed to writing programs.

1.1   APPLICATIONS OF COMPUTER GRAPHICS

The development of computer graphics has been driven both by the needs of the user community and by advances in hardware and software. The applications of computer graphics are many and varied; we can, however, divide them into four major areas:

1. Display of information
2. Design
3. Simulation and animation
4. User interfaces

Although many applications span two or more of these areas, the development of the field was based largely on separate work in each.

1.1.1 Display of Information

Classical graphics techniques arose as a medium to convey information among people. Although spoken and written languages serve a similar purpose, the human visual system is unrivaled both as a processor of data and as a pattern recognizer. More than 4000 years ago, the Babylonians displayed floor plans of buildings on stones. More than 2000 years ago, the Greeks were able to convey their architectural ideas graphically, even though the related mathematics was not developed until the Renaissance. Today, the same type of information is generated by architects, mechanical designers, and draftspeople using computer-based drafting systems.

For centuries, cartographers have developed maps to display celestial and geographical information. Such maps were crucial to navigators as these people explored the ends of the earth; maps are no less important today in fields such as geographic information systems. Now, maps can be developed and manipulated in real time over the Internet.

During the past 100 years, workers in the field of statistics have explored techniques for generating plots that aid the viewer in determining the information in a set of data. Now, we have computer plotting packages that provide a variety of plotting techniques and color tools that can handle multiple large data sets. Nevertheless, it is still the human ability to recognize visual patterns that ultimately allows us to interpret the information contained in the data. The field of information visualization is becoming increasingly more important as we have to deal with understanding complex phenomena, from problems in bioinformatics to detecting security threats.

Medical imaging poses interesting and important data analysis problems. Modern imaging technologies—such as computed tomography (CT), magnetic resonance imaging (MRI), ultrasound, and positron-emission tomography (PET)—generate three-dimensional data that must be subjected to algorithmic manipulation to provide useful information. Color Plate 20 shows an image of a person's head in which the skin is displayed as transparent and the internal structures are displayed as opaque. Although the data were collected by a medical imaging system, computer graphics produced the image that shows the structures.

Supercomputers now allow researchers in many areas to solve previously intractable problems. The field of scientific visualization provides graphical tools that help these researchers interpret the vast quantity of data that they generate. In fields such as fluid flow, molecular biology, and mathematics, images generated by conversion of data to geometric entities that can be displayed have yielded new insights into complex processes. For example, Color Plate 19 shows fluid dynamics in the mantle of the earth. The system used a mathematical model to generate the data. We present various visualization techniques as examples throughout the rest of the text.

1.1.2 Design

Professions such as engineering and architecture are concerned with design. Starting with a set of specifications, engineers and architects seek a cost-effective and aesthetic solution that satisfies the specifications. Design is an iterative process. Rarely in the real world is a problem specified such that there is a unique optimal solution. Design problems are either *overdetermined*, such that they possess no solution that satisfies all the criteria, much less an optimal solution, or *underdetermined*, such that they have multiple solutions that satisfy the design criteria. Thus, the designer works in an iterative manner. She generates a possible design, tests it, and then uses the results as the basis for exploring other solutions.

The power of the paradigm of humans interacting with images on the screen of a CRT was recognized by Ivan Sutherland over 50 years ago. Today, the use of interactive graphical tools in computer-aided design (CAD) pervades fields such as architecture and the design of mechanical parts and of very-large-scale integrated (VLSI) circuits. In many such applications, the graphics are used in a number of distinct ways. For example, in a VLSI design, the graphics provide an interactive interface between the user and the design package, usually by means of such tools as menus and icons. In addition, after the user produces a possible design, other tools analyze the design and display the analysis graphically. Color Plates 9 and 10 show two views of the same architectural design. Both images were generated with the same CAD system. They demonstrate the importance of having the tools available to generate different images of the same objects at different stages of the design process.

1.1.3 Simulation and Animation

Once graphics systems evolved to be capable of generating sophisticated images in real time, engineers and researchers began to use them as simulators. One of the most important uses has been in the training of pilots. Graphical flight simulators have proved both to increase safety and to reduce training expenses. The use of special VLSI chips has led to a generation of arcade games as sophisticated as flight simulators. Games and educational software for home computers are almost as impressive.

The success of flight simulators led to the use of computer graphics for animation in the television, motion picture, and advertising industries. Entire animated movies can now be made by computer at a cost less than that of movies made with traditional hand-animation techniques. The use of computer graphics with hand animation allows the creation of technical and artistic effects that are not possible with either alone. Whereas computer animations have a distinct look, we can also generate photorealistic images by computer. Images that we see on television, in movies, and in magazines often are so realistic that we cannot distinguish computer-generated or computer-altered images from photographs. In Chapter 6, we discuss many of the lighting effects used to produce computer animations. Color Plates 15 and 23 show realistic lighting effects that were created by artists and computer scientists using animation software. Although these images were created for commercial animations, interactive software to create such effects is widely available.

The field of virtual reality (VR) has opened up many new horizons. A human viewer can be equipped with a display headset that allows her to see separate images with her right eye and her left eye so that she has the effect of stereoscopic vision. In addition, her body location and position, possibly including her head and finger positions, are tracked by the computer. She may have other interactive devices available, including force-sensing gloves and sound. She can then act as part of a computer-generated scene, limited only by the image generation ability of the computer. For example, a surgical intern might be trained to do an operation in this way, or an astronaut might be trained to work in a weightless environment. Color Plate 22 shows one frame of a VR simulation of a simulated patient used for remote training of medical personnel.

Simulation and virtual reality have come together in many exciting ways in the film industry. Recently, stereo (3D) movies have become both profitable and highly acclaimed by audiences. Special effects created using computer graphics are part of virtually all movies, as are more mundane uses of computer graphics such as removal of artifacts from scenes. Simulations of physics are used to create visual effects ranging from fluid flow to crowd dynamics.

1.1.4 User Interfaces

Our interaction with computers has become dominated by a visual paradigm that includes windows, icons, menus, and a pointing device, such as a mouse. From a user's perspective, windowing systems such as the X Window System, Microsoft Windows, and the Macintosh Operating System differ only in details. More recently, millions of people have become users of the Internet. Their access is through graphical network browsers, such as Firefox, Chrome, Safari, and Internet Explorer, that use these same interface tools. We have become so accustomed to this style of interface that we often forget that what we are doing is working with computer graphics.

Although personal computers and workstations evolved by somewhat different paths, at present they are indistinguishable. When you add in smart phones, tablets, and game consoles, we have an incredible variety of devices with considerable computing power, all of which can access the World Wide Web through a browser. For lack of a better term, we will tend to use *computer* to include all these devices.

Color Plate 13 shows the interface used with a high-level modeling package. It demonstrates the variety of tools available in such packages and the interactive devices the user can employ in modeling geometric objects. Although we are familiar with this style of graphical user interface, devices such as smart phones and tablets have popularized touch-sensitive interfaces that allow the user to interact with every pixel on the display.

1.2 A GRAPHICS SYSTEM

A computer graphics system is a computer system; as such, it must have all the components of a general-purpose computer system. Let us start with the high-level view of a graphics system, as shown in the block diagram in Figure 1.1. There are six major elements in our system:

1. Input devices
2. Central Processing Unit
3. Graphics Processing Unit
4. Memory
5. Framebuffer
6. Output devices

This model is general enough to include workstations and personal computers, interactive game systems, mobile phones, GPS systems, and sophisticated image generation systems. Although most of the components are present in a standard computer, it is the way each element is specialized for computer graphics that characterizes this diagram as a portrait of a graphics system. As more and more functionality can be included in a single chip, many of the components are not physically separate. The CPU and GPU can be on the same chip and their memory can be shared. Nevertheless, the model still describes the software architecture and will be helpful as we study the various parts of computer graphics systems.

1.2.1 Pixels and the Framebuffer

Virtually all modern graphics systems are raster based. The image we see on the output device is an array—the **raster**—of picture elements, or **pixels**, produced by the graphics system. As we can see from Figure 1.2, each pixel corresponds to a location, or small area, in the image. Collectively, the pixels are stored in a part of

FIGURE 1.1   A graphics system.

FIGURE 1.2   Pixels. (a) Image of Yeti the cat. (b) Detail of area around one eye showing individual pixels.

memory called the **framebuffer**.[1] The framebuffer can be viewed as the core element of a graphics system. Its **resolution**—the number of pixels in the framebuffer—determines the detail that you can see in the image. The **depth**, or **precision**, of the framebuffer, defined as the number of bits that are used for each pixel, determines properties such as how many colors can be represented on a given system. For example, a 1-bit-deep framebuffer allows only two colors, whereas an 8-bit-deep framebuffer allows 2^8 (256) colors. In **full-color** systems, there are 24 (or more) bits per pixel. Such systems can display sufficient colors to represent most images realistically. They are also called **true-color** systems, or **RGB color** systems, because individual groups of bits in each pixel are assigned to each of the three primary colors—red, green, and blue—used in most displays. **High dynamic range** (HDR) systems use 12 or more bits for each color component. Until recently, framebuffers stored colors in integer formats. Recent framebuffers use floating point and thus support HDR colors more easily.

In a simple system, the framebuffer holds only the colored pixels that are displayed on the screen. In most systems, the framebuffer holds far more information, such as depth information needed for creating images from three-dimensional data. In these systems, the framebuffer comprises multiple buffers, one or more of which are **color buffers** that hold the colored pixels that are displayed. For now, we can use the terms *framebuffer* and *color buffer* synonymously without confusion.

1.2.2 The CPU and the GPU

In a simple system, there may be only one processor, the **central processing unit** (**CPU**), which must perform both the normal processing and the graphical process-

---

1. Some references use *frame buffer* rather than *framebuffer*.

ing. The main graphical function of the processor is to take specifications of graphical primitives (such as lines, circles, and polygons) generated by application programs and to assign values to the pixels in the framebuffer that best represent these entities. For example, a triangle is specified by its three vertices, but to display its outline by the three line segments connecting the vertices, the graphics system must generate a set of pixels that appear as line segments to the viewer. The conversion of geometric entities to pixel colors and locations in the framebuffer is known as **rasterization** or **scan conversion**. In early graphics systems, the framebuffer was part of the standard memory that could be directly addressed by the CPU. Today, virtually all graphics systems are characterized by special-purpose **graphics processing units** (**GPUs**), custom-tailored to carry out specific graphics functions. The GPU can be located on the motherboard of the system or on a graphics card. The framebuffer is accessed through the graphics processing unit and usually is on the same circuit board as the GPU.

GPUs have evolved to the point where they are as complex or even more complex than CPUs. They are characterized both by special-purpose modules geared toward graphical operations and by a high degree of parallelism—recent GPUs contain over 100 processing units, each of which is user programmable. GPUs are so powerful that they can often be used as mini supercomputers for general-purpose computing. We will discuss GPU architectures in more detail in Section 1.7.

1.2.3 Output Devices

Until recently, the dominant type of display (or **monitor**) was the **cathode-ray tube** (**CRT**). A simplified picture of a CRT is shown in Figure 1.3. When electrons strike the phosphor coating on the tube, light is emitted. The direction of the beam is controlled by two pairs of deflection plates. The output of the computer is converted, by digital-to-analog converters, to voltages across the x and y deflection plates. Light appears on the surface of the CRT when a sufficiently intense beam of electrons is directed at the phosphor.

If the voltages steering the beam change at a constant rate, the beam will trace a straight line, visible to the viewer. Such a device is known as the **random-scan**,

FIGURE 1.3   The cathode-ray tube (CRT).

calligraphic, or **vector** CRT, because the beam can be moved directly from any position to any other position. If intensity of the beam is turned off, the beam can be moved to a new position without changing any visible display. This configuration was the basis of early graphics systems that predated the present raster technology.

A typical CRT will emit light for only a short time—usually, a few milliseconds—after the phosphor is excited by the electron beam. For a human to see a steady, flicker-free image on most CRT displays, the same path must be retraced, or **refreshed**, by the beam at a sufficiently high rate, the **refresh rate**. In older systems, the refresh rate is determined by the frequency of the power system, 60 cycles per second or 60 hertz (Hz) in the United States and 50 Hz in much of the rest of the world. Modern displays are no longer coupled to these low frequencies and operate at rates up to about 85 Hz.

In a raster system, the graphics system takes pixels from the framebuffer and displays them as points on the surface of the display in one of two fundamental ways. In a **noninterlaced** system, the pixels are displayed row by row, or scan line by scan line, at the refresh rate. In an **interlaced** display, odd rows and even rows are refreshed alternately. Interlaced displays are used in commercial television. In an interlaced display operating at 60 Hz, the screen is redrawn in its entirety only 30 times per second, although the visual system is tricked into thinking the refresh rate is 60 Hz rather than 30 Hz. Viewers located near the screen, however, can tell the difference between the interlaced and noninterlaced displays. Noninterlaced displays are becoming more widespread, even though these displays must process pixels at twice the rate of the interlaced display.

Color CRTs have three different-colored phosphors (red, green, and blue), arranged in small groups. One common style arranges the phosphors in triangular groups called **triads**, each triad consisting of three phosphors, one of each primary. Most color CRTs have three electron beams, corresponding to the three types of phosphors. In the shadow-mask CRT (Figure 1.4), a metal screen with small holes—the **shadow mask**—ensures that an electron beam excites only phosphors of the proper color.

FIGURE 1.4   Shadow-mask CRT.

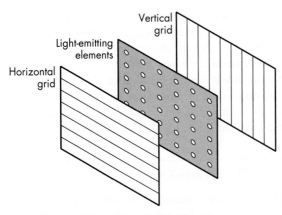

FIGURE 1.5   Generic flat-panel display.

Although CRTs are still common display devices, they are rapidly being replaced by flat-screen technologies. Flat-panel monitors are inherently raster based. Although there are multiple technologies available, including light-emitting diodes (LEDs), liquid-crystal displays (LCDs), and plasma panels, all use a two-dimensional grid to address individual light-emitting elements. Figure 1.5 shows a generic flat-panel monitor. The two outside plates each contain parallel grids of wires that are oriented perpendicular to each other. By sending electrical signals to the proper wire in each grid, the electrical field at a location, determined by the intersection of two wires, can be made strong enough to control the corresponding element in the middle plate. The middle plate in an LED panel contains light-emitting diodes that can be turned on and off by the electrical signals sent to the grid. In an LCD display, the electrical field controls the polarization of the liquid crystals in the middle panel, thus turning on and off the light passing through the panel. A plasma panel uses the voltages on the grids to energize gases embedded between the glass panels holding the grids. The energized gas becomes a glowing plasma.

Most projection systems are also raster devices. These systems use a variety of technologies, including CRTs and digital light projection (DLP). From a user perspective, they act as standard monitors with similar resolutions and precisions. Hard-copy devices, such as printers and plotters, are also raster based but cannot be refreshed.

Stereo (3D) television displays use alternate refresh cycles to switch the display between an image for the left eye and an image for the right eye. The viewer wears special glasses that are coupled to the refresh cycle. 3D movie projectors produce two images with different polarizations. The viewer wears polarized glasses so that each eye sees only one of the two projected images. As we shall see in later chapters, producing stereo images is basically a matter of changing the location of the viewer for each frame to obtain the left- and right-eye views.

1.2.4 Input Devices

Most graphics systems provide a keyboard and at least one other input device. The most common input devices are the mouse, the joystick, and the data tablet. Each provides positional information to the system, and each is usually equipped with one or more buttons to provide signals to the processor. Often called **pointing devices**, these devices allow a user to indicate a particular location on the display.

Modern systems, such as game consoles, provide a much richer set of input devices, with new devices appearing almost weekly. In addition, there are devices that provide three- (and more) dimensional input. Consequently, we want to provide a flexible model for incorporating the input from such devices into our graphics programs. We will discuss input devices and how to use them in Chapter 3.

1.3   IMAGES: PHYSICAL AND SYNTHETIC

For many years, the pedagogical approach to teaching computer graphics started with how to construct raster images of simple two-dimensional geometric entities (for example, points, line segments, and polygons) in the framebuffer. Next, most textbooks discussed how to define two- and three-dimensional mathematical objects in the computer and image them with the set of two-dimensional rasterized primitives.

This approach worked well for creating simple images of simple objects. In modern systems, however, we want to exploit the capabilities of the software and hardware to create realistic images of computer-generated three-dimensional objects—a task that involves many aspects of image formation, such as lighting, shading, and properties of materials. Because such functionality is supported directly by most present computer graphics systems, we prefer to set the stage for creating these images now, rather than to expand a limited model later.

Computer-generated images are synthetic or artificial, in the sense that the objects being imaged do not exist physically. In this chapter, we argue that the preferred method to form computer-generated images is similar to traditional imaging methods, such as cameras and the human visual system. Hence, before we discuss the mechanics of writing programs to generate images, we discuss the way images are formed by optical systems. We construct a model of the image formation process that we can then use to understand and develop computer-generated imaging systems.

In this chapter, we make minimal use of mathematics. We want to establish a paradigm for creating images and to present a computer architecture for implementing that paradigm. Details are presented in subsequent chapters, where we shall derive the relevant equations.

1.3.1   Objects and Viewers

We live in a world of three-dimensional objects. The development of many branches of mathematics, including geometry and trigonometry, was in response to the desire to systematize conceptually simple ideas, such as the measurement of the size of objects and the distance between objects. Often, we seek to represent our understanding of such spatial relationships with pictures or images, such as maps, paintings, and photographs. Likewise, the development of many physical devices—including cameras, microscopes, and telescopes—was tied to the desire to visualize spatial relationships among objects. Hence, there always has been a fundamental link between the physics and the mathematics of image formation—one that we can exploit in our development of computer image formation.

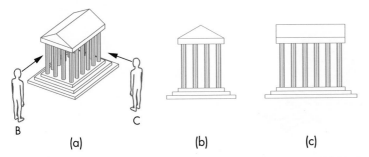

FIGURE 1.6   Image seen by three different viewers. (a) A's view. (b) B's view. (c) C's view.

Two basic entities must be part of any image formation process, be it mathematical or physical: *object* and *viewer*. The object exists in space independent of any image formation process and of any viewer. In computer graphics, where we deal with synthetic objects, we form objects by specifying the positions in space of various geometric primitives, such as points, lines, and polygons. In most graphics systems, a set of locations in space, or of **vertices**, is sufficient to define, or approximate, most objects. For example, a line can be specified by two vertices; a polygon can be specified by an ordered list of vertices; and a sphere can be specified by two vertices that specify its center and any point on its circumference. One of the main functions of a CAD system is to provide an interface that makes it easy for a user to build a synthetic model of the world. In Chapter 2, we show how WebGL allows us to build simple objects; in Chapter 9, we learn to define objects in a manner that incorporates relationships among objects.

Every imaging system must provide a means of forming images from objects. To form an image, we must have someone or something that is viewing our objects, be it a human, a camera, or a digitizer. It is the **viewer** that forms the image of our objects. In the human visual system, the image is formed on the back of the eye. In a camera, the image is formed in the film plane. It is easy to confuse images and objects. We usually see an object from our single perspective and forget that other viewers, located in other places, will see the same object differently. Figure 1.6(a) shows two viewers observing the same building. This image is what is seen by an observer A who is far enough away from the building to see both the building and the two other viewers B and C. From A's perspective, B and C appear as objects, just as the building does. Figure 1.6(b) and (c) shows the images seen by B and C, respectively. All three images contain the same building, but the image of the building is different in all three.

FIGURE 1.7   Camera system.

Figure 1.7 shows a camera system viewing a building. Here we can observe that both the object and the viewer exist in a three-dimensional world. However, the image that they define—what we find on the projection plane—is two-dimensional. The process by which the specification of the object is combined with the specification of the viewer to produce a two-dimensional image is the essence of image formation, and we will study it in detail.

FIGURE 1.8   A camera system with an object and a light source.

1.3.2 Light and Images

The preceding description of image formation is far from complete. For example, we have yet to mention light. If there were no light sources, the objects would be dark, and there would be nothing visible in our image. Nor have we indicated how color enters the picture or what the effects of the surface properties of the objects are.

Taking a more physical approach, we can start with the arrangement in Figure 1.8, which shows a simple physical imaging system. Again, we see a physical object and a viewer (the camera); now, however, there is a light source in the scene. Light from the source strikes various surfaces of the object, and a portion of the reflected light enters the camera through the lens. The details of the interaction between light and the surfaces of the object determine how much light enters the camera.

Light is a form of electromagnetic radiation. Taking the classical view, we look at electromagnetic energy as traveling as waves[2] that can be characterized either by their wavelengths or by their frequencies.[3] The electromagnetic spectrum (Figure 1.9) includes radio waves, infrared (heat), and a portion that causes a response in our visual systems. This **visible spectrum**, which has wavelengths in the range of 350 to 780 nanometers (nm), is called (visible) **light**. A given light source has a color determined by the energy that it emits at various wavelengths. Wavelengths in the middle of the range, around 520 nm, are seen as green; those near 450 nm are seen as blue; and those near 650 nm are seen as red. Just as with a rainbow, light at wavelengths between red and green we see as yellow, and at wavelengths shorter than blue we see as violet.

Light sources can emit light either as a set of discrete frequencies or over a continuous range. A laser, for example, emits light at a single frequency, whereas an incandescent lamp emits energy over a range of frequencies. Fortunately, in computer

2. In Chapter 12, we will introduce photon mapping that is based on light being emitted in discrete packets.

3. The relationship between frequency (f) and wavelength (λ) is $f\lambda = c$, where c is the speed of light.

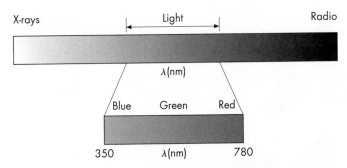

FIGURE 1.9   The electromagnetic spectrum.

graphics, except for recognizing that distinct frequencies are visible as distinct colors, we rarely need to deal with the physical properties of light.

Instead, we can follow a more traditional path that is correct when we are operating with sufficiently high light levels and at a scale where the wave nature of light is not a significant factor. **Geometric optics** models light sources as emitters of light energy, each of which have a fixed intensity. Modeled geometrically, light travels in straight lines, from the sources to those objects with which it interacts. An ideal **point source** emits energy from a single location at one or more frequencies equally in all directions. More complex sources, such as a lightbulb, can be characterized as emitting light over an area and by emitting more light in one direction than another. A particular source is characterized by the intensity of light that it emits at each frequency and by that light's directionality. We consider only point sources for now. More complex sources often can be approximated by a number of carefully placed point sources. Modeling of light sources is discussed in Chapter 6.

1.3.3 Imaging Models

There are multiple approaches to forming images from a set of objects, the light-reflecting properties of these objects, and the properties of the light sources in the scene. In this section, we introduce two physical approaches. Although these approaches are not suitable for the real-time graphics that we ultimately want, they will give us some insight into how we can build a useful imaging architecture. We return to these approaches in Chapter 12.

We can start building an imaging model by following light from a source. Consider the scene in Figure 1.10; it is illuminated by a single point source. We include the viewer in the figure because we are interested in the light that reaches her eye. The viewer can also be a camera, as shown in Figure 1.18. A **ray** is a semi-infinite line that emanates from a point and travels to infinity in a particular direction. Because light travels in straight lines, we can think in terms of rays of light emanating in all directions from our point source. A portion of these infinite rays contributes to the image on the film plane of our camera. For example, if the source is visible from the camera, some of the rays go directly from the source through the lens of the camera and strike the film plane. Most rays, however, go off to infinity, neither entering the

FIGURE 1.10   Scene with a single point light source.

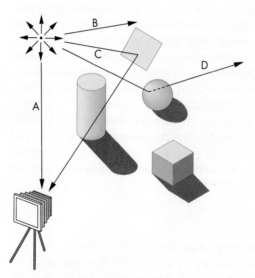

FIGURE 1.11   Ray interactions. Ray A enters camera directly. Ray B goes off to infinity. Ray C is reflected by a mirror. Ray D goes through a transparent sphere.

camera directly nor striking any of the objects. These rays contribute nothing to the image, although they may be seen by some other viewer. The remaining rays strike and illuminate objects. These rays can interact with the objects' surfaces in a variety of ways. For example, if the surface is a mirror, a reflected ray might—depending on the orientation of the surface—enter the lens of the camera and contribute to the image. Other surfaces scatter light in all directions. If the surface is transparent, the light ray from the source can pass through it and may interact with other objects, enter the camera, or travel to infinity without striking another surface. Figure 1.11 shows some of the possibilities.

Ray tracing and **photon mapping** are image formation techniques that are based on these ideas and that can form the basis for producing computer-generated images. We can use the ray-tracing idea to simulate physical effects as complex as we wish, as long as we are willing to carry out the requisite computing. Although tracing rays can provide a close approximation to the physical world, it is usually not well suited for real-time computation.

Other physical approaches to image formation are based on conservation of energy. The most important in computer graphics is **radiosity**. This method works best for surfaces that scatter the incoming light equally in all directions. Even in this case, radiosity requires more computation than can be done in real time. We defer discussion of these techniques until Chapter 12.

1.4 IMAGING SYSTEMS

We now introduce two imaging systems: the pinhole camera and the human visual system. The pinhole camera is a simple example of an imaging system that will enable us to understand the functioning of cameras and of other optical imagers. We emulate it to build a model of image formation. The human visual system is extremely complex but still obeys the physical principles of other optical imaging systems. We introduce it not only as an example of an imaging system but also because understanding its properties will help us to exploit the capabilities of computer graphics systems.

1.4.1 The Pinhole Camera

The pinhole camera in Figure 1.12 provides an example of image formation that we can understand with a simple geometric model. A **pinhole camera** is a box with a small hole in the center of one side; the film is placed inside the box on the side opposite the pinhole. Suppose that we orient our camera along the z-axis, with the pinhole at the origin of our coordinate system. We assume that the hole is so small that only a single ray of light, emanating from a point, can enter it. The film plane is

FIGURE 1.12   Pinhole camera.

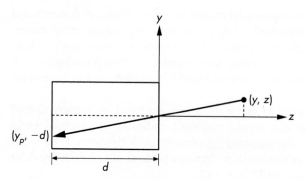

FIGURE 1.13   Side view of pinhole camera.

located a distance d from the pinhole. A side view (Figure 1.13) allows us to calculate where the image of the point (x, y, z) is on the film plane $z = -d$. Using the fact that the two triangles in Figure 1.13 are similar, we find that the y coordinate of the image is at y_p, where

$$y_p = -\frac{y}{z/d}.$$

A similar calculation, using a top view, yields

$$x_p = -\frac{x}{z/d}.$$

The point $(x_p, y_p, -d)$ is called the **projection** of the point (x, y, z). In our idealized model, the color on the film plane at this point will be the color of the point (x, y, z). The **field**, or **angle, of view** of our camera is the angle made by the largest object that our camera can image on its film plane. We can calculate the field of view with the aid of Figure 1.14.[4] If h is the height of the camera, the field of view (or angle of view) θ is

$$\theta = 2 \tan^{-1} \frac{h}{2d}.$$

The ideal pinhole camera has an infinite **depth of field**: Every point within its field of view is in focus. Every point in its field of view projects to a point on the back of the camera. The pinhole camera has two disadvantages. First, because the pinhole is so small—it admits only a single ray from a point source—almost no light enters the camera. Second, the camera cannot be adjusted to have a different field of view.

The jump to more sophisticated cameras and to other imaging systems that have lenses is a small one. By replacing the pinhole with a lens, we solve the two problems of the pinhole camera. First, the lens gathers more light than can pass through the

---

4. If we consider the problem in three, rather than two, dimensions, then the diagonal length of the film will substitute for h.

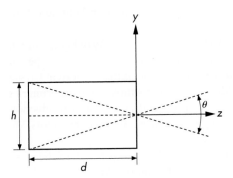

FIGURE 1.14 Field of view.

pinhole. The larger the aperture of the lens, the more light the lens can collect. Second, by picking a lens with the proper focal length—a selection equivalent to choosing d for the pinhole camera—we can achieve any desired field of view (up to 180 degrees). Lenses, however, do not have an infinite depth of field: Not all distances from the lens are in focus.

For our purposes, in this chapter we can work with a pinhole camera whose focal length is the distance d from the front of the camera to the film plane. Like the pinhole camera, computer graphics produces images in which all objects are in focus.

1.4.2 The Human Visual System

Our extremely complex visual system has all the components of a physical imaging system such as a camera or a microscope. The major components of the visual system are shown in Figure 1.15. Light enters the eye through the cornea, a transparent structure that protects the eye, and the lens. The iris opens and closes to adjust the amount of light entering the eye. The lens forms an image on a two-dimensional structure called the **retina** at the back of the eye. The rods and cones (so named because of their appearance when magnified) are light sensors and are located on the retina. They are excited by electromagnetic energy in the range of 350 to 780 nm.

The rods are low-level-light sensors that account for our night vision and are not color sensitive; the cones are responsible for our color vision. The sizes of the rods and cones, coupled with the optical properties of the lens and cornea, determine the **resolution** of our visual systems, or our **visual acuity**. Resolution is a measure of what size objects we can see. More technically, it is a measure of how close we can place two points and still recognize that there are two distinct points.

The sensors in the human eye do not react uniformly to light energy at different wavelengths. There are three types of cones and a single type of rod. Whereas intensity is a physical measure of light energy, **brightness** is a measure of how intense we perceive the light emitted from an object to be. The human visual system does not have the same response to a monochromatic (single-frequency) red light as to a monochromatic green light. If these two lights were to emit the same energy, they would appear to us to have different brightness, because of the unequal response

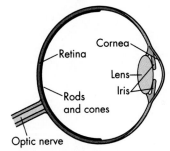

FIGURE 1.15 The human visual system.

of the cones to red and green light. We are most sensitive to green light, and least sensitive to red and blue.

Brightness is an overall measure of how we react to the intensity of light. Human color-vision capabilities are due to the different sensitivities of the three types of cones. The major consequence of having three types of cones is that, instead of having to work with all visible wavelengths individually, we can use three standard primaries to approximate any color that we can perceive. Consequently, most image production systems, including film and video, work with just three basic, or **primary**, colors. We discuss color in greater depth in Chapters 2 and 8.

The initial processing of light in the human visual system is based on the same principles used by most optical systems. However, the human visual system has a back end much more complex than that of a camera or telescope. The optic nerve is connected to the rods and cones in an extremely complex arrangement that has many of the characteristics of a sophisticated signal processor. The final processing is done in a part of the brain called the visual cortex, where high-level functions, such as object recognition, are carried out. We shall omit any discussion of high-level processing; instead, we can think simply in terms of an image that is conveyed from the rods and cones to the brain.

1.5 THE SYNTHETIC-CAMERA MODEL

Our models of optical imaging systems lead directly to the conceptual foundation for modern three-dimensional computer graphics. We look at creating a computer-generated image as being similar to forming an image using an optical system. This paradigm has become known as the **synthetic-camera model**. Consider the imaging system shown in Figure 1.16. We again see objects and a viewer. In this case, the viewer is a bellows camera.[5] The image is formed on the film plane at the back of the camera. So that we can emulate this process to create artificial images, we need to identify a few basic principles.

First, the specification of the objects is independent of the specification of the viewer. Hence, we should expect that, within a graphics library, there will be separate functions for specifying the objects and the viewer.

Second, we can compute the image using simple geometric calculations, just as we did with the pinhole camera. Consider the side view of the camera and a simple object in Figure 1.17. The view in part (a) of the figure is similar to that of the pinhole camera. Note that the image of the object is flipped relative to the object. Whereas with a real camera we would simply flip the film to regain the original orientation of the object, with our synthetic camera we can avoid the flipping by a simple trick. We draw another plane in front of the lens (Figure 1.17(b)) and work in three dimensions, as shown in Figure 1.18. We find the image of a point on the object

---

5. In a bellows camera, the front plane of the camera, where the lens is located, and the back of the camera, the film plane, are connected by flexible sides. Thus, we can move the back of the camera independently of the front of the camera, introducing additional flexibility in the image formation process. We use this flexibility in Chapter 5.

FIGURE 1.16 Imaging system.

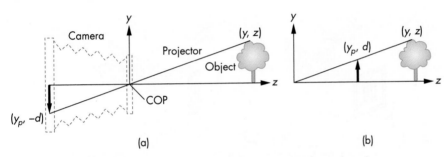

FIGURE 1.17 Equivalent views of image formation. (a) Image formed on the back of the camera. (b) Image plane moved in front of the camera.

on the virtual image plane by drawing a line, called a **projector**, from the point to the center of the lens, or the **center of projection** (**COP**). Note that all projectors are rays emanating from the center of projection. In our synthetic camera, the virtual image plane that we have moved in front of the lens is called the **projection plane**. The image of the point is located where the projector passes through the projection plane. In Chapter 5, we discuss this process in detail and derive the relevant mathematical formulas.

We must also consider the limited size of the image. As we saw, not all objects can be imaged onto the pinhole camera's film plane. The field of view expresses this limitation. In the synthetic camera, we can move this limitation to the front by placing a **clipping rectangle**, or **clipping window**, in the projection plane (Figure 1.19). This rectangle acts as a window through which a viewer, located at the center of projection, sees the world. Given the location of the center of projection, the location and orientation of the projection plane, and the size of the clipping rectangle, we can determine which objects will appear in the image.

FIGURE 1.18   Imaging with the synthetic camera.

(a)   (b)

FIGURE 1.19   Clipping. (a) Window in initial position. (b) Window shifted.

1.6   THE PROGRAMMER'S INTERFACE

There are numerous ways that a user can interact with a graphics system. With completely self-contained packages such as those used in the CAD community, a user develops images through interactions with the display using input devices such as a mouse and a keyboard. In a typical application, such as the painting program in Figure 1.20, the user sees menus and icons that represent possible actions. By clicking on these items, the user guides the software and produces images without having to write programs.

Of course, someone has to develop the code for these applications, and many of us, despite the sophistication of commercial products, still have to write our own graphics application programs (and even enjoy doing so).

The interface between an application program and a graphics system can be specified through a set of functions that resides in a graphics library. These speci-

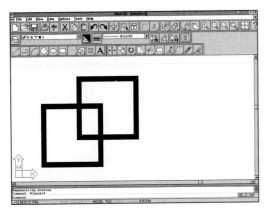

FIGURE 1.20   Interface for a painting program.

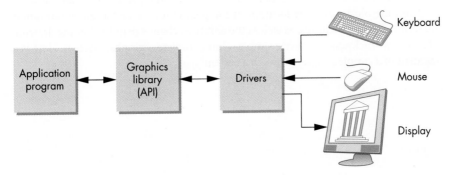

FIGURE 1.21   Application programmer's model of graphics system.

fications are called the **application programming interface (API)**. The application programmer's model of the system is shown in Figure 1.21. The application programmer sees only the API and is thus shielded from the details of both the hardware and the software implementation of the graphics library. The software **drivers** are responsible for interpreting the output of the API and converting these data to a form that is understood by the particular hardware. From the perspective of the writer of an application program, the functions available through the API should match the conceptual model that the user wishes to employ to specify images. By developing code that uses the API, the application programmer is able to develop applications that can be used with different hardware and software platforms.

1.6.1 The Pen-Plotter Model

Historically, most early graphics systems were two-dimensional systems. The conceptual model that they used is now referred to as the **pen-plotter model**, referring to the output device that was available on these systems. A **pen plotter** (Figure 1.22) produces images by moving a pen held by a gantry, a structure that can move the pen

FIGURE 1.22   Pen plotter.

in two orthogonal directions across the paper. The plotter can raise and lower the pen as required to create the desired image. Pen plotters are still in use; they are well suited for drawing large diagrams, such as blueprints. Various APIs—such as LOGO and PostScript—have their origins in this model. The HTML5 canvas upon which we will display the output from WebGL also has its origins in the pen-plotter model. Although they differ from one another, they have a common view of the process of creating an image as being similar to the process of drawing on a pad of paper. The user works on a two-dimensional surface of some size. She moves a pen around on this surface, leaving an image on the paper.

We can describe such a graphics system with two drawing functions:

```
moveto(x, y);
lineto(x, y);
```

Execution of the `moveto` function moves the pen to the location (x, y) on the paper without leaving a mark. The `lineto` function moves the pen to (x, y) and draws a line from the old to the new location of the pen. Once we add a few initialization and termination procedures, as well as the ability to change pens to alter the drawing color or line thickness, we have a simple—but complete—graphics system. Here is a fragment of a simple program in such a system:

```
moveto(0, 0);
lineto(1, 0);
lineto(1, 1);
lineto(0, 1);
lineto(0, 0);
```

This fragment would generate the output in Figure 1.23(a). If we added the code

```
moveto(0, 1);
lineto(0.5, 1.866);
lineto(1.5, 1.866);
lineto(1.5, 0.866);
lineto(1, 0);
moveto(1, 1);
lineto(1.5, 1.866);
```

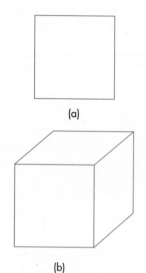

(a)

(b)

FIGURE 1.23 Output of pen-plotter program for (a) a square, and (b) a projection of a cube.

we would have the image of a cube formed by an oblique projection, as is shown in Figure 1.23(b).

For certain applications, such as page layout in the printing industry, systems built on this model work well. For example, the PostScript page description language, a sophisticated extension of these ideas, is a standard for controlling typesetters and printers.

An alternate raster-based (but still limited) two-dimensional model relies on writing pixels directly into a framebuffer. Such a system could be based on a single function of the form

```
writePixel(x, y, color);
```

where x,y is the location of the pixel in the framebuffer and color gives the color to be written there. Such models are well suited to writing the algorithms for rasterization and processing of digital images.

We are much more interested, however, in the three-dimensional world. The pen-plotter model does not extend well to three-dimensional graphics systems. For example, if we wish to use the pen-plotter model to produce the image of a three-dimensional object on our two-dimensional pad, either by hand or by computer, then we have to figure out where on the page to place two-dimensional points corresponding to points on our three-dimensional object. These two-dimensional points are, as we saw in Section 1.5, the projections of points in three-dimensional space. The mathematical process of determining projections is an application of trigonometry. We develop the mathematics of projection in Chapter 5; understanding projection is crucial to understanding three-dimensional graphics. We prefer, however, to use an API that allows users to work directly in the domain of their problems and to use computers to carry out the details of the projection process automatically, without the users having to make any trigonometric calculations within the application program. That approach should be a boon to users who have difficulty learning to draw various projections on a drafting board or sketching objects in perspective. More important, users can rely on hardware and software implementations of projections within the implementation of the API that are far more efficient than any possible implementation of projections within their programs would be.

Three-dimensional printers are revolutionizing design and manufacturing, allowing the fabrication of items as varied as mechanical parts, art, and biological items constructed from living cells. They illustrate the importance of separating the low-level production of the final piece from the high-level software used for design. At the physical level, they function much like our description of a pen plotter except that rather than depositing ink, they can deposit almost any material. The three-dimensional piece is built up in layers, each of which can be described using our pen-plotter model. However, the design is done in three dimensions with a high-level API that can output a file that is converted into a stack of layers for the printer.

1.6.2 Three-Dimensional APIs

The synthetic-camera model is the basis for a number of popular APIs, including OpenGL and Direct3D. If we are to follow the synthetic-camera model, we need functions in the API to specify the following:

- Objects
- A viewer
- Light sources
- Material properties

Objects are usually defined by sets of vertices. For simple geometric objects—such as line segments, rectangles, and polygons—there is a simple relationship between a list of **vertices**, or positions in space, and the object. For more complex objects, there may be multiple ways of defining the object from a set of vertices. A circle, for example, can be defined by three points on its circumference, or by its center and one point on the circumference.

Most APIs provide similar sets of primitive objects for the user. These primitives are usually those that can be displayed rapidly on the hardware. The usual sets include points, line segments, and triangles. WebGL programs specify primitives through lists of vertices. The following code fragment shows one way to specify three vertices in JavaScript for use with WebGL:

```
var vertices = [ ];
```

```
vertices[0] = [0.0, 0.0, 0.0]; // Vertex A
vertices[1] = [0.0, 1.0, 0.0]; // Vertex B
vertices[2] = [0.0, 0.0, 1.0]; // Vertex C
```

Or we could use

```
var vertices = [ ];
```

```
vertices.push([0.0, 0.0, 0.0]); // Vertex A
vertices.push([0.0, 1.0, 0.0]); // Vertex B
vertices.push([0.0, 0.0, 1.0]); // Vertex C
```

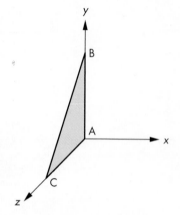

FIGURE 1.24   A triangle.

We could either send this array to the GPU each time that we want it to be displayed or store it on the GPU for later display. Note that these three vertices only give three locations in a three-dimensional space and do not specify the geometric entity that they define. The locations could describe a triangle, as in Figure 1.24, or we could use them to specify two line segments, using the first two locations to specify the first segment and the second and third locations to specify the second segment. We could also use the three points to display three pixels at locations in the framebuffer corresponding to the three vertices. We make this choice in our application by setting a parameter corresponding to the geometric entity we would like these locations to specify. For example, in WebGL we would use gl.TRIANGLES, gl.LINE_STRIP, or gl.POINTS for the three possibilities we just described. Although we are not yet ready to describe all the details of how we accomplish this task, we can note that, regardless of which geometric entity we wish our vertices to specify, we are specifying the geometry and leaving it to the graphics system to determine which pixels to color in the framebuffer.

Some APIs let the user work directly in the framebuffer by providing functions that read and write pixels. Additionally, some APIs provide curves and surfaces as primitives; often, however, these types are approximated by a series of simpler primitives within the application program. WebGL provides access to the framebuffer through texture maps.

FIGURE 1.25   Camera specification.

We can define a viewer or camera in a variety of ways. Available APIs differ both in how much flexibility they provide in camera selection and in how many different methods they allow. If we look at the camera in Figure 1.25, we can identify four types of necessary specifications:

1. **Position**   The camera location usually is given by the position of the center of the lens, which is the center of projection (COP).

2. **Orientation**   Once we have positioned the camera, we can place a camera coordinate system with its origin at the center of projection. We can then rotate the camera independently around the three axes of this system.

3. **Focal length**   The focal length of the lens determines the size of the image on the film plane or, equivalently, the portion of the world the camera sees.

4. **Film plane**   The back of the camera has a height and a width. On the bellows camera, and in some APIs, the orientation of the back of the camera can be adjusted independently of the orientation of the lens.

These specifications can be satisfied in various ways. One way to develop the specifications for the camera location and orientation is through a series of coordinate-system transformations. These transformations convert object positions represented in a coordinate system that specifies object vertices to object positions in a coordinate system centered at the COP. This approach is useful, both for doing implementation and for getting the full set of views that a flexible camera can provide. We use this approach extensively, starting in Chapter 5.

Having many parameters to adjust, however, can also make it difficult to get a desired image. Part of the problem lies with the synthetic-camera model. Classical viewing techniques, such as are used in architecture, stress the *relationship* between the object and the viewer, rather than the *independence* that the synthetic-camera model emphasizes. Thus, the classical two-point perspective of a cube in Figure 1.26 is a *two-point* perspective because of a particular relationship between the viewer and the planes of the cube (see Exercise 1.7). Although the WebGL API allows us to set transformations with complete freedom, we will provide additional helpful functions. For example, consider the two function calls

```
lookAt(cop, at, up);
perspective(fieldOfView, aspectRatio, near, far);
```

The first function call points the camera from the center of projection toward a desired point (the *at* point), with a specified *up* direction for the camera. The second selects a lens for a perspective view (the *field of view*) and how much of the world the camera should image (the *aspect ratio* and the *near* and *far* distances). These functions are built using the WebGL API but are so useful that we will add them to our libraries.

However, none of the APIs built on the synthetic-camera model provide functions for directly specifying a desired relationship between the camera and an object.

FIGURE 1.26   Two-point perspective of a cube.

Light sources are defined by their location, strength, color, and directionality. With WebGL, we can specify these parameters for each source. Material properties are characteristics, or attributes, of the objects, and such properties can also be specified through WebGL at the time that each object is defined. As we shall see in Chapter 6, we will be able to implement different models of light–material interactions with our shaders.

1.6.3 A Sequence of Images

In Chapter 2, we begin our detailed discussion of the WebGL API that we will use throughout this book. The images defined by your WebGL programs will be formed automatically by the hardware and software implementation of the image formation process.

Here we look at a sequence of images that shows what we can create using the WebGL API. We present these images as an increasingly more complex series of renderings of the same objects. The sequence not only loosely follows the order in which we present related topics but also reflects how graphics systems have developed over the past 40 years.

Color Plate 1 shows an image of an artist's creation of a sunlike object. Color Plate 2 shows the object rendered using only line segments. Although the object consists of many parts, and although the programmer may have used sophisticated data structures to model each part and the relationships among the parts, the rendered object shows only the outlines of the parts. This type of image is known as a **wireframe** image because we can see only the edges of surfaces: Such an image would be produced if the objects were constructed with stiff wires that formed a frame with no solid material between the edges. Before raster graphics systems became available, wireframe images were the only type of computer-generated images that we could produce.

In Color Plate 3, the same object has been rendered with flat polygons. Certain surfaces are not visible because there is a solid surface between them and the viewer; these surfaces have been removed by a hidden-surface-removal (HSR) algorithm. Most raster systems can fill the interior of polygons with a solid color in not much more time than they can render a wireframe image. Although the objects are three-dimensional, each surface is displayed in a single color, and the image fails to show the three-dimensional shapes of the objects. Early raster systems could produce images of this form.

In Chapters 2 and 4, we show you how to generate images composed of simple geometric objects—points, line segments, and triangles. In Chapters 4 and 5, you will learn how to transform objects in three dimensions and how to obtain a desired three-dimensional view of a model, with hidden surfaces removed.

Color Plate 4 illustrates smooth shading of the triangles that approximate the object; it shows that the object is three-dimensional and gives the appearance of a smooth surface. We develop shading models that are supported by WebGL in Chapter 6. These shading models are also supported in the hardware of most recent workstations; generating the shaded image on one of these systems takes approximately the same amount of time as does generating a wireframe image.

Color Plate 5 shows a more sophisticated wireframe model constructed using NURBS surfaces, which we introduce in Chapter 11. Such surfaces give the application programmer great flexibility in the design process but are ultimately rendered using line segments and polygons.

In Color Plates 6 and 7, we add surface texture to our object; texture is one of the effects that we discuss in Chapter 7. All recent graphics processors support texture mapping in hardware, so rendering of a texture-mapped image requires little additional time. In Color Plate 6, we use a technique called *bump mapping* that gives the appearance of a rough surface even though we render the same flat polygons as in the other examples. Color Plate 7 shows an *environment map* applied to the surface of the object, which gives the surface the appearance of a mirror. These techniques will be discussed in detail in Chapter 7.

Color Plate 8 shows a small area of the rendering of the object using an environment map. The image on the left shows the jagged artifacts known as aliasing errors that are due to the discrete nature of the framebuffer. The image on the right has been rendered using a smoothing or antialiasing method that we shall study in Chapters 7 and 8.

Not only do these images show what is possible with available hardware and a good API, but they are also simple to generate, as we shall see in subsequent chapters. In addition, just as the images show incremental changes in the renderings, the programs are incrementally different from one another.

1.6.4 The Modeling–Rendering Paradigm

Both conceptually and in practice it is often helpful to separate the modeling of the scene from the production of the image, or the **rendering** of the scene. Hence, we can look at image formation as the two-step process shown in Figure 1.27. Although the tasks are the same as those we have been discussing, this block diagram suggests that we might implement the modeler and the renderer with different software and hardware.

This paradigm first became important in CAD and animation where, due to the limitations of the hardware, the design or modeling of objects needed to be separated from the production, or the rendering, of the scene.

For example, consider the production of a single frame in an animation. We first want to design and position our objects. This step is highly interactive, and usually does not require all the detail in the objects nor to render the scene in great detail incorporating effects such as reflections and shadows. Consequently, we can carry out this step interactively with standard graphics hardware. Once we have designed

FIGURE 1.27   The modeling–rendering paradigm.

the scene, we want to render it, adding light sources, material properties, and a variety of other detailed effects, to form a production-quality image. This step can require a tremendous amount of computation, so we might prefer to use a render farm: a cluster of computers configured for numerical computing.

The interface between the modeler and renderer can be as simple as a file produced by the modeler that describes the objects and that contains additional information important only to the renderer, such as light sources, viewer location, and material properties. Pixar's RenderMan Interface is based on this approach and uses a file format that allows modelers to pass models to the renderer. One of the other advantages of this approach is that it allows us to develop modelers that, although they use the same renderer, are custom-tailored to particular applications. Likewise, different renderers can take as input the same interface file.

Although it is still used in the movie industry where we need to produce high-resolution images with many effects, with modern GPUs most applications do not need to separate modeling and rendering in quite the way we just described. However, there are a few places where will see this paradigm, albeit in a slightly different form. This paradigm has become popular as a method for generating images for multiplayer computer games. Models, including the geometric objects, lights, cameras, and material properties, are placed in a data structure called a **scene graph** that is passed to a renderer or game engine. We shall examine scene graphs in Chapter 9. As we shall see in Chapter 2, the standard way in which we use the GPU is to first form our geometry of objects in the CPU, and then send these data to the GPU for rendering. Hence, in a limited sense, the CPU is the modeler and the GPU is the renderer.

1.7 GRAPHICS ARCHITECTURES

On one side of the API is the application program. On the other is some combination of hardware and software that implements the functionality of the API. Researchers have taken various approaches to developing architectures to support graphics APIs.

Early graphics systems used general-purpose computers with the standard von Neumann architecture. Such computers are characterized by a single processing unit that processes a single instruction at a time. A simple model of these early graphics systems is shown in Figure 1.28. The display in these systems was based on a calligraphic CRT display that included the necessary circuitry to generate a line segment connecting two points. The job of the host computer was to run the application program and to compute the endpoints of the line segments in the image (in units of the

FIGURE 1.28   Early graphics system.

FIGURE 1.29 Display-processor architecture.

display). This information had to be sent to the display at a rate high enough to avoid flicker. In the early days of computer graphics, computers were so slow that refreshing even simple images, containing a few hundred line segments, would burden an expensive computer.

1.7.1 Display Processors

The earliest attempts to build special-purpose graphics systems were concerned primarily with relieving the general-purpose computer from the task of refreshing the display continuously. These **display processors** had conventional architectures (Figure 1.29) but included instructions to display primitives on the CRT. The main advantage of the display processor was that the instructions to generate the image could be assembled once in the host and sent to the display processor, where they were stored in the display processor's own memory as a **display list**, or **display file**. The display processor would then repetitively execute the program in the display list, at a rate sufficient to avoid flicker, independently of the host, thus freeing the host for other tasks. This architecture has become closely associated with the client–server architectures that are used in most systems.

1.7.2 Pipeline Architectures

The major advances in graphics architectures closely parallel the advances in workstations. In both cases, the ability to create special-purpose VLSI chips was the key enabling technological development. In addition, the availability of inexpensive solid-state memory led to the universality of raster displays. For computer graphics applications, the most important use of custom VLSI circuits has been in creating **pipeline** architectures.

The concept of pipelining is illustrated in Figure 1.30 for a simple arithmetic calculation. In our pipeline, there is an adder and a multiplier. If we use this configuration to compute $a + (b * c)$, the calculation takes one multiplication and one addition—the same amount of work required if we use a single processor to carry out both operations. However, suppose that we have to carry out the same computation with many values of a, b, and c. Now, the multiplier can pass on the results of its calculation to the adder and can start its next multiplication while the adder carries out the second step of the calculation on the first set of data. Hence, whereas it

FIGURE 1.30   Arithmetic pipeline.

takes the same amount of time to calculate the results for any one set of data, when we are working on two sets of data at one time, our total time for calculation is shortened markedly. Here the rate at which data flow through the system, the **throughput** of the system, has been doubled. Note that as we add more boxes to a pipeline, it takes more time for a single datum to pass through the system. This time is called the **latency** of the system; we must balance it against increased throughput in evaluating the performance of a pipeline.

We can construct pipelines for more complex arithmetic calculations that will afford even greater increases in throughput. Of course, there is no point in building a pipeline unless we will do the same operation on many data sets. But that is just what we do in computer graphics, where large sets of vertices and pixels must be processed in the same manner.

1.7.3 The Graphics Pipeline

We start with a set of objects. Each object comprises a set of graphical primitives. Each primitive comprises a set of vertices. We can think of the collection of primitive types and vertices as defining the **geometry** of the scene. In a complex scene, there may be thousands—even millions—of vertices that define the objects. We must process all these vertices in a similar manner to form an image in the framebuffer. If we think in terms of processing the geometry of our objects to obtain an image, we can employ the block diagram in Figure 1.31, which shows the four major steps in the imaging process:

1. Vertex processing

2. Clipping and primitive assembly

3. Rasterization

4. Fragment processing

In subsequent chapters, we discuss the details of these steps. Here we are content to preview these steps and show that they can be pipelined.

FIGURE 1.31   Geometric pipeline.

1.7.4 Vertex Processing

In the first block of our pipeline, each vertex is processed independently. The major function of this block is to carry out coordinate transformations. It can also compute a color for each vertex and change any other attributes of the vertex.

Many of the steps in the imaging process can be viewed as transformations between representations of objects in different coordinate systems. For example, in our discussion of the synthetic camera, we observed that a major part of viewing is to convert to a representation of objects from the system in which they were defined to a representation in terms of the coordinate system of the camera. A further example of a transformation arises when we finally put our images onto the output device. The internal representation of objects—whether in the camera coordinate system or perhaps in a system used by the graphics software—eventually must be represented in terms of the coordinate system of the display. We can represent each change of coordinate systems by a matrix. We can represent successive changes in coordinate systems by multiplying, or **concatenating**, the individual matrices into a single matrix. In Chapter 4, we examine these operations in detail. Because multiplying one matrix by another matrix yields a third matrix, a sequence of transformations is an obvious candidate for a pipeline architecture. In addition, because the matrices that we use in computer graphics will always be small (4×4), we have the opportunity to use parallelism within the transformation blocks in the pipeline.

Eventually, after multiple stages of transformation, the geometry is transformed by a projection transformation. We shall see in Chapter 5 that we can implement this step using 4×4 matrices, and thus projection fits in the pipeline. In general, we want to keep three-dimensional information as long as possible, as objects pass through the pipeline. Consequently, the projection transformation is somewhat more general than the projections in Section 1.5. In addition to retaining three-dimensional information, there is a variety of projections that we can implement. We shall see these projections in Chapter 5.

The assignment of vertex colors can be as simple as the program specifying a color or as complex as the computation of a color from a physically realistic lighting model that incorporates the surface properties of the object and the characteristic light sources in the scene. We shall discuss lighting models in Chapter 6.

1.7.5 Clipping and Primitive Assembly

The second fundamental block in the implementation of the standard graphics pipeline is for clipping and primitive assembly. We must do clipping because of the limitation that no imaging system can see the whole world at once. The human retina has a limited size corresponding to an approximately 90-degree field of view. Cameras have film of limited size, and we can adjust their fields of view by selecting different lenses.

We obtain the equivalent property in the synthetic camera by considering a **clipping volume**, such as the pyramid in front of the lens in Figure 1.18. The projections of objects within this volume appear in the image. Those that are outside do not and are said to be clipped out. Objects that straddle the edges of the clipping volume are partly visible in the image. Efficient clipping algorithms are developed in Chapter 8.

Clipping must be done on a primitive-by-primitive basis rather than on a vertex-by-vertex basis. Thus, within this stage of the pipeline, we must assemble sets of vertices into primitives, such as line segments and polygons, before clipping can take place. Consequently, the output of this stage is a set of primitives whose projections can appear in the image.

1.7.6 Rasterization

The primitives that emerge from the clipper are still represented in terms of their vertices and must be converted to pixels in the framebuffer. For example, if three vertices specify a triangle with a solid color, the rasterizer must determine which pixels in the framebuffer are inside the polygon. We discuss this rasterization (or scan conversion) process for line segments and polygons in Chapter 8. The output of the rasterizer is a set of **fragments** for each primitive. A fragment can be thought of as a potential pixel that carries with it information, including its color and location, that is used to update the corresponding pixel in the framebuffer. Fragments can also carry along depth information that allows later stages to determine whether a particular fragment lies behind other previously rasterized fragments for a given pixel.

1.7.7 Fragment Processing

The final block in our pipeline takes in the fragments generated by the rasterizer and updates the pixels in the framebuffer. If the application generated three-dimensional data, some fragments may not be visible because the surfaces that they define are behind other surfaces. The color of a fragment may be altered by texture mapping or bump mapping, as in Color Plates 6 and 7. The color of the pixel that corresponds to a fragment can also be read from the framebuffer and blended with the fragment's color to create translucent effects. These effects will be covered in Chapter 7.

1.8   PROGRAMMABLE PIPELINES

Graphics architectures have gone through multiple design cycles in which the importance of special-purpose hardware relative to standard CPUs has gone back and forth. However, the importance of the pipeline architecture has remained regardless of this cycle. None of the other approaches—ray tracing, radiosity, photon mapping—can achieve real-time behavior, that is, the ability to render complex dynamic scenes so that the viewer sees the display without defects. However, the term *real-time* is becoming increasingly difficult to define as graphics hardware improves. Although some approaches such as ray tracing can come close to real time, none can achieve the performance of pipeline architectures with simple application programs and simple GPU programs. Hence, the commodity graphics market is dominated by graphics cards that have pipelines built into the graphics processing unit. All of these commodity cards implement the pipeline that we have just described, albeit with more options, many of which we shall discuss in later chapters.

For many years, these pipeline architectures had a fixed functionality. Although the application program could set many parameters, the basic operations available within the pipeline were fixed. Recently, there has been a major advance in pipeline architectures. Both the vertex processor and the fragment processor are now programmable by the application programmer. One of the most exciting aspects of this advance is that many of the techniques that formerly could not be done in real time because they were not part of the fixed-function pipeline can now be done in real time. Bump mapping, which we illustrated in Color Plate 6, is but one example of an algorithm that is now programmable but formerly could only be done off-line.

Vertex shaders can alter the location or color of each vertex as it flows through the pipeline. Thus, we can implement a variety of light–material models or create new kinds of projections. Fragment shaders allow us to use textures in new ways and to implement other parts of the pipeline, such as lighting, on a per-fragment basis rather than per-vertex.

Programmability is now available at every level, including in handheld devices such as smart phones and tablets that include a color screen and a touch interface. Additionally, the speed and parallelism in programmable GPUs make them suitable for carrying out high-performance computing that does not involve graphics.

The latest versions of OpenGL have responded to these advances first by adding more and more programmability and options to the standard. Additionally, variants of OpenGL, like WebGL, have been created from the standard to better match the capabilities of the devices on which the API needs to run. For example, in mobile (i.e., handheld or embedded) devices, a version of OpenGL called OpenGL ES (where "ES" is an abbreviation for *embedded system*) is available on most smart phones and tablets. It has a reduced number of function calls but many of the same capabilities. Strictly speaking, WebGL is a version of OpenGL ES that works in web browsers, and may use OpenGL ES internally as its rendering engine. For those who started with the original fixed-function pipeline, it may take a little more time for our first programs, but the rewards will be significant.

1.9 PERFORMANCE CHARACTERISTICS

There are two fundamentally different types of processing in our architecture. At the front end, there is geometric processing, based on processing vertices through the various transformations: vertex shading, clipping, and primitive assembly. This processing is ideally suited for pipelining, and it usually involves floating-point calculations. The geometry engine developed by Silicon Graphics, Inc. (SGI) was a VLSI implementation for many of these operations in a special-purpose chip that became the basis for a series of fast graphics workstations. Later, floating-point accelerator chips put 4×4 matrix transformation units on the chip. Nowadays, graphics workstations and commodity graphics cards use graphics processing units (GPUs) that perform most of the graphics operations at the chip level. Pipeline architectures are the dominant type of high-performance system.

Beginning with rasterization and including many features that we discuss later, processing involves a direct manipulation of bits in the framebuffer. This back-end processing is fundamentally different from front-end processing, and, until recently, was implemented most effectively using architectures that had the ability to move blocks of bits quickly. The overall performance of a system was (and still is) characterized by how fast we can move geometric entities through the pipeline and by how many pixels per second we can alter in the framebuffer. Consequently, the fastest graphics workstations were characterized by geometric pipelines at the front ends and parallel bit processors at the back ends.

Until about 10 years ago, there was a clear distinction between front- and back-end processing and there were different components and boards dedicated to each. Now commodity graphics cards use GPUs that contain the entire pipeline within a single chip. The latest cards implement the entire pipeline using floating-point arithmetic and have floating-point framebuffers. These GPUs are so powerful that even the highest-level systems—systems that incorporate multiple pipelines—use these processors.

Since the operations performed when processing vertices and fragments are very similar, modern GPUs are **unified shading engines** that carry out both vertex and fragment shading concurrently. This processing might be limited to a single core in a small GPU (like in a mobile phone), or hundreds of processors in high-performance GPUs and gaming systems. This flexibility in processing allows GPUs to use their resources optimally regardless of an application's requirements.

Pipeline architectures dominate the graphics field, especially where real-time performance is of importance. Our presentation has made a case for using such an architecture to implement the hardware of a graphics system. Commodity graphics cards incorporate the pipeline within their GPUs. Today, even mobile phones can render millions of shaded texture-mapped triangles per second. However, we can also make as strong a case for pipelining being the basis of a complete software implementation of an API.

1.10 OPENGL VERSIONS AND WEBGL

So far we have not carefully distinguished between OpenGL and WebGL, other than to say WebGL is a version of OpenGL that runs in most modern browsers. To get a better understanding of the differences between various versions of OpenGL, it will help if we take a brief look at the history of OpenGL.

OpenGL is derived from IRIS GL, which had been developed as an API for SGI's revolutionary VLSI pipelined graphics workstations. IRIS GL was close enough to the hardware to allow applications to run efficiently and at the same time provided application developers with a high-level interface to graphics capabilities of the workstations. Because it was designed for a particular architecture and operating system, it was able to include both input and windowing functions in the API.

When OpenGL was developed as a cross-platform rendering API, the input and windowing functionality were eliminated. Consequently, although an application has to be recompiled for each architecture, the rendering part of the application code should be identical.

The first version of OpenGL (Version 1.0) was released in 1992. The API was based on the graphics pipeline architecture, but there was almost no ability to access the hardware directly. Early versions focused on **immediate mode graphics** in which graphic primitives were specified in the application and then immediately passed down the pipeline for display. Consequently, there was no memory of the primitives and their redisplay required them to be resent through the pipeline. New features were added incrementally in Versions 1.1–1.5. Other new features became available as extensions and, although not part of the standard, were supported on particular hardware. Version 2.0 was released in 2004 and Version 2.1 in 2006. Looking back, Version 2.0 was the key advance because it introduced the OpenGL Shading Language, which allowed application programmers to write their own shaders and exploit the power of GPUs. In particular, with better GPUs and more memory, geometry information could be stored or retained and **retained mode graphics** became increasingly more important.

Through Version 3.0 (2008), all versions of OpenGL were backward compatible so code developed on earlier versions was guaranteed to run on later versions. Hence, as new more complex versions were released, developers were forced to support older and less useful features. Version 3.0 announced that starting with Version 3.1, backward compatibility would no longer be provided by all implementations and, in particular, immediate mode was to be deprecated. Successive versions introduced more and more features. We are presently at Version 4.4. Although OpenGL has been ported to some other languages, the vast majority of applications are written in C and C++.

At the same time OpenGL was providing more and more capabilities to exploit the advances in GPU technology, there was an increasing demand for a simpler version that would run in embedded systems, smart phones, and other handheld devices. OpenGL ES 1.1 was released in 2008 and was based on OpenGL Version 1.5. OpenGL ES 2.0 is based on OpenGL Version 2.0 and supports only shader-based applications and not immediate mode. OpenGL ES Version 3.0 was released in 2013. We can now develop three-dimensional interactive applications for devices like smart phones whose hardware now contains GPUs.

Both the full OpenGL and the simpler OpenGL ES are designed to run locally and cannot take advantage of the Web. Thus, if we want to run an OpenGL application that we find on the Internet, we must download the binary file if it runs on the same architecture or download the source file and recompile. Even if we can run an application remotely and see its output on a local window, the application cannot use the GPU on the local system. WebGL is a JavaScript interface to OpenGL ES 2.0 that runs in modern web browsers. Thus, a user can visit the URL of a WebGL application on a remote system and, like other web applications, the program will run on the local system and make use of the local graphics hardware. WebGL and OpenGL ES 2.0 are fully shader based. Although WebGL does not have all the features of the latest versions of OpenGL, all the basic properties and capabilities of OpenGL are in WebGL. Consequently, we can almost always refer to OpenGL or WebGL without concern for the differences.

SUMMARY AND NOTES

In this chapter, we have set the stage for our top-down development of computer graphics. We presented the overall picture so that you can proceed to writing graphics application programs in the next chapter without feeling that you are working in a vacuum.

We have stressed that computer graphics is a method of image formation that should be related to classical methods of image formation—in particular, to image formation in optical systems such as cameras. In addition to explaining the pinhole camera, we have introduced the human visual system; both are examples of imaging systems.

We described multiple image formation paradigms, each of which has applicability in computer graphics. The synthetic-camera model has two important consequences for computer graphics. First, it stresses the independence of the objects and the viewer—a distinction that leads to a good way of organizing the functions that will be in a graphics library. Second, it leads to the notion of a pipeline architecture, in which each of the various stages in the pipeline performs distinct operations on geometric entities and then passes on the transformed objects to the next stage.

We also introduced the idea of tracing rays of light to obtain an image. This paradigm is especially useful in understanding the interaction between light and materials that is essential to physical image formation. Because ray tracing and other physically based strategies cannot render scenes in real time, we defer further discussion of them until Chapter 12.

The modeling–rendering paradigm is becoming increasingly important. A standard graphics workstation can generate millions of line segments or polygons per second at a resolution exceeding 2048×1546 pixels. Such a workstation can shade the polygons using a simple shading model and can display only visible surfaces at the same rate. However, realistic images may require a resolution of up to 6000×4000 pixels to match the resolution of film and may use light and material effects that cannot be implemented in real time. Even as the power of available hardware and software continues to grow, modeling and rendering have such different goals that we can expect the distinction between modeling and rendering to survive.

Our next step will be to explore the application side of graphics programming. We use the WebGL API, which is powerful, is supported on modern browsers, and has a distinct architecture that will allow us to use it to understand how computer graphics works, from an application program to a final image on a display.

SUGGESTED READINGS

There are many excellent graphics textbooks. The book by Newman and Sproull [New73] was the first to take the modern viewpoint of using the synthetic-camera model. The various editions of Foley et al. [Fol90, Fol94] and Hughes et al. [Hug13] have been the standard references. Other good texts include Hearn and Baker [Hea11], Hill [Hil07], and Shirley [Shi09].

Good general references include *Computer Graphics*, the quarterly journal of SIGGRAPH (the Association for Computing Machinery's Special Interest Group on Graphics), *IEEE Computer Graphics and Applications*, and *Visual Computer*. The proceedings of the annual SIGGRAPH conference include the latest techniques. These proceedings were formerly published as the summer issue of *Computer Graphics*. Now they are published as an issue of the *ACM Transactions on Graphics* and are available on DVD. Of particular interest to newcomers to the field are the state-of-the-art animations available from SIGGRAPH and the notes from tutorial courses taught at that conference, both of which are now available on DVD or in ACM's digital library.

Sutherland's doctoral dissertation, published as *Sketchpad: A Man–Machine Graphical Communication System* [Sut63], was probably the seminal paper in the development of interactive computer graphics. Sutherland was the first person to realize the power of the new paradigm in which humans interacted with images on a CRT display. Videotape copies of film of his original work are still available.

Tufte's books [Tuf83, Tuf90, Tuf97] show the importance of good visual design and contain considerable historical information on the development of graphics. The article by Carlbom and Paciorek [Car78] provides a good discussion of some of the relationships between classical viewing, as used in fields such as architecture, and viewing by computer.

Many books describe the human visual system. Pratt [Pra78] gives a good short discussion for working with raster displays. Also see Glassner [Gla95], Wyszecki and Stiles [Wys82], and Hall [Hal89].

EXERCISES

1.1   In representing a picture, one-bit- and eight-bit-deep frame buffers allow only two and 256 colors, respectively. How many bits does a full-color system allow?

1.2   In computer graphics, objects such as spheres are usually approximated by simpler objects constructed from flat polygons (polyhedra). Using lines of longitude and latitude, define a set of simple polygons that approximate a sphere centered at the origin. Can you use only quadrilaterals or only triangles?

1.3   A different method of approximating a sphere starts with a regular tetrahedron, which is constructed from four triangles. Find its vertices, assuming that it is centered at the origin and has one vertex on the y-axis. Derive an algorithm for obtaining increasingly closer approximations to a unit sphere, based on subdividing the faces of the tetrahedron.

1.4   Consider the clipping of a point in two dimensions against a circular clipping window. Show that you require only the coordinate of the point and the centre and radius of the circle to determine whether the point is not clipped or is clipped out completely.

1.5   For a line segment, show that clipping against the top of the clipping rectangle can be done independently of the clipping against the other sides. Use this result to show that a clipper can be implemented as a pipeline of four simpler clippers.

FIGURE 1.32   Perspective views of a cube.

1.6   Extend Exercise 1.4 to clipping against a three-dimensional sphere.

1.7   Consider the perspective views of the cube shown in Figure 1.32. The one on the left is called a *one-point perspective* because parallel lines in one direction of the cube—along the sides of the top—converge to a *vanishing point* in the image. In contrast, the image on the right is a *two-point perspective*. Characterize the particular relationship between the viewer, or a simple camera, and the cube that determines why one is a two-point perspective and the other a one-point perspective.

1.8   The memory in a frame buffer must be fast enough to allow the display to be refreshed at a rate sufficiently high to avoid flicker. A typical workstation display can have a resolution of 1024×1024 pixels. If it is refreshed 60 times per second, how fast must the memory be? That is, how much time can we take to read one pixel from memory? What is this number for a 600×800 display that operates at 50 Hz but is interlaced?

1.9   Movies are generally produced on 35-mm film that has a resolution of approximately 2000×3000 pixels. What implication does this resolution have for producing animated images for computers with resolution 600×800 pixels as compared with film?

1.10   Consider the design of a two-dimensional graphical API for a specific application, such as for VLSI design. List all the primitives and attributes that you would include in your system.

1.11   In a typical shadow-mask CRT, if we want to have a smooth display, the width of a pixel must be about three times the width of a triad. Assume that a monitor displays 600×800 pixels, has a CRT diameter of 50 cm, and has a CRT depth of 30 cm. Estimate the spacing between holes in the shadow mask.

1.12   An interesting exercise that should help you understand how rapidly graphics performance has improved is to go to the websites of some of the GPU manufacturers, such as NVIDIA, AMD, and Intel, and look at the specifications for their products. Often the specs for older cards and GPUs are still there. How rapidly has geometric performance improved? What about pixel processing? How has the cost per rendered triangle decreased?

CHAPTER 2

GRAPHICS PROGRAMMING

Our approach to computer graphics is programming oriented. Consequently, we want you to get started programming graphics as soon as possible. To this end, we will introduce a minimal application programming interface (API). This API will be sufficient to allow you to program many interesting two- and three-dimensional problems and to familiarize you with the basic graphics concepts.

We regard two-dimensional graphics as a special case of three-dimensional graphics. This perspective allows us to get started, even though we will touch on three-dimensional concepts lightly in this chapter. Our two-dimensional code will execute without modification on a three-dimensional system.

Our development will use a simple but informative problem: the Sierpinski gasket. It shows how we can generate an interesting and, to many people, unexpectedly sophisticated image using only a handful of graphics functions. We use WebGL as our API, but our discussion of the underlying concepts is broad enough to encompass most modern systems. In particular, our JavaScript code, which is required for WebGL, can easily be converted to C or C++ code for use with desktop OpenGL. The functionality that we introduce in this chapter is sufficient to allow you to write basic two- and three-dimensional programs that do not require user interaction.

2.1 THE SIERPINSKI GASKET

We will use as a sample problem the drawing of the Sierpinski gasket: an interesting shape that has a long history and is of interest in areas such as fractal geometry. The Sierpinski gasket is an object that can be defined recursively and randomly; in the limit, however, it has properties that are not at all random. We start with a two-dimensional version, but as we will see in Section 2.10, the three-dimensional version is almost identical.

Suppose that we start with three points in space. As long as the points are not collinear, they are the vertices of a unique triangle and also define a unique plane. We assume that this plane is the plane $z = 0$ and that these points, as specified in

69

some convenient coordinate system,[1] are $(x_1, y_1, 0)$, $(x_2, y_2, 0)$, and $(x_3, y_3, 0)$. The construction proceeds as follows:

1. Pick an initial point $\mathbf{p} = (x, y, 0)$ at random inside the triangle.

2. Select one of the three vertices at random.

3. Find the point $\mathbf{q}$ halfway between $\mathbf{p}$ and the randomly selected vertex.

4. Display $\mathbf{q}$ by putting some sort of marker, such as a small circle, at the corresponding location on the display.

5. Replace $\mathbf{p}$ with $\mathbf{q}$.

6. Return to step 2.

FIGURE 2.1   Generation of the Sierpinski gasket.

Thus, each time that we generate a new point, we display it on the output device. This process is illustrated in Figure 2.1, where $\mathbf{p}_0$ is the initial point, and $\mathbf{p}_1$ and $\mathbf{p}_2$ are the first two points generated by our algorithm.

Before we develop the program, you might try to determine what the resulting image will be. Try to construct it on paper; you might be surprised by your results.

A possible form for our graphics program might be this:

```
function sierpinski()
{
  initialize_the_system();
  p = find_initial_point();

  for (some_number_of_points) {
    q = generate_a_point(p);
    display_the_point(q);
    p = q;
  }

  cleanup();
}
```

This form can be converted into a real program fairly easily. However, even at this level of abstraction, we can see two other alternatives. Consider the pseudocode

```
function sierpinski()
{
  initialize_the_system();
  p = find_initial_point();

  for (some_number_of_points) {
    q = generate_a_point(p);
    store_the_point(q);
    p = q;
  }
```

---

1. In Chapter 4, we expand the concept of a coordinate system to the more general formulation of a *frame*.

```
    display_all_points();
    cleanup();
}
```

In this algorithm, we compute all the points first and put them into an array or some other data structure. We then display all the points through a single function call. This approach avoids the overhead of sending small amounts of data to the graphics processor for each point we generate at the cost having to store all the data. The strategy used in the first algorithm is known as **immediate mode graphics** and, until recently, was the standard method for displaying graphics, especially where interactive performance was needed. One consequence of immediate mode is that there is no memory of the geometric data. With our first example, if we want to display the points again, we would have to go through the entire creation and display process a second time.

In our second algorithm, because the data are stored in a data structure, we can redisplay the data, perhaps with some changes such as altering the color or changing the size of a displayed point, by resending the array without regenerating the points. The method of operation is known as **retained mode graphics** and goes back to some of the earliest special-purpose graphics display hardware. The architecture of modern graphics systems that employ a GPU leads to a third version of our program.

Our second approach has one major flaw. Suppose that we wish to redisplay the same objects in a different manner, as we might in an animation. The geometry of the objects is unchanged but the objects may be moving. Displaying all the points as we just outlined involves sending the data from the CPU to the GPU each time that we wish to display the objects in a new position. For large amounts of data, this data transfer is the major bottleneck in the display process. Consider the following alternative scheme:

```
function sierpinski()
{
    initialize_the_system();
    p = find_initial_point();

    for (some_number_of_points) {
        q = generate_a_point(p);
        store_the_point(q);
        p = q;
    }

    send_all_points_to_GPU();
    display_data_on_GPU();
    cleanup();
}
```

As before, we place data in an array, but now we have broken the display process into two parts: storing the data on the GPU and displaying the data that have been stored. If we only have to display our data once, there is no advantage over our previous method; but if we want to animate the display, our data are already on the GPU and redisplay does not require any additional data transfer, only a simple function call that alters the location of some spatial data describing the objects that have moved.

Although our final WebGL program will have a slightly different organization, we will follow this third strategy. We develop the full program in stages. First, we concentrate on the core: generating and displaying points. We must answer two questions:

- How do we represent points in space?
- Should we use two-dimensional, three-dimensional, or some other representation?

Once we answer these questions, we will be able to place our geometry on the GPU in a form that can be rendered. Then, we will be able to address how we view our objects using the power of programmable shaders.

2.2   PROGRAMMING TWO-DIMENSIONAL APPLICATIONS

For two-dimensional applications, such as the Sierpinski gasket, we could use a pen-plotter API, but such an approach would limit us. Instead, we choose to start with a three-dimensional world; we regard two-dimensional systems, such as the one on which we will produce our image, as special cases. Mathematically, we view the two-dimensional plane, or a simple two-dimensional curved surface, as a subspace of a three-dimensional space. Hence, statements—both practical and abstract—about the larger three-dimensional world hold for the simpler two-dimensional world.

We can represent a point in the plane $z = 0$ as $\mathbf{p} = (x, y, 0)$ in the three-dimensional world, or as $\mathbf{p} = (x, y)$ in the two-dimensional plane. WebGL, like most three-dimensional graphics systems, allows us to use either representation, with the underlying internal representation being the same, regardless of which form the programmer chooses. We can implement representations of points in a number of ways, but the simplest is to think of a three-dimensional point as being represented by a triplet $\mathbf{p} = (x, y, z)$ or a column matrix

$$\mathbf{p} = \begin{bmatrix} x \\ y \\ z \end{bmatrix},$$

whose components give the location of the point. For the moment, we can leave aside the question of the coordinate system in which $\mathbf{p}$ is represented.

We use the terms *vertex* and *point* in a somewhat different manner in WebGL. A **vertex** is a position in space; we use two-, three-, and four-dimensional spaces in computer graphics. We use vertices to specify the atomic geometric primitives that are recognized by our graphics system. The simplest geometric primitive is a point in space, which is usually specified by a single vertex. Two vertices can specify a line segment, a second primitive object; three vertices can specify either a triangle or a circle; four vertices can specify a quadrilateral; and so on. Two vertices can also specify either a circle or a rectangle. Likewise, three vertices can also specify three points or two connected line segments, and four vertices can specify a variety of objects including two triangles.

The heart of our Sierpinski gasket program is generating the points. In order to go from our third algorithm to a working WebGL program, we need to introduce a little more detail on WebGL. We want to start with as simple a program as possible. One simplification is to delay a discussion of coordinate systems and transformations among them by putting all the data we want to display inside a cube centered at the origin whose diagonal goes from $(-1, -1, -1)$ to $(1, 1, 1)$. This system, known as **clip coordinates**, is the one that our vertex shader uses to send information to the rasterizer. Objects outside this cube will be eliminated or **clipped** and cannot appear on the display. Later, we will learn to specify geometry in our application program in coordinates better suited for our application—**object coordinates**—and use transformations to convert the data to a representation in clip coordinates.

We could write the program using a simple array of two elements to hold the x and y values of each point. In JavaScript, we would construct such an array as follows:

```
var p = [x, y];
```

However, a JavaScript array is not just a collection of values as in C; it is an object with methods and properties, such as `length`. Thus, the code

```
var n = p.length;
```

sets `n` to 2. This difference is important when we send data to the GPU because the GPU expects just an array of numbers. Alternately, we can use a JavaScript typed array, such as

```
var p = new Float32Array([x, y]);
```

which is just a contiguous array of standard 32-bit floating-point numbers and thus can be sent to a GPU with WebGL. In either case, we can initialize the array component-wise as

```
p[0] = x;
p[1] = y;
```

We can generate far clearer code if we first define a two-dimensional point object and operations for this object. We have created such objects and methods and put them in a package `MV.js`. Within these objects, numerical data are stored using JavaScript arrays.

The functions and the three- and four-dimensional objects that we define in `MV.js` match the types in the OpenGL ES Shading Language (GLSL) that we use to write our shaders. Consequently, the use of `MV.js` should make all our coding examples clearer than if we had used ordinary JavaScript arrays. Although these functions have been defined to match GLSL, because JavaScript does not allow overloading of operators as do languages such as C++ and GLSL, we created functions for arithmetic operations using points, vectors, and other types. Nevertheless, code fragments using `MV.js`, such as

```
var a = vec2(1.0, 2.0);
var b = vec2(3.0, 4.0);
var c = add(a, b);  // returns a new vec2
```

can be used in the application and easily converted to code for a shader. We can access individual elements by indexing as we would an array (`a[0]` and `a[1]`). When we need to send data to the GPU, we will use the `flatten` function in `MV.js` to extract the data we need from our types and put them into formats required by the GPU.

The following code generates 5000 points starting with the vertices of a triangle that lies in the plane $z = 0$:

```
const numPoints = 5000;

var vertices = [
  vec2(-1.0, -1.0),
  vec2(0.0,  1.0),
  vec2(1.0, -1.0)
];

var u = scale(0.5, add(vertices[0], vertices[1]));
var v = scale(0.5, add(vertices[0], vertices[2]));
var p = scale(0.5, add(u, v));

points = [ p ];

for (var i = 1; i < numPoints; ++i) {
  var j = Math.floor(Math.random() * 3);

  p = scale(0.5, add(points[i-1], vertices[j]));
  points.push(p);
}
```

One feature of JavaScript arrays that we can use is the `push` method, which appends the passed object onto the end of the array. Using `push` avoids extraneous indexing and loops, thus simplifying our examples.

The initial point is the point we obtain by first finding the bisectors of two of the sides of the triangle determined by our three given vertices and then finding the bisector of the line segment connecting these two points. Such a point must lie inside the triangle as must all the points we generate by our algorithm. Consequently, none of our points will be clipped out.

The function `Math.random` is a standard random-number generator that produces a new random number between 0 and 1 each time it is called. We multiply each one by 3 and use the `Math.floor` function to reduce these random numbers to the three integers 0, 1, and 2. For a small number of iterations, the particular characteristics of the random-number generator are not crucial, and any other random-number generator should work at least as well as `Math.random`.

We intend to generate the points only once and then place them on the GPU. Hence, we make their creation part of an initialization function `init`. We specified our points in two dimensions. We could have also specified them in three dimensions by adding a z-coordinate, which is always zero, through the three-dimensional type in vec3. The changes to the code would be minimal. We would have the code lines

```
const numPoints = 5000;

var vertices = [
  vec3(-1.0, -1.0, 0.0),
  vec3(0.0, 1.0, 0.0),
  vec3(1.0, -1.0, 0.0)
];

var u = scale(0.5, add(vertices[0], vertices[1]));
var v = scale(0.5, add(vertices[0], vertices[2]));
var p = scale(0.5, add(u, v));

points = [ p ];

for (var i = 1; i < numPoints; ++i) {
  var j = Math.floor(Math.random() * 3);

  p = scale(0.5, add(points[i-1], vertices[j]));
  points.push(p);
}
```

as part of the initialization. We can see there is very little difference between this version and our original two-dimensional version. However, we still do not have a complete program; Figure 2.2 shows the output that we expect to see.

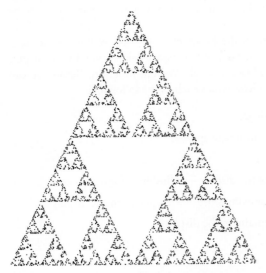

FIGURE 2.2   The Sierpinski gasket as generated with 5000 random points.

We can simplify the code even further using the mix function, which performs linear interpolation between two vectors. Mathematically, mix[2] can be written

$$\text{mix}(a, b, s) = s * a + (1 - s) * b.$$

Using mix, the code becomes

```
const numPoints = 5000;

var vertices = [
  vec3(-1.0, -1.0, 0.0),
  vec3(0.0, 1.0, 0.0),
  vec3(1.0, -1.0, 0.0)
];

var u = mix(vertices[0], vertices[1], 0.5);
var v = mix(vertices[0], vertices[2], 0.5);
var p = mix(u, v, 0.5);

points = [ p ];

for (var i = 0; points.length < numPoints; ++i) {
  var j = Math.floor(Math.random() * 3);

  p = mix(points[i], vertices[j], 0.5);
  points.push(p);
}
```

Note that because any three noncollinear points specify a unique plane, had we started with three points (x_1, y_1, z_1), (x_2, y_2, z_2), and (x_3, y_3, z_3) along with an initial point in the same plane, then the gasket would be generated in the plane specified by the original three vertices.

We have now written the core of the program. Although we have some data, we have not placed these data on the GPU nor have we asked the GPU to display anything. We have not even introduced a single WebGL function. Before we can display anything, we still have to address issues such as the following:

1. In what colors are we drawing?

2. Where on the display does our image appear?

3. How large will the image be?

4. How do we create an area of the display—a window—for our image?

5. How much of our infinite drawing surface will appear on the display?

6. How long will the image remain on the display?

---

2. Some other shader languages such as Cg use the name *lerp* rather than *mix*.

The answers to all these questions are important, although initially they may appear to be peripheral to our major concerns. As we will see, the basic code that we develop to answer these questions and to control the placement and appearance of our renderings will not change substantially across programs. Hence, the effort that we expend now will be repaid later.

2.3 THE WEBGL APPLICATION PROGRAMMING INTERFACE

We have the heart of a simple graphics program; now, we want to gain control over how our objects appear on the display. We also want to control the flow of the program, and we have to interact with the window system. Before completing our program, we describe the WebGL application programming interface (API) in more detail. Because vertices are represented in the same manner internally, whether they are specified as two- or three-dimensional entities, everything that we do here will be equally valid in three dimensions. Of course, we can do much more in three dimensions, but we are only getting started. In this chapter, we concentrate on how to specify primitives to be displayed.

As we saw in Chapter 1, WebGL is OpenGL ES 2.0 in JavaScript. More specifically, it renders within HTML5's Canvas element and thus allows us to run three-dimensional applications with most recent web browsers. Although WebGL is a smaller version of the full desktop OpenGL, its structure is similar to that of most modern graphics APIs. Hence, any effort that you put into learning WebGL will carry over to other software systems, including desktop OpenGL and DirectX. Even though WebGL is easy to learn compared to other APIs, it is nevertheless powerful. It supports the simple two- and three-dimensional programs that we will develop in Chapters 2 through 7; it also supports the advanced rendering techniques that we study in Chapters 9 through 12.

Our prime goal is to study computer graphics; we are using an API to help us attain that goal. Consequently, we do not present all WebGL functions, and we omit many details. However, our sample programs will be complete. More detailed information on WebGL and on other APIs is given in the Suggested Readings section at the end of the chapter.

2.3.1 Graphics Functions

Our basic model of a graphics package is a **black box**, a term that engineers use to denote a system whose properties are described only by its inputs and outputs; we may know nothing about its internal workings. We can think of the graphics system as a box whose inputs are function calls from an application program; measurements from input devices, such as the mouse and keyboard; and possibly other input, such as messages from the operating system. The outputs are primarily the graphics sent to our output devices. For now, we can take the simplified view of inputs as function calls and outputs as primitives displayed on our browser, as shown in Figure 2.3.

A graphics system performs multiple tasks to produce output and handle user input. An API for interfacing with this system can contain hundreds of individual functions. It will be helpful to divide these functions into seven major groups:

FIGURE 2.3   Graphics system as a black box.

1. Primitive functions

2. Attribute functions

3. Viewing functions

4. Transformation functions

5. Input functions

6. Control functions

7. Query functions

Although we will focus on WebGL, all graphics APIs support similar functionality. What differs among APIs is where these functions are supported. WebGL is designed around a pipeline architecture and modern versions are based on using programmable shaders. Consequently, WebGL and other APIs such as DirectX that support a similar architecture will have much in common whereas WebGL and an API for a ray tracer will have less overlap. Nevertheless, regardless of the underlying architecture and API, we still have to address all the seven tasks.

The **primitive functions** define the low-level objects or atomic entities that our system can display. Depending on the API, the primitives can include points, line segments, polygons, pixels, text, and various types of curves and surfaces. WebGL supports a very limited set of primitives directly, only points, line segments, and triangles. Support for other primitives comes from the application approximating them with the supported primitives. For the most important objects such as regular polyhedra, quadrics, and Bézier curves and surfaces that are not directly supported by WebGL, there are libraries that provide the necessary code. Support for expanded sets of primitives is usually done with great efficiency through programmable shaders.

If primitives are the *what* of an API—the primitive objects that can be displayed—then attributes are the *how*. That is, the attributes govern the way that a primitive appears on the display. **Attribute functions** allow us to perform operations ranging from choosing the color with which we display a line segment, to picking a pattern with which to fill the inside of a polygon, to selecting a typeface for the titles on a graph. In WebGL, we can set colors by passing the information from the application to the shader or by having a shader compute a color; for example, through a lighting model that uses data specifying light sources and properties of the surfaces in our model.

Our synthetic camera must be described if we are to create an image. As we saw in Chapter 1, we must describe the camera's position and orientation in our world and must select the equivalent of a lens. This process will not only fix the view but also allow us to clip out objects that are too close or too far away. The **viewing functions** allow us to specify various views, although APIs differ in the degree of flexibility they provide in choosing a view. WebGL does not provide any viewing functions but relies on the use of transformations either in the application or in the shaders to provide the desired view.

One of the characteristics of a good API is that it provides the user with a set of **transformation functions** that allows her to carry out transformations of objects, such as rotation, translation, and scaling. Our developments of viewing in Chapter 5 and of modeling in Chapter 9 will make heavy use of matrix transformations. In WebGL, we carry out transformations by forming them in our applications and then applying them either in the application or in the shaders.

For interactive applications, an API must provide a set of **input functions** to allow us to deal with the diverse forms of input that characterize modern graphics systems. We need functions to deal with devices such as keyboards, mice, and data tablets. In Chapter 3, we will introduce functions for working with different input modes and with a variety of input devices.

In any real application, we also have to worry about handling the complexities of working in a multiprocessing, multiwindow environment—usually an environment where we are connected to a network and there are other users. The **control functions** enable us to communicate with the window system, to initialize our programs, and to deal with any errors that take place during the execution of our programs.

If we are to write device-independent programs, we should expect the implementation of the API to take care of differences between devices, such as how many colors are supported or the size of the display. However, there are applications where we need to know some properties of the particular implementation. For example, we would probably choose to do things differently if we knew in advance that we were working with a display that could support only two colors rather than millions of colors. More generally, within our applications we can often utilize other information within the API, including camera parameters or values in the framebuffer. A good API provides this information through a set of **query functions**.

2.3.2 The Graphics Pipeline and State Machines

If we put together some of these perspectives on graphics APIs, we can obtain another view, one closer to the way WebGL, in particular, is actually organized and implemented. We can think of the entire graphics system as a **state machine**, a black box that contains a finite-state machine. This state machine has inputs that come from the application program. These inputs may change the state of the machine or can cause the machine to produce a visible output. From the perspective of the API, graphics functions are of two types: those that cause primitives to flow through a pipeline inside the state machine, and those that alter the state of the machine. In WebGL, there are only two functions that can produce output. Most set the state, either by enabling various WebGL features—hidden-surface removal, blending—or by setting parameters used for rendering.

Until recently, OpenGL defined many state variables and contained separate functions for setting the values of individual variables. The latest versions and WebGL have eliminated most of these variables and functions. Instead, the application program can define its own state variables and use them or send their values to the shaders.

One important consequence of the state machine view is that most parameters are persistent; their values remain unchanged until we explicitly change them through functions that alter the state. For example, once we set the color for clearing the screen, that color remains the *current clear color* until it is changed through a color-altering function. Another consequence of this view is that attributes that we may conceptualize as bound to objects—a red line or a blue circle—are in fact part of the state, and a line will be drawn in red only if the current color state calls for drawing in red. Although within our applications it is usually harmless, and often preferable, to think of attributes as bound to primitives, there can be annoying side effects if we neglect to make state changes when needed or lose track of the current state.

2.3.3 OpenGL and WebGL

Although WebGL is specifically designed to work within a web browser, it is based on OpenGL, which was developed for a workstation environment. It should be helpful at this point to look at the two environments in a bit more detail.

In desktop OpenGL, the core functions are in a library named GL (or OpenGL in Windows). Shaders are written in the OpenGL Shading Language (GLSL). In addition to the core OpenGL library, OpenGL needs at least one more library to provide the "glue" between OpenGL and the local window system. Although there are libraries that provide a basic standard interface between OpenGL and the multiple window systems, applications must be recompiled for each platform.

Because WebGL runs within the browser, we do not have to adapt to the local system. Both desktop OpenGL and WebGL make heavy use of defined constants to increase code readability and avoid the use of magic numbers. In all our WebGL applications, we will see these constants as strings such as gl.FILL and gl.POINTS, where gl is the name we assign to the WebGL context.

Neither OpenGL nor WebGL is object oriented. Consequently, OpenGL and, to a lesser extent, WebGL must support a variety of data types through multiple forms for many functions. For example, we will use various forms of the function gl.uniform to transfer data to shaders. If we transfer a single floating-point number such as a time value, we will use gl.uniform1f. We would use gl.uniform3fv to transfer a position in three dimensions through a pointer to a three-dimensional array of values. Later, we will use the form gl.uniformMatrix4fv to transfer a 4×4 matrix. Regardless of which form an application programmer chooses, the underlying representation is the same, just as the plane on which we are constructing the gasket can be looked at as either a two-dimensional space or the subspace of a three-dimensional space corresponding to the plane $z = 0$. Because JavaScript has only a single numerical type, WebGL applications can be simpler and we only need to worry about data types in operations which involve the transfer of data between the CPU and the GPU.

2.3.4 The WebGL Interface

WebGL can be integrated with other web applications, libraries, and tools. Because our focus is on graphics, we will start with a minimum number of web concepts and expand on them later. The first fundamental point is that WebGL applications are written in JavaScript.[3] JavaScript is an interpreted language that shares much of its syntax with high-level languages, such as C, C++, and Java, but has many features drawn from other languages. In particular, JavaScript is object oriented in a very different way from C++ or Java, has very few native types, and has functions as first-class objects. The key feature of JavaScript is that it is the language of the Web and thus all modern browsers will execute code written in JavaScript.[4]

The basic process of running a WebGL application is usually as follows. Suppose that we want to run a WebGL application that is located somewhere on the World Wide Web. The application is located on a computer called the **server**, and the computer where we run it is known as the **client**. We will discuss clients and servers more in Chapter 3. The browser is a client that can access the application through an address called its **Uniform Resource Locator** or **URL**.

Although our browser may recognize some other types of files, we will always start with a web page written in the **Hypertext Markup Language**. In particular, we use **HTML5**, which is the standard for modern browsers. We will usually refer to it just as HTML. The file describes a document or **web page**. Web pages obey the standard **Document Object Model** or **DOM**. Hence, each web page is a document object for which HTML is the standard description language. At its heart, an HTML document comprises **tags** and data. Tags denote the beginning and end of various elements such as text, images, and layout information, including fonts and colors. As we will see in our examples, both our JavaScript application and our shaders are page elements described between `<script>` and `</script>` tags. All browsers can execute the JavaScript code identified by a script tag. The HTML Canvas element provides a drawing surface for applications executed in the browser. In most recent browsers, the Canvas element provides the drawing surface for three-dimensional graphics applications using WebGL. Because all these files are in JavaScript, the browser can execute them with its JavaScript and WebGL engines.

We will discover other HTML elements in Chapter 3 when we discuss interactivity. These elements will describe graphical user interface (GUI) elements such as buttons and slide bars. This organization is illustrated in Figure 2.4.

Note that this process of reading and executing a web page also works locally. That is, we can load a local HTML file into our browser. On most systems, we can execute it directly because any HTML file will invoke a browser. At this point, if you have not done so already, you should test your browser by running one of the applications from the book's website.

2.3.5 Coordinate Systems

If we look back at our Sierpinski gasket code, you may be puzzled about how to interpret the values of x, y, and z in our specification of vertices. In what units are

---

3. There are packages available that can convert code from other languages, such as Java, to JavaScript.

4. The standard for JavaScript is set by the European Computer Manufacturers Association and the official name for JavaScript is ECMAScript.

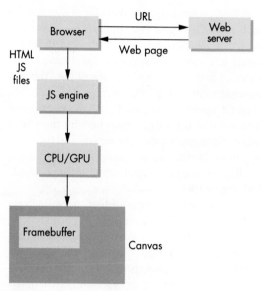

FIGURE 2.4   WebGL organization.

they? Are they in feet, meters, microns? Where is the origin? In each case, the simple answer is that it is up to you.

Originally, graphics systems required the user to specify all information, such as vertex locations, directly in units of the display device. If that were true for high-level application programs, we would have to talk about points in terms of screen locations in pixels or centimeters from a corner of the display. There are obvious problems with this method, not the least of which is the absurdity of using distances on the computer screen to describe phenomena where the natural unit might be light-years (such as in displaying astronomical data) or microns (for integrated circuit design). One of the major advances in graphics software systems occurred when the graphics systems allowed users to work in any coordinate system that they desired. The advent of **device-independent graphics** freed application programmers from worrying about the details of input and output devices. The user's coordinate system became known as the **world coordinate system**, or the **application** or **object coordinate system**. Within the slight limitations of floating-point arithmetic on our computers, we can use any numbers that fit our application.

For now we will refer to the units that the application program uses to specify vertex positions as **vertex coordinates**. In most applications, vertex coordinates will be the same as object or world coordinates, but, depending on what we choose to do or not do in our shaders, vertex coordinates can be one of the other internal coordinate systems used in the pipeline. We will discuss these other coordinate systems in Chapters 4 and 5.

Units on the display were first called **physical-device coordinates** or just **device coordinates**. For raster devices, such as most CRT and flat-panel displays, we use the term **window coordinates** or **screen coordinates**. Window coordinates are always

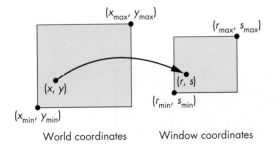

FIGURE 2.5   Mapping from vertex coordinates to window coordinates.

expressed in some integer type, because the center of any pixel in the framebuffer must be located on a fixed grid or, equivalently, because pixels are inherently discrete and we specify their locations using integers.

At some point, the values in vertex coordinates must be mapped to window coordinates, as shown in Figure 2.5. The graphics system, rather than the user, is responsible for this task, and the mapping is performed automatically as part of the rendering process. As we will see in the next few sections, to define this mapping the user needs to specify only a few parameters—such as the area of the world that she would like to see and the size of the display. However, between the application and the framebuffer are the two shaders and the rasterizer, and as we shall see when we discuss viewing, there are three other intermediate coordinate systems of importance.

2.4   PRIMITIVES AND ATTRIBUTES

Within the graphics community, there has been an ongoing debate about which primitives should be supported in an API. The debate is an old one and has never been fully resolved. On the minimalist side, the contention is that an API should contain a small set of primitives that all hardware can be expected to support. In addition, the primitives should be orthogonal, each giving a capability unobtainable from the others. Minimal systems typically support lines, triangles, and points, all of which can be generated efficiently in hardware. On the other end are systems that can also support a variety of primitives, such as text, circles, curves, surfaces, and solids. The argument here is that users need more complex primitives to build sophisticated applications easily. However, because few hardware systems can be expected to support the large set of primitives that is the union of all the desires of the user community, a program developed with such a system probably would not be portable, because few implementations could be expected to support the entire set of primitives.

As graphics hardware has improved and real-time performance has become measured in the tens of millions of triangles per second, the balance has tilted toward supporting a minimum set of primitives. One reason is that GPUs achieve their speed largely because they are optimized for points, lines, and triangles. We will develop code later that will approximate various curves and surfaces with primitives that are supported by GPUs.

FIGURE 2.6   Simplified WebGL pipeline.

We can separate primitives into two classes: **geometric primitives** and **image**, or **raster, primitives**. Geometric primitives are specified in the problem domain and include points, line segments, polygons, curves, and surfaces. These primitives pass through a geometric pipeline, as shown in Figure 2.6, where they are subject to a series of geometric operations that determine whether a primitive needs to be clipped, where on the display it appears if it is visible, and the rasterization of the primitive into pixels in the framebuffer. Because geometric primitives exist in a two- or three-dimensional space, they can be manipulated by operations such as rotation and translation. In addition, they can be used as building blocks for other geometric objects using these same operations. Raster primitives, such as arrays of pixels, lack geometric properties and cannot be manipulated in space in the same way as geometric primitives. They pass through a separate parallel pipeline on their way to the framebuffer. We will defer our discussion of raster primitives until Chapter 7 when we introduce texture mapping.

The basic WebGL geometric primitives are specified by sets of vertices. An application starts by computing vertex data—positions and other attributes—and putting the results into arrays that are sent to the GPU for display. When we want to display some geometry, we execute functions whose parameters specify how the vertices are to be interpreted. For example, we can display the `numPoints` vertices we computed for the Sierpinski gasket, starting with the first vertex, as points using the function call

```
gl.drawArrays(gl.POINTS, 0, numPoints);
```

after they have been placed on the GPU. Here `gl` is the WebGL context object and `drawArrays` is the WebGL function that initiates the rendering of primitives. We will discuss the WebGL context in more detail in Section 2.8.

All WebGL geometric primitives are variants of points, line segments, and triangular polygons. A point can be displayed as a single pixel or a small group of pixels. Finite sections of lines between two vertices, called **line segments**—in contrast to lines that are infinite in extent—are of great importance in geometry and computer graphics. You can use line segments to define approximations to curves, or you can use a sequence of line segments to connect data values for a graph. You can also use line segments to display the edges of closed objects, such as polygons, that have in-

FIGURE 2.7   Point and line-segment types.

teriors. Consequently, it is often helpful to think in terms of both vertices and line segments.

If we wish to display points or line segments, we have a few choices in WebGL (Figure 2.7). The primitives and their `type` specifications include the following:

Points (gl.POINTS) Each vertex is displayed at a size of at least one pixel.

Line segments (gl.LINES) The line-segment type causes successive pairs of vertices to be interpreted as the endpoints of individual segments. Note that successive segments usually are disconnected because the vertices are processed on a pairwise basis.

Polylines (gl.LINE_STRIP, gl.LINE_LOOP) If successive vertices (and line segments) are to be connected, we can use the line strip, or **polyline** form. Many curves can be approximated via a suitable polyline. If we wish the polyline to be closed, we can locate the final vertex in the same place as the first, or we can use the gl.LINE_LOOP type, which will draw a line segment from the final vertex to the first, thus creating a closed path.

FIGURE 2.8   Filled objects.

2.4.1 Polygon Basics

Line segments and polylines can model the edges of objects, but closed objects have interiors (Figure 2.8). Usually we reserve the name **polygon** for an object that has a border that can be described by a line loop but also has a well-defined interior.[5] Polygons play a special role in computer graphics because we can display them rapidly and use them to approximate arbitrary surfaces. The performance of graphics systems is characterized by the number of polygons per second that can be rendered.[6] We can render a polygon in a variety of ways: In WebGL, polygons are always filled. We can render its edges using line segments and render its interior with a pattern using textures, as shown in Figure 2.9. Although the outer edges of a polygon are defined easily by an ordered list of vertices, if the interior is not well defined, then the list of vertices may not be rendered at all or rendered in an undesirable manner. Three

FIGURE 2.9   Methods of displaying a polygon.

5. The term *fill area* is sometimes used instead of *polygon*.

6. Measuring polygon rendering speeds involves both the number of vertices and the number of pixels inside.

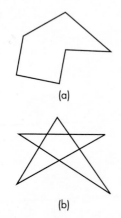

(a)

(b)

FIGURE 2.10   Polygons. (a) Simple. (b) Nonsimple.

FIGURE 2.11   Convexity.

properties will ensure that a polygon will be displayed correctly: It must be simple, convex, and flat.

In two dimensions, as long as no two edges of a polygon cross each other, we have a **simple** polygon. As we can see in Figure 2.10, simple two-dimensional polygons have well-defined interiors. Although the locations of the vertices determine whether or not a polygon is simple, the cost of testing is sufficiently high (see Exercise 2.12) that most graphics systems require that the application program do any necessary testing. We can ask what a graphics system will do if it is given a nonsimple polygon to display and whether there is a way to define an interior for a nonsimple polygon. We will examine these questions further in Chapter 8.

From the perspective of implementing a practical algorithm to fill the interior of a polygon, simplicity alone is often not enough. Some APIs guarantee a consistent fill from implementation to implementation only if the polygon is convex. An object is **convex** if all points on the line segment between any two points inside the object, or on its boundary, are inside the object. Thus, in Figure 2.11, p_1 and p_2 are arbitrary points inside a polygon and the entire line segment connecting them is inside the polygon. Although so far we have been dealing with only two-dimensional objects, this definition makes reference neither to the type of object nor to the number of dimensions. Convex objects include triangles, tetrahedra, rectangles, circles, spheres, and parallelepipeds (Figure 2.12). There are various tests for convexity (see Exercise 2.19). However, like simplicity testing, convexity testing is expensive and usually left to the application program.

In three dimensions, polygons present a few more difficulties because, unlike two-dimensional objects, all the vertices that specify the polygon need not lie in the same plane. One property that most graphics systems exploit, and that is the basis of WebGL polygons, is that any three vertices that are not collinear determine both a triangle and the plane in which that triangle lies. Hence, if we always use triangles, we are safe—we can be sure that these objects will be rendered correctly. Often, we are almost forced to use triangles because typical rendering algorithms are guaranteed to be correct only if the vertices form a flat convex polygon.

2.4.2 Polygons in WebGL

Returning to the WebGL types, the only polygons (Figure 2.13) that WebGL supports are triangles. Triangles can be displayed in three ways: as points corresponding to the

FIGURE 2.12   Convex objects.

FIGURE 2.13   Points and triangles types.

FIGURE 2.14   Triangle strip and triangle fan.

vertices using the point type, as edges using one of the line types, or with the interiors filled using a triangle type. If we want to draw a polygon that is filled and display its edges, then we have to render it twice, first as a filled polygon and then as a line loop with the same vertices.

Here are the triangle types:

Triangles (gl.TRIANGLES)   The edges are the same as they would be if we used line loops. Each successive group of three vertices specifies a new triangle.

Strips and fans (gl.TRIANGLE_STRIP, gl.TRIANGLE_FAN)   These objects are based on groups of triangles that share vertices and edges. In the triangle strip, for example, each additional vertex is combined with the previous two vertices to define a new triangle (Figure 2.14). A triangle fan is based on one fixed point. The next two points determine the first triangle, and subsequent triangles are formed from one new point, the previous point, and the first (fixed) point.

2.4.3 Approximating a Sphere

Fans and strips allow us to approximate many curved surfaces simply. For example, one way to construct an approximation to a sphere is to use a set of polygons defined by lines of longitude and latitude, as shown in Figure 2.15. We can do so very efficiently using triangle strips and fans. Consider a unit sphere. We can describe it by the following three equations:

$$x(\theta, \phi) = \sin \theta \cos \phi$$

$$y(\theta, \phi) = \cos \theta \cos \phi$$

$$z(\theta, \phi) = \sin \phi.$$

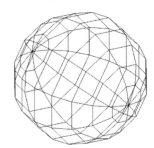

FIGURE 2.15   Sphere approximation showing triangle fans at poles.

Suppose that we decide how many circles of constant longitude and how many of constant latitude we want. If we consider two adjacent circles of constant latitude and two adjacent circles of constant longitude, they intersect in four places on each hemisphere. We can use these points to approximate the sphere in this region with a quadrilateral. In WebGL, we would then use two triangles to render the quadrilateral. Even better, we could approximate the sphere between two adjacent circles of constant latitude with a single triangle strip. However, we have a problem at the poles, where we can no longer use strips because all circles of longitude converge there. We can, however, use two triangle fans, one at each pole. Thus we do a a series of renders with `gl.drawArrays(gl.TRIANGLE_STRIP, ...)` and two with `gl.drawArrays(gl.TRIANGLE_FAN, ...)`.

2.4.4 Triangulation

We have been using the terms *polygon* and *triangle* somewhat interchangeably. If we are interested in objects with interiors, general polygons are problematic. A set of vertices may not all lie in the same plane or may specify a polygon that is neither simple nor convex. Such problems do not arise with triangles. As long as the three vertices of a triangle are not collinear, its interior is well defined and the triangle is simple, flat, and convex. Consequently, triangles are easy to render, and for these reasons triangles are the only fillable geometric entity that WebGL recognizes. In practice we need to deal with more general polygons. The usual strategy is to start with a list of vertices and generate a set of triangles consistent with the polygon defined by the list, a process known as **triangulation**.

Figure 2.16 shows a convex polygon and two different triangulations. Although every set of vertices can be triangulated, not all triangulations are equivalent. Consider the quadrilateral in Figure 2.17(a). If we triangulate it as in Figure 2.17(b), we create two long thin triangles rather than two triangles closer to being equilateral as in Figure 2.17(c). As we shall see when we discuss lighting in Chapter 6, long thin triangles can lead to visual artifacts when rendered. There are some simple algorithms that work for planar convex polygons. We can start with the first three vertices and form a triangle. We can then remove the second vertex from the list of vertices and repeat the process until we have only three vertices left, which form the final triangle. This process is illustrated in Figure 2.18, but it does not guarantee a good set of triangles nor can it handle concave polygons. In Chapter 8, we will discuss the triangulation of

(a)   (b)   (c)

FIGURE 2.16   (a) Two-dimensional polygon. (b) A triangulation. (c) Another triangulation.

FIGURE 2.17   (a) Quadrilateral. (b) A triangulation. (c) Another triangulation.

FIGURE 2.18   Recursive triangulation of a convex polygon.

simple but nonconvex polygons as part of rasterization. This technique allows us to render polygons more general than triangles.

We will delay a discussion of more general triangulation algorithms until we discuss curves and surfaces in Chapter 11. One reason for this delay is that there are a number of related processes that arise when we consider modeling surfaces. For example, laser scanning technology allows us to gather millions of unstructured three-dimensional vertices. We then have to form a surface from these vertices, usually in the form of a mesh of triangles. The **Delaunay triangulation** algorithm finds a best triangulation in the sense that when we consider the circle determined by any triangle, no other vertex lies in this circle. Triangulation is a special case of the more general problem of **tessellation**, which divides a polygon into a polygonal mesh, not all of which need be triangles. General tessellation algorithms are complex, especially when the initial polygon may contain holes.

2.4.5 Text

Graphical output in applications such as data analysis and display requires annotation, such as labels on graphs. Although in nongraphical programs textual output is the norm, text in computer graphics is problematic. In nongraphical applications, we are usually content with a simple set of characters, always displayed in the same manner. In computer graphics, however, we often wish to display text in a multitude of fashions by controlling type styles, sizes, colors, and other parameters. We also want to have available a choice of fonts. Type families are groups of fonts of a particular design, such as Times Roman, Computer Modern, or Helvetica.

Older graphics systems supported two types of text: stroke and raster. **Stroke text** (Figure 2.19) is constructed like other geometric objects. We use vertices to define line segments or curves that outline each character. If the characters are defined by closed boundaries, we can fill them. The advantage of stroke text is that it can be defined to have all the detail of any other object, and because it is defined in the same way as

Computer

Graphics

FIGURE 2.19   Stroke text (Post-Script font).

FIGURE 2.20   Raster text.

FIGURE 2.21   Raster-character replication.

other graphical objects are, it can be manipulated by our standard transformations and viewed like any other graphical primitive. Using transformations, we can make a stroke character bigger or rotate it, retaining its detail and appearance. Consequently, we need to define a character only once, and we can use transformations to generate it at the desired size and orientation.

Raster text (Figure 2.20) is simple and fast. Characters are defined as rectangles of bits called **bit blocks**. Each block defines a single character by the pattern of 0 and 1 bits in the block. A raster character can be placed in the framebuffer rapidly by a **bit-block-transfer (bitblt)** operation, which moves the block of bits using a single function call.

You can increase the size of raster characters by **replicating** or duplicating pixels, a process that gives larger characters a blocky appearance (Figure 2.21). Other transformations of raster characters, such as rotation, may not make sense, because the transformation may move the bits defining the character to locations that do not correspond to the location of pixels in the framebuffer.

As graphics systems focused on using the GPU for rendering lines and triangles, text primitives were eliminated. Because WebGL runs inside the browser, we can display better-looking text using a separate HTML canvas object rather than trying to generate text within the WebGL API.

2.4.6 Curved Objects

The primitives in our basic set have all been defined through vertices. With the exception of the point type, all consist of line segments or use line segments to define the boundary of a region that can be filled with a solid color or a pattern. We can take two approaches to creating a richer set of objects.

First, we can use the primitives that we have to approximate curves and surfaces. For example, if we want a circle, we can use a regular polygon of n sides. Likewise, we have approximated a sphere with triangles and quadrilaterals. More generally, we approximate a curved surface by a mesh of convex polygons—a tessellation—that can be produced either at the rendering stage or within the user program.

The other approach, which we will explore in Chapter 11, is to start with the mathematical definitions of curved objects and then build graphics functions to implement those objects. Objects such as quadric surfaces and parametric polynomial curves and surfaces are well understood mathematically, and we can specify them through sets of vertices. For example, we can specify a sphere by its center and a point on its surface, or we can specify a cubic polynomial curve using data at four points.

2.4.7 Attributes

Although we can describe a geometric object through a set of vertices, a given object can be displayed in many different ways. Properties that describe how an object should be rendered are called **attributes**. Available attributes depend on the type of object. For example, a line could be black or green. It could be solid or dashed. A polygon could be filled with a single color or with a pattern. We could display it as filled or only by its edges. Several of these attributes are shown in Figure 2.22 for lines and polygons.

Attributes such as the color of a cube may be associated with, or **bound** to, geometric objects. Often we will find it better to model an object such as the cube by its individual faces and to specify attributes for the faces. Hence, a cube would be green because its six faces are green. Each face could then be described by two triangles, so ultimately a green cube would be rendered as 12 green triangles.

If we go one step further, we see that each of the triangles is specified by three vertices. In a pipeline architecture, each vertex is processed independently through a vertex shader. Hence, we can associate properties with each vertex. For example, if we assign a different color to each vertex of a polygon, the rasterizer can interpolate these vertex colors to obtain different colors for each fragment. These **vertex attributes** may also be dependent on the application. For example, in a simulation of heat

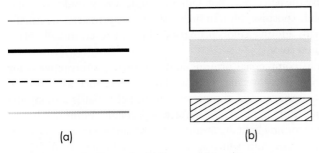

       (a)   (b)

FIGURE 2.22   Attributes for (a) lines and (b) polygons.

distribution of some object, the application might determine a temperature for each vertex defining the object. In Chapter 4, we will include vertex attribute data with our vertex locations in the array that is sent to the GPU.

Although the notion of current state works well for interactive applications, it is inconsistent with our physical intuition. A box is green or red. It either contains a pattern on its surfaces or it doesn't. Object-oriented graphics takes a fundamentally different approach in which attributes are part of a geometric object. In Chapter 9, we will discuss scene graphs, which are fundamental to systems such as Open Scene Graph, and we will see that they provide another higher-level object-oriented approach to computer graphics.

2.5   COLOR

Color is one of the most interesting aspects of both human perception and computer graphics. We can use the model of the human visual system from Chapter 1 to obtain a simple but useful color model. Full exploitation of the capabilities of the human visual system using computer graphics requires a far deeper understanding of the human anatomy, physiology, and psychophysics. We will present a more sophisticated development in Chapter 8.

A visible color can be characterized by a function $C(\lambda)$ that occupies wavelengths from about 350 to 780 nm, as shown in Figure 2.23. The value for a given wavelength λ in the visible spectrum gives the intensity of that wavelength in the color.

Although this characterization is accurate in terms of a physical color whose properties we can measure, it does not take into account how we *perceive* color. As noted in Chapter 1, the human visual system has three types of cones responsible for color vision. Hence, our brains do not receive the entire distribution $C(\lambda)$ for a given color but rather three values—the **tristimulus values**—that are the responses of the three types of cones to the color. This reduction of a color to three values leads to the **basic tenet of three-color theory**: *If two colors produce the same tristimulus values, then they are visually indistinguishable.*

A consequence of this tenet is that, in principle, a display needs only three primary colors to produce the three tristimulus values needed for a human observer. We vary the intensity of each primary to produce a color as we saw for the CRT in Chapter 1. The CRT is one example of the use of **additive color** where the primary colors add together to give the perceived color. Other examples that use additive color include projectors and slide (positive) film. In such systems, the primaries are usually red, green, and blue. With additive color, primaries add light to an initially black display, yielding the desired color.

For processes such as commercial printing and painting, a **subtractive color model** is more appropriate. Here we start with a white surface, such as a sheet of paper. Colored pigments remove color components from light that is striking the surface. If we assume that white light hits the surface, a particular point will be red if all components of the incoming light are absorbed by the surface except for wavelengths in the red part of the spectrum, which are reflected. In subtractive systems, the primaries are usually the **complementary colors**: cyan, magenta, and yellow (CMY;

FIGURE 2.23   A color distribution.

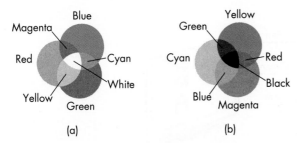

FIGURE 2.24   Color formation. (a) Additive color.
(b) Subtractive color.

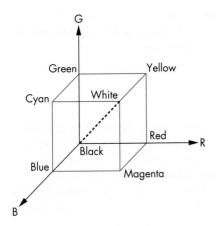

FIGURE 2.25   Color solid.

Figure 2.24). We will not explore subtractive color here. You need to know only that an RGB additive system has a dual with a CMY subtractive system (see Exercise 2.8).

We can view a color as a point in a **color solid**, as shown in Figure 2.25 and in Color Plate 21. We draw the solid using a coordinate system corresponding to the three primaries. The distance along a coordinate axis represents the amount of the corresponding primary in the color. If we normalize the maximum value of each primary to 1, then we can represent any color that we can produce with this set of primaries as a point in a unit cube. The vertices of the cube correspond to black (no primaries on); red, green, and blue (one primary fully on); the pairs of primaries, cyan (green and blue fully on), magenta (red and blue fully on), and yellow (red and green fully on); and white (all primaries fully on). The principal diagonal of the cube connects the origin (black) with white. All colors along this line have equal tristimulus values and appear as shades of gray.

There are many matters that we are not exploring fully here and will return to in Chapter 8. Most concern the differences among various sets of primaries or the limitations conferred by the physical constraints of real devices. In particular, the

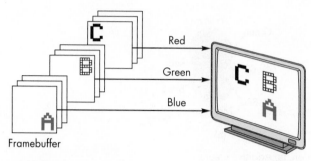

FIGURE 2.26   RGB color.

set of colors produced by one device—its **color gamut**—is not the same as for other devices, nor will it match the human's color gamut. In addition, the tristimulus values used on one device will not produce the same visible color as the same tristimulus values used on another device.

2.5.1 RGB Color

Now we can look at how color is handled in a graphics system from the programmer's perspective—that is, through the API. There are two different approaches. We will stress the **RGB color model** because an understanding of it will be crucial for our later discussion of shading. Historically, the **indexed color model** (Section 2.5.2) was easier to support in hardware because of its lower memory requirements and the limited colors available on displays, but in modern systems RGB color has become the norm.

In a three-primary-color, additive-color RGB system, there are conceptually separate buffers for red, green, and blue images. Each pixel has separate red, green, and blue components that correspond to locations in memory (Figure 2.26). In a typical system, there might be a 1280×1024 array of pixels, and each pixel might consist of 24 bits (3 bytes): 1 byte each for red, green, and blue. With present commodity graphics cards having up to 12 GB of memory, there is no longer a problem of storing and displaying the contents of the framebuffer at video rates.

As programmers, we would like to be able to specify any color that can be stored in the framebuffer. For our 24-bit example, there are 2^{24} possible colors, sometimes referred to as 16M colors, where M denotes 1024^2. Other systems may have as many as 12 (or more) bits per color or as few as 4 bits per color. Because our API should be independent of the particulars of the hardware, we would like to specify a color independently of the number of bits in the framebuffer and to let the drivers and hardware match our specification as closely as possible to the available display. A natural technique is to use the color cube and to specify color components as numbers between 0.0 and 1.0, where 1.0 denotes the maximum (or **saturated value**) of the corresponding primary, and 0.0 denotes a zero value of that primary.

In applications in which we want to assign a color to each vertex, we can put colors into a separate object, such as

```
var colors = [
  vec3(1.0, 0.0, 0.0),
  vec3(0.0, 1.0, 0.0),
  vec3(0.0, 0.0. 1.0)
];
```

which holds the colors red, green, and blue, and then put colors in an array as we did with vertex positions:

```
var colorsArray = [ ];

for (var index = 0; index < numPoints; ++index) {

  //determine which color[i] to assign to pointsArray[index]

  colorsArray.push(colors[i]);
}
```

Alternatively, we could create a single array that contains both vertex locations and vertex colors. These data can be sent to the shaders where colors will be applied to pixels in the framebuffer.

Later, we will be interested in a four-color (RGBA) system. The fourth color (A, or **alpha**) is stored in the framebuffer along with the RGB values; it can be set with four-dimensional versions of the color functions. In Chapter 7, we will see various uses for alpha, such as for creating fog effects or combining images. Here we need to specify the alpha value as part of the initialization of a WebGL program. If blending is enabled, then the alpha value will be treated by WebGL as either an **opacity** or **transparency** value. Transparency and opacity are complements of each other. An opaque object passes no light through it; a transparent object passes all light. Opacity values can range from fully transparent (A = 0.0) to fully opaque (A = 1.0). In WebGL, unlike in desktop OpenGL, if blending is not enabled, the value of A multiplies the R, G, and B values. Thus, values of A less than 1.0 mute the colors. Because the WebGL renders into an HTML canvas, we can use A to allow blending with non-WebGL canvas elements such as images.

One of the first tasks that we must do in a program is to clear an area of the screen—a drawing window—in which to display our output. We also must clear this window whenever we want to draw a new frame. By using the four-dimensional (RGBA) color system, the graphics and operating systems can interact to create effects where the drawing window interacts with other windows that may be beneath it by manipulating the opacity assigned to the window when it is cleared. The function call

```
gl.clearColor(1.0, 1.0, 1.0, 1.0);
```

specifies an RGBA clearing color that is white, because the first three components are set to 1.0, and is opaque, because the alpha component is 1.0. We can then use the function `gl.clear` to make the window on the screen solid and white.

2.5.2 Indexed Color

Early graphics systems had framebuffers that were limited in depth. For example, we might have had a framebuffer with a spatial resolution of 1280 × 1024, but each pixel was only 8 bits deep. We could divide each pixel's 8 bits into smaller groups of bits and assign red, green, and blue to each. Although this technique was adequate in a few applications, it usually did not give us enough flexibility with color assignment. Indexed color provided a solution that allowed applications to display a wide range of colors as long as the application did not need more colors than could be referenced by a pixel. Although indexed color is no longer part of recent versions of OpenGL, this technique can be programmed within an application.

We follow an analogy with an artist who paints in oils. The oil painter can produce an almost infinite number of colors by mixing together a limited number of pigments from tubes. We say that the painter has a potentially large color **palette**. At any one time, however, perhaps due to a limited number of brushes, the painter uses only a few colors. In this fashion, she can create an image that, although it contains a small number of colors, expresses her choices because she can select the few colors from a large palette.

Returning to the computer model, we can argue that if we can choose for each application a limited number of colors from a large selection (our palette), we should be able to create good-quality images most of the time.

We can select colors by interpreting our limited-depth pixels as indices into a table of colors rather than as color values. Suppose that our framebuffer has k bits per pixel. Each pixel value or index is an integer between 0 and $2^k - 1$. Suppose that we can display each color component with a precision of m bits; that is, we can choose from 2^m reds, 2^m greens, and 2^m blues. Hence, we can produce any of 2^{3m} colors on the display, but the framebuffer can specify only 2^k of them. We handle the specification through a user-defined **color lookup table** that is of size $2^k \times 3m$ (Figure 2.27). The user program fills the 2^k entries (rows) of the table with the desired colors, using m bits for each of red, green, and blue. Once the user has constructed the table, she can specify a color by its index, which points to the appropriate entry in the color lookup table (Figure 2.28). For $k = m = 8$, a common configuration, she can choose 256 out of 16 million colors. The 256 entries in the table constitute the user's color palette.

In systems that support color-index mode, the current color is established by a function that selects a particular color out of the table. Setting and changing the

Input	Red	Green	Blue
0	0	0	0
1	$2^m - 1$	0	0
.	0	$2^m - 1$	0
.	.	.	.
.	.	.	.
$2^k - 1$	.	.	.

$\leftarrow m \text{ bits} \rightarrow \quad \leftarrow m \text{ bits} \rightarrow \quad \leftarrow m \text{ bits} \rightarrow$

FIGURE 2.27   Color lookup table.

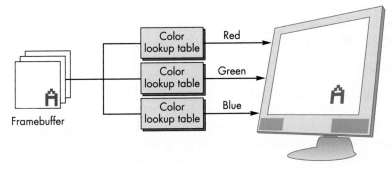

FIGURE 2.28   Indexed color.

entries in the color lookup table involves interacting with the window system. One difficulty arises if the window system and underlying hardware support only a limited number of colors, because the window system may have only a single color table that must be used for all its windows, or it might have to juggle multiple tables, one for each window on the screen.

Historically, color-index mode was important because it required less memory for the framebuffer and fewer other hardware components. However, cost is no longer an issue and color-index mode presents a few problems. When we work with dynamic images that must be shaded, usually we need more colors than are provided by color-index mode. In addition, the interaction with the window system is more complex than with RGB color. Consequently, for the most part, we will assume that we are using RGB color.

The major exception is when we consider a technique called **pseudocoloring**, where we start with a monochromatic image. For example, we might have scalar values of a physical entity such as temperature that we wish to display in color. We can create a mapping of these values to red, green, and blue that is identical to the color lookup tables used for indexed color. We will see an example of this technique in Chapter 7.

2.5.3 Setting of Color Attributes

For our simple example program, we use RGB color. We have three attributes to set. The first is the clear color, which is set to white by the WebGL function call:

```
gl.clearColor(1.0, 1.0, 1.0, 1.0);
```

Note this function uses RGBA color.

The color we use to render points is finalized in the fragment shader. We can set an RGB color in the application, using the functions in MV.js, such as

```
var pointColor = vec3(1.0, 0.0, 0.0);
```

or an RGBA color such as

```
var pointColor = vec4(1.0, 0.0, 0.0, 1.0);
```

and send this color to either shader. We could also set the color totally in the shader. We will see a few options later in this chapter. We can set the size of our rendered points to be 2 pixels high and 2 pixels wide by setting the built-in shader variable

```
gl_PointSize = 2.0;
```

in the vertex shader. Note that the point size attribute is one of the few state variables that can be set using a built-in shader variable. Hence, if two displays have different size pixels (due to their particular screen dimensions and resolutions), then the rendered images may appear slightly different. Certain graphics APIs, in an attempt to ensure that identical displays will be produced on all systems when the user program is the same, specify all attributes in a device-independent manner. Unfortunately, ensuring that two systems produce the same display has proved to be a difficult implementation problem. WebGL has chosen a more practical balance between desired behavior and realistic constraints.

2.6   VIEWING

We can now put a variety of graphical information into our world, and we can describe how we would like these objects to appear, but we do not yet have a method for specifying exactly which of these objects should appear on the screen. Just as what we record in a photograph depends on where we point the camera and what lens we use, we have to make similar viewing decisions in our program.

A fundamental concept that emerges from the synthetic-camera model that we introduced in Chapter 1 is that the specification of the objects in our scene is completely independent of our specification of the camera. Once we have specified both the scene and the camera, we can compose an image. The camera forms an image by exposing the film, whereas the computer system forms an image by carrying out a sequence of operations in its pipeline. The application program needs to worry only about the specification of the parameters for the objects and the camera, just as the casual photographer is concerned about the resulting picture, not about how the shutter works or the details of the photochemical interaction of film with light.

There are default viewing conditions in computer image formation that are similar to the settings on a basic camera with a fixed lens. However, a camera that has a fixed lens and sits in a fixed location forces us to distort our world to take a picture. We can create pictures of elephants only if we place the animals sufficiently far from the camera, or we can photograph ants only if we put the insects relatively close to the lens. We prefer to have the flexibility to change the lens to make it easier to form an image of a collection of objects. The same is true when we use our graphics system.

2.6.1 The Orthographic View

The simplest view, and WebGL's default, is the orthographic projection. We discuss this projection and others in detail in Chapter 4, but we introduce the orthographic projection here so that you can get started writing three-dimensional programs. Mathematically, the orthographic projection is what we would get if the camera in

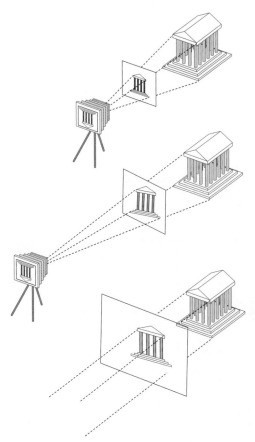

FIGURE 2.29   Creating an orthographic view by moving the camera away from
the projection plane.

our synthetic-camera model had an infinitely long telephoto lens and we could then
place the camera infinitely far from our objects. We can approximate this effect, as
shown in Figure 2.29, by leaving the image plane fixed and moving the camera far
from this plane. In the limit, all the projectors become parallel and the center of
projection is replaced by a **direction of projection**.

Rather than worrying about cameras an infinite distance away, suppose that we
start with projectors that are parallel to the positive z-axis and the projection plane
at $z = 0$, as shown in Figure 2.30. Note that not only are the projectors perpendicular
or orthogonal to the projection plane but also we can slide the projection plane along
the z-axis without changing where the projectors intersect this plane.

For orthographic viewing, we can think of there being a special orthographic
camera that resides in the projection plane, something that is not possible for other
views. Perhaps more accurately stated, there is a reference point in the projection
plane from which we can make measurements of a view volume and a direction of
projection. In WebGL, the reference point starts off at the origin and the camera

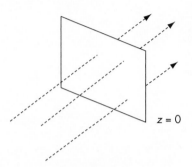

FIGURE 2.30   Orthographic projectors with projection plane $z = 0$.

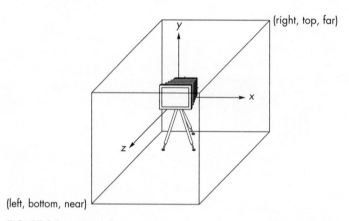

FIGURE 2.31   The default camera and an orthographic view volume.

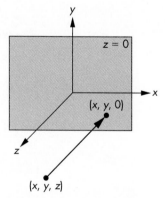

FIGURE 2.32   Orthographic projection.

points in the negative z direction, as shown in Figure 2.31. The orthographic projection takes a point (x, y, z) and projects it into the point $(x, y, 0)$, as shown in Figure 2.32. Note that if we are working in two dimensions with all vertices in the plane $z = 0$, a point and its projection are the same; however, we can employ the machinery of a three-dimensional graphics system to produce our image.

In WebGL, an orthographic projection with a right-parallelepiped viewing volume is the default. The volume is the cube defined by the planes

$$x = \pm 1 \qquad y = \pm 1 \qquad z = \pm 1.$$

The orthographic projection "sees" only those objects in the volume specified by this viewing volume. Unlike a real camera, the orthographic projection can include objects behind the camera. Thus, because the plane $z = 0$ is located between -1 and 1, the two-dimensional plane intersects the viewing volume.

In Chapters 4 and 5, we will learn to use transformations to create other views. For now, we will scale and position our objects so those that we wish to view are inside the default volume.

FIGURE 2.33 Viewing volume.

(a)

(b)

FIGURE 2.34 Two-dimensional viewing. (a) Objects before clipping. (b) Image after clipping.

2.6.2 Two-Dimensional Viewing

Remember that, in our view, two-dimensional graphics is a special case of three-dimensional graphics. Our viewing area is in the plane $z = 0$ within a three-dimensional **viewing volume**, as shown in Figure 2.33.

We could also consider two-dimensional viewing directly by taking a rectangular area of our two-dimensional world and transferring its contents to the display, as shown in Figure 2.34. The area of the world that we image is known as the **viewing rectangle**, or **clipping rectangle**. Objects inside the rectangle are in the image; objects outside are **clipped out** and are not displayed. Objects that straddle the edges of the rectangle are partially visible in the image. The size of the window on the display and where this window is placed on the display are independent decisions that we examine in Section 2.7.

2.7 CONTROL FUNCTIONS

We are almost done with our first program, but we must discuss the minimal interactions with the window and operating systems. If we look at the details for a specific environment, such as the X Window System on a Linux platform or Microsoft Windows on a PC, we see that the programmer's interface between the graphics system and the operating and window systems can be complex. Exploitation of the possibilities open to the application programmer requires knowledge specific to these systems. In addition, the details can be different for two different environments, and discussing these differences will do little to enhance our understanding of computer graphics.

Rather than deal with these issues in detail, we look at a minimal set of operations that must take place from the perspective of the graphics application program.

One approach that is used with desktop OpenGL is to employ a simple library that supports a set of operations common to all window systems. The OpenGL Utility Toolkit (GLUT) has been the most commonly used such library and was used in the previous editions of this book. Details specific to the underlying windowing or operating system are inside the implementation, rather than being part of its API. Operationally, we needed only to add another library to our standard library search path. Aside from the limitation inherent in this library (and other more modern replacements), applications still needed to be recompiled for each window system and could not run over the Web.

Because WebGL uses HTML and JavaScript, we do not have to make changes for different underlying window systems. Nevertheless, WebGL has to deal with many of the same issues as desktop OpenGL.

2.7.1 Interaction with the Window System

The term *window* is used in a number of different ways in the graphics and workstation literature. We use **window**, or **screen window**, to denote a rectangular area of our display. We are concerned only with raster displays. A window has a height and width, and because the window displays the contents of the framebuffer, positions in the window are measured in **window** or **screen coordinates** where the units are pixels. Window coordinates are three-dimensional, whereas screen coordinates are two-dimensional. Both systems use units measured in pixels for x and y, but window coordinates retain depth information.

In a modern environment, we can display many windows on the display. Each can have a different purpose, ranging from editing a file to monitoring our system. We use the term *window system* to refer to the multiwindow environment provided by systems such as the X Window System, Microsoft Windows, and Mac OS X. The window in which the graphics output appears is one of the windows managed by the window system. Hence, to the window system, the graphics window is a particular type of window—one in which graphics can be displayed or rendered.

References to positions in this window are relative to one corner of the window. We have to be careful about which corner is the origin. In science and engineering, the lower-left corner is the origin and has window coordinates (0,0). However, virtually all raster systems display their screens in the same way as commercial television systems do—from top to bottom, left to right. From this perspective, the top-left corner should be the origin. Our WebGL functions assume that the origin is bottom left, whereas information returned from the windowing system, such as the mouse position, often has the origin at the top left and thus requires us to convert the position from one coordinate system to the other.

Although our display may have a resolution of, say, 1280 × 1024 pixels, the window that we use can have any size. Thus, the framebuffer should have a resolution at least equal to the display size. Conceptually, if we use a window of 300 × 400 pixels, we can think of it as corresponding to a 300 × 400 framebuffer, even though it uses only a part of the real framebuffer.

Before we can open a window, there must be interaction between the windowing system and our application. In WebGL, this interaction is simple because almost all recent browsers have a canvas element that provides a drawing surface of a specified size. We can then use WebGL (or other methods) to draw on the canvas.

2.7.2 Aspect Ratio and Viewports

The **aspect ratio** of a rectangle is the ratio of the rectangle's width to its height. The independence of the object, viewing, and workstation window specifications can cause undesirable side effects if the aspect ratio of the viewing rectangle, specified by camera parameters, is not the same as the aspect ratio of the window specified for the canvas. If they differ, as depicted in Figure 2.35, objects are distorted on the screen. This distortion is a consequence of our default mode of operation, in which the entire clipping rectangle is mapped to the display window. The only way that we can map the entire contents of the clipping rectangle to the entire display window is to distort the contents of the former to fit inside the latter. We can avoid this distortion if we ensure that the clipping rectangle and display window have the same aspect ratio.

Another, more flexible, method is to use the concept of a viewport. A **viewport** is a rectangular area of the display window. By default, it is the entire window, but it can be set to any smaller size in pixels via the function

```
gl.viewport(x, y, w, h);
```

where (x,y) is the lower-left corner of the viewport (measured relative to the lower-left corner of the window), and w and h give the width and height, respectively. The

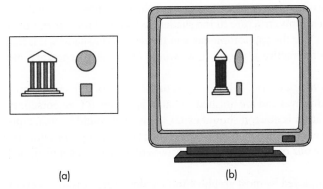

(a)   (b)

FIGURE 2.35   Aspect ratio mismatch. (a) Viewing rectangle. (b) Display window.

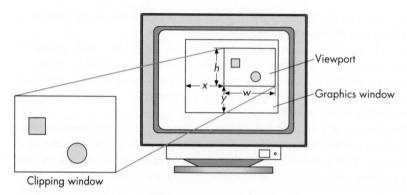

FIGURE 2.36   A mapping to the viewport.

values should be in pixels. Primitives are displayed in the viewport, as shown in Figure 2.36. For a given window, we can adjust the height and width of the viewport to match the aspect ratio of the clipping rectangle, thus preventing any object distortion in the image.

The viewport is part of the state. If we change the viewport between rendering objects or rerender the same objects with the viewport changed, we achieve the effect of multiple viewports with different images in different parts of the window. We will see further uses of the viewport in Chapter 3, where we consider interactive changes in the size and shape of the window.

2.7.3 Application Organization

In principle, we should be able to combine the simple initialization code with our code from Section 2.1 to form a complete WebGL program that generates the Sierpinski gasket. Unfortunately, life in a modern system is not that simple. There are two problems: One is generic to all graphics systems; the second has more to do with problems of interacting with the underlying windowing system.

Our basic mechanism for display will be to form a data structure that contains all the geometry and attributes we need to specify a primitive and how we would like it displayed. We then send this structure to the shaders, which will process our data and display the results. Once the application has sent the data to the shaders, it is free to do other tasks. In an interactive application, we would continue to generate more primitives.

Consider the following scenario. When we execute the core of our sample program, we draw a few primitives and are finished. What happens next? One possibility is that, since the application is done, it should exit. Clearly, that would be unacceptable if it means that the window in which the output is displayed disappears before we have had a chance to see our output. Fortunately, browsers use a more sophisticated mechanism.

The mechanism employed by most graphics and window systems is to use **event processing**, which gives us interactive control in our programs. **Events** are changes that are detected by the operating system and include such actions as a user pressing a key on the keyboard, the user clicking a mouse button or moving the mouse, or the user minimizing a window on the display. Events are varied and usually only a subset of them is important to graphics applications. An event may generate data that is stored with the occurrence of the event. For example, if a key is pressed, the code for the key will be stored.

When events occur they are placed in queue, the **event queue**, which can be examined by an application program or by the operating system. A given event can be ignored or cause an action to take place. For example, an application that does not use the keyboard will ignore all pressing and releasing of keys, whereas an application that uses the keyboard might use keyboard events to control the flow of the application.

The operating system and window system recognize many types of events, most of which are not relevant to our WebGL applications. Within WebGL, we will be able to identify the events to which we want to react through functions called **event listeners** or **callbacks**. A callback function is associated with a specific type of event. Hence a typical interactive application would use a mouse callback and perhaps a keyboard callback. We will look at interaction in detail in Chapter 3.

2.8 THE GASKET PROGRAM

Although our first application does not require us to write any callback functions, we introduce a structure that we will use for all our applications. Our application consists of two files: an HTML file and JavaScript file. Minimally, the HTML file will load some JavaScript files, including the JavaScript file for our application, a file with some commonly used utility functions, and the matrix package we use throughout this book. It also includes an HTML canvas object. Here is a basic file:

```
<html>

<script type="text/javascript" src="../Common/webgl-utils.js"></script>
<script type="text/javascript" src="../Common/initShaders.js"></script>
<script type="text/javascript" src="../Common/MV.js"></script>
<script type="text/javascript" src="gasket1.js"></script>

<body>
<canvas id="gl-canvas" width="512" height="512">
  <!-- The following message is displayed if the browser doesn't
    -- support HTML5 -->
  Sorry; your web browser does not support HTML5's canvas element.
</canvas>
</body>
</html>
```

The <html> tag indicates that the following code is written in HTML script. The <script> tags point to JavaScript files, which will be loaded by the browser. The first, webgl-utils.js, is a file containing the utilities needed to create the WebGL canvas object that we use in our application file gasket1.js. The file initShaders.js contains the code to read, compile, and link the shaders. This code uses many WebGL functions that are the same in every application. We will discuss the individual functions later, but because they do not have much to do with the graphics, we defer discussion of them. The functions in `MV.js` are for basic matrix and vector manipulation. The canvas element creates a drawing surface. We give it the identifier `gl-canvas` so we can refer to it in our application, and specify an initial height and width of the window in which our graphics will appear.

At this point you might be wondering where the shaders are. Shaders are programs that are compiled in the drivers. We create them as null-terminated strings of characters, usually with a standard text editor, which are eventually passed into WebGL. We have a couple of options as to where to place these programs. We could place each as a single string in the application. However, this approach is cumbersome for all but the simplest shaders. Alternately, we could put the shader source in files that are read in by the application. This approach is typically what is used with desktop OpenGL. Unfortunately, as a security measure, some browsers will not allow an application to read files. There is an example of initialization using this alternate approach on the book's website, and it differs only slightly from the approach used here, which will always work. In this approach, we include the shaders in the HTML file.

Now let's look at how to organize the application code. There are many ways we can do this, ranging from using a single file that contains everything including the shaders to using different files for each part of the application. Our approach will be to put the shaders and the description of the page in an HTML file and to put the WebGL application code in a separate JavaScript file. Thus, for example, if we use a button for input, the description of the button and its placement on the display will be in the HTML file, and the code that controls the result of clicking the button will be in the JavaScript file.

Because our applications run within the browser, how the code is executed differs from how a program written in a compiled language runs. As we have seen, the HTML file contains tags for multiple JavaScript files, one of which is the file containing our WebGL application. Normally, the process of reading these files is carried out asynchronously. The files contained in the `script` tags in the HTML file are read in order, as are the shaders. The browser then enters an execution phase that is event driven. We will discuss event handling in greater detail in Chapter 3, but at this point it is sufficient to know that if we have a function in the application file we want executed first, we can wait for the **onload event**, as in the code that begins

```
window.onload = function myFunction() { ... }
```

Or equivalently we can just name the function with the event handler[7]

```
onload = myFunction;
```

---

7. We also take advantage of the fact that JavaScript will automatically associate the `onload` function with the global `window` object.

and put myFunction somewhere in the application file. The onload event occurs when all the script files are read; it causes myFunction to be executed.

We will name our onload function init, and our applications will always have this function and at least a second function named render that will control the drawing onto the canvas. Depending on the application, we can add other functions and also will use various functions in MV.js and the utility library.

For a typical application, we can think of the code as consisting of three principal actions: initialization, generation of the geometry, and rendering of the geometry. Initialization includes reading, compiling, and linking the shaders, and forming the necessary data structures on the GPU. In interactive applications, we also need to set up our callback functions.

As we discussed in Section 2.1, generating and placing the data on the GPU and having the GPU render those data to an image on the display are separate operations. For complex applications, we can separate the algorithmic part of our application from all the initialization needed to set up our application. For our first examples, the code is so short that we can combine the generation with initialization.

We developed the algorithm to generate the Sierpinski gasket in Section 2.2. The corresponding code that will be included in init is

```
var vertices2 = [
  vec2(-1, -1),
  vec2(0, 1),
  vec2(1, -1)
];

var u = add(vertices[0], vertices[1]);
var v = add(vertices[0], vertices[2]);
var p = scale(0.5, add(u, v));

points = [ p ];

for (var i = 0; points.length < numPoints; ++i) {
  var j = Math.floor(Math.random() * 3);

  p = add(points[i], vertices[j]);
  p = scale(0.5, p);
  points.push(p);
}

gl.bufferData(gl.ARRAY_BUFFER, flatten(points), gl.STATIC_DRAW);
render();
```

All we have added to our previous code is a function to send the data to a buffer on the GPU, gl.bufferData. However, there is one slight complication that we must address: gl.bufferData accepts only arrays of native data type values (e.g., an array of floating-point values in memory) and not JavaScript objects. Specifically, we use JavaScript's **typed arrays** to pass data into WebGL functions that require native data type values. We have created a function flatten (defined in MV.js) that converts the JavaScript objects we use in our examples (e.g., vec2, or mat4) into the data format accepted by gl.bufferData.

In the example above, we specifically transform our point coordinate data stored in the JavaScript array points using flatten into a contiguous array of 32-bit floating-point values (internal to flatten, it temporarily creates a Float32Array), which can be sent directly to the GPU. This strategy allows us to use the matrix functions in MV.js and avoids the use of many for loops, which would be necessary if we tried to work with Float32Arrays directly.

As we will see in later chapters, we'll need to know the number of bytes used to store various types, like our vec2, for use in computing the byte offsets into GPU buffers like the ones created by gl.bufferData. To aid in that conversion, MV.js includes a JavaScript associative array named sizeof, which returns the size of any of our defined types. For example, to determine the starting byte offset of the third vec2 in a flattened array, you would write

```
var offset = 3 * sizeof['vec2'];
```

2.8.1 Sending Data to the GPU

Although we can create the points and put them in an array, we have to send these data to our GPU and render them. We start by creating a **vertex buffer object** (**VBO**) on the GPU in init and later place our data in that object. We create the buffer with the code

```
var buffer = gl.createBuffer();
gl.bindBuffer(gl.ARRAY_BUFFER, buffer);
```

The function gl.createBuffer creates the buffer and returns the identifier buffer. The gl.ARRAY_BUFFER parameter indicates that the data in the buffer will be vertex attribute data rather than indices to the data. The binding operation makes this buffer the **current buffer**. Subsequent functions that put data in a buffer will use this buffer until we bind a different buffer.

At this point, we have allocated the buffer on the GPU but have not placed any data in it. Hence, we have made this step part of our initialization. Later, we use

```
gl.bufferData(gl.ARRAY_BUFFER, flatten(pointsArray), gl.STATIC_DRAW);
```

to put data into the VBO. Once data are in GPU memory, we might, as in this example, simply display them once. But in more realistic applications we might alter the data, redisplay them many times, and even read data back from the GPU to the CPU. Modern GPUs can alter how they store data to increase efficiency depending on the type of application. The final parameter in gl.bufferData gives a hint of how the application plans to use the data. In our case, we are sending them once and displaying them so the choice of gl.STATIC_DRAW is appropriate.

2.8.2 Rendering the Points

When we want to display our points, we can use the function

```
gl.drawArrays(gl.POINTS, 0, numPoints);
```

which causes numPoints vertices to be rendered starting with the first vertex. The value of the first parameter, gl.POINTS, tells the GPU the data should be rendered as distinct points rather than as lines or triangles that could be displayed with the same data. Thus, a simple render function is

```
function render()
{
  gl.clear(gl.COLOR_BUFFER_BIT);
  gl.drawArrays(gl.POINTS, 0, numPoints);
}
```

We clear the framebuffer and then render the vertex data that are on the GPU. But this is just the beginning of the story. The rendering process must be carried out by the pipeline consisting of the vertex shader, the rasterizer, and the fragment shader in order to get the proper pixels displayed in the framebuffer. Because our example uses only points, we need only develop very simple shaders and put together the whole application. Even though our shaders will be almost trivial, we must provide both a vertex shader and a fragment shader to have a complete application. There are no default shaders. First, we will develop the shaders and then we will discuss how to connect them to our application in init. Also, because this example generates a static display, we only need to perform a single rendering.

2.8.3 The Vertex Shader

The only information that we put in our vertex buffer object is the location of each point. When we execute gl.drawArrays, each of the numPoints vertices generates an execution of a vertex shader that we must provide. If we leave the color determination to the fragment shader, all the vertex shader must do is pass the vertex's location to the rasterizer. Although we will see many more tasks that can be done in a vertex shader, the absolute minimum it must do is send a vertex location to the rasterizer.

We write our shader using the OpenGL ES Shading Language (GLSL), which is a C-like language with which we can write both vertex and fragment shaders. We will discuss GLSL in more detail later when we want to write more sophisticated shaders, but here is the code for a simple **pass-through** vertex shader:

```
attribute vec4 vPosition;

void main()
{
  gl_Position = vPosition;
}
```

Each shader is a complete program with main as its entry point. GLSL expands the C data types to include matrix and vector types. The type vec4 is equivalent to a C++ class for a four-element array of floats. We have provided similar types for the application side in MV.js and we will introduce more in Chapter 4. The input vertex's location is given by the four-dimensional vector vPosition, whose specification includes the keyword attribute to signify that its value is input to the shader from the application when the shader is initiated. There is one special built-in state variable in our shader, `gl_Position`, which is the position that is passed to the rasterizer and must be output by every vertex shader. Because `gl_Position` is built into WebGL, we need not declare it in the shader.

In general, a vertex shader will transform the representation of a vertex location from the coordinate system in which it is specified to a representation in clip coordinates for the rasterizer. However, because we specified the values in our application in clip coordinates, our shader does not have to make any changes to the values input to the shader and merely passes them through via `gl_Position`.

We still have to establish a connection between the array `pointsArray` in the application and the input array `vPosition` in the shader. We will do this after we compile and link our shaders. First, we look at the fragment shader.

2.8.4 The Fragment Shader

Each invocation of the vertex shader outputs a vertex, which then goes through primitive assembly and clipping before reaching the rasterizer. The rasterizer outputs fragments for each primitive inside the clipping volume. Each fragment invokes an execution of the fragment shader. At a minimum, each execution of the fragment shader must output a color for the fragment unless the fragment is to discarded. Here is a minimum GLSL fragment shader:

```
precision mediump float;

void main()
{
    gl_FragColor = vec4(1.0, 0.0, 0.0, 1.0);
}
```

All this shader does is assign a four-dimensional RGBA color to each fragment through the built-in variable `gl_FragColor`. The A component of the color is its opacity. We want our points to be opaque and not translucent, so we use A = 1.0. Setting R to 1.0 and the other two components to 0.0 colors each fragment red.

The setting of the precision for floating-point variables to `mediump` guarantees that our shader will run on all implementations that support WebGL. Most devices now support high precision, `highp`, and we can either request it directly or use compiler directives to test for support of high precision and then default to medium precision on systems that do not have the support.

2.8.5 Combining the Parts

We now have the pieces but need to put them together. In particular, we have to compile the shaders, connect variables in the application with their counterparts in the shaders, and link everything together. We start with the bare minimum. Shaders must be compiled and linked. Most of the time we will do these operations as part of initialization, so we can put the necessary code in a function `initShaders` that will remain almost unchanged from application to application.

Let's start by modifying our HTML file to include the shaders:

```
<html>

<script id="vertex-shader" type="x-shader/x-vertex">
attribute vec4 vPosition;

void main()
{
  gl_Position = vPosition;
}
</script>

<script id="fragment-shader" type="x-shader/x-fragment">
precision mediump float;

void main()
{
  gl_FragColor = vec4(1.0, 0.0, 0.0, 1.0);
}
</script>

<script type="text/javascript" src="../Common/webgl-utils.js"></script>
<script type="text/javascript" src="../Common/initShaders.js"></script>
<script type="text/javascript" src="../Common/MV.js"></script>
<script type="text/javascript" src="gasket1.js"></script>

<body>
<canvas id="gl-canvas" width="512" height="512">
  <!-- The following message is displayed if the browser doesn't
    -- support HTML5 -->
  Sorry; your web browser does not support HTML5's canvas element.
</canvas>
</body>
</html>
```

Because the browser supports WebGL, it understands the script for the vertex and fragment shaders. We give each shader an identifier (`vertex-shader` and `fragment-shader`) that we can use in the application to access these shaders.

2.8.6 The `initShaders` Function

The initialization, creation of geometry, and rendering code are all written in JavaScript whereas the shaders are written in GLSL. To obtain a module that we can execute, we have to connect these entities, a process that involves reading source code from files, compiling the individual parts, and linking everything together. We can control this process through our application using a set of WebGL functions that are discussed in Appendix A. Here, it will be sufficient to describe the steps briefly.

Our first step is to create a container called a **program object** to hold our shaders and two shader objects, one for each type of shader. The program object has an identifier we can use to refer to it in the application. After we create these objects, we can attach the shaders to the program object. Generally, the shader source code will be in standard text files. We read them into strings, which can be attached to the program object and compiled. If the compilation is successful, the application and shaders can be linked together. Assuming we have put the vertex shader source and the fragment shader source in the HTML file, we can execute the above steps using the function `initShaders.js`, which returns the program object, as in the code

```
program = initShaders("vertex-shader", "fragment-shader");
```

where `vertex-shader` and `fragment-shader` are the identifiers we assigned in the HTML file.

When we link the program object and the shaders, the names of shader variables are bound to indices in tables that are created in the linking process. The function `gl.getAttribLocation` returns the index of an attribute variable, such as the vertex location attribute `vPosition` in our vertex shader. From the perspective of the application program, the client, we have to do two things. We have to enable the vertex attributes that are in the shaders (`gl.enableVertexAttribArray`) and we must describe the form of the data in the vertex array (`gl.vertexAttribPointer`), as in the code

```
var vPosition = gl.getAttribLocation(program, "vPosition");
gl.vertexAttribPointer(vPosition, 2, gl.FLOAT, false, 0, 0);
gl.enableVertexAttribArray(vPosition);
```

In `gl.vertexAttribPointer`, the second and third parameters specify that the elements in array `pointsArray` are each two floating-point numbers. The fourth parameter says that we do not want the data normalized to the range (0.0, 1.0), while the fifth states that the values in the array are contiguous. The last parameter is the address in the buffer where the data begin. In this example, we have only a single data array `points`, so the zero value is correct. Note that we have chosen to use the name `vPosition` both in the vertex shader and in the name of the attribute location in the application. These names do not have to be the same, but using the same name emphasizes the connection between variables in the application and the corresponding variables in the shaders.

2.8.7 The `init` Function

Here's the complete `init` function:

```
function init()
{
  canvas = document.getElementById("gl-canvas");

  gl = WebGLUtils.setupWebGL(canvas);
  if (!gl) {
    alert("WebGL isn't available");
  }

  gl.viewport(0, 0, canvas.width, canvas.height);
  gl.clearColor(1.0, 1.0, 1.0, 1.0);
```

```
// Load shaders and initialize attribute buffers
program = initShaders(gl, "vertex-shader", "fragment-shader");
gl.useProgram(program);

var buffer = gl.createBuffer();
gl.bindBuffer(gl.ARRAY_BUFFER, buffer);

var vPosition = gl.getAttribLocation(program, "vPosition");
gl.vertexAttribPointer(vPosition, 2, gl.FLOAT, false, 0, 0);
gl.enableVertexAttribArray(vPosition);

render();
}
```

We have already seen most of its parts, but there are a couple of lines that we need to examine in more detail. The HTML file specifies a canvas of a desired size and assigns it an identifier `gl-canvas`. If the browser supports WebGL, the functions in `WebGLUtils.js` return a WebGL **context**. The WebGL context is a JavaScript object that contains all the WebGL functions and parameters. In the application, we create the WebGL context by

```
var canvas = document.getElementById("gl-canvas");
var gl = WebGLUtils.setupWebGL(canvas);
```

WebGL functions, such as `bindBuffer`, are contained in the `gl` object and are then called using the `gl.` prefix, as in `gl.bindBuffer`. WebGL parameters, such as `gl.FLOAT` and `gl.TRIANGLES`, are members of this object.

A complete listing of this program, the `initShader` function, as well as other example programs that we generate in subsequent chapters, are on the book's website. Details of `initShaders` are in Appendix A.

2.8.8 Reading the Shaders from the Application

If your browser allows it, most application programmers prefer to have the shaders read in by the application from text files rather than embedding them in the HTML file. We created a second version of `initShaders`, which is in a file `initShaders2.js` on the website. Using this version, the code

```
initShadersFromFiles(gl, "vshader.glsl", "fshader.glsl");
```

assumes that the shader source is in the files `vshader.glsl` and `fshader.glsl` in the same directory as the application JavaScript file. An example of using this option named `gasket1v2` is also on the website.

2.9   POLYGONS AND RECURSION

The output from our gasket program (Figure 2.2) shows considerable structure. If we were to run the program with more iterations, then much of the randomness in the image would disappear. Examining this structure, we see that regardless of how many points we generate, there are no points in the middle. If we draw line

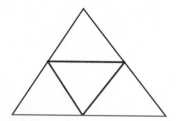

FIGURE 2.37   Bisecting the sides of a triangle.

segments connecting the midpoints of the sides of the original triangle, then we divide the original triangle into four triangles and the middle one contains no points (Figure 2.37).

Looking at the other three triangles, we see that we can apply the same observation to each of them; that is, we can subdivide each of these triangles into four triangles by connecting the midpoints of the sides, and each middle triangle will contain no points.

This structure suggests a second method for generating the Sierpinski gasket— one that uses polygons instead of points and does not require the use of a random-number generator. One advantage of using polygons is that we can fill solid areas on our display. Our strategy is to start with a single triangle, subdivide it into four smaller triangles by bisecting the sides, and then remove the middle triangle from further consideration. We repeat this procedure on the remaining triangles until the size of the triangles that we are removing is small enough—about the size of one pixel—that we can draw the remaining triangles.

We can implement the process that we just described through a recursive program. We start its development with a simple function that adds the locations of the three vertices that specify a triangle to an array `points`:[8]

```
function triangle(a, b, c)
{
  points.push(a);
  points.push(b);
  points.push(c);
}
```

Hence, each time that `triangle` is called, it copies three two-dimensional vertices to the data array.

Suppose that the vertices of our original triangle are again

```
var vertices = [
  vec2(-1.0, -1.0),
  vec2(0.0, 1.0),
  vec2(1.0, -1.0)
];
```

Then the midpoints of the sides can be computed using the `mix` function in `MV.js`:

```
var ab = mix(a, b, 0.5);
var ac = mix(a, c, 0.5);
var bc = mix(b, c, 0.5);
```

With these six locations, we can use `triangle` to place the data for the three triangles formed by (a, ab, ac), (c, ac, bc), and (b, bc, ab) in `pointsArray`.

---

8. In JavaScript, you could do this operation more succinctly as `points.push(a, b, c);`, pushing all of the elements in a single operation. We separated them here to make the code clearer.

However, we do not simply want to draw these triangles; we want to subdivide them. Hence, we make the process recursive. We specify a recursive function

```
divideTriangle(a, b, c, count);
```

that will draw the triangles only if count is zero. Otherwise, it will subdivide the triangle specified by a, b, and c, and decrease count. Here is the code:

```
function divideTriangle(a, b, c, count)
{
  if (count == 0) {
    triangle(a, b, c);
  }
  else {
    var ab = mix(0.5, a, b);
    var ac = mix(0.5, a, c);
    var bc = mix(0.5, b, c);

    --count;

    divideTriangle(a, ab, ac, count);
    divideTriangle(c, ac, bc, count);
    divideTriangle(b, bc, ab, count);
  }
}
```

We can initiate numTimesToSubdivide subdivisions by

```
divideTriangle(vertices[0], vertices[1], vertices[2],
               numTimesToSubdivide);
```

where numTimesToSubdivide is the number of times we want to subdivide the original triangle.

If we do not account for vertices shared by two vertices and treat each triangle independently, then each subdivison triples the number of vertices, giving us

$$numVertices = 3^{numTimesToSubdivide+1}.$$

The rest of the program is almost identical to our previous gasket program. We set up the buffer object exactly as we did previously, and we can then render all the triangles exactly as in our first example:

```
function render()
{
  gl.clear(gl.COLOR_BUFFER_BIT);
  gl.drawArrays(gl.TRIANGLES, 0, numVertices);
}
```

Output for five subdivision steps is shown in Figure 2.38. The complete program is given on the website (gasket2).

FIGURE 2.38 Triangles after five subdivisions.

2.10 THE THREE-DIMENSIONAL GASKET

We have argued that two-dimensional graphics is a special case of three-dimensional graphics, but we have not yet seen a complete three-dimensional program. Next, we convert our two-dimensional Sierpinski gasket program to a program that will generate a three-dimensional gasket; that is, one that is not restricted to a plane. We can follow either of the two approaches that we used for the two-dimensional gasket. Both extensions start in a similar manner, replacing the initial triangle with a tetrahedron (Figure 2.39).

FIGURE 2.39 Tetrahedron.

2.10.1 Use of Three-Dimensional Points

Because every tetrahedron is convex, the midpoint of a line segment between a vertex and any point inside a tetrahedron is also inside the tetrahedron. Hence, we can follow the same procedure as before, but this time, instead of the three vertices required to define a triangle, we need four initial vertices to specify the tetrahedron. Note that as long as no three vertices are collinear, we can choose the four vertices of the tetrahedron at random without affecting the character of the result.

The required changes are primarily in changing all the variables from two to three dimensions. We declare and initialize an array to hold the vertices as follows:

```
var vertices = [
  vec3(-0.5, -0.5, -0.5),
  vec3(0.5, -0.5, -0.5),
  vec3(0.0,  0.5,  0.0),
  vec3(0.0, -0.5,  0.5)
];
```

We again use an array `points` to store the vertices we will render, starting with a point inside the tetrahedron:

```
points = [ vec3(0.0, 0.0, 0.0) ];
```

We compute a new location as before but add a midpoint computation for the z component:

```
for (var i = 0; points.length < numPoints; ++i) {
  var j = Math.floor(Math.random() * 4);
  points.push(mix(points[i], vertices[j], 0.5));
}
```

We create vertex-array and buffer objects exactly as with the two-dimensional version and can use the same display function.

One problem with the three-dimensional gasket that we did not have with the two-dimensional gasket occurs because points are not restricted to a single plane; thus, it may be difficult to envision the three-dimensional structure from the two-dimensional image displayed, especially if we render each point in the same color.

To get around this problem, we can add a more sophisticated color setting process to our shaders, one that makes the color of each point depend on that point's location. We can map the color cube to the default view volume by noting that both are cubes, but whereas x, y, and z range from -1 to 1, each color component must be between 0 and 1. If we use the mapping

$$r = \frac{1+x}{2} \qquad g = \frac{1+y}{2} \qquad b = \frac{1+z}{2},$$

every point in the viewing volume maps to a distinct color. In the vertex shader, we set the color using the components of vPosition, so our vertex shader becomes

```
attribute vec4 vPosition;
varying vec4 fColor;

void main()
{
  fColor = vec4((1.0+vPosition.xyz)/2.0, 1.0);
  gl_Position = vPosition;
}
```

The variable fColor is a **varying variable** that is output to the rasterizer where it is interpolated to yield a color that is available for each fragment in the fragment shader. In this case, because we are rendering points, each vertex generates only a single fragment, so fColor will be the color assigned to the rendered vertex by the fragment shader.

```
precision mediump float;

varying vec4 fColor;

void main()
{
  gl_FragColor = fColor;
}
```

FIGURE 2.40   Three-dimensional Sierpinski gasket.

Figure 2.40 shows that if we generate enough points, the resulting figure will look like the initial tetrahedron with increasingly smaller tetrahedrons removed. This application is also on the website, called `gasket3`.

2.10.2 Naming Conventions

This use of varying variables illustrates the usefulness of having a convention for naming variables to avoid confusion between variables in the application and variables in the shaders. We will use v as the first character of variables that are used in the vertex shader and f as the first character of variables in the fragment shader. Using the name `fColor` for the varying variable in the vertex shader indicates that this variable will go through the rasterizer and be used in the fragment shader. Likewise, if we use the identifier `vColor` in the application, it will indicate that this variable is an attribute that will be used in the vertex shader. Uniform variables that we introduce later will be undecorated because they can appear and be used in either shader.

2.10.3 Use of Polygons in Three Dimensions

There is a more interesting approach to the three-dimensional Sierpinski gasket that uses both polygons and subdivision of a tetrahedron into smaller tetrahedrons. Suppose we start with a tetrahedron and find the midpoints of its six edges and connect these midpoints as shown in Figure 2.41. There are now four smaller tetrahedrons, one for each of the original vertices, and another area in the middle that we will discard.

FIGURE 2.41   Subdivided tetra-hedron.

Following our second approach to a single triangle, we will use recursive subdivision to subdivide the four tetrahedrons that we keep. Because the faces of a tetrahedron are the four triangles determined by its four vertices, at the end of the subdivisions we can render each of the final tetrahedrons by drawing four triangles.

Most of our code is almost the same as in two dimensions. Our triangle routine now uses points in three dimensions rather than in two dimensions, and we ignore the color for the moment.

```
function triangle(a, b, c)
{
  points.push(a);
  points.push(b);
  points.push(c);
}
```

We can draw each tetrahedron function:

```
function tetra(a, b, c, d)
{
  triangle(a, c, b);
  triangle(a, c, d);
  triangle(a, b, d);
  triangle(b, c, d);
}
```

We subdivide a tetrahedron in a manner similar to subdividing a triangle:

```
function divideTetra(a, b, c, d, count)
{
  if (count == 0) {
    tetra(a, b, c, d);
  }
  else {
    var ab = mix(a, b, 0.5);
    var ac = mix(a, c, 0.5);
    var ad = mix(a, d, 0.5);
    var bc = mix(b, c, 0.5);
    var bd = mix(b, d, 0.5);
    var cd = mix(c, d, 0.5);

    --count;

    divideTetra( a, ab, ac, ad, count);
    divideTetra(ab,  b, bc, bd, count);
    divideTetra(ac, bc,  c, cd, count);
    divideTetra(ad, bd, cd,  d, count);
  }
}
```

We can now start with four vertices (va, vb, vc, vd) and do numTimesToSubdivide subdivisions as follows:

```
divideTetra(vertices[0], vertices[1], vertices[2], vertices[3],
            numTimesToSubdivide);
```

There are two more problems that we must address before we have a useful three-dimensional program. The first is how to deal with color. If we use just a single color as in our first example, we won't be able to see any of the three-dimensional structure. Alternately, we could use the approach of our last example of letting the color of each fragment be determined by where the point is located in three dimensions. But we would prefer to use a small number of colors and color the face of each triangle with one of these colors. We can set this scheme by choosing some base colors in the application, such as

```
var baseColors = [
  vec3(1.0, 0.0, 0.0),
  vec3(0.0, 1.0, 0.0),
  vec3(0.0, 0.0, 1.0),
  vec3(0.0, 0.0, 0.0)
];
```

and then assigning colors to each point as it is generated. We add a color index to our triangle function that serves as an index into `baseColors`:

```
function tetra(a, b, c, d)
{
  triangle(a, c, b, 0);
  triangle(a, c, d, 1);
  triangle(a, b, d, 2);
  triangle(b, c, d, 3);
}
```

Then we form a color array in addition to our points array, adding a color index each time we add a vertex location:

```
function triangle(a, b, c, color)
{
  colors.push(baseColors[color]);
  points.push(a);
  colors.push(baseColors[color]);
  points.push(b);
  colors.push(baseColors[color]);
  points.push(c);
}
```

We need to send these colors to the GPU along with their associated vertices. There are multiple ways we can do this transfer. We could set up an array on the GPU large enough to hold both the vertices and the colors using `gl.bufferData` and then send the colors and vertices separately using `gl.bufferSubData`. If we take this approach, we could use the first half of the array for the vertex positions and the second half for the colors, or we could interleave the vertex positions and colors, accounting for this option with the first parameter in `gl.vertexAttribPointer`.

We will use a second approach, which uses separate buffers on the GPU for the colors and vertices. Here is the relevant code:

```
var cBuffer = gl.createBuffer();
gl.bindBuffer(gl.ARRAY_BUFFER, cBuffer);
gl.bufferData(gl.ARRAY_BUFFER, flatten(colorsArray), gl.STATIC_DRAW);

var vBuffer = gl.createBuffer();
gl.bindBuffer(gl.ARRAY_BUFFER, vBuffer);
gl.bufferData(gl.ARRAY_BUFFER, flatten(pointsArray), gl.STATIC_DRAW);
```

We also need two vertex arrays. If in the shader the color is named `vColor`, the second vertex array can be set up in the shader initialization

```
var vColor = gl.getAttribLocation(program, "vColor");
gl.vertexAttribPointer(vColor, 3, gl.FLOAT, false, 0, 0);
gl.enableVertexAttribArray(vColor);
```

In the vertex shader, we use `vColor` to set a color to be sent to the fragment shader. Here is the vertex shader:

```
precision mediump float;

attribute vec4 vPosition;
attribute vec4 vColor;
varying vec4 fColor;

void main()
{
  fColor = vColor;
  gl_Position = vPosition;
}
```

Note that we have some flexibility in mixing variables of different dimensions between the application and the shaders. We could work with `vec2`s for positions in the application and declare the corresponding variables in the shaders as `vec4`s. WebGL uses `vec4`s for storing positions with the default of (0, 0, 0, 1). Consequently, if we send a `vec2` for an x, y variable to a shader, it will be stored with the default of 0 for the z component and 1 for the w component.

2.10.4 Hidden-Surface Removal

If you execute the code in the previous section, you might be confused by the results. The program draws triangles in the order that they are specified in the program. This order is determined by the recursion in our program and not by the geometric relationships among the triangles. Each triangle is drawn (filled) in a solid color and is drawn over those triangles that have already been rendered to the display.

Contrast this order with the way that we would see the triangles if we were to construct the three-dimensional Sierpinski gasket out of small solid tetrahedra. We would see only those faces of tetrahedra that were in front of all other faces, as seen by a viewer. Figure 2.42 shows a simplified version of this **hidden-surface** problem. From the viewer's position, quadrilateral A is seen clearly, but triangle B is blocked from view, and triangle C is only partially visible. Without going into the details

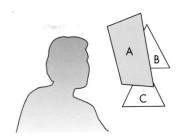

FIGURE 2.42 The hidden-surface problem.

of any specific algorithm, you should be able to convince yourself that, given the position of the viewer and the triangles, we should be able to draw the triangles such that the correct image is obtained. Algorithms for ordering objects so that they are drawn correctly are called **visible-surface algorithms** or **hidden-surface-removal algorithms**, depending on how we look at the problem. We discuss such algorithms in detail in Chapters 4 and 7.

For now, we can simply use a particular hidden-surface-removal algorithm, called the **z-buffer** algorithm, that is supported by WebGL. This algorithm can be turned on (enabled) and off (disabled) easily. In our main program, we just have to enable depth testing,

```
gl.enable(gl.DEPTH_TEST);
```

usually as part of `init`. Because the algorithm stores information in the depth buffer, we must clear this buffer whenever we wish to redraw the display; thus, we modify the clear procedure in the display function:

```
gl.clear(gl.COLOR_BUFFER_BIT | gl.DEPTH_BUFFER_BIT);
```

The render function is as follows:

```
function render()
{
  gl.clear(gl.COLOR_BUFFER_BIT | gl.DEPTH_BUFFER_BIT);
  gl.drawArrays(gl.TRIANGLES, 0, numVertices);
}
```

The results are shown in Figure 2.43 for a recursion of three steps. The complete program is on the website (**gasket4** and Color Plate 14).

FIGURE 2.43   Three-dimensional gasket after three recursion steps.

SUMMARY AND NOTES

In this chapter, we introduced just enough of the WebGL API to apply the basic concepts that we learned in Chapter 1. Although the application we used to develop our first program was two-dimensional, we took the path of looking at two-dimensional graphics as a special case of three-dimensional graphics. We then were able to extend the example to three dimensions with minimal work.

The Sierpinski gasket provides a nontrivial beginning application. A few extensions and mathematical issues are presented in the exercises at the end of this chapter. The texts in the Suggested Readings section provide many other examples of interesting curves and surfaces that can be generated with simple programs.

The historical development of graphics APIs and graphical models illustrates the importance of starting in three dimensions. The pen-plotter model from Chapter 1 was used for many years and is the basis of many important APIs, such as PostScript. Work to define an international standard for graphics APIs began in the 1970s and culminated with the adoption of GKS by the International Standards Organization (ISO) in 1984. However, GKS had its basis in the pen-plotter model, and as a two-dimensional API, it was of limited utility in the CAD community. Although the standard was extended to three dimensions with GKS-3D, the limitations imposed by the original underlying model led to a standard that was deficient in many aspects. The PHIGS and PHIGS+ APIs, started in the CAD community, are inherently three-dimensional and are based on the synthetic-camera model.

OpenGL is derived from the Iris GL API, which is based on implementing the synthetic-camera model with a pipeline architecture. Iris GL was developed for Silicon Graphics, Inc. (SGI) workstations, which incorporated a pipeline architecture originally implemented with special-purpose VLSI chips. Hence, although PHIGS and GL have much in common, GL was designed specifically for high-speed real-time rendering. OpenGL was a result of application users realizing the advantages of GL programming and wanting to carry these advantages to other platforms. Because it removed input and windowing functions from GL and concentrated on rendering, OpenGL emerged as a new API that was portable while retaining the features that make GL such a powerful API.

Although most application programmers who use OpenGL prefer to program in C, there is a fair amount of interest in higher-level interfaces. Using C++ rather than C requires minimal code changes but does not provide a true object-oriented interface to OpenGL. Among object-oriented programmers, there has been much interest in both OpenGL and higher-level APIs. Although there is no official Java binding for OpenGL, there have been multiple efforts to come up with one.

Within the game community, the dominance of Windows made it possible for game developers to write code for a single platform. DirectX runs only on Windows platforms and is optimized for speed on these systems. Although much DirectX code looks like OpenGL code, the coder can use device-dependent features that are available in commodity graphics cards. Consequently, applications written in DirectX do not have the portability and stability of OpenGL applications. Thus, we have seen DirectX dominating the game world, whereas scientific and engineering applications generally are written in OpenGL. For OpenGL programmers who want to use features specific to certain hardware, OpenGL has an extension mechanism for accessing these features, but at the cost of portability. Programming pipelines that are accessible through the OpenGL Shading Language and Cg are leading to small performance differences between OpenGL and DirectX for high-end applications.

We are now in the midst of major changes due to the combination of the Web and the proliferation of handheld devices, primarily smart phones. As we have seen, WebGL applications can run in almost all the latest browsers and on an increasing number of devices. As the speed and sophistication of GPUs and JavaScript engines continue to increase, we expect the majority of graphics applications will be ported to or developed with WebGL.

Our examples and programs have shown how we describe and display geometric objects in a simple manner. In terms of the modeling–rendering paradigm that we presented in Chapter 1, we have focused on the modeling. However, our models are completely unstructured. Representations of objects are lists of vertices and attributes. In Chapter 9, we will learn to construct hierarchical models that can represent relationships among objects. Nevertheless, at this point, you should be able to write interesting programs. Complete the exercises at the end of the chapter and extend a few of the two-dimensional problems to three dimensions.

SUGGESTED READINGS

The Sierpinski gasket provides a good introduction to the mysteries of fractal geometry; there are good discussions in several texts [Bar93, Hil09, Man82, Pru90].

The pen-plotter API is used by PostScript [Ado85] and LOGO [Pap81]. LOGO provides turtle graphics, an API that is both simple to learn and capable of describing several of the two-dimensional mathematical curves that we use in Chapter 11 (see Exercise 2.4). It is also used for the agent-based modeling applications in NetLogo [Rai11] and StarLogo [Col01].

GKS [ANSI85], GKS-3D [ISO88], PHIGS [ANSI88], and PHIGS+ [PHI89] are both US and international standards. Their formal descriptions can be obtained from the American National Standards Institute (ANSI) and from ISO. Numerous textbooks use these APIs [Ang90, End84, Fol94, Hea04, Hop83, Hop91].

The X Window System [Sch88] has become the standard on UNIX workstations and has influenced the development of window systems on other platforms. The RenderMan interface is described in [Ups89].

The standard reference for OpenGL is the *OpenGL Programming Guide* [Shr13]. There is also a formal specification of OpenGL [Seg92]. The OpenGL Shading Language is described in [Ros09], [Shr13], and [Bai12]. The standards documents as well as many other references and pointers to code examples are on the OpenGL (*www.opengl.org*) and Khronos (*www.kronos.org*) websites.

Starting with the second edition and continuing through the present edition, the *OpenGL Programming Guide* uses the GLUT library that was developed by Mark Kilgard [Kil94b]. The *Programming Guide* provides many more code examples using OpenGL. GLUT was developed for use with the X Window System [Kil96], but there are also versions for Windows and the Macintosh. Much of this information and many of the example programs are available over the Internet.

OpenGL: A Primer [Ang08], the companion book to previous editions of this text, contains details of the OpenGL functions used here and also provides more example programs. Windows users can find more examples in [Wri07] and [Fos97]. Details for Mac OS X users are [Koe08].

The *Open GL ES 2.0 Programming Guide* [Mun09] provides the background for WebGL. Many tutorials for WebGL are referenced from the Khronos WebGL site (*www.khronos.org/webgl*). Recently, books covering WebGL are starting to appear, including [Can12], [Par12], and a WebGL programming guide [Mat13].

The graphics part of the DirectX API was originally known as Direct3D. The present version is Version 11.

Two standard references for JavaScript aimed at those with programming experience are Flanagan [Fla11] and Crowford [Cro08].

EXERCISES

2.1   A slight variation on generating the Sierpinski gasket with triangular polygons yields the *fractal mountains* used in computer-generated animations. After you find the midpoint of each side of the triangle, perturb this location before subdivision. Generate these triangles without fill. Later, you can do this exercise in three dimensions and add shading. After a few subdivisions, you should have generated sufficient detail that your triangles look like a mountain.

2.2   The Sierpinski gasket, as generated in Exercise 2.1, demonstrates many of the geometric complexities that are studied in fractal geometry [Man82]. Suppose that you construct the gasket with mathematical lines that have length but no width. In the limit, what percentage of the area of the original triangle remains after the central triangle has been removed after each subdivision? Consider the perimeters of the triangles remaining after each central triangle is removed. In the limit, what happens to the total perimeter length of all remaining triangles?

2.3   In the Section 2.1, the procedure to draw the well-known interesting shape Sierpinski gasket is explained. It has a long history and is of interest in areas such as fractal geometry. In Section 2.1, the procedure is explained for a planer system, while in Section 2.10, the gasket is explained for a three-dimensional system. Write a small construction that will generate a Sierpinski gasket for a three-dimensional version. In the two-dimensional gasket, we use a triangle. What changes do we have to make for its equivalent three-dimensional version? State the problems of the three-dimensional gasket over the two-dimensional gasket, and how we can overcome them.

2.4   *Turtle graphics* is an alternative positioning system that is based on the concept of a turtle moving around the screen with a pen attached to the bottom of its shell. The turtle's position can be described by a triplet (x, y, θ), giving the

FIGURE 2.44   Generation of the Koch snowflake.

location of the center and the orientation of the turtle. A typical API for such a system includes functions such as the following:

```
init(x,y,theta); // initialize position and orientation of turtle
forward(distance);
right(angle);
left(angle);
pen(up_down);
```

Implement a turtle graphics library using WebGL.

2.5   Use your turtle graphics library from Exercise 2.4 to generate the Sierpinski gasket and fractal mountains of Exercises 2.1 and 2.2.

2.6   Space-filling curves have interested mathematicians for centuries. In the limit, these curves have infinite length, but they are confined to a finite rectangle and never cross themselves. Many of these curves can be generated iteratively. Consider the "rule" pictured in Figure 2.44 that replaces a single line segment with four shorter segments. Write a program that starts with a triangle and iteratively applies the replacement rule to all the line segments. The object that you generate is called the Koch snowflake. For other examples of space-filling curves, see [Hil07] and [Bar93].

2.7   You can generate a simple maze starting with a rectangular array of cells. Each cell has four sides. You remove sides (except from the perimeter of all the cells) until all the cells are connected. Then you create an entrance and an exit by removing two sides from the perimeter. A simple example is shown in Figure 2.45. Write a program using WebGL that takes as input the two integers N and M and then draws an $N \times M$ maze.

2.8   Describe how you would adapt the RGB color model in WebGL to allow you to work with an additive color model.

2.9   We saw that a fundamental operation in graphics systems is to map a point (x, y) that lies within a clipping rectangle to a point (x_s, y_s) that lies in the viewport of a window on the screen. Assume that the two rectangles are defined by the viewport specified by

```
gl.viewport(u, v, w, h);
```

and a viewing rectangle specified by

$$x_{min} \leq x \leq x_{max} \qquad y_{min} \leq y \leq y_{max}.$$

Find the mathematical equations that map (x, y) into (x_s, y_s).

FIGURE 2.45   Maze.

2.10 Many graphics APIs use relative positioning. In such a system, the API contains functions such as

```
shift_rel (x,y);
row_rel (x,y);
col_rel (x,y);
```

for drawing lines and polygons. The `shift_rel` function shifts an internal position, or cursor, to a new position; the `row_rel` function moves the cursor along a row and defines a line segment between the old cursor position and the new position; `col_rel` function moves the cursor in a column and defines a line segment between the old cursor position and the new position. Give an idea how these functions work.

2.11 In practice, testing each point in a polygon to determine whether it is inside or outside the polygon is done by a point-by-point testing. Describe some general strategies to test the same for a mesh.

2.12 Devise a test to determine whether a two-dimensional polygon is simple.

2.13 Figure 2.46 shows a set of polygons called a *mesh*; these polygons share some edges and vertices. Devise one or more simple data structures that represent the mesh. A good data structure should include information on shared vertices and edges. Using WebGL, find an efficient method for displaying a mesh represented by your data structure. *Hint:* Start with an array or linked list that contains the locations of the vertices.

2.14 In Section 2.3.1, we saw all graphics APIs support similar functionality but the difference among APIs is where these functions are supported. Discuss where to use primitive functions and attribute functions. Find the relation between these sets of functions.

2.15 In WebGL, we can associate a color with each vertex. If the endpoints of a line segment have different colors assigned to them, WebGL will interpolate between the colors as it renders the line segment. It will do the same for polygons. Use this property to display the *Maxwell triangle*: an equilateral triangle whose vertices are red, green, and blue. What is the relationship between the Maxwell triangle and the color cube?

2.16 We can simulate many realistic effects using computer graphics by incorporating simple physics in the model. Simulate a ball moving in a plane surface in two dimensions. You can model the ball with a closed polygon that has a sufficient number of sides to look smooth.

2.17 An interesting but difficult extension of Exercise 2.16 is to simulate a game of bat and ball. You will need to have a bat that strikes the ball at a different angle, and the path of the ball will be set accordingly. Simulate a system that will use these graphical models to implement this game.

2.18 A certain graphics system with a CRT display is advertised to display any eight out of 64 colors. What does this statement tell you about the framebuffer and about the quality of the monitor?

2.19 Devise a test for the convexity of a two-dimensional polygon.

FIGURE 2.46 Polygonal mesh.

2.20 Another approach to the three-dimensional gasket is based on subdividing only the faces of an initial tetrahedron. Write a program that takes this approach. How do the results differ from the program that we developed in Section 2.10?

2.21 We have used tetrahedron in the representation of three-dimensional gaskets. We may subdivide the tetrahedron into smaller tetrahedrons corresponding to the original vertices by decreasing the volume by a factor f. What is the ratio of the new surface area if the original tetrahedron is subdivided into eight tetrahedrons?

2.22 Creating simple games is a good way to become familiar with interactive graphics programming. Program the game of tic-tac-toe. You can look at each square as an object that can be filled with cross or circle by the user. You can start with a program in which the user plays both sides.

2.23 There are different types of software available that allow comparing the results of solutions for the same problem using different theories or principles. Implement a system which allows the user to display the result of a problem using multiple techniques. The result may include charts with values.

2.24 In our two-dimensional Sierpinski gasket examples, we mentioned a starting point inside the initial triangle. Using small program code, show what changes we have to make for initializing the variables in its three-dimensional version.

CHAPTER 3

INTERACTION AND ANIMATION

We now turn to the development of interactive graphics programs. Interactive computer graphics opens up a myriad of applications, ranging from interactive design of buildings, to control of large systems through graphical interfaces, to virtual reality systems, to computer games.

Our examples in Chapter 2 were all static. We described a scene, sent data to the GPU, and then rendered these data. However, in most real applications we need a dynamic display because the objects we want to display change their positions, colors, or shapes. Our first task will be to introduce a simple method for creating animated applications; that is, applications in which the display changes with time, even without input from the user.

Next, we turn our focus to adding interactivity to WebGL, a task that requires us to look in more detail at how the graphics interact with the browser environment. As part of the development, we will have a preliminary discussion of buffers, a topic we will return to in Chapter 7. We then introduce the variety of devices available for interaction. We consider input devices from two different perspectives: the way that the physical devices can be described by their physical properties, and the way that these devices appear to the application program. We then consider client–server networks and client–server graphics. Finally, we use these ideas to develop event-driven input for our graphics programs.

3.1 ANIMATION

Our examples in Chapter 2 were all static; we rendered the scene once and did nothing else. Now suppose that we want to change what we see. For example, suppose that we display a simple object such as a square and we want to rotate this square at a constant rate. A simple but slow and inelegant approach would be to have our application generate new vertex data periodically, send these data to the GPU, and do another render each time that we send new data. This approach would negate many of the advances using shaders, because it would have a potential bottleneck due to the repetitive sending of data from the CPU to the GPU. We can do much better if we start thinking in terms of a recursive rendering process where the render function can

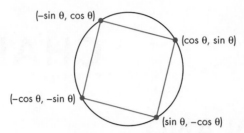

FIGURE 3.1   Square constructed from four points on a circle.

call itself. We will illustrate various options using a simple program that produces a rotating square.

3.1.1 The Rotating Square

Consider the two-dimensional point

$$x = \cos \theta \qquad y = \sin \theta.$$

This point lies on a unit circle regardless of the value of θ. The three points $(-\sin \theta, \cos \theta)$, $(-\cos \theta, -\sin \theta)$, and $(\sin \theta, -\cos \theta)$ also lie on the unit circle. These four points are equidistant along the circumference of the circle, as shown in Figure 3.1. Thus, if we connect the points to form a polygon, we will have a square centered at the origin whose sides are of length $\sqrt{2}$.

We can start with $\theta = 0$, which gives us the four vertices $(0, 1)$, $(1, 0)$, $(-1, 0)$ and $(0, -1)$. We can send these vertices to the GPU by first setting up an array

```
var vertices = [
  vec2(0, 1),
  vec2(1, 0),
  vec2(-1, 0),
  vec2(0, -1)
];
```

and then sending the array

```
var bufferId = gl.createBuffer();
gl.bindBuffer(gl.ARRAY_BUFFER, vBuffer);
gl.bufferData(gl.ARRAY_BUFFER, flatten(vertices), gl.STATIC_DRAW);
```

We can render these data using a render function as in Chapter 2

```
function render()
{
  gl.clear(gl.COLOR_BUFFER_BIT);
  gl.drawArrays(gl.TRIANGLE_STRIP, 0, 4);
}
```

and the simple pass-through shaders we used in Chapter 2.

Now suppose that we want to display the square with a different value of θ. We could compute new vertices with positions determined by the two equations we started with for a general θ and then send these vertices to the GPU, followed by another rendering. If we want to see the square rotating, we could put the code in a loop that increments θ by a fixed amount each time. But such a strategy would be extremely inefficient. Not only would we be sending vertices to the GPU repeatedly, something that would be far more problematic if we were to replace the square by an object with hundreds or thousands of vertices, but we would also be doing the trigonometric calculations in the CPU rather than the GPU where these calculations could be done much faster.

A better solution is to send the original data to the GPU as we did initially and then alter θ in the render function and send the new θ to the GPU. In order to transfer data from the CPU to variables in the shader, we must introduce a new type of shader variable. In a given application, a variable may change in a variety of ways. When we send vertex attributes to a shader, these attributes can be different for each vertex in a primitive. We may also want parameters that will remain the same for all vertices in a primitive or equivalently for all the vertices that are displayed when we execute a function such as `gl.drawArrays`. Such variables are called **uniform qualified variables**.

Consider the vertex shader

```
attribute vec4 vPosition;
uniform float theta;

void main()
{
  gl_Position.x = -sin(theta) * vPosition.x + cos(theta) * vPosition.y;
  gl_Position.y =  sin(theta) * vPosition.y + cos(theta) * vPosition.x;
  gl_Position.z = 0.0;
  gl_Position.w = 1.0;
}
```

The variable `theta` has the qualifier `uniform` so the shader expects its value to be provided by the application. With this value, the shader outputs a vertex position that is rotated by θ.

In order to get a value of θ to the shader, we must perform two steps. First, we must provide a link between `theta` in the shader and a variable in the application. Second, we must send the value from the application to the shader.

Suppose that we use a variable also named `theta` in the application[1]

```
var theta = 0.0;
```

---

1. We could use any valid name, but we will use the same name in our examples to make it easier to recognize the tie between a particular shader variable and the corresponding application variable.

When the shaders and application are compiled and linked by `initShaders`, tables are created that we can query to make the necessary correspondence using the function `gl.getUniformLocation`, as in the code

```
var thetaLoc = gl.getUniformLocation(program, "theta");
```

Note that this function is analogous to the way we linked attributes in the vertex shader with variables in the application. We can then send the value of `theta` from the application to the shader by

```
gl.uniform1f(thetaLoc, theta);
```

There are multiple forms of `gl.uniform` corresponding to the types of values we are sending—scalars, vectors, or matrices—and to whether we are sending the values or pointers to the values. Here, the `1f` indicates that we are sending the value of a floating-point variable. We will see other forms starting in Chapter 4, where we will be sending vectors and matrices to shaders. Although our example sends data to a vertex shader, we can also use uniforms to send data to fragment shaders.

Returning to our example, we send new values of `theta` to the vertex shader in the `render` function

```
function render()
{
  gl.clear(gl.COLOR_BUFFER_BIT);
  theta += 0.1;
  gl.uniform1f(thetaLoc, theta);
  gl.drawArrays(gl.TRIANGLE_STRIP, 0, 4);

  render();
}
```

which increases θ, renders, and calls itself. Unfortunately, this approach will not quite work. In fact, we will see only the initial display of the square. To fix the problem, we need to examine how and when the display is changed.

3.1.2 The Display Process

Before proceeding, it would be helpful to overview how the browser and the window system interact with a physical display device. Consider a typical flat-panel display and a static image that comprises multiple windows. This image is stored as pixels in a buffer maintained by the window system and is periodically and automatically redrawn on the display. The **refresh** or **repaint** operation draws a new image (or frame), at a rate of approximately 60 frames per second (fps) (or 60 hertz or 60 Hz). The actual rate is set by the window system, and you may be able to adjust it.

Historically, the frame rate was tied to the alternating current (AC) power transmission frequency of 60 Hz in North America and 50 Hz in Europe. The refresh was required by the short persistence of the phosphors in CRTs. Although now CRT monitors are no longer the dominant technology and the electronics are no longer coupled to the line frequency, there is still a minimum rate for each display technology that must be high enough to avoid visual artifacts (most noticeably flicker, if the rate is too low). From our perspective, this process is not synchronized with the execution of our program and usually we do not need to worry about it. As we noted in Chapter 1, the redraw can be **progressive** and redraw the entire display each time, or it can be interlaced, redrawing odd and even lines on alternate frames.

Consider a browser window on the display. Although this window is being redrawn by the display process, its contents are unchanged unless some action takes place that changes pixels in the display buffer. The action (or event) can be caused by some action on the part of the user, such as clicking a mouse button or pressing a key, or the action can be caused by an event such as a new frame in a video needing to be displayed. We will discuss events and event processing in detail later in this chapter, but for now we should note that the browser runs asynchronously, executing one piece of code until some event interrupts the flow or the code runs to completion, in which case the browser waits for another event.

Now suppose that the browser window is a WebGL window. As we saw from our examples, we input a series of JavaScript files including the file with the application. The **onload** event starts the execution of our application with the `init` function. In our applications so far, the execution ended in the `render` function. That invokes the `gl.drawArrays` function. At this point, execution of our code is complete and the results are displayed. However, the code for rendering the square,

```
function render()
{
  gl.clear(gl.COLOR_BUFFER_BIT);
  theta += 0.1;
  gl.uniform1f(thetaLoc, theta);
  gl.drawArrays(gl.TRIANGLE_STRIP, 0, 4);

  render();
}
```

has a fundamental difference; namely, that it calls itself, and this recursion puts the drawing inside an infinite loop. Thus, we cannot reach the end of our code and we never see changes to the display. Nevertheless, the executions of `gl.drawArrays` cause changes in another buffer.

3.1.3 Double Buffering

Suppose that the color buffer in the framebuffer is a single buffer that holds the colored pixels produced by our application. Then each time the browser repaints the display, we would see its present contents. If the objects we are rendering are not changing, then, other than possibly seeing a little flicker if the redraw rate is slow or noticing the slight shifting of the image in an interlaced display, we would see an unchanging image in the window.

However, if we change the contents of the framebuffer during a refresh, we may see undesirable artifacts of how we generate the display. In addition, if we are rendering more geometry than can be rendered in a single refresh cycle, we will see different parts of objects on successive refreshes. If an object is moving, its image may be distorted on the display.

Consider what might happen with the repetitive clearing and redrawing of an area of the screen, as we are attempting in our rotating-square program. Even though the square is a simple object and is easily rendered in a single refresh cycle, there is no coupling between when new squares are drawn into the framebuffer and when the framebuffer is redisplayed by the hardware. Thus, depending on exactly when the framebuffer is displayed, only part of the square may be in the buffer. This model is known as **single buffering** because there is only one buffer—the color buffer in the framebuffer—for rendering and display.

Double buffering provides a solution to these problems. Suppose that we have two color buffers at our disposal, conventionally called the front and back buffers. The **front buffer** is always the one displayed, whereas the **back buffer** is the one into which we draw. WebGL requires double buffering. A typical rendering starts with a clearing of the back buffer, rendering into the back buffer, and finishing with a buffer swap. The remaining issue is how and when the buffer swap is triggered. In the example we started with, in which we tried to use a recursive call to the render function, we failed to provide a buffer swap so we would not see a change in the display. We will examine two approaches: using timers and using the function `requestAnimFrame`.

Note that double buffering does not solve all the problems that we encounter with animated displays. If the display is complex, we still may need multiple frames to draw the image into the framebuffer. Double buffering does not speed up this process; it only ensures that we never see a partial display. However, we are often able to have visibly acceptable displays at rates as low as 10 to 20 frames per second if we use double buffering.

3.1.4 Using a Timer

One way to generate a buffer swap and to control the rate at which the display is repainted is to use the `setInterval` method to call the render function repeatedly after a specified number of milliseconds. Thus, if we replace the execution of `render` at the end of `init` with

```
setInterval(render, 16);
```

`render` will be called after 16 milliseconds (when the timer interval has elapsed), or about 60 times per second. An interval of 0 milliseconds will cause the render function to be executed as fast as possible. Each time the time-out function completes, it forces the buffers to be swapped, and thus we get an updated display.

Suppose that you want to check if indeed the interval between renderings is the interval specified in `setInterval`, or perhaps to check how long it takes to execute some code. We can measure times in milliseconds by adding a timer to our code using the `Date` object. The `getTime` method returns the number of milliseconds since midnight GMT on January 1, 1970. Here is a simple use of a timer to output the time between renderings. Before we render, we save an initial time

```
var t1, t2;

var date = new Date;
t1 = date.getTime();
```

and then in **render**

```
t2 = date.getTime();
console.log(t2 - t1);
t1 = t2;
```

3.1.5 Using `requestAnimFrame`

Because `setInterval` and related JavaScript functions, such as `setTimeout`, are independent of the browser, it can be difficult to get a smooth animation. One solution to this problem is to use the function `requestAnimFrame`, which is supported by most browsers. Consider the simple rendering function

```
function render()
{
  gl.clear(gl.COLOR_BUFFER_BIT);
  theta += 0.1;
  gl.uniform1f(thetaLoc, theta);
  gl.drawArrays(gl.TRIANGLE_STRIP, 0, 4);
  requestAnimFrame(render);
}
```

The function `requestAnimFrame` requests the browser to display the rendering the next time it wants to refresh the display and then call the render function recursively. For a simple display, such as our square, we will get a smooth display at about 60 fps.

Finally, we can use `requestAnimFrame` within `setInterval` to get a different frame rate, as in the render function, of about 10 fps:

```
function render()
{
  setTimeout(function() {
    requestAnimFrame(render);
    gl.clear(gl.COLOR_BUFFER_BIT);
    theta += 0.1;
    gl.uniform1f(thetaLoc, theta);
    gl.drawArrays(gl.TRIANGLE_STRIP, 0, 4);
  }, 100);
}
```

Although this solution should work pretty well for most simple animations, let's take a somewhat different look at the problem by focusing on the framebuffer and, at least initially, not worrying about the browser, the window system, or anything else going on.

3.2   INTERACTION

One of the most important advances in computer technology was enabling users to interact with computer displays. More than any other event, Ivan Sutherland's Sketchpad project launched the present era of *interactive* computer graphics. The basic paradigm that he introduced is deceptively simple. The user sees an image on the display. She reacts to this image by means of an interactive device, such as a mouse. The image changes in response to her input. She reacts to this change, and so on. Whether we are writing programs using the tools available in a modern window system or using the human–computer interface in an interactive museum exhibit, we are making use of this paradigm.

In the 50 years since Sutherland's work, there have been many advances in both hardware and software, but the viewpoint and ideas that he introduced still dominate interactive computer graphics. These influences range from how we conceptualize the human–computer interface to how we can employ graphical data structures that allow for efficient implementations.

In this chapter, we take an approach slightly different from that in the rest of the book. Although rendering is the prime concern of most modern APIs, interactivity is an important component of most applications. OpenGL, and thus WebGL, do not support interaction directly. The major reason for this omission is that the system architects who designed OpenGL wanted to increase its portability by allowing the system to work in a variety of environments. Consequently, window and input functions were left out of the API. Although this decision makes renderers portable, it makes discussions of interaction that do not include specifics of the window system more difficult. In addition, because any application program must have at least a minimal interface to the window environment, we cannot entirely avoid such issues if we want to write complete, nontrivial programs. If interaction is omitted from the API, the application programmer is forced to worry about the often arcane details of her particular environment.

Nevertheless, it is hard to imagine any application that does not involve some sort of interaction, whether it is as simple as entering data or something more complex that uses gestures with multiple fingers on a touch screen. For desktop OpenGL, there are some toolkits that provide an API that supports operations common to all window systems, such as opening windows and getting data from a mouse or keyboard. Such toolkits require recompilation of an application to run with a different window system, but the application source code need not be changed.

There is much greater compatibility across platforms with WebGL. Because WebGL is contained within HTML5, we can employ a variety of tools and make use of a variety of packages, all of which will run on any system that supports WebGL. We will follow the same approach as in Chapter 2 and focus on creating interactive applications with JavaScript rather than using a higher-level package. We believe that this approach will make it clearer how interactivity works and will be more robust because it will not make use of software packages that are under continual change.

Before proceeding, we want to lessen some of the confusion with regard to multiple ways the terms *window* and *window system* are used. We use the term *window system*, as we did in Chapter 2, to include the total environment provided by systems such as Linux using the X Window System, all the versions of Microsoft Windows, and Mac OS X. When you open a window in your browser, this window is also a window within the larger operating system, although one with special properties that allow it to display information specified, for example, by files written in HTML. When we run a WebGL program through our browser, the window it runs in is under control of the browser, which itself is under control of the local windowing system. Matters can get more complex since our interaction with the browser window might cause more windows to appear, such as pop-ups, or windows might be destroyed. All these actions require complex interactions among operating systems, browsers, application programs, and various buffers. Any detailed discussion will take us away from our desire to stay close to graphics.

Without getting into detail about the interaction among the various entities, we can work with the following high-level model: The WebGL application programs that we develop will render into a window opened by a browser that supports WebGL.

We start by describing several interactive devices and the variety of ways that we can interact with them. Then we put these devices in the setting of a client–server network and introduce an API for minimal interaction. Finally, we generate sample programs.

3.3 INPUT DEVICES

We can think about input devices in two distinct ways. The obvious one is to look at them as physical devices, such as a keyboard or a mouse, and to discuss how they work. Certainly, we need to know something about the physical properties of our input devices, so such a discussion is necessary if we are to obtain a full understanding of input. However, from the perspective of an application programmer, we should not need to know the details of a particular physical device to write an application program. Rather, we prefer to treat input devices as *logical* devices whose properties are specified in terms of what they do from the perspective of the application program. A **logical device** is characterized by its high-level interface with the application program rather than by its physical characteristics. Logical devices are familiar to all writers of high-level programs.

Consider this fragment of C++ code,

```
int x;
cin >> x;
cout << x;
```

in which we read and then write an integer. Obviously, we could have just as easily written this fragment in C or Java. Although we would typically run the program on a workstation, entering the data from a keyboard and seeing the output on the display, we could also use mechanisms such as redirection to have the input come from the output from another program or have the output placed in a disk file. Even if we use the keyboard and display, the use of the default input and output streams `cin` and `cout` requires no knowledge of the properties of the physical devices, such as the keyboard codes or the resolution of the display. Rather, `cin` and `cout` are logical functions that are defined by how they handle input or output character strings from the perspective of the C++ program. More generally, data input and output in C are done through functions such as `printf`, `scanf`, `getchar`, and `putchar`, whose arguments use the standard C data types, and through input (`cin`) and output (`cout`) streams in C++.

When we output a string of characters using `printf` or `cout`, the physical device on which the output appears could be a printer, a terminal, or a disk file. The output could even be the input to another program. The details of the format required by the destination device are of minor concern to the writer of the application program.

In computer graphics, the use of logical devices is somewhat more complex because the forms that input can take are more varied than the strings of bits or characters to which we are usually restricted in nongraphical applications. For example, we can use the mouse—a physical device—to select a location on the screen or to indicate which item in a menu we wish to select. These are two different logical functions. In the first case, an (x, y) pair (in some coordinate system) is returned to the user program; in the second, the application program may receive an integer identifier that corresponds to an entry in the menu. The separation of physical from logical devices not only allows us to use the same physical device in multiple, markedly different, logical ways but also allows the same program to work without modification if the mouse is replaced by another physical device, such as a data tablet or trackball.

There is a second issue that arises from our code fragment; namely, how and when does the input data get to a program variable and, likewise, how does the data from a program variable get to a display device. These issues relate to interaction between the physical devices and the operating system and will also be examined later.

3.4   PHYSICAL INPUT DEVICES

From the physical perspective, each input device has properties that make it more suitable for certain tasks than for others. We take the view used in most of the workstation literature that there are two primary types of physical devices: pointing devices and keyboard devices. The **pointing device** allows the user to indicate a position on a display and almost always incorporates one or more buttons to allow the user to send signals or interrupts to the computer. The **keyboard device** is almost always a physical keyboard but can be generalized to include any device that returns character codes. For example, a tablet computer uses recognition software to decode the user's writing with a stylus but in the end produces character codes identical to those of the standard keyboard.

3.4.1 Keyboard Codes

For many years, the standard code for representing characters was the American Standard Code for Information Interchange (ASCII), which assigns a single byte to each character. ASCII used only the first 127 codes and was later expanded to a larger 8-bit character set known as Latin 1 that can represent most European languages. However, 8 bits is insufficient to support other languages that are needed for a true worldwide Internet. Consequently, Unicode was developed as 16-bit (2-byte) code that is rich enough to support virtually all languages and is the standard for all modern browsers. Because Latin 1 is a superset of ASCII and Unicode is a superset of Latin 1, code developed based on earlier byte-oriented character sets should work in any browser.

3.4.2 The Light Pen

The **light pen** has a long history in computer graphics. It was the device used in Sutherland's original Sketchpad. The light pen contains a light-sensing device, such as a photocell (Figure 3.2). If the light pen is positioned on the face of the CRT at a location opposite where the electron beam strikes the phosphor, the light emitted exceeds a threshold in the photodetector and a signal is sent to the computer. Because each redisplay of the framebuffer starts at a precise time, we can use the time at which this signal occurs to determine a position on the CRT screen (see Exercise 3.14). The light pen was originally used on random scan devices so the time of the interrupt could easily be matched to a piece of code in the display list, thus making the light pen ideal for selecting application-defined objects. With raster scan devices, the position on the display can be determined by the time the scan begins and the time it takes to scan each line. Hence, we have a direct-positioning device.

The light pen has some deficiencies, including its cost and the difficulty of obtaining a position that corresponds to a dark area of the screen. For all practical purposes, the light pen has been superseded by the mouse and track pad. However, tablet PCs are used in a manner that mimics how the light pen was used originally: The user has a stylus with which she can move randomly about the tablet (display) surface.

FIGURE 3.2   Light pen.

3.4.3 The Mouse and the Trackball

The mouse (Figure 3.3) and trackball (Figure 3.4) are similar in use and often in construction as well. When turned over, a typical mechanical mouse looks like a trackball. In both devices, the motion of the ball is converted to signals sent back to the computer by pairs of encoders inside the device that are turned by the motion of the ball. The encoders measure motion in two orthogonal directions. Note that the wheel found on many recent mice acts as an independent one-dimensional mouse-like device.

FIGURE 3.3   Mouse.

There are many variants of these devices. Some use optical detectors rather than mechanical detectors to measure motion. Small trackballs are popular with portable computers because they can be incorporated directly into the keyboard. There are also various pressure-sensitive devices used in keyboards that perform similar functions to the mouse and trackball but that do not move; their encoders measure the pressure exerted on a small knob that often is located between two keys in the middle of the keyboard.

FIGURE 3.4   Trackball.

We can view the output of the mouse or trackball as two independent values provided by the device. These values can be considered as positions and converted—either within the graphics system or by the user program—to a two-dimensional location in either screen or world coordinates. If it is configured in this manner,

FIGURE 3.5   Cursor positioning.

we can use the device to position a marker (cursor) automatically on the display; however, we rarely use these devices in this direct manner.

It is not necessary that the outputs of the mouse or trackball encoders be interpreted as positions. Instead, either the device driver or a user program can interpret the information from the encoder as two independent velocities (see Exercise 3.4). The computer can then integrate these values to obtain a two-dimensional position. Thus, as a mouse moves across a surface, the integrals of the velocities yield x, y values that can be converted to indicate the position for a cursor on the screen, as shown in Figure 3.5. By interpreting the distance traveled by the ball as a velocity, we can use the device as a variable-sensitivity input device. Small deviations from rest cause slow or small changes; large deviations cause rapid or large changes. With either device, if the ball does not rotate, then there is no change in the integrals and a cursor tracking the position of the mouse will not move. In this mode, these devices are **relative-positioning** devices because changes in the position of the ball yield a position in the user program; the absolute location of the ball (or the mouse) is not used by the application program.

Relative positioning, as provided by a mouse or trackball, is not always desirable. In particular, these devices are not suitable for an operation such as tracing a diagram. If, while the user is attempting to follow a curve on the screen with a mouse, she lifts and moves the mouse, the absolute position on the curve being traced is lost.

3.4.4 Data Tablets, Touch Pads, and Touch Screens

Data tablets (or just **tablets**) provide absolute positioning. A typical data tablet (Figure 3.6) has rows and columns of wires embedded under its surface. The position of the stylus is determined through electromagnetic interactions between signals traveling through the wires and sensors in the stylus. Touch-sensitive transparent screens that can be placed over the face of a CRT have many of the same properties as the data tablet. Small, rectangular, pressure-sensitive **touch pads** are embedded in the keyboards of most portable computers. These touch pads can be configured as either relative- or absolute-positioning devices. Some are capable of detecting simultaneous motion input from multiple fingers touching different spots on the pad and can use this information to enable more complex behaviors.

Tablet devices and smart phones are characterized by **touch screens**. A touch screen is both a display and an input device. Positions are detected by changes in pressure on the display's surface, which might be initiated by a single or multiple pressure points, engaged by fingers or perhaps a stylus. Since the input device is overlaid on the displayed image, the user can interact directly with the displayed

FIGURE 3.6   Data tablet.

image. Thus, if we display a button, the user can push it. If we display the image of an object, the user can move it around the screen by touching the object and then moving her finger or stylus.

Additionally, most touch devices are capable of tracking multiple pressure points that allows **gestural input**. For example, a common gesture is a "pinch," using two fingers to initially make contact with the touch device at two separate locations and drawing the two fingers together to the same point on the touch device.

FIGURE 3.7   Joystick.

3.4.5 The Joystick

One other device, the **joystick** (Figure 3.7), is particularly worthy of mention. The motion of the stick in two orthogonal directions is encoded, interpreted as two velocities, and integrated to identify a screen location. The integration implies that if the stick is left in its resting position, there is no change in the cursor position, and that the farther the stick is moved from its resting position, the faster the screen location changes. Thus, the joystick is a variable-sensitivity device. The other advantage of the joystick is that the device can be constructed with mechanical elements, such as springs and dampers, that give resistance to a user who is pushing the stick. Such a mechanical feel, which is not possible with the other devices, makes the joystick well suited for applications such as flight simulators and game controllers.

3.4.6 Multidimensional Input Devices

For three-dimensional graphics, we might prefer to use three-dimensional input devices. Although various such devices are available, none have yet won the widespread acceptance of the popular two-dimensional input devices. A **spaceball** looks like a joystick with a ball on the end of the stick (Figure 3.8); however, the stick does not move. Rather, pressure sensors in the ball measure the forces applied by the user. The spaceball can measure not only the three direct forces (up–down, front–back, left–right) but also three independent twists. The device measures six independent values and thus has six **degrees of freedom**. Such an input device could be used, for example, both to position and to orient a camera.

FIGURE 3.8   Spaceball.

Other three-dimensional devices, such as laser scanners, measure three-dimensional positions directly. Numerous tracking systems used in virtual reality applications sense the position of the user. Virtual reality and robotics applications often need more degrees of freedom than the two to six provided by the devices that we have described. Devices such as data gloves can sense motion of various parts of the human body, thus providing many additional input signals. Recently, in addition to being wireless, input devices such as Nintendo's Wii incorporate gyroscopic sensing of position and orientation.

Many of the devices becoming available can take advantage of the enormous amount of computing power that can be used to drive them. For example, motion-capture (**mocap**) systems use arrays of standard digital cameras placed around an environment to capture reflected lights from small spherical dots that can be placed on humans at crucial locations, such as the arm and leg joints. In a typical system, eight cameras will see the environment and capture the location of the dots at high frame rates, producing large volumes of data. The computer, often just a standard PC, can process the two-dimensional pictures of the dots to determine, in each frame, where in three-dimensional space each dot must be located to have produced the captured data.

3.4.7 Logical Devices

We can now return to looking at input from inside the application program; that is, from the logical point of view. Two major characteristics describe the logical behavior of an input device: (1) the measurements that the device returns to the user program, and (2) the time when the device returns those measurements.

Some earlier APIs defined six classes of logical input devices. Because input in a modern window system cannot always be disassociated completely from the properties of the physical devices, modern systems no longer take this approach. Nevertheless, we describe the six classes briefly because they illustrate the variety of input forms available to a developer of graphical applications. We will see how WebGL can provide the functionality of each of these classes.

1. **String**   A string device is a logical device that provides ASCII strings to the user program. This logical device is usually implemented by means of a physical keyboard. In this case, the terminology is consistent with that used in most window systems, which usually do not distinguish between the logical string device and a physical keyboard.

2. **Locator**   A locator device provides a position in world coordinates to the user program. It is usually implemented by means of a pointing device, such as a mouse or a trackball. In WebGL, we usually use the pointing device in this manner, although we have to do the conversion from screen coordinates to world coordinates within our own programs.

3. **Pick**   A pick device returns the identifier of an object on the display to the user program. It is usually implemented with the same physical device as a locator, but has a separate software interface to the user program. We will examine a few alternatives for implementing picking in WebGL through the use of a pointing device.

4. **Choice**   Choice devices allow the user to select one of a discrete number of options. In WebGL, we can use various widgets provided by the window system. A **widget** is a graphical interactive device, provided by either the window system or a toolkit. Typical widgets include menus, slide bars, and graphical buttons. Most widgets are implemented as special types of windows. For example, a menu with n selections acts as a choice device, allowing us to select one of n alternatives. Widget sets are the key element defining a **graphical user interface**, or **GUI**. We will be able to use simple buttons, menus, and scroll bars in our examples without using a separate GUI package.

5. **Valuator**   Valuators provide analog input to the user program. On older graphics systems, there were boxes or dials to provide valuator input. Here again, widgets within various toolkits usually provide this facility through graphical devices such as slide bars and radio boxes.

6. **Stroke**   A stroke device returns an array of locations. Although we can think of a stroke device as similar to multiple uses of a locator, it is often implemented such that an action—say, pushing down a mouse button—starts the transfer of data into the specified array, and a second action, such as releasing the button, ends this transfer.

We can augment this list to include types of input from modern devices like touch pads and panels that accept multiple, simultaneous physical interactions and aggregate those actions into logical inputs representing gestures. Considering a "two-finger pinch" gesture, the device would register two initial "touches" at distinct locations. As the user completes the pinch gesture, the device would need to aggregate the motion of the user's fingers moving toward the same location on the touch device. If an application were provided this "raw" input, it would be challenging to intrepret the input data to determine the actual user gesture. Fortunately, most windowing systems for these types of devices do the processing either in the touch device's hardware or the device driver.

3.4.8 Input Modes

The manner by which input devices provide input to an application program can be described in terms of two entities: a measure process and a device trigger. The **measure** of a device is what the device returns to the user program. The **trigger** of a device is a physical input on the device with which the user can signal the computer. For example, the measure of a keyboard should include a single character or a string of characters, and the trigger can be the Return or Enter key. For a locator, the measure includes the position of the locator, and the associated trigger can be a button on the physical device. The measure processes are initiated by the browser when the application code has been loaded.

The application program can obtain the measure of a device in three distinct modes. Each mode is defined by the relationship between the measure process and the trigger. Once a measure process is started, the measure is taken and placed in a buffer, even though the contents of the buffer may not yet be available to the program. For example, the position of a mouse is tracked continuously by the underlying window system and a cursor is displayed regardless of whether the application program needs mouse input.

In **request mode**, the measure of the device is not returned to the program until the device is triggered. This input mode is standard in nongraphical applications. For example, if a typical C program requires character input, we use a function such as `scanf` in C or `cin` in C++. When the program needs the input, it halts when it encounters the `scanf` or `cin` statement and waits while we type characters at our terminal. We can backspace to correct our typing, and we can take as long as we like. The data are placed in a keyboard buffer whose contents are returned to our program only after a particular key, such as the Enter key (the trigger), is pressed. For a logical device, such as a locator, we can move our pointing device to the desired location and then trigger the device with its button; the trigger will cause the location to be returned to the application program. The relationship between measure and trigger for request mode is shown in Figure 3.9.

FIGURE 3.9   Request mode.

FIGURE 3.10   Sample mode.

Sample-mode input is immediate. As soon as the function call in the user program is encountered, the measure is returned. Hence, no trigger is needed (Figure 3.10). In sample mode, the user must have positioned the pointing device or entered data using the keyboard before the function call, because the measure is extracted immediately from the buffer.

One characteristic of both request- and sample-mode input in APIs that support them is that the user must identify which device is to provide the input. Consequently, we ignore any other information that becomes available from any input device other than the one specified. Both request and sample modes are useful for situations where the program guides the user, but are not useful in applications where the user controls the flow of the program. For example, a flight simulator or computer game might have multiple input devices—such as a joystick, dials, buttons, and switches—most of which can be used at any time. Writing programs to control the simulator with only sample- and request-mode input is nearly impossible because we do not know what devices the pilot will use at any point in the simulation. More generally, sample- and request-mode input are not sufficient for handling the variety of possible human–computer interactions that arise in a modern computing environment.

Our third mode, **event mode**, can handle these other interactions. We introduce it in three steps. First, we show how event mode can be described as another mode within our measure–trigger paradigm. Second, we discuss the basics of clients and servers where event mode is the preferred interaction mode. Third, we show the event-mode interface to WebGL through event handlers.

Suppose that we are in an environment with multiple input devices, each with its own trigger and each running a measure process. Each time that a device is triggered, an **event** is generated. The device measure, including the identifier for the device, is placed in an **event queue**. This process of placing events in the event queue is completely independent of what the application program does with these events. One way that the application program can work with events is shown in Figure 3.11. The application program can examine the front event in the queue or, if the queue is empty, can wait for an event to occur. If there is an event in the queue, the program can look at the first event's type and then decide what to do. If, for example, the first event is from the keyboard but the application program is not interested in keyboard input, the event can be discarded and the next event in the queue can be examined.

FIGURE 3.11   Event–mode model.

Another approach is to associate a function called a **callback** with a specific type of event. Event types can be subdivided into a few categories. **Mouse events** include moving the mouse (or other pointing device) and depressing or releasing one or more mouse buttons. **Window events** include opening or closing a window, replacing a window with an icon, and resizing a window with the pointing device. **Keyboard events** include pressing or releasing a key. Other event types are associated with the operating system and the browser, such as idle time-outs and indicators as to when a page has been loaded.

From the perspective of the window system, the operating system queries or polls the event queue regularly and executes the callbacks corresponding to events in the queue. We take this approach because it is the one currently used with the major window systems and has proved effective in client–server environments.

3.5 CLIENTS AND SERVERS

So far, our approach to input has been isolated from all other activities that might be happening in our computing environment. We have looked at our graphics system as a monolithic box with limited connections to the outside world, rather than through our carefully controlled input devices and a display. Networks and multiuser computing have changed this picture dramatically and to such an extent that, even if we had a single-user isolated system, its software probably would be configured as a simple client–server network.

If computer graphics is to be useful for a variety of real applications, it must function well in a world of distributed computing and networks. In this world, our building blocks are entities called **servers** that can perform tasks for **clients**. Clients and servers can be distributed over a network (Figure 3.12) or contained entirely within a single computational unit. Familiar examples of servers include print servers, which can allow sharing of a high-speed printer among users; compute servers, such as remotely located high-performance computers, accessible from user programs; file servers that allow users to share files and programs, regardless of the machine they are logged into; and terminal servers that handle dial-in access. Users and user programs that make use of these services are clients or client programs. Servers can also exist at a lower level of granularity within a single operating system. For example, the operating system might provide a clock service that multiple client programs can use.

It is less obvious what we should call a workstation connected to the network: It can be both a client and a server, or, perhaps more to the point, a workstation may run client programs and server programs concurrently.

The model that we use here was popularized by the X Window System. We use much of that system's terminology, which is now common to most window

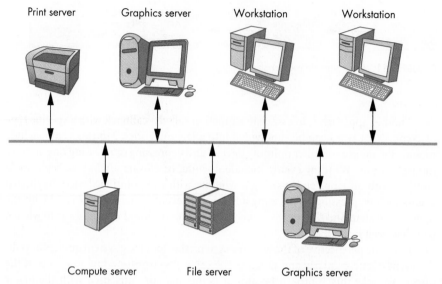

FIGURE 3.12   Network.

systems and fits well with graphical applications. A workstation with a raster display, a keyboard, and a pointing device, such as a mouse, is a **graphics server**. The server can provide output services on its display and input services through the keyboard and pointing device. These services are potentially available to clients anywhere on the network.

Application programs written in C or C++ that use desktop OpenGL for graphics applications are clients that use the graphics server. Within an isolated system, this distinction may not be apparent as we write, compile, and run the software on a single machine. However, we also can run the same application program using other graphics servers on the network. Note that in a modern system, the GPU acts as the graphics server for display, whereas the CPU is the client for those services.

As we saw in Chapter 2, WebGL works within a browser. The browser accesses applications on web servers and the browser is a **web client**. We can regard the World Wide Web as a vast storehouse of information stored as web pages in web servers using standard encodings, such as HTML for documents or JPEG for images.

3.6 PROGRAMMING EVENT-DRIVEN INPUT

In this section, we develop event-driven input through a set of simple examples that use the callback mechanism that we introduced in Section 3.4. We examine various events that are recognized by WebGL through HTML5 and, for those of interest to our application, we write callback functions that govern how the application program responds to the events. Note that because input is not part of WebGL, we will obtain input through callbacks that are supported by the browser and thus are not restricted to use by graphics applications.

3.6.1 Events and Event Listeners

Because WebGL is concerned with rendering and not input, we use JavaScript and HTML for the interactive part of our application. An event is classified by its type and **target**. The target is an object, such as a button, that we create through the HTML part of our code and appears on the display. A target can also be a physical object such as a mouse. Thus, a "click" is an event type whose target could be a button object or a mouse object. The measure of the device is associated with the particular object.

The notion of event types works well not only with WebGL but also within the HTML environment. Event types can be thought of as members of a higher-level classification of events onto **event categories**. Our primary concern will be with the category of device-dependent input events, which includes all the types associated with devices such as a mouse and a keyboard. Within this category, event types include **mousedown**, **keydown**, and **mouse click**. Each event has a name that is recognized by JavaScript and usually begins with the prefix on, such as onload and onclick. For a device-independent type such as onclick, the target might be a physical mouse or a button on the display that was created as part of our HTML document. The target of the onload event that we have seen in our examples is our canvas.

We can respond to events in a number of ways. In our examples, we invoked our initialization function by

```
window.onload = init;
```

Here the event type is load with a target of our window. The callback function is init.[2] Callbacks that we associate with events are called **event listeners** or **event handlers**.

3.6.2 Adding a Button

Suppose we want to alter our rotating cube so we can rotate it either clockwise or counterclockwise and switch between these modes through a graphical button that can be clicked using the mouse. We can add a button element in the HTML file with the single line of code

```
<button id="DirectionButton">Change Rotation Direction</button>
```

which gives an identifier to the new element and puts a label ("Change Rotation Direction") on the display inside the button. In the JavaScript file, we define a boolean variable for the direction that gets used in the render function to select a positive or negative rotation:

---

2. Note that one reason for using an event here is the asynchronous nature of code running in the browser. By forcing our program to wait for the entire program to be loaded by the browser, we gain control over when our application can proceed.

```
var direction = true;

theta += (direction ? 0.1 : -0.1);
```

Finally, we need to couple the button element with a variable in our program and add an event listener:

```
var myButton = document.getElementById("DirectionButton");
myButton.addEventListener("click", function() { direction = !direction;
});
```

We can also use the alternate form

```
document.getElementById("DirectionButton").onclick =
  function() { direction = !direction; };
```

The click event is not the only one that can be coupled to our button. We could also use the mousedown event

```
myButton.addEventListener("mousedown",
                          function() { direction = !direction; });
```

assuming that during initialization we define

```
var direction = true;
```

Although in this example we can use either event, in a more complex application we might prefer to use the mousedown event to be specific as to which device can cause the event. We can achieve even more specificity using additional information in the measure returned by the event. For example, if we are using a multibutton mouse, we can restrict the change to a particular button, as in

```
myButton.addEventListener("click", function() {
  if (event.button == 0) { direction = !direction; }
});
```

where on a three-button mouse button 0 is the left mouse button, button 1 is the middle button, and button 2 is the right button.

If we have a single-button mouse, we can use the meta keys on the keyboard to give us more flexibility. For example, if we want to use the Shift key with our click event, our code might look like

```
myButton.addEventListener("click", function() {
  if (event.shiftKey == 0) { direction = !direction; }
});
```

We can also put all the button code in the HTML file instead of dividing it between the HTML file and the JavaScript file. For our button, we could simply have the code

```
<button onclick="direction = !direction"></button>
```

in the HTML file. However, we prefer to separate the description of the object on the page from the action associated with the object, with the latter being in the JavaScript file.

3.6.3 Menus

Menus are specified by **select elements** in HTML that we can define in our HTML file. A menu can have an arbitrary number of entries, each of which has two parts: the text that is visible on the display and a number that we can use on our application to couple that entry to a callback. We can demonstrate menus with our rotating square by adding a menu with three entries to our HTML file:

```
<select id="mymenu" size="3">
<option value="0">Toggle Rotation Direction X</option>
<option value="1">Spin Faster</option>
<option value="2">Spin Slower</option>
</select>
```

As with a button, we create an identifier that we can refer to in our application. Each line in the menu has a `value` that is returned when that row is clicked with the mouse. Let's first modify our render function slightly so we can alter the speed of rotation by having a variable `delay` that we use with a timer to control the rate of animation:

```
var delay = 100;

function render()
{
  setTimeout(function() {
    requestAnimFrame(render);
    gl.clear(gl.COLOR_BUFFER_BIT);
    theta += (direction ? 0.1 : -0.1);
    gl.uniform1f(thetaLoc, theta);
    gl.drawArrays(gl.TRIANGLE_STRIP, 0, 4);
  }, delay);
}
```

The click event returns the line of the menu that was pointed to through the `selectedIndex` member of `m`:

```
var m = document.getElementById("mymenu");

m.addEventListener("click", function() {
  switch (m.selectedIndex) {
    case 0:
      direction = !direction;
      break;
    case 1:
      delay /= 2.0;
      break;
```

```
    case 2:
      delay *= 2.0;
      break;
  }
});
```

3.6.4 Using Keycodes

We can also use key press events to control our rotating square. Suppose that we want to use the numeric keys 1, 2, and 3 rather than the menu. These keys have codes 49, 50, and 51 in Unicode (and ASCII). Now we can use the keydown event and a simple listener.

In the following code, you will see that we are responding to a window event that occurs on the page, not in the WebGL window. Hence, we use the global objects `window` and `event`, which are defined by the browser and available to all JavaScript programs.

```
window.addEventListener("keydown", function() {
  switch (event.keyCode) {
    case 49:  // '1' key
      direction = !direction;
      break;
    case 50:  // '2' key
      delay /= 2.0;
      break;
    case 51:  // '3' key
      delay *= 2.0;
      break;
  }
});
```

This listener requires us to know the Unicode mapping of keycodes to characters. Instead, we could do this mapping with a listener of the form

```
window.onkeydown = function(event) {
  var key = String.fromCharCode(event.keyCode);
  switch (key) {
    case '1':
      direction = !direction;
      break;
    case '2':
      delay /= 2.0;
      break;
    case '3':
      delay *= 2.0;
      break;
  }
};
```

3.6.5 Sliders

Rather than incrementing or decrementing a value in our program through repetitive uses of a button or key, we can add a **slider element** to our display, as in Figure 3.13. We move the slider with our mouse, and the movements generate events whose measure includes a value dependent on the position of the slider. Thus, when the slider is at the left end, the value will be at its minimum and when the slider is on the right, the value will be at its maximum.

FIGURE 3.13 Slide bar.

In a similar manner to buttons and menus, we can create a visual element on our web page in the HTML file and handle the input from the events in the JavaScript file. For sliders, we specify the minimum and maximum values corresponding to the left and right extents of the slider and the initial value of the slider. We also specify the minimum change necessary to generate an event. We usually also want to display some text on either side of the slider that specifies the minimum and maximum values.

Suppose that we want to create a slider to set the delay between 0 and 100 milliseconds. A basic slider can be created in the HTML file by using the HTML **range element**, as shown below:

```
<input id="slide" type="range"
  min="0" max="100" step="10" value="50" />
```

We use `id` to identify this element to the application. The `type` parameter identifies which HTML input element we are creating. The `min`, `max`, and `value` parameters give the minimum, maximum, and initial values associated with the slider. Finally, `step` gives the amount of change needed to generate an event. We can display the minimum and maximum values on the sides and put the slider below the element that precedes it on the page by

```
<div>
speed 0 <input id="slide" type="range"
  min="0" max="100" step="10" value="50" />
100 </div>
```

In the application, we can get the value of speed from the slider with the two lines

```
document.getElementById("slide").onchange =
  function() { delay = event.srcElement.value; };
```

As with buttons and menus, we use `getElementById` to couple the slider with the application. The value of the slider is returned in `event.srcElement.value` each time an event is generated. All the input elements we have described so far—menus, buttons, and sliders—are displayed using defaults for the visual appearance. We can beautify the visual display in many ways, ranging from using HTML and CSS to using various packages.

3.7   POSITION INPUT

In our examples so far when we used the mouse, all we made use of was the fact that the event occurred and perhaps which button generated the event. There is more information available when we create a click event or mousedown event. In particular, we can access the location of the mouse when the event occurred.

When a click or mouse event occurs, the returned event object includes the values `event.ClientX` and `event.ClientY`, which give the position of the mouse in window coordinates. Recall that positions in the window have dimensions `canvas.width` × `canvas.height`. Positions are measured in pixels with the origin at the upper-left corner so that positive y values are down. For this position to be useful in our application, we must transform these values to the same units as the application.

In this chapter, we are using clip coordinates for our applications, which range from $(-1, 1)$ in both directions and the positive y direction is up. If (x_w, y_w) is the position in the window with width w and height h, then the position in clip coordinates is obtained by flipping the y value and rescaling, yielding the equations

$$x = -1 + \frac{2 * x_w}{w}, \qquad y = -1 + \frac{2 * (w - y_w)}{w}.$$

We can use the mouse position in many ways. Let's start by simply converting each position to clip coordinates and placing it on the GPU. We use a variable `index` to keep track of how many points we have placed on the GPU and initialize our arrays as in previous examples. Consider the event listener

```
canvas.addEventListener("click", function() {
  gl.bindBuffer(gl.ARRAY_BUFFER, vBuffer);
  var t = vec2(-1 + 2*event.clientX/canvas.width,
               -1 + 2*(canvas.height-event.clientY)/canvas.height);
  gl.bufferSubData(gl.ARRAY_BUFFER, sizeof['vec2']*index, t);
  index++;
});
```

The click event returns the object `event` that has members `event.clientX` and `event.clientY`, which is the position in the WebGL window with the y value measured from the top of the window.

If all we want to do is display the locations, we can use the render function

```
function render()
{
  gl.clear(gl.COLOR_BUFFER_BIT);
  gl.drawArrays(gl.POINTS, 0, index);
  window.requestAnimFrame(render, canvas);
}
```

Note that our listener can use the mousedown event instead of the click event, and the display will be the same.[3]

We can also demonstrate many of the elements of painting applications by making a few minor changes. For example, if we use

```
gl.drawArrays(gl.TRIANGLE_STRIP, 0, index);
```

in our render function, the first three points define the first triangle and each successive mouse click will add another triangle. We can also add color. For example, suppose that we specify the seven colors

```
var colors = [
  vec4(0.0, 0.0, 0.0, 1.0),   // black
  vec4(1.0, 0.0, 0.0, 1.0),   // red
  vec4(1.0, 1.0, 0.0, 1.0),   // yellow
  vec4(0.0, 1.0, 0.0, 1.0),   // green
  vec4(0.0, 0.0, 1.0, 1.0),   // blue
  vec4(1.0, 0.0, 1.0, 1.0),   // magenta
  vec4(0.0, 1.0, 1.0, 1.0)    // cyan
];
```

Then each time we add a point, we also add a color, chosen either randomly or by cycling through the seven colors, as in the code

```
gl.bindBuffer(gl.ARRAY_BUFFER, cBufferId);
var t = vec4(colors[index%7]);
gl.bufferSubData(gl.ARRAY_BUFFER, sizeof['vec4']*index, t);
```

The website contains a number of sample programs that illustrate interaction. There are three versions of the rotating square application. The first, rotatingSquare1, only displays the square without interaction. The second, rotatingSquare2, adds buttons and menus. The third, rotatingSquare3, adds a slider. The application square places a colored square at each location where the mouse is clicked. The application triangle draws a triangle strip using the first three mouse clicks to specify the first triangle; then successive mouse clicks each add another triangle.

3.8 WINDOW EVENTS

Most window systems allow the user to resize the window interactively, usually by using the mouse to drag a corner of the window to a new location. This event is an example of a **window event**. Other examples include exposing an element that was hidden under another element and minimizing or restoring a window. In each case, we can use an event listener to alter the display.

---

3. If we want to display points at a larger size, we can set the value of gl_PointSize in the vertex shader.

Let's consider the **resize** or **reshape** event. If such an event occurs, the application program can decide what to do. If the window size changes, we have to consider three questions:

1. Do we redraw all the objects that were on the canvas before it was resized?

2. What do we do if the aspect ratio of the new window is different from that of the old window?

3. Do we change the sizes or attributes of new primitives if the size of the new window is different from that of the old?

There is no single answer to any of these questions. If we are displaying the image of a real-world scene, our resize function probably should make sure that no shape distortions occur. But this choice may mean that part of the resized window is unused or that part of the scene cannot be displayed in the window. If we want to redraw the objects that were in the window before it was resized, we need a mechanism for storing and recalling them.

Suppose that when we resize the window, we want to display the same contents as before and also maintain proportions on the canvas. Resizing refers to the entire browser window, which includes the canvas to which we are rendering and other elements, such as menus or buttons specified in our HTML file. The resize event returns the height and width of the resized window (`innerHeight` and `innerWidth`). The original canvas was specified with height and width given by `canvas.height` and `canvas.width`. As long as the smaller of the new window height and width is greater than the larger of the original canvas height and width, we need not modify our rendering. Once this condition is violated, we change the viewport to be small enough to fit in the resized window but maintain proportions. The following code assumes a square canvas must be maintained:

```
window.onresize = function() {
  var min = innerWidth;

  if (innerHeight < min) {
    min = innerHeight;
  }
  if (min < canvas.width || min < canvas.height) {
    gl.viewport(0, canvas.height-min, min, min);
  }
};
```

We could use our graphics primitives and our mouse callbacks to construct various graphical input devices. For example, we could construct a more visually pleasing slide bar using filled rectangles for the device, text for any labels, and the mouse to get the position. However, much of the code would be tedious to develop. There are many JavaScript packages that provide sets of widgets, but because our philosophy is not to restrict our discussion to any particular package, we will not discuss the specifics of such widget sets.

3.9 PICKING

Picking is the logical input operation that allows the user to identify an object on the display. Although the action of picking uses the pointing device, the information that the user wants returned to the application program is not a position. A pick device is considerably more difficult to implement on a modern system than is a locator.

Such was not always the case. Old display processors could accomplish picking easily by means of a light pen. Each redisplay of the screen would start at a precise time. The light pen would generate an interrupt when the redisplay passed its sensor. By comparing the time of the interrupt with the time that the redisplay began, the processor could identify an exact place in the display list and subsequently could determine which object was being displayed.

One reason for the difficulty of picking in modern systems is the forward nature of the rendering pipeline. Primitives are defined in an application program and move forward through a sequence of geometric operations, rasterization, and fragment operations on their way to the framebuffer. Although much of this process is reversible in a mathematical sense, the hardware is not reversible. Hence, converting from a location on the display to the corresponding primitive is not a direct calculation. There are also potential uniqueness problems (see Exercises 3.7 and 3.8).

There are at least four ways to deal with this difficulty. One process, known as **selection**, involves adjusting the clipping region and viewport such that we can keep track of which primitives in a small clipping region are rendered into a region near the cursor. The names assigned to these primitives go into a **hit list** that can be examined later by the user program. Older versions of OpenGL supported this approach, but it has been deprecated in shader-based versions, and most application programmers prefer one of the other approaches.

If we start with our synthetic-camera model, we can build an approach based on the idea that if we generate a ray from the center of projection through the location of the mouse on the projection plane, we can, at least in principle, check for which objects this ray intersects. The closest object we intersect is the one selected. This approach is best suited to a ray-tracing renderer but can be implemented with a pipeline architecture, although with a performance penalty.

A simple approach is to use (**axis-aligned**) **bounding boxes**, or **extents**, for objects of interest. The extent of an object is the smallest rectangle, aligned with the coordinates axes, that contains the object. For two-dimensional applications, it is relatively easy to determine the rectangle in screen coordinates that corresponds to a rectangle point in object or world coordinates. For three-dimensional applications, the bounding box is a right parallelepiped. If the application program maintains a simple data structure to relate objects and bounding boxes, approximate picking can be done within the application program.

Another simple approach involves using an extra color buffer, which is not displayed, and an extra rendering. Suppose that we render our objects into this second color buffer, each in a distinct color. The application programmer is free to determine an object's contents by simply changing colors wherever a new object definition appears in the program.

We can perform picking in four steps that are initiated by a user-defined pick function in the application. First, we draw the objects into the second buffer with the pick colors. Second, we get the position of the mouse using the mouse callback. Third, we use the function `gl.readPixels` to find the color at the position in the second buffer corresponding to the mouse position. Finally, we search a table of colors to find which object corresponds to the color read. We must follow this process by a normal rendering into the framebuffer. We will develop this approach in Chapter 7.

3.10   BUILDING MODELS INTERACTIVELY

One example of computer-aided design (CAD) is building geometric structures interactively. In Chapter 4, we will look at ways in which we can model geometric objects comprised of polygons. Here, we want to examine the interactive part.

Let's start by writing an application that will let the user specify a series of axis-aligned rectangles interactively. Each rectangle can be defined by two mouse positions at diagonally opposite corners. Consider the event listener

```
canvas.addEventListener("mousedown", function() {
  gl.bindBuffer(gl.ARRAY_BUFFER, vBuffer);
  if (first) {
    first = false;
    var t1 = vec2(-1 + 2*event.clientX/canvas.width,
                  -1 + 2*(canvas.height-event.clientY)/canvas.height);
  }
  else {
    first = true;
    var t2 = vec2(-1 + 2*event.clientX/canvas.width-1,
                  -1 + 2*(canvas.height-event.clientY)/canvas.height);
    var t3 = vec2(t1[0], t2[1]);
    var t4 = vec2(t2[0], t1[1]);

    gl.bufferSubData(gl.ARRAY_BUFFER, sizeof['vec2']*(index+0),
                     flatten(t1));
    gl.bufferSubData(gl.ARRAY_BUFFER, sizeof['vec2']*(index+1),
                     flatten(t3));
    gl.bufferSubData(gl.ARRAY_BUFFER, sizeof['vec2']*(index+2),
                     flatten(t2));
    gl.bufferSubData(gl.ARRAY_BUFFER, sizeof['vec2']*(index+3),
                     flatten(t4));

    index += 4;
  }
});
```

and the render function

```
function render()
{
  gl.clear(gl.COLOR_BUFFER_BIT);
  for (var i = 0; i < index; i += 4) {
```

```
    gl.drawArrays(gl.TRIANGLE_FAN, i, 4);
  }

  window.requestAnimFrame(render);
}
```

We use the boolean variable `first` to keep track of whether the mouse click is generating a new rectangle or generating the diagonally opposite corner of a rectangle from the previous mouse click. The position of the mouse from the first click is stored. When the second click occurs, the two positions are used to compute the positions of the two other vertices of the rectangle, and then all four positions are put on the GPU. The order in which they are put on the GPU is determined by the render function's use of a triangle fan, rather than the triangle strip we used in previous examples. We will see the advantage of this form when we extend our example to polygons with more than four vertices. The rest of the program is similar to our previous examples.

We add a color selection menu to the HTML files:

```
<select id="mymenu" size="7">
<option value="0">Black</option>
<option value="1">Red</option>
<option value="2">Yellow</option>
<option value="3">Green</option>
<option value="4">Blue</option>
<option value="5">Magenta</option>
<option value="6">Cyan</option>
</select>
```

The event listener for this menu simply stores the index of the color, thus making it the current color that will be used until another color is selected. Here is the code for color selection:

```
var cIndex = 0;
var colors = [
  vec4(0.0, 0.0, 0.0, 1.0),  // black
  vec4(1.0, 0.0, 0.0, 1.0),  // red
  vec4(1.0, 1.0, 0.0, 1.0),  // yellow
  vec4(0.0, 1.0, 0.0, 1.0),  // green
  vec4(0.0, 0.0, 1.0, 1.0),  // blue
  vec4(1.0, 0.0, 1.0, 1.0),  // magenta
  vec4(0.0, 1.0, 1.0, 1.0)   // cyan
];

var m = document.getElementById("mymenu");
m.addEventListener("click", function() { cIndex = m.selectedIndex; });
```

The color index can be used in multiple ways. If we want each rectangle to be a solid color, we can set up a vertex array for the colors and then augment the event listener for the vertex positions by adding the code

```
gl.bindBuffer(gl.ARRAY_BUFFER, cBufferId);
var t = vec4(colors[cIndex]);
```

```
gl.bufferSubData(gl.ARRAY_BUFFER, sizeof['vec4']*(index-4), flatten(t));
gl.bufferSubData(gl.ARRAY_BUFFER, sizeof['vec4']*(index-3), flatten(t));
gl.bufferSubData(gl.ARRAY_BUFFER, sizeof['vec4']*(index-2), flatten(t));
gl.bufferSubData(gl.ARRAY_BUFFER, sizeof['vec4']*(index-1), flatten(t));
```

Note that this code is coming after we have already incremented `index` when we put the four vertex positions on the GPU. If we want each rectangle to be displayed in a solid color, we could store these colors in an array; then in the render function we could send each polygon's color to the shaders as a uniform variable. Using a vertex array does, however, let us assign a different color to each vertex and then have the rasterizer interpolate these colors over the rectangle.

Now let's consider what changes are needed to allow the user to work with a richer set of objects. Suppose that we want to be able to design a polygon with an arbitrary number of vertices. Although we can easily store as many vertices as we like in our event listener, there are some issues. For example,

1. How do we indicate the beginning and end of a polygon when the number of vertices is arbitrary?

2. How do we render when each polygon can have a different number of vertices?

We can solve the first problem by adding a button that will end the present polygon and start a new one. Solving the second problem involves adding some additional structure to our code. The difficulty is that, while it is easy to keep adding vertices to our vertex array, the shaders do not have the information as to where one polygon ends and the next begins. We can, however, store such information in an array in our program.

We will make use of `gl.TRIANGLE_FAN` in the render function because it will render a list of successive vertices into a polygon without having to reorder the vertices as we did with `gl.TRIANGLE_STRIP`. However, having all the triangles that comprise a polygon share the first vertex does not lead to a particularly good triangulation of the set of vertices. In Chapter 12, we will consider better triangulation algorithms.

First, we consider a single polygon with an arbitrary number of vertices. The event listener for the mouse can add colors and positions to vertex arrays each time the mouse is clicked in the canvas.

```
canvas.addEventListener("mousedown", function() {
  var t = vec2(2*event.clientX/canvas.width-1,
               2*(canvas.height-event.clientY)/canvas.height-1);
  gl.bindBuffer(gl.ARRAY_BUFFER, vBuffer);
  gl.bufferSubData(gl.ARRAY_BUFFER, sizeof['vec2']*index, flatten(t));

  t = vec4(colors[cIndex]);
  gl.bindBuffer(gl.ARRAY_BUFFER, cBuffer);
  gl.bufferSubData(gl.ARRAY_BUFFER, sizeof['vec4']*index, flatten(t));

  index++;
});
```

We add a button

```
<button id="Button1">End Polygon</button>
```

in the HTML file and the corresponding event listener

```
getElementById("Button1").onclick = function() {
  render();
  index = 0;
});
```

and the render function

```
function render()
{
  gl.clear(gl.COLOR_BUFFER_BIT);
  gl.drawArrays(gl.TRIANGLE_FAN, 0, index);
}
```

to the application file.

As simple as this code is, there are a couple of interesting points. Note that the render function is called from the button listener, which then resets the index that counts vertices. We can change the color from the color menu between adding vertices. The rasterizer will blend the colors for the next couple of vertices when a color is changed.

To get multiple polygons, we need to keep track of the beginning of each polygon and how many vertices are in each one. We add the three variables

```
var numPolygons = 0;
var numIndices = [ 0 ];
var start = [ 0 ];
```

The variable `numPolygons` stores the number of polygons we have entered so far. The array `numIndices` stores the number of vertices for each polygon, and the array `start` stores the index of the first vertex in each polygon. The only change we have to make to the mouse listener is to increase the number of vertices in the present polygon

```
numIndices[numPolygons]++;
```

The button callback

```
getElementById("Button1") = function() {
  numPolygons++;
  numIndices[numPolygons] = 0;
  start[numPolygons] = index;
  render();
});
```

starts a new polygon before rendering. Finally, the rendering function is

```
function render()
{
  gl.clear(gl.COLOR_BUFFER_BIT);
  for (var i = 0; i < numPolygons; ++i) {
    gl.drawArrays(gl.TRIANGLE_FAN, start[i], numIndices[i]);
  }
}
```

The programs `cad1` and `cad2` on the website show some of the elements that go into a simple painting program; `cad1` draws a new rectangle specified by each pair of mouse clicks, and `cad2` allows the user to draw polygons with an arbitrary number of vertices.

3.11 DESIGN OF INTERACTIVE PROGRAMS

Defining what characterizes a good interactive program is difficult, but recognizing and appreciating a good interactive program is easy. A good program includes features such as these:

- A smooth display, showing neither flicker nor any artifacts of the refresh process
- A variety of interactive devices on the display
- A variety of methods for entering and displaying information
- An easy-to-use interface that does not require substantial effort to learn
- Feedback to the user
- Tolerance for user errors
- A design that incorporates consideration of both the visual and motor properties of the human

The importance of these features and the difficulty of designing a good interactive program should never be underestimated. The field of human–computer interaction (HCI) is an active one and we will not shortchange you by condensing it into a few pages. Our concern in this book is computer graphics; within this topic, our primary interest is rendering. However, there are a few topics common to computer graphics and HCI that we can pursue to improve our interactive programs.

SUMMARY AND NOTES

In this chapter, we have touched on a number of topics related to interactive computer graphics. These interactive aspects make the field of computer graphics exciting and fun.

Our discussion of animation showed both the ease with which we can animate a scene with WebGL and some of the limitations on how we can control the animation in a web environment.

We have been heavily influenced by the client–server perspective. Not only does it allow us to develop programs within a networked environment but it also makes it possible to design programs that are portable yet can still take advantage of special features that might be available in the hardware. These concepts are crucial for object-oriented graphics and graphics for the Internet.

From the application programmer's perspective, various characteristics of interactive graphics are shared by most systems. We see the graphics part of the system as a server, consisting of a raster display, a keyboard, and a pointing device. In almost all workstations, we have to work within a multiprocessing, windowed environment. Most likely, many other processes are executing concurrently with the execution of your graphics program. However, the window system allows us to write programs for a specific window that act as though that window were the display device of a single-user system.

The overhead of setting up a program to run in this environment is small. Each application program contains a set of function calls that is virtually the same in every program. The use of logical devices within the application program frees the programmer from worrying about the details of particular hardware.

Within the environment that we have described, event-mode input is the norm. Although the other forms are available—request mode is the normal method used for keyboard input—event-mode input gives us far more flexibility in the design of interactive programs.

The speed of the latest generation of graphics processors not only allows us to carry out interactive applications that were not possible even a few years ago but also makes us rethink (as we should periodically) whether the techniques we are using are still the best ones. For example, whereas hardware features such as logical operations and overlay planes made possible many interactive techniques, now with a fast GPU we can often simply draw the entire display fast enough that these features are no longer necessary.

Because our API, WebGL, is independent of any operating or window system, we were able to use the simple event-handling capabilities in JavaScript to get input from a mouse and the keyboard. Because we want to keep our focus on computer graphics, this approach was justified but nevertheless led to applications with a limited and inelegant interface. To get a better graphical user interface (GUI), the best approach would be to use some combination of HTML, CSS, and available GUI packages. Some references are in the Suggested Readings section that follows.

Interactive computer graphics is a powerful tool with unlimited applications. At this point, you should be able to write fairly sophisticated interactive programs. Probably the most helpful exercise that you can do now is to write one. The exercises at the end of the chapter provide suggestions.

SUGGESTED READINGS

Many of the conceptual foundations for the windows-icons-menus-pointing interfaces that we now consider routine were developed at the Xerox Palo Alto Research Center (PARC) during the 1970s (see [Sch97]). The mouse also was developed there

[Eng68]. The familiar interfaces of today—such as the Macintosh Operating System, the X Window System, and Microsoft Windows—all have their basis in this work.

The volume by Foley and associates [Fol94] contains a thorough description of the development of user interfaces with an emphasis on the graphical aspects. The books by Schneiderman [Sch97] and Nielson [Nie94] provide an introduction to HCI.

The X Window System [Sch88] was developed at the Massachusetts Institute of Technology and is the de facto standard in the UNIX workstation community. The development of the Linux version for PCs has allowed the X Window System to run on these platforms too.

The input and interaction modes that we discussed in this chapter grew out of the standards that led to GKS [ANSI85] and PHIGS [ANSI88]. These standards were developed for both calligraphic and raster displays; thus, they do not take advantage of the possibilities available on raster-only systems (see [Pik84] and [Gol83]).

Using desktop OpenGL requires the application developer to choose between a platform-dependent interfacing method that gives access to the full capabilities of the local system or a simplified toolkit that supports the functionality common to all systems. Previous editions of this text [Ang10] used the GLUT toolkit [Kil94b] exclusively. Additional details on GLUT are found in *OpenGL: A Primer* [Ang08]. See [Kil94a, OSF89] for details on interfacing directly with the X Window System and various X Window toolkits. Tookits including freeglut and GLEW are available for extending GLUT to recent versions of OpenGL; see [Shr13] and the OpenGL website, *www.opengl.org*.

The approach we have taken here is to use the event-handling functionality built into JavaScript [Fla11]. We avoid use of HTML, CSS, or any of the many GUI packages available. Consequently, our code is simple, portable, and limited. The most popular package for interfacing is jQuery [McF12], which provides more widgets and a better interface to the capabilities of HTML and CSS. For an introduction to HTML and CSS, see [Duk11].

To end where we began, Sutherland's Sketchpad is described in [Sut63].

EXERCISES

3.1 Rewrite the Sierpinski gasket program from Chapter 2 such that the left mouse button will start the generation of points on the screen, the right mouse button will halt the generation of new points, and the middle mouse button will terminate the program. Include a resize callback.

3.2 Construct slide bars to allow users to define colors in the CAD program. Your interface should let the user see a color before that color is used.

3.3 Add an elapsed-time indicator in the CAD program (Section 3.10) using a clock of your own design.

3.4 Creating simple games is a good way to become familiar with interactive graphics programming. Program a game of tic-tac-toe. You can look at each circle or cross as an object that can be given by the user. You can start with a program in which the user plays both sides

3.5   Write a program that allows a user to play a simple version of solitaire. First, design a simple set of cards using only our basic primitives. Your program can be written in terms of picking rectangular objects.

3.6   Simulating a pool or billiards game presents interesting problems. As in Exercise 2.17, you must compute trajectories and detect collisions. The interactive aspects include initiating movement of the balls via a graphical cue stick, ensuring that the display is smooth, and creating a two-person game.

3.7   The mapping from a point in object or world coordinates to one in screen coordinates is well defined. It is not invertible because we go from three dimensions to two dimensions. Suppose, however, that we are working with a two-dimensional application. Is the mapping invertible? What problem can arise if you use a two-dimensional mapping to return to a position in object or world coordinates by a locator device?

3.8   What is the use of single buffering?

3.9   In a typical application program, the programmer must decide whether or not to use display lists. Consider at least two applications. For each, list at least two factors in favor of display lists and two against.

3.10   Write an interactive program that will allow you to guide a graphical rat through the maze you generated in Exercise 2.7. You can use the left and right buttons to turn the rat and the middle button to move him forward.

3.11   Spaceballs, such as those used in games, often use pressure sensors in the ball to measure the forces applied by the user. Where are such input devices used?

3.12   The orientation of an airplane is described by a coordinate system as shown in Figure 3.14. The forward–backward motion of the joystick controls the up–down rotation with respect to the axis running along the length of the airplane, called the **pitch**. The right–left motion of the joystick controls the rotation about this axis, called the **roll**. Write a program that uses the mouse to control pitch and roll for the view seen by a pilot. You can do this exercise in two dimensions by considering a set of objects to be located far from the airplane, then having the mouse control the two-dimensional viewing of these objects.

3.13   Consider a table with a two-dimensional sensing device located at the end of two linked arms, as shown in Figure 3.15. Suppose that the lengths of the two arms are fixed and the arms are connected by simple (one degree of freedom) pivot joints. Determine the relationship between the joint angles θ and ϕ and the position of the sensor.

3.14   Suppose that a CRT has a square face of 40×40 centimeters and is refreshed in a noninterlaced manner at a rate of 60 Hz. Ten percent of the time that the system takes to draw each scan line is used to return the CRT beam from the right edge to the left edge of the screen (the horizontal retrace time), and 10 percent of the total drawing time is allocated for the beam to return from the lower-right corner of the screen to the upper-left corner after each refresh is

FIGURE 3.14   Airplane coordinate system.

FIGURE 3.15   Two-dimensional sensing arm.

FIGURE 3.16   Symbols for logical circuits.

complete (the vertical retrace time). Assume that the resolution of the display is 1024×1024 pixels. Find a relationship between the time at which a light pen detects the beam and the light pen's position. Give the result using both centimeters and screen coordinates for the location on the screen.

3.15   Circuit-layout programs are variants of paint programs. Consider the design of logical circuits using the boolean AND, OR, and NOT functions. Each of these functions is provided by one of the three types of integrated circuits (gates), the symbols for which are shown in Figure 3.16. Write a program that allows the user to design a logical circuit by selecting gates from a menu and positioning them on the screen. Consider methods for connecting the outputs of one gate to the inputs of others.

3.16   Extend Exercise 3.15 to allow the user to specify a sequence of input signals. Have the program display the resulting values at selected points in the circuit.

3.17   Extend Exercise 3.15 to have the user enter a logical expression. Have the program generate a logical diagram from that expression.

3.18   Use the methods of Exercise 3.15 to form flowcharts for programs or images of graphs that you have studied in a data structures class.

3.19   Plotting packages offer a variety of methods for displaying data. Write an interactive plotting application for two-dimensional curves. Your application should allow the user to choose the mode (polyline display of the data, bar chart, or pie chart), colors, and line styles.

3.20   The required refresh rate for CRT displays of 50 to 85 Hz is based on the use of short-persistence phosphors that emit light for extremely short intervals when excited. Long-persistence phosphors are available. Why are long-persistence phosphors not used in most workstation displays? In what types of applications might such phosphors be useful?

3.21   Modify the polygon program in Section 3.10 using a linked list rather than an array to store the objects. Your program should allow the user to both add and delete objects interactively.

3.22   Another CAD application that can be developed in WebGL is a paint program. You can display the various objects that can be painted—lines, rectangles, circles, and triangles, for example—and use picking to select which to draw. The mouse can then enter vertex data and select attributes such as colors from a menu. Write such an application.

CHAPTER 4

GEOMETRIC OBJECTS AND TRANSFORMATIONS

We are now ready to concentrate on three-dimensional graphics. Much of this chapter is concerned with matters such as how to represent basic geometric types, how to convert between various representations, and what statements we can make about geometric objects independent of a particular representation.

We begin with an examination of the mathematical underpinnings of computer graphics. This approach should avoid much of the confusion that arises from a lack of care in distinguishing among a geometric entity, its representation in a particular reference system, and a mathematical abstraction of it.

We use the notions of affine and Euclidean vector spaces to create the necessary mathematical foundation for later work. One of our goals is to establish a method for dealing with geometric problems that is independent of coordinate systems. The advantages of such an approach will be clear when we worry about how to represent the geometric objects with which we would like to work. The coordinate-free approach will prove to be far more robust than one based on representing the objects in a particular coordinate system or frame. This coordinate-free approach also leads to the use of homogeneous coordinates, a system that not only enables us to explain this approach but also leads to efficient implementation techniques.

We use the terminology of abstract data types to reinforce the distinction between an object and its representation. Our development will show that the mathematics arise naturally from our desire to manipulate a few basic geometric objects. Much of what we present here is an application of vector spaces, geometry, and linear algebra. Appendixes B and C summarize the formalities of vector spaces and matrix algebra, respectively.

In a vein similar to the approach we took in Chapter 2, we develop a simple application program to illustrate the basic principles and to see how the concepts are realized within an API. In this chapter, our example is focused on the representation and transformations of a cube. We also consider how to specify transformations interactively and apply them smoothly. Because transformations are key to both modeling and implementation, we will develop transformation capabilities that can be carried out in both the application code and the shaders.

4.1   SCALARS, POINTS, AND VECTORS

In computer graphics, we work with a set of geometric objects usually including lines, polygons, and polyhedra. Such objects exist in a three-dimensional world and have properties that can be described using concepts such as length and angle. As we discovered working in two dimensions, we can define most geometric objects using a limited set of simple entities. These basic geometric objects and the relationships among them can be described using three fundamental types: scalars, points, and vectors.

Although we will consider each type from a geometric perspective, each of these types also can be defined formally as obeying a set of axioms (see Appendix B). Although ultimately we will use the geometric instantiation of each type, we want to take great care in distinguishing between the abstract definition of each entity and any particular example, or implementation, of it. By taking care here, we can avoid many subtle pitfalls later. Although we will work in three-dimensional spaces, virtually all our results will hold in n-dimensional spaces.

4.1.1 Geometric Objects

Our simplest geometric object is a point. In a three-dimensional geometric system, a **point** is a location in space. The only property that a point possesses is that point's location; a mathematical point has neither a size nor a shape.

Points are useful in specifying geometric objects but are not sufficient by themselves. We need real numbers to specify quantities such as the distance between two points. Real numbers—and complex numbers, which we will use occasionally—are examples of **scalars**. Scalars are objects that obey a set of rules that are abstractions of the operations of ordinary arithmetic. Thus, addition and multiplication are defined and obey the usual rules such as commutativity and associativity. Every scalar has multiplicative and additive inverses, which implicitly define subtraction and division.

We need one additional type—the **vector**—to allow us to work with directions.[1] Physicists and mathematicians use the term *vector* for any quantity with direction and magnitude. Physical quantities, such as velocity and force, are vectors. A vector does not, however, have a fixed location in space.

In computer graphics, we often connect points with directed line segments, as shown in Figure 4.1. A directed line segment has both magnitude—its length—and direction—its orientation—and thus is a vector. Because vectors have no fixed position, the directed line segments shown in Figure 4.2 are identical because they have the same direction and magnitude. We will often use the terms *vector* and *directed line segment* synonymously.

FIGURE 4.1   Directed line segment that connects points.

FIGURE 4.2   Identical vectors.

---

1. The types such as vec3 used by GLSL are not geometric types but rather storage types. Hence, we can use a vec3 to store information about a point, a vector, or a color. Although the choice of names by GLSL can cause some confusion, we have kept GLSL's usage in MV.js, lest we cause more confusion.

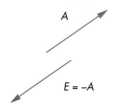

FIGURE 4.3 (a) Parallel line segments. (b) Addition of line segments.

Vectors can have their lengths increased or decreased without changing their directions. Thus, in Figure 4.3(a), line segment A has the same direction as line segment B, but B has twice the length that A has, so we can write $B = 2A$.

We can also combine directed line segments by the **head-to-tail rule**, as shown in Figure 4.3(b). Here, we connect the head of vector A to the tail of vector C to form a new vector D, whose magnitude and direction are determined by the line segment from the tail of A to the head of C. We call this new vector, D, the **sum** of A and C and write $D = A + C$. Because vectors have no fixed positions, we can move any two vectors as necessary to form their sum graphically. Note that we have described two fundamental operations: the addition of two vectors and the multiplication of a vector by a scalar.

If we consider two directed line segments, A and E, as shown in Figure 4.4, with the same length but opposite directions, their sum as defined by the head-to-tail addition has no length. This sum forms a special vector called the **zero vector**, which we denote **0**, that has a magnitude of zero. Because it has no length, the orientation of this vector is undefined. We say that E is the **inverse** of A and we can write $E = -A$. Using inverses of vectors, scalar–vector expressions such as $A + 2B - 3C$ make sense.

Although we can multiply a vector by a scalar to change its length, there are no obvious sensible operations between two points that produce another point. Nor are there operations between a point and a scalar that produce a point. There is, however, an operation between points and directed line segments (vectors), as illustrated in Figure 4.5. We can use a directed line segment to move from one point to another. We call this operation **point–vector addition**, and it produces a new point. We write this operation as $P = Q + v$. We can see that the vector v displaces the point Q to the new location P.

Looking at Figure 4.5 slightly differently, we can see that any two points define a directed line segment or vector from one point to the second. We call this operation **point–point subtraction**, and we can write it as $v = P - Q$. Because vectors can be multiplied by scalars, some expressions involving scalars, vectors, and points make sense, such as $P + 3v$, or $2P - Q + 3v$ (because it can be written as $P + (P - Q) + 3v$, the sum of a point and two vectors), whereas others, such as $P + 3Q - v$, do not.

FIGURE 4.4 Inverse vectors.

FIGURE 4.5 Point–vector addition.

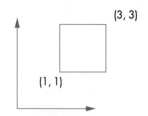

FIGURE 4.6   Object and coordinate system.

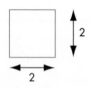

FIGURE 4.7   Object without coordinate system.

4.1.2 Coordinate-Free Geometry

Points exist in space regardless of any reference or coordinate system. Thus, we do not need a coordinate system to specify a point or a vector. This fact may seem counter to your experiences, but it is crucial to understanding geometry and how to build graphics systems. Consider the two-dimensional example shown in Figure 4.6. Here we see a coordinate system defined by two axes, an origin, and a simple geometric object, a square. We can refer to the point at the lower-left corner of the square as having coordinates (1, 1) and note that the sides of the square are orthogonal to each other and that the point at (3, 1) is 2 units from the point at (1, 1). Now suppose that we remove the axes as shown in Figure 4.7. We can no longer specify where the points are. But those locations were relative to an arbitrary location of the origin and the orientation of the axes. What is more important is that the fundamental geometric relationships are preserved. The square is still a square, orthogonal lines are still orthogonal, and distances between points remain the same.

Of course, we may find it inconvenient, at best, to refer to a specific point as "that point over there" or "the blue point to the right of the red one." Coordinate systems and frames (see Section 4.3) solve this reference problem, but for now we want to see just how far we can get following a coordinate-free approach that does not require an arbitrary reference system.

4.1.3 The Mathematical View: Vector and Affine Spaces

If we view scalars, points, and vectors as members of mathematical sets, then we can look at a variety of abstract spaces for representing and manipulating these sets of objects. Mathematicians have explored such spaces for applied problems ranging from the solution of differential equations to the approximation of mathematical functions. The formal definitions of the spaces of interest to us—vector spaces, affine spaces, and Euclidean spaces—are given in Appendix B. We are concerned with only those examples in which the elements are geometric types.

We start with a set of scalars, any pair of which can be combined to form another scalar through two operations, called *addition* and *multiplication*. If these operations obey the closure, associativity, commutativity, and inverse properties described in Appendix B, the elements form a **scalar field**. Familiar examples of scalars include the real numbers and the complex numbers.

Perhaps the most important mathematical space is the (**linear**) **vector space**. A vector space contains two distinct types of entities: vectors and scalars. In addition to the rules for combining scalars, within a vector space, we can combine scalars and vectors to form new vectors through **scalar–vector multiplication** and vectors with vectors through **vector–vector addition**. Examples of mathematical vector spaces include n-tuples of real numbers and the geometric operations on our directed line segments.

In a linear vector space, we do not necessarily have a way of measuring a vector quantity. A **Euclidean space** is an extension of a vector space that adds a measure of size or distance and allows us to define such things as the magnitude of a vector. For a Euclidean space of line segments, the magnitude of a segment is its length.

An **affine space** is an extension of the vector space that includes an additional type of object: the point. Although there are no operations between two points or between a point and a scalar that yield points, there is an operation of *point–vector addition* that produces a new point. Alternately, we can say there is an operation called *point–point subtraction* that produces a vector from two points. Examples of affine spaces include the geometric operations on points and directed line segments that we introduced in Section 4.1.1.

In these abstract spaces, objects can be defined independently of any particular representation; they are simply members of various sets. One of the major vector-space concepts is that of representing a vector in terms of one or more sets of basis vectors. Representation (Section 4.3) provides the tie between abstract objects and their implementation. Conversion between representations leads us to geometric transformations.

4.1.4 The Computer Science View

Although the mathematician may prefer to think of scalars, points, and vectors as members of sets that can be combined according to certain axioms, the computer scientist prefers to see them as **abstract data types** (**ADTs**). An ADT is a set of operations on data; the operations are defined independently of how the data are represented internally or of how the operations are implemented. The notion of *data abstraction* is fundamental to computer science. For example, the operation of adding an element to a list can be defined independently of how the list is stored or of how real numbers are represented on a particular computer. People familiar with this concept should have no trouble distinguishing between objects (and operations on objects) and objects' representations (or implementations) in a particular system. From a computational point of view, we should be able to declare geometric objects through code such as

```
vector u, v;
point p, q;
scalar a, b;
```

regardless of the internal representation or implementation of the objects on a particular system. In object-oriented languages, such as C++, we can use language features, including classes and overloading of operators, so we can write lines of code, such as

```
q = p + a * v;
```

using our geometric data types. In JavaScript, even without operator overloading, we can have equivalent constructs, such as

```
var p = new Point;
var q = new Point;
var a = new Scalar;
var v = new Vector;
q = p.add(v.mult(a));
```

Of course, first we must define functions that perform the necessary operations. In order to write them, we must look at the mathematical functions that we wish to implement. First, we will define our objects. Then we will look to certain abstract mathematical spaces to help us with the operations among them.

4.1.5 Geometric ADTs

The three views of scalars, points, and vectors leave us with a mathematical and computational framework for working with our geometric entities. In summary, for computer graphics our scalars are the real numbers using ordinary addition and multiplication. Our geometric points are locations in space, and our vectors are directed line segments. These objects obey the rules of an affine space. We can also create the corresponding ADTs in a program.

Our next step is to show how we can use our types to form geometrical objects and to perform geometric operations among them. We will use the following notation:

- Greek letters α, β, γ, ... denote scalars;
- uppercase letters P, Q, R, ... denote points;
- lowercase letters u, v, w, ... denote vectors.

We have not as yet introduced any reference system, such as a coordinate system; thus, for vectors and points, this notation refers to the abstract objects, rather than to these objects' representations in a particular reference system. We use boldface letters for the latter in Section 4.3. The **magnitude** of a vector v is a real number denoted by $|v|$. The operation of vector–scalar multiplication (see Appendix B) has the property that

$$|\alpha v| = |\alpha||v|,$$

and the direction of αv is the same as the direction of v if α is positive and the opposite direction if α is negative.

We have two equivalent operations that relate points and vectors. First, there is the subtraction of two points, P and Q—an operation that yields a vector v denoted by

$$v = P - Q.$$

As a consequence of this operation, given any point Q and vector v, there is a unique point, P, that satisfies the preceding relationship. We can express this statement as follows: Given a point Q and a vector v, there is a point P such that

$$P = Q + v.$$

FIGURE 4.8   Point–point subtraction.

Thus, P is formed by a point–vector addition operation. Figure 4.8 shows a visual interpretation of this operation. The head-to-tail rule gives us a convenient way of visualizing vector–vector addition. We obtain the sum $u + v$ as shown in Figure 4.9(a) by drawing the sum vector as connecting the tail of u to the head of v. However, we

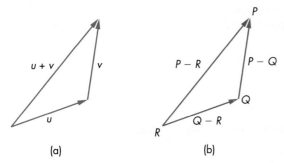

FIGURE 4.9   Use of the head-to-tail rule. (a) For vectors. (b) For points.

can also use this visualization, as demonstrated in Figure 4.9(b), to show that for any three points P, Q, and R,

$$(P - Q) + (Q - R) = P - R.$$

4.1.6 Lines

The sum of a point and a vector (or the subtraction of two points) leads to the notion of a line in an affine space. Consider all points of the form

$$P(\alpha) = P_0 + \alpha d,$$

FIGURE 4.10   Line in an affine space.

where P_0 is an arbitrary point, d is an arbitrary vector, and α is a scalar that can vary over some range of values. Given the rules for combining points, vectors, and scalars in an affine space, for any value of α, evaluation of the function $P(\alpha)$ yields a point. For geometric vectors (directed line segments), these points lie on a line, as shown in Figure 4.10. This form is known as the **parametric form** of the line because we generate points on the line by varying the parameter α. For $\alpha = 0$, the line passes through the point P_0, and as α is increased, all the points generated lie in the direction of the vector d. If we restrict α to nonnegative values, we get the **ray** emanating from P_0 and going in the direction of d. Thus, a line is infinitely long in both directions, a line segment is a finite piece of a line between two points, and a ray is infinitely long in one direction.

4.1.7 Affine Sums

Whereas in an affine space the addition of two vectors, the multiplication of a vector by a scalar, and the addition of a vector and a point are defined, the addition of two arbitrary points and the multiplication of a point by a scalar are not. However, there is an operation called **affine addition** that has certain elements of these latter two operations. For any point Q, vector v, and positive scalar α,

$$P = Q + \alpha v$$

FIGURE 4.11   Affine addition.

describes all points on the line from Q in the direction of v, as shown in Figure 4.11. However, we can always find a point R such that

$$v = R - Q;$$

thus,

$$P = Q + \alpha(R - Q) = \alpha R + (1 - \alpha)Q.$$

This operation looks like the addition of two points and leads to the equivalent form

$$P = \alpha_1 R + \alpha_2 Q,$$

where

$$\alpha_1 + \alpha_2 = 1.$$

FIGURE 4.12   Line segment that connects two points.

4.1.8 Convexity

A **convex** object is one for which any point lying on the line segment connecting any two points in the object is also in the object. We saw the importance of convexity for polygons in Chapter 2. We can use affine sums to help us gain a deeper understanding of convexity. For $0 \le \alpha \le 1$, the affine sum defines the line segment connecting R and Q, as shown in Figure 4.12; thus, this line segment is a convex object. We can extend the affine sum to include objects defined by n points $P_1, P_2, \ldots, P_n$. Consider the form

$$P = \alpha_1 P_1 + \alpha_2 P_2 + \cdots + \alpha_n P_n.$$

We can show, by induction (see Exercise 4.32), that this sum is defined if and only if

$$\alpha_1 + \alpha_2 + \cdots + \alpha_n = 1.$$

The set of points formed by the affine sum of n points, under the additional restriction

$$\alpha_i \ge 0, \quad i = 1, 2, \ldots, n,$$

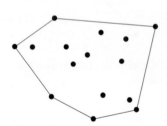

FIGURE 4.13   Convex hull.

is called the **convex hull** of the set of points (Figure 4.13). It is easy to verify that the convex hull includes all line segments connecting pairs of points in $\{P_1, P_2, \ldots, P_n\}$. Geometrically, the convex hull is the set of points that we form by stretching a tight-fitting surface over the given set of points—**shrink-wrapping** the points. It is the smallest convex object that includes the set of points. The notion of convexity is extremely important in the design of curves and surfaces; we will return to it in Chapter 11.

4.1.9 Dot and Cross Products

Many of the geometric concepts relating the orientation between two vectors are in terms of the **dot (inner)** and **cross (outer) products** of two vectors. The dot product of u and v is written $u \cdot v$ (see Appendix B). If $u \cdot v = 0$, u and v are said to be

orthogonal. In a Euclidean space, the magnitude of a vector is defined. The square of the magnitude of a vector is given by the dot product

$$|u|^2 = u \cdot u.$$

The cosine of the angle between two vectors is given by

$$\cos \theta = \frac{u \cdot v}{|u||v|}.$$

In addition, $|u| \cos \theta = u \cdot v / |v|$ is the length of the orthogonal projection of u onto v, as shown in Figure 4.14. Thus, the dot product expresses the geometric result that the shortest distance from a point (the end of the vector u) to the line segment v is obtained by drawing the vector orthogonal to v from the end of u. We can also see that the vector u is composed of the vector sum of the orthogonal projection of u on v and a vector orthogonal to v.

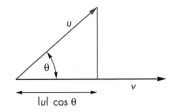

FIGURE 4.14   Dot product and projection.

In a vector space, a set of vectors is **linearly independent** if we cannot write one of the vectors in terms of the others using scalar–vector multiplication and vector addition. A vector space has a **dimension**, which is the maximum number of linearly independent vectors that we can find. Given any three linearly independent vectors in a three-dimensional space, we can use the dot product to construct three vectors, each of which is orthogonal to the other two. This process is outlined in Appendix B. We can also use two nonparallel vectors, u and v, to determine a third vector n that is orthogonal to them (Figure 4.15). This vector is the **cross product**

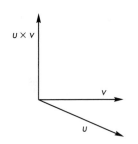

FIGURE 4.15   Cross product.

$$n = u \times v.$$

Note that we can use the cross product to derive three mutually orthogonal vectors in a three-dimensional space from any two nonparallel vectors. Starting again with u and v, we first compute n as before. Then, we can compute w by

$$w = u \times n,$$

and u, n, and w are mutually orthogonal.

The cross product is derived in Appendix C, using the representation of the vectors that gives a direct method for computing it. The magnitude of the cross product gives the magnitude of the sine of the angle θ between u and v,

$$|\sin \theta| = \frac{|u \times v|}{|u||v|}.$$

Note that the vectors u, v, and n form a **right-handed coordinate system**; that is, if u points in the direction of the thumb of the right hand and v points in the direction of the index finger, then n points in the direction of the middle finger.

4.1.10 Planes

A **plane** in an affine space can be defined as a direct extension of the parametric line. From simple geometry, we know that three points not on the same line determine a unique plane. Suppose that P, Q, and R are three such points in an affine space. The

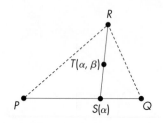

FIGURE 4.16   Formation of a plane.

line segment that joins P and Q is the set of points of the form

$$S(\alpha) = \alpha P + (1 - \alpha)Q \quad 0 \le \alpha \le 1.$$

Suppose that we take an arbitrary point on this line segment and form the line segment from this point to R, as shown in Figure 4.16. Using a second parameter β, we can describe points along this line segment as

$$T(\beta) = \beta S + (1 - \beta)R \quad 0 \le \beta \le 1.$$

Such points are determined by α and β and form the triangle determined by P, Q, and R. If we remove the restrictions on the range of α and β and combine the preceding two equations, we obtain one form of the equation of a plane:

$$T(\alpha, \beta) = \beta[\alpha P + (1 - \alpha)Q] + (1 - \beta)R.$$

We can rearrange this equation in the following form:

$$T(\alpha, \beta) = \alpha\beta P + \beta(1 - \alpha)(Q - P) + (1 - \beta)(R - P).$$

Noting that $Q - P$ and $R - P$ are arbitrary vectors, we have shown that a plane can also be expressed in terms of a point, P_0, and two nonparallel vectors, u and v, as

$$T(\alpha, \beta) = P_0 + \alpha u + \beta v.$$

If we write T as

$$T(\alpha, \beta) = \beta\alpha P + \beta(1 - \alpha)Q + (1 - \beta)R,$$

this form is equivalent to expressing T as

$$T(\alpha, \beta', \gamma) = \alpha'P + \beta'Q + \gamma'R,$$

as long as

$$\alpha' + \beta' + \gamma' = 1.$$

The representation of a point by $(\alpha', \beta', \gamma')$ is called its **barycentric coordinate** representation of T with respect to P, Q, and R.

We can also observe that for $0 \le \alpha, \beta \le 1$, all the points $T(\alpha, \beta)$ lie in the triangle formed by P, Q, and R. If a point P lies in the plane, then

$$P - P_0 = \alpha u + \beta v.$$

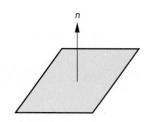

FIGURE 4.17   Normal to a plane.

We can find a vector n that is orthogonal to both u and v, as shown in Figure 4.17. If we use the cross product

$$n = u \times v,$$

then the equation of the plane becomes

$$n \cdot (P - P_0) = 0.$$

The vector n is perpendicular, or orthogonal, to the plane; it is called the **normal** to the plane. The forms $P(\alpha)$, for the line, and $T(\alpha, \beta)$, for the plane, are known as **parametric forms** because they give the value of a point in space for each value of the parameters α and β.

FIGURE 4.18 Curves in three dimensions.

4.2 THREE-DIMENSIONAL PRIMITIVES

In a three-dimensional world, we can have a far greater variety of geometric objects than we can in two dimensions. When we worked in a two-dimensional plane in Chapter 2, we considered objects that were simple curves, such as line segments, and flat objects with well-defined interiors, such as simple polygons. In three dimensions, we retain these objects, but they are no longer restricted to lie in the same plane. Hence, curves become curves in space (Figure 4.18), and objects with interiors can become surfaces in space (Figure 4.19). In addition, we can have objects with volumes, such as parallelepipeds and ellipsoids (Figure 4.20).

FIGURE 4.19 Surfaces in three dimensions.

We face two problems when we expand our graphics system to incorporate all these possibilities. First, the mathematical definitions of these objects can become complex. Second, we are interested in only those objects that lead to efficient implementations in graphics systems. The full range of three-dimensional objects cannot be supported on existing graphics systems, except by approximate methods.

Three features characterize three-dimensional objects that fit well with existing graphics hardware and software:

1. The objects are described by their surfaces and can be thought of as being hollow.

2. The objects can be specified through a set of vertices in three dimensions.

3. The objects either are composed of or can be approximated by flat, convex polygons.

FIGURE 4.20 Volumetric objects.

We can understand why we set these conditions if we consider what most modern graphics systems do best: They render triangles or meshes of triangles. Commodity graphics cards can render over 100 million small, flat triangles per second. Performance measurements for graphics systems usually are quoted for small three-dimensional triangles that can be generated by triangle strips. In addition, these triangles are shaded, lit, and texture mapped, features that are implemented in the hardware of modern graphics cards.

The first condition implies that we need only two-dimensional primitives to model three-dimensional objects because a surface is a two- rather than a three-dimensional entity. The second condition is an extension of our observations in Chapters 1 and 2. If an object is specified by vertices, we can use a pipeline architecture to process these vertices at high rates, and we can use the hardware to generate the images of the objects only during rasterization. The final condition is an extension from our discussion of two-dimensional polygons. Most graphics systems are optimized for the processing of points, line segments, and triangles. In three dimensions, a single triangle usually is specified by an ordered list of three vertices.

However, for general polygons specified with more than three vertices, the vertices do not have to lie in the same plane. If they do not, there is no simple way to define the interior of the object. Consequently, most graphics systems require that the application either specify simple planar polygons or triangles. If a system allows polygons and the application does not specify a flat polygon, then the results of rasterizing the polygon are not guaranteed to be what the programmer might desire. Because triangular polygons are always flat, either the modeling system is designed to always produce triangles, or the graphics system provides a method to divide, or **tessellate**, an arbitrary polygon into triangular polygons. If we apply this same argument to a curved object, such as a sphere, we realize that we should use an approximation to the sphere composed of small, flat polygons. Hence, even if our modeling system provides curved objects, we assume that a triangle mesh approximation is used for rendering.

The major exception to this approach is **constructive solid geometry** (**CSG**). In such systems, we build objects from a small set of volumetric objects through a set of operations such as union and intersection. We consider CSG models in Chapter 9. Although this approach is an excellent one for modeling, rendering CSG models is more difficult than is rendering surface-based polygonal models. Although this situation may not hold in the future, we discuss in detail only surface rendering.

All the primitives with which we work can be specified through a set of vertices. As we move away from abstract objects to real objects, we must consider how we represent points in space in a manner that can be used within our graphics systems.

4.3   COORDINATE SYSTEMS AND FRAMES

So far, we have considered vectors and points as abstract objects, without representing them in an underlying reference system. In a three-dimensional vector space, we can represent any vector w uniquely in terms of any three linearly independent vectors v_1, v_2, and v_3 (see Appendix B), as

$$w = \alpha_1 v_1 + \alpha_2 v_2 + \alpha_3 v_3.$$

The scalars α_1, α_2, and α_3 are the **components** of w with respect to the **basis** v_1, v_2, and v_3. These relationships are shown in Figure 4.21. We can write the **representation** of w with respect to this basis as the column matrix

$$\mathbf{a} = \begin{bmatrix} \alpha_1 \\ \alpha_2 \\ \alpha_3 \end{bmatrix},$$

where boldface letters denote a representation in a particular basis, as opposed to the original abstract vector w. We can also write this relationship as

$$w = \mathbf{a}^T \begin{bmatrix} v_1 \\ v_2 \\ v_3 \end{bmatrix} = \mathbf{a}^T \mathbf{v},$$

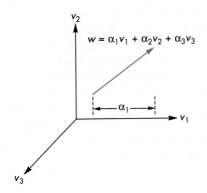

FIGURE 4.21   Vector derived from three basis vectors.

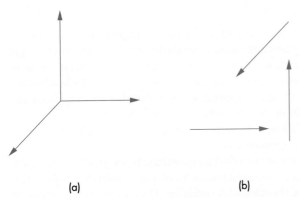

(a)   (b)

FIGURE 4.22   Coordinate systems. (a) Vectors emerging from a common point.
(b) Vectors moved.

where

$$\mathbf{v} = \begin{bmatrix} v_1 \\ v_2 \\ v_3 \end{bmatrix}.$$

We usually think of the basis vectors v_1, v_2, v_3, as defining a **coordinate system**. However, for dealing with problems using points, vectors, and scalars, we need a more general method. Figure 4.22 shows one aspect of the problem. The three vectors form a coordinate system that is shown in Figure 4.22(a) as we would usually draw it, with the three vectors emerging from a single point. We could use these three basis vectors as a basis to represent any vector in three dimensions. Vectors, however, have direction and magnitude but lack a position attribute. Hence, Figure 4.22(b) is equivalent, because we have moved the basis vectors, leaving their magnitudes and directions unchanged. Most people find this second figure confusing, even though mathematically it expresses the same information as the first figure. We are still left with the problem of how to represent points—entities that have fixed positions.

Because an affine space contains points, once we fix a particular reference point—the origin—in such a space, we can represent all points unambiguously. The usual convention for drawing coordinate axes as emerging from the origin, as shown in Figure 4.22(a), makes sense in the affine space where both points and vectors have representations. However, this representation requires us to know *both* the reference point and the basis vectors. The origin and the basis vectors determine a **frame**. Loosely, this extension fixes the origin of the vector coordinate system at some point P_0. Within a given frame, every vector can be written uniquely as

$$w = \alpha_1 v_1 + \alpha_2 v_2 + \alpha_3 v_3 = \mathbf{a}^T \mathbf{v},$$

just as in a vector space; in addition, every point can be written uniquely as

$$P = P_0 + \beta_1 v_1 + \beta_2 v_2 + \beta_3 v_3 = P_0 + \mathbf{b}^T \mathbf{v}.$$

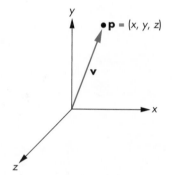

FIGURE 4.23   A dangerous representation of a vector.

Thus, the representation of a particular vector in a frame requires three scalars; the representation of a point requires three scalars and the knowledge of where the origin is located. As we will see in Section 4.3.4, by abandoning the more familiar notion of a coordinate system and a basis in that coordinate system in favor of the less familiar notion of a frame, we avoid the difficulties caused by vectors having magnitude and direction but no fixed position. In addition, we are able to represent points and vectors in a manner that will allow us to use matrix representations while maintaining a distinction between the two geometric types.

Because points and vectors are two distinct geometric types, graphical representations that equate a point with a directed line segment drawn from the origin to that point (Figure 4.23) should be regarded with suspicion. Thus, a correct interpretation of Figure 4.23 is that a given vector can be defined as going from a fixed reference point (the origin) to a particular point in space. Note that a vector, like a point, exists regardless of the reference system, but as we will see with both points and vectors, eventually we have to work with their representation in a particular reference system.

4.3.1 Representations and N-Tuples

Suppose that vectors e_1, e_2, and e_3 form a basis. The representation of any vector, v, is given by the component $(\alpha_1, \alpha_2, \alpha_3)$ of a vector $\mathbf{a}$ where

$$v = \alpha_1 e_1 + \alpha_2 e_2 + \alpha_3 e_3.$$

The basis vectors[2] must themselves have representations, which we can denote $\mathbf{e}_1$, $\mathbf{e}_2$, and $\mathbf{e}_3$, given by

---

2. Many textbooks on vectors refer to these vectors as the unit basis $\mathbf{i}$, $\mathbf{j}$, $\mathbf{k}$ and write other vectors in the form $v = \alpha_1 \mathbf{i} + \alpha_2 \mathbf{j} + \alpha_3 \mathbf{k}$.

$$\mathbf{e_1} = (1, 0, 0)^T$$

$$\mathbf{e_2} = (0, 1, 0)^T$$

$$\mathbf{e_3} = (0, 0, 1)^T.$$

In other words, the 3-tuple $(1, 0, 0)$ is the representation of the first basis vector. Consequently, rather than thinking in terms of abstract vectors, we can work with 3-tuples and write the representation of any vector v as a column matrix $\mathbf{a}$ or the 3-tuple $(\alpha_1, \alpha_2, \alpha_3)$, where

$$\mathbf{a} = \alpha_1 \mathbf{e_1} + \alpha_2 \mathbf{e_2} + \alpha_3 \mathbf{e_3}.$$

The basis 3-tuples $\mathbf{e_1}$, $\mathbf{e_2}$, and $\mathbf{e_3}$ are vectors in the familiar Euclidean space $\mathbf{R}^3$. The vector space $\mathbf{R}^3$ is equivalent (or **homomorphic**) to the vector space of our original geometric vectors. From a practical perspective, it is almost always easier to work with 3-tuples (or more generally n-tuples) than with other representations.

4.3.2 Change of Coordinate Systems

Frequently, we are required to find how the representation of a vector changes when we change the basis vectors. For example, in WebGL, we specify our geometry using the coordinate system or frame that is natural for the model, which is known as the **object** or **model frame**. Models are then brought into the **world frame**.[3] At some point, we want to know how these objects appear to the camera. It is natural at that point to convert representations from the world frame to the **camera** or **eye frame**. The conversion from the object frame to the eye frame is done by the model-view matrix.

Let's consider changing representations for vectors first. Suppose that $\{v_1, v_2, v_3\}$ and $\{u_1, u_2, u_3\}$ are two bases. Each basis vector in the second set can be represented in terms of the first basis (and vice versa). Hence, there exist nine scalar components, $\{\gamma_{ij}\}$, such that

$$u_1 = \gamma_{11}v_1 + \gamma_{12}v_2 + \gamma_{13}v_3$$

$$u_2 = \gamma_{21}v_1 + \gamma_{22}v_2 + \gamma_{23}v_3$$

$$u_3 = \gamma_{31}v_1 + \gamma_{32}v_2 + \gamma_{33}v_3.$$

The 3×3 matrix

$$\mathbf{M} = \begin{bmatrix} \gamma_{11} & \gamma_{12} & \gamma_{13} \\ \gamma_{21} & \gamma_{22} & \gamma_{23} \\ \gamma_{31} & \gamma_{32} & \gamma_{33} \end{bmatrix}$$

is defined by these scalars, and

---

3. In our simple examples, the object and world frames are often the same.

$$\begin{bmatrix} u_1 \\ u_2 \\ u_3 \end{bmatrix} = \mathbf{M} \begin{bmatrix} v_1 \\ v_2 \\ v_3 \end{bmatrix},$$

or

$\mathbf{u} = \mathbf{Mv}.$

The matrix $\mathbf{M}$ contains the information to go from a representation of a vector in one basis to its representation in the second basis. The inverse of $\mathbf{M}$ gives the matrix representation of the change from $\{u_1, u_2, u_3\}$ to $\{v_1, v_2, v_3\}$. Consider a vector w that has the representation $\{\alpha_1, \alpha_2, \alpha_3\}$ with respect to $\{v_1, v_2, v_3\}$; that is,

$w = \alpha_1 v_1 + \alpha_2 v_2 + \alpha_3 v_3.$

Equivalently,

$w = \mathbf{a}^T \mathbf{v},$

where

$$\mathbf{a} = \begin{bmatrix} \alpha_1 \\ \alpha_2 \\ \alpha_3 \end{bmatrix} \qquad \mathbf{v} = \begin{bmatrix} v_1 \\ v_2 \\ v_3 \end{bmatrix}.$$

Assume that $\mathbf{b}$ is the representation of w with respect to $\{u_1, u_2, u_3\}$; that is,

$w = \beta_1 u_1 + \beta_2 u_2 + \beta_3 u_3,$

or

$$w = \mathbf{b}^T \begin{bmatrix} u_1 \\ u_2 \\ u_3 \end{bmatrix} = \mathbf{b}^T \mathbf{u},$$

where

$$\mathbf{b} = \begin{bmatrix} \beta_1 \\ \beta_2 \\ \beta_3 \end{bmatrix}.$$

Then, using our representation of the second basis in terms of the first, we find that

$$w = \mathbf{b}^T \begin{bmatrix} u_1 \\ u_2 \\ u_3 \end{bmatrix} = \mathbf{b}^T \mathbf{M} \begin{bmatrix} v_1 \\ v_2 \\ v_3 \end{bmatrix} = \mathbf{a}^T \begin{bmatrix} v_1 \\ v_2 \\ v_3 \end{bmatrix}.$$

Thus,

$\mathbf{a} = \mathbf{M}^T \mathbf{b}.$

The matrix

$$\mathbf{T} = (\mathbf{M}^T)^{-1}$$

takes us from **a** to **b**, through the simple matrix equation

$$\mathbf{b} = \mathbf{Ta}.$$

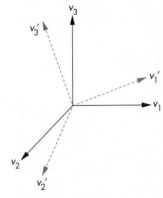

FIGURE 4.24 Rotation and scaling of a basis.

Thus, rather than working with our original vectors, typically directed line segments, we can work instead with their representations, which are 3-tuples or elements of $\mathbf{R}^3$. This result is important because it moves us from considering abstract vectors to working with column matrices of scalars—the vectors' representations. The important point to remember is that whenever we work with columns of real numbers as "vectors," there is an underlying basis of which we must not lose track, lest we end up working in the wrong coordinate system.

   These changes in basis leave the origin unchanged. We can use them to represent rotation and scaling of a set of basis vectors to derive another basis set, as shown in Figure 4.24. However, a simple translation of the origin or change of frame, as shown in Figure 4.25, cannot be represented in this way. After we complete a simple example, we introduce homogeneous coordinates, which allow us to change frames yet still use matrices to represent the change.

4.3.3 Example: Change of Representation

Suppose that we have a vector w whose representation in some basis is

$$\mathbf{a} = \begin{bmatrix} 1 \\ 2 \\ 3 \end{bmatrix}.$$

We can denote the three basis vectors as v_1, v_2, and v_3. Hence,

$$w = v_1 + 2v_2 + 3v_3.$$

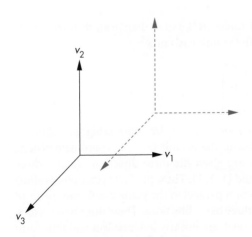

FIGURE 4.25 Translation of a basis.

Now suppose that we want to make a new basis from the three vectors v_1, v_2, and v_3 where

$$u_1 = v_1$$

$$u_2 = v_1 + v_2$$

$$u_3 = v_1 + v_2 + v_3.$$

The matrix $\mathbf{M}$ is

$$\mathbf{M} = \begin{bmatrix} 1 & 0 & 0 \\ 1 & 1 & 0 \\ 1 & 1 & 1 \end{bmatrix}.$$

The matrix that converts a representation in v_1, v_2, and v_3 to one in which the basis vectors are u_1, u_2, and u_3 is

$$\mathbf{T} = (\mathbf{M}^T)^{-1} = \begin{bmatrix} 1 & 1 & 1 \\ 0 & 1 & 1 \\ 0 & 0 & 1 \end{bmatrix}^{-1}$$

$$= \begin{bmatrix} 1 & -1 & 0 \\ 0 & 1 & -1 \\ 0 & 0 & 1 \end{bmatrix}.$$

In the new system, the representation of w is

$$\mathbf{b} = \mathbf{T}\mathbf{a} = \begin{bmatrix} -1 \\ -1 \\ 3 \end{bmatrix}.$$

That is,

$$w = -u_1 - u_2 + 3u_3.$$

If we are working in the space of 3-tuples ($\mathbf{R}^3$), rather than in an abstract setting, then we can associate v_1, v_2, and v_3 with the unit basis in $\mathbf{R}^3$:

$$\mathbf{e}_1 = \begin{bmatrix} 1 \\ 0 \\ 0 \end{bmatrix} \qquad \mathbf{e}_2 = \begin{bmatrix} 0 \\ 1 \\ 0 \end{bmatrix} \qquad \mathbf{e}_3 = \begin{bmatrix} 0 \\ 0 \\ 1 \end{bmatrix}.$$

We can make this example a little more concrete by considering the following variant. Suppose that we are working with the default (x, y, z) coordinate system, which happens to be orthogonal. We are given the three direction vectors whose representations are $(1, 0, 0)$, $(1, 1, 0)$, and $(1, 1, 1)$. Thus, the first vector points along the x-axis, the second points in a direction parallel to the plane $z = 0$, and the third points in a direction symmetric to the three basis directions. These three new vectors, although they are not mutually orthogonal, are linearly independent and thus form a basis for a new coordinate system that we can call the x', y', z' system. The original directions have representations in the x', y', z' system given by the columns of the matrix **T**.

4.3.4 Homogeneous Coordinates

The potential confusion between a vector and a point that we illustrated in Figure 4.23 still exists with a three-dimensional representation. Suppose that we start with the frame defined by the point P_0 and the vectors v_1, v_2, and v_3. Usually, our first inclination is to represent a point P located at (x, y, z) with the column matrix

$$\mathbf{p} = \begin{bmatrix} x \\ y \\ z \end{bmatrix},$$

where x, y, and z are the components of the basis vectors for this point, so that

$$P = P_0 + xv_1 + yv_2 + zv_3.$$

If we represent the point this way, then its representation is of the same form as the vector

$$w = xv_1 + yv_2 + zv_3.$$

Homogeneous coordinates avoid this difficulty by using a four-dimensional representation for both points and vectors in three dimensions. In the frame specified by (v_1, v_2, v_3, P_0), any point P can be written uniquely as

$$P = \alpha_1 v_1 + \alpha_2 v_2 + \alpha_3 v_3 + P_0.$$

If we agree to define the "multiplication" of a point by the scalars 0 and 1 as

$$0 \cdot P = \mathbf{0}$$
$$1 \cdot P = P,$$

then we can express this relation formally, using a matrix product, as

$$P = \begin{bmatrix} \alpha_1 & \alpha_2 & \alpha_3 & 1 \end{bmatrix} \begin{bmatrix} v_1 \\ v_2 \\ v_3 \\ P_0 \end{bmatrix}.$$

Strictly speaking, this expression is not a dot or inner product, because the elements of the matrices are dissimilar; nonetheless, the expression is computed as though it were an inner product by multiplying corresponding elements and summing the results. The four-dimensional row matrix on the right side of the equation is the **homogeneous-coordinate representation** of the point P in the frame determined by v_1, v_2, v_3, and P_0. Equivalently, we can say that P is represented by the column matrix

$$\mathbf{p} = \begin{bmatrix} \alpha_1 \\ \alpha_2 \\ \alpha_3 \\ 1 \end{bmatrix}.$$

In the same frame, any vector w can be written as

$$w = \delta_1 v_1 + \delta_2 v_2 + \delta_3 v_3$$

$$= [\, \delta_1 \quad \delta_2 \quad \delta_3 \quad 0 \,]^T \begin{bmatrix} v_1 \\ v_2 \\ v_3 \\ P_0 \end{bmatrix}.$$

Thus, w can be represented by the column matrix

$$\mathbf{w} = \begin{bmatrix} \delta_1 \\ \delta_2 \\ \delta_3 \\ 0 \end{bmatrix}.$$

There are numerous ways to interpret this formulation geometrically. We simply note that we can carry out operations on points and vectors using their homogeneous-coordinate representations and ordinary matrix algebra. Consider, for example, a change of frames—a problem that caused difficulties when we used three-dimensional representations. If (v_1, v_2, v_3, P_0) and (u_1, u_2, u_3, Q_0) are two frames, then we can express the basis vectors and reference point of the second frame in terms of the first as

$$u_1 = \gamma_{11} v_1 + \gamma_{12} v_2 + \gamma_{13} v_3$$

$$u_2 = \gamma_{21} v_1 + \gamma_{22} v_2 + \gamma_{23} v_3$$

$$u_3 = \gamma_{31} v_1 + \gamma_{32} v_2 + \gamma_{33} v_3$$

$$Q_0 = \gamma_{41} v_1 + \gamma_{42} v_2 + \gamma_{43} v_3 + P_0.$$

These equations can be written in the form

$$\begin{bmatrix} u_1 \\ u_2 \\ u_3 \\ Q_0 \end{bmatrix} = \mathbf{M} \begin{bmatrix} v_1 \\ v_2 \\ v_3 \\ P_0 \end{bmatrix},$$

where now $\mathbf{M}$ is the 4×4 matrix

$$\mathbf{M} = \begin{bmatrix} \gamma_{11} & \gamma_{12} & \gamma_{13} & 0 \\ \gamma_{21} & \gamma_{22} & \gamma_{23} & 0 \\ \gamma_{31} & \gamma_{32} & \gamma_{33} & 0 \\ \gamma_{41} & \gamma_{42} & \gamma_{43} & 1 \end{bmatrix}.$$

M is called the **matrix representation** of the change of frames.

We can also use **M** to compute the changes in the representations directly. Suppose that **a** and **b** are the homogeneous-coordinate representations either of two points or of two vectors in the two frames. Then

$$\mathbf{b}^T \begin{bmatrix} u_1 \\ u_2 \\ u_3 \\ Q_0 \end{bmatrix} = \mathbf{b}^T \mathbf{M} \begin{bmatrix} v_1 \\ v_2 \\ v_3 \\ P_0 \end{bmatrix} = \mathbf{a}^T \begin{bmatrix} v_1 \\ v_2 \\ v_3 \\ P_0 \end{bmatrix}.$$

Hence,

$$\mathbf{a} = \mathbf{M}^T \mathbf{b}.$$

When we work with representations, as is usually the case, we are interested in $\mathbf{M}^T$, which is of the form

$$\mathbf{M}^T = \begin{bmatrix} \alpha_{11} & \alpha_{12} & \alpha_{13} & \alpha_{14} \\ \alpha_{21} & \alpha_{22} & \alpha_{23} & \alpha_{24} \\ \alpha_{31} & \alpha_{32} & \alpha_{33} & \alpha_{34} \\ 0 & 0 & 0 & 1 \end{bmatrix}$$

and is determined by 12 coefficients.

There are other advantages to using homogeneous coordinates that we explore extensively in later chapters. Perhaps the most important is that all affine (line-preserving) transformations can be represented as matrix multiplications in homogeneous coordinates. Although we have to work in four dimensions to solve three-dimensional problems when we use homogeneous-coordinate representations, less arithmetic work is involved. The uniform representation of all affine transformations makes carrying out successive transformations (concatenation) far easier than in three-dimensional space. In addition, modern hardware implements homogeneous-coordinate operations directly, using parallelism to achieve high-speed calculations.

4.3.5 Example: Change in Frames

Consider again the example of Section 4.3.3. If we again start with the basis vectors v_1, v_2, and v_3 and convert to a basis determined by the same u_1, u_2, and u_3, then the three equations are the same:

$$u_1 = v_1,$$

$$u_2 = v_1 + v_2,$$

$$u_3 = v_1 + v_2 + v_3.$$

The reference point does not change, so we add the equation

$$Q_0 = P_0.$$

Thus, the matrices in which we are interested are the matrix

$$\mathbf{M} = \begin{bmatrix} 1 & 0 & 0 & 0 \\ 1 & 1 & 0 & 0 \\ 1 & 1 & 1 & 0 \\ 0 & 0 & 0 & 1 \end{bmatrix},$$

its transpose, and their inverses.

Suppose that in addition to changing the basis vectors, we also want to move the reference point to the point that has the representation (1, 2, 3, 1) in the original system. The displacement vector $v = v_1 + 2v_2 + 3v_3$ moves P_0 to Q_0. The fourth component identifies this entity as a point. Thus, we add to the three equations from the previous example the equation

$$Q_0 = P_0 + v_1 + 2v_2 + 3v_3,$$

and the matrix $\mathbf{M}^T$ becomes

$$\mathbf{M}^T = \begin{bmatrix} 1 & 1 & 1 & 1 \\ 0 & 1 & 1 & 2 \\ 0 & 0 & 1 & 3 \\ 0 & 0 & 0 & 1 \end{bmatrix}.$$

Its inverse is

$$\mathbf{T} = (\mathbf{M}^T)^{-1} = \begin{bmatrix} 1 & -1 & 0 & 1 \\ 0 & 1 & -1 & 1 \\ 0 & 0 & 1 & -3 \\ 0 & 0 & 0 & 1 \end{bmatrix}.$$

This pair of matrices allows us to move back and forth between representations in the two frames. Note that $\mathbf{T}$ takes the *point* (1, 2, 3) in the original frame, whose representation is

$$\mathbf{p} = \begin{bmatrix} 1 \\ 2 \\ 3 \\ 1 \end{bmatrix},$$

to

$$\mathbf{p}' = \begin{bmatrix} 0 \\ 0 \\ 0 \\ 1 \end{bmatrix},$$

the origin in the new system. However, the *vector* (1, 2, 3), which is represented as

$$\mathbf{a} = \begin{bmatrix} 1 \\ 2 \\ 3 \\ 0 \end{bmatrix}$$

in the original system, is transformed to

$$\mathbf{b} = \begin{bmatrix} -1 \\ -1 \\ 3 \\ 0 \end{bmatrix},$$

a transformation that is consistent with the results from our example of change in coordinate systems and that also demonstrates the importance of distinguishing between points and vectors.

4.3.6 Working with Representations

Application programs almost always work with representations rather than abstract points. Thus, when we specify a point—for example, by putting its coordinates in an array—we are doing so with respect to some frame. In our earlier examples, we avoided dealing with changes in frames by specifying data in clip coordinates, a normalized system that WebGL uses for its rendering. However, applications programmers prefer to work in frames that have a relationship to the problem on which they are working and thus want to place the origin, orient the axes, and scale the units so they make sense in the problem space. Because WebGL eventually needs its data in clip coordinates, at least one change of representation is required. As we shall see, in fact there are additional frames that we will find useful for modeling and rendering. Hence, we will carry out a sequence of changes in representation.

Changes of representation are thus specified by a matrix of the form

$$\mathbf{a} = \mathbf{Cb},$$

where $\mathbf{a}$ and $\mathbf{b}$ are the two representations of a point or vector in homogeneous coordinates. As we have seen in Section 4.3.4, this matrix must be a homogeneous form, so $\mathbf{C}$ is the transpose of a matrix $\mathbf{M}$ and is given by

$$\mathbf{C} = \mathbf{M}^T = \begin{bmatrix} \alpha_{11} & \alpha_{12} & \alpha_{13} & \alpha_{14} \\ \alpha_{21} & \alpha_{22} & \alpha_{23} & \alpha_{24} \\ \alpha_{31} & \alpha_{32} & \alpha_{33} & \alpha_{34} \\ 0 & 0 & 0 & 1 \end{bmatrix}.$$

The problem is how to find $\mathbf{C}$ when we are working with representations. It turns out to be quite easy. Suppose that we are working in some frame and we specify another frame by its representation in this frame. Thus, if in the original system we specify a frame by the representations of three vectors, u, v, and n, and give the origin of the new frame as the point p, then in homogeneous coordinates all four of these entities are 4-tuples or elements of $\mathbf{R}^4$.

Let's consider the inverse problem. The matrix

$$\mathbf{T} = \mathbf{C}^{-1}$$

converts from representations in the (u, v, n, p) frame to representations in the original frame. Thus, we must have

$$\mathbf{T} \begin{bmatrix} 1 \\ 0 \\ 0 \\ 0 \end{bmatrix} = \mathbf{u} = \begin{bmatrix} u_1 \\ u_2 \\ u_3 \\ 0 \end{bmatrix}.$$

Likewise,

$$\mathbf{T} \begin{bmatrix} 0 \\ 1 \\ 0 \\ 0 \end{bmatrix} = \mathbf{v} = \begin{bmatrix} v_1 \\ v_2 \\ v_3 \\ 0 \end{bmatrix}$$

$$\mathbf{T} \begin{bmatrix} 0 \\ 0 \\ 1 \\ 0 \end{bmatrix} = \mathbf{n} = \begin{bmatrix} n_1 \\ n_2 \\ n_3 \\ 0 \end{bmatrix}$$

$$\mathbf{T} \begin{bmatrix} 0 \\ 0 \\ 0 \\ 1 \end{bmatrix} = \mathbf{p} = \begin{bmatrix} p_1 \\ p_2 \\ p_3 \\ 1 \end{bmatrix}.$$

Putting these results together, we find

$$\mathbf{TI} = \mathbf{T} = \begin{bmatrix} u & v & n & p \end{bmatrix} = \begin{bmatrix} u_1 & v_1 & n_1 & p_1 \\ u_2 & v_2 & n_2 & p_2 \\ u_3 & v_3 & n_3 & p_3 \\ 0 & 0 & 0 & 1 \end{bmatrix},$$

or

$$\mathbf{C} = \begin{bmatrix} u & v & n & p \end{bmatrix}^{-1} = \begin{bmatrix} u_1 & v_1 & n_1 & p_1 \\ u_2 & v_2 & n_2 & p_2 \\ u_3 & v_3 & n_3 & p_3 \\ 0 & 0 & 0 & 1 \end{bmatrix}^{-1}.$$

Thus, the representation of a frame in terms of another frame gives us the inverse of the matrix we need to convert from representations in the first frame to representations in the second. Of course, we must compute this inverse, but computing the inverse of a 4×4 matrix of this form should not present a problem. We can use a standard matrix package or include the equations for each component of the inverse within an inverse function, as we have done in `MV.js`.

4.4 FRAMES IN WEBGL

As we have seen, WebGL is based on a pipeline model, the first part of which is a sequence of operations on vertices, many of which are geometric. We can characterize such operations by a sequence of transformations or, equivalently, as a sequence of changes of frames for the objects specified by an application program.

In earlier versions of OpenGL with a fixed-function pipeline and immediate-mode rendering, six frames were specified in the pipeline. With programmable shaders, we have a great deal of flexibility to add additional frames or avoid some traditional frames. Although, as we demonstrated in our first examples, we could use some knowledge of how the pipeline functions to avoid using all these frames, that would not be the best way to build our applications. Rather, each of the six frames we will discuss will prove to be useful, either for developing our applications or for implementation of the pipeline. Some will be applied in the application code, others in our shaders. Some may not be visible to the application. In each of these frames, a vertex has different coordinates. The following is the usual order in which the frames occur in the pipeline:

1. Model coordinates

2. Object (or world) coordinates

3. Eye (or camera) coordinates

4. Clip coordinates

5. Normalized device coordinates

6. Window (or screen) coordinates

Let's consider what happens when an application program specifies a vertex. This vertex may be specified directly in the application program or indirectly through an instantiation of some object. In most applications, we tend to specify or use an object with a convenient size, orientation, and location in its own frame, called the **model frame**. For example, a cube would typically have its faces aligned with axes of the frame, its center at the origin, and a side length of 1 or 2 units. The coordinates in the corresponding function calls are in model coordinates.

An individual scene may comprise hundreds or even thousands of individual objects. The application program generally applies a sequence of transformations to each object to size, orient, and position it within a frame that is appropriate for the particular application. For example, if we were using an instance of a square for a window in an architectural application, we would scale it to have the correct proportions and units, which would probably be in feet or meters. The origin of application coordinates might be a location in the center of the bottom floor of the building. This application frame is called the **object** or **world frame**, and the values are in **object** or **world coordinates**. Note that if we do not model with predefined objects or apply any transformations before we specify our geometry, model and object coordinates are the same.

Model and object coordinates are the natural frames for the application programmer to work with to specify objects. However, the image that is produced depends on what the camera or viewer sees. Virtually all graphics systems use a frame whose origin is the center of the camera's lens[4] and whose axes are aligned with the sides of the camera. This frame is called the **camera frame** or **eye frame**. Because there is an affine transformation that corresponds to each change of frame, there are 4×4 matrices that represent the transformation from model coordinates to world coordinates and from world coordinates to eye coordinates. These transformations usually are concatenated together into the **model-view transformation**, which is specified by the model-view matrix. Usually, the use of the model-view matrix instead of the individual matrices should not pose any problems for the application programmer. In Chapter 6, where we discuss lighting and shading, we will see situations where we must separate the two transformations.

The final three representations are used primarily in the implementation of the pipeline, but, for completeness, we introduce them here. Once objects are in eye coordinates, WebGL must check whether they lie within the view volume. If an object does not, it is clipped from the scene prior to rasterization. WebGL can carry out this process most efficiently if it first carries out a projection transformation that brings all potentially visible objects into a cube centered at the origin in **clip coordinates**. We will study this transformation in Chapter 5. After this transformation, vertices are still represented in homogeneous coordinates. The division by the w component, called **perspective division**, yields three-dimensional representations in **normalized device coordinates**. The final transformation takes a position in normalized device coordinates and, taking into account the viewport, creates a three-dimensional representation in **window coordinates**. Window coordinates are measured in units of pixels on the display but retain depth information. If we remove the depth coordinate, we are working with two-dimensional **screen coordinates**.

The application programmer usually works with two frames: the model frame and the object frame. By concatenating the transformation that takes the model frame to the object frame with the transformation that takes the object frame to the eye frame, we form the model-view matrix that positions the objects relative to the eye frame. Thus, the model-view matrix converts the homogeneous-coordinate representations of points and vectors from their representations in the application space to their representations in the eye frame.

Because WebGL does not a use a fixed-function pipeline, we are not required to use the model-view matrix. Nevertheless, the model-view matrix provides the transformation that most applications require, and we will almost always include it in our examples. One of the issues we will discuss in some detail is where we specify our transformations and where they are applied. For example, we could specify a transformation in the application and apply it to the data there. We could also define

---

4. For a perspective view, the center of the lens is the center of projection (COP), whereas for an orthogonal view, the direction of projection is aligned with the sides of the camera.

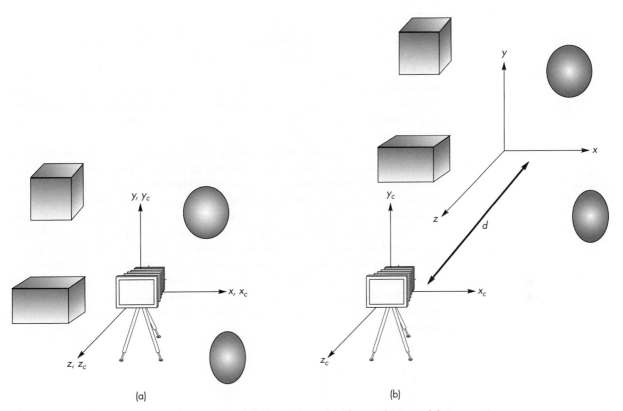

FIGURE 4.26   Camera and object frames. (a) In default positions. (b) After applying model-view matrix.

the parameters of a transformation in the application and send these parameters to the shaders and let the GPU carry out the transformations. We examine these approaches in the following sections.

Let's assume that we specify our objects directly in object coordinates and the model-view matrix is initialized to an identity matrix. At this point, the object frame and eye frame are identical. Thus, if we do not change the model-view matrix, we are working in eye coordinates. As we saw in Chapter 2, the camera is at the origin of its frame, as shown in Figure 4.26(a). The three basis vectors in eye space correspond to (1) the up direction of the camera, the y direction; (2) the direction the camera is pointing, the negative z direction; and (3) a third orthogonal direction, x, placed so that the x, y, z directions form a right-handed coordinate system. We obtain other frames in which to place objects by performing homogeneous coordinate transformations that specify new frames relative to the camera frame. In Section 4.5, we will learn how to specify these transformations; in Section 4.3, we used them to position the camera relative to our objects.

Because frame changes are represented by model-view matrices that can be stored, we can save frames and move between frames by changing the current model-view matrix. In Chapter 9, we will see that creating a data structure such as a stack to store transformations will be helpful in working with complex models.

When first working with multiple frames, there can be some confusion about which frames are fixed and which are varying. Because the model-view matrix positions the camera *relative* to the objects, it is usually a matter of convenience as to which frame we regard as fixed. Most of the time, we will regard the camera as fixed and the other frames as moving relative to the camera, but you may prefer to adopt the view that the objects are fixed and the camera moves. The notion of a fixed viewer who moves the objects to obtain the desired view has its history in art, whereas the view that the objects are fixed comes from physics.

Before beginning a detailed discussion of transformations and how we use them in WebGL, we present two simple examples. In the default settings shown in Figure 4.26(a), the camera and object frames coincide with the camera pointing in the negative z direction. In many applications, it is natural to specify objects near the origin, such as a square centered at the origin or perhaps a group of objects whose center of mass is at the origin. It is also natural to set up our viewing conditions so that the camera sees only those objects that are in front of it. Consequently, to form images that contain all these objects, we must either move the camera away from the objects or move the objects away from the camera. Equivalently, we move the camera frame relative to the object frame. If we regard the camera frame as fixed and the model-view matrix as positioning the object frame relative to the camera frame, then the model-view matrix

$$\mathbf{A} = \begin{bmatrix} 1 & 0 & 0 & 0 \\ 0 & 1 & 0 & 0 \\ 0 & 0 & 1 & -d \\ 0 & 0 & 0 & 1 \end{bmatrix}$$

moves a point (x, y, z) in the object frame to the point $(x, y, z - d)$ in the camera frame. Thus, by making d a suitably large positive number, we "move" the objects in front of the camera by moving the object frame relative to the camera frame, as shown in Figure 4.26(b). Note that as far as the user—who is working in object coordinates—is concerned, she is positioning objects as before. The model-view matrix takes care of the relative positioning of the object and eye frames. This strategy is almost always better than attempting to alter the positions of the objects by changing their vertex positions to place them in front of the camera.

Let's look at another example. When we define our objects using vertices, we are working in the application frame (or object frame). The vertex positions specified there are the representation of points in that frame. Thus, we do not use the object frame directly but rather implicitly by representing points (and vectors) in it. Consider the situation illustrated in Figure 4.27.

Here we see the camera positioned in the object frame. Using homogeneous coordinates, it is centered at a point $p = (1, 0, 1, 1)^T$ in object coordinates and points at the origin in the world frame. Thus, the vector whose representation in the object frame is $\mathbf{n} = (-1, 0, -1, 0)^T$ is orthogonal to the back of the camera and points toward the origin. The camera is oriented so that its up direction is the same as the up direction in world coordinates and has the representation $\mathbf{v} = (0, 1, 0, 0)^T$. We can form an orthogonal coordinate system for the camera by using the cross product to

FIGURE 4.27 Camera at (1, 0, 1) pointing toward the origin.

determine a third orthogonal direction for the camera, which is $\mathbf{u} = (1, 0, -1, 0)^T$. We can now proceed as we did in Section 4.3.6 and derive the matrix $\mathbf{M}$ that converts the representation of points and vectors in the object frame to their representations in the camera frame. The transpose of this matrix in homogeneous coordinates is obtained by the inverse of a matrix containing the coordinates of the camera,

$$
(\mathbf{M}^T)^{-1} = \begin{bmatrix} & u^T & \\ & v^T & \\ & n^T & \\ 0 & 0 & 0 & 1 \end{bmatrix} = \begin{bmatrix} 1 & 0 & -1 & 1 \\ 0 & 1 & 0 & 0 \\ -1 & 0 & -1 & 1 \\ 0 & 0 & 0 & 1 \end{bmatrix}^{-1} = \begin{bmatrix} \frac{1}{2} & 0 & -\frac{1}{2} & 0 \\ 0 & 1 & 0 & 0 \\ -\frac{1}{2} & 0 & -\frac{1}{2} & 1 \\ 0 & 0 & 0 & 1 \end{bmatrix}.
$$

Note that the origin in the original frame is now a distance of $\sqrt{2}$ in the n direction from the origin in the camera frame or, equivalently, at the point whose representation is (0, 0, 1, 1) in the camera frame.

In WebGL, we can set a model-view matrix by sending an array of 16 elements to the vertex shader. For situations in which we have the representation of one frame in terms of another through the specification of the basis vectors and the origin, it is a direct exercise to find the required coefficients. However, such is not usually the case. For most geometric problems, we usually go from one frame to another by a sequence of geometric transformations such as rotations, translations, and scales. We will follow this approach in subsequent sections. But first, we will introduce some helpful JavaScript functions that are included in our matrix package.

4.5   MATRIX AND VECTOR TYPES

In Chapter 2, we saw how using some new data types could clarify our application code and were necessary for GLSL. Let's expand and formalize these notions by introducing the JavaScript types that we will use in our applications. The code is in the package MV.js that can be included in your application through the HTML line

```
<script type="text/javascript" src="../Common/MV.js"></script>
```

The matrix types are for 3×3 and 4×4 matrices, whereas the vector types are for 2-, 3-, and 4-element arrays. Note that the matrix types are stored as one-dimensional arrays, but we rarely need to use that fact. Rather, we manipulate matrices and vector types through a set of functions. The package contains functions to create these entities, such as

```
var a = vec3();          // create a vec3 with all components set to 0
var b = vec3(1, 2, 3);   // create a vec3 with the components 1, 2, 3
var c = vec3(b);         // copy the vec3 'b' by copying vec3 'c'

var d = mat3();          // create a mat3 identity matrix
var e = mat3(0, 1, 2,
             3, 4, 5,
             6, 7, 8);   // create a mat3 from 9 elements
var f = mat3(e);         // create the mat3 'f' by copying mat3 'e'
```

Because JavaScript does not support operator overloading as does C++ and GLSL,[5] we use functions to perform the basic matrix–vector operations. The following code illustrates some of the functionality:

```
a = add(b,c);      // adds vectors 'b' and 'c' and puts result in 'a'
d = mat4();        // sets 'd' to an identity matrix
d = transpose(e);  // sets 'd' to the transpose of 'e'
f = mult(e, d);    // sets 'f' to the product of 'e' and 'd'
```

Other functions in the package compute matrix inverses, dot and cross products, and the standard transformation and viewing matrices that we will develop in this and the next chapter.

In light of our previous distinctions between points and vectors, the use of a single type to represent both may be a bit disconcerting. However, this problem occurs in many fields. Most scientists and engineers use the terms *vectors* and *matrices* to refer to one-dimensional and two-dimensional arrays, respectively, rather than using the terms *row* and *column* matrix to describe one-dimensional arrays. GLSL uses the `vec2`, `vec3`, and `vec4` types to store any quantity that has two, three, or four elements, including vectors (directions) and points in homogeneous coordinates, colors (either RGB or RGBA), and, as we shall see later, texture coordinates.

One advantage of using separate matrix and vector types in our application is that the code that manipulates points, vectors, and transformations in our applications will look similar to code that carries out the same operations in the shaders using GLSL. We will see that we often have a choice as to where we carry out our algorithms, in the application or in one of the shaders. By using similar types, we will be able to transfer an algorithm easily from an application to one of the shaders.

---

5. See the sixth edition [Ang11] for an example of a matrix–vector package that uses operator overloading.

4.5.1 Row versus Column Major Matrix Representations

Consider a matrix as we might specify by

```
var m = mat3(
  0, 1, 2,
  3, 4, 5,
  6, 7, 8
);
```

Most engineers and scientists would equate this specification with the matrix

$$\mathbf{M} = \begin{bmatrix} 0 & 1 & 2 \\ 3 & 4 & 5 \\ 6 & 7 & 8 \end{bmatrix}.$$

When we use this method of specifying m, we are specifying our matrix in **row major order**; that is, the elements of the first row, followed by the elements of the second row, and so on. We can just as well say that m corresponds to the matrix

$$\mathbf{M} = \begin{bmatrix} 0 & 3 & 6 \\ 1 & 4 & 7 \\ 2 & 5 & 8 \end{bmatrix}.$$

which would be specifying m in **column major order**. As long as we are consistent, we can use either form, but unfortunately there is a problem. Whereas most of us are more comfortable with row major form, WebGL is based, as are all versions of OpenGL, on column major form. Thus, when we send a matrix to the GPU, we are sending a 16-element array that must be in column major order for the WebGL functions on the GPU to work correctly. Rather than forcing you to work in column major form, MV.js uses the more familiar row major form in its matrix functions, and the flatten function automatically transpose a matrix to change the array from row major order to column major order when it is sent to the GPU.

4.6 MODELING A COLORED CUBE

We now have most of the basic conceptual and practical knowledge we need to build three-dimensional graphical applications. We will use it to produce a program that draws a rotating cube. One frame of an animation might be as shown in Figure 4.28. However, before we can rotate the cube, we will consider how we can model it efficiently. Although three-dimensional objects can be represented, like two-dimensional objects, through a set of vertices, we will see that data structures help us to incorporate the relationships among the vertices, edges, and faces of geometric objects. Such data structures are supported in WebGL through a facility called **vertex arrays,** which we introduce at the end of this section.

FIGURE 4.28   One frame of cube animation.

After we have modeled the cube, we can animate it by using affine transformations. We introduce these transformations in Section 4.7 and then use them to alter a model-view matrix. In Chapter 5, we use these transformations again as part of the viewing process. Our pipeline model will serve us well. Vertices will flow through a number of transformations in the pipeline, all of which will use our homogeneous-coordinate representation. At the end of the pipeline awaits the rasterizer. At this point, we can assume it will do its job automatically, provided we perform the preliminary steps correctly.

4.6.1 Modeling the Faces

The cube is as simple a three-dimensional object as we might expect to model and display. There are a number of ways, however, to model it. A CSG system would regard it as a single primitive. At the other extreme, the hardware processes the cube as an object defined by eight vertices. Our decision to use surface-based models implies that we regard a cube either as the intersection of six planes or as the six polygons, called **facets**, that define its faces. A carefully designed data structure should support both a high-level application specification of the cube and a low-level model needed for the implementation.

We start by assuming that the vertices of the cube are available through an array `vertices`. We will work with homogeneous coordinates, using our vector types as either

```
var vertices = [
  vec3(-0.5, -0.5,  0.5),
  vec3(-0.5,  0.5,  0.5),
  vec3(0.5,   0.5,  0.5),
  vec3(0.5,  -0.5,  0.5),
  vec3(-0.5, -0.5, -0.5),
  vec3(-0.5,  0.5, -0.5),
  vec3(0.5,   0.5, -0.5),
  vec3(0.5,  -0.5, -0.5)
];
```

or

```
var vertices = [
  vec4(-0.5, -0.5,  0.5, 1.0),
  vec4(-0.5,  0.5,  0.5, 1.0),
  vec4(0.5,   0.5,  0.5, 1.0),
  vec4(0.5,  -0.5,  0.5, 1.0),
  vec4(-0.5, -0.5, -0.5, 1.0),
  vec4(-0.5,  0.5, -0.5, 1.0),
  vec4(0.5,   0.5, -0.5, 1.0),
  vec4(0.5,  -0.5, -0.5, 1.0)
];
```

We can then use the list of points to specify the faces of the cube. For example, one face is specified by the sequence of vertices 0, 3, 2, 1, where each integer is the index of a vertex. Thus, this face starts with the zeroth element of the array `vertices`, namely, `vec3(-0.5, -0.5, 0.5)`, and goes on to the third, second, and first elements of `vertices`. We can specify the other five faces similarly.

4.6.2 Inward- and Outward-Pointing Faces

We have to be careful about the order in which we specify our vertices when we are defining a three-dimensional polygon. We used the order 0, 3, 2, 1 for the first face. The order 1, 0, 3, 2 would be the same, because the final vertex in a polygon specification is always linked back to the first. However, the order 0, 1, 2, 3 is different. Although it describes the same boundary, the edges of the polygon are traversed in the reverse order—0, 3, 2, 1—as shown in Figure 4.29. The order is important because each polygon has two sides. Our graphics systems can display either or both of them. From the camera's perspective, we need a consistent way to distinguish between the two faces of a polygon. The order in which the vertices are specified provides this information.

FIGURE 4.29 Traversal of the edges of a polygon.

We call a face **outward facing** if the vertices are traversed in a counterclockwise order when the face is viewed from the outside. This method is also known as the **right-hand rule** because if you orient the fingers of your right hand in the direction the vertices are traversed, the thumb points outward.

In our example, the order 0, 3, 2, 1 specifies an outward face of the cube, whereas the order 0, 1, 2, 3 specifies the back face of the same polygon. Note that each face of an enclosed object, such as our cube, is an inside or outside face, regardless of where we view it from, as long as we view the face from outside the object. By specifying front and back carefully, we will be able to eliminate (or **cull**) faces that are not visible or to use different attributes to display front and back faces. We will consider culling further in Chapter 6.

4.6.3 Data Structures for Object Representation

The cube is comprised of six faces and 24 vertices. We can put all the specifications into a two-dimensional array of positions

```
var faces = new Array(6);

for (var i = 0; i < faces.length; ++i) {
  faces[i] = new Array(4);
}
```

or we could use a single array of 24 vertices,

```
var faces = new Array(24);
```

where `vertices[i]` contains the x, y, z coordinates of the ith vertex in the list. Both of these methods work, but they both fail to capture the essence of the cube's **topology**, as opposed to the cube's **geometry**. If we think of the cube as a polyhedron, we have an object that is composed of six faces. The faces are each quadrilaterals that meet at vertices; each vertex is shared by three faces. In addition, pairs of vertices define edges of the quadrilaterals; each edge is shared by two faces. These statements describe the topology of a six-sided polyhedron. All are true,

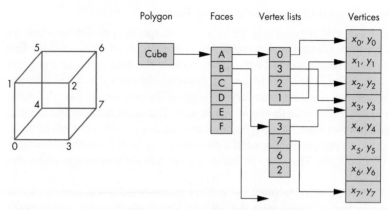

FIGURE 4.30   Vertex-list representation of a cube.

regardless of the location of the vertices—that is, regardless of the geometry of the object.[6]

Throughout the rest of this book, we will see that there are numerous advantages to building for our objects data structures that separate the topology from the geometry. In this example, we use a structure, the vertex list, that is both simple and useful and can be expanded later.

The data specifying the location of the vertices contain the geometry and can be stored as a simple list or array, such as in `vertices[8]`—the **vertex list**. The top-level entity is a cube; we regard it as being composed of six faces. Each face consists of four ordered vertices. Each vertex can be specified indirectly through its index. This data structure is shown in Figure 4.30. One of the advantages of this structure is that each geometric location appears only once, instead of being repeated each time it is used for a face. If, in an interactive application, the location of a vertex is changed, the application needs to change that location only once, rather than searching for multiple occurrences of the vertex. We will now examine two ways to draw a cube based on the separation of the geometry from the topology.

4.6.4 The Colored Cube

We can use the vertex-list representation to define a cube with color attributes. We use a function quad that takes as input the indices of four vertices in outward-pointing order and adds data to two arrays, as in Chapter 2, to store the vertex positions and the corresponding colors for each face in the arrays

```
var numVertices  = 36;

var points = [ ];
var colors = [ ];
```

---

6. We are ignoring special cases (singularities) that arise, for example, when three or more vertices lie along the same line or when the vertices are moved so that we no longer have nonintersecting faces.

Note that because we can only display triangles, the quad function must generate two triangles for each face and thus six vertices (or four if we use a triangle strip or triangles fan for each face). If we want each vertex to have its own color, then we need 24 vertices and 24 colors for our data. Using this quad function, we can specify our cube through the function

```
function colorCube()
{
  quad(1, 0, 3, 2);
  quad(2, 3, 7, 6);
  quad(3, 0, 4, 7);
  quad(6, 5, 1, 2);
  quad(4, 5, 6, 7);
  quad(5, 4, 0, 1);
}
```

We will assign the colors to the vertices using the colors of the corners of the color solid from Chapter 2 (black, white, red, green, blue, cyan, magenta, yellow). We assign a color for each vertex using the index of the vertex. Alternately, we could use the first index of the first vertex specified by quad to fix the color for the entire face. Here are the RGBA colors:

```
var vertexColors = [
  [ 0.0, 0.0, 0.0, 1.0 ],  // black
  [ 1.0, 0.0, 0.0, 1.0 ],  // red
  [ 1.0, 1.0, 0.0, 1.0 ],  // yellow
  [ 0.0, 1.0, 0.0, 1.0 ],  // green
  [ 0.0, 0.0, 1.0, 1.0 ],  // blue
  [ 1.0, 0.0, 1.0, 1.0 ],  // magenta
  [ 1.0, 1.0, 1.0, 1.0 ],  // white
  [ 0.0, 1.0, 1.0, 1.0 ]   // cyan
];
```

Here is the quad function that uses the first three vertices to specify one triangle and the first, third, and fourth to specify the second:

```
function quad(a, b, c, d)
{
  var indices = [ a, b, c, a, c, d ];

  for (var i = 0; i < indices.length; ++i) {
    points.push(vertices[indices[i]]);
    colors.push(vertexColors[indices[i]]);
  }
}
```

Our program is almost complete, but first we examine how the colors and other vertex attributes can be assigned to fragments by the rasterizer.

4.6.5 Color Interpolation

Although we have specified colors for the vertices of the cube, the graphics system must decide how to use this information to assign colors to points inside the polygon. There are many ways to use the colors of the vertices to fill in, or **interpolate**, colors across a polygon. Probably the most common method used in computer graphics is based on the barycentric coordinate representation of triangles that we introduced in Section 4.1. One of the major reasons for this approach is that triangles are the key object that we work with in rendering.

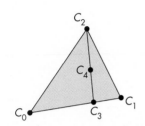

FIGURE 4.31 Interpolation using barycentric coordinates.

Consider the polygon shown in Figure 4.31. The colors C_0, C_1, and C_2 are the ones assigned to the vertices in the application program. Assume that we are using RGB color and that the interpolation is applied individually to each primary color. We first use linear interpolation to interpolate colors, along the edges between vertices 0 and 1, creating RGB colors along the edges through the parametric equations as follows:

$$C_{01}(\alpha) = (1 - \alpha)C_0 + \alpha C_1.$$

As α goes from 0 to 1, we generate colors, $C_{01}(\alpha)$ along this edge. For a given value of α, we obtain the color C_3. We can now interpolate colors along the line connecting C_3 with the color C_2 at the third vertex,

$$C_{32}(\beta) = (1 - \beta)C_3 + \beta C_2,$$

which, for a given value of β, gives the color C_4 at an interior point. As the barycentric coordinates α and β range from 0 to 1, we get interpolated colors for all the interior points and thus a color for each fragment generated by the rasterizer. The same interpolation method can be used on any vertex attribute.[7]

We now have an object that we can display much as we did with the three-dimensional Sierpinski gasket in Section 2.9, using a basic orthographic projection. In Section 4.7, we introduce transformations, enabling us to animate the cube and also to construct more complex objects. First, however, we introduce a WebGL feature that not only reduces the overhead of generating our cube but also gives us a higher-level method of working with the cube and with other polyhedral objects.

4.6.6 Displaying the Cube

The parts of the application program to display the cube and the shaders are almost identical to the code we used to display the three-dimensional gasket in Chapter 2. The differences are entirely in how we place data in the arrays for the vertex positions and vertex colors. The WebGL parts, including the shaders, are the same.

However, the display of the cube is not very informative. Because the sides of the cube are aligned with the clipping volume, we see only the front face. The display also occupies the entire window. We could get a more interesting display by changing the data so that it corresponds to a rotated cube. We could scale the data to get a smaller cube. For example, we could scale the cube by half by changing the vertex data, but

---

7. Modern graphics cards support interpolation methods that are correct under perspective viewing.

that would not be a very flexible solution. We could put the scale factor in the quad function. A better solution might be to change the vertex shader to

```
attribute vec4 vPosition;
attribute vec4 vColor;
varying vec4 fColor;

void main()
{
  fColor = vColor;
  gl_Position = 0.5 * vPosition;
}
```

Note that we also changed the vertex shader to use input data in four-dimensional homogeneous coordinates. The fragment shader is now

```
varying vec4 fColor;

void main()
{
  gl_FragColor = fColor;
}
```

Rather than looking at these ad hoc approaches, we will develop a transformation capability that will enable us to rotate, scale, and translate data either in the application or in the shaders. We will also examine in greater detail how we convey data among the application and shaders that enable us to carry out transformations in the GPU and alter transformations dynamically.

4.6.7 Drawing with Elements

WebGL provides an even simpler way to represent and draw meshes. Suppose that we have the vertices and colors in arrays as before, but now, instead of executing code that copies the vertices and colors into new arrays in the correct order for drawing, we create an array of indices in the correct order. Consider the array

```
var indices = [
  1, 0, 3,
  3, 2, 1,
  2, 3, 7,
  7, 6, 2,
  3, 0, 4,
  4, 7, 3,
  6, 5, 1,
  1, 2, 6,
  4, 5, 6,
  6, 7, 4,
  5, 4, 0,
  0, 1, 5
];
```

The elements of this array are the indices of the 12 triangles that form the cube. Thus, (1, 0, 3) and (3, 2, 1) are the two triangles that form one face, and `indices` contains all the information on the topology of the cube. WebGL contains the drawing function `gl.drawElements` that couples an array of indices to arrays of vertices and other attributes. Consequently, by using `drawElements` for the cube, we no longer need the quad function nor the `points` and `colors` arrays. Instead, we send `vertices` and `vertexColors` to the GPU

```
gl.bufferData(gl.ARRAY_BUFFER, flatten(vertices), gl.STATIC_DRAW);
gl.bufferData(gl.ARRAY_BUFFER, flatten(vertexColors), gl.STATIC_DRAW);
```

and the indices

```
var iBuffer = gl.createBuffer();
gl.bindBuffer(gl.ELEMENT_ARRAY_BUFFER, iBuffer);
gl.bufferData(gl.ELEMENT_ARRAY_BUFFER, new Uint8Array(indices),
              gl.STATIC_DRAW);
```

Note that we use the parameter `gl.ELEMENT_ARRAY_BUFFER` to identify the array we are sending as an array of indices rather than of data. Also, because WebGL expects the indices to be sent as integers rather than as floating-point numbers, we convert to a typed array. Finally, in the render function, we draw the cube by

```
gl.drawElements(gl.TRIANGLES, numVertices, gl.UNSIGNED_BYTE, 0);
```

The parameters are much like in `gl.drawElements`. The last parameter is the starting index.

We will use both forms. For complex meshes in which different vertices may terminate different numbers of edges, using element arrays is usually preferable.

4.7   AFFINE TRANSFORMATIONS

A **transformation** is a function that takes a point (or vector) and maps it into another point (or vector). We can picture such a function by looking at Figure 4.32 or by writing down the functional form

$$Q = T(P)$$

for points, or

$$v = R(u)$$

for vectors. If we use homogeneous coordinate representations, then we can represent both vectors and points as four-dimensional column matrices, and we can define the transformation with a single function,

$$\mathbf{q} = f(\mathbf{p}),$$

$$\mathbf{v} = f(\mathbf{u}),$$

FIGURE 4.32   Transformation.

that transforms the representations of both points and vectors in a given frame.

This formulation is too general to be useful, as it encompasses all single-valued mappings of points and vectors. In practice, even if we were to have a convenient description of the function f, we would have to carry out the transformation on every point on a curve. For example, if we transform a line segment, a general transformation might require us to carry out the transformation for every point between the two endpoints.

Consider instead a restricted class of transformations. Let's assume that we are working in four-dimensional, homogeneous coordinates. In this space, both points and vectors are represented as 4-tuples.[8] We can obtain a useful class of transformations if we place restrictions on f. The most important restriction is linearity. A function f is a **linear function** if and only if, for any scalars α and β and any two vertices (or vectors) p and q,

$$f(\alpha p + \beta q) = \alpha f(p) + \beta f(q).$$

The importance of such functions is that if we know the transformations of p and q, we can obtain the transformations of linear combinations of p and q by taking linear combinations of their transformations. Hence, we avoid having to calculate transformations for every linear combination.

Using homogeneous coordinates, we work with the representations of points and vectors. A linear transformation then transforms the representation of a given point (or vector) into another representation of that point (or vector) and can always be written in terms of the two representations, $\mathbf{u}$ and $\mathbf{v}$, as a matrix multiplication,

$$\mathbf{v} = \mathbf{Cu},$$

where $\mathbf{C}$ is a square matrix. Comparing this expression with the expression we obtained in Section 4.3 for changes in frames, we observe that as long as $\mathbf{C}$ is nonsingular, each linear transformation corresponds to a change in frame. Hence, we can view a linear transformation in two equivalent ways: (1) as a change in the underlying representation, or frame, that yields a new representation of our vertices, or (2) as a transformation of the vertices within the same frame.

When we work with homogeneous coordinates, $\mathbf{C}$ is a 4×4 matrix that leaves unchanged the fourth (w) component of a representation. The matrix $\mathbf{C}$ is of the form

$$\mathbf{C} = \begin{bmatrix} \alpha_{11} & \alpha_{12} & \alpha_{13} & \alpha_{14} \\ \alpha_{21} & \alpha_{22} & \alpha_{23} & \alpha_{24} \\ \alpha_{31} & \alpha_{32} & \alpha_{33} & \alpha_{34} \\ 0 & 0 & 0 & 1 \end{bmatrix}$$

---

8. We consider only those functions that map vertices to other vertices and that obey the rules for manipulating points and vectors that we have developed in this chapter and in Appendix B.

and is the transpose of the matrix $\mathbf{M}$ that we derived in Section 4.3.4. The 12 values can be set arbitrarily, and we say that this transformation has 12 **degrees of freedom**. However, points and vectors have slightly different representations in our affine space. Any vector is represented as

$$\mathbf{u} = \begin{bmatrix} \alpha_1 \\ \alpha_2 \\ \alpha_3 \\ 0 \end{bmatrix}.$$

Any point can be written as

$$\mathbf{p} = \begin{bmatrix} \beta_1 \\ \beta_2 \\ \beta_3 \\ 1 \end{bmatrix}.$$

If we apply an arbitrary $\mathbf{C}$ to a vector,

$$\mathbf{v} = \mathbf{Cu},$$

we see that only 9 of the elements of $\mathbf{C}$ affect $\mathbf{u}$, and thus there are only 9 degrees of freedom in the transformation of vectors. Affine transformations of points have the full 12 degrees of freedom.

We can also show that affine transformations preserve lines. Suppose that we write a line in the form

$$P(\alpha) = P_0 + \alpha d,$$

where P_0 is a point and d is a vector. In any frame, the line can be expressed as

$$\mathbf{p}(\alpha) = \mathbf{p}_0 + \alpha \mathbf{d},$$

where $\mathbf{p}_0$ and $\mathbf{d}$ are the representations of P_0 and d in that frame. For any affine transformation matrix $\mathbf{C}$,

$$\mathbf{Cp}(\alpha) = \mathbf{Cp}_0 + \alpha \mathbf{Cd}.$$

Thus, we can construct the transformed line by first transforming $\mathbf{p}_0$ and $\mathbf{d}$ and using whatever line generation algorithm we choose when the line segment must be displayed. If we use the two-point form of the line,

$$\mathbf{p}(\alpha) = \alpha \mathbf{p}_0 + (1 - \alpha) \mathbf{p}_1,$$

a similar result holds. We transform the representations of $\mathbf{p}_0$ and $\mathbf{p}_1$ and then construct the transformed line. Because there are only 12 elements in $\mathbf{C}$ that we can select arbitrarily, there are 12 degrees of freedom in the affine transformation of a line or line segment.

We have expressed these results in terms of abstract mathematical spaces. However, their importance in computer graphics is practical. We need only transform the homogeneous-coordinate representation of the endpoints of a line segment to determine completely a transformed line. Thus, we can implement our graphics systems as a pipeline that passes endpoints through affine transformation units and generates the interior points at the rasterization stage.

Fortunately, most of the transformations that we need in computer graphics are affine. These transformations include rotation, translation, and scaling. With slight modifications, we can also use these results to describe the standard parallel and perspective projections discussed in Chapter 4.

4.8 TRANSLATION, ROTATION, AND SCALING

We have been going back and forth between looking at geometric objects as abstract entities and working with their representation in a given frame. When we work with application programs, we have to work with representations. In this section, first we show how we can describe the most important affine transformations independently of any representation. Then we find matrices that describe these transformations by acting on the representations of our points and vectors. In Section 4.11, we will see how these transformations can be implemented in WebGL.

We look at transformations as ways of moving the points that describe one or more geometric objects to new locations. Although there are many transformations that will move a particular point to a new location, there will almost always be only a single way to transform a collection of points to new locations while preserving the spatial relationships among them. Hence, although we can find many matrices that will move one corner of our color cube from P_0 to Q_0, only one of them, when applied to all the vertices of the cube, will result in a displaced cube of the same size and orientation.

4.8.1 Translation

Translation is an operation that displaces points by a fixed distance in a given direction, as shown in Figure 4.33. To specify a translation, we need only specify a displacement vector d, because the transformed points are given by

$$P' = P + d$$

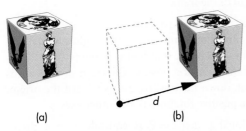

(a) (b)

FIGURE 4.33 Translation. (a) Object in original position. (b) Object translated.

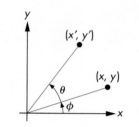

FIGURE 4.34   Two-dimensional rotation.

for all points P on the object. Note that this definition of translation makes no reference to a frame or representation. Translation has three degrees of freedom because we can specify the three components of the displacement vector arbitrarily.

4.8.2 Rotation

Rotation is more complicated to specify than translation because we must specify more parameters. We start with the simple example of rotating a point about the origin in a two-dimensional plane, as shown in Figure 4.34. Having specified a particular point—the origin—we are in a particular frame. A two-dimensional point at (x, y) in this frame is rotated about the origin by an angle θ to the position (x', y'). We can obtain the standard equations describing this rotation by representing (x, y) and (x', y') in polar form:

$$x = \rho \cos \phi$$

$$y = \rho \sin \phi$$

$$x' = \rho \cos(\theta + \phi)$$

$$y' = \rho \sin(\theta + \phi).$$

Expanding these terms using the trigonometric identities for the sine and cosine of the sum of two angles, we find

$$x' = \rho \cos \phi \cos \theta - \rho \sin \phi \sin \theta = x \cos \theta - y \sin \theta,$$

$$y' = \rho \cos \phi \sin \theta + \rho \sin \phi \cos \theta = x \sin \theta + y \cos \theta.$$

These equations can be written in matrix form as

$$\begin{bmatrix} x' \\ y' \end{bmatrix} = \begin{bmatrix} \cos \theta & -\sin \theta \\ \sin \theta & \cos \theta \end{bmatrix} \begin{bmatrix} x \\ y \end{bmatrix}.$$

We expand this form to three dimensions in Section 4.9.

Note three features of this transformation that extend to other rotations:

1. There is one point—the origin, in this case—that is unchanged by the rotation. We call this point the **fixed point** of the transformation. Figure 4.35 shows a two-dimensional rotation about a fixed point in the center of the object rather than about the origin of the frame.

2. Knowing that the two-dimensional plane is part of three-dimensional space, we can reinterpret this rotation in three dimensions. In a right-handed system, when we draw the x- and y-axes in the standard way, the positive z-axis comes out of the page. Our definition of a positive direction of rotation is counterclockwise when we look down the positive z-axis toward the origin. We use this definition to define positive rotations about other axes.

3. Rotation in the two-dimensional plane $z = 0$ is equivalent to a three-dimensional rotation about the z-axis. Points in planes of constant z all rotate in a similar manner, leaving their z values unchanged.

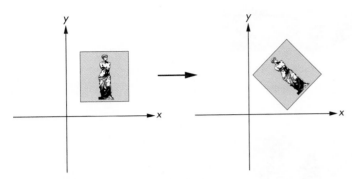

FIGURE 4.35   Rotation about a fixed point.

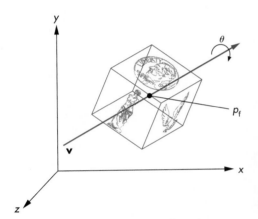

FIGURE 4.36   Three-dimensional rotation.

We can use these observations to define a general three-dimensional rotation that is independent of the frame. We must specify the three entities shown in Figure 4.36: a fixed point (P_f), a rotation angle (θ), and a line or vector about which to rotate. For a given fixed point, there are three degrees of freedom: the two angles necessary to specify the orientation of the vector and the angle that specifies the amount of rotation about the vector.

Rotation and translation are known as **rigid-body transformations**. No combination of rotations and translations can alter the shape or volume of an object; they can alter only the object's location and orientation. Consequently, rotation and translation alone cannot give us all possible affine transformations. The transformations shown in Figure 4.37 are affine, but they are not rigid-body transformations.

4.8.3 Scaling

Scaling is an affine non-rigid-body transformation by which we can make an object bigger or smaller. Figure 4.38 illustrates both uniform scaling in all directions and scaling in a single direction. We need nonuniform scaling to build up the full set of

FIGURE 4.37   Non-rigid-body transformations.

FIGURE 4.38   Uniform and nonuniform scaling.

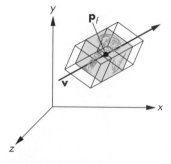

FIGURE 4.39   Effect of scale factor.

affine transformations that we use in modeling and viewing by combining a properly chosen sequence of scalings, translations, and rotations.

Scaling transformations have a fixed point, as we can see from Figure 4.39. Hence, to specify a scaling, we can specify the fixed point, a direction in which we wish to scale, and a scale factor (α). For $\alpha > 1$, the object gets longer in the specified direction; for $0 \leq \alpha < 1$, the object gets shorter in that direction. Negative values of α give us **reflection** (Figure 4.40) about the fixed point, in the scaling direction. Scaling has six degrees of freedom. Three independent values are needed to specify an arbitrary fixed point, and three more are needed to specify the magnitude and direction of scaling.

FIGURE 4.40   Reflection.

4.9   TRANSFORMATIONS IN HOMOGENEOUS COORDINATES

All graphics APIs force us to work within some reference system. Hence, we cannot work with high-level expressions such as

$$Q = P + \alpha v.$$

Instead, we work with representations in homogeneous coordinates and with expressions such as

$$\mathbf{q} = \mathbf{p} + \alpha \mathbf{v}.$$

Within a frame, each affine transformation is represented by a 4×4 matrix of the form

$$\mathbf{A} = \begin{bmatrix} \alpha_{11} & \alpha_{12} & \alpha_{13} & \alpha_{14} \\ \alpha_{21} & \alpha_{22} & \alpha_{23} & \alpha_{24} \\ \alpha_{31} & \alpha_{32} & \alpha_{33} & \alpha_{34} \\ 0 & 0 & 0 & 1 \end{bmatrix}.$$

4.9.1 Translation

Translation displaces points to new positions defined by a displacement vector. If we move the point $\mathbf{p}$ to $\mathbf{p}'$ by displacing by a distance $\mathbf{d}$, then

$$\mathbf{p}' = \mathbf{p} + \mathbf{d}.$$

Looking at their homogeneous-coordinate forms,

$$\mathbf{p} = \begin{bmatrix} x \\ y \\ z \\ 1 \end{bmatrix}, \qquad \mathbf{p'} = \begin{bmatrix} x' \\ y' \\ z' \\ 1 \end{bmatrix}, \qquad \mathbf{d} = \begin{bmatrix} \alpha_x \\ \alpha_y \\ \alpha_z \\ 0 \end{bmatrix},$$

we see that these equations can be written component by component as

$$x' = x + \alpha_x,$$

$$y' = y + \alpha_y,$$

$$z' = z + \alpha_z.$$

This method of representing translation using the addition of column matrices does not combine well with our representations of other affine transformations. However, we can also get this result using the matrix multiplication

$$\mathbf{p'} = \mathbf{T}\mathbf{p},$$

where

$$\mathbf{T} = \begin{bmatrix} 1 & 0 & 0 & \alpha_x \\ 0 & 1 & 0 & \alpha_y \\ 0 & 0 & 1 & \alpha_z \\ 0 & 0 & 0 & 1 \end{bmatrix}.$$

$\mathbf{T}$ is called the **translation matrix**. We sometimes write it as $\mathbf{T}(\alpha_x, \alpha_y, \alpha_z)$ to emphasize the three independent parameters.

It might appear that using a fourth fixed element in the homogeneous representation of a point is not necessary. However, if we use the three-dimensional forms

$$\mathbf{q} = \begin{bmatrix} x \\ y \\ z \end{bmatrix}, \qquad \mathbf{q'} = \begin{bmatrix} x' \\ y' \\ z' \end{bmatrix},$$

it is not possible to find a 3×3 matrix $\mathbf{D}$ such that $\mathbf{q'} = \mathbf{D}\mathbf{q}$ for the given displacement vector $\mathbf{d}$. For this reason, the use of homogeneous coordinates is often seen as a clever trick that allows us to convert the addition of column matrices in three dimensions to matrix–matrix multiplication in four dimensions.

We can obtain the inverse of a translation matrix either by applying an inversion algorithm or by noting that if we displace a point by the vector d, we can return to the original position by a displacement of $-d$. By either method, we find that

$$\mathbf{T}^{-1}(\alpha_x, \alpha_y, \alpha_z) = \mathbf{T}(-\alpha_x, -\alpha_y, -\alpha_z) = \begin{bmatrix} 1 & 0 & 0 & -\alpha_x \\ 0 & 1 & 0 & -\alpha_y \\ 0 & 0 & 1 & -\alpha_z \\ 0 & 0 & 0 & 1 \end{bmatrix}.$$

4.9.2 Scaling

For both scaling and rotation, there is a fixed point that is unchanged by the transformation. We can start with the fixed point at the origin; later we show how we can concatenate transformations to obtain scaling and rotation transformations for an arbitrary fixed point.

A scaling matrix with a fixed point at the origin allows for independent scaling along the coordinate axes. The three equations are

$$x' = \beta_x x,$$

$$y' = \beta_y y,$$

$$z' = \beta_z z.$$

These three equations can be combined in homogeneous form as

$$\mathbf{p}' = \mathbf{S}\mathbf{p},$$

where

$$\mathbf{S} = \mathbf{S}(\beta_x, \beta_y, \beta_z) = \begin{bmatrix} \beta_x & 0 & 0 & 0 \\ 0 & \beta_y & 0 & 0 \\ 0 & 0 & \beta_z & 0 \\ 0 & 0 & 0 & 1 \end{bmatrix}.$$

As is true of the translation matrix and, indeed, of all homogeneous-coordinate transformations, the final row of the matrix does not depend on the particular transformation, but rather forces the fourth component of the transformed point to retain the value 1.

We obtain the inverse of a scaling matrix by applying the reciprocals of the scale factors:

$$\mathbf{S}^{-1}(\beta_x, \beta_y, \beta_z) = \mathbf{S}\left(\frac{1}{\beta_x}, \frac{1}{\beta_y}, \frac{1}{\beta_z}\right).$$

4.9.3 Rotation

We first look at rotation with a fixed point at the origin. There are three degrees of freedom corresponding to our ability to rotate independently about the three coordinate axes. We have to be careful, however, because matrix multiplication is not a commutative operation (Appendix C). Rotation about the x-axis by an angle θ followed by rotation about the y-axis by an angle ϕ does not give us the same result as the one that we obtain if we reverse the order of the rotations.

We can find the matrices for rotation about the individual axes directly from the results of the two-dimensional rotation that we developed in Section 4.8.2. We saw that the two-dimensional rotation was actually a rotation in three dimensions about the z-axis and that the points remained in planes of constant z. Thus, in three dimensions, the equations for rotation about the z-axis by an angle θ are

$$x' = x \cos \theta - y \sin \theta,$$

$$y' = x \sin \theta + y \cos \theta,$$

$$z' = z,$$

or, in matrix form,

$$\mathbf{p}' = \mathbf{R}_z \mathbf{p},$$

where

$$\mathbf{R}_z = \mathbf{R}_z(\theta) = \begin{bmatrix} \cos \theta & -\sin \theta & 0 & 0 \\ \sin \theta & \cos \theta & 0 & 0 \\ 0 & 0 & 1 & 0 \\ 0 & 0 & 0 & 1 \end{bmatrix}.$$

We can derive the matrices for rotation about the x- and y-axes through an identical argument. If we rotate about the x-axis, then the x values are unchanged, and we have a two-dimensional rotation in which points rotate in planes of constant x; for rotation about the y-axis, the y values are unchanged. The matrices are

$$\mathbf{R}_x = \mathbf{R}_x(\theta) = \begin{bmatrix} 1 & 0 & 0 & 0 \\ 0 & \cos \theta & -\sin \theta & 0 \\ 0 & \sin \theta & \cos \theta & 0 \\ 0 & 0 & 0 & 1 \end{bmatrix},$$

$$\mathbf{R}_y = \mathbf{R}_y(\theta) = \begin{bmatrix} \cos \theta & 0 & \sin \theta & 0 \\ 0 & 1 & 0 & 0 \\ -\sin \theta & 0 & \cos \theta & 0 \\ 0 & 0 & 0 & 1 \end{bmatrix}.$$

The signs of the sine terms are consistent with our definition of a positive rotation in a right-handed system.

Suppose we let $\mathbf{R}$ denote any of our three rotation matrices. A rotation by θ can always be undone by a subsequent rotation by $-\theta$; hence,

$$\mathbf{R}^{-1}(\theta) = \mathbf{R}(-\theta).$$

In addition, noting that all the cosine terms are on the diagonal and the sine terms are off-diagonal, we can use the trigonometric identities

$$\cos(-\theta) = \cos \theta$$

$$\sin(-\theta) = -\sin \theta$$

to find

$$\mathbf{R}^{-1}(\theta) = \mathbf{R}^T(\theta).$$

In Section 4.10.1, we show how to construct any desired rotation matrix, with a fixed point at the origin, as a product of individual rotations about the three axes:

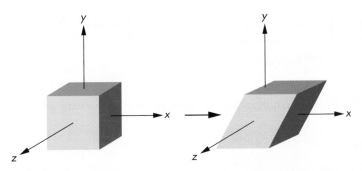

FIGURE 4.41 Shear.

$$\mathbf{R} = \mathbf{R}_z \mathbf{R}_y \mathbf{R}_x.$$

Using the fact that the transpose of a product is the product of the transposes in the reverse order, we see that for any rotation matrix,

$$\mathbf{R}^{-1} = \mathbf{R}^T.$$

A matrix whose inverse is equal to its transpose is called an **orthogonal matrix**. Normalized orthogonal matrices correspond to rotations about the origin.

4.9.4 Shear

Although we can construct any affine transformation from a sequence of rotations, translations, and scalings, there is one more affine transformation—the **shear** transformation—that is of such importance that we regard it as a basic type rather than deriving it from the others. Consider a cube centered at the origin, aligned with the axes, and viewed from the positive z-axis, as shown in Figure 4.41. If we pull the top to the right and the bottom to the left, we shear the object in the x direction. Note that neither the y nor the z values are changed by the shear, so we can call this operation "x shear" to distinguish it from shears of the cube in other possible directions. Using simple trigonometry in Figure 4.42, we see that each shear is characterized by a single angle θ; the equations for this shear are

FIGURE 4.42 Computation of the shear matrix.

$$x' = x + y \cot \theta,$$

$$y' = y,$$

$$z' = z,$$

leading to the shearing matrix

$$\mathbf{H}_x(\theta) = \begin{bmatrix} 1 & \cot \theta & 0 & 0 \\ 0 & 1 & 0 & 0 \\ 0 & 0 & 1 & 0 \\ 0 & 0 & 0 & 1 \end{bmatrix}.$$

FIGURE 4.43   Application of transformations one at a time.

We can obtain the inverse by noting that we need to shear only in the opposite direction; hence,

$$\mathbf{H}_x^{-1}(\theta) = \mathbf{H}_x(-\theta).$$

A shear in the x direction followed by a shear in the z direction leaves the y values unchanged and can be regarded as a shear in the x–z plane.

4.10   CONCATENATION OF TRANSFORMATIONS

In this section, we create examples of affine transformations by multiplying together, or **concatenating**, sequences of the basic transformations that we just introduced. Using this strategy is preferable to attempting to define an arbitrary transformation directly. The approach fits well with our pipeline architectures for implementing graphics systems.

Suppose that we carry out three successive transformations on the homogeneous representations of a point $\mathbf{p}$, creating a new point $\mathbf{q}$. Because the matrix product is associative, we can write the sequence as

$$\mathbf{q} = \mathbf{CBAp},$$

without parentheses. Note that here the matrices $\mathbf{A}$, $\mathbf{B}$, and $\mathbf{C}$ can be arbitrary 4×4 matrices, although in practice they will most likely be affine. The order in which we carry out the transformations affects the efficiency of the calculation. In one view, shown in Figure 4.43, we can carry out $\mathbf{A}$, followed by $\mathbf{B}$, followed by $\mathbf{C}$—an order that corresponds to the grouping

$$\mathbf{q} = (\mathbf{C}(\mathbf{B}(\mathbf{Ap}))).$$

If we are to transform a single point, this order is the most efficient because each matrix multiplication involves multiplying a column matrix by a square matrix. If we have many points to transform, then we can proceed in two steps. First, we calculate

$$\mathbf{M} = \mathbf{CBA}.$$

Then, we use this matrix on each point

$$\mathbf{q} = \mathbf{Mp}.$$

FIGURE 4.44   Pipeline transformation.

This order corresponds to the pipeline shown in Figure 4.44, where we compute $\mathbf{M}$ first, then load it into a pipeline transformation unit through a shader. If we simply count operations, we see that although we do a little more work in computing $\mathbf{M}$ initially, this extra work is insignificant compared with the savings we obtain by using a single matrix multiplication for each point, because **M** may be applied to tens of thousands of points. We now derive examples of computing **M**.

4.10.1 Rotation About a Fixed Point

Our first example shows how we can alter the transformations that we defined with a fixed point at the origin (rotation, scaling, shear) to have an arbitrary fixed point. We demonstrate for rotation about the z-axis; the technique is the same for the other cases.

Consider a cube with its center at $\mathbf{p}_f$ and its sides aligned with the axes. We want to rotate the cube without changing x and y values, but this time about its center $\mathbf{p}_f$, which becomes the fixed point of the transformation, as shown in Figure 4.45. If $\mathbf{p}_f$ were the origin, we would know how to solve the problem: We would simply use $\mathbf{R}_z(\theta)$. This observation suggests the strategy of first moving the cube to the origin. We can then apply $\mathbf{R}_z(\theta)$ and finally move the object back such that its center is again at $\mathbf{p}_f$. This sequence is shown in Figure 4.46. In terms of our basic affine transformations, the first is $\mathbf{T}(-\mathbf{p}_f)$, the second is $\mathbf{R}_z(\theta)$, and the final is $\mathbf{T}(\mathbf{p}_f)$.

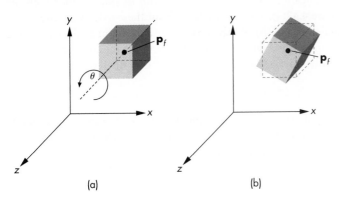

(a) (b)

FIGURE 4.45 Rotation of a cube about its center.

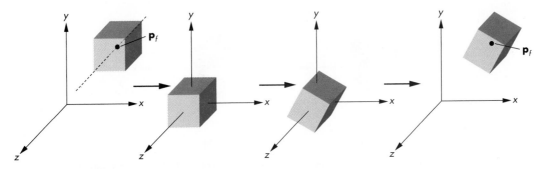

FIGURE 4.46 Sequence of transformations.

Concatenating them together, we obtain the single matrix

$$\mathbf{M} = \mathbf{T}(\mathbf{p}_f)\mathbf{R}_z(\theta)\mathbf{T}(-\mathbf{p}_f).$$

If we multiply out the matrices, we find that

$$\mathbf{M} = \begin{bmatrix} \cos\theta & -\sin\theta & 0 & x_f - x_f\cos\theta + y_f\sin\theta \\ \sin\theta & \cos\theta & 0 & y_f - x_f\sin\theta - y_f\cos\theta \\ 0 & 0 & 1 & 0 \\ 0 & 0 & 0 & 1 \end{bmatrix}.$$

4.10.2 General Rotation

Rotation about the origin has three degrees of freedom. Consequently, we can specify an arbitrary rotation about the origin in terms of three successive rotations about the three axes. The order is not unique (see Exercise 4.10), although the resulting rotation matrix is. One way to form the desired rotation matrix is by first doing a rotation about the z-axis, then doing a rotation about the y-axis, and concluding with a rotation about the x-axis.

Consider the cube, again centered at the origin with its sides aligned with the axes, as shown in Figure 4.47(a). We can rotate it about the z-axis by an angle α to orient it, as shown in Figure 4.47(b). We then rotate the cube by an angle β about the y-axis, as shown in a top view in Figure 4.48. Finally, we rotate the cube by an angle γ about the x-axis, as shown in a side view in Figure 4.49. Our final rotation matrix is

$$\mathbf{R} = \mathbf{R}_x\mathbf{R}_y\mathbf{R}_z.$$

A little experimentation should convince you that we can achieve any desired orientation by proper choice of α, β, and γ, although, as we will see in the example of Section 4.10.4, finding these angles can be tricky.

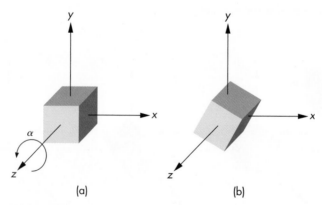

FIGURE 4.47   Rotation of a cube about the z-axis. (a) Cube before rotation. (b) Cube after rotation.

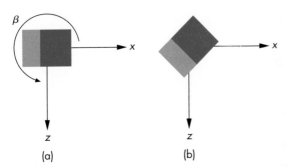

FIGURE 4.48   Rotation of a cube about the *y*-axis.

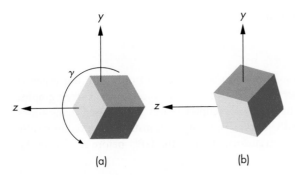

FIGURE 4.49   Rotation of a cube about the *x*-axis.

4.10.3 The Instance Transformation

Our example of a cube that can be rotated to any desired orientation suggests a generalization appropriate for modeling. Consider a scene composed of many simple objects, such as those shown in Figure 4.50. One option is to specify each of these objects, through its vertices, in the desired location with the desired orientation and size. An alternative and preferred method is to specify each of the object types once at a convenient size, in a convenient place, and with a convenient orientation. Each occurrence of an object in the scene is an **instance** of that object's prototype, and we can obtain the desired size, orientation, and location by applying an affine transformation—the **instance transformation**—to the prototype. We can build a simple database to describe a scene from a list of object identifiers (such as 1 for a cube and 2 for a sphere) and instance transformations to be applied to each object.

The instance transformation is applied in the order shown in Figure 4.51. Objects are usually defined in their own frames, with the origin at the center of mass and the sides aligned with the model frame axes. First, we scale the object to the desired size. Then we orient it with a rotation matrix. Finally, we translate it to the desired orientation. Hence, the instance transformation is of the form

$$\mathbf{M} = \mathbf{TRS}.$$

FIGURE 4.50   Scene of simple objects.

FIGURE 4.51 Instance transformation.

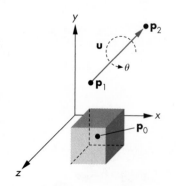

FIGURE 4.52 Rotation of a cube about an arbitrary axis.

Modeling with the instance transformation works well not only with our pipeline architectures but also with other methods for retaining objects such as scene graphs, which we will introduce in Chapter 9. A complex object that is used many times need only be loaded onto the GPU once. Displaying each instance of it requires only sending the appropriate instance transformation to the GPU before rendering the object.

4.10.4 Rotation About an Arbitrary Axis

Our final rotation example illustrates not only how we can achieve a rotation about an arbitrary point and line in space but also how we can use direction angles to specify orientations. Consider rotating a cube, as shown in Figure 4.52. We need three entities to specify this rotation. There is a fixed point $\mathbf{p}_0$ that we assume is the center of the cube, a vector about which we rotate, and an angle of rotation. Note that none of these entities relies on a frame and that we have just specified a rotation in a coordinate-free manner. Nonetheless, to find an affine matrix to represent this transformation, we have to assume that we are in some frame.

The vector about which we wish to rotate the cube can be specified in various ways. One way is to use two points, $\mathbf{p}_1$ and $\mathbf{p}_2$, defining the vector

$$\mathbf{u} = \mathbf{p}_2 - \mathbf{p}_1.$$

Note that the order of the points determines the positive direction of rotation for θ and that even though we can draw $\mathbf{u}$ as passing through $\mathbf{p}_0$, only the orientation of $\mathbf{u}$ matters. Replacing $\mathbf{u}$ with a unit-length vector

$$\mathbf{v} = \frac{\mathbf{u}}{|\mathbf{u}|} = \begin{bmatrix} \alpha_x \\ \alpha_y \\ \alpha_z \end{bmatrix}$$

in the same direction simplifies the subsequent steps. We say that **v** is the result of **normalizing u**. We have already seen that moving the fixed point to the origin is a helpful technique. Thus, our first transformation is the translation $\mathbf{T}(-\mathbf{p}_0)$, and the final one is $\mathbf{T}(\mathbf{p}_0)$. After the initial translation, the required rotation problem is as shown in Figure 4.53. Our previous example (see Section 4.10.2) showed that we could get an arbitrary rotation from three rotations about the individual axes. This problem is more difficult because we do not know what angles to use for the individual rotations. Our strategy is to carry out two rotations to align the axis of rotation, **v**, with the z-axis. Then we can rotate by θ about the z-axis, after which we can undo the two rotations that did the aligning. Our final rotation matrix will be of the form

$$\mathbf{R} = \mathbf{R}_x(-\theta_x)\mathbf{R}_y(-\theta_y)\mathbf{R}_z(\theta)\mathbf{R}_y(\theta_y)\mathbf{R}_x(\theta_x).$$

This sequence of rotations is shown in Figure 4.54. The difficult part of the process is determining θ_x and θ_y.

We proceed by looking at the components of **v**. Because **v** is a unit-length vector,

$$\alpha_x^2 + \alpha_y^2 + \alpha_z^2 = 1.$$

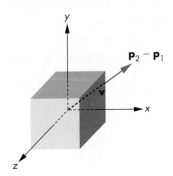

FIGURE 4.53 Movement of the fixed point to the origin.

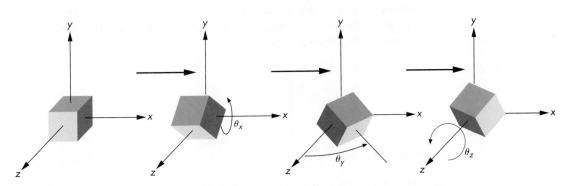

FIGURE 4.54 Sequence of rotations.

FIGURE 4.55   Direction angles.

FIGURE 4.56   Computation of the x rotation.

FIGURE 4.57   Computation of the y rotation.

We draw a line segment from the origin to the point $(\alpha_x, \alpha_y, \alpha_z)$. This line segment has unit length and the orientation of **v**. Next, we draw the perpendiculars from the point $(\alpha_x, \alpha_y, \alpha_z)$ to the coordinate axes, as shown in Figure 4.55. The three **direction angles**—ϕ_x, ϕ_y, ϕ_z—are the angles between the line segment (or **v**) and the axes. The **direction cosines** are given by

$$\cos \phi_x = \alpha_x,$$

$$\cos \phi_y = \alpha_y,$$

$$\cos \phi_z = \alpha_z.$$

Only two of the direction angles are independent, because

$$\cos^2 \phi_x + \cos^2 \phi_y + \cos^2 \phi_z = 1.$$

We can now compute θ_x and θ_y using these angles. Consider Figure 4.56. It shows that the effect of the desired rotation on the point $(\alpha_x, \alpha_y, \alpha_z)$ is to rotate the line segment into the plane $y = 0$. If we look at the projection of the line segment (before the rotation) on the plane $x = 0$, we see a line segment of length d on this plane. Another way to envision this figure is to think of the plane $x = 0$ as a wall and consider a distant light source located far down the positive x-axis. The line that we see on the wall is the shadow of the line segment from the origin to $(\alpha_x, \alpha_y, \alpha_z)$. Note that the length of the shadow is less than the length of the line segment. We can say the line segment has been **foreshortened** to $d = \sqrt{\alpha_y^2 + \alpha_z^2}$. The desired angle of rotation is determined by the angle that this shadow makes with the z-axis. However, the rotation matrix is determined by the sine and cosine of θ_x. Thus, we never need to compute θ_x; rather, we need only compute

$$\mathbf{R}_x(\theta_x) = \begin{bmatrix} 1 & 0 & 0 & 0 \\ 0 & \alpha_z/d & -\alpha_y/d & 0 \\ 0 & \alpha_y/d & \alpha_z/d & 0 \\ 0 & 0 & 0 & 1 \end{bmatrix}.$$

We compute $\mathbf{R}_y$ in a similar manner. Figure 4.57 shows the rotation. This angle is clockwise about the y-axis; therefore, we have to be careful about the sign of the sine terms in the matrix, which is

$$\mathbf{R}_y(\theta_y) = \begin{bmatrix} d & 0 & -\alpha_x & 0 \\ 0 & 1 & 0 & 0 \\ \alpha_x & 0 & d & 0 \\ 0 & 0 & 0 & 1 \end{bmatrix}.$$

Finally, we concatenate all the matrices to find

$$\mathbf{M} = \mathbf{T}(\mathbf{p}_0)\mathbf{R}_x(-\theta_x)\mathbf{R}_y(-\theta_y)\mathbf{R}_z(\theta)\mathbf{R}_y(\theta_y)\mathbf{R}_x(\theta_x)\mathbf{T}(-\mathbf{p}_0).$$

Let's look at a specific example. Suppose that we wish to rotate an object by 45 degrees about the line passing through the origin and the point $(1, 2, 3)$. We leave the fixed point at the origin. The first step is to find the point along the line that is a unit distance from the origin. We obtain it by normalizing $(1, 2, 3)$ to $(1/\sqrt{14}, 2/\sqrt{14}, 3/\sqrt{14})$, or $(1/\sqrt{14}, 2/\sqrt{14}, 3/\sqrt{14}, 1)$ in homogeneous coordinates. The first part of the rotation takes this point to $(0, 0, 1, 1)$. We first rotate about the x-axis by the angle $\cos^{-1}\frac{3}{\sqrt{14}}$. This matrix carries $(1/\sqrt{14}, 2/\sqrt{14}, 3/\sqrt{14}, 1)$ to $(1/\sqrt{14}, 0, \sqrt{13/14}, 1)$, which is in the plane $y = 0$. The y rotation must be by the angle $-\cos^{-1}(\sqrt{13/14})$. This rotation aligns the object with the z-axis, and now we can rotate about the z-axis by the desired 45 degrees. Finally, we undo the first two rotations. If we concatenate these five transformations into a single rotation matrix $\mathbf{R}$, we find that

$$\mathbf{R} = \mathbf{R}_x\left(-\cos^{-1}\frac{3}{\sqrt{13}}\right)\mathbf{R}_y\left(\cos^{-1}\sqrt{\frac{13}{14}}\right)\mathbf{R}_z(45)\,\mathbf{R}_y\left(-\cos^{-1}\sqrt{\frac{13}{14}}\right)$$

$$\times \mathbf{R}_x\left(\cos^{-1}\frac{3}{\sqrt{13}}\right)$$

$$= \begin{bmatrix} \frac{2+13\sqrt{2}}{28} & \frac{2-\sqrt{2}-3\sqrt{7}}{14} & \frac{6-3\sqrt{2}+4\sqrt{7}}{28} & 0 \\ \frac{2-\sqrt{2}+3\sqrt{7}}{14} & \frac{4+5\sqrt{2}}{14} & \frac{6-3\sqrt{2}-\sqrt{7}}{14} & 0 \\ \frac{6-3\sqrt{2}-4\sqrt{7}}{28} & \frac{6-3\sqrt{2}+\sqrt{7}}{14} & \frac{18+5\sqrt{2}}{28} & 0 \\ 0 & 0 & 0 & 1 \end{bmatrix}.$$

This matrix does not change any point on the line passing through the origin and the point $(1, 2, 3)$. If we want a fixed point other than the origin, we form the matrix

$$\mathbf{M} = \mathbf{T}(\mathbf{p}_f)\mathbf{R}\mathbf{T}(-\mathbf{p}_f).$$

This example is not trivial. It illustrates the powerful technique of applying many simple transformations to get a complex one. The problem of rotation about an arbitrary point or axis arises in many applications. The major variations lie in the manner in which the axis of rotation is specified. However, we can usually employ techniques similar to the ones that we have used here to determine direction angles or direction cosines.

4.11 TRANSFORMATION MATRICES IN WEBGL

We can now focus on the implementation of a homogeneous-coordinate transformation package and that package's interface to the user. We have introduced a set of frames, including the world frame and the camera frame, that should be important for developing applications. In a shader-based implementation of OpenGL, the existence or nonexistence of these frames is entirely dependent on what the application

FIGURE 4.58   Current transformation matrix (CTM).

programmer decides to do.[9] In a modern implementation of OpenGL, the application programmer can choose not only which frames to use but also where to carry out the transformations between frames. Some will best be carried out in the application, others in a shader.

As we develop a method for specifying and carrying out transformations, we should emphasize the importance of *state*. Although very few state variables are predefined in WebGL, once we specify various attributes and matrices, they effectively define the state of the system. Thus, when a vertex is processed, how it is processed is determined by the values of these state variables.

The two transformations that we will use most often are the model-view transformation and the projection transformation. The model-view transformation brings representations of geometric objects from the application or object frame to the camera frame. The projection matrix will both carry out the desired projection and change the representation to clip coordinates. We will use only the model-view matrix in this chapter. The model-view matrix normally is an affine transformation matrix and has only 12 degrees of freedom, as discussed in Section 4.7. The projection matrix, as we will see in Chapter 5, is also a 4×4 matrix but is not affine.

4.11.1 Current Transformation Matrices

The generalization common to most graphics systems is of a **current transformation matrix** (**CTM**). The CTM is part of the pipeline (Figure 4.58); thus, if **p** is a vertex specified in the application, then the pipeline produces **Cp**. Note that Figure 4.58 does not indicate where in the pipeline the current transformation matrix is applied. If we use a CTM, we can regard it as part of the state of the system.

First, we will introduce a simple set of functions that we can use to form and manipulate 4×4 affine transformation matrices. Let **C** denote the CTM (or any other 4×4 affine matrix). Initially, we will set it to the 4×4 identity matrix; it can be reinitialized as needed. If we use the symbol $\leftarrow$ to denote replacement, we can write this initialization operation as

$$\mathbf{C} \leftarrow \mathbf{I}.$$

The functions that alter **C** are of three forms: those that load it with some matrix and those that modify it by premultiplication or postmultiplication by a matrix. The three transformations supported in most systems are translation, scaling with a fixed point of the origin, and rotation with a fixed point of the origin. Symbolically, we can write

---

9. In earlier versions of OpenGL that relied on the fixed-function pipeline, the model-view and projection matrices were part of the specification and their state was part of the environment.

these operations in postmultiplication form as

$\mathbf{C} \leftarrow \mathbf{CT}$

$\mathbf{C} \leftarrow \mathbf{CS}$

$\mathbf{C} \leftarrow \mathbf{CR}$

and in load form as

$\mathbf{C} \leftarrow \mathbf{T}$

$\mathbf{C} \leftarrow \mathbf{S}$

$\mathbf{C} \leftarrow \mathbf{R}.$

Most systems allow us to load the CTM with an arbitrary matrix $\mathbf{M}$,

$\mathbf{C} \leftarrow \mathbf{M},$

or to postmultiply by an arbitrary matrix $\mathbf{M}$,

$\mathbf{C} \leftarrow \mathbf{CM}.$

Although we will occasionally use functions that set a matrix, most of the time we will alter an existing matrix; that is, the operation

$\mathbf{C} \leftarrow \mathbf{CR},$

is more common than the operation

$\mathbf{C} \leftarrow \mathbf{R}.$

4.11.2 Basic Matrix Functions

Using our matrix types, we can create and manipulate three- and four-dimensional matrices. Because we will work mostly in three dimensions using four-dimensional homogeneous coordinates, we will illustrate only that case. We can create an identity matrix by

```
var a = mat4();
```

or fill it with components by

```
var a = mat4(0, 1, 2, 3, 4, 5, 6, 7, 8, 9, 10, 11, 12, 13, 14, 15);
```

or by vectors as in

```
var a = mat4(
  vec4(0, 1, 2, 3),
  vec4(4, 5, 6, 7),
  vec4(8, 9, 10, 11),
  vec4(12, 13, 14, 15)
);
```

We can copy into an existing matrix using

```
b = mat4(a);
```

We also can find the determinant, inverse, and transpose of a matrix a:

```
var det = determinant(a);
b = inverse(a);   // 'b' becomes inverse of 'a'
b = transpose(a); // 'b' becomes transpose of 'a'
```

We can multiply two matrices together by

```
c = mult(a b); // c = a * b
```

If d and e are vec3s, we can multiply d by a matrix a:

```
e = mult(a, d);
```

We can also reference or change individual elements using standard indexing, as in

```
a[1][2] = 0;
var d = vec4(a[2]);
```

4.11.3 Rotation, Translation, and Scaling

In our applications and shaders, the matrix that is most often applied to all vertices is the product of the model-view matrix and the projection matrix. We can think of the CTM as the product of these matrices (Figure 4.59), and we can manipulate each individually by working with the desired matrix.

Using our matrix and vector types, we can form affine matrices for rotation, translation, and scaling using the following six functions:

```
var a = rotate(angle, direction);
var b = rotateX(angle);
var c = rotateY(angle);
var d = rotateZ(angle);
var e = scale(scaleVector);
var f = translate(translateVector);
```

For rotation, the angles are specified in degrees and the rotations are around a fixed point at the origin. In the translation function, the variables are the components of the displacement vector; for scaling, the variables determine the scale factors along the coordinate axes and the fixed point is the origin.

FIGURE 4.59   Model-view and projection matrices.

4.11.4 Rotation About a Fixed Point

In Section 4.10.1, we showed that we can perform a rotation about a fixed point, other than the origin, by first moving the fixed point to the origin, then rotating about the origin, and finally moving the fixed point back to its original location. Using the example from Section 4.11, the following sequence sets the matrix mode, then forms the required matrix for a 45-degree rotation about the line through the origin and the point (1, 2, 3) with a fixed point of (4, 5, 6):

```
var R = mat4();
var ctm = mat4();

var thetaX = Math.acos(3.0/Math.sqrt(14.0));
var thetaY = Math.sqrt(13.0/14.0);
var d = vec3(4.0, 5.0, 6.0);

R = mult(R, rotateX(thetaX));
R = mult(R, rotateY(thetaY));
R = mult(R, rotateZ(-45.0));
R = mult(R, rotateY(-thetaY));
R = mult(R, rotateX(-thetaX));

ctm = translate(ctm, d);
ctm = mult(ctm, R);
ctm = translate(ctm, negate(d));
```

Because we want to do arbitrary rotations so often, it is a good exercise (Exercise 4.34) to write the function `mat4.rotate(m, theta, d)` that will form an arbitrary rotation matrix for a rotation of `theta` degrees about a line in the direction of the vector $d = (dx, dy, dz)$.

4.11.5 Order of Transformations

You might be bothered by what appears to be a reversal of the required function calls. The rule in WebGL is this: *The transformation specified last is the one applied first.* A little examination shows that this order is a consequence of multiplying the CTM on the right by the specified affine transformation and thus is both correct and reasonable. The sequence of operations that we specified was

$$\mathbf{C} \leftarrow \mathbf{I}$$

$$\mathbf{C} \leftarrow \mathbf{CT}(4.0, 5.0, 6.0)$$

$$\mathbf{C} \leftarrow \mathbf{CR}(45.0, 1.0, 2.0, 3.0)$$

$$\mathbf{C} \leftarrow \mathbf{CT}(-4.0, -5.0, -6.0).$$

In each step, we postmultiply at the end of the existing CTM, forming the matrix

$$\mathbf{C} = \mathbf{T}(4.0, 5.0, 6.0)\ \mathbf{R}(45.0, 1.0, 2.0, 3.0)\ \mathbf{T}(-4.0, -5.0, -6.0),$$

which is the matrix that we expect from Section 4.10.4. Each vertex **p** that is specified *after* the model-view matrix has been set will be multiplied by **C**, thus forming the new vertex

q = **Cp**.

There are other ways to think about the order of operations. One way is in terms of a stack. Altering the CTM is similar to pushing matrices onto a stack; when we apply the final transformation, the matrices are popped off the stack in the reverse order in which they were placed there. The analogy is conceptual rather than exact because when we use a transformation function, the matrix is altered immediately.

4.12   SPINNING OF THE CUBE

We will now examine how we can manipulate the color cube interactively. We will take the cube that we defined in Section 4.6 and rotate it using either three buttons of the mouse or three buttons on the display.

There are three fundamentally different ways of doing the updates to the display. In the first, we will form a new model-view matrix in the application and apply it to the vertex data to get new vertex positions. We must then send the new data to the GPU. This approach is clearly inefficient as it involves sending vertex arrays from the CPU to the GPU. We leave this approach as an exercise (Exercise 4.35). You may want to implement this approach to test it against the other two approaches.

In the second, we compute a new model-view matrix for each rotation and send it to the vertex shader and apply it there. In the third approach, we send only the angles to the vertex shader and recompute the model-view matrix there.

In all three approaches, both the interface and the method of updating the rotation are the same. The model-view matrix is the concatenation of rotations about the x-, y-, and z-axes. One of the three angles is incremented by a fixed amount each iteration. The user selects which angle is to be incremented. We can create three buttons in the HTML file:

```
<button id="ButtonX">Rotate X</button>
<button id="ButtonY">Rotate Y</button>
<button id="ButtonZ">Rotate Z</button>
```

We set up the axes and the array of angles in the initialization

```
var theta = [0, 0, 0];
```

We will use 0, 1, and 2 to denote rotation about the x-, y-, and z-axes, respectively:

```
var xAxis = 0;
var yAxis = 1;
var zAxis = 2;
var axis = 0;
```

Event listeners for the button events are

```
var a = document.getElementById("ButtonX")
a.addEventListener("onclick", function() { axis = xAxis; }, false);
var b = document.getElementById("ButtonY")
b.addEventListener("onclick", function() { axis = yAxis; }, false);
var c = document.getElementById("ButtonZ")
c.addEventListener("onclick", function() { axis = zAxis; }, false);
```

Alternately, we can respond to the buttons by

```
document.getElementById("xButton").onclick = function() { axis = xAxis;
};
document.getElementById("yButton").onclick = function() { axis = yAxis;
};
document.getElementById("zButton").onclick = function() { axis = zAxis;
};
```

We can also use a three-button mouse to select the axis by

```
var d = document.getElementById("gl-canvas");
d.addEventListener("onclick", function() {
  switch (event.button) {
    case 0:
      axis = xAxis;
      break;
    case 1:
      axis = yAxis;
      break;
    default:
      axis = zAxis;
      break;
  }
}, false);
```

The event object is produced whenever a button is depressed.

The render function increments the angle associated with the chosen axis by 2 degrees each time:

```
theta[axis] += 2;
```

In the first two strategies, we compute a model-view matrix in the application code

```
modelViewMatrix = mat4();
modelViewMatrix = mult(modelViewMatrix, rotateX(thetaArray[xAxis]));
modelViewMatrix = mult(modelViewMatrix, rotateY(thetaArray[yAxis]));
modelViewMatrix = mult(modelViewMatrix, rotateZ(thetaArray[zAxis]));
```

In the first approach, which we left as an exercise, we use this matrix to change the positions of all the points and then resend the points to the GPU. In the second approach, we send this matrix to the vertex shader and compute and apply the model-view matrix in the vertex shader. Here is a simple vertex shader that converts the vertex positions to clip coordinates and passes the color attribute values on to the rasterizer:

```
attribute vec4 vPosition;
attribute vec4 vColor;
varying   vec4 fColor;
uniform   mat4 modelViewMatrix;

void main()
{
  fColor = vcolor;
  gl_Position =  modelViewMatrix * vPosition;
}
```

The difference between this vertex shader and those in our previous examples is that we have used a uniform variable for the model-view matrix.

4.12.1 Uniform Matrices

We set up uniform matrices in much the same way as we did for uniform scalars in Chapter 3. There are forms of `gl.uniform` corresponding to all the types supported by GLSL, including floats, ints, and two-, three-, and four-dimensional vectors and matrices. For the 4 × 4 rotation matrix `ctm`, we use the form

```
gl.uniformMatrix4fv(modelViewMatrix, false, flatten(ctm));
```

Here, `modelViewMatrix` is determined by

```
var modelViewMatrixLoc = gl.getUniformLocation(program,
                                     "modelViewMatrix");
```

for the vertex shader

```
attribute vec4 vPosition;
attribute vec4 vColor;
varying   vec4 fColor;
uniform   mat4 modelViewMatrix;

void main()
{
  fColor = vColor;
  gl_Position = modelViewMatrix * vPosition;
}
```

The second parameter in `gl.uniformMatrix4fv` declares that the data should be sent in row major order. WebGL requires that this parameter be set to `false`. Hence, the shader expects column major data. In addition, the shader expects a stream of 32-bit floating-point numbers, not our matrix or vector types that include more information. The `flatten` function converts `ctm` to the required `Float32Array` in column major order so the matrix can be used correctly in the shader. The render function is now

```
function render()
{
  gl.clear(gl.COLOR_BUFFER_BIT | gl.DEPTH_BUFFER_BIT);

  theta[axis] += 2.0;
  ctm = rotateX(theta[xAxis]);
  ctm = mult(ctm, rotateY(theta[yAxis]));
  ctm = mult(ctm, rotateZ(theta[zAxis]));

  gl.uniformMatrix4fv(modelViewMatrix, false, flatten(ctm));
  gl.drawArrays(gl.TRIANGLES, 0, numVertices);

  requestAnimFrame(render);
}
```

Our third approach is to send only the rotation angles and let the vertex shader compute the model-view matrix:

```
attribute vec4 vPosition;
attribute vec4 vColor;
varying   vec4 fColor;
uniform   vec3 theta;

void main()
{
  vec3 angles = radians(theta);
  vec3 c = cos(angles);
  vec3 s = sin(angles);

  mat4 rx = mat4(1.0,   0.0,   0.0, 0.0,
                 0.0,   c.x,   s.x, 0.0,
                 0.0,  -s.x,   c.x, 0.0,
                 0.0,   0.0,   0.0, 1.0);

  mat4 ry = mat4(c.y, 0.0, -s.y, 0.0,
                 0.0, 1.0,  0.0, 0.0,
                 s.y, 0.0,  c.y, 0.0,
                 0.0, 0.0,  0.0, 1.0);

  mat4 rz = mat4(c.z, -s.z, 0.0, 0.0,
                 s.z,  c.z, 0.0, 0.0,
                 0.0,  0.0, 1.0, 0.0,
                 0.0,  0.0, 0.0, 1.0);

  fColor = vColor;
  gl_Position = rz * ry * rx * vPosition;
}
```

The angles are sent from the application as part of the render function

```
function render()
{
  gl.clear(gl.COLOR_BUFFER_BIT | gl.DEPTH_BUFFER_BIT);

  theta[axis] += 2.0;

  gl.uniform3fv(thetaLoc, flatten(theta));
  gl.drawArrays(gl.TRIANGLES, 0, numVertices);

  requestAnimFrame(render);
}
```

Here we again use `flatten` to obtain a Float32Array.

It might not be apparent which of these strategies is best. Although the third approach requires sending only three values to the vertex shader, as opposed to 16 in the second approach, the third approach has the shader computing the sines and cosines for every vertex. Nevertheless, the third approach may be the best with modern GPUs. The trigonometric calculations are hard-coded into the GPU and require almost no time. In addition, parallelism within the GPU will have multiple vertices being processed concurrently. By carrying out the computation of the model-view matrix on the GPU, we free up the CPU to do other tasks required by the application. However, we cannot reach a general conclusion since performance depends on many factors, including the specifics of the application, the number of processors on the GPU, and how many pixels have to be generated.

4.13   INTERFACES TO THREE-DIMENSIONAL APPLICATIONS

In Section 4.12, we used a three-button mouse to control the direction of rotation of our cube. This interface is limited. Rather than use all three mouse buttons to control rotation, we might want to use mouse buttons to control functions, such as pulling down a menu, that we would have had to assign to keys in our previous example.

In Section 4.10, we noted that there were many ways to obtain a given orientation. Rather than do rotations about the x-, y-, and z-axes in that order, we could do a rotation about the x-axis, followed by a rotation about the y-axis, and finish with another rotation about the x-axis. If we do our orientation this way, we can obtain our desired orientation using only two mouse buttons, although we still need to carry out three rotations. However, there is still a problem: Each rotation is in a single direction. It would be easier to orient an object if we could rotate either forward or backward about an axis and stop the rotation once we reached a desired orientation.

Using the the keyboard in combination with the mouse, we could, for example, use the left mouse button for a forward rotation about the x-axis and the Control key in combination with the left mouse button for a backward rotation about the x-axis. Various other combinations of keys would enable us to use a single-button mouse to control the rotation.

However, neither of these options provides a good user interface, which should be more intuitive and less awkward. Let's consider a few options that provide a more interesting and smoother interaction.

4.13.1 Using Areas of the Screen

Suppose that we want to use one mouse button for orienting an object, one for getting closer to or farther from the object, and one for translating the object to the left or right. We can use the motion callback to achieve all these functions. The callback returns which button has been activated and where the mouse is located. We can use the location of the mouse to control how fast and in which direction we rotate or translate and to move in or out.

As just noted, we need the ability to rotate around only two axes to achieve any orientation. We could then use the left mouse button and the mouse position to control orientation. We can use the distance from the center of the screen to control the x and y rotations. Thus, if the left mouse button is held down but the mouse is located in the center of the screen, there will be no rotation; if the mouse is moved up, the object will be rotated about the y-axis in a clockwise manner; and if the mouse is moved down, the object will be rotated about the y-axis in a counterclockwise manner. Likewise, motion to the right or left will cause rotation about the x-axis. The distance from the center can control the speed of rotation. Motion toward the corners can cause simultaneous rotations about the x- and y-axes.

Using the right mouse button in a similar manner, we can translate the object right to left and up to down. We might use the middle mouse button to move the object toward or away from the viewer by having the mouse position control a translation in the z direction. The code for such an interface is straightforward; we leave it as an exercise (Exercise 4.22).

4.13.2 A Virtual Trackball

The use of the mouse position to control rotation about two axes provides us with most of the functionality of a trackball. We can go one step further and create a graphical or virtual trackball using our mouse and the display. One of the benefits of such a device is that we can create a frictionless trackball that, once we start it rotating, will continue to rotate until stopped by the user. Thus, the device will support continuous rotations of objects but will still allow changes in the speed and orientation of the rotation. We can also do the same for translation and other parameters that we can control from the mouse.

We start by mapping the position of a trackball to that of a mouse. Consider the trackball shown in Figure 4.60. We assume that the ball has a radius of 1 unit. We can map a position on its surface to the plane $y = 0$ by doing an orthogonal projection to the plane, as shown in Figure 4.61. The position (x, y, z) on the surface of the ball is mapped to $(x, 0, z)$ on the plane. This projection is reversible because we know that the three-dimensional point that is projected to the point on the plane must satisfy the equation of the sphere

$$x^2 + y^2 + z^2 = 1.$$

FIGURE 4.60   Trackball frame.

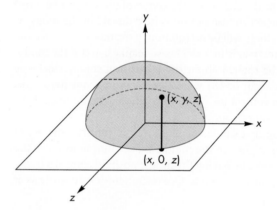

FIGURE 4.61   Projection of the trackball position to the plane.

Thus, given the point on the plane $(x, 0, z)$, the corresponding point on the hemisphere must be (x, y, z), where

$$y = \sqrt{1 - x^2 - z^2}.$$

We can compute the three-dimensional information and track it as the mouse moves. Suppose that we have two positions on the hemisphere, $\mathbf{p}_1$ and $\mathbf{p}_2$; then the vectors from the origin to these points determine the orientation of a plane, as shown in Figure 4.62, whose normal is defined by their cross product

$$\mathbf{n} = \mathbf{p}_1 \times \mathbf{p}_2.$$

The motion of the trackball that moves from $\mathbf{p}_1$ to $\mathbf{p}_2$ can be achieved by a rotation about $\mathbf{n}$. The angle of rotation is the angle between the vectors $\mathbf{p}_1$ and $\mathbf{p}_2$, which we can compute using the magnitude of the cross product. Because both $\mathbf{p}_1$ and $\mathbf{p}_2$ have unit length,

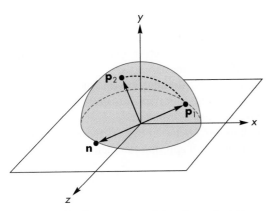

FIGURE 4.62   Computation of the plane of rotation.

$$|\sin \theta| = |\mathbf{n}|.$$

If we are tracking the mouse at a high rate, then the changes in position that we detect will be small; rather than use an inverse trigonometric function to find θ, we can use the approximation

$$\sin \theta \approx \theta.$$

We can implement the virtual trackball through the use of listeners and the render function. We can think of the process in terms of three logical variables, or flags, that control the tracking of the mouse and the display redrawing. These are set initially as follows:

```
var trackingMouse = false;
var trackballMove = false;
var redrawContinue = false;
```

If `redrawContinue` is true, the idle function posts a redisplay. If `tracking-Mouse` is true, we update the trackball position as part of the motion callback. If `trackballMove` is true, we update the rotation matrix that we use in our render routine.

The changes in these variables are controlled through the mouse callback. When we push a mouse button—either a particular button or any button, depending on exactly what we want—we start updating the trackball position by initializing it and then letting the motion callback update it and post redisplays in response to changes in the position of the mouse. When the mouse button is released, we stop tracking the mouse. We can use the two most recent mouse positions to define a velocity vector so that we can continually update the rotation matrix. Thus, once the mouse button is released, the object will continue to rotate at a constant velocity—an effect that we could achieve with an ideal frictionless trackball but not directly with either a real mouse or a real trackball.

4.13.3 Smooth Rotations

Our approach to orienting objects has been based on angles (the Euler angles) measured with respect to the three coordinate axes. This perspective led to our forming rotation matrices by concatenating simple rotations about the x-, y-, and z-axes to obtain a desired rotation about an arbitrary axis. Although in principle we can rotate about an arbitrary axis, we usually employ our concatenation strategy rather than computing this axis and the corresponding angle of rotation.[10]

Consider what happens if we wish to move between two orientations as part of an animation. In principle, we can determine an appropriate rotation matrix as the product of rotations about the three axes,

$$\mathbf{R}(\theta) = \mathbf{R}_x(\theta_x)\,\mathbf{R}_y(\theta_y)\,\mathbf{R}_z(\theta_z).$$

If we want to create a sequence of images that move between the two orientations, we can change the individual angles in small increments, either individually or simultaneously. Such a sequence would not appear smooth to a viewer; she would detect the individual rotations about each of the three axes.

With a device such as the trackball, we saw that we could rotate the cube smoothly about any axis. We did so by exploiting the equivalence between the two orientations of the cube and two points on a unit circle. A smooth rotation between the two orientations corresponds to a great circle on the surface of a sphere. This circle corresponds to a single rotation about a suitable axis that is the normal to the plane determined by the two points on the sphere and that sphere's center. If we increase this angle smoothly, our viewer will see a smooth rotation.

In one sense, what has failed us is our mathematical formulation, which relies on the use of coordinate axes. However, a deeper and less axis-dependent method is embedded within the matrix formulation. Suppose that we start with an arbitrary rotation matrix $\mathbf{R}$. All points on a line in the direction $\mathbf{d}$ are unaffected by the rotation. Thus, for any such point $\mathbf{p}$,

$$\mathbf{Rp} = \mathbf{p}.$$

In terms of the matrix $\mathbf{R}$, the column matrix $\mathbf{p}$ is an **eigenvector** of the matrix corresponding to the **eigenvalue** 1 (see Appendix C). In addition, for the direction $\mathbf{d}$,

$$\mathbf{Rd} = \mathbf{d},$$

so that its direction is unaffected by the rotation. Consequently, $\mathbf{d}$ is also an eigenvector of $\mathbf{R}$ corresponding to another eigenvalue of 1. The point $\mathbf{p}$ must be the fixed point of the rotation, and the vector $\mathbf{d}$ must be the normal to a plane perpendicular to the direction of rotation. In terms of the trackball, computing the axis of rotation was equivalent to finding a particular eigenvector of the desired rotation matrix. We could also go the other way. Given an arbitrary rotation matrix, by finding its eigenvalues and eigenvectors, we also determine the axis of rotation and the fixed point.

---

10. This section and the next may be skipped on a first reading.

4.13.4 Incremental Rotation

Suppose that we are given two orientations of an object, such as a camera, and we want to go smoothly from one to the other. One approach is to find the great circle path as we did with the virtual trackball and make incremental changes in the angle that rotates us along this path. Thus, we start with the axis of rotation, a start angle, a final angle, and a desired increment in the angle determined by the number of steps we wish to take. The main loop in the code will be of the form

```
var ctm = mat4();
// initialize ctm here
for (i = 0, i < imax; ++i) {
  thetax += dx;
  thetay += dy;
  thetaz += dz;

  ctm = mult(ctm, rotateX(thetaX));
  ctm = mult(ctm, rotateY(thetaY));
  ctm = mult(ctm, rotateZ(thetaZ));

  drawObject();
}
```

One problem with this approach is that the calculation of the rotation matrix requires the evaluation of the sines and cosines of three angles. We would do better if we compute the rotation matrix once and reuse it. We could also use the small angle approximations

$$\sin \theta \approx \theta \qquad \cos \theta \approx 1.$$

If we form an arbitrary rotation matrix through the Euler angles,

$$\mathbf{R} = \mathbf{R}_z(\psi) \, \mathbf{R}_y(\phi) \, \mathbf{R}_x(\theta),$$

then we can use the approximations to write $\mathbf{R}$ as

$$\mathbf{R} = \begin{bmatrix} \cos \psi & -\sin \psi & 0 & 0 \\ \sin \psi & \cos \psi & 0 & 0 \\ 0 & 0 & 1 & 0 \\ 0 & 0 & 0 & 1 \end{bmatrix} \begin{bmatrix} \cos \phi & 0 & \sin \phi & 0 \\ 0 & 1 & 0 & 0 \\ -\sin \phi & 0 & \cos \phi & 0 \\ 0 & 0 & 0 & 1 \end{bmatrix}$$

$$\times \begin{bmatrix} 1 & 0 & 0 & 0 \\ 0 & \cos \theta & -\sin \theta & 0 \\ 0 & \sin \theta & \cos \theta & 0 \\ 0 & 0 & 0 & 1 \end{bmatrix}$$

$$\approx \begin{bmatrix} 1 & -\psi & \phi & 0 \\ \psi & 1 & -\theta & 0 \\ -\phi & \theta & 1 & 0 \\ 0 & 0 & 0 & 1 \end{bmatrix}.$$

This method is subject to accumulated errors if we raise $\mathbf{R}$ to a high power. See Exercise 4.24.

4.14 QUATERNIONS

Quaternions are an extension of complex numbers that provide an alternative method for describing and manipulating rotations. Although less intuitive than our original approach, quaternions provide advantages for animation and both hardware and software implementations of rotation.

4.14.1 Complex Numbers and Quaternions

In two dimensions, the use of complex numbers to represent operations such as rotation is well known to most students of engineering and science. For example, suppose that we let $\mathbf{i}$ denote the pure imaginary number such that $\mathbf{i}^2 = -1$. Recalling Euler's identity,

$$e^{\mathbf{i}\upsilon} = \cos\theta + \mathbf{i}\sin\theta,$$

we can write the polar representation of a complex number $\mathbf{c}$ as

$$\mathbf{c} = a + \mathbf{i}b = re^{\mathbf{i}\theta},$$

where $r = \sqrt{a^2 + b^2}$ and $\theta = \tan^{-1} b/a$.

If we rotate $\mathbf{c}$ about the origin by ϕ to $\mathbf{c}'$, then we can find $\mathbf{c}'$ using a rotation matrix, or we can use the polar representation to write

$$\mathbf{c}' = re^{\mathbf{i}(\theta+\phi)} = re^{\mathbf{i}\theta}e^{\mathbf{i}\phi}.$$

Thus, $e^{\mathbf{i}\phi}$ is a rotation operator in the complex plane and provides an alternative to using transformations that may prove more efficient in practice.

However, we are really interested in rotations in a three-dimensional space. In three dimensions, the problem is more difficult because, to specify a rotation about the origin, we need to specify both a direction (a vector) and the amount of rotation about it (a scalar). One solution is to use a representation that consists of both a vector and a scalar. Usually, this representation is written as the **quaternion**

$$a = (q_0, q_1, q_2, q_3) = (q_0, \mathbf{q}),$$

where $\mathbf{q} = (q_1, q_2, q_3)$. The operations among quaternions are based on the use of three "complex" numbers $\mathbf{i}$, $\mathbf{j}$, and $\mathbf{k}$ with the properties

$$\mathbf{i}^2 = \mathbf{j}^2 = \mathbf{k}^2 = \mathbf{ijk} = -1.$$

These numbers are analogous to the unit vectors in three dimensions, and we can write $\mathbf{q}$ as

$$\mathbf{q} = q_1\mathbf{i} + q_2\mathbf{j} + q_3\mathbf{k}.$$

Now we can use the relationships among $\mathbf{i}, \mathbf{j}$, and $\mathbf{k}$ to derive quaternion addition and multiplication. If the quaternion b is given by

$$b = (p_0, \mathbf{p}),$$

then using the dot and cross products for vectors,

$$a + b = (p_0 + q_0, \mathbf{p} + \mathbf{q})$$

$$ab = (p_0 q_0 - \mathbf{q} \cdot \mathbf{p}, q_0\mathbf{p} + p_0\mathbf{q} + \mathbf{q} \times \mathbf{p}).$$

We can also define a magnitude for quaternions in the normal manner as

$$|a|^2 = q_0^2 + q_1^2 + q_2^2 + q_3^2 = q_0^2 + \mathbf{q} \cdot \mathbf{q}.$$

Quaternions have a multiplicative identity, the quaternion $(1, \mathbf{0})$, and it is easy to verify that the inverse of a quaternion is given by

$$a^{-1} = \frac{1}{|a|^2}(q_0, -\mathbf{q}).$$

4.14.2 Quaternions and Rotation

So far, we have only defined a new mathematical object. For it to be of use to us, we must relate it to our geometric entities and show how it can be used to carry out operations such as rotation. Suppose that we use the vector part of a quaternion to represent a point in space

$$p = (0, \mathbf{p}).$$

Thus, the components of $\mathbf{p} = (x, y, z)$ give the location of the point. Consider the quaternion

$$r = \left(\cos\frac{\theta}{2}, \sin\frac{\theta}{2}\mathbf{v} \right),$$

where $\mathbf{v}$ has unit length. We can then show that the quaternion r is a unit quaternion ($|r| = 1$), and therefore

$$r^{-1} = \left(\cos\frac{\theta}{2}, -\sin\frac{\theta}{2}\mathbf{v} \right).$$

If we consider the quaternion

$$p' = rpr^{-1},$$

where r is the rotation quaternion and p is the quaternion representation of a point, it has the form $(0, \mathbf{p}')$, where

$$\mathbf{p}' = \cos^2 \frac{\theta}{2}\mathbf{p} + \sin^2 \frac{\theta}{2}(\mathbf{p} \cdot \mathbf{v})\mathbf{v} + 2 \sin \frac{\theta}{2} \cos \frac{\theta}{2}(\mathbf{v} \times \mathbf{p}) - \sin^2 \frac{\theta}{2}(\mathbf{v} \times \mathbf{p}) \times \mathbf{v}$$

and thus p' is the representation of a point. What is less obvious is that p' is the result of rotating the point $\mathbf{p}$ by θ degrees about the vector $\mathbf{v}$. However, we can verify that this indeed is the case by comparing terms in p' with those of the general rotation. Before doing so, consider the implication of this result. Because we get the same result, the quaternion product formed from r and p is an alternate to transformation matrices as a representation of rotation about an arbitrary axis with a fixed point at the origin. If we count operations, quaternions are faster and have been built into both hardware and software implementations.

Let's consider a few examples. Suppose we consider the rotation about the z-axis by θ with a fixed point at the origin. The desired unit vector v is $(0, 0, 1)$, yielding the quaternion

$$r = \cos \frac{\theta}{2} + \sin \frac{\theta}{2}(0, 0, 1).$$

The rotation of an arbitrary point $\mathbf{p} = (x, y, z)$ yields the quaternion

$$p' = rpr^{-1} = r(0, \mathbf{p})r^{-1} = (0, \mathbf{p}'),$$

where

$$\mathbf{p}' = (x \cos \theta - y \sin \theta, x \sin \theta + y \cos \theta, z).$$

Thus, we get the expected result but with fewer operations. If we consider a sequence of rotations about the coordinate axes that in matrix form yields the matrix $\mathbf{R} = \mathbf{R}_x(\theta_x)\mathbf{R}_y(\theta_y)\mathbf{R}_z(\theta_z)$, we instead can use the product of the corresponding quaternions to form $r_x r_y r_z$.

Returning to the rotation about an arbitrary axis, in Section 4.10.4, we derived a matrix of the form

$$\mathbf{M} = \mathbf{T}(\mathbf{p}_0) \, \mathbf{R}_x(-\theta_x) \, \mathbf{R}_y(-\theta_y) \, \mathbf{R}_z(\theta_z) \, \mathbf{R}_y(\theta_y) \, \mathbf{R}_x(\theta_x) \, \mathbf{T}(-\mathbf{p}_0).$$

Because of the translations at the beginning and end, we cannot use quaternions for the entire operation. We can, however, recognize that the elements of $p' = rpr^{-1}$ can be used to find the elements of the homogeneous-coordinate rotation matrix embedded in $\mathbf{M}$. Thus, if again $r = (\cos \frac{\theta}{2}, \sin \frac{\theta}{2}\mathbf{v})$, then

$$\mathbf{R} = \begin{bmatrix} 1 - 2\sin^2 \frac{\theta}{2}(v_y^2 + v_z^2) & 2\sin^2 \frac{\theta}{2}v_x v_y - 2\cos \frac{\theta}{2}\sin \frac{\theta}{2}v_z \\ 2\sin^2 \frac{\theta}{2}v_x v_y + 2\cos \frac{\theta}{2}\sin \frac{\theta}{2}v_z & 1 - 2\sin^2 \frac{\theta}{2}(v_x^2 + v_z^2) \\ 2\sin^2 \frac{\theta}{2}v_x v_z - 2\cos \frac{\theta}{2}\sin \frac{\theta}{2}v_y & 2\sin^2 \frac{\theta}{2}v_y v_z + 2\cos \frac{\theta}{2}\sin \frac{\theta}{2}v_x \\ 0 & 0 \end{bmatrix}$$

$$\begin{bmatrix} 2\sin^2 \frac{\theta}{2}v_x v_z + 2\cos \frac{\theta}{2}\sin \frac{\theta}{2}v_y & 0 \\ 2\sin^2 \frac{\theta}{2}v_y v_z - 2\cos \frac{\theta}{2}\sin \frac{\theta}{2}v_x & 0 \\ 1 - 2\sin^2 \frac{\theta}{2}(v_x^2 + v_y^2) & 0 \\ 0 & 1 \end{bmatrix}.$$

This matrix can be made to look more familiar if we use the trigonometric identities

$$\cos\theta = \cos^2\frac{\theta}{2} - \sin^2\frac{\theta}{2} = 1 - 2\sin^2\frac{\theta}{2}$$

$$\sin\theta = 2\cos\frac{\theta}{2}\sin\frac{\theta}{2},$$

and recall that **v** is a unit vector so that

$$v_x^2 + v_y^2 + v_z^2 = 1.$$

Thus, we can use quaternion products to form r and then form the rotation part of **M** by matching terms between **R** and r. We then use our normal transformation operations to add in the effect of the two translations.

Alternately, we can use the our vector types to create quaternions either in the application (Exercise 4.28) or in the shaders (Exercise 4.33). In either case, we can carry out the rotation directly without converting back to a rotation matrix.

In addition to the efficiency of using quaternions instead of rotation matrices, quaternions can be interpolated to obtain smooth sequences of rotations for animation. Quaternions have been used in animations to get smooth camera motion as the camera tracks a path. However, we have to be careful because as we rotate around a great circle using quaternions, we do not preserve the up direction.

4.14.3 Quaternions and Gimbal Lock

Quaternions have one additional advantage over rotation matrices. They avoid a problem known as **gimbal lock**, which arises from our use of Euler angles to specify a rotation.

In order to get some insight into the problem, let's consider a simple real-world problem. Suppose that we are somewhere in the Northern Hemisphere on a clear night and looking at the North Star. We can describe its position uniquely by the angle between our line of sight and the ground (the elevation) and the angle between our line of sight and some fixed longitude (the azimuth). Now suppose that we are transported to the North Pole and we look straight up at the North Star. The elevation is now 90 degrees but the azimuth is irrelevant; whatever direction we turn, we still see the North Star directly overhead. Mathematically, we have lost a degree of freedom in our positioning at the North Pole and may have difficulty finding a path to another star specified by its azimuth and elevation, because the singularity has caused us not to have an initial azimuth due to the ambiguity at the pole. The name *gimbal lock* comes from the gimbal device that is used in gyroscopes. The problem has arisen in spacecraft and robots.

We can demonstrate this problem mathematically for our rotations. Consider our standard formula, which builds a general rotation matrix from successive rotations about the x-, y-, and z-axes

$$\mathbf{R} = \mathbf{R}_z(\psi)\,\mathbf{R}_y(\phi)\,\mathbf{R}_x(\theta).$$

Suppose that the rotation about the y-axis is by 90 degrees so $\mathbf{R}_y(\phi)$ is the matrix

$$
\mathbf{R}_y(\phi) = \begin{bmatrix} 0 & 0 & 1 & 0 \\ 0 & 1 & 0 & 0 \\ -1 & 0 & 0 & 0 \\ 0 & 0 & 0 & 1 \end{bmatrix}
$$

This matrix swaps the negative x- and z-axes and consequently leads to a problem with the other two rotations. If we multiply out the three matrices with this $\mathbf{R}_y(\phi)$, we obtain the matrix

$$
\mathbf{R} = \begin{bmatrix} \cos\psi & -\sin\psi & 0 & 0 \\ \sin\psi & \cos\psi & 0 & 0 \\ 0 & 0 & 1 & 0 \\ 0 & 0 & 0 & 1 \end{bmatrix} \begin{bmatrix} 0 & 0 & 1 & 0 \\ 0 & 1 & 0 & 0 \\ -1 & 0 & 0 & 0 \\ 0 & 0 & 0 & 1 \end{bmatrix} \begin{bmatrix} 1 & 0 & 0 & 0 \\ 0 & \cos\theta & -\sin\theta & 0 \\ 0 & \sin\theta & \cos\theta & 0 \\ 0 & 0 & 0 & 1 \end{bmatrix}
$$

$$
= \begin{bmatrix} 0 & \sin(\theta - \psi) & \cos(\theta - \psi) & 0 \\ 0 & \cos(\theta - \psi) & -\sin(\theta - \psi) & 0 \\ -1 & 0 & 0 & 0 \\ 0 & 0 & 0 & 1 \end{bmatrix}.
$$

This matrix is a rotation matrix that includes the swapping of the x and z directions. However, because the sine and cosine terms depend on only the difference between θ and ψ, we have lost a degree of freedom and there are infinite ways to combine θ and ψ to get the same rotation. If we use quaternions instead of the concatenation of rotation matrices defined by Euler angles, this problem never arises and accounts for the importance of quaternions in animation, robotics, and aerospace.

SUMMARY AND NOTES

In this chapter, we have presented two different, but ultimately complementary, points of view regarding the mathematics of computer graphics. One is that mathematical abstraction of the objects with which we work in computer graphics is necessary if we are to understand the operations that we carry out in our programs. The other is that transformations—and the techniques for carrying them out, such as the use of homogeneous coordinates—are the basis for implementations of graphics systems.

Our mathematical tools come from the study of vector analysis and linear algebra. For computer graphics purposes, however, the order in which we have chosen to present these tools is the reverse of the order that most students learn them. In particular, linear algebra is studied first, and then vector-space concepts are linked to the study of n-tuples in $\mathbf{R}^n$. In contrast, our study of representation in mathematical spaces led to our use of linear algebra as a tool for implementing abstract types.

We pursued a coordinate-free approach for two reasons. First, we wanted to show that all the basic concepts of geometric objects and of transformations are independent of the ways the latter are represented. Second, as object-oriented languages become more prevalent, application programmers will work directly with the objects, instead of with those objects' representations. The references in the Suggested Readings section contain examples of geometric programming systems that illustrate the potential of this approach.

Homogeneous coordinates provided a wonderful example of the power of mathematical abstraction. By going to an abstract mathematical space—the affine space—we were able to find a tool that led directly to efficient software and hardware methods.

Finally, we provided the set of affine transformations supported in WebGL and discussed ways that we could concatenate them to provide all affine transformations. The strategy of combining a few simple types of matrices to build a desired transformation is a powerful one; you should use it for a few of the exercises at the end of this chapter. In Chapter 5, we build on these techniques to develop viewing for three-dimensional graphics; in Chapter 9, we use our transformations to build hierarchical models.

SUGGESTED READINGS

There are many texts on vector analysis and linear algebra, although most treat the topics separately. Within the geometric design community, the vector-space approach of coordinate-free descriptions of curves and surfaces has been popular; see the book by Faux and Pratt [Fau80]. See DeRose [DeR88, DeR89] for an introduction to geometric programming. Homogeneous coordinates arose in geometry [Max51] and were later discovered by the graphics community [Rob63, Rie81]. Their use in hardware started with Silicon Graphics' Geometry Engine [Cla82]. Modern hardware architectures use application-specific integrated circuits (ASICs) that include homogeneous-coordinate transformations.

Quaternions were introduced to computer graphics by Shoemake [Sho85] for use in animation. See the book by Kuipers [Kui99] for many examples of the use of rotation matrices and quaternions. Geometric algebra [Hes99] provides a unified approach to linear algebra and quaternions.

Software tools such as Mathematica [Wol91] and MATLAB [Mat95] are excellent aids for learning to manipulate transformation matrices.

EXERCISES

4.1   Justify the following sequence of statements:

    a.   No combination of rotations and translations can alter the shape of an object

    b.   For a fixed point, there are three degrees of freedom

    c.   There is one point that remains unchanged by a rotation

4.2   In this chapter, we have represented mathematical terms like scalars, points, and vectors in different computer science languages as abstract data types (ADTs). Write a program template in C++ that will take input for an instance of point, input a vector value to add to that point, and generate a new point.

4.3   Write a library of functions that will allow you to do geometric programming. Your library should contain functions for manipulating the basic geometric types (points, lines, vectors) and operations on those types, including dot and cross products. It should allow you to change frames. You can also create functions to interface with WebGL so that you can display the results of geometric calculations.

4.4   If we are interested in only two-dimensional graphics, we can use three-dimensional homogeneous coordinates by representing a point as $\mathbf{p} = [x\,y\,1]^T$ and a vector as $\mathbf{v} = [a\,b\,0]^T$. Find the 3×3 rotation, translation, scaling, and shear matrices. How many degrees of freedom are there in an affine transformation for transforming two-dimensional points?

4.5   A mathematical point has neither a size nor a shape. Scalars are real numbers or complex numbers. Mathematicians use the term vector for any quantity with direction and magnitude but no fixed location in space. How are these three geometric objects used in two- and three-dimensional geometric systems? How do these geometric objects combine and increase their operational strength?

4.6   How can we generate a desired rotation matrix about an origin for a geometric object? How may we generate different rotation matrices for a geometric object?

4.7   Show the different effects of scale factor on scaling an object. What is the domain of values for a scale factor?

4.8   Derive the homogeneous coordinate transformation from the rotation, translation, and scaling transformations.

4.9   In two dimensions, we can specify a line by the equation $y = mx + h$. Find an affine transformation to reflect two-dimensional points about this line. Extend your result to reflection about a plane in three dimensions.

4.10   In Section 4.10, we showed that an arbitrary rotation matrix could be composed from successive rotations about the three axes. How many ways can we compose a given rotation if we can do only three simple rotations? Are all three of the simple rotation matrices necessary?

4.11   All three-dimensional objects cannot be supported on existing graphics systems. Show how to use two-dimensional primitives to model three-dimensional objects.

4.12   Find an approach for dealing with geometric problems that is independent of coordinate systems.

4.13   Define vector and scalar in a geometric system. What is the property of the vector scalar multiplication?

4.14   Determine the rotation matrix for a rotation of the form $\mathbf{R}_x\mathbf{R}_y\mathbf{R}_z$. Assume that the fixed point is the origin and the angles are θ_x, θ_y, and θ_z.

4.15   What are the two fundamental operations between vector and scalars that are described in this chapter?

4.16   Consider the solution of either constant-coefficient linear differential or difference equations (recurrences). Show that the solutions of the homogeneous equations form a vector space. Relate the solution for a particular inhomogeneous equation to an affine space.

4.17 Write a program to generate a Sierpinski gasket as follows. Start with a white triangle. At each step, use transformations to generate three similar triangles that are drawn over the original triangle, leaving the center of the triangle white and the three corners black.

4.18 Start with a cube centered at the origin and aligned with the coordinate axes. Find a rotation matrix that will orient the cube symmetrically, as shown in Figure 4.63.

FIGURE 4.63   Symmetric orientation of cube.

4.19 We can perform different types of operations on vectors, like increase or decrease their length without changing their direction. Given a set of vectors, find a method to combine these segments.

4.20 Three vertices determine a triangle if they do not lie in the same line. Devise a test for collinearity of three vertices.

4.21 We defined an instance transformation as the product of a translation, a rotation, and a scaling. Can we accomplish the same effect by applying these three types of transformations in a different order?

4.22 Write a program that allows you to orient the cube with one mouse button, to translate it with a second, and to zoom in and out with a third.

4.23 Given two nonparallel, three-dimensional vectors u and v, how can we form an orthogonal coordinate system in which u is one of the basis vectors?

4.24 An incremental rotation about the z-axis can be approximated by the matrix

$$\begin{bmatrix} 1 & -\theta & 0 & 0 \\ \theta & 1 & 0 & 0 \\ 0 & 0 & 1 & 0 \\ 0 & 0 & 0 & 1 \end{bmatrix}.$$

What negative aspects are there if we use this matrix for a large number of steps? Can you suggest a remedy? *Hint:* Consider points a distance of 1 from the origin.

4.25 Find the quaternion for 45-degree rotations about the z-axis with the fixed point at origin.

4.26 Determine the rotation matrix $\mathbf{R} = \mathbf{R}(\theta_x)\,\mathbf{R}(\theta_y)\,\mathbf{R}(\theta_z)$. Find the corresponding quaternion.

4.27 Redo the trackball program using quaternions instead of rotation matrices.

4.28 Using the `vec4` class, create a set of quaternion operations that can be carried out in an application. For example, you might start with the prototypes

```
typedef vec4 quaternion;
quaternion multq(const quaternion &, const quaternion &);
quaternion addq(const quaternion &, const quaternion &);
quaternion inverseq(const quaternion &);
point4 rotateq(float theta, const point4 &);
```

4.29 Write a vertex shader that takes as input an angle and an axis of rotation and rotates vertices about this axis.

4.30 In principle, an object-oriented system could provide scalars, vectors, and points as basic types. None of the popular APIs does so. What do you think are the different approaches to represent a point in terms of another point, vector, and scalar?

4.31 To specify a scaling, we can specify the fixed point, a direction in which we wish to scale, and a scale factor (α). For what value of α will

   a. the object grow longer in the specified direction?
   b. the object grow shorter in the specified direction?

4.32 Show that the sum

$$P = \alpha_1 P_1 + \alpha_2 P_2 + \cdots + \alpha_n P_n$$

is defined if and only if

$$\alpha_1 + \alpha_2 + \cdots + \alpha_n = 1.$$

Hint: Start with the first two terms and write them as
$$P = \alpha_1 P_1 + \alpha_2 P_2 + \cdots = \alpha_1 P_1 + (\alpha_2 + \alpha_1 - \alpha_1)P_2 + \cdots$$
$$= \alpha_1(P_1 - P_2) + (\alpha_1 + \alpha_2)P_2 + \cdots,$$

and then proceed inductively.

4.33 Write a vertex shader whose input is a quaternion and that rotates the input vertex using quaternion rotation.

4.34 Write a function `rotate(float theta, vec3d)` that will rotate by `theta` degrees about the axis d with a fixed point at the origin.

4.35 Implement rotation of the cube by computing and applying the rotation matrix in the application. Test this approach against the two approaches taken in Section 4.12.

CHAPTER 5

VIEWING

We have completed our discussion of the first half of the synthetic-camera model—specifying objects in three dimensions. We now investigate the multitude of ways in which we can describe our virtual camera. Along the way, we examine related topics, such as the relationship between classical viewing techniques and computer viewing and how projection is implemented using projective transformations.

There are three parts to our approach. First, we look at the types of views that we can create and why we need more than one type of view. Then we examine how an application program can specify a particular view within WebGL. We will see that the viewing process has two parts. In the first, we use the model-view matrix to switch vertex representations from the object frame in which we defined our objects to their representation in the eye frame, in which the camera is at the origin. This representation of the geometry will allow us to use canonical viewing procedures. The second part of the process deals with the type of projection we prefer (parallel or perspective) and the part of the world we wish to image (the clipping or view volume). These specifications will allow us to form a projection matrix that is concatenated with the model-view matrix. Finally, we derive the projection matrices that describe the most important parallel and perspective views and investigate how to carry out these projections in WebGL.

5.1 CLASSICAL AND COMPUTER VIEWING

Before looking at the interface between computer graphics systems and application programs for three-dimensional viewing, we take a slight diversion to consider classical viewing. There are two reasons for examining classical viewing. First, many of the jobs that were formerly done by hand drawing—such as animation in movies, architectural rendering, drafting, and mechanical-parts design—are now routinely done with the aid of computer graphics. Practitioners of these fields need to be able to produce classical views—such as isometrics, elevations, and various perspectives—and thus must be able to use the computer system to produce such renderings. Second, the relationships between classical and computer viewing show many advantages of, and a few difficulties with, the approach used by most APIs.

FIGURE 5.1   Viewing.

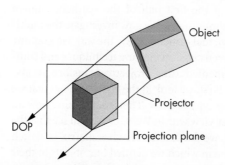

FIGURE 5.2   Movement of the center of projection (COP) to infinity.

When we introduced the synthetic-camera model in Chapter 1, we pointed out the similarities between classical and computer viewing. The basic elements in both cases are the same. We have objects, a viewer, projectors, and a projection plane (Figure 5.1). The projectors meet at the **center of projection** (**COP**). The COP corresponds to the center of the lens in the camera or in the eye, and in a computer graphics system, it is the origin of the **camera frame** for perspective views. All standard graphics systems follow the model that we described in Chapter 1, which is based on geometric optics. The projection surface is a plane, and the projectors are straight lines. This situation is the one we usually encounter and is straightforward to implement, especially with our pipeline model.

Both classical and computer graphics allow the viewer to be an infinite distance from the objects. Note that as we move the COP to infinity, the projectors become parallel and the COP can be replaced by a **direction of projection** (**DOP**), as shown in Figure 5.2. Note also that as the COP moves to infinity, we can leave the projection plane fixed and the size of the image remains about the same, even though the COP is infinitely far from the objects. Views with a finite COP are called **perspective views**; views with a COP at infinity are called **parallel views**. For parallel views, the origin of the camera frame usually lies in the projection plane.

Color Plates 9 and 10 show a parallel and a perspective rendering, respectively. These plates illustrate the importance of having both types of views available in applications such as architecture; in an API that supports both types of viewing, the user can switch easily between various viewing modes. Most modern APIs support both parallel and perspective viewing. The class of projections produced by these systems is known as **planar geometric projections** because the projection surface is a plane and the projectors are lines. Both perspective and parallel projections preserve lines; they do not, in general, preserve angles. Although the parallel views are the limiting case of perspective viewing, both classical and computer viewing usually treat them as separate cases. For classical views, the techniques that people use to construct the two types by hand are different, as anyone who has taken a drafting class surely knows. From the computer perspective, there are differences in how we specify the two types of views. Rather than looking at a parallel view as the limit of the perspective view, we derive the limiting equations and use those equations directly to form the corresponding projection matrix. In modern pipeline architectures, the projection matrix corresponding to either type of view can be loaded into the pipeline.

Although computer graphics systems have two fundamental types of viewing (parallel and perspective), classical graphics appears to permit a host of different views, ranging from multiview orthographic projections to one-, two-, and three-point perspectives. This seeming discrepancy arises in classical graphics as a result of the desire to show a specific relationship among an object, the viewer, and the projection plane, as opposed to the computer graphics approach of complete independence of all specifications.

5.1.1 Classical Viewing

When an architect draws an image of a building, she knows which side she wishes to display and thus where she should place the viewer in relationship to the building. Each classical view is determined by a specific relationship between the objects and the viewer.

In classical viewing, there is the underlying notion of a **principal face**. The types of objects viewed in real-world applications, such as architecture, tend to be composed of a number of planar faces, each of which can be thought of as a principal face. For a rectangular object, such as a building, there are natural notions of the front, back, top, bottom, right, and left faces. In addition, many real-world objects have faces that meet at right angles; thus, such objects often have three orthogonal directions associated with them.

Figure 5.3 shows some of the main types of views. We start with the most restrictive view for each of the parallel and perspective types, and then move to the less restrictive conditions.

5.1.2 Orthographic Projections

Our first classical view is the **orthographic projection** shown in Figure 5.4. In all orthographic (or orthogonal) views, the projectors are perpendicular to the projection plane. In a **multiview orthographic projection**, we make multiple projections, in each case with the projection plane parallel to one of the principal faces of the object.

Front elevation   Elevation oblique   Plan oblique

Isometric   One-point perspective   Three-point perspective

FIGURE 5.3   Classical views.

FIGURE 5.4   Orthographic projection.

Usually, we use three views—such as the front, top, and right—to display the object. The reason that we produce multiple views should be clear from Figure 5.5. For a box-like object, only the faces parallel to the projection plane appear in the image. A viewer usually needs more than two views to visualize what an object looks like from its multiview orthographic projections. Visualization from these images can require skill on the part of the viewer. The importance of this type of view is that it preserves both distances and angles in faces parallel to the view plane, and because there is no distortion of either distance or shape in images of these faces, multiview orthographic projections are well suited for working drawings.

5.1.3 Axonometric Projections

If we want to see more principal faces of our box-like object in a single view, we must remove one of our restrictions. In **axonometric** views, the projectors are still orthogonal to the projection plane, as shown in Figure 5.6, but the projection plane

FIGURE 5.5   Temple and three multiview orthographic projections.

FIGURE 5.6   Axonometric projections. (a) Construction of trimetric-view projections. (b) Top view. (c) Side view.

can have any orientation with respect to the object. If the projection plane is placed symmetrically with respect to the three principal faces that meet at a corner of our rectangular object, then we have an **isometric** view. If the projection plane is placed symmetrically with respect to two of the principal faces, then the view is **dimetric**. The general case is a **trimetric** view. These views are shown in Figure 5.7. Note that in an isometric view, a line segment's length in the image space is shorter than its length measured in the object space. This **foreshortening** of distances is the same in the three principal directions, so we can still make distance measurements. In the dimetric view, however, there are two different foreshortening ratios; in the trimetric

Dimetric   Trimetric   Isometric

FIGURE 5.7   Axonometric views.

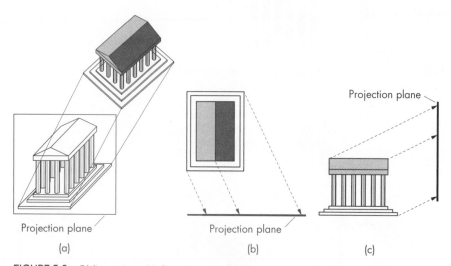

FIGURE 5.8   Oblique view. (a) Construction. (b) Top view. (c) Side view.

view, there are three. Also, although parallel lines are preserved in the image, angles are not. A circle is projected into an ellipse. This distortion is the price we pay for the ability to see more than one principal face in a view that can be produced easily either by hand or by computer. Axonometric views are used extensively in architectural and mechanical design.

5.1.4 Oblique Projections

The **oblique** views are the most general parallel views. We obtain an oblique projection by allowing the projectors to make an arbitrary angle with the projection plane, as shown in Figure 5.8. Consequently, angles in planes parallel to the projection plane are preserved. A circle in a plane parallel to the projection plane is projected into a circle, yet we can see more than one principal face of the object. Oblique views are the most difficult to construct by hand. They are also somewhat unnatural. Most physical viewing devices, including the human visual system, have a lens that is in a fixed relationship with the image plane—usually, the lens is parallel to the plane. Although these devices produce perspective views, if the viewer is far from the object, the views are approximately parallel, but orthogonal, because the projection plane is parallel to the lens. The bellows camera that we used to develop the synthetic-camera model in Section 1.6 has the flexibility to produce approximations to parallel oblique views. One use of such a camera is to create images of buildings in which the sides of the building are parallel rather than converging, as they would be in an image created with an orthogonal view with the camera on the ground.

From the application programmer's point of view, there is no significant difference among the different parallel views. The application programmer specifies a type of view—parallel or perspective—and a set of parameters that describe the camera. The problem for the application programmer is how to specify these parameters in the viewing procedures so as best to view an object or to produce a specific classical view.

5.1.5 Perspective Viewing

All perspective views are characterized by **diminution** of size. When objects are moved farther from the viewer, their images become smaller. This size change gives perspective views their natural appearance; however, because the amount by which a line is foreshortened depends on how far the line is from the viewer, we cannot make measurements from a perspective view. Hence, the major use of perspective views is in applications such as architecture and animation, where it is important to achieve natural-looking images.

In the classical perspective views, the viewer is located symmetrically with respect to the projection plane and is on the perpendicular from the center of projection, as shown in Figure 5.9. Thus, the pyramid determined by the window in the projection plane and the center of projection is a symmetric or right pyramid. This symmetry is caused by the fixed relationship between the back (retina) and lens of the eye for human viewing, or between the back and lens of a camera for standard cameras, and by similar fixed relationships in most physical situations. Some cameras, such as the

FIGURE 5.9 Perspective viewing.

(a)   (b)   (c)

FIGURE 5.10   Classical perspective views. (a) Three-point. (b) Two-point.
(c) One-point.

bellows camera, have movable film backs and can produce general perspective views. The model used in computer graphics includes this general case.

The classical perspective views are usually known as **one-**, **two-**, and **three-point perspectives**. The differences among the three cases are based on how many of the three principal directions in the object are parallel to the projection plane. Consider the three perspective projections of the building shown in Figure 5.10. Any corner of the building includes the three principal directions. In the most general case— the three-point perspective—parallel lines in each of the three principal directions converge to a finite **vanishing point** (Figure 5.10(a)). If we allow one of the principal directions to become parallel to the projection plane, we have a two-point projection (Figure 5.10(b)), in which lines in only two of the principal directions converge. Finally, in the one-point perspective (Figure 5.10(c)), two of the principal directions are parallel to the projection plane, and we have only a single vanishing point. As with parallel viewing, it should be apparent from the programmer's point of view that the three situations are merely special cases of general perspective viewing, which we implement in Section 5.4.

5.2   VIEWING WITH A COMPUTER

We can now return to three-dimensional graphics from a computer perspective. Because viewing in computer graphics is based on the synthetic-camera model, we should be able to construct any of the classical views. However, there is a fundamental difference. All the classical views are based on a particular relationship among the objects, the viewer, and the projectors. In computer graphics, we stress the independence of the object specifications and camera parameters. Hence, to create one of the classical views, the application program must use information about the objects to create and place the proper camera.

Using WebGL, we will have many options on how and where we carry out viewing. All our approaches will use the powerful transformation capabilities of the GPU. Because every transformation is equivalent to a change of frames, we can develop viewing in terms of the frames and coordinate systems we introduced in Chapter 4. In particular, we will work with object coordinates, camera coordinates, and clip coordinates.

A good starting point is the output of the vertex shader. In Chapters 2 and 4, we used the fact that as long as the vertices output by the vertex shader were within the clipping volume, they continued onto the rasterizer. Hence, in Chapter 2 we were able to specify vertex positions inside the default viewing cube. In Chapter 4, we learned how to scale positions using affine transformations so they would be mapped inside the cube. We also relied on the fact that objects that are sent to the rasterizer are projected with a simple orthographic projection.

Hidden-surface removal, however, occurs after the fragment shader. Consequently, although an object might be blocked from the camera by other objects, even with hidden-surface removal enabled, the rasterizer will still generate fragments for blocked objects within the clipping volume. However, we need more flexibility in both how we specify objects and how we view them. There are four major additions to address:

1. We need the ability to work in the units of the application.

2. We need to position the camera independently of the objects.

3. We want to be able to specify a clipping volume in units related to the application.

4. We want to be able to do either parallel or perspective projections.

We can accomplish all these additions by careful use of transformations: the first three using affine transformations, and the last using a process called perspective normalization. All of these transformations must be carried out either in the application code or in the vertex shader.

We approach all these tasks through the transformation capabilities we developed in Chapter 4. Of the frames we discussed for WebGL, three are important in the viewing process: the object frame, the camera frame, and the clip coordinate frame. In Chapters 2, 3, and 4, we were able to avoid explicitly specifying the first two by using a default in which all three frames were identical. We either directly specified vertex positions in clip coordinates or used an affine transformation to scale objects we wanted to be visible to lie within the clipping cube in clip coordinates. The camera was fixed to be at the origin and pointing in the negative z direction in clip coordinates.[1]

To obtain a more flexible way to do viewing, we will separate the process into two fundamental operations. First, we must position and orient the camera. This operation is the job of the model-view transformation. After vertices pass through this transformation, they will be represented in eye or camera coordinates. The second step is the application of the projection transformation. This step applies the specified projection—orthographic or perspective—to the vertices and puts objects within the specified clipping volume into the same clipping cube in clip coordinates. One of the functions of either projection will be to allow us to specify a view volume in camera coordinates rather than having to scale our object to fit into the default view volume. These transformations are shown in Figure 5.11.

---

1. The default camera can "see" objects behind it if they are in the clipping volume.

FIGURE 5.11   Viewing transformations.

What we have called the current transformation matrix will be the product of two matrices: the model-view matrix and the projection matrix. The model-view matrix will take vertices in object coordinates and convert them to a representation in camera coordinates and thus must encapsulate the positioning and orientation of the camera. The projection matrix will both carry out the desired projection—either orthogonal or perspective—and convert a viewing volume specified in camera coordinates to fit inside the viewing cube in clip coordinates.

5.3   POSITIONING OF THE CAMERA

In this section, we deal with positioning and orientation of the camera; in Section 5.4, we discuss how we specify the desired projection. Although we focus on an API that will work well with WebGL, we also briefly examine a few other APIs to specify a camera.

5.3.1 Positioning of the Camera Frame

As we saw in Chapter 4, we can specify vertices in any units we choose, and we can define a model-view matrix by a sequence of affine transformations that repositions these vertices. The model-view transformation is the concatenation of a modeling transformation that takes instances of objects in model coordinates and brings them into the object frame with a viewing transformation that transforms object coordinates to eye coordinates. Because we usually do not need to access object coordinates, we can use the model-view matrix rather than separate modeling and viewing matrices.

Initially, we start with the model-view matrix set to an identity matrix, so the camera frame and the object frame are identical. Hence, the camera is initially pointing in the negative z direction (Figure 5.12). In most applications, we model our objects as being located around the origin, so a camera located at the default position with the default orientation does not see all the objects in the scene. Thus, either we must move the camera away from the objects that we wish to have in our image, or the objects must be moved in front of the camera. These are equivalent operations, as either can be looked at as positioning the frame of the camera with respect to the frame of the objects.

It might help to think of a scene in which we have initially specified several objects by specifying all vertices and putting their positions into an array. We start with the model-view matrix set to an identity matrix. Changes to the model-view matrix move the object frame relative to the camera and affect the camera's view of all ob-

FIGURE 5.12   Initial camera position.

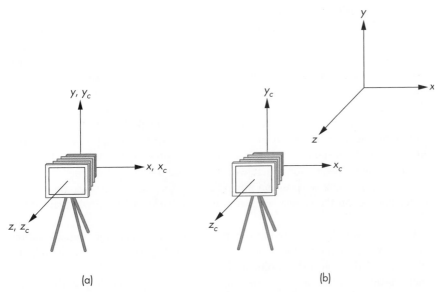

FIGURE 5.13 Movement of the camera and object frames. (a) Initial configuration. (b) Configuration after change in the model-view matrix.

jects defined *afterward*, because their vertices are specified relative to the repositioned object frame. Equivalently, in terms of the flow of an application program, the projection and model-view matrices are part of its state. We will either apply them to the vertex positions in the application or, more likely, we will send them to the vertex shader where they will be applied automatically whenever vertex data are sent to the shader.

In either case, the sequence illustrated in Figure 5.13 shows the process. In part (a), we have the initial configuration. A vertex specified at $\mathbf{p}$ has the same representation in both frames. In part (b), we have changed the model-view matrix to $\mathbf{C}$ by a sequence of transformations. The two frames are no longer the same, although $\mathbf{C}$ contains the information to move from the camera frame to the object frame or, equivalently, contains the information that moves the camera away from its initial position at the origin of the object frame. A vertex specified at $\mathbf{q}$ *after* the change to the model-view matrix is at $\mathbf{q}$ in the object frame. However, its position in the camera frame is $\mathbf{Cq}$ and can be stored internally within the application or sent to the GPU, where it will be converted to camera coordinates. The viewing transformation will assume that vertex data it starts with are in camera coordinates.

An equivalent view is that the camera is still at the origin of its own frame, and the model-view matrix is applied to primitives specified in this system. In practice, you can use either view. But be sure to take great care regarding where in your program the primitives are specified relative to changes in the model-view matrix.

At any given time, the model-view matrix encapsulates the relationship between the camera frame and the object frame. Although combining the modeling and viewing transformations into a single matrix may initially cause confusion, on closer examination this approach is a good one. If we regard the camera as an object with geometric properties, then transformations that alter the position and orientation of objects should also affect the position and orientation of the camera relative to these objects.

The next problem is how we specify the desired position of the camera and then implement camera positioning in WebGL. We outline three approaches, one in this section and two in Section 5.3.2. Two others are given as exercises (Exercises 5.2 and 5.3).

Our first approach is to specify the position indirectly by applying a sequence of rotations and translations to the model-view matrix. This approach is a direct application of the instance transformation that we presented in Chapter 4, but we must be careful for two reasons. First, we usually want to specify the camera's position and orientation *before* we position any objects in the scene.[2] Second, the order of transformations on the camera may appear to be backward from what you might expect.

Consider an object centered at the origin. The camera is in its initial position, also at the origin, pointing down the negative z-axis. Suppose that we want an image of the faces of the object that point in the positive z direction. We must move the camera *away* from the origin. If we allow the camera to remain pointing in the negative z direction, then we want to move the camera backward along the positive z-axis, and the proper transformation is

$$\mathbf{T} = \begin{bmatrix} 1 & 0 & 0 & 0 \\ 0 & 1 & 0 & 0 \\ 0 & 0 & 1 & -d \\ 0 & 0 & 0 & 1 \end{bmatrix},$$

where d is a positive number.

Many people find it helpful to interpret this operation as moving the camera frame relative to the object frame. This point of view has its basis in physics, where the objects are fixed in space and the viewer can be moved to obtain the desired view. This model carries over into many design applications, where we usually think of objects as being positioned in a fixed frame, and it is the viewer who must move to the right position to achieve the desired view.

However, in classical viewing, the viewer dominates. Conceptually, we do viewing by picking up the object, orienting it as desired, and bringing it to the desired location. One consequence of the classical approach is that distances are measured from the viewer to the object, rather than—as in most physically based systems—from the object to the viewer. Classical viewing often resulted in a left-handed camera frame. Early computer graphics systems followed the classical approach by having modeling in right-handed coordinates and viewing in left-handed coordinates—a decision that, although technically correct, caused confusion among users.

---

2. In an animation, where in the program we specify the position of the camera depends on whether we wish to attach the camera to a particular object or to place the camera in a fixed position in the scene (see Exercise 5.3).

In WebGL, the internal frames are right handed. Fortunately, because the application program works primarily in object coordinates, the application programmer usually does not see any of the internal representations and thus does not have to worry about these alternate perspectives on viewing. However, WebGL views the camera as fixed, and thus the objects are repositioned and reoriented by the model-view matrix. Generally, we will work with right-handed systems when we create our objects. The only place we usually need to be careful is when we are working in camera coordinates and must measure distances from the camera to the objects, which is consistent with classical viewing.

Suppose that we want to look at the same object from the positive *x*-axis. Now, not only do we have to move away from the object, but we also have to rotate the camera about the *y*-axis, as shown in Figure 5.14. We must do the translation after we rotate the camera by 90 degrees about the *y*-axis. In the program, the calls must be in the reverse order, as we discussed in Section 4.10, so we expect to see code like the following:

FIGURE 5.14   Positioning of the camera.

```
modelViewMatrix = mult(translate(0, 0, -d), rotateY(-90));
```

In terms of the two frames, first we rotate the object frame relative to the camera frame, and then we move the two frames apart.

In Chapters 2 and 4, we were able to show simple three-dimensional examples by using an identity matrix as the default projection matrix. That default setting has the effect of creating an orthographic projection with the camera at the origin, pointed in the negative *z* direction. In our cube example in Chapter 4, we rotated the cube to see the desired faces. As we just discussed, rotating the cube is equivalent to rotating the frame of the cube with respect to the frame of the camera; we could have achieved the same view by rotating the camera relative to the cube. We can extend this strategy of translating and rotating the camera to create other orthographic views. Perspective views require changes to the default projection.

Consider creating an isometric view of the cube. Suppose that again we start with a cube centered at the origin and aligned with the axes. Because the default camera is in the middle of the cube, we want to move the cube away from the camera by a translation. We obtain an isometric view when the camera is located symmetrically with respect to three adjacent faces of the cube; for example, anywhere along the line from the origin through the point (1, 1, 1). We can rotate the cube and then move it away from the camera to achieve the desired view or, equivalently, move the camera away from the cube and then rotate it to point at the cube.

Starting with the default camera, suppose that we are now looking at the cube from somewhere on the positive *z*-axis. We can obtain one of the eight isometric views—there is one for each vertex—by first rotating the cube about the *x*-axis until we see the two faces symmetrically, as shown in Figure 5.15(a). Clearly, we obtain this view by rotating the cube by 45 degrees. The second rotation is about the *y*-axis. We rotate the cube until we get the desired isometric. The required angle of rotation is −35.26 degrees about the *y*-axis. This second angle of rotation may not seem obvious. Consider what happens to the cube after the first rotation. From our position on the positive *z*-axis, the cube appears as shown in Figure 5.15(a). The original corner

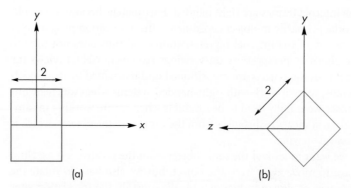

FIGURE 5.15 Cube after rotation about x-axis. (a) View from positive z-axis. (b) View from positive x-axis.

vertex at $(-1, 1, 1)$ has been transformed to $(-1, 0, \sqrt{2})$. If we look at the cube from the x-axis, as in Figure 5.15(b), we see that we want to rotate the right vertex to the y-axis. The right triangle that determines this angle has sides of 1 and $\sqrt{2}$, which correspond to an angle of 35.26 degrees. However, we need a clockwise rotation, so the angle must be negative. Finally, we move the camera away from the origin. Thus, our strategy is first to rotate the frame of the camera relative to the frame of the object and then to separate the two frames; the model-view matrix is of the form

$$\mathbf{M} = \mathbf{T}\mathbf{R}_x\mathbf{R}_y.$$

We obtain this model-view matrix for an isometric by multiplying the matrices in homogeneous coordinates. The concatenation of the rotation matrices yields

$$\mathbf{R} = \mathbf{R}_x\mathbf{R}_y = \begin{bmatrix} 1 & 0 & 0 & 0 \\ 0 & \sqrt{6}/3 & -\sqrt{3}/3 & 0 \\ 0 & \sqrt{3}/3 & \sqrt{6}/3 & 0 \\ 0 & 0 & 0 & 1 \end{bmatrix} \begin{bmatrix} \sqrt{2}/2 & 0 & \sqrt{2}/2 & 0 \\ 0 & 1 & 0 & 0 \\ -\sqrt{2}/2 & 0 & \sqrt{2}/2 & 0 \\ 0 & 0 & 0 & 1 \end{bmatrix}$$

$$= \begin{bmatrix} \sqrt{2}/2 & 0 & \sqrt{2}/2 & 0 \\ \sqrt{6}/6 & \sqrt{6}/3 & -\sqrt{6}/6 & 0 \\ -\sqrt{3}/3 & \sqrt{3}/3 & \sqrt{3}/3 & 0 \\ 0 & 0 & 0 & 1 \end{bmatrix}.$$

It is simple to verify that the original vertex $(-1, 1, 1)$ is correctly transformed to $(0, 0, \sqrt{3})$ by this matrix. If we concatenate in the translation by $(0, 0, -d)$, the matrix becomes

$$\mathbf{T}\mathbf{R} = \begin{bmatrix} \sqrt{2}/2 & 0 & \sqrt{2}/2 & 0 \\ \sqrt{6}/6 & \sqrt{6}/3 & -\sqrt{6}/6 & 0 \\ -\sqrt{3}/3 & \sqrt{3}/3 & \sqrt{3}/3 & -d \\ 0 & 0 & 0 & 1 \end{bmatrix}.$$

In WebGL, the code for setting the model-view matrix is as follows:

```
var modelViewMatrix = translate(0, 0, -d);
modelViewMatrix = mult(modelViewMatrix, rotateX(35.26));
modelViewMatrix = mult(modelViewMatrix, rotateY(45));
```

We have gone from a representation of our objects in object coordinates to one in camera coordinates. Rotation and translation do not affect the size of an object nor, equivalently, the size of its orthographic projection. However, these transformations can affect whether or not objects are clipped. Because the clipping volume is measured relative to the camera, if, for example, we translate the object away from the camera, it may no longer lie within the clipping volume. Hence, even though the projection of the object is unchanged and the camera still points at it, the object would not be in the image.

5.3.2 Two Viewing APIs

The construction of the model-view matrix for an isometric view is a little unsatisfying. Although the approach was intuitive, an interface that requires us to compute the individual angles before specifying the transformations is a poor one for an application program. We can take a different approach to positioning the camera—an approach that is similar to that used by PHIGS, one of the original standard APIs for three-dimensional graphics. Our starting point is again the object frame. We describe the camera's position and orientation in this frame. The precise type of image that we wish to obtain—perspective or parallel—is determined separately by the specification of the projection matrix. This second part of the viewing process is often called the **normalization transformation**. We approach this problem as one of a change in frames. Again, we think of the camera as positioned initially at the origin, pointed in the negative z direction. Its desired location is centered at a point called the **view reference point** (**VRP**; Figure 5.16), whose position is given in the object frame. The user executes a function such as

FIGURE 5.16   Camera frame.

```
var viewReferencePoint = vec4(x, y, z, 1);
```

to specify this position. Next, we want to specify the orientation of the camera. We can divide this specification into two parts: specification of the **view-plane normal** (**VPN**) and specification of the **view-up vector** (**VUP**). The VPN (**n** in Figure 5.16) gives the orientation of the projection plane or back of the camera. The orientation of a plane is determined by that plane's normal, and thus part of the API is a function such as

```
var viewPlaneNormal = vec4(nx, ny, nz, 0);
```

The orientation of the plane does not specify what direction is up from the camera's perspective. Given only the VPN, we can rotate the camera with its back in this plane. The specification of the VUP fixes the camera and is performed by a function such as

```
var viewUp = vec4(vupX, vupY, vupZ, 0);
```

FIGURE 5.17   Determination of
the view-up vector.

We project the VUP vector on the view plane to obtain the up direction vector **v** (Figure 5.17). Use of the projection allows the user to specify any vector not parallel to **v**, rather than being forced to compute a vector lying in the projection plane. The vector **v** is orthogonal to **n**. We can use the cross product to obtain a third orthogonal direction **u**. This new orthogonal coordinate system usually is referred to as either the **viewing-coordinate system** or the **u-v-n system**. With the addition of the VRP, we have the desired camera frame. The matrix that does the change of frames is the **view orientation matrix** and is equivalent to the viewing component of the model-view matrix.

We can derive this matrix using rotations and translations in homogeneous coordinates. We start with the specifications of the view reference point,

$$\mathbf{p} = \begin{bmatrix} x \\ y \\ z \\ 1 \end{bmatrix},$$

the view-plane normal,

$$\mathbf{n} = \begin{bmatrix} n_x \\ n_y \\ n_z \\ 0 \end{bmatrix},$$

and the view-up vector,

$$\mathbf{v_{up}} = \begin{bmatrix} v_{up_x} \\ v_{up_y} \\ v_{up_z} \\ 0 \end{bmatrix}.$$

We construct a new frame with the view reference point as its origin, the view-plane normal as one coordinate direction, and two other orthogonal directions that we call **u** and **v**. Our default is that the original x, y, z axes become u, v, n, respectively. The view reference point can be handled through a simple translation $\mathbf{T}(-x, -y, -z)$ from the viewing frame to the original origin. The rest of the model-view matrix is determined by a rotation so that the model-view matrix **V** is of the form

$$\mathbf{V} = \mathbf{TR}.$$

The direction **v** must be orthogonal to **n**; hence,

$$\mathbf{n} \cdot \mathbf{v} = 0.$$

Figure 5.16 shows that **v** is the projection of $\mathbf{v_{up}}$ into the plane formed by **n** and $\mathbf{v_{up}}$ and thus must be a linear combination of these two vectors,

$$\mathbf{v} = \alpha \mathbf{n} + \beta \mathbf{v_{up}}.$$

If we temporarily ignore the length of the vectors, then we can set $\beta = 1$ and solve for

$$\alpha = -\frac{\mathbf{v_{up}} \cdot \mathbf{n}}{\mathbf{n} \cdot \mathbf{n}}$$

and

$$\mathbf{v} = \mathbf{v_{up}} - \frac{\mathbf{v_{up}} \cdot \mathbf{n}}{\mathbf{n} \cdot \mathbf{n}} \mathbf{n}.$$

We can find the third orthogonal direction by taking the cross product

$$\mathbf{u} = \mathbf{v} \times \mathbf{n}.$$

These vectors do not generally have unit length. We can normalize each independently, obtaining three unit-length vectors $\mathbf{u}'$, $\mathbf{v}'$, and $\mathbf{n}'$. The matrix

$$\mathbf{A} = \begin{bmatrix} u'_x & v'_x & n'_x & 0 \\ u'_y & v'_y & n'_y & 0 \\ u'_z & v'_z & n'_z & 0 \\ 0 & 0 & 0 & 1 \end{bmatrix}$$

is a rotation matrix that orients a vector in the $\mathbf{u'v'n'}$ system with respect to the original system. However, we really want to go in the opposite direction to obtain the representation of vectors from the original system in the $\mathbf{u'v'n'}$ system. We want $\mathbf{A}^{-1}$, but because $\mathbf{A}$ is a rotation matrix, the desired matrix $\mathbf{R}$ is

$$\mathbf{R} = \mathbf{A}^{-1} = \mathbf{A}^T.$$

Finally, multiplying by the translation matrix $\mathbf{T}$, we have

$$\mathbf{V} = \mathbf{RT} = \begin{bmatrix} u'_x & u'_y & u'_z & -xu'_x - yu'_y - zu'_z \\ v'_x & v'_y & v'_z & -xv'_x - yv'_y - zv'_z \\ n'_x & n'_y & n'_z & -xn'_x - yn'_y - zn'_z \\ 0 & 0 & 0 & 1 \end{bmatrix}.$$

Note that, in this case, the translation matrix is on the right, whereas in our first derivation it was on the left. One way to interpret this difference is that in our first derivation, we first rotated one of the frames and then pushed the frames apart in a direction represented in the camera frame. In the second derivation, the camera position was specified in the object frame. Another way to understand this difference is to note that the matrices $\mathbf{RT}$ and $\mathbf{TR}$ have similar forms. The rotation parts of the product—the upper-left 3×3 submatrices—are identical, as are the bottom rows. The top three elements in the right column differ because the frame of the rotation affects the translation coefficients in $\mathbf{RT}$ and does not affect them in $\mathbf{TR}$. For our isometric example,

$$\mathbf{n} = \begin{bmatrix} -1 \\ 1 \\ 1 \\ 0 \end{bmatrix} \qquad \mathbf{v_{up}} = \begin{bmatrix} 0 \\ 1 \\ 0 \\ 0 \end{bmatrix}.$$

The camera position must be along a diagonal in the original frame. If we use

$$\mathbf{p} = \frac{\sqrt{3}}{3} \begin{bmatrix} -d \\ d \\ d \\ 1 \end{bmatrix},$$

we obtain the same model-view matrix that we derived in Section 5.3.1.

5.3.3 The Look-At Function

The use of the VRP, VPN, and VUP is but one way to provide an API for specifying the position of a camera. In many situations, a more direct method is appropriate. Consider the situation illustrated in Figure 5.18. Here a camera is located at a point **e** called the **eye point**, specified in the object frame, and it is pointed at a second point **a**, called the **at point**. These points determine a VPN and a VRP. The VPN is given by the vector formed by point subtraction between the eye point and the at point,

$$\mathbf{vpn} = \mathbf{a} - \mathbf{e},$$

and normalizing it,

$$\mathbf{n} = \frac{\mathbf{vpn}}{|\mathbf{vpn}|}.$$

The view reference point is the eye point. Hence, we need only add the desired up direction for the camera, and a function to construct the desired matrix `lookAt` could be of the form

```
m = lookAt(eye, at, up)
```

FIGURE 5.18   Look-at positioning.

where `eye`, `at`, and `up` are three-dimensional vector types. Note that once we have computed the vector **vpn**, we can proceed as we did with forming the transformation in the previous section. A slightly simpler computation would be to form a vector perpendicular to **n** and $\mathbf{v}_{up}$ by taking their cross product and normalizing it,

$$\mathbf{u} = \frac{\mathbf{v}_{up} \times \mathbf{n}}{|\mathbf{v}_{up} \times \mathbf{n}|}.$$

Finally, we get the normalized projection of the up vector onto the camera plane by taking a second cross product,

$$\mathbf{v} = \frac{\mathbf{n} \times \mathbf{u}}{|\mathbf{n} \times \mathbf{u}|}.$$

Note that we can use the standard rotations, translations, and scalings as part of defining our objects. Although these transformations will also alter the model-view matrix, it is often helpful conceptually to consider the use of `lookAt` as positioning the objects and subsequent operations that affect the model-view matrix as positioning the camera.

Note that whereas functions, such as `lookAt`, that position the camera alter the model-view matrix and are specified in object coordinates, functions that we introduce to form the projection matrix will be specified in eye coordinates.

5.3.4 Other Viewing APIs

In many applications, neither of the viewing interfaces that we have presented is appropriate. Consider a flight simulation application. The pilot using the simulator usually uses three angles—**roll**, **pitch**, and **yaw**—to specify her orientation. These angles are specified relative to the center of mass of the vehicle and to a coordinate system aligned along the axes of the vehicle, as shown in Figure 5.19. Hence, the pilot sees an object in terms of the three angles and in terms of the distance from the object to the center of mass of her vehicle. A viewing transformation can be constructed (Exercise 5.2) from these specifications using a translation and three simple rotations.

Viewing in many applications is most naturally specified in polar—rather than rectilinear—coordinates. Applications involving objects that rotate about other objects fit this category. For example, consider the specification of a star in the sky. Its

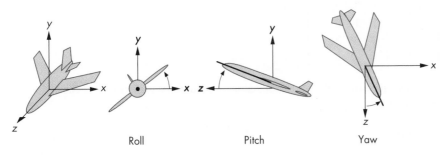

Roll   Pitch   Yaw

FIGURE 5.19 Roll, pitch, and yaw.

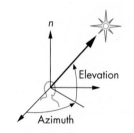

FIGURE 5.20 Elevation and azimuth.

direction from a viewer is given by its elevation and azimuth (Figure 5.20). The **elevation** is the angle above the plane of the viewer at which the star appears. By defining a normal at the point that the viewer is located and using this normal to define a plane, we define the elevation, regardless of whether or not the viewer is actually standing on a plane. We can form two other axes in this plane, creating a viewing-coordinate system. The **azimuth** is the angle measured from an axis in this plane to the projection onto the plane of the line between the viewer and the star. The camera can still be rotated by a **twist angle** about the direction it is pointed.

5.4 PARALLEL PROJECTIONS

A parallel projection is the limit of a perspective projection in which the center of projection is infinitely far from the objects being viewed, resulting in projectors that are parallel rather than converging at the center of projection. Equivalently, a parallel projection is what we would get if we had a telephoto lens with an infinite focal length. Rather than first deriving the equations for a perspective projection and computing their limiting behavior, we will derive the equations for parallel projections directly using the fact that we know in advance that the projectors are parallel and point in a direction of projection.

5.4.1 Orthogonal Projections

FIGURE 5.21 Orthogonal projection.

Orthogonal or **orthographic** projections are a special case of parallel projections, in which the projectors are perpendicular to the view plane. In terms of a camera, orthogonal projections correspond to a camera with a back plane parallel to the lens, which has an infinite focal length. Figure 5.21 shows an orthogonal projection with the projection plane $z = 0$. As points are projected into this plane, they retain their x and y values. The equations of projection are

$$x_p = x$$

$$y_p = y$$

$$z_p = 0.$$

We can write this result using our original homogeneous coordinates:

$$\begin{bmatrix} x_p \\ y_p \\ z_p \\ 1 \end{bmatrix} = \begin{bmatrix} 1 & 0 & 0 & 0 \\ 0 & 1 & 0 & 0 \\ 0 & 0 & 0 & 0 \\ 0 & 0 & 0 & 1 \end{bmatrix} \begin{bmatrix} x \\ y \\ z \\ 1 \end{bmatrix}.$$

To prepare ourselves for a more general orthogonal projection, we can write this expression as

$$\mathbf{q} = \mathbf{MIp},$$

where

$$\mathbf{p} = \begin{bmatrix} x \\ y \\ z \\ 1 \end{bmatrix},$$

I is a 4×4 identity matrix, and

$$\mathbf{M} = \begin{bmatrix} 1 & 0 & 0 & 0 \\ 0 & 1 & 0 & 0 \\ 0 & 0 & 0 & 0 \\ 0 & 0 & 0 & 1 \end{bmatrix}.$$

The projection described by **M** is carried out by the hardware after the vertex shader. Hence, only those objects inside the cube of side length 2 centered at the origin will be projected and possibly visible. If we want to change which objects are visible, we can replace the identity matrix by a transformation **N** that we can carry out either in the application or in the vertex shader, which will give us control over the clipping volume. For example, if we replace **I** with a scaling matrix, we can see more or fewer objects.

5.4.2 Parallel Viewing with WebGL

We will focus on a single orthogonal viewing function in which the view volume is a right parallelepiped, as shown in Figure 5.22. The sides of the clipping volume are the four planes

$x = right \qquad x = left$

$y = top \qquad y = bottom.$

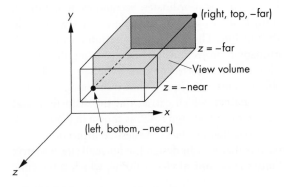

FIGURE 5.22 Orthographic viewing.

The near (front) clipping plane is located a distance `near` from the origin, and the far (back) clipping plane is at a distance `far` from the origin. All these values are in camera coordinates. We will derive a function

```
ortho = function(left, right, bottom, top, near, far) { ... }
```

that will form the projection matrix $\mathbf{N}$.

Although mathematically we get a parallel view by moving the camera to infinity, because the projectors are parallel, we can slide this camera in the direction of projection without changing the projection. Consequently, it is helpful to think of an orthogonal camera located initially at the origin in camera coordinates with the view volume determined by

$$x = \pm 1 \qquad y = \pm 1 \qquad z = \pm 1$$

as the default behavior. Equivalently, we are applying an identity projection matrix for $\mathbf{N}$. We will derive a nonidentity matrix $\mathbf{N}$ using translation and scaling that will transform vertices in camera coordinates to fit inside the default view volume, a process called **projection normalization.** This matrix is what will be produced by `ortho`. Note that we are forced to take this approach because the final projection carried out by the GPU is fixed. Nevertheless, the normalization process is efficient and will allow us to carry out parallel and perspective projections with the same pipeline.

5.4.3 Projection Normalization

When we introduced projection in Chapter 1 and looked at classical projection earlier in this chapter, we viewed it as a technique that took the specification of points in three dimensions and mapped them to points on a two-dimensional projection surface. Such a transformation is not invertible, because all points along a projector map into the same point on the projection surface.

In computer graphics systems, we adopt a slightly different approach. First, we work in four dimensions using homogeneous coordinates. Second, we retain depth information—distance along a projector—as long as possible so that we can do hidden-surface removal later in the pipeline. Third, we use projection normalization to convert all projections into orthogonal projections by first distorting the objects such that the orthogonal projection of the distorted objects is the same as the desired projection of the original objects. This technique is shown in Figure 5.23. The concatenation of the **normalization matrix**, which carries out the distortion, and the simple orthogonal projection matrix from Section 5.4.2, as shown in Figure 5.24, yields a homogeneous-coordinate matrix that produces the desired projection.

One advantage of this approach is that we can design the normalization matrix so that view volume is distorted into the **canonical view volume**, which is the cube defined by the planes

$$x = \pm 1 \qquad y = \pm 1 \qquad z = \pm 1.$$

FIGURE 5.23   Predistortion of objects. (a) Perspective view. (b) Orthographic projection of distorted object.

FIGURE 5.24   Normalization transformation.

Besides the advantage of having both perspective and parallel views supported by the same pipeline by loading in the proper normalization matrix, the canonical view volume simplifies the clipping process because the sides are aligned with the coordinate axes.

The normalization process defines what most systems call the **projection matrix**. The projection matrix brings objects into four-dimensional clip coordinates, and the subsequent perspective division converts vertices to a representation in three-dimensional normalized device coordinates. Values in normalized device coordinates are later mapped to window coordinates by the viewport transformation. Here we are concerned with the first step—deriving the projection matrix.

5.4.4 Orthogonal Projection Matrices

Although parallel viewing is a special case of perspective viewing, we start with orthogonal parallel viewing and later extend the normalization technique to perspective viewing.

In WebGL, the default projection matrix is the identity matrix, or equivalently, what we would get from the following code:

```
var N = ortho(-1.0, 1.0, -1.0, 1.0, -1.0, 1.0);
```

The view volume is in fact the canonical view volume. Points within the cube defined by the sides $x = \pm 1$, $y = \pm 1$, and $z = \pm 1$ are mapped to the same cube. Points outside this cube remain outside the cube. As trivial as this observation may seem, it indicates that we can get the desired projection matrix for the general orthogonal view by finding a matrix that maps the right parallelepiped specified by `ortho` to this same cube.

Before we do so, recall that the last two parameters in `ortho` are distances to the near and far planes measured from a camera at the origin pointed in the negative z direction. Thus, the near plane is at $z = 1.0$, which is behind the camera, and the far plane is at $z = -1.0$, which is in front of the camera. Although the projectors are parallel and an orthographic projection is conceptually similar to having a camera with a long telephoto lens located far from the objects, the importance of the near and far distances in `ortho` is that they determine which objects are clipped out.

Now suppose that, instead, we set the `ortho` parameters by the following function call:

```
var N = ortho(left, right, bottom, top, near, far);
```

We now have specified a right parallelepiped view volume whose right side (relative to the camera) is the plane $x = left$, whose left side is the plane $x = right$, whose top is the plane $y = top$, and whose bottom is the plane $y = bottom$. The front is the near clipping plane $z = -near$, and the back is the far clipping plane $z = -far$. The projection matrix that WebGL sets up is the matrix that transforms this volume to the cube centered at the origin with sides of length 2, which is shown in Figure 5.25. This matrix converts the vertices that specify our objects to vertices within this canonical view volume, by scaling and translating them. Consequently, vertices are transformed such that vertices within the specified view volume are transformed to vertices within the canonical view volume, and vertices outside the specified view volume are transformed to vertices outside the canonical view volume. Putting everything together, we see that the projection matrix is determined by the type of view and the view volume specified in `ortho`, and that these specifications are relative to the camera. The positioning and orientation of the camera are determined by the model-view matrix. These two matrices are concatenated together, and objects have their vertices transformed by this matrix product.

We can use our knowledge of affine transformations to find this projection matrix. There are two tasks that we need to perform. First, we must move the center of the specified view volume to the center of the canonical view volume (the origin) by doing a translation. Second, we must scale the sides of the specified view volume to

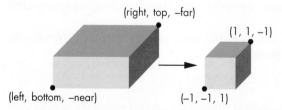

FIGURE 5.25   Mapping a view volume to the canonical view volume.

FIGURE 5.26   Affine transformations for normalization.

each have a length of 2 (see Figure 5.25). Hence, the two transformations are

$$\mathbf{T} = \mathbf{T}(-(right + left)/2, -(top + bottom)/2, (far + near)/2)$$

and

$$\mathbf{S} = \mathbf{S}(2/(right - left), 2/(top - bottom), 2/(near - far)),$$

and they can be concatenated together (Figure 5.26) to form the projection matrix

$$\mathbf{N} = \mathbf{ST} = \begin{bmatrix} \frac{2}{right-left} & 0 & 0 & -\frac{left+right}{right-left} \\ 0 & \frac{2}{top-bottom} & 0 & -\frac{top+bottom}{top-bottom} \\ 0 & 0 & -\frac{2}{far-near} & -\frac{far+near}{far-near} \\ 0 & 0 & 0 & 1 \end{bmatrix}.$$

This matrix maps the near clipping plane, $z = -near$, to the plane $z = -1$ and the far clipping plane, $z = -far$, to the plane $z = 1$. Because the camera is pointing in the negative z direction, the projectors are directed from infinity on the negative z-axis toward the origin.

5.4.5 Oblique Projections

Using `ortho`, we have only a limited class of parallel projections; namely, only those for which the projectors are orthogonal to the projection plane. As we saw earlier in this chapter, oblique parallel projections are useful in many fields.[3] We could develop an oblique projection matrix directly; instead, however, we follow the process that we used for the general orthogonal projection. We convert the desired projection to a canonical orthogonal projection of distorted objects.

An oblique projection can be characterized by the angle that the projectors make with the projection plane, as shown in Figure 5.27. In APIs that support general parallel viewing, the view volume for an oblique projection has the near and far clipping planes parallel to the view plane, and the right, left, top, and bottom planes parallel to the direction of projection, as shown in Figure 5.28. We can derive the equations for oblique projections by considering the top and side views in Figure 5.29, which shows a projector and the projection plane $z = 0$. The angles θ and ϕ characterize the

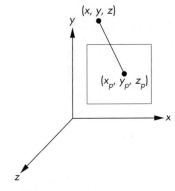

FIGURE 5.27   Oblique projection.

---

3. Note that without oblique projections we cannot draw coordinate axes in the way that we have been doing in this book (see Exercise 5.15).

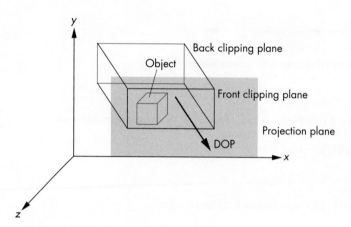

FIGURE 5.28   Oblique clipping volume.

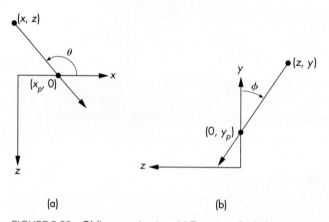

(a)   (b)

FIGURE 5.29   Oblique projection. (a) Top view. (b) Side view.

degree of obliqueness. In drafting, projections such as the cavalier and cabinet projections are determined by specific values of these angles. However, these angles are not the only possible interface (see Exercises 5.9 and 5.10).

If we consider the top view, we can find x_p by noting that

$$\tan \theta = \frac{z}{x_p - x},$$

and thus

$$x_p = x + z \cot \theta.$$

Likewise,

$$y_p = y + z \cot \phi.$$

Using the equation for the projection plane

$$z_p = 0,$$

we can write these results in terms of a homogeneous-coordinate matrix

$$\mathbf{P} = \begin{bmatrix} 1 & 0 & \cot\theta & 0 \\ 0 & 1 & \cot\phi & 0 \\ 0 & 0 & 0 & 0 \\ 0 & 0 & 0 & 1 \end{bmatrix}.$$

Following our strategy of the previous example, we can break $\mathbf{P}$ into the product

$$\mathbf{P} = \mathbf{M}_{orth}\mathbf{H}(\theta, \phi) = \begin{bmatrix} 1 & 0 & 0 & 0 \\ 0 & 1 & 0 & 0 \\ 0 & 0 & 0 & 0 \\ 0 & 0 & 0 & 1 \end{bmatrix} \begin{bmatrix} 1 & 0 & \cot\theta & 0 \\ 0 & 1 & \cot\phi & 0 \\ 0 & 0 & 1 & 0 \\ 0 & 0 & 0 & 1 \end{bmatrix},$$

where $\mathbf{H}(\theta, \phi)$ is a shearing matrix. Thus, we can implement an oblique projection by first doing a shear of the objects by $\mathbf{H}(\theta, \phi)$ and then doing an orthographic projection. Figure 5.30 shows the effect of $\mathbf{H}(\theta, \phi)$ on a cube inside an oblique view volume. The sides of the clipping volume become orthogonal to the view plane, but the sides of the cube become oblique as they are affected by the same shear transformation. However, the orthographic projection of the distorted cube is identical to the oblique projection of the undistorted cube.

We are not finished, because the view volume created by the shear is not our canonical view volume. We have to apply the same scaling and translation matrices

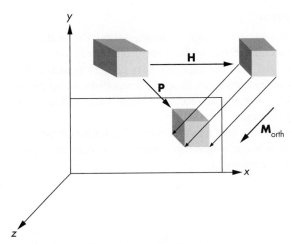

FIGURE 5.30 Effect of shear transformation.

that we used in Section 5.4.4. Hence, the transformation

$$\mathbf{ST} = \begin{bmatrix} \frac{2}{right-left} & 0 & 0 & -\frac{right+left}{right-left} \\ 0 & \frac{2}{top-bottom} & 0 & -\frac{top+bottom}{top-bottom} \\ 0 & 0 & -\frac{2}{far-near} & -\frac{far+near}{near-far} \\ 0 & 0 & 0 & 1 \end{bmatrix}$$

must be inserted after the shear and before the final orthographic projection, so the final matrix is

$$\mathbf{N} = \mathbf{M}_{\text{orth}}\mathbf{ST}\,\mathbf{H}.$$

The values of *left*, *right*, *bottom*, and *top* are the vertices of the right parallelepiped view volume created by the shear. These values depend on how the sides of the original view volume are communicated through the application program; they may have to be determined from the results of the shear to the corners of the original view volume. One way to do this calculation is shown in Figure 5.29.

The specification for an oblique projection can be through the angles θ and ψ that projectors make with the projection plane. The parameters *near* and *far* are not changed by the shear. However, the x and y values where the sides of the view volume intersect the near plane are changed by the shear and become *left*, *right*, *top*, and *bottom*. If these points of intersection are $(x_{\min}, near)$, $(x_{\max}, near)$, $(y_{\min}, near)$, and $(y_{\max}, near)$, then our derivation of shear in Chapter 4 yields the relationships

$$left = x_{\min} - near * \cot\theta$$

$$right = x_{\max} - near * \cot\theta$$

$$top = y_{\max} - near * \cot\phi$$

$$bottom = y_{\min} - near * \cot\phi.$$

5.4.6 An Interactive Viewer

In this section, we extend the rotating cube program to include both the model-view matrix and an orthogonal projection matrix whose parameters can be set interactively. As in our previous examples with the cube, we have choices as to where to apply our transformations. In this example, we will send the model-view and projection matrices to the vertex shader. For an interface, we will use a set of slide bars to change parameters to alter both matrices.

The colored cube is centered at the origin in object coordinates, so wherever we place the camera, the at point is at the origin. Let's position the camera in polar coordinates so the eye point has coordinates

$$\mathbf{eye} = \begin{bmatrix} r\cos\theta \\ r\sin\theta\cos\phi \\ r\sin\theta\sin\phi \end{bmatrix},$$

where the radius r is the distance from the origin. We can let the up direction be the y direction in object coordinates. These values specify a model-view matrix through the `lookAt` function. In this example, we will send both a model-view and a projection matrix to the vertex shader with the render function

```
function render()
{
  gl.clear(gl.COLOR_BUFFER_BIT | gl.DEPTH_BUFFER_BIT);

  eye = vec3(radius * Math.sin(theta) * Math.cos(phi),
             radius * Math.sin(theta) * Math.sin(phi),
             radius * Math.cos(theta));
  modelViewMatrix = lookAt(eye, at, up);

  projectionMatrix = ortho(left, right, bottom, ytop, near, far);
  gl.uniformMatrix4fv(modelViewMatrixLoc, false,
                      flatten(modelViewMatrix));
  gl.uniformMatrix4fv(projectionMatrixLoc, false,
                      flatten(projectionMatrix));

  gl.drawArrays(gl.TRIANGLES, 0, numVertices);
  requestAnimFrame(render);
}
```

where up and `at` and other fixed values are set as part of the initialization

```
const at = vec3(0.0, 0.0, 0.0);
const up = vec3(0.0, 1.0, 0.0);
```

Note that we use the name `ytop` instead of `top` to avoid a naming conflict with the window object member names. The corresponding vertex shader is

```
attribute  vec4 vPosition;
attribute  vec4 vColor;
varying    vec4 fcolor;

uniform mat4 modelViewMatrix;
uniform mat4 projectionMatrix;

void main()
{
  fcolor = vColor;
  gl_Position = projectionMatrix * modelViewMatrix * vPosition;
}
```

and the fragment shader is

```
varying vec4 color;

void main()
{
  gl_FragColor = fcolor;
}
```

The sliders are specified in the HTML file. For example, to control the near and far distances we can use

```
<div>
  depth .05
  <input id="depthSlider" type="range"
    min=".05" max="3" step="0.1" value ="2" />
  3
</div>
```

and the corresponding event handler in the JavaScript file:

```
document.getElementById("depthSlider").onchange = function() {
  far = event.srcElement.value/2;
  near = -event.srcElement.value/2;
};
```

Note that as we move the camera around, the size of the image of the cube does not change, which is a consequence of using an orthogonal projection. However, depending on the radius and the near and far distances, some or even all of the cube can be clipped out. This behavior is a consequence of the parameters in `ortho` being measured relative to the camera. Hence, if we move the camera back by increasing the radius, the back of the cube will be clipped out first. Eventually, as the radius becomes larger, the entire cube will be clipped out. In a similar manner, if we reduce the near and far distance, we can make the cube disappear from the display.

Now consider what happens as we change the parameters in `ortho`. As we increase `right` and `left`, the cube elongates in the x direction. A similar phenomenon occurs when we increase `bottom` and `ytop` in the y direction. Although this distortion of the cube's image may be annoying, it is a consequence of using an x–y rectangle in `ortho` that is not square. This rectangle is mapped to the full viewport, which has been unchanged. We can alter the program so that we increase or decrease all of `left`, `right`, `bottom`, and `top` simultaneously, or we can alter the viewport as part of any change to `ortho` (see Exercise 5.28). Two examples are on the website for interactive viewing of the colored cube; `ortho` uses buttons to alter the view, whereas `ortho2` uses slide bars.

5.5 PERSPECTIVE PROJECTIONS

We now turn to perspective projections, which are what we get with a camera whose lens has a finite focal length or, in terms of our synthetic-camera model, when the center of projection is finite.

As with parallel projections, we will separate perspective viewing into two parts: the positioning of the camera and the projection. Positioning will be done the same way, and we can use the `lookAt` function. The projection part is equivalent to selecting a lens for the camera. As we saw in Chapter 1, it is the combination of the lens and the size of the film (or the back of the camera) that determines how much of the world in front of a camera appears in the image. In computer graphics, we

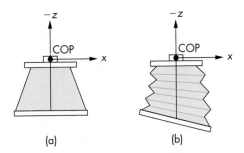

FIGURE 5.31 Two cameras. (a) Back parallel to front. (b) Back not parallel to front.

make an equivalent choice when we select the type of projection and the viewing parameters.

With a physical camera, a wide-angle lens gives the most dramatic perspectives, with objects near the camera appearing large compared to objects far from the lens. A telephoto lens gives an image that appears flat and is close to a parallel view.

First, we consider the mathematics for a simple projection. We can extend our use of homogeneous coordinates to the projection process, which allows us to characterize a particular projection with a 4×4 matrix.

5.5.1 Simple Perspective Projections

Suppose that we are in the camera frame with the camera located at the origin, pointed in the negative z direction. Figure 5.31 shows two possibilities. In Figure 5.31(a), the back of the camera is orthogonal to the z direction and is parallel to the lens. This configuration corresponds to most physical situations, including those of the human visual system and of simple cameras. The situation shown in Figure 5.31(b) is more general: the back of the camera can have any orientation with respect to the front. We consider the first case in detail because it is simpler. However, the derivation of the general result follows the same steps and should be a direct exercise (Exercise 5.6).

As we saw in Chapter 1, we can place the projection plane in front of the center of projection. If we do so for the configuration of Figure 5.31(a), we get the views shown in Figure 5.32. A point in space (x, y, z) is projected along a projector into the point (x_p, y_p, z_p). All projectors pass through the origin, and, because the projection plane is perpendicular to the z-axis,

$$z_p = d.$$

Because the camera is pointing in the negative z direction, the projection plane is in the negative half-space $z < 0$, and the value of d is negative.

From the top view shown in Figure 5.32(b), we see two similar triangles whose tangents must be the same. Hence,

$$\frac{x}{z} = \frac{x_p}{d},$$

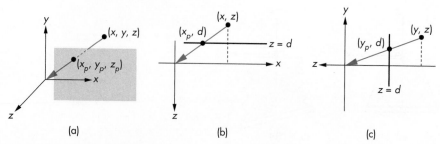

FIGURE 5.32   Three views of perspective projection. (a) Three-dimensional view. (b) Top view. (c) Side view.

and

$$x_p = \frac{x}{z/d}.$$

Using the side view shown in Figure 5.32(c), we obtain a similar result for y_p:

$$y_p = \frac{y}{z/d}.$$

These equations are nonlinear. The division by z describes **nonuniform foreshortening**: The images of objects farther from the center of projection are reduced in size (diminution) compared to the images of objects closer to the COP.

We can look at the projection process as a transformation that takes points (x, y, z) to other points (x_p, y_p, z_p). Although this **perspective transformation** preserves lines, it is not affine. It is also irreversible. Because all points along a projector project into the same point, we cannot recover a point from its projection. In Sections 5.7 and 5.8, we will develop an invertible variant of the projection transformation that preserves relative distances that are needed for hidden-surface removal.

We can extend our use of homogeneous coordinates to handle projections. When we introduced homogeneous coordinates, we represented a point in three dimensions (x, y, z) by the point $(x, y, z, 1)$ in four dimensions. Suppose that, instead, we replace (x, y, z) by the four-dimensional point

$$\mathbf{p} = \begin{bmatrix} wx \\ wy \\ wz \\ w \end{bmatrix}.$$

As long as $w \neq 0$, we can recover the three-dimensional point from its four-dimensional representation by dividing the first three components by w. In this new homogeneous-coordinate form, points in three dimensions become lines through the origin in four dimensions. Transformations are again represented by 4×4 matrices, but now the final row of the matrix can be altered—and thus w can be changed by such a transformation.

Obviously, we would prefer to keep $w = 1$ to avoid the divisions otherwise necessary to recover the three-dimensional point. However, by allowing w to change, we can represent a larger class of transformations, including perspective projections. Consider the matrix

$$\mathbf{M} = \begin{bmatrix} 1 & 0 & 0 & 0 \\ 0 & 1 & 0 & 0 \\ 0 & 0 & 1 & 0 \\ 0 & 0 & 1/d & 0 \end{bmatrix}.$$

The matrix $\mathbf{M}$ transforms the point

$$\mathbf{p} = \begin{bmatrix} x \\ y \\ z \\ 1 \end{bmatrix}$$

to the point

$$\mathbf{q} = \begin{bmatrix} x \\ y \\ z \\ z/d \end{bmatrix}.$$

At first glance, $\mathbf{q}$ may not seem sensible; however, when we remember that we have to divide the first three components by the fourth to return to our original three-dimensional space, we obtain the results

$$x_p = \frac{x}{z/d}$$

$$y_p = \frac{y}{z/d}$$

$$z_p = \frac{z}{z/d} = d,$$

which are the equations for a simple perspective projection. In homogeneous coordinates, dividing $\mathbf{q}$ by its w component replaces $\mathbf{q}$ by the equivalent point

$$\mathbf{q}' = \begin{bmatrix} \frac{x}{z/d} \\ \frac{y}{z/d} \\ d \\ 1 \end{bmatrix} = \begin{bmatrix} x_p \\ y_p \\ z_p \\ 1 \end{bmatrix}.$$

We have shown that we can do at least a simple perspective projection, by defining a 4×4 projection matrix that we apply after the model-view matrix. However, we must perform a **perspective division** at the end. This division can be made a part of the pipeline, as shown in Figure 5.33.

FIGURE 5.33   Projection pipeline.

5.6   PERSPECTIVE PROJECTIONS WITH WEBGL

The projections that we developed in Section 5.5 did not take into account the properties of the camera: the focal length of its lens or the size of the film plane. Figure 5.34 shows the angle of view for a simple pinhole camera, like the one that we discussed in Chapter 1. Only those objects that fit within the angle (or field) of view of the camera appear in the image. If the back of the camera is rectangular, only objects within an infinite pyramid—the **view volume**—whose apex is at the COP can appear in the image. Objects not within the view volume are said to be **clipped** out of the scene. Hence, our description of simple projections has been incomplete; we did not include the effects of clipping.

With most graphics APIs, the application program specifies clipping parameters through the specification of a projection. The infinite pyramid in Figure 5.34 becomes a finite clipping volume by adding front and back clipping planes, in addition to the angle of view, as shown in Figure 5.35. The resulting view volume is a **frustum**—a truncated pyramid. We have fixed only one parameter by specifying that the COP is at the origin in the camera frame. In principle, we should be able to specify each of the six sides of the frustum to have almost any orientation. If we did so, however, we would make it difficult to specify a view in the application and complicate the implementation. In practice, we rarely need this flexibility, and usually we can get by with only two perspective viewing functions. Other APIs differ in their function calls but incorporate similar restrictions.

FIGURE 5.34   Specification of a view volume.

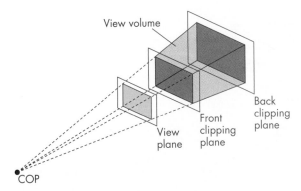

FIGURE 5.35 Front and back clipping planes.

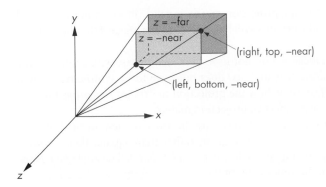

FIGURE 5.36 Specification of a frustum.

5.6.1 Perspective Functions

We will develop two functions for specifying perspective views and one for specifying parallel views. Alternatively, we can form the projection matrix directly, either by loading it or by applying rotations, translations, and scalings to an initial identity matrix. We can specify a perspective camera view by the function

```
frustum = function(left, right, bottom, top, near, far)
```

whose parameters are similar to those in `ortho`. These parameters are shown in Figure 5.36 in the camera frame. The near and far distances are measured from the COP (the origin in eye coordinates) to the front and back clipping planes, both of which are parallel to the plane $z = 0$. Because the camera is pointing in the negative z direction, the front (near) clipping plane is the plane $z = -near$ and the back (far) clipping plane is the plane $z = -far$. The left, right, top, and bottom values are measured in the near (front clipping) plane. The plane $x = left$ is to the left of the camera as viewed from the COP in the direction the camera is pointing. Similar statements hold for `right`, `bottom`, and `top`. Although in virtually all applications $far > near > 0$, as

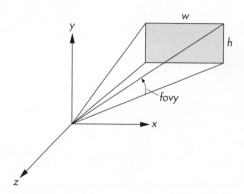

FIGURE 5.37   Specification using the field of view.

long as *near* $\neq$ *far*, the resulting projection matrix is valid, although objects behind the center of projection—the origin—will be inverted in the image if they lie between the near and far planes.

Note that these specifications do not have to be symmetric with respect to the z-axis and that the resulting frustum also does not have to be symmetric (a right frustum). In Section 5.7, we show how the projection matrix for this projection can be derived from the simple perspective projection matrix.

In many applications, it is natural to specify the angle of view, or field of view. However, if the projection plane is rectangular, rather than square, then we see a different angle of view in the top and side views (Figure 5.37). The angle *fovy* is the angle between the top and bottom planes of the clipping volume. The function

```
perspective = function(fovy, aspect, near, far)
```

allows us to specify the angle of view in the up (y) direction, as well as the aspect ratio—width divided by height—of the projection plane. The near and far planes are specified as in `frustum`.

5.7   PERSPECTIVE PROJECTION MATRICES

For perspective projections, we follow a path similar to the one that we used for parallel projections: We find a transformation that allows us, by distorting the vertices of our objects, to do a simple canonical projection to obtain the desired image. Our first step is to decide what this canonical viewing volume should be. We then introduce a new transformation, the **perspective normalization transformation**, that converts a perspective projection to an orthogonal projection. Finally, we derive the perspective projection matrix that we will use in WebGL.

5.7.1   Perspective Normalization

In Section 5.5, we introduced a simple perspective projection matrix. For the projection plane at $z = -1$ and the center of the projection at the origin, the projection

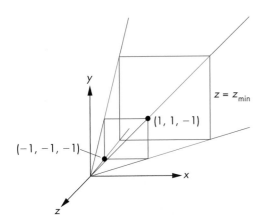

FIGURE 5.38   Simple perspective projection.

matrix is

$$\mathbf{M} = \begin{bmatrix} 1 & 0 & 0 & 0 \\ 0 & 1 & 0 & 0 \\ 0 & 0 & 1 & 0 \\ 0 & 0 & -1 & 0 \end{bmatrix}.$$

To form an image, we also need to specify a clipping volume. Suppose that we fix the angle of view at 90 degrees by making the sides of the viewing volume intersect the projection plane at a 45-degree angle. Equivalently, the view volume is the infinite view pyramid formed by the planes

$$x = \pm z,$$

$$y = \pm z,$$

shown in Figure 5.38. We can make the volume finite by specifying the near plane to be $z = -near$ and the far plane to be $z = -far$, where both *near* and *far*, the distances from the center of projection to the near and far planes, satisfy

$$0 < near < far.$$

Consider the matrix

$$\mathbf{N} = \begin{bmatrix} 1 & 0 & 0 & 0 \\ 0 & 1 & 0 & 0 \\ 0 & 0 & \alpha & \beta \\ 0 & 0 & -1 & 0 \end{bmatrix},$$

which is similar in form to $\mathbf{M}$ but is nonsingular. For now, we leave α and β unspecified (but nonzero). If we apply $\mathbf{N}$ to the homogeneous-coordinate point $\mathbf{p} = [\, x \quad y \quad z \quad 1\,]^T$, we obtain the new point $\mathbf{q} = [\, x' \quad y' \quad z' \quad w'\,]^T$, where

$$x' = x$$

$$y' = y$$

$$z' = \alpha z + \beta$$

$$w' = -z.$$

After dividing by w', we have the three-dimensional point

$$x'' = -\frac{x}{z}$$

$$y'' = -\frac{y}{z}$$

$$z'' = -\left(\alpha + \frac{\beta}{z}\right).$$

If we apply an orthographic projection along the z-axis to $\mathbf{N}$, we obtain the matrix

$$\mathbf{M}_{\text{orth}}\mathbf{N} = \begin{bmatrix} 1 & 0 & 0 & 0 \\ 0 & 1 & 0 & 0 \\ 0 & 0 & 0 & 0 \\ 0 & 0 & -1 & 0 \end{bmatrix},$$

which is a simple perspective projection matrix, and the projection of the arbitrary point $\mathbf{p}$ is

$$\mathbf{p}' = \mathbf{M}_{\text{orth}}\mathbf{N}\mathbf{p} = \begin{bmatrix} x \\ y \\ 0 \\ -z \end{bmatrix}.$$

After we do the perspective division, we obtain the desired values for x_p and y_p:

$$x_p = -\frac{x}{z}$$

$$y_p = -\frac{y}{z}.$$

We have shown that we can apply a transformation $\mathbf{N}$ to points, and after an orthogonal projection, we obtain the same result as we would have for a perspective projection. This process is similar to how we converted oblique projections to orthogonal projections by first shearing the objects.

The matrix $\mathbf{N}$ is nonsingular and transforms the original viewing volume into a new volume. We choose α and β such that the new volume is the canonical clipping volume. Consider the sides

$$x = \pm z.$$

They are transformed by $x'' = -x/z$ to the planes

$x'' = \pm 1$.

Likewise, the sides $y = \pm z$ are transformed to

$y'' = \pm 1$.

The front clipping plane $z = -near$ is transformed to the plane

$$z'' = -\left(\alpha - \frac{\beta}{near}\right).$$

Finally, the far plane $z = -far$ is transformed to the plane

$$z'' = -\left(\alpha - \frac{\beta}{far}\right).$$

We obtain two equations in two unknowns by requiring that we map the plane $z = -near$ to the plane $z'' = -1$ and the plane $z = -far$ to the plane $z'' = 1$. These requirements yield

$$\alpha = -\frac{near + far}{near - far}$$

$$\beta = -\frac{2 * near * far}{near - far},$$

and we have our desired canonical clipping volume. Figure 5.39 shows this transformation and the distortion to a cube within the volume. Thus, **N** has transformed the viewing frustum to a right parallelepiped, and an orthographic projection in the transformed volume yields the same image as does the perspective projection. The matrix **N** is called the **perspective normalization matrix**. The mapping

$$z'' = -\left(\alpha + \frac{\beta}{z}\right)$$

is nonlinear but preserves the ordering of depths. Thus, if z_1 and z_2 are the depths of two points within the original viewing volume and

$z_1 > z_2,$

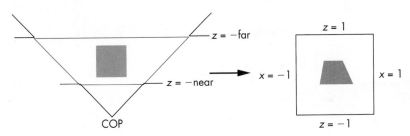

FIGURE 5.39 Perspective normalization of view volume.

then the transformed values satisfy

$$z_1'' > z_2''.$$

Consequently, hidden-surface removal works in the normalized volume, although the nonlinearity of the transformation can cause numerical problems because the depth buffer usually has a limited depth resolution. Note that although the original projection plane we placed at $z = -1$ has been transformed by $\mathbf{N}$ to the plane $z'' = \beta - \alpha$, there is little consequence to this result because we follow $\mathbf{N}$ by an orthographic projection.

Although we have shown that both perspective and parallel transformations can be converted to orthographic transformations, the benefits of this conversion are greatest in implementation. As long as we can put a carefully chosen projection matrix in the pipeline before the vertices are defined, we need only one viewing pipeline for all possible views. In Chapter 8, where we discuss implementation in detail, we will see how converting all view volumes to right parallelepipeds by our normalization process simplifies both clipping and hidden-surface removal.

5.7.2 WebGL Perspective Transformations

The function `frustum` does not restrict the view volume to a symmetric (or right) frustum. The parameters are as shown in Figure 5.40. We can form the perspective matrix by first converting this frustum to the symmetric frustum with 45-degree sides (see Figure 5.39). The process is similar to the conversion of an oblique parallel view to an orthogonal view. First, we do a shear to convert the asymmetric frustum to a symmetric one. Figure 5.40 shows the desired transformation. The shear angle is determined as in Section 4.9 by our desire to skew (shear) the point $((\textit{left} + \textit{right})/2, (\textit{top} + \textit{bottom})/2, -\textit{near})$ to $(0, 0, -\textit{near})$. The required shear matrix is

$$\mathbf{H}(\theta, \phi) = \mathbf{H}\left(\cot^{-1}\left(\frac{\textit{left} + \textit{right}}{-2 * \textit{near}}\right), \cot^{-1}\left(\frac{\textit{top} + \textit{bottom}}{-2 * \textit{near}}\right)\right).$$

The resulting frustum is described by the planes

FIGURE 5.40 WebGL perspective.

$$x = \pm \frac{right - left}{-2 * near}$$

$$y = \pm \frac{top - bottom}{-2 * near}$$

$$z = -near$$

$$z = -far.$$

The next step is to scale the sides of this frustum to

$$x = \pm z$$

$$y = \pm z,$$

without changing either the near plane or the far plane. The required scaling matrix is $\mathbf{S}(-2 * near/(right - left), -2 * near/(top - bottom), 1)$. Note that this transformation is determined uniquely without reference to the location of the far plane $z = -far$ because, in three dimensions, an affine transformation is determined by the results of the transformation on four points. In this case, these points are the four vertices where the sides of the frustum intersect the near plane.

To get the far plane to the plane $z = -1$ and the near plane to $z = 1$ after applying a projection normalization, we use the projection normalization matrix

$$\mathbf{N} = \begin{bmatrix} 1 & 0 & 0 & 0 \\ 0 & 1 & 0 & 0 \\ 0 & 0 & \alpha & \beta \\ 0 & 0 & -1 & 0 \end{bmatrix},$$

with α and β as in Section 5.7.1. The resulting projection matrix is in terms of the near and far distances,

$$\mathbf{P} = \mathbf{NSH} = \begin{bmatrix} \frac{2*near}{right-left} & 0 & \frac{right+left}{right-left} & 0 \\ 0 & \frac{2*near}{top-bottom} & \frac{top+bottom}{top-bottom} & 0 \\ 0 & 0 & -\frac{far+near}{far-near} & \frac{-2*far*near}{far-near} \\ 0 & 0 & -1 & 0 \end{bmatrix}.$$

We obtain the projection matrix corresponding to `perpsective(fovy, aspect, near, far)` by using symmetry in $\mathbf{P}$,

$$left = -right$$

$$bottom = -top,$$

and simple trigonometry to determine

$$top = near * \tan(fovy)$$

$$right = top * aspect,$$

simplifying **P** to

$$\mathbf{P} = \mathbf{NSH} = \begin{bmatrix} \frac{near}{right} & 0 & 0 & 0 \\ 0 & \frac{near}{top} & 0 & 0 \\ 0 & 0 & \frac{-(far+near)}{far-near} & \frac{-2*far*near}{far-near} \\ 0 & 0 & -1 & 0 \end{bmatrix}.$$

5.7.3 Perspective Example

We have to make almost no changes to our previous example to move from an orthogonal projection to a perspective projection. We can substitute `frustum` for `ortho` and the parameters are the same. However, for a perspective view we should have

$far > near > 0.$

Note that if we want to see the foreshortening we associate with perspective views, we can either move the cube off the z-axis or add additional cubes to the right or left. An example using buttons to vary the viewing parameters is on the website (`perspective1`), as is one using sliders (`perspective2`).

5.8   HIDDEN-SURFACE REMOVAL

Before introducing a few additional examples and extensions of viewing, we need to deepen our understanding of the hidden-surface-removal process. Let's start with the cube we have been using in our examples. When we look at a cube that has opaque sides, depending on its orientation, we see only one, two, or three front-facing sides. From the perspective of our basic viewing model, we can say that we see only these faces because they block the projectors from reaching any other surfaces.

From the perspective of computer graphics, however, all six faces of the cube have been specified and travel down the graphics pipeline; thus, the graphics system must be careful about which surfaces it displays. Conceptually, we seek algorithms that either remove those surfaces that should not be visible to the viewer, called **hidden-surface-removal algorithms**, or find which surfaces are visible, called **visible-surface algorithms**. There are many approaches to the problem, several of which we investigate in Chapter 8. WebGL has a particular algorithm associated with it, the **z-buffer algorithm**, to which we can interface through three function calls. Hence, we introduce that algorithm here, and we return to the topic in Chapter 8.

Hidden-surface-removal algorithms can be divided into two broad classes. **Object-space algorithms** attempt to order the surfaces of the objects in the scene such that rendering surfaces in a particular order provides the correct image. For example, for our cube, if we were to render the back-facing surfaces first, we could "paint" over them with the front surfaces and produce the correct image. This class of algorithms does not work well with pipeline architectures in which objects are passed down the pipeline in an arbitrary order. In order to decide on a proper order in which

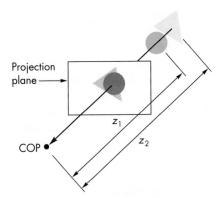

FIGURE 5.41   The z-buffer algorithm.

to render the objects, the graphics system must have all the objects available so it can sort them into the desired back-to-front order.

Image-space algorithms work as part of the projection process and seek to determine the relationship among object points on each projector. The z-buffer algorithm is of the latter type and fits in well with the rendering pipeline in most graphics systems because we can save partial information as each object is rendered.

The basic idea of the z-buffer algorithm is shown in Figure 5.41. A projector from the COP passes through two surfaces. Because the circle is closer to the viewer than to the triangle, it is the circle's color that determines the color placed in the color buffer at the location corresponding to where the projector pierces the projection plane. The difficulty is determining how we can make this idea work regardless of the order in which the triangle and the circle pass through the pipeline.

Let's assume that all the objects are polygons. If, as the polygons are rasterized, we can keep track of the distance from the COP or the projection plane to the closest point on each projector that has already been rendered, then we can update this information as successive polygons are projected and filled. Ultimately, we display only the closest point on each projector. The algorithm requires a **depth buffer**, or **z-buffer**, to store the necessary depth information as polygons are rasterized. Because we must keep depth information for each pixel in the color buffer, the z-buffer has the same spatial resolution as the color buffers. Its depth resolution is usually 32 bits with recent graphics cards that store this information as floating-point numbers. The z-buffer is one of the buffers that constitute the framebuffer and is usually part of the memory on the graphics card.

The depth buffer is initialized to a value that corresponds to the farthest distance from the viewer. When each polygon inside the clipping volume is rasterized, the depth of each fragment—how far the corresponding point on the polygon is from the viewer—is calculated. If this depth is greater than the value at that fragment's location in the depth buffer, then a polygon that has already been rasterized is closer to the viewer along the projector corresponding to the fragment. Hence, for this fragment we ignore the color of the polygon and go on to the next fragment for this polygon, where we make the same test. If, however, the depth is less than what is already in the

z-buffer, then along this projector the polygon being rendered is closer than any we have seen so far. Thus, we use the color of the polygon to replace the color of the pixel in the color buffer and update the depth in the z-buffer.[4]

For the example shown in Figure 5.41, we see that if the triangle passes through the pipeline first, its colors and depths will be placed in the color and z-buffers. When the circle passes through the pipeline, its colors and depths will replace the colors and depths of the triangle where they overlap. If the circle is rendered first, its colors and depths will be placed in the buffers. When the triangle is rendered, in the areas where there is overlap with the circle, the depth of the triangle is greater than the depth of the circle, so at the corresponding pixels no changes will be made to the color or depth buffers.

Major advantages of this algorithm are that its complexity is proportional to the number of fragments generated by the rasterizer and that it can be implemented with a small number of additional calculations over what we have to do to project and display polygons without hidden-surface removal. We will return to this issue in Chapter 8.

A depth buffer is part of the framebuffer. Consequently, the application programmer need only enable hidden-surface removal by using

```
gl.enable(gl.DEPTH_TEST);
```

and clear it, usually at the same time as the color buffer

```
g.clear(gl.COLOR_BUFFER_BIT | gl.DEPTH_BUFFER_BIT);
```

5.8.1 Culling

For a convex object, such as the cube, faces whose normals point away from the viewer are never visible and can be eliminated or culled before the rasterizer. We can turn on culling in WebGL by enabling it as follows:

```
gl.enable(gl.CULL_FACE);
```

We can select which faces we want to cull using the function

```
gl.cullFace(face);
```

where `face` is either `gl.BACK` or `gl.FRONT`. The default is to cull back faces. However, back face culling is guaranteed to produce a correct image only if we have a single convex object. Often we can use culling in addition to the z-buffer algorithm (which works with any collection of objects for which we have depth information). For example, suppose that we have a scene composed of a collection of n cubes. If we use only the z-buffer algorithm, we pass $6n$ polygons through the pipeline. If we enable culling, half the polygons can be eliminated early in the pipeline, and thus only $3n$ polygons pass through all stages of the pipeline.

---

4. The color of the polygon is determined by shading (Chapter 6) and texture mapping (Chapter 7) if these features are enabled.

We can use culling to render faces that have different properties on the front and back faces, such as their colors, by doing two renderings: one with the back faces culled and a second with the front faces culled. We consider culling further in Chapter 8.

5.9 DISPLAYING MESHES

We now have the tools to walk through a scene interactively by having the camera parameters change in response to user input. Before introducing a simple interface, let's consider another example of data display: mesh plots. A **mesh** is a set of polygons that share vertices and edges. A general mesh, as shown in Figure 5.42, may contain polygons with any number of vertices and requires a moderately sophisticated data structure to store and display efficiently. Rectangular and triangular meshes, such as those introduced in Chapter 2 for modeling a sphere, are much simpler to work with and are useful for a wide variety of applications. Here we introduce rectangular meshes for the display of height data. Height data determine a surface, such as terrain, either through a function that gives the heights above a reference value, such as elevations above sea level, or through samples taken at various points on the surface.

Suppose that the heights are given by y through a function

$$y = f(x, z),$$

where x and z are the points on a two-dimensional surface such as a rectangle. Thus, for each x, z, we get exactly one y, as shown in Figure 5.43. Such surfaces are sometimes called $2\frac{1}{2}$-**dimensional surfaces** or **height fields**. Although all surfaces cannot be represented this way, they have many applications. For example, if we use an x, z coordinate system to give positions on the surface of the earth, then we can use such a function to represent the height or altitude at each location. In many situations the function f is known only discretely, and we have a set of samples or measurements of experimental data of the form

$$y_{ij} = f(x_i, z_j).$$

FIGURE 5.42   Mesh.

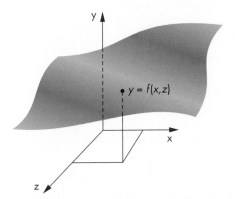

FIGURE 5.43   Height field.

We assume that these data points are equally spaced such that

$$x_i = x_0 + i\Delta x, \quad i = 0, \dots, nRows$$

$$z_j = z_0 + j\Delta z, \quad j = 0, \dots, nColumns,$$

where Δx and Δz are the spacing between the samples in the x and z directions, respectively. If f is known analytically, then we can sample it to obtain a set of discrete data with which to work.

Probably the simplest way to display the data is to draw a line strip for each value of x and another for each value of z, thus generating $nRows + nColumns$ line strips. Suppose that the height data are in a two-dimensional array `data`. We can form a single array with the data converted to vertices arranged first by rows and then by columns with the code

```
for (var i = 0; i < nRows-1; ++i) {
  for (var j = 0; j < nColumns-1; ++j) {
    pointsArray[index] = vec4(2*i/nRows-1, data[i][j], 2*j/nColumns-1,
                              1.0);
    index++;
  }
}

for (var j = 0; j < nColumns-1; ++j) {
  for (var i = 0; i < nRows-1; ++i) {
    pointsArray[index] = vec4(2*i/nRows-1, data[i][j], 2*j/nColumns-1,
                              1.0);
    index++;
  }
}
```

We usually will want to scale the data over a convenient range, such as $(-1, 1)$, and scale the x and z values to make them easier to display as part of the model-view matrix or, equivalently, by adjusting the size of the view volume.

We set up the vertex buffer object as in our previous examples. The rendering process renders all the rows and then all the columns as follows:

```
function render()
{
  gl.clear(gl.COLOR_BUFFER_BIT);

  // Put code for model-view and projection matrices here

  for (var i = 0; i < nRows; ++i) {
    gl.drawArrays(gl.LINE_STRIP, i*nColumns, nColumns);
  }

  for (var i = 0; i < nColumns; ++i) {
    gl.drawArrays(gl.LINE_STRIP, i*nRows+Index/2, nRows);
  }
```

FIGURE 5.44   Mesh plot of Honolulu data using line strips.

```
  requestAnimFrame(render);
}
```

You should now be able to complete a program to display the data. Figure 5.44 shows a rectangular mesh from height data for a part of Honolulu, Hawaii. These data are available on the website for the book.

There are a few problems with this simple approach. Let's look at a particular data set generated from the sombrero (Mexican hat or **sinc**) function.

$$f(r) = \sin(\pi r)/\pi r$$

where $r = \sqrt{x^2 + z^2}$. The function has a number of interesting properties. It is 0 at multiples of π and goes to zero as r goes to infinity. At the origin, both the numerator and denominator are zero, but we can use some elementary calculus to show that this ratio becomes 1. In Appendix D, we will see how this function arises in our analysis of aliasing.

We can form a two-dimensional array using this function to determine values where r is the distance to a point in the x, y plane with the code

```
var data = new Array(nRows);

for (var i = 0; i < nRows; ++i) {
  data[i] = new Array(nColumns);
}

for (var i = 0; i < nRows; ++i) {
  var x = Math.PI * (4*i/nRows-2.0);

  for (var j = 0; j < nColumns; ++j) {
    var y = Math.PI * (4*j/nRows-2.0);
    var r = Math.sqrt(x*x + y*y);
    // Using limit for 0/0 at r = 0
    data[i][j] = (r != 0 ? Math.sin(r)/r : 1.0);
  }
}
```

FIGURE 5.45   Mesh plot of sombrero function.

which forms a two-dimensional array as an array of one-dimensional arrays.

Figure 5.45 shows the result with the viewer looking down at the function. Because we are only rendering line segments, then where there is a fold we can see the lines from both the front and back surfaces.

5.9.1 Displaying Meshes as Surfaces

Let's consider an approach in which we display the mesh using polygons. In this section, we will use filled polygons to hide the back surfaces but still display the mesh as line segments. Then in Chapter 6, we will learn how to display the mesh with lights and material properties.

We start by reorganizing the data so that each successive four points in the vertex array define a rectangular polygon using the values `data[i][j]`, `data[i+1][j]`, `data[i+1][j+1]`, and `data[i][j+1]`. The corresponding code is

```
for (var i = 0; i < nRows-1; ++i) {
  for (var j = 0; j < nColumns-1; ++j)  {
    pointsArray.push(vec4(2*i/nRows-1, data[i][j], 2*j/nColumns-1, 1.0);
    pointsArray.push(vec4(2*(i+1)/nRows-1, data[i+1][j], 2*j/nColumns-1,
                     1.0);
    pointsArray.push(vec4(2*(i+1)/nRows-1, data[i+1][j+1],
                     2*(j+1)/nColumns-1, 1.0);
    pointsArray.push(vec4(2*i/nRows-1, data[i][j+1], 2*(j+1)/nColumns-1,
                     1.0);
  }
}
```

Using the render function:

```
function render()
{
  gl.clear(gl.COLOR_BUFFER_BIT);

  for (var i = 0; i < index; i+= 4) {
    gl.drawArrays(gl.LINE_LOOP, i, 4);
  }
```

```
requestAnimFrame(render);
}
```

Except at the edges, we get the same display as in Figure 5.45 with the back faces still showing. However, note that the same data that define a line loop (`data[i][j]`, `data[i+1][j]`, `data[i+1][j+1]`, and `data[i][j+1]`) also define a triangle fan with two triangles that cover the same area. Consequently, if we first render the four vertices as a triangle fan in the background color and then render the same vertices in a different color as a line loop with hidden-surface removal enabled, the two filled triangles will hide any surfaces behind them. Here is the basic code:

```
white = vec3(1.0, 1.0, 1.0, 1.0);
black = vec3(0.0, 0.0, 0.0, 1.0);
var colorLoc = gl.getUniformLocation(program, "color");

function render()
{
  gl.clear(gl.COLOR_BUFFER_BIT | gl.DEPTH_BUFFER_BIT);

  gl.uniform4fv(colorLoc, flatten(white));
  for (var i = 0; i < index; i+= 4) {
    gl.drawArrays(gl.TRIANGLE_FAN, i, 4);
  }

  gl.uniform4fv(colorLoc, flatten(black));
  for (var i = 0; i < index; i+= 4) {
    gl.drawArrays(gl.LINE_LOOP, i, 4);
  }

  requestAnimFrame(render);
}
```

Figure 5.46 shows the results of this approach. We see only the front surfaces, but the lines appear somewhat broken. Fortunately, we can take care of this problem very easily.

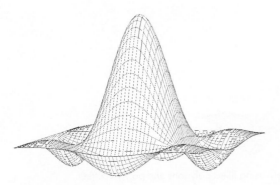

FIGURE 5.46   Mesh plot of sombrero using filled polygons.

5.9.2 Polygon Offset

There is one additional trick that we used in the display of Figure 5.44. If we draw both a polygon and a line loop with the code in the previous section, then each triangle is rendered twice in the same plane, once filled and once by its edges. Even though the second rendering of just the edges is done after the rendering of the filled triangles, numerical inaccuracies in the renderer often cause parts of second rendering to lie behind the corresponding fragments in the first rendering. We can avoid this problem by enabling the **polygon offset mode** and setting the offset parameters using gl.polygonOffset. Polygon offset moves fragments slightly away from the viewer, so that all the desired lines should be visible. In initialization, we can set up polygon offset by

```
gl.enable(gl.POLYGON_OFFSET_FILL);
gl.polygonOffset(1.0, 2.0);
```

The two parameters in gl.polygonOffset are combined with the slope of the polygon and an implementation-dependent constant that guarantees a difference in depth between the fragments from the polygon and the fragments from the line segments. Consequently, you may have to do a little experimentation to find the best values. The results for the sombrero function are shown in Figure 5.47. The programs hat and hata on the website show the sombrero function rendered with lines and triangles, respectively.

There are some modifications we can make to our program. First, if we use all the data, the resulting plot may contain many small polygons. The resulting density of lines in the display may be annoying and can contain moiré patterns. Hence, we might prefer to subsample the data either by using every kth point for some k, or by averaging groups of data points to obtain a new set of samples with smaller *nRows* and *nColumns*. We also note that by rendering one rectangle at a time, although all the data are on the GPU, we are making many function calls in the render function. A more efficient approach would be to use triangle strips that each cover at least one row of the data. The exercises at the end of the chapter outline some of these alternatives.

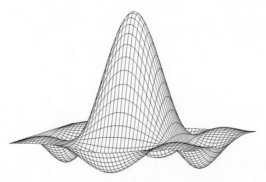

FIGURE 5.47   Mesh plot of sombrero using filled polygons and polygon offset.

5.9.3 Walking through a Scene

The next step is to specify the camera and add interactivity. In this version, we use orthographic viewing and we allow the viewer to move the camera using buttons of the display, but we have the camera always pointing at the center of the cube. The lookAt function provides a simple way to reposition and reorient the camera. The changes that we have to make to our previous program in Section 5.3 are minor.

In our examples, we are using direct positioning of the camera through lookAt. There are other possibilities. One is to use rotation and translation matrices to alter the model-view matrix incrementally. If we want to move the viewer through the scene without having her looking at a fixed point, this option may be more appealing. We could also keep a position variable in the program and change it as the viewer moves. In this case, the model-view matrix would be computed from scratch rather than changed incrementally. Which option we choose depends on the particular application, and often on other factors as well, such as the possibility that numerical errors might accumulate if we were to change the model-view matrix incrementally many times.

The basic mesh rendering can be extended in many ways. In Chapter 6, we will learn to add lights and surface properties to create a more realistic image; in Chapter 7, we will learn to add a texture to the surface. The texture map might be an image of the terrain from a photograph or other data that can be obtained by digitization of a map. If we combine these techniques, we can generate a display in which we can make the image depend on the time of day by changing the position of the light source. It is also possible to obtain smoother surfaces by using the data to define a smoother surface with the aid of one of the curved surface types that we will introduce in Chapter 11.

5.10   PROJECTIONS AND SHADOWS

The creation of simple shadows is an interesting application of projection matrices. Although shadows are not geometric objects, they are important components of realistic images and give many visual cues to the spatial relationships among the objects in a scene. Starting from a physical point of view, shadows require a light source to be present. A point is in shadow if it is not illuminated by any light source or, equivalently, if a viewer at that point cannot see any light sources. However, if the only light source is at the center of projection, there are no visible shadows because any shadows are behind visible objects. This lighting strategy has been called the "flashlight in the eye" model and corresponds to the simple lighting we have used thus far.

To add physically correct shadows, we must understand the interaction between light and materials, a topic that we investigate in Chapter 6. There we show that global calculations are difficult; normally, they cannot be done in real time. Nevertheless, the importance of shadows in applications such as flight simulators has led to a number of special approaches that can be used in many circumstances.

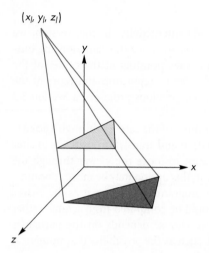

(x_l, y_l, z_l)

y

x

z

FIGURE 5.48   Shadow from a single polygon.

5.10.1 Projected Shadows

Consider the shadow generated by the point source in Figure 5.48. We assume for simplicity that the shadow falls on a flat ground that can be described by the equation

$$y = 0.$$

Not only is the shadow a flat polygon, called a **shadow polygon**, but it is also a projection of the original polygon onto the surface. Specifically, the shadow polygon is the projection of the polygon onto the surface with the center of projection at the light source. Thus, if we do a projection onto the plane of a surface in a frame in which the light source is at the origin, we obtain the vertices of the shadow polygon. These vertices must then be converted back to a representation in the object frame. Rather than do the work as part of an application program, we can find a suitable projection matrix and use it to compute the vertices of the shadow polygon.

Suppose that we start with a light source at (x_l, y_l, z_l), as shown in Figure 5.49(a). If we reorient the figure such that the light source is at the origin, as shown in Figure 5.49(b), using a translation matrix $\mathbf{T}(-x_l, -y_l, -z_l)$, then we have a simple perspective projection through the origin. The projection matrix is

$$\mathbf{M} = \begin{bmatrix} 1 & 0 & 0 & 0 \\ 0 & 1 & 0 & 0 \\ 0 & 0 & 1 & 0 \\ 0 & \frac{1}{-y_l} & 0 & 0 \end{bmatrix}.$$

Finally, we translate everything back with $\mathbf{T}(x_l, y_l, z_l)$. The concatenation of this matrix and the two translation matrices projects the vertex (x, y, z) to

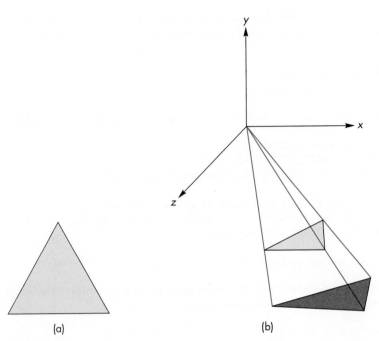

FIGURE 5.49   Shadow polygon projection. (a) From a light source. (b) With source moved to the origin.

$$x_p = x_l - \frac{x - x_l}{(y - y_l)/y_l}$$

$$y_p = 0$$

$$z_p = z_l - \frac{z - z_l}{(y - y_l)/y_l}.$$

However, with a WebGL program, we can alter the model-view matrix to form the desired polygon. If the light source is fixed, we can compute the shadow projection matrix once as part of initialization. Otherwise, we need to recompute it, perhaps in the render function, if the light source is moving.

Let's project a single square polygon parallel onto the plane $y = 0$. We can specify the square through the vertices

```
pointsArray = [
  vec4(-0.5, 0.5, -0.5, 1.0),
  vec4(-0.5, 0.5,  0.5, 1.0),
  vec4( 0.5, 0.5,  0.5, 1.0),
  vec4( 0.5, 0.5, -0.5, 1.0)
];
```

Note that the vertices are ordered so that we can render them using a triangle fan. We initialize a red color for the square and a black color for its shadow that we will send to the fragment shader.

```
red = vec3(1.0, 0.0, 0.0);
black = vec3(0.0, 0.0, 0.0);
```

We initialize a vertex array and a buffer object, as we did in our previous examples:

```
var vBuffer = gl.createBuffer();
gl.bindBuffer(gl.ARRAY_BUFFER, vBuffer);
gl.bufferData(gl.ARRAY_BUFFER, flatten(pointsArray), gl.STATIC_DRAW);

var vPosition = gl.getAttribLocation(program, "vPosition");
gl.vertexAttribPointer(vPosition, 4, gl.FLOAT, false, 0, 0);
gl.enableVertexAttribArray(vPosition);

fColorLoc = gl.getUniformLocation(program, "fColor");
```

We also want to initialize the matrix **M** that we apply to the light position, the initial light position, and the position and orientation of the viewer:

```
light = vec3(0.0, 2.0, 0.0);

light = vec3(a, b, c);    // Location of light
m = mat4();     // Shadow projection matrix initially an identity matrix

m[11] = 0.0;
m[5] = -1.0/light.y;

at = vec3(0.0, 0.0, 0.0);
up = vec3(0.0, 1.0, 0.0);
eye = vec3(1.0, 1.0, 1.0);
```

In our example, we will move the light source but not the square, so the model-view matrix for the shadow will change but not the projection matrix. We can set up these matrices in the initialization

```
modelViewMatrixLoc = gl.getUniformLocation(program, "modelViewMatrix");
projectionMatrixLoc = gl.getUniformLocation(program,
                                                "projectionMatrix");

projectionMatrix = ortho(left, right, bottom, ytop, near, far);
gl.uniformMatrix4fv(projectionMatrixLoc, false,
                    flatten(projectionMatrix));
```

The render function is

```
function render()
{
  theta += 0.1;
```

```
if (theta > 2*Math.PI) {
  theta -= 2*Math.PI;
}

gl.clear(gl.COLOR_BUFFER_BIT | gl.DEPTH_BUFFER_BIT);

// Model-view matrix for square

modelViewMatrix = lookAt(eye, at, up);

// Send color and matrix for square then render

gl.uniformMatrix4fv(modelViewMatrixLoc, false,
                    flatten(modelViewMatrix));
gl.uniform4fv(fColorLoc, flatten(red));
gl.drawArrays(gl.TRIANGLE_FAN, 0, 4);

// Rotate light source

light[0] = Math.sin(theta);
light[2] = Math.cos(theta);

// Model-view matrix for shadow then render

modelViewMatrix = mult(modelViewMatrix, translate(light[0], light[1],
                       light[2]));
modelViewMatrix = mult(modelViewMatrix, m);
modelViewMatrix = mult(modelViewMatrix, translate(-light[0],
                       -light[1], -light[2]));

// Send color and matrix for shadow

gl.uniformMatrix4fv(modelViewMatrixLoc, false,
                    flatten(modelViewMatrix));
gl.uniform4fv(fColorLoc, flatten(black));
gl.drawArrays(gl.TRIANGLE_FAN, 0, 4);

  requestAnimFrame(render);
}
```

Note that although we are performing a projection with respect to the light source, the matrix that we use is the model-view matrix. We render the same polygon twice: the first time as usual and the second time with an altered model-view matrix that transforms the vertices. The same viewing conditions are applied to both the polygon and its shadow polygon. The full program, shadow, is on the website.

For a simple environment, such as an airplane flying over flat terrain casting a single shadow, this technique works well. It is also easy to convert from point sources to distant (parallel) light sources (see Exercise 5.17). When objects can cast shadows on other objects, this method becomes impractical. However, the basic ideas of projective shadows lead to the more general method of shadow maps.

5.11   SHADOW MAPS

Consider Figure 5.50 that is similar to Figure 5.48 but shows a viewer at (x_v, y_v, z_v) looking at the point (x, y, z). The point is in shadow because it is behind the blue polygon as seen by a viewer at the *light source*. Suppose we place a camera at the light source and render the scene with hidden-surface removal enabled. Then we will form an image as in Figure 5.49(a), but we can use the fact that the depth buffer will contain the distances from the light source not only to the polygon but to every other object visible to the source, including the ground and, in particular, the point (x, y, z). It follows that (x, y, z) is in shadow because the distance to it from the light source is greater than the distance to it that is the stored in the depth buffer. The complication here is that (x, y, z) is in object coordinates and our rendering from the light source is in a frame specified by the location and direction of the light source. Hence, to compute the distances correctly for each point in the framebuffer, we must compute its location in the light source frame. The required transformation is the one we derived for projecting polygonal shadows.

The process then goes as follows. We render the scene from a camera at the light source and store the resulting depth buffer, which is called the **shadow buffer**. If there are multiple light sources, we render the scene from the location of each one and store its depth buffer. Note that since we are only interested in the depth buffer, we can do each rendering without colors, lighting, or textures. We then render the scene normally from the location of the camera. For each fragment, we transform its depth to light space and compare that distance to the corresponding location in the

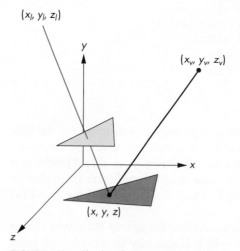

FIGURE 5.50   Shadow from a single polygon.

depth buffer(s). If it is less than the distances in any of the depth buffers, we use the computer color; otherwise we use the shadow color.

In Chapter 7, we will learn how to render to off-screen buffers, which will allow us to compute each shadow map in the same amount of time as a normal rendering. The main problem with shadow mapping is aliasing. The shadow map is limited by the resolution of the depth buffer, and the transformation between light coordinates and object coordinates can exacerbate the visual effects of this limited resolution. In Chapter 12, we address more general, but slower, rendering methods that will create shadows automatically as part of the rendering process.

SUMMARY AND NOTES

We have come a long way. We can now write complete nontrivial three-dimensional applications. Probably the most instructive activity that you can do now is to write such an application. Developing skill with manipulating the model-view and projection functions takes practice.

We have presented the mathematics of the standard projections. Although most APIs free the application programmer from writing projection functions, understanding the mathematics leads to understanding a pipeline implementation based on concatenation of 4×4 matrices. Until recently, application programs had to do the projections within the applications, and most hardware systems did not support perspective projections.

There are three major themes in the remainder of this book. The first major theme is realism. Although more complex objects allow us to build more realistic models, we also explore more complex rendering options. In Chapter 6, we consider the interaction of light with the materials that characterize our objects. We look more deeply at hidden-surface-removal methods, at shading models, and in Chapter 7 at techniques such as texture mapping that allow us to create complex images from simple objects using advanced rendering techniques.

Second, we look more deeply at implementation in Chapter 8. At this point, we will have introduced the major functional units of the graphics pipeline. We discuss the details of the algorithms used in each unit. We will also see additional possibilities for creating images by working directly in the framebuffer.

Third, we explore modeling further by expanding our basic set of primitives. In Chapter 9, we incorporate more complex relationships between simple objects through hierarchical models. In Chapter 10, we explore approaches to modeling that allow us to describe objects through procedures rather than as geometric objects. This approach allows us to model objects with only as much detail as is needed, to incorporate physical laws into our models, and to model natural phenomena that cannot be described by polygons. In Chapter 11, we leave the world of flat objects, adding curves and curved surfaces. These objects are defined by vertices, and we can implement them by breaking them into small flat primitives so we can use the same viewing pipeline.

SUGGESTED READINGS

Carlbom and Paciorek [Car78] discuss the relationships between classical and computer viewing. Rogers and Adams [Rog90] give many examples of the projection matrices corresponding to the standard views used in drafting. Foley et al. [Fol90], Watt [Wat00], and Hearn and Baker [Hea04] derive canonical projection transformations. All follow a PHIGS orientation, so the API is slightly different from the one used here, although Foley derives the most general case. The references differ in whether they use column or row matrices, in where the COP is located, and in whether the projection is in the positive or negative *z* direction. See the *OpenGL Programming Guide* [Shr13] for a further discussion of the use of the model-view and projection matrices in OpenGL.

Shadow projections were proposed by Blinn. Shadow maps are due to Williams [78]. See[Bi88] and [Hug13] for details on these methods and others.

EXERCISES

5.1 All perspective views are characterized by diminution of size. When objects are moved farther from the viewer, their images become smaller. How does the classical perspective view work?

5.2 Consider an airplane whose position is specified by the roll, pitch, and yaw and by the distance from an object. Find a model-view matrix in terms of these parameters.

5.3 Consider a satellite orbiting the earth. Its position above the earth is specified in polar coordinates. Find a model-view matrix that keeps the viewer looking at the earth. Such a matrix could be used to show the earth as it rotates.

5.4 Show how hidden-surface-removal algorithms or visible-surface algorithms work.

5.5 Can we obtain an isometric view of the sphere by a single rotation about a suitably chosen axis? Explain your answer.

5.6 Derive the perspective projection matrix when the COP can be at any point and the projection plane can be at any orientation.

5.7 Show why the projection of the original polygon onto the surface is called shadow polygon.

5.8 Any attempt to take the projection of a point in the same plane as the COP will lead to a division by zero. What is the projection of a line segment that has endpoints on either side of the projection plane?

5.9 Compare and contrast angle elevation and azimuth.

5.10 Derive an oblique projection matrix from specification of front and back clipping planes and top-right and bottom-left intersections of the sides of the clipping volume with the front clipping plane.

5.11 Our approach of normalizing all projections seems to imply that we could predistort all objects and support only orthographic projections. Explain any problems we would face if we took this approach to building a graphics system.

5.12 How do the WebGL projection matrices change if the COP is not at the origin? Assume that the COP is at $(0, 0, d)$ and the projection plane is $z = 0$.

5.13 We can create an interesting class of three-dimensional objects by extending two-dimensional objects into the third dimension by extrusion. For example, a circle becomes a cylinder, a line becomes a quadrilateral, and a quadrilateral in the plane becomes a parallelepiped. Use this technique to convert the two-dimensional maze from Exercise 2.7 to a three-dimensional maze.

5.14 Extend the maze program of Exercise 5.13 to allow the user to walk through the maze. A click on the middle mouse button should move the user forward; a click on the right or left button should turn the user 90 degrees to the right or left, respectively.

5.15 If we were to use orthogonal projections to draw the coordinate axes, the x- and y-axes would lie in the plane of the paper, but the z-axis would point out of the page. Instead, we can draw the x- and y-axes meeting at a 90-degree angle, with the z-axis going off at -135 degrees from the x-axis. Find the matrix that projects the original orthogonal-coordinate axes to this view.

5.16 Write a program to display a rotating cube in a box with three light sources. Each light source should project the cube onto one of the three visible sides of the box.

5.17 Find the projection of a point onto the plane $ax + by + cz + d = 0$ from a light source located at infinity in the direction (d_x, d_y, d_z).

5.18 Using one of the three-dimensional interfaces discussed in Chapter 3, write a program to move the camera through a scene composed of simple objects.

5.19 Write a program to fly through the three-dimensional Sierpinski gasket formed by subdividing tetrahedra. Can you prevent the user from flying through walls?

5.20 In animation, often we can save effort by working with two-dimensional patterns that are mapped onto flat polygons that are always parallel to the camera, a technique known as **billboarding**. Write a program that will keep a simple polygon facing the camera as the camera moves.

5.21 Stereo images are produced by creating two images with the viewer in two slightly different positions. Consider a viewer who is at the origin but whose eyes are separated by Δx units. What are the appropriate viewing specifications to create the two images?

5.22 In Section 5.9, we displayed a mesh by drawing two line strips. How would you alter this approach so it does not draw the extra line from the end of one row (or column) to the beginning of the next row (or column)?

5.23 Derive a method for displaying a mesh using a triangle strip for each row of rectangles. Can you extend your method to draw the entire mesh with a single triangle strip?

5.24 Why is scan line z-buffer more effective than depth buffer or z-buffer algorithm?

5.25 What is the use of projection normalization?

5.26 Render a rectangular mesh as a single triangle strip by creating a degenerate triangle at the end of each row.

5.27 Write a program that will fly around above a mesh. Your program should allow the user to look around at the hills and valleys rather than always looking at a single point.

5.28 Write a reshape function that does not distort the shape of objects as the window is altered.

CHAPTER 6

LIGHTING AND SHADING

We have learned to build three-dimensional graphical models and to display them. However, if you render one of our models, you might be disappointed to see images that look flat and thus fail to illustrate the three-dimensional nature of the model. This appearance is a consequence of our unnatural assumption that each surface is lit such that it appears to a viewer in a single color. Under this assumption, the orthographic projection of a sphere is a uniformly colored circle, and a cube appears as a flat hexagon. If we look at a photograph of a lit sphere, we see not a uniformly colored circle but rather a circular shape with many gradations or **shades** of color. It is these gradations that give two-dimensional images the appearance of being three-dimensional.

What we have left out is the interaction between light and the surfaces in our models. This chapter begins to fill that gap. We develop separate models of light sources and of the most common light–material interactions. Our aim is to add shading to a fast pipeline graphics architecture. Consequently, we develop only local lighting models. Such models, as opposed to global lighting models, allow us to compute the shade to assign to a point on a surface, independent of any other surfaces in the scene. The calculations depend only on the material properties assigned to the surface, the local geometry of the surface, and the locations and properties of the light sources. In this chapter, we introduce the lighting models used most often in WebGL applications. We will see that we have choices as to where to apply a given lighting model: in the application, in the vertex shader, or in the fragment shader.

Following our previous development, we investigate how we can apply shading to polygonal models. We develop a recursive approximation to a sphere that will allow us to test our shading algorithms. We then discuss how light and material properties are specified in WebGL applications and can be added to our sphere-approximating program.

We conclude the chapter with a short discussion of the two most important methods for handling global lighting effects: ray tracing and radiosity.

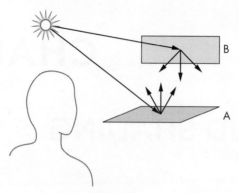

FIGURE 6.1   Reflecting surfaces.

6.1   LIGHT AND MATTER

In Chapters 1 and 2, we presented the rudiments of human color vision, delaying until now any discussion of the interaction between light and surfaces. Perhaps the most general approach to rendering is based on physics, where we use principles such as conservation of energy to derive equations that describe how light is reflected from surfaces.

From a physical perspective, a surface can either emit light by self-emission, as a lightbulb does, or reflect light from other surfaces that illuminate it. Some surfaces may both reflect light and emit light from internal physical processes. When we look at a point on an object, the color that we see is determined by multiple interactions among light sources and reflective surfaces. These interactions can be viewed as a recursive process. Consider the simple scene in Figure 6.1. Some light from the source that reaches surface A is scattered. Some of this reflected light reaches surface B, and some of it is then scattered back to A, where some of it is again reflected back to B, and so on. This recursive scattering of light between surfaces accounts for subtle shading effects, such as the bleeding of colors between adjacent surfaces. Mathematically, the limit of this recursive process can be described using an integral equation, the **rendering equation**, which in principle we could use to find the shading of all surfaces in a scene. Unfortunately, this equation cannot be solved analytically in the general case. Numerical methods are not fast enough for real-time rendering. There are various approximate approaches, such as radiosity and ray tracing, each of which is an excellent approximation to the rendering equation for particular types of surfaces. Although ray tracing can render moderately complex scenes in real time, these methods cannot render scenes at the rate at which we can pass polygons through the modeling-projection pipeline. Consequently, we focus on a simpler rendering model, based on the Phong reflection model, that provides a compromise between physical correctness and efficient calculation. We will introduce global methods in Section 6.12 and then consider the rendering equation, radiosity, and ray tracing in greater detail in Chapter 12.

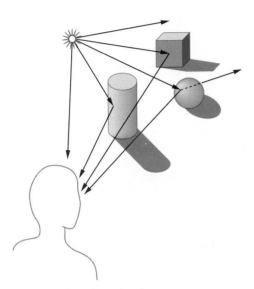

FIGURE 6.2   Light and surfaces.

Rather than looking at a global energy balance, we follow rays of light from light-emitting (or self-luminous) surfaces that we call **light sources**. We then model what happens to these rays as they interact with reflecting surfaces in the scene. This approach is similar to ray tracing, but we consider only single interactions between light sources and surfaces. There are two independent parts of the problem. First, we must model the light sources in the scene. Then we must build a reflection model that deals with the interactions between materials and light.

To get an overview of the process, we can start following rays of light from a point source, as shown in Figure 6.2. As we noted in Chapter 1, our viewer sees only the light that leaves the source and reaches her eyes—perhaps through a complex path and multiple interactions with objects in the scene. If a ray of light enters her eye directly from the source, she sees the color of the source. If the ray of light hits a surface visible to our viewer, the color she sees is based on the interaction between the source and the surface material: She sees the color of the light reflected from the surface toward her eyes.

In terms of computer graphics, we replace the viewer by the projection plane, as shown in Figure 6.3. Conceptually, the clipping window in this plane is mapped to the display; thus, we can think of the projection plane as ruled into rectangles, each corresponding to a pixel. The color of the light source and of the surfaces determines the color of one or more pixels in the framebuffer.

We need to consider only those rays that leave the source and reach the viewer's eye, either directly or through interactions with objects. In the case of computer viewing, these are the rays that reach the center of projection (COP) after passing through the clipping rectangle. Note that in scenes for which the image shows a lot of the background, most rays leaving a source do not contribute to the image and are thus of no interest to us. We make use of this observation in Section 6.12.

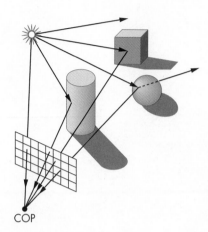

FIGURE 6.3   Light, surfaces, and computer imaging.

FIGURE 6.4   Light–material interactions. (a) Specular surface. (b) Diffuse surface. (c) Translucent surface.

Figure 6.2 shows both single and multiple interactions between rays and objects. It is the nature of these interactions that determines whether an object appears red or brown, light or dark, dull or shiny. When light strikes a surface, some of it is absorbed and some of it is reflected. If the surface is opaque, reflection and absorption account for all the light striking the surface. If the surface is translucent, some of the light is transmitted through the material and emerges to interact with other objects. These interactions depend on wavelength. An object illuminated by white light appears red because it absorbs most of the incident light but reflects light in the red range of frequencies. A shiny object appears so because its surface is smooth. Conversely, a dull object has a rough surface. The shading of objects also depends on the orientation of their surfaces, a factor that we shall see is characterized by the normal vector at each point. These interactions between light and materials can be classified into the three groups depicted in Figure 6.4.

(a) **Specular surfaces** appear shiny because most of the light that is reflected or **scattered** is in a narrow range of angles close to the angle of reflection. Mirrors are **perfectly specular surfaces**; the light from an incoming light ray may be partially absorbed, but all reflected light from a given angle emerges at a single angle, obeying the rule that the angle of incidence is equal to the angle of reflection.

(b) **Diffuse surfaces** are characterized by reflected light being scattered in all directions. Walls painted with matte or flat paint are diffuse reflectors, as are many natural materials, such as terrain viewed from an airplane or a satellite. **Perfectly diffuse surfaces** scatter light equally in all directions, and thus a flat, perfectly diffuse surface appears the same to all viewers.

(c) **Translucent surfaces** allow some light to penetrate the surface and to emerge from another location on the object. This process of **refraction** characterizes glass and water. Some incident light may also be reflected at the surface.

We shall model all these surfaces in Sections 6.3 and 6.4. First, we consider light sources.

6.2 LIGHT SOURCES

Light can leave a surface through two fundamental processes: self-emission and reflection. We usually think of a light source as an object that emits light only through internal energy sources. However, a light source, such as a lightbulb, can also reflect some light that is incident on it from the surrounding environment. We will usually omit the emissive term in our simple models. When we discuss lighting in Section 6.7, we will see that we can easily add a self-emission term.

FIGURE 6.5   Light source.

If we consider a source such as the one in Figure 6.5, we can look at it as an object with a surface. Each point (x, y, z) on the surface can emit light that is characterized by the direction of emission (θ, ϕ) and the intensity of energy emitted at each wavelength λ. Thus, a general light source can be characterized by a six-variable **illumination function**, $I(x, y, z, \theta, \phi, \lambda)$. Note that we need two angles to specify a direction, and we are assuming that each frequency can be considered independently. From the perspective of a surface illuminated by this source, we can obtain the total contribution of the source (Figure 6.6) by integrating over its surface, a process that accounts for the emission angles that reach this surface and must also account for the distance between the source and the surface. For a distributed light source, such as a lightbulb, the evaluation of this integral is difficult, whether we use analytic or

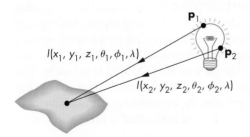

FIGURE 6.6   Adding the contribution from a source.

numerical methods. Often, it is easier to model the distributed source with polygons, each of which is a simple source, or with an approximating set of point sources.

We consider four basic types of sources: ambient lighting, point sources, spotlights, and distant light. These four lighting types are sufficient for rendering most simple scenes.

6.2.1 Color Sources

Not only do light sources emit different amounts of light at different frequencies, but their directional properties can vary with frequency as well. Consequently, a physically correct model can be complex. However, our model of the human visual system is based on three-color theory that tells us we perceive three tristimulus values, rather than a full-color distribution. For most applications, we can thus model light sources as having three components—red, green, and blue—and we can use each of the three color sources to obtain the corresponding color components that a human observer sees.

We describe a source through a three-component intensity or **luminance** function,

$$\mathbf{I} = \begin{bmatrix} I_r \\ I_g \\ I_b \end{bmatrix},$$

each of whose components is the intensity of the independent red, green, and blue components. Thus, we use the red component of a light source for the calculation of the red component of the image. Because light–material computations involve three similar but independent calculations, we will tend to present a single scalar equation, with the understanding that it can represent any of the three color components.

6.2.2 Ambient Light

In many rooms, such as classrooms or kitchens, the lights have been designed and positioned to provide uniform illumination throughout the room. Often such illumination is achieved through large sources that have diffusers whose purpose is to scatter light in all directions. We could create an accurate simulation of such illumination, at least in principle, by modeling all the distributed sources and then integrating the illumination from these sources at each point on a reflecting surface. Making such a model and rendering a scene with it would be a daunting task for a graphics system, especially one for which real-time performance is desirable. Alternatively, we can look at the desired effect of the sources: to achieve a uniform light level in the room. This uniform lighting is called **ambient light**. If we follow this second approach, we can postulate an ambient intensity at each point in the environment. Thus, ambient illumination is characterized by an intensity, $\mathbf{I}_a$, that is identical at every point in the scene.

Our ambient source has three color components:

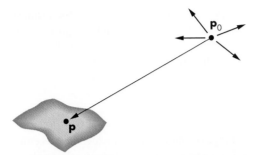

FIGURE 6.7   Point source illuminating a surface.

$$\mathbf{I}_a = \begin{bmatrix} I_{ar} \\ I_{ag} \\ I_{ab} \end{bmatrix}.$$

We will use the *scalar* I_a to denote any one of the red, green, or blue components of $\mathbf{I}_a$. Although every point in our scene receives the same illumination from $\mathbf{I}_a$, each surface can reflect this light differently.

6.2.3 Point Sources

An ideal **point source** emits light equally in all directions. We can characterize a point source located at a point $\mathbf{p}_0$ by a three-component color matrix:

$$\mathbf{I}(\mathbf{p_0}) = \begin{bmatrix} I_r(\mathbf{p_0}) \\ I_g(\mathbf{p_0}) \\ I_b(\mathbf{p_0}) \end{bmatrix}.$$

The intensity of illumination received from a point source is proportional to the inverse square of the distance between the source and surface. Hence, at a point $\mathbf{p}$ (Figure 6.7), the intensity of light received from the point source is given by the matrix

$$\mathbf{i}(\mathbf{p}, \mathbf{p_0}) = \frac{1}{|\mathbf{p} - \mathbf{p_0}|^2}\mathbf{I}(\mathbf{p_0}).$$

As with ambient light, we will use $I(\mathbf{p_0})$ to denote any of the components of $\mathbf{I}(\mathbf{p_0})$.

The use of point sources in most applications is determined more by their ease of use than by their resemblance to physical reality. Scenes rendered with only point sources tend to have high contrast; objects appear either bright or dark. In the real world, it is the large size of most light sources that contributes to softer scenes, as we can see from Figure 6.8, which shows the shadows created by a source of finite size. Some areas are fully in shadow, or in the **umbra**, whereas others are in partial shadow, or in the **penumbra**. We can mitigate the high-contrast effect from point-source illumination by adding ambient light to a scene.

The distance term also contributes to the harsh renderings with point sources. Although the inverse-square distance term is correct for point sources, in practice it

FIGURE 6.8   Shadows created by finite-size light source.

is usually replaced by a term of the form $(a + bd + cd^2)^{-1}$, where d is the distance between $\mathbf{p}$ and $\mathbf{p}_0$. The constants a, b, and c can be chosen to soften the lighting. Note that if the light source is far from the surfaces in the scene, the intensity of the light from the source is sufficiently uniform that the distance term is constant over each surface.

6.2.4 Spotlights

Spotlights are characterized by a narrow range of angles through which light is emitted. We can construct a simple spotlight from a point source by limiting the angles at which light from the source can be seen. We can use a cone whose apex is at $\mathbf{p}_s$, which points in the direction $\mathbf{l}_s$, and whose width is determined by an angle θ, as shown in Figure 6.9. If $\theta = 180$, the spotlight becomes a point source.

More realistic spotlights are characterized by the distribution of light within the cone—usually with most of the light concentrated in the center of the cone. Thus, the intensity is a function of the angle ϕ between the direction of the source and a vector $\mathbf{s}$ to a point on the surface (as long as this angle is less than θ; Figure 6.10). Although this function could be defined in many ways, it is usually defined by $\cos^e \phi$, where the exponent e (Figure 6.11) determines how rapidly the light intensity drops off.

As we shall see throughout this chapter, cosines are convenient functions for lighting calculations. If $\mathbf{u}$ and $\mathbf{v}$ are any unit-length vectors, we can compute the cosine of the angle θ between them with the dot product

$$\cos \theta = \mathbf{u} \cdot \mathbf{v},$$

a calculation that requires only three multiplications and two additions.

6.2.5 Distant Light Sources

Most shading calculations require the direction from the point on the surface to the light-source position. As we move across a surface, calculating the intensity at each point, we should recompute this vector repeatedly—a computation that is a significant part of the shading calculation. However, if the light source is far from the surface, the vector does not change much as we move from point to point, just as the light from the sun strikes all objects that are in close proximity to one another at the same angle. Figure 6.12 illustrates that we are effectively replacing a point source of light with a source that illuminates objects with parallel rays of light—a parallel source. In practice, the calculations for distant light sources are similar to the calculations for parallel projections; they replace the *location* of the light source with the *direction* of the light source. Hence, in homogeneous coordinates, a point light source at $\mathbf{p}_0$ is represented internally as a four-dimensional column matrix:

FIGURE 6.9   Spotlight.

FIGURE 6.10   Attenuation of a spotlight.

FIGURE 6.11   Spotlight exponent.

FIGURE 6.12   Parallel light source.

$$\mathbf{p}_0 = \begin{bmatrix} x \\ y \\ z \\ 1 \end{bmatrix}.$$

In contrast, the distant light source is described by a direction vector whose representation in homogeneous coordinates is the matrix

$$\mathbf{p}_0 = \begin{bmatrix} x \\ y \\ z \\ 0 \end{bmatrix}.$$

The graphics system can carry out rendering calculations more efficiently for distant light sources than for near ones. Of course, a scene rendered with distant light sources looks different from a scene rendered with near sources. Fortunately, our models will allow both types of sources.

6.3 THE PHONG REFLECTION MODEL

Although we could approach light–material interactions through physical models, we have chosen to use a model that leads to efficient computations, especially when we use it with our pipeline-rendering model. The reflection model that we present was introduced by Phong and later modified by Blinn. It has proved to be efficient and a close enough approximation to physical reality to produce good renderings under a variety of lighting conditions and material properties.

The Phong model uses the four vectors shown in Figure 6.13 to calculate a color for an arbitrary point $\mathbf{p}$ on a surface. If the surface is curved, all four vectors can change as we move from point to point. The vector $\mathbf{n}$ is the normal at $\mathbf{p}$; we discuss its calculation in Section 6.4. The vector $\mathbf{v}$ is in the direction from $\mathbf{p}$ to the viewer or COP. The vector $\mathbf{l}$ is in the direction of a line from $\mathbf{p}$ to an arbitrary point on the source for a distributed light source or, as we are assuming for now, to the point light source. Finally, the vector $\mathbf{r}$ is in the direction that a perfectly reflected ray from $\mathbf{l}$ would take. Note that $\mathbf{r}$ is determined by $\mathbf{n}$ and $\mathbf{l}$. We calculate it in Section 6.4.

The Phong model supports three types of material–light interactions—ambient, diffuse, and specular—that we introduced in Section 6.1. Suppose that we have a set of point sources. We assume that each source can have separate ambient, diffuse, and specular components for each of the three primary colors. Although this assumption may appear unnatural, remember that our goal is to create realistic shading effects in as close to real time as possible. We use a local model to simulate effects that can be global in nature. Thus, our light-source model has ambient, diffuse, and specular terms. We need nine coefficients to characterize these terms at any point $\mathbf{p}$ on the surface. We can place these nine coefficients in a 3×3 illumination matrix for the ith light source:

$$\mathbf{L}_i = \begin{bmatrix} L_{ira} & L_{iga} & L_{iba} \\ L_{ird} & L_{igd} & L_{ibd} \\ L_{irs} & L_{igs} & L_{ibs} \end{bmatrix}.$$

FIGURE 6.13 Vectors used by the Phong model.

The first row of the matrix contains the ambient intensities for the red, green, and blue terms from source i. The second row contains the diffuse terms; the third contains the specular terms. We assume that any distance attenuation terms have not yet been applied. This matrix is only a simple way of storing the nine lighting terms we need. In practice, we will use constructs such as

```
light_i_ambient = vec4();
light_i_diffuse = vec4();
light_i_specular = vec4();
```

for each source in our code. The four-dimensional form will be useful when we consider lighting with materials that are not opaque.

We construct the model by assuming that we can compute how much of each of the incident lights is reflected at the point of interest. For example, for the red diffuse term from source i, L_{ird}, we can compute a reflection term R_{ird}, and the latter's contribution to the intensity at $\mathbf{p}$ is $R_{ird}L_{ird}$. The value of R_{ird} depends on the material properties, the orientation of the surface, the direction of the light source, and the distance between the light source and the viewer. Thus, for each point, we have nine coefficients that we can place in a matrix of reflection terms of the form

$$\mathbf{R}_i = \begin{bmatrix} R_{ira} & R_{iga} & R_{iba} \\ R_{ird} & R_{igd} & R_{ibd} \\ R_{irs} & R_{igs} & R_{ibs} \end{bmatrix}.$$

We can then compute the contribution for each color source by adding the ambient, diffuse, and specular components. For example, the red intensity that we see at $\mathbf{p}$ from source i is

$$I_{ir} = R_{ira}L_{ira} + R_{ird}L_{ird} + R_{irs}L_{irs}$$

$$= I_{ira} + I_{ird} + I_{irs}.$$

We obtain the total intensity by adding the contributions of all sources and, possibly, a global ambient term. Thus, the red term is

$$I_r = \sum_i (I_{ira} + I_{ird} + I_{irs}) + I_{ar},$$

where I_{ar} is the red component of the global ambient light.

We can simplify our notation by observing that the necessary computations are the same for each source and for each primary color. They differ depending on whether we are considering the ambient, diffuse, or specular terms. Hence, we can omit the subscripts i, r, g, and b. We write

$$I = I_a + I_d + I_s = L_a R_a + L_d R_d + L_s R_s,$$

with the understanding that the computation will be done for each of the primaries and each source; the global ambient term can be added at the end. As with the lighting terms, when we get to code we will use statements such as

```
reflect_i_ambient = vec4();
reflect_i_diffuse = vec4();
reflect_i_specular = vec4();
```

Note that these terms are all for a single surface and in general we will have different reflectivity properties for each material.

6.3.1 Ambient Reflection

The intensity of ambient light I_a is the same at every point on the surface. Some of this light is absorbed and some is reflected. The amount reflected is given by the ambient reflection coefficient, $R_a = k_a$. Because only a positive fraction of the light is reflected, we must have

$$0 \leq k_a \leq 1,$$

and thus

$$I_a = k_a L_a.$$

Here L_a can be any of the individual light sources, or it can be a global ambient term.

A surface has, of course, three ambient coefficients—k_{ar}, k_{ag}, and k_{ab}—and they can differ. Hence, for example, a sphere appears yellow under white ambient light if its blue ambient coefficient is small and its red and green coefficients are large.

6.3.2 Diffuse Reflection

A perfectly diffuse reflector scatters the light that it reflects equally in all directions. Hence, such a surface appears the same to all viewers. However, the amount of light reflected depends both on the material—because some of the incoming light is absorbed—and on the position of the light source relative to the surface. Diffuse reflections are characterized by rough surfaces. If we were to magnify a cross section of a diffuse surface, we might see an image like that shown in Figure 6.14. Rays of light that hit the surface at only slightly different angles are reflected back at markedly different angles. Perfectly diffuse surfaces are so rough that there is no preferred angle of reflection. Such surfaces, sometimes called **Lambertian surfaces**, can be modeled mathematically with Lambert's law.

Consider a diffuse planar surface, as shown in Figure 6.15, illuminated by the sun. The surface is brightest at noon and dimmest at dawn and dusk because, according to Lambert's law, we see only the vertical component of the incoming light. One way to understand this law is to consider a small parallel light source striking a plane, as shown in Figure 6.16. As the source is lowered in the (artificial) sky, the same amount of light is spread over a larger area, and the surface appears dimmer. Returning to the point source of Figure 6.15, we can characterize diffuse reflections mathematically. Lambert's law states that

$$R_d \propto \cos \theta,$$

FIGURE 6.14   Rough surface.

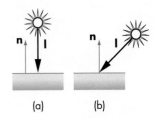

(a)   (b)

FIGURE 6.15   Illumination of a diffuse surface. (a) At noon. (b) In the afternoon.

FIGURE 6.16   Vertical contributions by Lambert's law. (a) At noon. (b) In the afternoon.

where θ is the angle between the normal at the point of interest $\mathbf{n}$ and the direction of the light source $\mathbf{l}$. If both $\mathbf{l}$ and $\mathbf{n}$ are unit-length vectors,[1] then

$$\cos \theta = \mathbf{l} \cdot \mathbf{n}.$$

If we add in a reflection coefficient k_{d} representing the fraction of incoming diffuse light that is reflected, we have the diffuse reflection term:

$$I_{\mathrm{d}} = k_{\mathrm{d}}(\mathbf{l} \cdot \mathbf{n})L_{\mathrm{d}}.$$

If we wish to incorporate a distance term, to account for attenuation as the light travels a distance d from the source to the surface, we can again use the quadratic attenuation term:

$$I_{\mathrm{d}} = \frac{k_{\mathrm{d}}}{a + bd + cd^2}(\mathbf{l} \cdot \mathbf{n})L_{\mathrm{d}}.$$

There is a potential problem with this expression because $(\mathbf{l} \cdot \mathbf{n})L_{\mathrm{d}}$ will be negative if the light source is below the horizon. In this case, we want to use zero rather than a negative value. Hence, in practice we use $\max((\mathbf{l} \cdot \mathbf{n})L_{\mathrm{d}}, 0)$.

6.3.3 Specular Reflection

If we employ only ambient and diffuse reflections, our images will be shaded and will appear three-dimensional, but all the surfaces will look dull, somewhat like chalk. What we are missing are the highlights that we see reflected from shiny objects. These highlights usually show a color different from the color of the reflected ambient and

---

1. Direction vectors, such as $\mathbf{l}$ and $\mathbf{n}$, are used repeatedly in shading calculations through the dot product. In practice, both the programmer and the graphics software should seek to normalize all such vectors as soon as possible.

diffuse light. For example, a red plastic ball viewed under white light has a white highlight that is the reflection of some of the light from the source in the direction of the viewer (Figure 6.17).

Whereas a diffuse surface is rough, a specular surface is smooth. The smoother the surface is, the more it resembles a mirror. Figure 6.18 shows that as the surface gets smoother, the reflected light is concentrated in a smaller range of angles centered about the angle of a perfect reflector—a mirror or a perfectly specular surface. Modeling specular surfaces realistically can be complex because the pattern by which the light is scattered is not symmetric. It depends on the wavelength of the incident light, and it changes with the reflection angle.

Phong proposed an approximate model that can be computed with only a slight increase over the work done for diffuse surfaces. The model adds a term for specular reflection. Hence, we consider the surface as being rough for the diffuse term and smooth for the specular term. The amount of light that the viewer sees depends on the angle ϕ between $\mathbf{r}$, the direction of a perfect reflector, and $\mathbf{v}$, the direction of the viewer. The Phong model uses the equation

$$I_s = k_s L_s \cos^\alpha \phi.$$

The coefficient k_s $(0 \leq k_s \leq 1)$ is the fraction of the incoming specular light that is reflected. The exponent α is a **shininess** coefficient. Figure 6.19 shows how, as α is increased, the reflected light is concentrated in a narrower region centered on the angle of a perfect reflector. In the limit, as α goes to infinity, we get a mirror; values in the range 100 to 500 correspond to most metallic surfaces, and smaller values (< 100) correspond to materials that show broad highlights.

The computational advantage of the Phong model is that if we have normalized $\mathbf{r}$ and $\mathbf{v}$ to unit length, we can again use the dot product, and the specular term becomes

$$I_s = k_s L_s \max((\mathbf{r} \cdot \mathbf{v})^\alpha, 0).$$

We can add a distance term, as we did with diffuse reflections. What is referred to as

FIGURE 6.17   Specular highlights.

FIGURE 6.18   Specular surface.

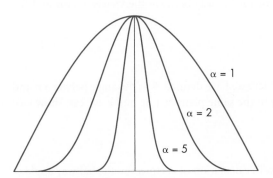

FIGURE 6.19   Effect of shininess coefficient.

the **Phong model**, including the distance term, is written as

$$I = \frac{1}{a + bd + cd^2} \left(k_d L_d \max(\mathbf{l} \cdot \mathbf{n}, 0) + k_s L_s \max((\mathbf{r} \cdot \mathbf{v})^{\alpha}, 0) \right) + k_a L_a.$$

This formula is computed for each light source and for each primary.

It might seem to make little sense either to associate a different amount of ambient light with each source or to allow the components for specular and diffuse lighting to be different. Because we cannot solve the full rendering equation, we must use various tricks in an attempt to obtain realistic renderings.

Consider, for example, an environment with many objects. When we turn on a light, some of that light hits a surface directly. These contributions to the image can be modeled with specular and diffuse components of the source. However, much of the rest of the light from the source is scattered from multiple reflections from other objects and makes a contribution to the light received at the surface under consideration. We can approximate this term by having an ambient component associated with the source. The shade that we should assign to this term depends on *both* the color of the source and the color of the objects in the room—an unfortunate consequence of our use of approximate models. To some extent, the same analysis holds for diffuse light. Diffuse light reflects among the surfaces, and the color that we see on a particular surface depends on other surfaces in the environment. Again, by using carefully chosen diffuse and specular components with our light sources, we can approximate a global effect with local calculations.

We have developed the Phong model in object space. The actual shading, however, is not done until the objects have passed through the model-view and projection transformations. These transformations can affect the cosine terms in the model (see Exercise 6.20). Consequently, to make a correct shading calculation, we must either preserve spatial relationships as vertices and vectors pass through the pipeline, perhaps by sending additional information through the pipeline from object space, or go backward through the pipeline to obtain the required shading information.

6.3.4 The Modified Phong Model

If we use the Phong model with specular reflections in our rendering, the dot product $\mathbf{r} \cdot \mathbf{v}$ should be recalculated at every point on the surface. We can obtain an interesting approximation by using the unit vector halfway between the viewer vector and the light-source vector:

$$\mathbf{h} = \frac{\mathbf{l} + \mathbf{v}}{|\mathbf{l} + \mathbf{v}|}.$$

Figure 6.20 shows all five vectors. Here we have defined ψ as the angle between $\mathbf{n}$ and $\mathbf{h}$, the **halfway angle**. When $\mathbf{v}$ lies in the same plane as $\mathbf{l}$, $\mathbf{n}$, and $\mathbf{r}$, we can show (see Exercise 6.7) that

$$2\psi = \phi.$$

If we replace $\mathbf{r} \cdot \mathbf{v}$ with $\mathbf{n} \cdot \mathbf{h}$, we avoid calculation of $\mathbf{r}$. However, the halfway angle ψ is smaller than ϕ, and if we use the same exponent e in $(\mathbf{n} \cdot \mathbf{h})^e$ that we used in $(\mathbf{r} \cdot \mathbf{v})^e$,

FIGURE 6.20   Determination of the halfway vector.

then the size of the specular highlights will be smaller. We can mitigate this problem by replacing the value of the exponent e with a value e' so that $(\mathbf{n} \cdot \mathbf{h})^{e'}$ is closer to $(\mathbf{r} \cdot \mathbf{v})^e$. It is clear that avoiding recalculation of $\mathbf{r}$ is desirable. However, to appreciate fully where savings can be made, you should consider all the cases of flat and curved surfaces, near and far light sources, and near and far viewers (see Exercise 6.8).

When we use the halfway vector in the calculation of the specular term, we are using the **Blinn-Phong**, or **modified Phong, lighting model**. This model was the default in systems with a fixed-function pipeline and was built into hardware before programmable shaders became available. We will use this model in our first shaders that carry out lighting.

Color Plate 17 shows a group of Utah teapots (Section 11.10) that have been rendered using the modified Phong model. Note that it is only our ability to control material properties that makes the teapots appear different from one another. The various teapots demonstrate how the modified Phong model can create a variety of surface effects, ranging from dull surfaces to highly reflective surfaces that look like metal.

6.4 COMPUTATION OF VECTORS

The illumination and reflection models that we have derived are sufficiently general that they can be applied to curved or flat surfaces, to parallel or perspective views, and to distant or near surfaces. Most of the calculations for rendering a scene involve the determination of the required vectors and dot products. For each special case, simplifications are possible. For example, if the surface is a flat polygon, the normal is the same at all points on the surface. If the light source is far from the surface, the light direction is the same at all points.

In this section, we examine how the vectors are computed for the general case. In Section 6.5, we see what additional techniques can be applied when our objects are composed of flat polygons. This case is especially important because most renderers render curved surfaces by approximating those surfaces with many small, flat polygons.

6.4.1 Normal Vectors

For smooth surfaces, the vector normal to the surface exists at every point and gives the local orientation of the surface. Its calculation depends on how the surface is represented mathematically. Two simple cases—the plane and the sphere—illustrate both how we compute normals and where the difficulties lie.

A plane can be described by the equation

$$ax + by + cz + d = 0.$$

As we saw in Chapter 4, this equation could also be written in terms of the normal to the plane, $\mathbf{n}$, and a point, $\mathbf{p}_0$, known to be on the plane

$$\mathbf{n} \cdot (\mathbf{p} - \mathbf{p}_0) = 0,$$

where $\mathbf{p}$ is any point (x, y, z) on the plane. Comparing the two forms, we see that the vector $\mathbf{n}$ is given by

$$\mathbf{n} = \begin{bmatrix} a \\ b \\ c \end{bmatrix},$$

or, in homogeneous coordinates,

$$\mathbf{n} = \begin{bmatrix} a \\ b \\ c \\ 0 \end{bmatrix}.$$

However, suppose that instead we are given three noncollinear points—$\mathbf{p}_0$, $\mathbf{p}_1$, $\mathbf{p}_2$—that are in this plane and thus are sufficient to determine it uniquely. The vectors $\mathbf{p}_2 - \mathbf{p}_0$ and $\mathbf{p}_1 - \mathbf{p}_0$ are parallel to the plane, and we can use their cross product to find the normal

$$\mathbf{n} = (\mathbf{p}_2 - \mathbf{p}_0) \times (\mathbf{p}_1 - \mathbf{p}_0).$$

We must be careful about the order of the vectors in the cross product: Reversing the order changes the surface from outward pointing to inward pointing, and that reversal can affect the lighting calculations. As we shall see in Section 6.5, forcing users to compute normals creates more flexibility in how we apply our lighting model.

For curved surfaces, how we compute normals depends on how we represent the surface. In Chapter 11, we discuss three different methods for representing curves and surfaces. We can investigate a few of the possibilities by considering how we represent a unit sphere centered at the origin. The usual equation for this sphere is the **implicit equation**

$$f(x, y, z) = x^2 + y^2 + z^2 - 1 = 0,$$

or in vector form,

$$f(\mathbf{p}) = \mathbf{p} \cdot \mathbf{p} - 1 = 0.$$

The normal is given by the **gradient vector**, which is defined by the column matrix

$$\mathbf{n} = \begin{bmatrix} \frac{\partial f}{\partial x} \\ \frac{\partial f}{\partial y} \\ \frac{\partial f}{\partial z} \end{bmatrix} = \begin{bmatrix} 2x \\ 2y \\ 2z \end{bmatrix} = 2\mathbf{p}.$$

The sphere could also be represented in **parametric form**. In this form, the x, y, and z values of a point on the sphere are represented independently in terms of two parameters u and v:

$$x = x(u, v)$$

$$y = y(u, v)$$

$$z = z(u, v).$$

As we shall see in Chapter 11, this form is preferable in computer graphics, especially for representing curves and surfaces; although, for a particular surface, there may be multiple parametric representations. One parametric representation for the sphere is

$$x(u, v) = \cos u \sin v$$

$$y(u, v) = \cos u \cos v$$

$$z(u, v) = \sin u.$$

As u and v vary in the range $-\pi/2 < u < \pi/2$, $-\pi < v < \pi$, we get all the points on the sphere. When we are using the parametric form, we can obtain the normal from the **tangent plane**, shown in Figure 6.21, at a point $\mathbf{p}(u, v) = [x(u, v) \quad y(u, v) \quad z(u, v)]^T$ on the surface. The tangent plane gives the local orientation of the surface at a point; we can derive it by taking the linear terms of the Taylor series expansion of the surface at $\mathbf{p}$. The result is that at $\mathbf{p}$, lines in the directions of the vectors represented by

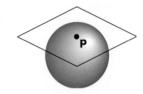

FIGURE 6.21 Tangent plane to sphere.

$$\frac{\partial \mathbf{p}}{\partial u} = \begin{bmatrix} \frac{\partial x}{\partial u} \\ \frac{\partial y}{\partial u} \\ \frac{\partial z}{\partial u} \end{bmatrix} \qquad \frac{\partial \mathbf{p}}{\partial v} = \begin{bmatrix} \frac{\partial x}{\partial v} \\ \frac{\partial y}{\partial v} \\ \frac{\partial z}{\partial v} \end{bmatrix}$$

lie in the tangent plane. We can use their cross product to obtain the normal

$$\mathbf{n} = \frac{\partial \mathbf{p}}{\partial u} \times \frac{\partial \mathbf{p}}{\partial v}.$$

For our sphere, we find that

$$\mathbf{n} = \cos u \begin{bmatrix} \cos u \sin v \\ \cos u \cos v \\ \sin u \end{bmatrix} = (\cos u)\mathbf{p}.$$

We are interested in only the direction of $\mathbf{n}$; thus, we can divide by $\cos u$ to obtain the unit normal to the sphere,

$$\mathbf{n} = \mathbf{p}.$$

In Section 6.9, we use this result to shade a polygonal approximation to a sphere.

Within a graphics system, we usually work with a collection of vertices, and the normal vector must be approximated from some set of points close to the point where the normal is needed. The pipeline architecture of real-time graphics systems makes this calculation difficult because we process one vertex at a time, and thus the graphics system may not have the information available to compute the approximate normal at a given point. Consequently, graphics systems often leave the computation of normals to the user program.

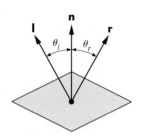

FIGURE 6.22   A mirror.

In WebGL, we will usually compute the vertex normals in the application and put them in a vertex array buffer just as we do for vertex positions. In the vertex shaders, the normals are then available as an attribute-qualified variable.

6.4.2 Angle of Reflection

Once we have calculated the normal at a point, we can use this normal and the direction of the light source to compute the direction of a perfect reflection. An ideal mirror is characterized by the following statement: *The angle of incidence is equal to the angle of reflection.* These angles are as pictured in Figure 6.22. The **angle of incidence** is the angle between the normal and the light source (assumed to be a point source); the **angle of reflection** is the angle between the normal and the direction in which the light is reflected. In two dimensions, there is but a single angle satisfying the angle condition. In three dimensions, however, our statement is insufficient to compute the required angle: There are an infinite number of angles satisfying our condition. We must add the following statement: *At a point* **p** *on the surface, the incoming light ray, the reflected light ray, and the normal at the point must all lie in the same plane.* These two conditions are sufficient for us to determine **r** from **n** and **l**. Our primary interest is the direction, rather than the magnitude, of **r**. However, many of our rendering calculations will be easier if we deal with unit-length vectors. Hence, we assume that both **l** and **n** have been normalized such that

$$|\mathbf{l}| = |\mathbf{n}| = 1.$$

We also want

$$|\mathbf{r}| = 1.$$

If $\theta_i = \theta_r$, then

$$\cos \theta_i = \cos \theta_r.$$

Using the dot product, the angle condition is

$$\cos \theta_i = \mathbf{l} \cdot \mathbf{n} = \cos \theta_r = \mathbf{n} \cdot \mathbf{r}.$$

The coplanar condition implies that we can write **r** as a linear combination of **l** and **n**:

$$\mathbf{r} = \alpha \mathbf{l} + \beta \mathbf{n}.$$

Taking the dot product with **n**, we find that

$$\mathbf{n} \cdot \mathbf{r} = \alpha \mathbf{l} \cdot \mathbf{n} + \beta = \mathbf{l} \cdot \mathbf{n}.$$

We can get a second condition between α and β from our requirement that **r** also be of unit length; thus,

$$1 = \mathbf{r} \cdot \mathbf{r} = \alpha^2 + 2\alpha\beta\mathbf{l} \cdot \mathbf{n} + \beta^2.$$

Solving these two equations, we find that

$$\mathbf{r} = 2(\mathbf{l} \cdot \mathbf{n})\mathbf{n} - \mathbf{l}.$$

Some of the shaders we develop will use this calculation to compute a reflection vector for use in the application; others that need the reflection vector only in a shader can use the GLSL `reflect` function to compute it. Methods such as environment maps will use the reflected-view vector (see Exercise 6.24) that is used to determine what a viewer would see if she looked at a reflecting surface, such as a highly polished sphere.

6.5 POLYGONAL SHADING

Assuming that we can compute normal vectors, given a set of light sources and a viewer, the lighting models that we have developed can be applied at every point on a surface. Unfortunately, even if we have simple equations to determine normal vectors, as we did in our example of a sphere (Section 6.4), the amount of computation required can be large. We have already seen many of the advantages of using polygonal models for our objects. A further advantage is that for flat polygons, we can significantly reduce the work required for shading. Most graphics systems, including WebGL, exploit the efficiencies possible for rendering flat polygons by decomposing curved surfaces into many small, flat polygons.

Consider a polygonal mesh, such as that shown in Figure 6.23, where each polygon is flat and thus has a well-defined normal vector. We consider three ways to shade the polygons: flat shading, smooth or Gouraud shading, and Phong shading.

6.5.1 Flat Shading

The three vectors—**l**, **n**, and **v**—can vary as we move from point to point on a surface. For a flat polygon, however, **n** is constant. If we assume a distant viewer, **v** is constant over the polygon. Finally, if the light source is distant, **l** is constant. Here *distant* could be interpreted in the strict sense of meaning that the source is at infinity. The necessary adjustments, such as changing the *location* of the source to the *direction* of the source, could then be made to the shading equations and to their implementation. *Distant* could also be interpreted in terms of the size of the polygon relative to how far the polygon is from the source or viewer, as shown in Figure 6.24. Graphics systems and user programs often exploit this definition.

If the three vectors are constant, then the shading calculation needs to be carried out only once for each polygon, and each point on the polygon is assigned the same shade. This technique is known as **flat**, or **constant, shading**.

FIGURE 6.23   Polygonal mesh.

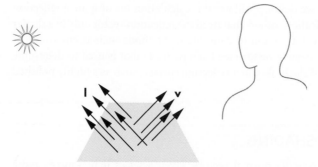

FIGURE 6.24   Distant source and viewer.

FIGURE 6.25   Flat shading of polygonal mesh.

FIGURE 6.26   Step chart.

Flat shading will show differences in shading among the polygons in our mesh. If the light sources and viewer are near the polygon, the vectors **l** and **v** will be different for each polygon. However, if our polygonal mesh has been designed to model a smooth surface, flat shading will almost always be disappointing because we can see even small differences in shading between adjacent polygons, as shown in Figure 6.25. The human visual system has a remarkable sensitivity to small differences in light intensity, due to a property known as **lateral inhibition**. If we see an increasing sequence of intensities, as is shown in Figure 6.26, we perceive the increases in brightness as overshooting on one side of an intensity step and undershooting on the other, as shown in Figure 6.27. We see stripes, known as **Mach bands**, along the edges. This phenomenon is a consequence of how the cones in the eye are connected to the optic nerve, and there is little that we can do to avoid it, other than to look for smoother shading techniques that do not produce large differences in shades at the edges of polygons.

6.5.2 Smooth and Gouraud Shading

In our rotating-cube example of Section 4.9, we saw that the rasterizer interpolates colors assigned to vertices across a polygon. Suppose that the lighting calculation

FIGURE 6.27   Perceived and actual intensities at an edge.

is made at each vertex using the material properties and the vectors **n**, **v**, and **l** computed for each vertex. Thus, each vertex will have its own color that the rasterizer can use to interpolate a shade for each fragment. Note that if the light source is distant, and either the viewer is distant or there are no specular reflections, then smooth (or interpolative) shading shades a polygon in a constant color.

If we consider our mesh, the idea of a normal existing at a vertex should cause concern to anyone worried about mathematical correctness. Because multiple polygons meet at interior vertices of the mesh, each of which has its own normal, the normal at the vertex is discontinuous. Although this situation might complicate the mathematics, Gouraud realized that the normal at the vertex could be *defined* in such a way as to achieve smoother shading through interpolation. Consider an interior vertex, as shown in Figure 6.28, where four polygons meet. Each has its own normal. In **Gouraud shading**, we define the normal at a vertex to be the normalized average of the normals of the polygons that share the vertex. For our example, the **vertex normal** is given by

FIGURE 6.28   Normals near interior vertex.

$$\mathbf{n} = \frac{\mathbf{n}_1 + \mathbf{n}_2 + \mathbf{n}_3 + \mathbf{n}_4}{|\mathbf{n}_1 + \mathbf{n}_2 + \mathbf{n}_3 + \mathbf{n}_4|}.$$

From a WebGL perspective, Gouraud shading is deceptively simple. We need only set the vertex normals correctly. Often, the literature makes no distinction between smooth and Gouraud shading. However, the lack of a distinction causes a problem: How do we find the normals that we should average together? If our program is linear, specifying a list of vertices (and other properties), we do not have the necessary information about which polygons share a vertex. What we need, of course, is a data structure for representing the mesh. Traversing this data structure can generate the vertices with the averaged normals. Such a data structure should contain, at a minimum, polygons, vertices, normals, and material properties. One possible structure is the one shown in Figure 6.29. The key information that must be represented in the data structure is which polygons meet at each vertex.

Color Plates 3 and 4 show simple shading effects available in WebGL. In Color Plate 3, there is a single light source, but each polygon has been rendered with a single shade (constant shading), computed using the Phong model. In Color Plate 4, normals have been assigned to all the vertices. WebGL has then computed shades for the vertices and has interpolated these shades over the faces of the polygons.

Color Plate 21 contains another illustration of the smooth shading. We used this color cube as an example in both Chapters 4 and 5, and the programs are on the

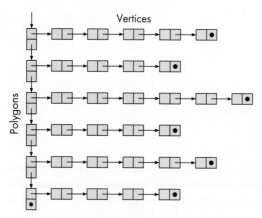

FIGURE 6.29   Mesh data structure.

FIGURE 6.30   Edge normals.

website. The eight vertices are colored black, white, red, green, blue, cyan, magenta, and yellow. Once smooth shading is enabled, WebGL interpolates the colors across the faces of the polygons automatically.

6.5.3 Phong Shading

Even the smoothness introduced by Gouraud shading may not prevent the appearance of Mach bands. Phong proposed that instead of interpolating vertex intensities, as we do in Gouraud shading, we interpolate normals across each polygon. Consider a polygon that shares edges and vertices with other polygons in the mesh, as shown in Figure 6.30. We can compute vertex normals by interpolating over the normals of the polygons that share the vertex. Next, we can use interpolation, as we did in Chapter 4, to interpolate the normals over the polygon. Consider Figure 6.31. We can use the interpolated normals at vertices A and B to interpolate normals along the edge between them:

$$\mathbf{n}_C(\alpha) = (1 - \alpha)\mathbf{n}_A + \alpha\mathbf{n}_B.$$

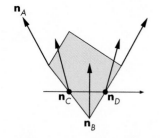

FIGURE 6.31   Interpolation of normals in Phong shading.

We can do a similar interpolation on all the edges. The normal at any interior point can be obtained from points on the edges by

$$\mathbf{n}(\alpha, \beta) = (1 - \beta)\mathbf{n}_C + \beta\mathbf{n}_D.$$

Once we have the normal at each point, we can make an independent shading calculation. Usually, this process can be combined with rasterization of the polygon. Until recently, Phong shading could only be carried out off-line because it requires the interpolation of normals across each polygon. In terms of the pipeline, Phong shading requires that the lighting model be applied to each fragment, hence, the name **per-fragment shading**. We will implement Phong shading through a fragment shader.

6.6 APPROXIMATION OF A SPHERE BY RECURSIVE SUBDIVISION

We have used the sphere as an example curved surface to illustrate shading calculations. However, the sphere is not an object supported within WebGL, so we will generate approximations to a sphere using triangles through a process known as **recursive subdivision**, a technique we introduced in Chapter 2 for constructing the Sierpinski gasket. Recursive subdivision is a powerful technique for generating approximations to curves and surfaces to any desired level of accuracy. The sphere approximation provides a basis for us to write simple programs that illustrate the interactions between shading parameters and polygonal approximations to curved surfaces.

Our starting point is a tetrahedron, although we could start with any regular polyhedron whose facets could be divided initially into triangles.[2] The regular tetrahedron is composed of four equilateral triangles, determined by four vertices. We start with the four vertices $(0, 0, 1)$, $(0, 2\sqrt{2}/3, -1/3)$, $(-\sqrt{6}/3, -\sqrt{2}/3, -1/3)$, and $(\sqrt{6}/3, -\sqrt{2}/3, -1/3)$. All four lie on the unit sphere, centered at the origin. (Exercise 6.6 suggests one method for finding these points.)

We get a first approximation by drawing a wireframe for the tetrahedron. We specify the four vertices by

```
var va = vec4(0.0, 0.0, -1.0, 1);
var vb = vec4(0.0, 0.942809, 0.333333, 1);
var vc = vec4(-0.816497, -0.471405, 0.333333, 1);
var vd = vec4(0.816497, -0.471405, 0.333333, 1);
```

These are the same points we used in Chapter 2 to draw the three-dimensional Sierpinski gasket. The order of vertices obeys the right-hand rule, so we can convert the code to draw shaded polygons with little difficulty. If we add the usual code for initialization, setting up a vertex buffer object and drawing the array, our program will generate an image such as that in Figure 6.32: a simple regular polyhedron, but a poor approximation to a sphere.

FIGURE 6.32 Tetrahedron.

2. The regular icosahedron is composed of 20 equilateral triangles. It makes a nice starting point for generating spheres.

(a)   (b)   (c)

FIGURE 6.33   Subdivision of a triangle by (a) bisecting angles, (b) computing the centroid, and (c) bisecting sides.

We can get a closer approximation to the sphere by subdividing each facet of the tetrahedron into smaller triangles. Subdividing into triangles will ensure that all the new facets will be flat. There are at least three ways to do the subdivision, as shown in Figure 6.33. We can bisect each of the angles of the triangle and draw the three bisectors, which meet at a common point, thus generating three new triangles. We can also compute the center of mass (centroid) of the vertices by simply averaging them and then draw lines from this point to the three vertices, again generating three triangles. However, these techniques do not preserve the equilateral triangles that make up the regular tetrahedron. Instead—recalling a construction for the Sierpinski gasket of Chapter 2—we can connect the bisectors of the sides of the triangle, forming four equilateral triangles, as shown in Figure 6.33(c). We use this technique for our example.

There are two main differences between the gasket program and the sphere program. First, when we subdivide a face of the tetrahedron, we do not throw away the middle triangle formed from the three bisectors of the sides. Second, although the vertices of a triangle lie on the circle, the bisector of a line segment joining any two of these vertices does not. We can push the bisectors to lie on the unit circle by normalizing their representations to have a unit length.

We initiate the recursion by

```
tetrahedron(va, vb, vc, vd, numTimesToSubdivide);
```

which divides the four sides,

```
function tetrahedron(a, b, c, d, n)
{
  divideTriangle(a, b, c, n);
  divideTriangle(d, c, b, n);
  divideTriangle(a, d, b, n);
  divideTriangle(a, c, d, n);
}
```

with the midpoint subdivision:

```
function divideTriangle(a, b, c, count)
{
  if (count > 0) {
    var ab = normalize(mix(a, b, 0.5), true);
    var ac = normalize(mix(a, c, 0.5), true);
    var bc = normalize(mix(b, c, 0.5), true);
```

```
    divideTriangle(a, ab, ac, count - 1);
    divideTriangle(ab, b, bc, count - 1);
    divideTriangle(bc, c, ac, count - 1);
    divideTriangle(ab, bc, ac, count - 1);
  }
  else {
    triangle(a, b, c);
  }
}
```

Note that we use the `mix` function to find the midpoint of two vertices. The `true` parameter in `normalize` indicates that we are normalizing the homogeneous representation of a point and that the fourth component of 1 should not be used in the normalization. The triangle function adds the vertex positions to a vertex array:

```
function triangle(a, b, c){
  pointsArray.push(a);
  pointsArray.push(a);
  pointsArray.push(a);
  index += 3;
}
```

FIGURE 6.34   Sphere approximations using subdivision.

Figure 6.34 shows an approximation to the sphere drawn with this code. We now add lighting and shading to our sphere approximation.

6.7 SPECIFYING LIGHTING PARAMETERS

For many years, the Blinn-Phong lighting model was the standard in computer graphics. It was implemented in hardware and was specified as part of the OpenGL fixed functionality pipeline. With programmable shaders, we are free to implement other lighting models. We can also choose where to apply a lighting model: in the application, in the vertex shader, or in the fragment shader. Consequently, we must define a group of lighting and material parameters and then either use them in the application code or send them to the shaders.

6.7.1 Light Sources

In Section 6.2, we introduced four types of light sources: ambient, point, spotlight, and distant. However, because spotlights and distant light sources can be derived from a point source, we will focus on point sources and ambient light. An ideal point source emits light uniformly in all directions. To obtain a spotlight from a point source, we need only limit the directions of the point source and make the light emissions follow a desired profile. To get a distant source from a point source, we need to allow the location of the source to go to infinity so the position of the source becomes the direction of the source. Note that this argument is similar to the argument that parallel viewing is the limit of perspective viewing as the center of projection moves to infinity. As we argued in deriving the equations for parallel projections, we will find it easier to derive the equations for lighting with distant sources directly rather than by taking limits.

Although the contribution of ambient light is the same everywhere in a scene, ambient light is dependent on the sources in the environment. For example, consider a closed room with a single white point source. When the light is turned off, there is no light in the room of any kind. When the light is turned on, at any point in the room that can see the light source, there is a contribution from the light hitting surfaces directly to the diffuse or specular reflection we see at that point. There is also a contribution from the white light bouncing off multiple surfaces in the room that is almost the same at every point in the room. It is this latter contribution that we call ambient light. Its color depends not only on the color of the source but also on the reflective properties of the surfaces in the room. Thus, if the room has red walls, we would expect the ambient component to have a dominant red component. Nevertheless, the ambient component to the shade we see on a surface is ultimately tied to the light sources in the environment and hence becomes part of the specification of the sources.

For every light source, we must specify its color and either its location or its direction. As in Section 6.2, the color of a source will have three separate color components—diffuse, specular, and ambient—that we can specify for a single light as

```
var lightAmbient = vec4(0.2, 0.2, 0.2, 1.0);
var lightDiffuse = vec4(1.0, 1.0, 1.0, 1.0);
var lightSpecular = vec4(1.0, 1.0, 1.0, 1.0);
```

We can specify the position of the light using a `vec4`. For a point source, its position will be in homogeneous coordinates, so a light might be specified as

```
var lightPosition = vec4(1.0, 2.0, 3.0,1.0);
```

If the fourth component is changed to zero as in

```
var lightPosition = vec4(1.0, 2.0, 3.0, 0.0);
```

the source becomes a directional source in the direction (1.0, 2.0, 3.0).

For a positional light source, we may also want to account for the attenuation of light received due to its distance from the source. Although, for an ideal source, the attenuation is inversely proportional to the square of the distance d, we can gain more flexibility by using the distance attenuation model,

$$f(d) = \frac{1}{a + bd + cd^2},$$

which contains constant, linear, and quadratic terms. We can use three floats for these values,

```
var attenuationConstant, attenuationLinear, attenuationQuadratic;
```

and use them in the application or send them to the shaders as uniform variables.

We can also convert a positional source to a spotlight by setting its direction, the angle of the cone or the spotlight cutoff, and the drop-off rate or spotlight exponent. These three parameters can be specified by three floats.

6.7.2 Materials

Material properties should match up directly with the supported light sources and with the chosen reflection model. We may also want the flexibility to specify different material properties for the front and back faces of a surface.

For example, we might specify ambient, diffuse, and specular reflectivity coefficients (k_a, k_d, k_s) for each primary color through three colors, using either RGB or RGBA colors, as for the opaque surface

```
var materialAmbient = vec4(1.0, 0.0, 1.0, 1.0);
var materialDiffuse = vec4(1.0, 0.8, 0.0, 1.0);
var materialSpecular = vec4(1.0, 0.8, 0.0, 1.0);
```

Here we have defined a small amount of gray ambient reflectivity, yellow diffuse properties, and white specular reflections. Note that often the diffuse and specular reflectivity are the same. For the specular component we also need to specify its shininess:

```
var materialShininess = 100.0;
```

If we have different reflectivity properties for the front and back faces, we can also specify three additional parameters,

```
var backAmbient, backDiffuse, backSpecular;
```

which can be used to render the back faces.

We also want to allow for scenes in which a light source is within the view volume and thus might be visible, For example, for an outdoor night scene, the moon might be visible to the viewer and thus should appear in the image. We could model the moon with a simple polygonal approximation to a circle. However, when we render the moon, its color should be constant and not be affected by other light sources. We can create such effects by including an emissive component that models self-luminous sources. This term is unaffected by any of the light sources, and it does not affect any other surfaces. It adds a fixed color to the surfaces and is specified in a manner similar to other material properties. For example,

```
var emission = vec4(0.0, 0.3, 0.3, 1.0);
```

specifies a small amount of blue-green (cyan) emission.

6.8   IMPLEMENTING A LIGHTING MODEL

So far, we have only looked at parameters that we might use in a light model. We have yet to build a particular model. Nor have we worried about where to apply a lighting model. We focus on a simple version of the Blinn-Phong model using a single point source. Because light from multiple sources is additive, we can repeat the calculation for each source and add up the individual contributions. We have three choices as to where we do the calculation: in the application, in the vertex shader, or in the fragment shader. Although the basic model can be the same for each, there will be major differences both in efficiency and appearance depending on where the calculation is done.

6.8.1 Applying the Lighting Model in the Application

We have used two methods to assign colors to filled triangles. In the first, we sent a single color for each polygon to the shaders as a uniform variable and used this color for each fragment. In the second, we assigned a color to each vertex as a vertex attribute. The rasterizer then interpolated these vertex colors across the polygon. Both of these approaches can be applied to lighting. In constant or flat shading, we apply a lighting model once for each polygon and use the computed color for the entire polygon. In the interpolative shading, we apply the model at each vertex to compute a vertex color attribute. The vertex shader can then output these colors, and the rasterizer will interpolate them to determine a color for each fragment.

Let's explore a simple example with ambient, diffuse, and specular lighting. Assume the following parameters have been specified for a single point light source:

```
var ambientColor, diffuseColor, specularColor;
var lightPosition;
```

Also assume a single material whose parameters are

```
var reflectAmbient, reflectDiffuse, reflectSpecular;
```

The color we need to compute is the sum of the ambient, diffuse, and specular contributions,

```
var color, ambient, diffuse, specular;
```

where each of these is a `vec3` or `vec4` and `color` is the sum of the computed ambient, diffuse, and specular terms. Each component of the ambient term is the product of the corresponding terms from the ambient light source and the material reflectivity. Thus, if we define

```
var ambientProduct;
```

we can use the function `mult` that multiplies two `vec4`s component by component; hence

```
ambientProduct = mult(lightAmbient, materialAmbient);
diffuseProduct = mult(lightDiffuse, materialDiffuse);
specularProduct = mult(lightSpecular, materialSpecular);
```

We need the normal to compute the diffuse term. Because we are working with triangles, we have three vertices, and these vertices determine a unique plane and its normal. Suppose that these vertices have indices a, b, and c in the array `vertices`. The cross product of b − a and c − a is perpendicular to the plane determined by the three vertices. Thus, we get the desired unit normal by

```
var t1 = subtract(vertices[b], vertices[a]);
var t2 = subtract(vertices[c], vertices[a]);
var normal = vec4(normalize(cross(t1, t2)));
```

Note that the direction of the normal depends on the order of the vertices and assumes we are using the right-hand rule to determine an outward face.

Next we need to take the dot product of the unit normal with the vector in the direction of the light source. There are four cases we must consider:

- Constant shading with a distant source
- Interpolative shading with a distant source
- Constant shading with a finite source
- Interpolative shading with a finite source

For constant shading, we only need compute a single diffuse color for each triangle. For a distant source, we have the direction of the source, which is the same for all points on the triangle. Hence, we can simply take the dot product of the unit normal with a normalized source direction. The diffuse contribution is then

```
var d = dot(normal, lightPosition);
diffuse = mult(lightDiffuse, reflectDiffuse);
diffuse = scale(d, diffuse);
```

There is one additional step we should take. The diffuse term only makes sense if the face is oriented toward the light source or, equivalently, the dot product is non-negative, so we must modify the calculation to

```
var d = Math.max(dot(normal, lightPostiion), 0.0);
```

For a distant light source, the diffuse contribution is the same at each vertex of a polygon, so we need perform only one diffuse lighting calculation per polygon. Consequently, interpolative and constant diffuse shading produce the same contribution for each fragment.

For a finite or near source, we have two choices: Either we compute a single diffuse contribution for the entire polygon and use constant shading, or we compute the diffuse term at each vertex and use interpolative shading. Because we are working with triangles, the normal is the same at each vertex, but with a near source, the vector from any point on the polygon to the light source will be different. If we want to compute only a single diffuse color, we can use the point at the center of the triangle to compute the direction:

```
var v = add(a, add(b, c));
v = scale(1/3, v);
lightPosition = subtract(lightPosition, v);
var d = Math.max(dot(normal, lightPosition), 0);
diffuseProduct = mult(lightDiffuse, reflectDiffuse);
diffuse = mult(d, diffuseProduct);
```

The calculation for the specular term appears to be similar to the calculation for the diffuse term, but there is one tricky issue: We need to compute the halfway vector. For a distance source, the light position becomes a direction, so

```
half = normalize(add(lightPosition, viewDirection));
```

The view direction is a vector from a point on the surface to the eye. The default is that the camera is at the origin in object space, so for a vertex v, the vector is

```
origin = vec4(0.0, 0.0, 0.0, 1.0);
viewDirection =  subtract(v, origin);
```

Thus, even though each triangle has a single normal, there is a different halfway vector for each vertex and, consequently, the specular term will vary across the surface as the rasterizer interpolates the vertex shades. The specular term for vertex v can be computed as

```
var s = dot(half, n);

if (s > 0.0) {
  specularProduct = mult(lightSpecular, materialSpecular);
  specular = scale(Math.pow(s, materialShininess, specularProduct));
  specular[3] = 1.0;
}
else {
  specular = vec4(0.0, 0.0, 0.0, 1.0);
}
```

Note that scaling of a `vec4` has no effect because the perspective division will cancel out the scaling. We can set the `w` component to 1 as above to avoid the problem. Alternately, we can use the **selection** and **swizzling** operators in GLSL to scale only the first three components, as in the code

```
specular.xyz = scale(Math.pow(s, materialShininess, specular).xyz);
```

Here the swizzle on the right picks out the first three components, and the swizzle on the left specifies that we are changing only the first three components of `specular`. We need to add one final step. Just as with the diffuse term, if the surface does not face the light source, there will be no contribution. So we add the test

```
if (d < 0) {
  specular = vec4(0.0, 0.0, 0.0, 1.0);
}
```

where d was computed in the calculation of the diffuse term.

6.8.2 Efficiency

For a static scene, the lighting computation is done once, so we can send the vertex positions and vertex colors to the GPU once. Consider what happens if we add lighting to our rotating cube program. Each time the cube rotates about a coordinate axis, the normal to four of the faces changes, as does the position of each of the six vertices. Hence, we must recompute the diffuse and specular components at each of the vertices. If we do all the calculations in the CPU, both the vertex positions and colors must then be sent to the GPU. For large data sets, this process is extremely inefficient. Not only are we doing a lot of computation in the CPU but we are also causing a potential bottleneck by sending so much vertex data to the GPU. Consequently, we will almost always want to do lighting calculation in the shaders.

Before examining shaders for lighting, there are a few other efficiency measures we can employ, either in the application or in a shader. We can obtain many efficiencies if we assume that either or both the viewer and the light source are far from the polygon we are rendering. Hence, even if the source is a point source with a finite location, it might be far enough away that the distances from the vertices to the source are all about the same. In this case, the diffuse term at each vertex would be identical, and we would need only one calculation per polygon. Note that a definition of far and near in this context depends both on the distance to the light source and on the size of the polygon. A small polygon will not show much variation in the diffuse component even if the source is fairly close to the polygon. The same argument holds for the specular term when we consider the distance between vertices and the viewer. We can add parameters that allow the application to specify whether it should use these simplified calculations.

In Chapter 5, we saw that a surface has both a front face and a back face. For polygons, we determine front and back by the order in which the vertices are specified, using the right-hand rule. For most objects, we see only the front faces, so we are not concerned with how WebGL shades the back-facing surfaces. For example, for convex objects, such as a sphere or a parallelepiped (Figure 6.35), the viewer can never see a back face, regardless of where she is positioned. However, if we remove a side from a cube or slice the sphere, as shown in Figure 6.36, a properly placed viewer may see a back face; thus, we must shade both the front and back faces correctly. In many situations we can ignore all back faces by either culling them out in the application or not rendering any face whose normal does not point toward the viewer. If we render back faces, they may have different material properties than the front faces, so we must specify a set of back face properties.

Light sources are special types of geometric objects and have geometric attributes, such as position, just like polygons and points. Hence, light sources can be affected by transformations. We can specify them at the desired position or specify them in a convenient position and move them to the desired position by the model-view transformation. The basic rule governing object placement is that vertices are converted to eye coordinates by the model-view transformation in effect at the time the vertices are defined. Thus, by careful placement of the light-source specifications relative to the definition of other geometric objects, we can create light sources that remain stationary while the objects move, light sources that move while objects remain stationary, and light sources that move with the objects.

We also have choices as to which coordinate system to use for lighting computations. For now we will do our lighting calculations in object coordinates. Depending on whether the light source or objects are moving, it may be more efficient to use eye coordinates. Later, when we add texture mapping to our skills, we will introduce lighting methods that use local coordinate systems.

6.8.3 Lighting in the Vertex Shader

When we presented transformations, we saw that a transformation such as the model-view transformation could be carried out either in the application or in the

FIGURE 6.35   Shading of convex objects.

FIGURE 6.36   Visible back surfaces.

vertex shader, but for most applications it was far more efficient to implement the transformation in the shader. The same is true for lighting. To implement lighting in the vertex shader, we must carry out three steps.

First, we must choose a lighting model. Do we use the Blinn-Phong or some other model? Do we include distance attenuation? Do we want two-sided lighting? Once we make these decisions, we can write a vertex shader to implement the model. Finally, we have to transfer the necessary data to the shader. Some data can be transferred using uniform variables, while other data can be transferred as vertex attributes.

Let's go through the process for the model we just developed, the Blinn-Phong model without distance attenuation and with a single point light source. We can transfer the ambient, diffuse, and specular components of the source plus its position as uniform variables. We can do likewise for the material properties. Rather than writing the application code first, because we know how to transfer information to a shader, we will first write the vertex shader.

The vertex shader must output a vertex position in clip coordinates and a vertex color to the rasterizer. If we send a model-view matrix and a projection matrix to the shader, then the computation of the vertex position is identical to our examples in Chapters 4 and 5. Hence, this part of the code will look something like

```
attribute vec4 vPosition;
uniform mat4 modelViewMatrix;
uniform mat4 projectionMatrix;

void main()
{
  gl_Position = projectionMatrix * modelViewMatrix * vPosition;
}
```

Note that because GLSL supports operator overloading, the code is much simpler and clearer than in the application. The output color is the sum of the ambient, diffuse, and specular contributions,

```
varying vec4 fColor
vec4 ambient, diffuse, specular;

fColor = ambient + diffuse + specular;
```

so the part we must address is computation of these three terms.

Rather than sending all the reflectivity and light colors separately to the shader, we send only the product term for each contribution. Thus, in the ambient computation, we use the products of the red, green, and blue ambient light with the red, green, and blue ambient reflectivities. We can compute these products and send them to the shader as the uniform vector

```
uniform vec4 ambientProduct;
```

We can do the same for the diffuse and specular products:

```
uniform vec4 diffuseProduct;
uniform vec4 specularProduct;
```

The ambient term is then simply

```
ambient = ambientProduct;
```

The diffuse term requires a normal for each vertex. Because triangles are flat, the normal is the same for each vertex in a triangle, so we can send the normal to the shader as a uniform variable.[3] We can use the `normalize` function to get a unit-length normal from the `vec4` type we used in the application:

```
attribute vec4 vNormal;

vec3 N = normalize(vNormal.xyz);
```

The unit vector in the direction of the light source is given by

```
vec3 L = normalize(lightPosition - vPosition).xyz;
```

The diffuse term is then

```
diffuse = max(dot(L, N), 0.0) * diffuseProduct;
```

The specular term is computed in a similar manner. Because the viewer is at the origin in object coordinates, the normalized vector in the direction of the viewer is

```
vec3 E = -normalize(vPosition.xyz);
```

and the halfway vector is

```
vec3 H = normalize(L+E);
```

The specular term is then

```
specular = pow(max(dot(N, H), 0.0), shininess) * specularProduct;
```

However, if the light source is behind the surface, there cannot be a specular term, so we add a simple test:

```
specular = max(pow(max(dot(N, H), 0.0), shininess) * specularProduct,
               0.0);
```

Here is the full shader:

```
attribute vec4 vPosition;
attribute vec4 vNormal;

varying vec4 fColor;
```

---

3. In Section 6.9, we will consider methods that assign a different normal to each vertex of a polygon.

```
uniform vec4 ambientProduct, diffuseProduct, specularProduct;
uniform mat4 modelViewMatrix;
uniform mat4 projectionMatrix;
uniform vec4 lightPosition;
uniform float shininess;

void main()
{
  vec3 pos = -(modelViewMatrix * vPosition).xyz;
  vec3 light = lightPosition.xyz;
  vec3 L = normalize(light - pos);

  vec3 E = normalize(-pos);
  vec3 H = normalize(L + E);

  // Transform vertex normal into eye coordinates

  vec3 N = normalize((modelViewMatrix * vNormal).xyz);

  // Compute terms in the illumination equation

  vec4 ambient = ambientProduct;

  float Kd = max(dot(L, N), 0.0);
  vec4  diffuse = Kd * diffuseProduct;

  float Ks = pow(max(dot(N, H), 0.0), shininess);
  vec4  specular = Ks * specularProduct;

  if (dot(L, N) < 0.0) {
    specular = vec4(0.0, 0.0, 0.0, 1.0);
  }

  fColor = ambient + diffuse + specular;
  fColor.a = 1.0;

  gl_Position = projectionMatrix * modelViewMatrix * vPosition;
}
```

Because the colors are set in the vertex shader, the simple fragment shader that we have used previously,

```
varying vec4 fColor;

void main()
{
  gl_FragColor = fColor;
}
```

will take the interpolated colors from the rasterizer and assign them to fragments.

Let's return to the cube shading example. The main change we have to make is to set up uniform variables for the light and material parameters. Thus, for the ambient component we might have an ambient light term and an ambient reflectivity, given as

```
var lightAmbient = vec4(0.2, 0.2, 0.2, 1.0);
var materialAmbient = vec4(1.0, 0.0, 1.0, 1.0);
```

We compute the ambient product

```
var ambientProduct = mult(lightAmbient, materialAmbient);
```

We get these values to the shader by

```
gl.uniform4fv(gl.getUniformLocation(program, "ambientProduct"),
              ambientProduct);
```

We can do the same for the rest of the uniform variables in the vertex shader. Note that the normal vector depends on more than one vertex and so cannot be computed in the shader, because the shader has the position information only for the vertex that initiated its execution.

There is an additional issue we must address because the cube is rotating. As the cube rotates, the positions of all the vertices and all the normals to the surface change. When we first developed the program, we applied the rotation transformation in the application, and each time that the rotation matrix was updated we resent the vertices to the GPU. Later, we argued that it was far more efficient to send the rotation matrix to the shader and let the transformation be carried out in the GPU. The same is true with this example. We can send a projection matrix and a model-view matrix as uniform variables. This example has only one object, the cube, and thus the rotation matrix and the model-view matrix are identical. If we rotate the cube, we must also rotate the normal by the same amount. If we want to apply the rotation to the normal vector in the GPU, then we need to make the following change to the shader:

```
vec3 N = normalize((modelViewMatrix * vNormal).xyz);
```

The complete program is on the website.

Note that rotating the normal is a special case of transforming the normal vector. If we apply a general transformation to the cube, we must compute a matrix called the **normal matrix** to apply to the normal vector so that the angle between a vector from the origin to a vertex and the normal is unchanged. We can derive this transformation as follows.

When we compute lighting, we need the cosine of the angle between the light direction l and the normal to the surface n, and the cosine of the angle between the view direction v and n, which we obtain through the dot products $l \cdot n$ and $v \cdot n$. However, when we transform to a different frame, say, from the object frame to the camera frame, we go from v' to $\mathbf{M}v$, where $\mathbf{M}$ is usually the model-view matrix. We must also transform n by some matrix $\mathbf{N}$ such that these cosines are unchanged. Otherwise, our lighting calculations will be wrong. Consider the angle between the view direction and the normal. Let's assume that both v and n are three-dimensional vectors, not in homogeneous form. Then we require

$$v \cdot n = v^T n = v' \cdot n' = (\mathbf{M}v)^T (\mathbf{N}n) = v^T \mathbf{M}^T \mathbf{N}n.$$

Hence, we must have

$$\mathbf{M}^T \mathbf{N} = \mathbf{I},$$

and thus

$$\mathbf{N} = (\mathbf{M}^T)^{-1}.$$

Generally, $\mathbf{M}$ is the upper-left 3×3 submatrix of the model-view matrix. In this example, we can use the fact that we are only doing a rotation about the origin, and under this condition the normal matrix is the same rotation matrix that transforms the vertex positions.

However, if there are multiple objects in the scene or the viewing parameters change, we have to be a little careful with this construct. Suppose that there is a second nonrotating cube in the scene and we also use nondefault viewing parameters. Now we have two different model-view matrices, one for each cube. One is constant and the other is changing as one of the cubes rotates. What is really changing is the modeling part of the model-view matrix and not the viewing part that positions the camera. We can handle this complication in a number of ways. We could compute the two model-view matrices in the application and send them to the vertex shader each time there is a rotation. We could also use separate modeling and viewing transformations and send only the modeling matrix—the rotation matrix—to the shader after initialization. We would then form the model-view matrix in the shader. We could also just send the rotation angles to the shader and do all the work there. If the light source is also changing its position, we have even more options.

6.9   SHADING OF THE SPHERE MODEL

The rotating cube is a simple example to demonstrate lighting, but because there are only six faces and they meet at right angles, it is not a good example for testing the smoothness of a lighting model. Consider instead the sphere model that we developed in Section 6.6. Although the model comprises many small triangles, unlike the cube, we do not want to see the edges. Rather, we want to shade the polygons so that we cannot see the edges where triangles meet, and the smoother the shading, the fewer polygons we need to model the sphere.

To shade the sphere model, we can start with the same shaders we used for the rotating cube. The differences are in the application program. We replace the generation of the cube with the tetrahedron subdivision from Section 6.6, adding the computation of the normals, which are sent to the vertex shader as attribute-qualified variables. The result is shown in Figure 6.37. Note that even as we increase the number of subdivisions so that the interiors of the spheres appear smooth, we can still see edges of polygons around the outside of the sphere image. This type of outline is called a **silhouette edge**.

FIGURE 6.37   Shaded sphere model.

The differences in this example between constant shading and smooth shading are minor. Because each triangle is flat, the normal is the same at each vertex. If the source is far from the object, the diffuse component will be constant for each triangle. Likewise, if the camera is far from the viewer, the specular term will be constant for each triangle. However, because two adjacent triangles will have different normals and thus are shaded with different colors, even if we create many triangles, we still can see the lack of smoothness.

One way to get an idea of how smooth a display we can produce with relatively few triangles is to use the actual normals of the sphere for each vertex in the approximation. In Section 6.4, we found that for the sphere centered at the origin, the normal at a point $\mathbf{p}$ is simply $\mathbf{p}$. Hence, in the `triangle` function the position of a vertex gives the normal:

```
function triangle(a, b, c)
{
  normalsArray.push(a);
  normalsArray.push(b);
  normalsArray.push(c);

  pointsArray.push(a);
  pointsArray.push(b);
  pointsArray.push(c);
}
```

FIGURE 6.38 Shading of the sphere with the true normals.

The results of this definition of the normals are shown in Figure 6.38.

Although using the true normals produces a rendering more realistic than flat shading, the example is not a general one because we have used normals that are known analytically. We also have not provided a true Gouraud-shaded image. Suppose we want a Gouraud-shaded image of our approximate sphere. At each vertex, we need to know the normals of all polygons incident at the vertex. Our code does not have a data structure that contains the required information. Try Exercises 6.9 and 6.10, in which you construct such a structure. Note that six polygons meet at a vertex created by subdivision, whereas only three polygons meet at the original vertices of the tetrahedron. If we start with a rectangular or triangular mesh, it is easier to construct a data structure that allows us to obtain normals from adjacent polygons at each vertex. See Exercise 6.11.

6.10 PER-FRAGMENT LIGHTING

There is another option we can use to obtain a smoother shading. We can do the lighting calculation on a per-fragment basis rather than on a per-vertex basis. When we did all our lighting calculations in the vertex shader, visually there was no advantage over doing the same computation in the application and then sending the computed vertex colors to the vertex shader, which would then pass them on to the rasterizer. Thus, whether we did lighting in the vertex shader or in the application, the rasterizer interpolated the same vertex colors to obtain fragment colors.

With a fragment shader, we can do an independent lighting calculation for each fragment. The fragment shader needs to get the interpolated values of the normal vector, light source position, and eye position from the rasterizer. The vertex shader can compute these values and output them to the rasterizer. In addition, the vertex shader must output the vertex position in clip coordinates. Here is the vertex shader:

```
attribute vec4 vPosition;
attribute vec4 vNormal;
varying vec3 N, L, E;
uniform mat4 modelViewMatrix;
uniform mat4 projectionMatrix;
uniform vec4 lightPosition;

void main()
{
  vec3 pos = -(modelViewMatrix * vPosition).xyz;
  vec3 light = lightPosition.xyz;
  L = normalize(light - pos);
  E =  -pos;
  N = normalize((modelViewMatrix * vNormal).xyz);

  gl_Position = projectionMatrix * modelViewMatrix * vPosition;
}
```

The fragment shader can now apply the Blinn-Phong lighting model to each fragment using the light and material parameters passed in from the application as uniform variables and the interpolated vectors from the rasterizer. The following shader corresponds to the vertex shader we used in the previous example:

```
uniform vec4 ambientProduct;
uniform vec4 diffuseProduct;
uniform vec4 specularProduct;
uniform float shininess;
varying vec3 N, L, E;

void main()
{
  vec4 fColor;

  vec3 H = normalize(L + E);
  vec4 ambient = ambientProduct;

  float Kd = max(dot(L, N), 0.0);
  vec4  diffuse = Kd * diffuseProduct;

  float Ks = pow(max(dot(N, H), 0.0), shininess);
  vec4  specular = Ks * sSpecularProduct;

  if (dot(L, N) < 0.0) {
    specular = vec4(0.0, 0.0, 0.0, 1.0);
  }
```

```
    fColor = ambient + diffuse + specular;
    fColor.a = 1.0;

    gl_FragColor = fColor;
}
```

Note that we normalize vectors in the fragment shader rather than in the vertex shaders. If we were to normalize a variable such as the normals in the vertex shader, that would not guarantee that the interpolated normals produced by the rasterizer would have the unit magnitude needed for the lighting computation.

Because we can only render triangles in WebGL, unless we use Gouraud shading with the true normals, the normals will be the same whether we use per-vertex or per-fragment shading. If the light source and viewer are relatively far from the surface, so that each triangle makes only a small contribution to the rendered image, we might not notice a significant difference between per-vertex and per-fragment shading. However, we may notice differences in efficiency that depend on both the application and the particular GPU.

Color Plate 18 shows a teapot rendered with both per-vertex and per-fragment lighting and a narrow specular highlight. With per-fragment lighting, the specular highlight is more concentrated. There are four versions of the shaded sphere on the website. The first, `shadedSphere1`, uses the true vertex normals and per-vertex shading. The second, `shadedSphere2`, uses the true normal and per-fragment shading. The third and fourth, `shadedSphere3` and `shadedSphere4`, use the normal computed from the three vertices of each triangle and do per-vertex and per-fragment shading, respectively. The program `shadedCube` is a rotating cube with the normals computed from the vertices of each triangle.

6.11 NONPHOTOREALISTIC SHADING

Programmable shaders make it possible not only to incorporate more realistic lighting models in real time but also to create interesting nonphotorealistic effects. Two such examples are the use of only a few colors and emphasizing the edges in objects. Both these effects are techniques that we might want to use to obtain a cartoonlike effect in an image.

Suppose that we use only two colors in a vertex shader:

```
vec4 color1 = vec4(1.0, 1.0, 0.0, 1.0); // yellow
vec4 color2 = vec4(1.0, 0.0, 0.0, 1.0); // red
```

We could then switch between the colors based, for example, on the magnitude of the diffuse color. Using the light and normal vectors, we could assign colors as

```
gl_FragColor = (dot(lightv, norm)) > 0.5 ? color1 : color2;
```

Although we could have used two colors in simpler ways, by using the diffuse color to determine a threshold, the color of the object changes with its shape and the position of the light source.

We can also try to draw the silhouette edge of an object. One way to identify such edges is to look at sign changes in `dot(lightv, norm)`. This value should be positive for any vertex facing the viewer and negative for a vertex pointed away from the viewer. Thus, we can test for small values of this value and assign a color such as black to the vertex:

```
vec4 color3 = vec4(0.0, 0.0, 0.0, 1.0); // black

if (abs(dot(viewv, norm) < 0.01)) {
 gl_FragColor = color3;
}
```

Color Plate 11 shows the results of these methods applied to the teapot model.

6.12 GLOBAL ILLUMINATION

There are limitations imposed by the local lighting model that we have used. Consider, for example, an array of spheres illuminated by a distant source, as shown in Figure 6.39(a). The spheres close to the source block some of the light from the source from reaching the other spheres. However, if we use our local model, each sphere is shaded independently; all appear the same to the viewer (Figure 6.39(b)). In addition, if these spheres are specular, some light is scattered among spheres. Thus, if the spheres are very shiny, we should see the reflection of multiple spheres in some of the spheres and possibly even the multiple reflections of some spheres in themselves. Our lighting model cannot handle this situation. Nor can it produce shadows, except by using the tricks for some special cases, as we saw in Chapter 5.

All these phenomena—shadows, reflections, blockage of light—are global effects and require a global lighting model. Although such models exist and can be quite elegant, in practice they are incompatible with the pipeline model. With the pipeline model, we must render each polygon independently of the other polygons, and we want our image to be the same regardless of the order in which the application produces the polygons. Although this restriction limits the lighting effects that we can simulate, we can render scenes very rapidly.

There are two alternative rendering strategies—ray tracing and radiosity—that can handle global effects. Each is best at different lighting conditions. Ray tracing starts with the synthetic-camera model but determines, for each projector that strikes a polygon, whether that point is indeed illuminated by one or more sources before

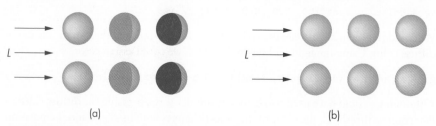

FIGURE 6.39   Array of shaded spheres. (a) Global lighting model. (b) Local lighting model.

computing the local shading at each point. Thus, in Figure 6.40, we see three polygons and a light source. The projector shown intersects one of the polygons. A local renderer might use the modified Phong model to compute the shade at the point of intersection. The ray tracer would find that the light source cannot strike the point of intersection directly, but that light from the source is reflected from the third polygon and this reflected light illuminates the point of intersection. In Chapter 12, we shall show how to find this information and make the required calculations.

A radiosity renderer is based upon energy considerations. From a physical point of view, all the light energy in a scene is conserved. Consequently, there is an energy balance that accounts for all the light that radiates from sources and is reflected by various surfaces in the scene. A radiosity calculation thus requires the solution of a large set of equations involving all the surfaces. As we shall see in Chapter 12, a ray tracer is best suited to a scene consisting of highly reflective surfaces, whereas a radiosity renderer is best suited for a scene in which all the surfaces are perfectly diffuse.

Although a pipeline renderer cannot take into account many global phenomena exactly, this observation does not mean we cannot produce realistic imagery with WebGL or another API that is based upon a pipeline architecture. What we can do is use our knowledge of WebGL and of the effects that global lighting produces to approximate what a global renderer would do. For example, our use of projective shadows in Chapter 5 shows that we can produce simple shadows. Many of the most exciting advances in computer graphics over the past few years have been in the use of pipeline renderers for global effects. We shall study many such techniques in the next few chapters, including mapping methods, multipass rendering, and transparency.

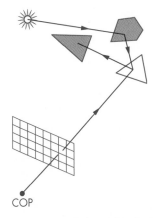

FIGURE 6.40 Polygon blocked from light source.

SUMMARY AND NOTES

We have developed a lighting model that fits well with our pipeline approach to graphics. With it, we can create a variety of lighting effects and we can employ different types of light sources. Although we cannot create all the global effects of a ray tracer, a typical graphics workstation can render a polygonal scene using the modified Phong reflection model and smooth shading in about the same amount of time as it can render a scene without shading. From the perspective of an application program, adding shading requires setting parameters that describe the light sources and materials and that can be implemented with programmable shaders. In spite of the limitations of the local lighting model that we have introduced, our simple renderer performs remarkably well; it is the basis of the reflection model supported by most APIs.

Programmable shaders have changed the picture considerably. Not only can we create new methods of shading each vertex, we can use fragment shaders to do the lighting calculation for each fragment, thus avoiding the need to interpolate colors across each polygon. Methods such as Phong shading that were not possible within the standard pipeline can now be programmed by the user and will execute in about the same amount of time as the modified Phong shader. It is also possible to create a myriad of new shading effects, including shadows and reflections.

The recursive subdivision technique that we used to generate an approximation to a sphere is a powerful one that will reappear in various guises in Chapter 11, where we use variants of this technique to render curves and surfaces. It will also arise when we introduce modeling techniques that rely on the self-similarity of many natural objects.

This chapter concludes our development of polygonal-based graphics. You should now be able to generate scenes with lighting and shading. Techniques for creating even more sophisticated images, such as texture mapping and compositing, involve using the pixel-level capabilities of graphics systems—topics that we consider in Chapter 7.

Now is a good time for you to write an application program. Experiment with various lighting and shading parameters. Try to create light sources that move, either independently or with the objects in the scene. You will probably face difficulties in producing shaded images that do not have small defects, such as cracks between polygons through which light can enter. Many of these problems are artifacts of small numerical errors in rendering calculations. There are many tricks of the trade for mitigating the effects of these errors. Some you will discover on your own; others are given in the Suggested Readings for this chapter.

We turn to rasterization issues in Chapter 8. Although we have seen some of the ways in which the different modules in the rendering pipeline function, we have not yet seen the details. As we develop these details, you will see how the pieces fit together such that each successive step in the pipeline requires only a small increment of work.

SUGGESTED READINGS

The use of lighting and reflection in computer graphics has followed two parallel paths: the physical and the computational. From the physical perspective, Kajiya's rendering equation [Kaj86] describes the overall energy balance in an environment and requires knowledge of the reflectivity function for each surface. Reflection models, such as the Torrance-Sparrow model [Tor67] and Cook-Torrance model [Coo82], are based on modeling a surface with small planar facets. See Hall [Hal89] and Foley [Fol90] for discussions of such models.

Phong [Pho75] is credited with putting together a computational model that included ambient, diffuse, and specular terms. The use of the halfway vector was first suggested by Blinn [Bli77]. The basic model of transmitted light was used by Whitted [Whi80]. It was later modified by Heckbert and Hanrahan [Hec84]. Gouraud [Gou71] introduced interpolative shading.

The *OpenGL Programming Guide* [Shr13] contains many good hints on the effective use of OpenGL's rendering capabilities and discusses the fixed-function lighting pipeline that uses functions that have been deprecated in shader-based OpenGL.

EXERCISES

6.1   When we build three-dimensional graphical models, we may be disappointed to see images looking flat and not illustrating the three-dimensional nature of the model. Give an example to shows such defects, and describe a way to overcome such limitations.

6.2   When we develop separate models of light sources and interaction of light materials for a model, our aim is to add shading to a fast pipeline graphics architecture. For such a system, we develop only the local lighting models. Explain the characteristic of the local lighting models that support these features over the global lighting models.

6.3   The Phong reflection model uses four vectors to calculate a color for an arbitrary point on a surface. Why do we use these four vectors?

6.4   What are the different types of material-light interaction the Phong model supports?

6.5   A simple version of the Blinn-Phong model uses a single point source. State the effect of light from multiple sources on such a model, and how to implement it.

6.6   Find four points equidistant from one another on a unit sphere. These points determine a tetrahedron. *Hint:* You can arbitrarily let one of the points be at $(0, 1, 0)$ and let the other three be in the plane $y = -d$, for some positive value of d.

6.7   Show that if **v** lies in the same plane as **l**, **n**, and **r**, then the halfway angle satisfies

$$2\psi = \phi.$$

What relationship is there between the angles if **v** is not coplanar with the other vectors?

6.8   Consider all the combinations of near or far viewers, near or far light sources, flat or curved surfaces, and diffuse and specular reflections. For which cases can you simplify the shading calculations? In which cases does the use of the halfway vector help? Explain your answers.

6.9   Construct a data structure for representing the subdivided tetrahedron. Traverse the data structure such that you can Gouraud-shade the approximation to the sphere based on subdividing the tetrahedron.

6.10   Repeat Exercise 6.9 but start with an icosahedron instead of a tetrahedron.

6.11   Construct a data structure for representing meshes of quadrilaterals. Write a program to shade the meshes represented by your data structure.

6.12   Write a program that does recursive subdivisions on quadrilaterals and quadrilateral meshes.

6.13   Consider two translucent materials that meet along a planar boundary. Suppose that the speed of light in the two materials is v_1 and v_2, respectively. Show that Snell's law is a statement that light travels from a point in one material to a point in the second material in the minimum time.

6.14   Show the changes we make to diffuse contribution when the face is oriented toward the light source.

6.15   Although we have yet to discuss framebuffer operations, you can start constructing a ray tracer using a single routine of the form `write_pixel(x, y, color)` that places the value of `color` (either an RGB color or an intensity) at the pixel located at `(x, y)` in the framebuffer. Write a pseudocode routine `ray` that recursively traces a cast ray. You can assume that you have a function available that will intersect a ray with an object. Consider how to limit how far the original ray will be traced.

6.16   If you have a pixel-writing routine available on your system, write a ray tracer that will ray-trace a scene composed of only spheres. Use the mathematical equations for the spheres rather than a polygonal approximation.

6.17   Add light sources and shading to the maze program in Exercise 5.13.

6.18   Using the sphere generation program as a starting point, construct an interactive program that will allow you to position one or more light sources and to alter material properties. Use your program to try to generate images of surfaces that match familiar materials, such as various metals, plastic, and carbon.

6.19   As geometric data pass through the viewing pipeline, a sequence of rotations, translations, and scalings, and a projection transformation are applied to the vectors that determine the cosine terms in the Phong reflection model. Which, if any, of these operations preserve(s) the angles between the vectors? What are the implications of your answer for the implementation of shading?

6.20   Estimate the amount of extra calculations required for Phong shading as compared to Gouraud shading. Take into account the results of Exercise 6.19.

6.21   How to derive a transformation to compute a matrix to apply to the normal vector so that the angle between a vector from the origin to a vertex and the normal is unchanged?

6.22   Redo the implementation of the Blinn-Phong shading model so the calculations are carried out in eye coordinates.

6.23   Compare the principles of the local lighting model and the global lighting model. State the different rendering strategies implemented by the global lighting model to overcome the limitation of the local lighting model.

6.24   Consider a highly reflective sphere centered at the origin with a unit radius. If a viewer is located at **p**, describe the points she would see reflected in the sphere at a point on its surface.

CHAPTER 7

DISCRETE TECHNIQUES

Thus far, we have worked directly with geometric objects such as lines, polygons, and polyhedra. Although we understood that, if visible, these entities would eventually be rasterized into pixels in the framebuffer, other than assigning a color to each fragment, we did not have to concern ourselves with working with pixels directly. Over the last 30 years, the major advances in hardware and software have evolved to allow the application program to access the framebuffer both directly and indirectly. Many of the most exciting methods that have evolved over the past two decades rely on interactions between the application program and various buffers. Texture mapping, antialiasing, blending, and alpha blending are only a few of the techniques that become possible when the API allows us to work with discrete buffers. At the same time, GPUs have evolved to include a large amount of memory to support discrete techniques. This chapter introduces these techniques, focusing on those that are supported by WebGL and by similar APIs.

We start by looking at the framebuffer in more detail and the basis for working with arrays of pixels. We then consider mapping methods. These techniques are applied during the rendering process, and they enable us to give the illusion of a surface of great complexity, even though the surface might be as simple as a single polygon. All these techniques use arrays of pixels to define how the shading process that we studied in Chapter 6 is augmented to create these illusions.

We will then look at techniques that involve buffers other than the framebuffer supplied by the window system. We will see how these buffers can be used for new applications, many of which use the power of modern GPUs to perform tasks that go far beyond classical computer graphics.

We will also examine techniques that use the fragment shader for combining or blending images. Here we use the fourth "color" in RGBA mode, and we will see that we can use this channel to blend images and to create effects such as transparency. Appendix D provides the mathematical foundation for many of the sampling and aliasing problems that arise whenever we work with discrete elements.

FIGURE 7.1   Buffer.

FIGURE 7.2   WebGL framebuffer.

7.1   BUFFERS

We have already used two types of standard buffers: color buffers and depth buffers. There may be others supported by the hardware and software for special purposes. What all buffers have in common is that they are inherently discrete: They have limited resolution, both spatially and in depth. We can define a (two-dimensional)[1] **buffer** as a block of memory with $n \times m$ k-bit elements (Figure 7.1).

We have used the term *framebuffer* to mean the set of buffers that the graphics system uses for rendering, including the front and back color buffers, the depth buffer, and other buffers the hardware may provide. These buffers generally reside on the graphics card. Later in this chapter, we will extend the notion of a framebuffer to include other buffers that a system might provide for off-screen rendering operations. For now, we will work with just the standard framebuffer as used by WebGL and other APIs.

At a given spatial location in the framebuffer, the k bits can include 32-bit RGBA colors, integers representing depths, or bits that can be used for masks. Groups of bits can store 1-byte representations of color components, integers for depths, or floating-point numbers for colors or depths. Figure 7.2 shows a framebuffer, such as required by WebGL, and its constituent parts. If we consider the entire framebuffer, the values of n and m match the spatial resolution of the display. The depth of the framebuffer—the value of k—can exceed a few hundred bits. Even for the simple cases that we have seen so far, we have 64 bits for the front and back color buffers and 24 or 32 bits for the depth buffer. The numerical accuracy or **precision** of a given buffer is determined by its depth. Thus, if a framebuffer has 32 bits each for its front and back color buffers, each RGBA color component is stored with a precision of 8 bits.

When we work with the framebuffer, we usually work with one constituent buffer at a time. Thus, we shall use the term *buffer* in what follows to mean a particular buffer within the framebuffer. Each of these buffers is $n \times m$ and is k bits deep. However, k can be different for each buffer. For a color buffer, its k is determined by how many colors the system can display, usually 24 bits for RGB displays and 32 bits for RGBA displays. For the depth buffer, its k is determined by the depth precision

---

1. We can also have one-, three-, and four-dimensional buffers.

that the system can support, often 32 bits to match the size of a floating-point number or an integer. Many systems use a 24-bit depth buffer, which is combined with an 8-bit stencil buffer.[2] We use the term **bitplane** to refer to any of the k $n \times m$ planes in a buffer, and **pixel** to refer to all k of the bits at a particular spatial location. With this definition, a pixel can be a byte, an integer, or even a floating-point number, depending on which buffer is used and how data are stored in the buffer.

The applications programmer generally will not know how information is stored in the framebuffer, because the framebuffer is part of the implementation, which the programmer sees as a black box. When we render our geometry, we access the framebuffer indirectly via the rendering pipeline. We can color individual pixels through the fragment shader, but even this method is indirect because we operate only on the fragments produced by the rasterizer.

Some APIs, including earlier versions of OpenGL, provided functions for both reading and writing blocks of pixels directly in a color buffer. Many of these functions have been deprecated in favor of using the texture functions for image input. We can still read blocks of pixels from a color buffer with WebGL, but this function is not very efficient due to the forward nature of pipeline architectures and our desire to minimize data transfers between the CPU and the GPU. More generally, we will see that we must work with at least three types of memory: processor memory in the CPU, texture memory attached to the GPU, and memory in the GPU.

When the application program reads or writes pixels, not only are data transferred between ordinary processor memory and graphics memory on the graphics card, but usually these data must be reformatted to be compatible with the framebuffer. Consequently, what are ordinarily thought of as digital images, for example, JPEG, PNG, or TIFF images, exist only on the application side of the process. Not only must the application programmer worry how to decode particular images so they can be sent to the framebuffer through WebGL functions, but the programmer also must be aware of the time that is spent in the movement of digital data between processor memory and the framebuffer. If the application programmer also knows the internal format of data stored in any of the buffers, she can often write application programs that execute more efficiently.

7.2   DIGITAL IMAGES

Before we look at how the graphics system can work with digital images, let's first examine what we mean by a digital image. Note that many references use the term *image* rather than *digital image*. This terminology can be confused with the term *image* as we have used it to refer to the result of combining geometric objects and a camera, through the projection process, to obtain what we have called an image. In this chapter, the context should be clear so that there should not be any confusion. Within our programs, we generally work with images that are arrays of pixels. These images can be of a variety of sizes and data types, depending on the type of image

---

2. Stencil buffers are used for masking operations. See [Shr13].

with which we are working. For example, if we are working with RGB images, we usually represent each of the color components with 1 byte whose values range from 0 to 255. Thus, we might declare a 512 × 512 image in our application program as

```
var texSize = 512;

myImage = new Array(texSize);

for (var i = 0; i < texSize; ++i) {
  myimage[i] = new Array(texSize);

  for (var j = 0; j < texSize; ++j) {
    myImage[i][j] = new Uint8Array(3);
  }
}
```

or, if we are using a floating-point representation, we would use

```
myImage[i][j] = new Float32Array(3);
```

If we are working with monochromatic or **luminance** images, each pixel represents a gray level from black (0) to white (255), so we would use

```
myImage[i][j] = new Uint8Array(1);
```

However, because a JavaScript `Array` is an object with methods such as `length`, the resulting `myImage` is more than a set of numbers that we can send to WebGL. Alternately, we could define an image as a typed array with 3 × `texSize` × `texSize` elements such as

```
var myImage = new Uint8Array(3*texSize*texSize);
```

In this case, to reference the pixel at row i, column j, we would use `myImage[texSize*i+j]`, rather than `myImage[i][j]` for a luminance image.

One way to form digital images is through code in the application program. For example, suppose that we want to create a 512 × 512 RGBA image that consists of an 8 × 8 checkerboard of alternating red and black squares, such as we might use for a game. The following code will work:

```
var texSize = 64;
var numRows = 8;
var numCols = 8;
var numComponents = 4;

var myImage = new Uint8Array(numComponents*texSize*texSize);

for (var i = 0; i < texSize; ++i) {
  for (var j = 0; j < texSize; ++j) {
    var patchx = Math.floor(i/(texSize/numRows));
    var patchy = Math.floor(j/(texSize/numCols));
    c = (patchx%2 !== patchy%2 ? 255 : 0);
```

```
    var index = numComponents(i*texSize + j);
    myImage[index+0] = c;
    myImage[index+1] = 0;
    myImage[index+2] = 0;
    myImage[index+3] = 255;
    }
}
```

Note that we are using a one-dimensional typed array, so we form a long stream of bytes for our image and we are using unsigned bytes for each color component. This format is the one that is most compatible with present hardware, although some GPUs support floating-point buffers. We will use this form for setting up texture images in the next section.

We could use a similar strategy to form a two-dimensional array of colors. If we want the same size checkerboard using `vec4`s, we could use the code

```
var texSize = 64;
var numRows = 8;
var numCols = 8;

var myImage = new Array();

for (var i = 0; i < texSize, ++i) {
  myImage[i] = new Array(texSize);
}

var red = vec4.(1.0, 0.0, 0.0, 1.0);
var black = vec4(0.0, 0.0, 0.0, 1.0);

for (var i = 0; i < texSize; ++i) {
  for (var j = 0; j < texSize; ++j) {
    var patchx = Math.floor(i/(texSize/numRows));
    var patchy = Math.floor(j/(texSize/numCols));
    myImage[i][j] = (patchx%2 !== patchy%2 ? vec4(red) : vec4(black));
  }
}
```

and use the `flatten` function to convert `myImage` to a typed array.

Usually, writing code to form images is limited to those that contain regular patterns. More often, we obtain images directly from data. For example, if we have an array of real numbers that we have obtained from an experiment or a simulation, we can scale them over the range 0 to 255 and then convert these data to form an unsigned-byte luminance image or scale them over 0.0 to 1.0 for a floating-point image.

There is a third method of obtaining images that has become much more prevalent because of the influence of the Internet. Images are produced by scanning continuous images, such as photographs, or produced directly using digital cameras. Each image is in one of many possible standard formats. Some of the most popular formats are GIF, TIFF, PNG, PDF, and JPEG. These formats include direct coding of the values in some order, compressed but lossless coding, and compressed lossy coding. Each format arose from the particular needs of a group of applications. For example, PostScript (PS) images are defined by the PostScript language used to control printers. These images are an exact encoding of the image data—either RGB or luminance—into the 7-bit ASCII character set. Consequently, PostScript images can be understood by a large class of printers and other devices but tend to be very large. Encapsulated PostScript (EPS) are similar but include additional information that is useful for previewing images. GIF images are color index images and thus store a color table and an array of indices for the image.

TIFF images can have two forms. In one form, all the image data are coded directly. A header describes how the data are arranged. In the second form, the data are compressed. Compression is possible because most images contain much redundant data. For example, large areas of most images show very little variation in color or intensity. This redundancy can be removed by algorithms that result in a compressed version of the original image that requires less storage. Compressed TIFF images are formed by the Lempel-Ziv algorithm that provides optimal lossless compression, allowing the original image to be compressed and recovered exactly. JPEG images are compressed by an algorithm that allows small errors in the compression and reconstruction of the image. Consequently, JPEG images have very high **compression ratios**, that is, the ratio of the number of bits in the original file to the number of bits in the compressed data file, with little or no visible distortion. Figure 7.3 shows three versions of a single 1200×1200 luminance image: uncompressed, as a TIFF image (panel (a)); and as two JPEG images, compressed with different ratios (panel (b) and panel (c)). The corresponding file sizes are 1,440,198; 80,109; and 38,962 bytes, respectively. Thus, the TIFF image has 1 byte for each pixel plus 198 bytes of header and trailer information. For the JPEG images, the compression ratios are approximately 18:1 and 37:1. Even with the higher compression ratio, there is little visible distortion in the image. If we store the original image as a PostScript image, the file will be approximately twice as large as the TIFF image because each byte will be converted into two 7-bit ASCII characters, each pair requiring 2 bytes of storage. If we store the image as a compressed TIFF file, we use only about one-half of the storage. Using a zip file—a popular format used for compressing arbitrary files—would give about the same result. This amount of compression is image dependent. Although this compression method is lossless, the compression ratio is far worse than is obtainable with lossy JPEG images, which are visibly almost indistinguishable from the original. This closeness accounts for the popularity of the JPEG format for sending images over the Internet. Most digital cameras produce images in JPEG and RAW formats. The RAW format gives the unprocessed RGB data plus a large amount of header information, including the date, the resolution, and even the GPS location at which the picture was taken.

The large number of image formats poses problems for a graphics API. Although some image formats are simple, others are quite complex. The WebGL API avoids the problem by supporting only blocks of pixels, as compared to images formatted for files. Because WebGL is supported through the browser and HTML, we can access images in the standard web formats, such as GIF, JPEG, PNG, and BMP, as texture images.

FIGURE 7.3 (a) Original TIFF luminance image. (b) JPEG image compressed by a factor of 18. (c) JPEG image compressed by a factor of 37.

We can also obtain digital images directly from our graphics system by forming images of three-dimensional scenes using the geometric pipeline and then reading these images back. We will see how to do the required operations later in this chapter.

7.3 MAPPING METHODS

One of the most powerful uses of discrete data is for surface rendering. The process of modeling an object by a set of geometric primitives and then rendering these primitives has its limitations. Consider, for example, the task of creating a virtual orange by computer. Our first attempt might be to start with a sphere. From our discussion in Chapter 6, we know that we can build an approximation to a sphere out of triangles and render these triangles using material properties that match those of a real orange. Unfortunately, such a rendering would be far too regular to look much like an orange. We could instead follow the path that we shall explore in Chapter 11:

We could try to model the orange with some sort of curved surface and then render the surface. This procedure would give us more control over the shape of our virtual orange, but the image that we would produce still would not look right. Although it might have the correct overall properties, such as shape and color, it would lack the fine surface detail of the real orange. If we attempt to add this detail by adding more polygons to our model, even with hardware capable of rendering tens of millions of polygons per second, we can still overwhelm the pipeline.

An alternative is not to attempt to build increasingly more complex models, but rather to build a simple model and to add detail as part of the rendering process. As we saw in Chapter 6, as the implementation renders a surface—be it a polygon or a curved surface—it generates sets of fragments, each of which corresponds to a pixel in the framebuffer. Fragments carry color, depth, and other information that can be used to determine how they contribute to the pixels to which they correspond. As part of the rasterization process, we must assign a shade or color to each fragment. We started in Chapter 6 by using the modified Phong model to determine vertex colors that could be interpolated across surfaces. However, these colors can be modified during fragment processing after rasterization. The mapping algorithms can be thought of as either modifying the shading algorithm based on a two-dimensional array, the map, or modifying the shading by using the map to alter the surface using three major techniques:

- Texture mapping
- Bump mapping
- Environment mapping

Texture mapping uses an image (or texture) to influence the color of a fragment. Textures can be specified using a fixed pattern, such as the regular patterns often used to fill polygons; by a procedural texture generation method; or through a digitized image. In all cases, we can characterize the resulting image as the mapping of a texture to a surface, as shown in Figure 7.4, which is carried out as part of the rendering of the surface.

Whereas texture maps give detail by painting patterns onto smooth surfaces, **bump maps** distort the normal vectors during the shading process to make the surface appear to have small variations in shape, such as the bumps on a real orange. **Reflection maps**, or **environment maps**, allow us to create images that have the

FIGURE 7.4   Texture mapping a pattern to a surface.

appearance of reflected materials without having to trace reflected rays. In this technique, an image of the environment is painted onto the surface as that surface is being rendered.

The three methods have much in common. All three alter the shading of individual fragments as part of fragment processing. All rely on the map being stored as a one-, two-, or three-dimensional digital image. All keep the geometric complexity low while creating the illusion of complex geometry. However, all are also subject to aliasing errors.

There are various examples of two-dimensional mappings in the color plates. Color Plate 7 was created using an environment map and shows how a single texture map can create the illusion of a highly reflective surface while avoiding global calculations. Color Plate 10 uses texture mapping to create a brick pattern. In virtual reality, visualization simulations, and interactive games, real-time performance is required. Hardware support for texture mapping in modern systems allows the detail to be added, without significantly degrading the rendering time.

However, in terms of the standard pipeline, there are significant differences among the three techniques. Two-dimensional texture mapping is supported by WebGL. Environment maps are a special case of standard texture mapping but can be altered to create a variety of new effects in the fragment shader. Bump mapping requires us to process each fragment independently, something we can do with a fragment shader.

7.4 TWO-DIMENSIONAL TEXTURE MAPPING

Textures are patterns. They can range from regular patterns, such as stripes and checkerboards, to the complex patterns that characterize natural materials. In the real world, we can distinguish among objects of similar size and shape by their textures. If we want to create more detailed virtual images, we can extend our present capabilities by mapping a texture to the objects that we create.

Textures can be one-, two-, three-, or four-dimensional. For example, a one-dimensional texture might be used to create a pattern for coloring a curve. A three-dimensional texture might describe a solid block of material from which we could sculpt an object. Because the use of surfaces is so important in computer graphics, mapping two-dimensional textures to surfaces is by far the most common use of texture mapping and will be the only form of texture mapping that we shall consider in detail. However, the processes by which we map these entities is much the same regardless of the dimensionality of the texture, and we lose little by concentrating on two-dimensional texture mapping. At present, WebGL supports only two-dimensional texture mapping and an extension of two-dimensional texture mapping called a cube map.

Although there are multiple approaches to texture mapping, all require a sequence of steps that involve mappings among three or four different coordinate systems. At various stages in the process, we will be working with screen coordinates, where the final image is produced; object coordinates, where we describe the objects upon which the textures will be mapped; texture coordinates, which we use to locate positions in the texture; and parametric coordinates, which we use to specify parametric surfaces. Methods differ according to the types of surfaces we are using and the type of rendering architecture we have. Our approach will be to start with a fairly general discussion of texture, introducing the various mappings, and then to show how texture mapping is handled by a real-time pipeline architecture, such as that employed by WebGL.

In most applications, textures start out as two-dimensional images of the sorts we introduced in Section 7.2. Thus, they might be formed by application programs or scanned in from a photograph, but, regardless of their origin, they are eventually brought into processor memory as arrays. We call the elements of these arrays **texels**, or texture elements, rather than pixels to emphasize how they will be used. However, at this point, we prefer to think of this array as a continuous rectangular two-dimensional texture pattern $T(s, t)$. The independent variables s and t are known as **texture coordinates**.[3] With no loss of generality, we can scale our texture coordinates to vary over the interval [0.0, 1.0].

A **texture map** associates a texel with each point on a geometric object that is itself mapped to screen coordinates for display. If the object is represented in homogeneous or (x, y, z, w) coordinates, then there are functions such that

$$x = x(s, t)$$

$$y = y(s, t)$$

$$z = z(s, t)$$

$$w = w(s, t).$$

One of the difficulties we must confront is that, although these functions exist conceptually, finding them may not be possible in practice. In addition, we are worried about the inverse problem: Given a point (x, y, z) or (x, y, z, w) on an object, how do we find the corresponding texture coordinates, or equivalently, how do we find the "inverse" functions

$$s = s(x, y, z, w)$$

$$t = t(x, y, z, w)$$

to use to find the texel $T(s, t)$?

If we define the geometric object using parametric (u, v) surfaces, such as we did for the sphere in Section 6.6, there is an additional mapping function that gives object coordinate values (x, y, z) or (x, y, z, w) in terms of u and v. Although this mapping is known for simple surfaces, such as spheres and triangles, and for the surfaces that we shall discuss in Chapter 11, we also need the mapping from parametric coordinates (u, v) to texture coordinates and sometimes the inverse mapping from texture coordinates to parametric coordinates.

We also have to consider the projection process that takes us from object coordinates to screen coordinates, going through eye coordinates, clip coordinates, and window coordinates along the way. We can abstract this process through a function

---

3. In four dimensions, the coordinates are in (s, t, r, q) or (s, t, p, q) space.

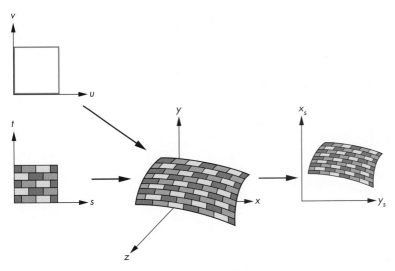

FIGURE 7.5   Texture maps for a parametric surface.

that takes a texture coordinate pair (s, t) and tells us where in the color buffer the corresponding value of $T(s, t)$ will make its contribution to the final image. Thus, there is a mapping of the form

$$x_s = x_s(s, t)$$

$$y_s = y_s(s, t)$$

into coordinates, where (x_s, y_s) is a location in the color buffer.

Depending on the algorithm and the rendering architecture, we might also want the function that takes us from a pixel in the color buffer to the texel that makes a contribution to the color of that pixel.

One way to think about texture mapping is in terms of two concurrent mappings: the first from texture coordinates to object coordinates, and the second from parametric coordinates to object coordinates, as shown in Figure 7.5. A third mapping takes us from object coordinates to screen coordinates.

Conceptually, the texture-mapping process is simple. A small area of the texture pattern maps to the area of the geometric surface, corresponding to a pixel in the final image. If we assume that the values of T are RGB color values, we can use these values either to modify the color of the surface that might have been determined by a lighting model or to assign a color to the surface based only on the texture value. This color assignment is carried out as part of the computation of fragment colors.

On closer examination, we face a number of difficulties. First, we must determine the map from texture coordinates to object coordinates. A two-dimensional texture usually is defined over a rectangular region in texture space. The mapping from this rectangle to an arbitrary region in three-dimensional space may be a complex function or may have undesirable properties. For example, if we wish to map a rectangle to a sphere, we cannot do so without distortion of shapes and distances. Second, owing

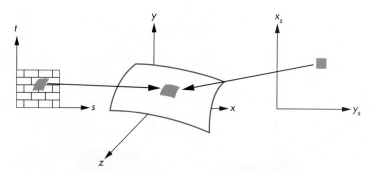

FIGURE 7.6   Preimages of a pixel.

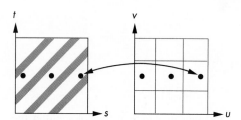

FIGURE 7.7   Aliasing in texture generation.

to the nature of the rendering process, which works on a pixel-by-pixel basis, we are more interested in the inverse map from screen coordinates to texture coordinates. It is when we are determining the shade of a pixel that we must determine what point in the texture image to use—a calculation that requires us to go from screen coordinates to texture coordinates. Third, because each pixel corresponds to a small rectangle on the display, we are interested in mapping not points to points, but rather areas to areas. Here again is a potential aliasing problem that we must treat carefully if we are to avoid artifacts, such as wavy sinusoidal or moiré patterns.

Figure 7.6 shows several of the difficulties. Suppose that we are computing a color for the square pixel centered at screen coordinates (x_s, y_s). The center (x_s, y_s) corresponds to a point (x, y, z) in object space, but, if the object is curved, the projection of the corners of the pixel backward into object space yields a curved **preimage** of the pixel. In terms of the texture image $T(s, t)$, projecting the pixel back yields a preimage in texture space that is the area of the texture that ideally should contribute to the shading of the pixel.

Let's put aside for a moment the problem of how we find the inverse map and look at the determination of colors. One possibility is to use the location that we get by back projection of the pixel center to find a texture value. Although this technique is simple, it is subject to serious aliasing problems, which are especially visible if the texture is periodic. Figure 7.7 illustrates the aliasing problem. Here, we have a repeated texture and a flat surface. The back projection of the center of each pixel happens to fall in between the dark lines, and the texture value is always the lighter color. More generally, not taking into account the finite size of a pixel can lead to moiré patterns in the image. A better strategy—but one more difficult to implement—is to assign a texture value based on averaging of the texture map over the preimage. Note that this method is imperfect, too. For the example in Figure 7.7, we would assign an average shade, but we would still not get the striped pattern of the texture. Ultimately, we still have aliasing defects due to the limited resolution of both the framebuffer and the texture map. These problems are most visible when there are regular high-frequency components in the texture.

Now we can turn to the mapping problem. In computer graphics, most curved surfaces are represented parametrically. A point $\mathbf{p}$ on the surface is a function of two parameters u and v. For each pair of values, we generate the point

$$\mathbf{p}(u, v) = \begin{bmatrix} x(u, v) \\ y(u, v) \\ z(u, v) \end{bmatrix}.$$

In Chapter 11, we study in detail the derivation of such surfaces. Given a parametric surface, we can often map a point in the texture map $T(s, t)$ to a point on the surface $\mathbf{p}(u, v)$ by a linear map of the form

$$u = as + bt + c$$
$$v = ds + et + f.$$

As long as $ae \neq bd$, this mapping is invertible. Linear mapping makes it easy to map a texture to a group of parametric surface patches. For example, if, as shown in Figure 7.8, the patch determined by the corners (s_{min}, t_{min}) and (s_{max}, t_{max}) corresponds to the surface patch with corners (u_{min}, v_{min}) and (u_{max}, v_{max}), then the mapping is

$$u = u_{min} + \frac{s - s_{min}}{s_{max} - s_{min}}(u_{max} - u_{min})$$

$$v = v_{min} + \frac{t - t_{min}}{t_{max} - t_{min}}(v_{max} - v_{min}).$$

This mapping is easy to apply, but it does not take into account the curvature of the surface. Equal-sized texture patches must be stretched to fit over the surface patch.

Another approach to the mapping problem is to use a two-step mapping. The first step maps the texture to a simple three-dimensional intermediate surface, such as a sphere, cylinder, or cube. In the second step, the intermediate surface containing

FIGURE 7.8   Linear texture mapping.

FIGURE 7.9   Texture mapping with a cylinder.

the mapped texture is mapped to the surface being rendered. This two-step mapping process can be applied to surfaces defined in either geometric or parametric coordinates. The following example is essentially the same in either system.

Suppose that our texture coordinates vary over the unit square and that we use the surface of a cylinder of height h and radius r as our intermediate object, as shown in Figure 7.9. Points on the cylinder are given by the parametric equations

$$x = r \cos(2\pi u)$$

$$y = r \sin(2\pi u)$$

$$z = v/h,$$

as u and v vary over (0, 1). Hence, we can use the mapping

$$s = u \qquad t = v.$$

By using only the curved part of the cylinder, and not the top and bottom, we are able to map the texture without distorting its shape. However, if we map to a closed object, such as a sphere, we must introduce shape distortion. This problem is similar to the problem of creating a two-dimensional image of the earth for a map. If you look at the various maps of the earth in an atlas, all distort shapes and distances. Both texture-mapping and map-design techniques must choose among a variety of representations, based on where we wish to place the distortion. For example, the familiar Mercator projection puts the most distortion at the poles. If we use a sphere of radius r as the intermediate surface, a possible mapping is

$$x = r \cos(2\pi u)$$

$$y = r \sin(2\pi u) \cos(2\pi v)$$

$$z = r \sin(2\pi u) \sin(2\pi v).$$

but is subject to distortion that is most pronounced at the poles.

We can also use a rectangular box, as shown in Figure 7.10. Here, we map the texture to a box that can be unraveled, like a cardboard packing box. This mapping often is used with environment maps (Section 7.7).

The second step is to map the texture values on the intermediate object to the desired surface. Figure 7.11 shows three possible strategies. In panel (a), we take the texture value at a point on the intermediate object, go from this point in the direction

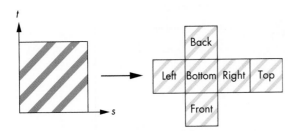

FIGURE 7.10   Texture mapping with a box.

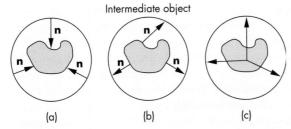

FIGURE 7.11   Second mapping. (a) Using the normal from the intermediate surface. (b) Using the normal from the object surface. (c) Using the center of the object.

of the normal until we intersect the object, and then place the texture value at the point of intersection. We could also reverse this method, starting at a point on the surface of the object and going in the direction of the normal at this point until we intersect the intermediate object, where we obtain the texture value, as shown in panel (b). A third option, if we know the center of the object, is to draw a line from the center through a point on the object and to calculate the intersection of this line with the intermediate surface, as shown in panel (c). The texture at the point of intersection with the intermediate object is assigned to the corresponding point on the desired object.

7.5   TEXTURE MAPPING IN WEBGL

Desktop OpenGL supports a variety of texture-mapping options. Even the first versions of OpenGL contained the functionality to map one- and two-dimensional textures to one- through four-dimensional graphical objects. Although mapping, of three- and four-dimensional textures are now part of desktop OpenGL, because WebGL supports only two-dimensional textures, we will focus on mapping two-dimensional textures to surfaces. Nevertheless, the basics of texture mapping are the same in WebGL and desktop OpenGL.

WebGL's texture maps rely on its pipeline architecture. We have seen that there are actually two parallel pipelines: the geometric pipeline and the pixel pipeline. For

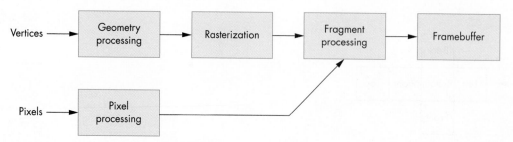

FIGURE 7.12   Pixel and geometry pipelines.

texture mapping, the pixel pipeline merges with fragment processing after rasterization, as shown in Figure 7.12. This architecture determines the type of texture mapping that is supported. In particular, texture mapping is done as part of fragment processing. Each fragment that is generated can then be tested for visibility with the z-buffer. We can think of texture mapping as a part of the shading process, but a part that is done on a fragment-by-fragment basis. Texture coordinates are handled much like normals and colors. They can be associated with vertices as an additional vertex attribute and the required texture values can be obtained by the rasterizer interpolating the texture coordinates at the vertices across polygons. They can also be generated in one of the shaders.

Texture mapping requires interaction among the application program, the vertex shader, and the fragment shader. There are three basic steps. First, we must form a texture image and place it in texture memory on the GPU. Second, we must assign texture coordinates to each fragment. Finally, we must apply the texture to each fragment. Each of these steps can be accomplished in multiple ways, and there are many parameters that we can use to control the process. As texture mapping has become more important and GPUs have evolved to support more texture-mapping options, APIs have added more and more texture-mapping functions.

7.5.1 Texture Objects

In early versions of OpenGL, there was only a single texture, the **current texture**, that existed at any time. Each time that a different texture was needed—for example, if we wanted to apply different textures to different surfaces in the same scene—we had to set up a new texture map. This process was very inefficient. Each time another texture image was needed, it had to be loaded into texture memory, replacing the texels that were already there.

In a manner analogous to having multiple program objects, **texture objects** allow the application program to define objects that consist of the texture array and the various texture parameters that control its application to surfaces. As long as there is sufficient memory to retain them, these objects reside in texture memory in the GPU.

For a single texture, we start by creating a texture object,

```
var texture = gl.createTexture();
```

and then bind it as the current two-dimensional texture object by executing the function

```
gl.bindTexture(gl.TEXTURE_2D, texture);
```

Subsequent texture functions specify the texture image and its parameters, which become part of this texture object. Another execution of `gl.bindTexture` with an existing name makes that texture object the current texture object. We can delete an unused texture object with the function `gl.deleteTexture`.

7.5.2 The Texture Image Array

Two-dimensional texture mapping starts with an array of texels, which is a two-dimensional pixel rectangle. Suppose that we have a 64×64 RGBA image `myTexels` that was generated by the code

```
var texSize = 64;
var numRows = 8;
var numCols = 8;

var myTexels = new Uint8Array(4*texSize*texSize);

for (var i = 0; i < texSize; ++i) {
  for (var j = 0; j < texSize; ++j) {
    var patchx = Math.floor(i/(texSize/numRows));
    var patchy = Math.floor(j/(texSize/numCols));

    var c = (patchx%2 !== patchy%2 ? 255 : 0);

    myTexels[4*i*texSize+4*j]   = c;
    myTexels[4*i*texSize+4*j+1] = c;
    myTexels[4*i*texSize+4*j+2] = c;
    myTexels[4*i*texSize+4*j+3] = 255;
  }
}
```

Thus, the colors in `myTexels` form an 8×8 black-and-white checkerboard. We specify that this array is to be used as a two-dimensional texture after the call to `gl.bindTexture` by

```
gl.texImage2D(gl.TEXTURE_2D, 0, gl.RGBA, texSize, texSize, 0, gl.RGBA,
              gl.UNSIGNED_BYTE, myTexels);
```

More generally, two-dimensional textures are specified through the function

```
gl.texImage2D(target, level,  iformat,
              width, height, border, format, type, texelArray)
```

The `target` parameter lets us choose a single image, as in our example, or set up a cube map (Section 7.8). The `level` parameter is used for mipmapping (Section 7.5.4), where 0 denotes the highest level (resolution) or that we are not using mipmapping. The third parameter specifies how we would like the texture stored in texture memory. The fourth and fifth parameters (width and height) specify the size of the image in memory. The `border` parameter is no longer used and should be set to 0. The `format` and `type` parameters describe how the pixels in the `texArray` in processor memory are stored, so that WebGL can read those pixels and store them in texture memory. In WebGL, `texelArray` should be a single `Uint8Array` typed array.

Alternatively, we can use an image stored in one of the standard web formats for our texels. Suppose we have an RGB gif image `logo.gif`. Then we can use this image as a texture with the code

```
var myTexels = new Image();
image.src = "logo.gif";
gl.pixelStorei(gl.UNPACK_FLIP_Y_WEBGL, true);
gl.texImage2D(gl.TEXTURE_2D, 0, gl.RGB, gl.RGB,
              gl.UNSIGNED_BYTE, myTexels);
```

The function `gl.pixelStorei` is needed to flip the image from top to bottom due to the different coordinate systems used for the image and by our application. We can also identify the image in the HTML with the `img` tag

```
<img id="logo" src="logo.gif"></img>
```

and then access it in our application by

```
var image = document.getElementById("logo");
```

7.5.3 Texture Coordinates and Samplers

The key element in applying a texture in the fragment shader is the mapping between the location of a fragment and the corresponding location within the texture image where we will get the texture color for that fragment. Because each fragment has a location in the framebuffer that is one of its attributes, we need not refer to this position explicitly in the fragment shader. The potential difficulty is identifying the desired location in the texture image. In many applications, we could compute this location from a mathematical model of the objects. In others, we might use some sort of approximation. WebGL does not have any preferred method and simply requires that we provide the location to the fragment shader or compute it within the shader.

Rather than having to use integer texel locations that depend on the dimensions of the texture image, we use two floating-point texture coordinates, s and t, both of which range over the interval [0.0, 1.0] as we traverse the texture image. For our example of a 64×64 two-dimensional texture image `myImage`, the value $(0.0, 0.0)$ corresponds to the texel `myImage[0][0]`, and $(1.0, 1.0)$ corresponds to the texel `myImage[63][63]`, as shown in Figure 7.13. In terms of the one-dimensional array `myTexels` that we use in `gl.texImage2D`, the corresponding points are

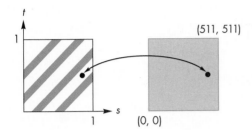

FIGURE 7.13 Mapping to texture coordinates.

`myTexels[0]` and `myTexels[64*64-1]`. Any values of s and t in the unit interval map to a unique texel.

It is up to the application and the shaders to determine the appropriate texture coordinates for a fragment. The most common method is to treat texture coordinates as a vertex attribute. Thus, we could provide texture coordinates just as we provide vertex colors in the application. We then would pass these coordinates to the vertex shader and let the rasterizer interpolate the vertex texture coordinates to fragment texture coordinates.

Let's consider a simple example of using our checkerboard texture image for each side of the cube. The example is particularly simple because we have an obvious mapping between each face of the cube and the texture coordinates for each vertex; namely, we assign texture coordinates (0.0, 0.0), (0.0, 1.0), (1.0, 1.0), and (1.0, 0.0) to the four corners of each face.

Recall that we form 36 triangles for the six faces. We add an array to hold the texture coordinates and another for the texture coordinates at the corners of a quadrilateral:

```
var texCoordsArray = [ ];

var texCoord = [
  vec2(0, 0),
  vec2(0, 1),
  vec2(1, 1),
  vec2(1, 0)
];
```

Here is the code of the `quad` function that colors each face with a solid color determined by the first index:

```
function quad(a, b, c, d)
{
  pointsArray.push(vertices[a]);
  colorsArray.push(vertexColors[a]);
  texCoordsArray.push(texCoord[0]);

  pointsArray.push(vertices[b]);
  colorsArray.push(vertexColors[a]);
  texCoordsArray.push(texCoord[1]);
```

```
  pointsArray.push(vertices[c]);
  colorsArray.push(vertexColors[a]);
  texCoordsArray.push(texCoord[2]);

  pointsArray.push(vertices[a]);
  colorsArray.push(vertexColors[a]);
  texCoordsArray.push(texCoord[0]);

  pointsArray.push(vertices[c]);
  colorsArray.push(vertexColors[a]);
  texCoordsArray.push(texCoord[2]);

  pointsArray.push(vertices[d]);
  colorsArray.push(vertexColors[a]);
  texCoordsArray.push(texCoord[3]);
}
```

We also need to perform initialization so we can pass the texture coordinates as a vertex attribute with the identifier vTexCoord in the vertex shader:

```
var tBuffer = gl.createBuffer();
gl.bindBuffer(gl.ARRAY_BUFFER, Buffer);
gl.bufferData(gl.ARRAY_BUFFER, flatten(texCoordsArray), gl.STATIC_DRAW);

var vTexCoord = gl.getAttribLocation(program, "vTexCoord");
gl.vertexAttribPointer(vTexCoord, 2, gl.FLOAT, false, 0, 0);
gl.enableVertexAttribArray(vTexCoord);
```

Turning to the vertex shader, we add the texture coordinate attribute and output the texture coordinates. Here is the vertex shader for the rotating cube with texture coordinates:

```
attribute vec4 vPosition;
attribute vec4 vColor;
attribute vec2 vTexCoord;
varying vec4 fColor;
varying vec2 fTexCoord;

uniform vec3 theta;

void main()
{
  // Compute the sines and cosines of theta for each of
  // the three axes in one computation.
  vec3 angles = radians(theta);
  vec3 c = cos(angles);
  vec3 s = sin(angles);

  // Remember: These matrices are column major
  mat4 rx = mat4(1.0,  0.0,  0.0, 0.0,
```

```
           0.0,   c.x,   s.x,  0.0,
           0.0,  -s.x,   c.x,  0.0,
           0.0,   0.0,   0.0,  1.0);

  mat4 ry = mat4(c.y,  0.0,  -s.y,  0.0,
                 0.0,  1.0,   0.0,  0.0,
                 s.y,  0.0,   c.y,  0.0,
                 0.0,  0.0,   0.0,  1.0);

  mat4 rz = mat4(c.z,  -s.z,  0.0,  0.0,
                 s.z,   c.z,  0.0,  0.0,
                 0.0,   0.0,  1.0,  0.0,
                 0.0,   0.0,  0.0,  1.0);

  fColor = vColor;
  fTexColor = vTexCoord;
  gl_Position = rz * ry * rx * vPosition;
}
```

The output texture coordinates `fTexCoord` are interpolated by the rasterizer and are input to the fragment shader.

Note that the vertex shader is only concerned with the texture coordinates and has nothing to do with the texture object we created earlier. We should not be surprised because the texture itself is not needed until we are ready to assign a color to a fragment, which occurs in the fragment shader. Note also that many of the parameters that determine how we can apply the texture, a number of which we have yet to discuss, are inside the texture object and thus will allow us to use very simple fragment shaders.

The key to putting everything together is a new type of variable called a **sampler**, which we usually use only in a fragment shader. A sampler variable provides access to a texture object, including all its parameters. There are two types of sampler variables for the types of textures supported in WebGL: the two-dimensional (`sampler2D`) and the cube map (`samplerCube`). What a sampler does is return a value or sample of the texture image for the input texture coordinates. How this value is determined depends on parameters associated with the texture object. For now, we can use the defaults that return the value of the single texel determined by the texture coordinates passed to the sampler.

We link the texture object `texture` we create in the application to the sampler in the fragment shader by

```
var texture = createTexture();
gl.uniform1i(gl.getUniformLocation(program, "texMap"), 0);
```

where `texMap` is the name of the sampler in the fragment shader. The second parameter to `gl.uniform1i` refers to the default texture unit. We will discuss multiple texture units in Section 7.5.6.

The fragment shader is almost trivial. The interpolated vertex colors and the texture coordinates are input variables. If we want the texture values to multiply the colors as if we were using the checkerboard texture to simulate glass that alternates between clear and opaque, we could multiply the colors from the application by the values in the texture image as in the following fragment shader:

```
varying vec2 vTexCoord;
varying vec4 fColor;
uniform sampler2D texMap;

void main()
{
   gl_FragColor = fColor * texture2D(texMap, fTexCoord);
}
```

In this case the texture map acts as a mask. Where the texel is white, we use the value of color for the fragment color and if the texel is black, the fragment color is set to black. We could also use the texture to fully determine the color of each fragment by using

```
gl_FragColor = texture2D(texture, fTexCoord);
```

In the example shown in Figure 7.14(a), we use the whole texture on a rectangle. If we used only part of the range of s and t—for example, (0.0, 0.5)—we would use only part of myTexels for the texture map, and would get an image like that in Figure 7.14(b). WebGL interpolates s and t across the quadrilateral, then maps these values back to the appropriate texel in myTexels. The quadrilateral example is simple because there is an obvious mapping of texture coordinates to vertices. For general polygons, the application programmer must decide how to assign the texture coordinates. Figure 7.15 shows a few of the possibilities with the same texture map. Panels (a) and (b) use the same triangle but different texture coordinates. Note the artifacts of the interpolation and how quadrilaterals are treated as two triangles as they are rendered in panel (c).

The basics of WebGL texture mapping are simple: Specify an array of colors for the texture values, assign texture coordinates, and use a sampler in the fragment shader. Unfortunately, there are a few nasty details that we must discuss before we

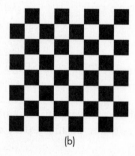

(a)   (b)

FIGURE 7.14   Mapping of a checkerboard texture to a quadrilateral. (a) Using the entire texel array. (b) Using part of the texel array.

(a)   (b)   (c)

FIGURE 7.15   Mapping of texture to polygons. (a and b) Mapping of a checkerboard texture to a triangle. (c) Mapping of a checkerboard texture to a trapezoid.

can use texture effectively. Solving the resulting problems involves making trade-offs between the quality of the images and efficiency.

One problem is how to interpret a value of s or t outside of the range (0.0, 1.0). Generally, we want the texture either to repeat if we specify values outside this range or to clamp the values to 0.0 or 1.0—that is, we want to use the values at 0.0 and 1.0 for values below and above the interval (0.0, 1.0), respectively. For repeated textures, we set these parameters via

```
gl.texParameteri(gl.TEXTURE_2D, gl.TEXTURE_WRAP_S, gl.REPEAT);
```

For t, we use `gl.TEXTURE_WRAP_T`; for clamping, we use `gl.CLAMP_TO_EDGE`. By executing these functions after the `gl.bindTexture`, the parameters become part of the texture object.

7.5.4 Texture Sampling

Aliasing of textures is a major problem. When we map texture coordinates to the array of texels, we rarely get a point that corresponds to the center of a texel. One option is to use the value of the texel that is closest to the texture coordinate output by the rasterizer. This option is known as **point sampling**, but it is the one most subject to visible aliasing errors. A better strategy, although one that requires more work, is to use a weighted average of a group of texels in the neighborhood of the texel determined by point sampling. This option is known as **linear filtering**. Thus, in Figure 7.16 we see the location within a texel that is given by bilinear interpolation from the texture coordinates at the vertices and the four texels that would be used to obtain a smoother value. If we are using linear filtering, there is a problem at the edges of the texel array because we need additional texel values outside the array.

There is a further complication, however, in deciding how to use the texel values to obtain a texture value. The size of the pixel that we are trying to color on the screen may be smaller or larger than one texel, as shown in Figure 7.17.

In the first case, the texel is larger than one pixel (**magnification**); in the second, it is smaller (**minification**). In both cases, the fastest strategy is to use the value of

FIGURE 7.16   Texels used with linear filtering.

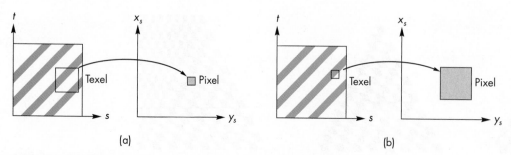

FIGURE 7.17   Mapping texels to pixels. (a) Magnification. (b) Minification.

the nearest point sampling. We can specify this option for both magnification and minification of textures as follows:

```
gl.texParameteri(gl.TEXTURE_2D, gl.TEXTURE_MAG_FILTER, gl.NEAREST);
gl.texParameteri(gl.TEXTURE_2D, gl.TEXTURE_MIN_FILTER, gl.NEAREST);
```

Alternatively, we can use filtering to obtain a smoother, less aliased image if we specify `gl.LINEAR` instead of `gl.NEAREST`.

WebGL has another way to deal with the minification problem; it is called **mipmapping**. For objects that project to an area of screen space that is small compared with the size of the texel array, we do not need the resolution of the original texel array. WebGL allows us to create a series of texture arrays at reduced sizes; it will then automatically use the appropriate size texture in this pyramid of textures, the one for which the size of the texel is approximately the size of a pixel. For a 64×64 original array, we can set up 32×32, 16×16, 8×8, 4×4, 2×2, and 1×1 arrays for the current texture object by executing the function call

```
gl.generateMipmap(gl.TEXTURE_2D);
```

Note that because each successive mipmap texture halves the resolution until we get to a 1×1 image, WebGL mipmapping requires that the top-level image have row and column dimensions that are powers of 2.

We can also set up the maps directly using the `level` parameter in `gl.Tex-Image2D`. This parameter is the level in the mipmap hierarchy for the specified texture array. Thus, level 0 refers to the original image, level 1 to the image at half resolution, and so on. However, we can give a pointer to any image in different calls to `gl.TexImage2D` and thus can have entirely different images used at different levels of the mipmap hierarchy. These mipmaps are invoked automatically if we specify

```
gl.tTexParameteri(gl.TEXTURE_2D, gl.TEXTURE_MIN_FILTER,
                 gl.NEAREST_MIPMAP_NEAREST);
```

This option asks WebGL to use point sampling with the best mipmap. We can also do filtering within the best mipmap (`gl.NEAREST_MIPMAP_LINEAR`), point sampling using linear filtering between mipmaps (`gl.LINEAR_MIPMAP_NEAREST`), or both (`gl.LINEAR_MIPMAP_LINEAR`).

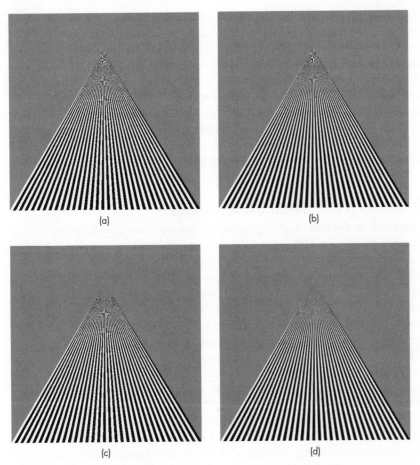

FIGURE 7.18 Texture mapping to a quadrilateral. (a) Point sampling. (b) Linear filtering. (c) Mipmapping point sampling. (d) Mipmapping linear filtering.

Figure 7.18 shows the differences in mapping a texture using the nearest texel, linear filtering, and mipmapping, the latter using the nearest texel and using linear filtering. The object is a quadrilateral that appears almost as a triangle when shown in perspective. The texture is a black-and-white checkerboard. Note that this texture map, because of its regularity, shows dramatic aliasing effects. The use of the nearest texel shows moiré patterns and jaggedness in the lines. Using linear filtering makes the lines smoother, but there are still clear moiré patterns at the far end. The texels between the black-and-white checks are gray because of the filtering. In Figure 7.18(c) we see where the texture mapping switches from one level to another. Mipmapping using the nearest mipmap in the hierachy also replaces many of the blacks and whites of the two-color patterns with grays that are the average of the two color values. For the parts of the object that are farthest from the viewer, the texels are gray and blend with the background. The mipmapped texture using the nearest texel in the proper mipmap still shows the jaggedness that is smoothed out when we use linear filtering with the mipmap. Advances in the speed of GPUs and the inclusion of large amounts of texture memory in these GPUs often allows applications to use filtering and mipmapping without a significant performance penalty.

A final issue with using textures in WebGL is the interaction between texture and shading. For RGB colors, there are multiple options. The texture can modulate the shade that we would have assigned without texture mapping by multiplying the color components of the texture by the color components from the shader. We could let the color of the texture totally determine the color of a fragment—a technique called **decaling**. These and other options are easily implemented in the fragment shader.

7.5.5 Working with Texture Coordinates

Our examples so far have implicitly assumed that we know how to assign texture coordinates. If we work with rectangular polygons of the same size, then it is fairly easy to assign coordinates. We can also use the fact that texture coordinates can be stored as one-, two-, three-, or four-dimensional arrays, just as vertices are. Thus, texture coordinates can be transformed by matrices and manipulated in the same manner as we transformed positions with the model-view and projection matrices. We can use a texture matrix to scale and orient textures and to create effects in which the texture moves with the object, the camera, or the lights.

However, if the set of polygons is an approximation to a curved object, then assigning texture coordinates is far more difficult. Consider the polygonal approximation of the Utah teapot[4] in Figure 7.19. The model is built from data that describe small surface patches. The patches are of different sizes, with smaller patches in areas of high curvature. When we use the same number of line strips to display each patch, as in Figure 7.19, we see different size quadrilaterals. This problem extends to the texture-mapped image in Figure 7.20, which shows our checkerboard texture mapped to the teapot without making any adjustment for the different sizes of the patches. As we can see, by assigning the same set of texture coordinates to each patch, the texture-mapping process adjusts to the individual sizes of the triangles we use for rendering by scaling the texture map as needed. Hence, in areas such as the handle, where many small triangles are needed to give a good approximation to the curved surface, the black-and-white boxes are small compared to those on the body of the teapot. In some applications, these patterns are acceptable. However, if all surfaces of the teapot were made from the same material, we would expect to see the same pattern on all its parts. In principle, we could use the texture matrix to scale texture coordinates to achieve the desired display. However, in practice, it is almost impossible to determine the necessary information from the model to form the matrix.

One solution to this problem is to generate texture coordinates for each vertex in terms of the distance from a plane in either eye coordinates or object coordinates. Mathematically, each texture coordinate is given as a linear combination of the homogeneous-coordinate values. Thus, for s and t,

---

4. We will discuss the Utah teapot in detail in Chapter 11.

FIGURE 7.19   Polygonal model of Utah teapot.

FIGURE 7.20   Texture-mapped Utah teapot.

$$s = a_s x + b_s y + c_s z + d_s w$$

$$t = a_t x + b_t y + c_t z + d_t w.$$

Figure 7.21(a) shows the teapot with texture-coordinate generation in object space. Figure 7.21(b) uses the same equations but with the calculations in eye space. By doing the calculation in object space, the texture is fixed to the object and thus will rotate with the object. Using eye space, the texture pattern changes as we apply transformations to the object and give the illusion of the object moving through a texture field. One of the important applications of this technique is in terrain generation and mapping. We can map surface features as textures directly onto a three-dimensional mesh.

7.5.6 Multitexturing

So far, we have looked at applying a single texture to an object. However, there are many surface rendering effects that can best be implemented by more than a single application of a texture. For example, suppose that we want to apply a shadow to an object whose surface shades are themselves determined by a texture map. We could use a texture map for the shadow, but if there were only a single texture application, this method would not work.

If, instead, we have multiple texture units as in Figure 7.22, then we can accomplish this task. Each unit acts as an independent texturing stage starting with the results of the previous stage. This facility is supported in recent versions of OpenGL, including WebGL.

(a)

(b)

FIGURE 7.21   Teapot using texture coordinate generation. (a) In object coordinates. (b) In eye coordinates.

FIGURE 7.22   Sequence of texture units.

Suppose that we want to use two texture units. We can define two texture objects as part of our initialization. We then activate each in turn and decide how its texture should be applied. Let's start with the first image as the checkerboard we have already used:

```
var texSize = 64;
var numRows = 8;
var numCols = 8;

var image1 = new Uint8Array(4*texSize*texSize);

for (var i = 0; i < texSize; ++i) {
  for (var j = 0; j < texSize; ++j) {
    var patchx = Math.floor(i/(texSize/numRows));
    var patchy = Math.floor(j/(texSize/numCols));

    var c = (patchx%2 !== patchy%2 ? 255 : 0);

    image1[4*i*texSize+4*j]   = c;
    image1[4*i*texSize+4*j+1] = c;
```

```
    image1[4*i*texSize+4*j+2] = c;
    image1[4*i*texSize+4*j+3] = 255;
  }
}
```

A second image varies sinusoidally between black and white:

```
var image2 = new Uint8Array(4*texSize*texSize);

// Create a checkerboard pattern
for (var i = 0; i < texSize; ++i) {
  for (var j = 0; j < texSize; ++j) {
    var c = 127 + 127 * Math.sin(0.1*i*j);
    image2[4*i*texSize+4*j]   = c;
    image2[4*i*texSize+4*j+1] = c;
    image2[4*i*texSize+4*j+2] = c;
    image2[4*i*texSize+4*j+3] = 255;
  }
}
```

We form two standard texture objects:

```
texture1 = gl.createTexture();
gl.bindTexture(gl.TEXTURE_2D, texture1);
gl.pixelStorei(gl.UNPACK_FLIP_Y_WEBGL, true);
gl.texImage2D(gl.TEXTURE_2D, 0, gl.RGBA, texSize, texSize, 0,
              gl.RGBA, gl.UNSIGNED_BYTE, image1);
gl.generateMipmap(gl.TEXTURE_2D);
gl.texParameteri(gl.TEXTURE_2D, gl.TEXTURE_MIN_FILTER,
gl.NEAREST_MIPMAP_LINEAR);
gl.texParameteri(gl.TEXTURE_2D, gl.TEXTURE_MAG_FILTER, gl.NEAREST);

texture2 = gl.createTexture();
gl.bindTexture(gl.TEXTURE_2D, texture2);
gl.pixelStorei(gl.UNPACK_FLIP_Y_WEBGL, true);
gl.texImage2D(gl.TEXTURE_2D, 0, gl.RGBA, texSize, texSize, 0,
              gl.RGBA, gl.UNSIGNED_BYTE, image2);
gl.generateMipmap(gl.TEXTURE_2D);
gl.texParameteri(gl.TEXTURE_2D, gl.TEXTURE_MIN_FILTER,
gl.NEAREST_MIPMAP_LINEAR);
gl.texParameteri(gl.TEXTURE_2D, gl.TEXTURE_MAG_FILTER, gl.NEAREST);
```

We can assign each texture object to a different texture unit, and the fragment shader can use two samplers to access them. Suppose that in the fragment shader, we have the two samplers specified as

```
uniform sampler2D Tex0;
uniform sampler2D Tex1;
```

In the application we can assign the texture objects to the first two texture units and connect the samplers in the shader to the application by

```
gl.activeTexture(gl.TEXTURE0);
gl.bindTexture(gl.TEXTURE_2D, texture1);
gl.uniform1i(gl.getUniformLocation(program, "Tex0"), 0);

gl.activeTexture(gl.TEXTURE1);
gl.bindTexture(gl.TEXTURE_2D, texture2);
gl.uniform1i(gl.getUniformLocation(program, "Tex1"), 1);
```

All we have left to do is decide how the shader will use these textures. Suppose we simply want to multiply the effect of the checkerboard texture from our previous example by the sinusoidal pattern in the second texture. Then the fragment color is given by

```
gl_FragColor = color * texture2D(Tex0, texCoord)
                     * texture2D(Tex1, texCoord);
```

The results are shown in Color Plate 16. Note that because `texCoord` is simply a varying variable passed into the fragment shader, we could alter its values or even use a different variable for the texture coordinates. We will see examples of using more than a single pair of texture coordinates in the shader when we consider imaging operations later in this chapter.

7.6   TEXTURE GENERATION

One of the most powerful uses of texture mapping is to provide detail without generating numerous geometric objects. Virtually all graphics systems can do two-dimensional texture mapping in real time; for every frame, the texture is mapped to objects as part of the rendering process at almost the same rate as non-texture-mapped objects are processed. Graphics boards for personal computers contain sufficient memory to allow game developers to create games that store large numbers of texture maps that are used to construct complex animated environments.

If, for example, we want to simulate grass in a scene, we can texture-map an image of grass that we might have obtained by, say, scanning a photograph, faster than we can generate two- or three-dimensional objects that look like grass. In mapping applications, rather than generating realistic surface detail for terrain, we can digitize a real map and paint it on a three-dimensional surface model by texture mapping.

We can also look for procedural methods for determining texture patterns. Of particular interest are patterns that we see in nature, such as the textures of sand, grass, or minerals. These textures show both structure (regular patterns) and considerable randomness. Most approaches to algorithmically generating such textures start with a random-number generator and process its output, as shown in Figure 7.23. We shall study procedural noise in detail in Chapter 10.

The generation of a three-dimensional texture field $T(s, t, r)$ is a direct extension of two-dimensional texture generation techniques. Although it is not yet supported in WebGL except as an extension, there are some practical advantages to using three-dimensional textures that merit taking a brief look at them. Most important is that by associating each (s, t, r) value directly with an (x, y, z) point, we can avoid the map-

FIGURE 7.23   Texture generation.

ping problem entirely. The user need only define a function $T(s, t, r)$ with the desired properties. Conceptually, this process is similar to sculpting the three-dimensional object from a solid block whose volume is colored by the specified texture. This technique has been used to generate objects that look as if they have been carved from solid rock. The texture generation process defines a function $T(s, t, r)$ that displays the graininess we associate with materials such as marble and granite.

There are other advantages to using three-dimensional textures. Suppose that we have a two-dimensional texture that we obtained by photographing or modeling some natural material, such as stone. Now suppose that we want to create a cube that looks like it was formed from this stone. If we use two-dimensional texture mapping, we have to map the same pattern to the six sides of the cube. To make the cube look real, we must try to make the texture map appear continuous at the edges of the cube, where two texture maps meet. When we work with natural patterns, it is virtually impossible to ensure that we can do this matching. Note that the problem is even more serious at the vertices of the cube, where three texture maps meet (see Exercise 7.22). Often we can use filtering and texture borders to give visually acceptable results. However, if we use three-dimensional textures, this problem does not arise.

7.7   ENVIRONMENT MAPS

Highly reflective surfaces are characterized by specular reflections that mirror the environment. Consider, for example, a shiny metal ball in the middle of a room. We can see the contents of the room, in a distorted form, on the surface of the ball. Obviously, this effect requires global information, as we cannot shade the ball correctly without knowing about the rest of the scene. A physically based rendering method, such as a ray tracer, can produce this kind of image, although in practice ray-tracing calculations usually are too time consuming to be practical for real-time applications. We can, however, use variants of texture mapping that can give approximate results that are visually acceptable through **environment maps** or **reflection maps**.

The basic idea is simple. Consider the mirror in Figure 7.24, which we can look at as a polygon whose surface is a highly specular material. From the point of view of a renderer, the position of the viewer and the normal to the polygon are known, so that the angle of reflection is determined as in Chapter 6. If we follow along this angle until we intersect the environment, we obtain the shade that is reflected in the mirror. Of course, this shade is the result of a shading process that involves the light sources and materials in the scene. We can obtain an approximately correct value of this shade as part of a two-step rendering pass, similar in some respects to the two-step texture-mapping process that we outlined in Section 7.4. In the first pass, we

FIGURE 7.24   Scene with a mirror.

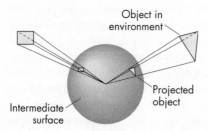

FIGURE 7.25   Mapping of the environment.

render the scene without the mirror polygon, with the camera placed at the center of the mirror pointed in the direction of the normal of the mirror. Thus, we obtain an image of the objects in the environment as "seen" by the mirror. This image is not quite correct (Exercise 7.1), but is usually good enough. We can then use this image to obtain the shades (texture values) to place on the mirror polygon for the normal second rendering with the mirror placed back in the scene.

There are two difficulties with this approach. First, the images that we obtain in the first pass are not quite correct, because they have been formed without one of the objects—the mirror—in the environment. Second, we must confront the mapping issue. Onto what surface should we project the scene in the first pass, and where should we place the camera? Potentially, we want all the information in the scene, since we may want to do something like have our mirror move. Then we would see different parts of the environment on successive frames, and thus a simple projection will not suffice.

There have been a variety of approaches to this projection problem. The classic approach is to project the environment onto a sphere centered at the center of projection. In Figure 7.25, we see some polygons that are outside the sphere and their projections onto the sphere. Note that a viewer located at the center of the sphere cannot tell whether she is seeing the polygons in their original positions or their projections on the sphere. This illusion is similar to what we see in a planetarium. The "stars" that appear to be an infinite distance away are actually the projection of lights onto the hemisphere that encloses the audience.

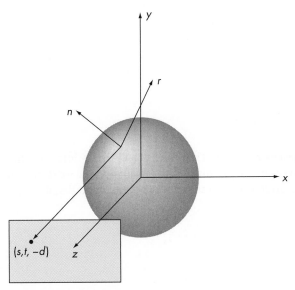

FIGURE 7.26 Reflection map.

In the original version of environment mapping, the surface of the sphere was then converted to a rectangle using lines of longitude and latitude for the mapping. Although conceptually simple, there are problems at the poles where the shape distortion becomes infinite. Computationally, this mapping does not preserve areas very well and requires evaluating a large number of trigonometric functions.

Desktop OpenGL supports a variation of this method called **sphere mapping**. The application program supplies a circular image that is the orthographic projection of the sphere onto which the environment has been mapped. The advantage of this method is that the mapping from the reflection vector to two-dimensional texture coordinates on this circle is simple and can be implemented in either hardware or software. The difficult part is obtaining the required circular image. It can be approximated by taking a perspective projection with a very wide-angle lens or by remapping some other type of projection, such as the cube projection that we discuss next. We load the texture image in texture memory through `glTexImage2D`.

The equations for generating the texture coordinates can be understood with the help of Figure 7.26. It is probably easiest if we work backward from the viewer to the image. Suppose that the texture map is in the plane $z = -d$, where d is positive and we project backward orthogonally toward a unit sphere centered at the origin. Thus, if the texture coordinates in the plane are (s, t), then the projector intersects the sphere at $(s, t, \sqrt{1.0 - s^2 - t^2})$. For the unit sphere centered at the origin, the coordinates of any point on the sphere are also the components of the unit normal at that point. We can then compute the direction of reflection, as in Chapter 6, by

$$\mathbf{r} = 2(\mathbf{n} \cdot \mathbf{v})\mathbf{n} - \mathbf{v},$$

where

$$\mathbf{v} = \begin{bmatrix} s \\ t \\ 0 \end{bmatrix}$$

$$\mathbf{n} = \begin{bmatrix} s \\ t \\ \sqrt{1.0 - s^2 - t^2} \end{bmatrix}.$$

The vector $\mathbf{r}$ points into the environment. Thus, any object that $\mathbf{r}$ intersects has texture coordinates (s, t). However, this argument is backward because we start with an object defined by vertices. Given $\mathbf{r}$, we can solve for s and t and find that if

$$\mathbf{r} = \begin{bmatrix} r_x \\ r_y \\ r_z \end{bmatrix},$$

then

$$s = \frac{r_x}{f} + \frac{1}{2}$$

$$t = \frac{r_y}{f} + \frac{1}{2},$$

where

$$f = 2\sqrt{r_x^2 + r_y^2 + (r_z + 1)^2}.$$

If we put everything into eye coordinates, we compute $\mathbf{r}$ using the unit vector from the origin to the vertex for $\mathbf{v}$ and the vertex normal for $\mathbf{n}$.

This process reveals some issues that show that this method is only approximate. The reflection map is only correct for the vertex at the origin. In principle, each vertex should have its own reflection map. Actually, each point on the object should have its own map and not an approximate value computed by interpolation. The errors are most significant the farther the object is from the origin. Nevertheless, reflection mapping gives visually acceptable results in most situations, especially when there is animation as in films and games.

If we want to compute an environment map using the graphics system, we prefer to use the standard projections that are supported by the graphics systems. For an environment such as a room, the natural intermediate object is a box. We compute six projections, corresponding to the walls, floor, and ceiling, using six virtual cameras located at the center of the box, each pointing in a different direction. At this point, we can treat the six images as a single environment map and derive the textures from it, as in Figure 7.27. Color Plates 23 and 24 demonstrate the use of cube maps to produce images for a multiprojector environment dome, such as used in a planetarium. Color Plate 23(a) shows a cube environment with both an object and an identifier on each face. Color Plate 23(b) shows five virtual cameras at the origin, oriented to capture all faces of the cube other than the bottom face, which was not needed for this

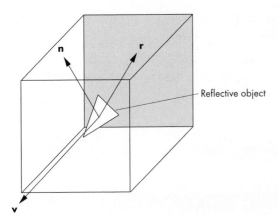

FIGURE 7.27   Reflective cube map.

application. Color Plate 23(a) shows the five texture maps displayed as an unfolded box. Color Plate 24(b) shows the textures mapped to a hemisphere.

Regardless of how the images are computed, once we have them, we can specify a cube map in WebGL with six function calls, one for each face of a cube centered at the origin. Thus, if we have a 512×512 RGBA image `imagexp` for the positive-x face, we have the following:

```
gl.texImage2D(gl.TEXTURE_CUBE_MAP_POSITIVE_X, 0, gl.RGBA, 512, 512, 0,
              gl.RGBA, gl.UNSIGNED_BYTE, imagexp);
```

For reflection maps, the calculation of texture coordinates can be done automatically. However, cube maps are fundamentally different from sphere maps, which are much like standard two-dimensional texture maps with special coordinate calculations. Here, we must use three-dimensional texture coordinates, which are often computed in the shader. In the next section, we will see that these cube map calculations are simple.

These techniques are examples of **multipass rendering** (or **multirendering**), where, in order to compute a single image, we compute multiple images, each using the rendering pipeline. Multipass methods are becoming increasingly more important as the power of graphics cards has increased to the point where we can render a scene multiple times from different perspectives in less time than is needed for reasonable refresh rates. Equivalently, most of these techniques can be done within the fragment shader.

7.8 REFLECTION MAP EXAMPLE

Let's look at a simple example of a reflection map based on our rotating cube example. In this example, we will use a cube map in which each of the six texture maps is a single texel. Our rotating cube will be totally reflective and placed inside a box, each of whose sides is one of the six colors red, green, blue, cyan, magenta, or yellow. Here's how we can set up the cube map as part of initialization using texture unit 0:

```
var red = new Uint8Array([255, 0, 0, 255]);
var green = new Uint8Array([0, 255, 0, 255]);
var blue = new Uint8Array([0, 0, 255, 255]);
var cyan = new Uint8Array([0, 255, 255, 255]);
var magenta = new Uint8Array([255, 0, 255, 255]);
var yellow = new Uint8Array([255, 255, 0, 255]);

var cubeMap;

gl.bindTexture(gl.TEXTURE_CUBE_MAP, cubeMap);
gl.activeTexture(gl.TEXTURE0);

cubeMap = gl.createTexture();
gl.texImage2D(gl.TEXTURE_CUBE_MAP_POSITIVE_X ,0,gl.RGBA,
              1,1,0,gl.RGBA,gl.UNSIGNED_BYTE, red);
gl.texImage2D(gl.TEXTURE_CUBE_MAP_NEGATIVE_X ,0,gl.RGBA,
              1,1,0,gl.RGBA,gl.UNSIGNED_BYTE, green);
gl.texImage2D(gl.TEXTURE_CUBE_MAP_POSITIVE_Y ,0,gl.RGBA,
              1,1,0,gl.RGBA,gl.UNSIGNED_BYTE, blue);
gl.texImage2D(gl.TEXTURE_CUBE_MAP_NEGATIVE_Y ,0,gl.RGBA,
              1,1,0,gl.RGBA,gl.UNSIGNED_BYTE, cyan);
gl.texImage2D(gl.TEXTURE_CUBE_MAP_POSITIVE_Z ,0,gl.RGBA,
              1,1,0,gl.RGBA,gl.UNSIGNED_BYTE, yellow);
gl.texImage2D(gl.TEXTURE_CUBE_MAP_NEGATIVE_Z ,0,gl.RGBA,
              1,1,0,gl.RGBA,gl.UNSIGNED_BYTE, magenta);
gl.texParameteri(gl.TEXTURE_CUBE_MAP, gl.TEXTURE_MIN_FILTER,
                 gl.NEAREST);
```

The texture map will be applied using a cube map sampler in the fragment shader. We set up the required uniform variable as in our other examples:

```
gl.uniform1i(gl.getUniformLocation(program, "texture"), 0);
```

Now that we have set up the cube map, we can turn to the determination of the texture coordinates. The required computations for a reflection or environment map are shown in Figure 7.28. We assume that the environment has already been mapped to the cube. The difference between a reflection map and a simple cube texture map is that we use the reflection vector to access the texture for a reflection map rather than the view vector. We can compute the reflection vector at each vertex in our vertex program and then let the fragment program interpolate these values over the primitive.

However, to compute the reflection vector, we need the normal to each side of the rotating cube. We can compute normals in the application and send them to the vertex shader as a vertex attribute through the quad function

```
var pointsArray = [ ];
var normalsArray = [ ];

function quad(a, b, c, d)
{
  var t1 = subtract(vertices[b], vertices[a]);
  var t2 = subtract(vertices[c], vertices[b]);
```

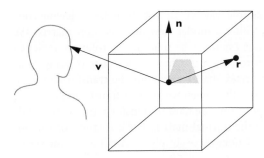

FIGURE 7.28   Reflection cube map.

```
var normal = cross(t1, t2);
normal = normalize(normal);

pointsArray.push(vertices[a]);
normalsArray.push(normal);

pointsArray.push(vertices[b]);
normalsArray.push(normal);

pointsArray.push(vertices[c]);
normalsArray.push(normal);

pointsArray.push(vertices[a]);
normalsArray.push(normal);

pointsArray.push(vertices[c]);
normalsArray.push(normal);

pointsArray.push(vertices[d]);
normalsArray.push(normal);
}
```

Then we put the position and normal data in two vertex arrays:

```
var nBuffer = gl.createBuffer();
gl.bindBuffer(gl.ARRAY_BUFFER, nBuffer);
gl.bufferData(gl.ARRAY_BUFFER, flatten(normalsArray), gl.STATIC_DRAW);

var normal = gl.getAttribLocation(program, "Normal");
gl.vertexAttribPointer(normal, 4, gl.FLOAT, false, 0, 0);
gl.enableVertexAttribArray(normal);

var vBuffer = gl.createBuffer();
gl.bindBuffer(gl.ARRAY_BUFFER, vBufferI);
gl.bufferData(gl.ARRAY_BUFFER, flatten(pointsArray), gl.STATIC_DRAW);

var vPosition = gl.getAttribLocation(program, "vPosition");
gl.vertexAttribPointer(vPosition, 4, gl.FLOAT, false, 0, 0);
gl.enableVertexAttribArray(vPosition);
```

To illustrate the cube map in a simple way, we can use the default viewing conditions so that we need not specify either a model-view or projection matrix. We will rotate the cube as in our previous examples by sending the rotation angles to the vertex shader, using these angles to compute a model-view matrix using rotation matrices, and then having the vertex shader carry out the transformation of vertex positions. Recall from Chapter 6 that when we apply a transformation such as the model-view matrix to vertex positions, we have to transform the corresponding normals by a transformation by the normal matrix. For a rotation of the object, the normal matrix is a rotation. Under these simplified conditions, our vertex shader is

```
varying vec3 R;
attribute vec4 vPosition;
attribute vec4 Normal;

uniform mat4 ModelView;
uniform vec3 theta;

void main()
{
  vec3 angles = radians(theta);
  vec3 c = cos(angles);
  vec3 s = sin(angles);

  mat4 rx = mat4(1.0,  0.0,   0.0, 0.0,
                 0.0,  c.x,   s.x, 0.0,
                 0.0, -s.x,   c.x, 0.0,
                 0.0,  0.0,   0.0, 1.0);

  mat4 ry = mat4(c.y, 0.0, -s.y, 0.0,
                 0.0, 1.0,  0.0, 0.0,
                 s.y, 0.0,  c.y, 0.0,
                 0.0, 0.0,  0.0, 1.0);

  mat4 rz = mat4(c.z, -s.z, 0.0, 0.0,
                 s.z,  c.z, 0.0, 0.0,
                 0.0,  0.0, 1.0, 0.0,
                 0.0,  0.0, 0.0, 1.0);

  mat4 ModelView = rz * ry * rx;
  vec4 eyePos  = ModelView * vPosition;

  vec4 N = ModelView * Normal;
  R = reflect(eyePos.xyz, N.xyz);

  gl_Position = ModelView * vPosition;
}
```

It computes the reflection vector in eye coordinates as a varying variable. If we want the color to be totally determined by the texture, the fragment shader is simply

```
varying vec3 R;
uniform samplerCube texMap;

void main()
{
  vec4 texColor = textureCube(texMap, R);
  gl_FragColor = texColor;
}
```

Although the texture coordinates are three-dimensional, the sampler uses one of the six two-dimensional texture images to determine the color. Suppose that the reflection vector R in our sampler points in the direction (x, y, z). We can see from Figure 7.28 that the largest magnitude component of R determines which texture to use. For example, if R points in the direction $(.3, .4, −.5)$, it will intersect the negative z surface first and the sample will convert $(.3, .4)$ to the proper texture coordinates on the correct texture image.

We can create more complex lighting by having the color determined in part by the specular, diffuse, and ambient lighting, as we did for the modified Phong lighting model. However, we must be careful about which frame we want to use in our shaders. The difference between this example and previous ones is that the environment map usually is computed in world coordinates. Object positions and normals are specified in object coordinates and are brought into the world frame by modeling transformations in the application. We usually never see the object-coordinate representation of objects because the model-view transformation converts object coordinates directly to eye coordinates. In many applications, we define our objects directly without modeling transformations so that model and object coordinates are the same. However, we want to write our program in a manner that allows for modeling transformations when we do reflection mapping. One way to accomplish this task is to compute the modeling matrix in the application and pass it to the fragment program as a uniform variable. Also note that we need the inverse transpose of the modeling matrix to transform the normal. However, if we pass in the inverse matrix as another uniform variable, we can postmultiply the normal to obtain the desired result. Color Plate 12 shows the use of a reflection map to determine the colors on the teapot. The teapot is set inside a cube, each of whose sides is one of the colors red, green, blue, cyan, magenta, or yellow.

7.9 BUMP MAPPING

Bump mapping is a texture-mapping technique that can give the appearance of great complexity in an image without increasing the geometric complexity. Unlike simple texture mapping, bump mapping will show changes in shading as the light source or object moves, making the object appear to have variations in surface smoothness.

Let's start by returning to our example of creating an image of an orange. If we take a photograph of a real orange, we can apply this image as a texture map to a surface. However, if we move the lights or rotate the object, we immediately notice that we have the image of a model of an orange rather than the image of a real orange. The problem is that a real orange is characterized primarily by small variations in its surface rather than by variations in its color, and the former are not captured by texture mapping. The technique of **bump mapping** varies the apparent shape of the surface by perturbing the normal vectors as the surface is rendered; the colors that are generated by shading then show a variation in the surface properties. Unlike techniques such as environment mapping that can be implemented without programmable shaders, bump mapping cannot be done in real time without them. In particular, because bump mapping is done on a fragment-by-fragment basis, we must be able to program the fragment shader.

7.9.1 Finding Bump Maps

We start with the observation that the normal at any point on a surface characterizes the orientation of the surface at that point. If we perturb the normal at each point on the surface by a small amount, then we create a surface with small variations in its shape. If this perturbation to the normal can be applied only during the shading process, we can use a smooth model of the surface, which must have a smooth normal, but we can shade it in a way that gives the appearance of a complex surface. Because the perturbations are applied to the normal vectors, the rendering calculations are correct for the altered surface, even though the more complex surface defined by the perturbed normals need never be created.

We can perturb the normals in many ways. The following procedure for parametric surfaces is an efficient one. Let $\mathbf{p}(u, v)$ be a point on a parametric surface. The partial derivatives at the point

$$
\mathbf{p}_u = \begin{bmatrix} \frac{\partial x}{\partial u} \\ \frac{\partial y}{\partial u} \\ \frac{\partial z}{\partial u} \end{bmatrix} \qquad \mathbf{p}_v = \begin{bmatrix} \frac{\partial x}{\partial v} \\ \frac{\partial y}{\partial v} \\ \frac{\partial z}{\partial v} \end{bmatrix}
$$

lie in the plane tangent to the surface at the point. Their cross product can be normalized to give the unit normal at that point:

$$
\mathbf{n} = \frac{\mathbf{p}_u \times \mathbf{p}_v}{|\mathbf{p}_u \times \mathbf{p}_v|}.
$$

Suppose that we displace the surface in the normal direction by a function called the **bump**, or **displacement**, **function**, $d(u, v)$, which we can assume is known and small ($|d(u, v)| \ll 1$). The displaced surface is given by

$$
\mathbf{p}' = \mathbf{p} + d(u, v)\mathbf{n}.
$$

We would prefer not to create the displaced surface because such a surface would have a higher geometric complexity than the undisplaced surface and would thus slow down the rendering process. We just want to make it look as though we have displaced the original surface. We can achieve the desired look by altering the normal $\mathbf{n}$, instead of $\mathbf{p}$, and using the perturbed normal in our shading calculations.

The normal at the perturbed point $\mathbf{p}'$ is given by the cross product

$$
\mathbf{n}' = \mathbf{p}'_u \times \mathbf{p}'_v.
$$

We can compute the two partial derivatives by differentiating the equation for $\mathbf{p}'$, obtaining

$$\mathbf{p}'_u = \mathbf{p}_u + \frac{\partial d}{\partial u}\mathbf{n} + d(u, v)\mathbf{n}_u$$

$$\mathbf{p}'_v = \mathbf{p}_v + \frac{\partial d}{\partial v}\mathbf{n} + d(u, v)\mathbf{n}_v.$$

If d is small, we can neglect the term on the right of these two equations and take their cross product, noting that $\mathbf{n} \times \mathbf{n} = \mathbf{0}$, to obtain the approximate perturbed normal:

$$\mathbf{n}' \approx \mathbf{n} + \frac{\partial d}{\partial u}\mathbf{n} \times \mathbf{p}_v + \frac{\partial d}{\partial v}\mathbf{n} \times \mathbf{p}_u.$$

The two terms on the right are the displacement, the difference between the original and perturbed normals. The cross product of two vectors is orthogonal to both of them. Consequently, both cross products yield vectors that lie in the tangent plane at $\mathbf{p}$, and their sum must also be in the tangent plane.

Although $\mathbf{p}'_u$ and $\mathbf{p}'_v$ lie in the tangent plane perpendicular to $\mathbf{n}'$, they are not necessarily orthogonal to each other. We can obtain an orthogonal basis and a corresponding rotation matrix using the cross product. First, we normalize $\mathbf{n}'$ and $\mathbf{p}'_u$, obtaining the vectors

$$\mathbf{m} = \frac{\mathbf{n}'}{|\mathbf{n}'|}$$

$$\mathbf{t} = \frac{\mathbf{p}'_u}{|\mathbf{p}'_u|}.$$

We obtain the third orthogonal vector, $\mathbf{b}$, by

$$\mathbf{b} = \mathbf{m} \times \mathbf{t}.$$

The vector $\mathbf{t}$ is called the **tangent vector** at $\mathbf{p}$, and $\mathbf{b}$ is called the **binormal vector** at $\mathbf{p}$. The matrix

$$\mathbf{M} = [\mathbf{t} \quad \mathbf{b} \quad \mathbf{m}]^T$$

is the rotation matrix that will convert representations in the original space to representations in terms of the three vectors. The new space is sometimes called **tangent space**. Because the tangent and binormal vectors can change for each point on the surface, tangent space is a local coordinate system.

To better understand the implication of having introduced another frame, one that is local to the point on the surface, let's consider a bump from the plane $z = 0$. The surface can be written in implicit form as

$$f(x, y) = ax + by + c = 0.$$

If we let $u = x$ and $v = y$, then, if $a \neq 0$, we have

$$\mathbf{p}(u, v) = \begin{bmatrix} u \\ -\dfrac{b}{a}v - \dfrac{c}{a} \\ 0 \end{bmatrix}.$$

The vectors $\partial\mathbf{p}/\partial u$ and $\partial\mathbf{p}/\partial v$ can be normalized to give the orthogonal vectors

$$\frac{\mathbf{p}'_u}{|\mathbf{p}'_u|} = [\, 1 \quad 0 \quad 0\,]^T \qquad \frac{\mathbf{p}'_v}{|\mathbf{p}'_v|} = [\, 0 \quad 1 \quad 0\,]^T.$$

Because these vectors turned out to be orthogonal, they serve as the tangent binormal vectors. The unit normal is

$$\mathbf{n} = [\, 0 \quad 0 \quad 1\,]^T.$$

For this case, the displacement function is a function $d(x, y)$. To specify the bump map, we need two functions that give the values of $\partial d/\partial x$ and $\partial d/\partial y$. If these functions are known analytically, we can evaluate them either in the application or in the shader. More often, however, we have a sampled version of $d(x, y)$ as an array of pixels $\mathbf{D} = [d_{ij}]$. The required partial derivatives can be approximated by the difference between adjacent elements:

$$\frac{\partial d}{\partial x} \propto d_{ij} - d_{i-1,j} \qquad \frac{\partial d}{\partial y} \propto d_{ij} - d_{i,j-1}.$$

These arrays can be precomputed in the application and stored as a texture called a **normal map**. The fragment shader can obtain the values using a sampler.

Before we develop the necessary shaders, consider what is different for the general case when the surface is not described by the plane $z = 0$. In our simple case, the tangent space axes aligned with the object or world axes. In general, the normal from a surface will not point in the z direction nor along any particular axis. In addition, the tangent and binormal vectors, although orthogonal to each other and the normal, will have no particular orientation with respect to the world or object axes. The displacement function is measured along the normal, so its partial derivatives are in an arbitrary plane. However, in tangent space this displacement is along the z-coordinate axis. Hence, the importance of the matrix $\mathbf{M}$ composed of the normal, tangent, and binormal vectors is that it allows us to go to the local coordinate system in which the bump map calculations match what we just did. The usual implementation of bump mapping is to find this matrix and transform object-space vectors into vectors in a tangent-space local coordinate system. Because tangent space is local, the change in representation can be different for every fragment. With polygonal meshes, the calculation can be simpler if we use the same normal across each polygon and the application can send the tangent and binormal to the vertex shader once for each polygon.

We are almost ready to write vertex and fragment shaders for bump mapping. The entities that we need for lighting—the surface normal, the light vector(s), the half-angle vector, and the vertex location—are usually in eye or object coordinates at the point in the process when we do lighting. Whether we use a normal map or compute the perturbation of the normal procedurally in a fragment shader, the displacements are in texture-space coordinates. For correct shading, we have to convert

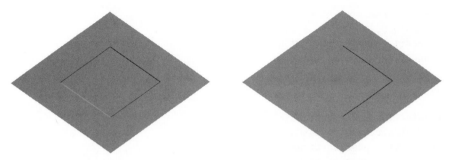

FIGURE 7.29 Two views of a bump-mapped square with a moving light source.

either the normal map to object-space coordinates or the object-space coordinates to texture-space coordinates. In general, the latter requires less work because it can be carried out on a per-vertex basis in the vertex shader rather than on a per-fragment basis. As we have seen, the matrix needed to convert from object space to texture space is precisely the matrix composed of the normal, tangent, and binormal.

We can send the normal to the vertex shader as a vertex attribute if it changes at each vertex, or, if we are working with a single flat polygon at a time, we can use a uniform variable. The application can also provide tangent vectors in a similar manner. The binormal can then be computed in the shader using the cross product function. These computations are done in the vertex shader, which produces a light vector and view vector in tangent coordinates for use in the fragment shader. Because the normal vector in tangent coordinates always points in the positive z direction, the view and light vectors are sufficient for doing lighting in tangent space.

7.9.2 Bump Map Example

Our example is a single square in the plane $y = 0$ with a light source above the plane that rotates in the plane $y = 10.0$. We will include only diffuse lighting to minimize the amount of code we need. Our displacement is a small square in the center of the original square. Before developing the code, the output is shown in Figure 7.29. The image on the left is with the light source in its original position; the image on the right is with the light source rotated 45 degrees in the $x - z$ plane at the same height above the surface.

First, let's look at the application program. We will use two triangles for the square polygon, and each of the six vertices will have a texture so that part of the code will be much the same as in previous examples:

```
var pointsArray = [ ];
var texCoordsArray = [ ];

var texCoord = [
  vec2(0, 0),
  vec2(0, 1),
  vec2(1, 1),
  vec2(1, 0)
];
```

```
var vertices = [
  vec4(0.0, 0.0, 0.0, 1.0),
  vec4(1.0,  0.0,  0.0, 1.0),
  vec4(1.0,  0.0,  1.0, 1.0),
  vec4(0.0, 0.0,  1.0, 1.0)
];

pointsArray.push(vertices[0]);
texCoordsArray.push(texCoord[0]);
pointsArray.push(vertices[1]);
texCoordsArray.push(texCoord[1]);
pointsArray.push(vertices[2]);
texCoordsArray.push(texCoord[2]);
pointsArray.push(vertices[2]);  ;
texCoordsArray.push(texCoord[2]);
pointsArray.push(vertices[3]);
texCoordsArray.push(texCoord[3]);
pointsArray.push(vertices[0]);
texCoordsArray.push(texCoord[0]);
```

We send these data to the GPU as vertex attributes.

The displacement map is generated as an array in the application. The displacement data are in the array `data`. The normal map is computed by taking differences to approximate the partial derivatives for two of the components and using 1.0 for the third to form the array `normals`. Because these values are stored as colors in a texture image, the components are scaled to the interval (0.0, 1.0).

```
// Bump data

var data = new Array()
for (var i = 0; i <= texSize; ++i) {
  data[i] = new Array();

  for (var j = 0; j <= texSize; ++j) {
    data[i][j] = 0.0;
  }
}

for (var i = texSize/4; i < 3*texSize/4; ++i) {
  for (var j = texSize/4; j < 3*texSize/4; ++j) {
    data[i][j] = 1.0;
  }
}

// Bump map normals

var normalst = new Array()
for (var i = 0; i < texSize; ++i) {
  normalst[i] = new Array();
```

```
    for (var j = 0; j < texSize; ++j) {
      normalst[i][j] = new Array();

      normalst[i][j][0] = data[i][j]-data[i+1][j];
      normalst[i][j][1] = data[i][j]-data[i][j+1];
      normalst[i][j][2] = 1;
    }
  }

// Scale to texture coordinates

for (var i = 0; i < texSize; ++i) {
  for (var j = 0; j < texSize; ++j) {
    var d = 0;

    for (var k = 0; k < 3 ; ++k) {
      d += normalst[i][j][k] * normalst[i][j][k];
    }

    d = Math.sqrt(d);
    for (k = 0; k < 3; ++k) {
      normalst[i][j][k] = 0.5 * normalst[i][j][k]/d + 0.5;
    }
  }
}

// Normal texture array

var normals = new Uint8Array(3*texSize*texSize);

for (var i = 0; i < texSize; ++i) {
  for (var j = 0; j < texSize; ++j) {
    for (var k = 0; k < 3; ++k) {
      normals[3*texSize*i+3*j+k] = 255 * normalst[i][j][k];
    }
  }
}
```

The array `normals` is then sent to the GPU by building a texture object. We send a projection matrix, a model-view matrix, the light position, and the diffuse lighting parameters to the shaders as uniform variables. Because the surface is flat, the normal is constant and can be sent to the shader as a uniform variable. Likewise, the tangent vector is constant and can be any vector in the same plane as the polygon and can also be sent to the vertex shader as a uniform variable.

We now turn to the vertex shader. In this simple example, we want to do the calculations in texture space. Hence, we must transform both the light vector and eye vector to this space. The required transformation matrix is composed of the normal, tangent, and binormal vectors.

The normal and tangent are specified in object coordinates and must first be converted to eye coordinates. The required transformation matrix is the normal matrix, which is the inverse transpose of the upper-left 3×3 submatrix of the model-view matrix. We assume this matrix is computed in the application and sent to the shader as another uniform variable. We can then use the transformed normal and tangent to give the binormal in eye coordinates. Finally, we use these three vectors to transform the view vector and light vector to texture space. Here is the vertex shader:

```
// Bump map vertex shader

varying vec3 L; // light vector in texture-space coordinates
varying vec3 V; // view vector in texture-space coordinates

attribute vec2 vTexCoord;
attribute vec4 vPosition;

uniform vec4 Normal;
uniform vec4 LightPosition;
uniform mat4 ModelView;
uniform mat4 Projection;
uniform mat3 NormalMatrix;
uniform vec3 objTangent; // Tangent vector in object coordinates

varying vec2 fTexCoord;

void main()
{
  fTexCoord = vTexCoord;

  vec3 eyePosition = (ModelView * vPosition).xyz;
  vec3 eyeLightPos = (ModelView * LightPosition).xyz;

  // Normal, tangent, and binormal in eye coordinates

  vec3 N = normalize(NormalMatrix * Normal.xyz);
  vec3 T = normalize(NormalMatrix * objTangent);
  vec3 B = cross(N, T);

  // Light vector in texture space

  L.x = dot(T, eyeLightPos - eyePosition);
  L.y = dot(B, eyeLightPos - eyePosition);
  L.z = dot(N, eyeLightPos - eyePosition);

  L = normalize(L);

  // View vector in texture space
```

```
   V.x = dot(T, -eyePosition);
   V.y = dot(B, -eyePosition);
   V.z = dot(N, -eyePosition);

   V = normalize(V);

   gl_Position = Projection * ModelView * vPosition;
}
```

Our strategy for the fragment shader is to send the normalized perturbed normals as a texture map from the application to the shader as a normal map. The fragment shader is given here:

```
precision mediump float;

varying vec3 L;
varying vec3 V;
varying vec2 fTexCoord;

uniform sampler2D texMap;
uniform vec4 DiffuseProduct;

void main()
{
  vec4 N = texture2D(texMap, fTexCoord);
  vec3 NN =  normalize(2.0*N.xyz - 1.0);
  vec3 LL = normalize(L);
  float Kd = max(dot(NN, LL), 0.0);

  gl_FragColor = vec4(Kd * DiffuseProduct.xyz, 1.0);
}
```

The values in the texture map are scaled back to the interval $(-1.0, 1.0)$. The diffuse product is a vector computed in the application, each of whose components is the product of a diffuse light component and a diffuse material component.

Note that this example does not use the texture-space view vectors computed in the vertex shader. These vectors would be necessary if we wanted to add a specular term. We have only touched the surface (so to speak) of bump mapping. Many of its most powerful applications result when it is combined with procedural texture generation, which we explore further in Chapter 9.

7.10 BLENDING TECHNIQUES

Thus far, we have assumed that we want to form a single image and that the objects that form this image have surfaces that are opaque. WebGL provides a mechanism, through **alpha (α) blending**, that can, among other effects, create images with translucent objects. The **alpha channel** is the fourth color in RGBA (or RGBα) color mode. Like the other colors, the application program can control the value of A (or

FIGURE 7.30 Translucent and opaque polygons.

α) for each pixel. However, in RGBA mode, if blending is enabled, the value of α controls how the RGB values are written into the framebuffer. Because fragments from multiple objects can contribute to the color of the same pixel, we say that these objects are **blended** or **composited** together. We can use a similar mechanism to blend together images.

7.10.1 Opacity and Blending

The **opacity** of a surface is a measure of how much light penetrates through that surface. An opacity of 1 ($\alpha = 1$) corresponds to a completely opaque surface that blocks all light incident on it. A surface with an opacity of 0 is transparent; all light passes through it. The **transparency** or **translucency** of a surface with opacity α is given by $1 - \alpha$.

Consider the three uniformly lit polygons shown in Figure 7.30. Assume that the middle polygon is opaque, and the front polygon, nearest to the viewer, is transparent. If the front polygon were perfectly transparent, the viewer would see only the middle polygon. However, if the front polygon is only partially opaque (partially transparent), similar to colored glass, the color the viewer sees is a blending of the colors of the front and middle polygons. Because the middle polygon is opaque, the viewer does not see the back polygon. If the front polygon is red and the middle is blue, she sees magenta, due to the blending of the colors. If we let the middle polygon be only partially opaque, she sees the blending of the colors of all three polygons.

In computer graphics, we usually render polygons one at a time into the framebuffer. Consequently, if we want to use blending, we need a way to apply opacity as part of fragment processing. We can use the notion of source and destination pixels. As a polygon is processed, pixel-sized fragments are computed and, if they are visible, are assigned colors based on the shading model in use. Until now, we have used the color of a fragment—as computed by the shading model and by any mapping techniques—to determine the color of the pixel in the framebuffer at the location in screen coordinates of the fragment. If we regard the fragment as the source pixel and the framebuffer pixel as the destination, we can combine these values in various ways. Using α values is one way of controlling the blending on a fragment-by-fragment basis. Combining the colors of polygons is similar to joining two pieces of colored glass into a single piece of glass that has a higher opacity and a color different from either of the original pieces.

If we represent the source and destination pixels with the four-element (RGBα) arrays

$$\mathbf{s} = [\, s_r \quad s_g \quad s_b \quad s_a \,]$$
$$\mathbf{d} = [\, d_r \quad d_g \quad d_b \quad d_a \,],$$

then a blending operation replaces $\mathbf{d}$ with

$$\mathbf{d}' = [\, b_r s_r + c_r d_r \quad b_g s_g + c_g d_g \quad b_b s_b + c_b d_b \quad b_a s_a + c_a d_a \,].$$

The arrays of constants $\mathbf{b} = [\, b_r \quad b_g \quad b_b \quad b_a \,]$ and $\mathbf{c} = [\, c_r \quad c_g \quad c_b \quad c_a \,]$ are the **source** and **destination blending factors**, respectively. As occurs with RGB colors, a value of α over 1.0 is limited (or clamped) to the maximum of 1.0, and negative values are clamped to 0.0. We can choose both the values of α and the method of combining source and destination values to achieve a variety of effects.

7.10.2 Image Blending

The most straightforward use of α blending is to combine and display several images that exist as pixel maps or, equivalently, as sets of data that have been rendered independently. In this case, we can regard each image as a radiant object that contributes equally to the final image. Usually, we wish to keep our RGB colors between 0 and 1 in the final image, without having to clamp those values greater than 1. Hence, we can either scale the values of each image or use the source and destination blending factors.

Suppose that we have n images that should contribute equally to the final display. At a given pixel, image i has components $\mathbf{C}_i \alpha_i$. Here, we are using $\mathbf{C}_i$ to denote the color triplet (R_i, G_i, B_i). If we replace $\mathbf{C}_i$ by $\frac{1}{n}\mathbf{C}_i$ and α_i by $\frac{1}{n}$, then we can simply add each image into the framebuffer (assuming the framebuffer is initialized to black with an $\alpha = 0$). Alternately, we can use a source blending factor of $\frac{1}{n}$ by setting the α value for each pixel in each image to $\frac{1}{n}$, and using 1 for the destination blending factor and α for the source blending factor. Although these two methods produce the same image, the second may be more efficient if the hardware supports blending. Note that if n is large, blending factors of the form $\frac{1}{n}$ can lead to significant loss of color resolution. Recent framebuffers support floating-point arithmetic and thus can avoid this problem.

7.10.3 Blending in WebGL

The mechanics of blending in WebGL are straightforward, with one caveat. Because the default framebuffer is an HTML canvas element, it can interact with other HTML elements. The default canvas has an α channel that is used when we specify RGBA colors. So far when we used RGBA colors, we always used an α of 1 and we did not try to add anything to the canvas other than the contents of the framebuffer.

However, if we set the α of a fragment to a value other than 1, this value will be placed in the α channel of the WebGL canvas. Consequently, even if we do not place any other canvas elements on the same location, the color we see will be muted by this α. For example, if the fragment has RGBA values of $(1.0, 0.5, 0.2, 0.5)$, the color we see will have an RGB of $(0.5, 0.25, 0.1)$.

One of the potential uses of the ability to mix other canvas elements with the contents of the WebGL framebuffer is that we can add GUI elements and text to our images. We will not purse this path and instead focus on blending in the framebuffer through WebGL functions.

We enable blending by

```
gl.enable(gl.BLEND);
```

Then we set up the desired source and destination factors by

```
gl.blendFunc(sourceFactor, destinationFactor);
```

WebGL has a number of blending factors defined, including the values 1 (`gl.ONE`) and 0 (`gl.ZERO`), the source α and $1 - \alpha$ (`gl.SRC_ALPHA` and `gl.ONE_MINUS_SRC_ALPHA`), and the destination α and $1 - \alpha$ (`gl.DST_ALPHA` and `gl.ONE_MINUS_DST_ALPHA`). The application program specifies the desired options and then uses RGBA color.

The major difficulty with blending is that for most choices of the blending factors the order in which we render the polygons affects the final image. For example, many applications use the source α as the source blending factor and $1 - \alpha$ for the destination factor. The resulting color and opacity are

$$(R_{d'}, G_{d'}, B_{d'}, \alpha_{d'}) = (\alpha_s R_s + (1 - \alpha_s)R_d, \alpha_s G + (1 - \alpha_s)G_d,$$

$$\alpha_s B_s + (1 - \alpha_s)B_d, \alpha_s \alpha_d + (1 - \alpha_s)\alpha_d).$$

This formula ensures that neither colors nor opacities can saturate. However, the resulting color and α values depend on the order in which the polygons are rendered. Consequently, unlike in most WebGL programs, where the user does not have to worry about the order in which polygons are rasterized, to get a desired effect we must now control this order within the application.

A more subtle but visibly apparent problem occurs when we combine opaque and translucent objects in a scene. Normally, when we use blending, we do not enable hidden-surface removal, because polygons behind any polygon already rendered would not be rasterized and thus would not contribute to the final image. In a scene with both opaque and transparent polygons, any polygon behind an opaque polygon should not be rendered, but translucent polygons in front of opaque polygons should be blended. There is a simple solution to this problem that does not require the application program to order the polygons. We can enable hidden-surface removal as usual and make the z-buffer read-only for any polygon that is translucent. We do so by calling

```
gl.depthMask(gl.FALSE);
```

When the depth buffer is read-only, a translucent polygon is discarded when it lies behind any opaque polygon that has already been rendered. A translucent polygon that lies in front of any polygon that has already been rendered is blended with the color of those polygons. However, because the z-buffer is read-only for this polygon, the depth values in the buffer are unchanged. Opaque polygons set the depth mask to true and are rendered normally. Note that because the result of blending depends on the order in which we blend individual elements, we may notice defects in images in which we render translucent polygons in an arbitrary order. If we are willing to sort the translucent polygons, then we can render all the opaque polygons first and then render the translucent polygons in a back-to-front order with the z-buffer in read-only mode.

7.10.4 Antialiasing Revisited

One of the major uses of the α channel is for antialiasing. Because a line must have a finite width to be visible, the default width of a line that is rendered should be one pixel. We cannot produce a thinner line. Unless the line is horizontal or vertical, such a line partially covers a number of pixels in the framebuffer, as shown in Figure 7.31. Suppose that, as part of the geometric-processing stage of the rendering process, while we process a fragment, we set the α value for the corresponding pixel to a number between 0 and 1 that is the fraction of that pixel covered by the fragment. We can then use this α value to modulate the color as we render the fragment to the framebuffer. We can use a destination blending factor of $1 - \alpha$ and a source destination factor of α. However, if there is overlap of fragments within a pixel, then there are numerous possibilities, as we can see from Figure 7.32. In panel (a), the fragments do not overlap; in panel (b), they do overlap. Consider the problem from the perspective of a renderer that works one polygon at a time. For our simple example, suppose that we start with an opaque background and that the framebuffer starts with the background color $\mathbf{C}_0$. We can set $\alpha_0 = 0$, because no part of the pixel has yet been covered with fragments from polygons. The first polygon is rendered. The color of the destination pixel is set to

$$\mathbf{C}_d = (1 - \alpha_1)\mathbf{C}_0 + \alpha_1\mathbf{C}_1,$$

and its α value is set to

$$\alpha_d = \alpha_1.$$

FIGURE 7.31   Raster line.

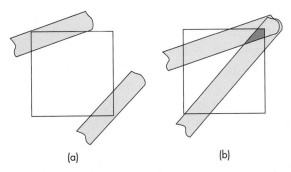

(a)   (b)

FIGURE 7.32   Fragments. (a) Nonoverlapping. (b) Overlapping.

Thus, a fragment that covers the entire pixel ($\alpha_1 = 1$) will have its color assigned to the destination pixel, and the destination pixel will be opaque. If the background is black, the destination color will be $\alpha_1 \mathbf{C}_1$. Now consider the fragment from the second polygon that subtends the same pixel. How we add in its color and α value depends on how we wish to interpret the overlap. If there is no overlap, we can assign the new color by blending the color of the destination with the color of the fragment, resulting in the color and α:

$$\mathbf{C}_d = (1 - \alpha_2)((1 - \alpha_1)\mathbf{C}_0 + \alpha_1 \mathbf{C}_1) + \alpha_2 \mathbf{C}_2$$

$$\alpha_d = \alpha_1 + \alpha_2.$$

This color is a blending of the two colors and does not need to be clamped. The resulting value of α represents the new fraction of the pixel that is covered. However, the resulting color is affected by the order in which the polygons are rendered. The more difficult questions are what to do if the fragments overlap and how to tell whether there is an overlap. One tactic is to take a probabilistic view. If fragment 1 occupies a fraction α_1 of the pixel, fragment 2 occupies a fraction α_2 of the same pixel, and we have no other information about the location of the fragments within the pixel, then the average area of overlap is $\alpha_1 \alpha_2$. We can represent the average case as shown in Figure 7.33. Hence, the new destination α should be

$$\alpha_d = \alpha_1 + \alpha_2 - \alpha_1 \alpha_2.$$

How we should assign the color is a more complex problem, because we have to decide whether the second fragment is in front of the first or vice versa, or even whether the two should be blended. We can define an appropriate blending for whichever assumption we wish to make. Note that, in a pipeline renderer, polygons can be generated in an order that has nothing to do with their distances from the viewer. However, if we couple α blending with hidden-surface removal, we can use the depth information to make front-versus-back decisions.

FIGURE 7.33 Average overlap.

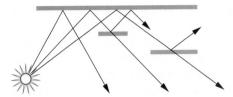

FIGURE 7.34   Scene with translucent objects.

7.10.5 Back-to-Front and Front-to-Back Rendering

Although using the α channel gives us a way of creating the appearance of translucency, it is difficult to handle transparency in a physically correct manner without taking into account how an object is lit and what happens to rays and projectors that pass through translucent objects. In Figure 7.34, we can see several of the difficulties. We ignore refraction of light through translucent surfaces—an effect that cannot be handled easily with a pipeline polygon renderer. Suppose that the rear polygon is opaque, but reflective, and that the two polygons closer to the viewer are translucent. By following various rays from the light source, we can see a number of possibilities. Some rays strike the rear polygon, and the corresponding pixels can be colored with the shade at the intersection of the projector and the polygon. For these rays, we should also distinguish between points illuminated directly by the light source and points for which the incident light passes through one or both translucent polygons. For rays that pass through only one translucent surface, we have to adjust the color based on the color and opacity of the polygon. We should also add a term that accounts for the light striking the front polygon that is reflected toward the viewer. For rays passing through both translucent polygons, we have to consider their combined effect.

For a pipeline renderer, the task is even more difficult—if not impossible—because we have to determine the contribution that each polygon makes as it is passes through the pipeline, rather than considering the contributions of all polygons to a given pixel at the same time. In applications where handling of translucency must be done in a consistent and realistic manner, we often must sort the polygons from front to back within the application. Then depending on the application, we can do a front-to-back or back-to-front rendering using WebGL's blending functionality (see Exercise 7.23).

7.10.6 Scene Antialiasing and Multisampling

Rather than antialiasing individual lines and polygons, as we discussed in Section 7.10.4, we can antialias the entire scene using a technique called **multisampling**. In this mode, every pixel in the framebuffer contains a number of **samples**. Each sample is capable of storing a color, depth, and other values. When a scene is rendered, it is as if the scene is rendered at an enhanced resolution. However, when the image must be displayed in the framebuffer, all the samples for each pixel are combined to produce the final pixel color.

Just as line and polygon antialiasing can be enabled and disabled during the rendering of a frame, so too with multisampling. To turn on multisampling and begin antialiasing all the primitives rendered in the frame, we call `glEnable(gl.SAMPLE_COVERAGE)` or `glEnable(gl.SAMPLE_ALPHA_TO_COVERAGE)`. In both cases, the rendering is done using multiple samples for each pixel, and the renderer keeps track of which samples render into the pixel. In effect, we render at a higher resolution than the display and use the information from the multiple samples to get an anti-aliased value. The difference between the two variants is that the second combines multisampling with the alpha values of the fragments that contribute to the pixel.

7.10.7 Image Processing

We can use pixel mapping to perform various image-processing operations. Suppose that we start with a discrete image. Perhaps this image was generated by a rendering, or perhaps we obtained it by digitizing a continuous image using a scanner. We can represent the image with an $N \times M$ matrix,

$$\mathbf{A} = [\, a_{ij} \,],$$

of scalar levels. If we process each color component of a color image independently, we can regard the entries in $\mathbf{A}$ either as individual color components or as gray (luminance) levels. A **linear filter** produces a filtered matrix $\mathbf{B}$ whose elements are

$$b_{ij} = \sum_{k=-m}^{m} \sum_{l=-n}^{n} h_{kl}\, a_{i+k,\,j+l}.$$

We say that $\mathbf{B}$ is the result of **convolving** $\mathbf{A}$ with a filter matrix $\mathbf{H}$. In general, the values of m and n are small, and we can represent $\mathbf{H}$ by a small $(2m + 1 \times 2n + 1)$ **convolution matrix**.

We can view the filtering operation as shown in Figure 7.35 for $m = n = 1$. For each pixel in $\mathbf{A}$, we place the convolution matrix over a_{ij} and take a weighted average of the surrounding points. The values in the matrix are the weights. For example, for $m = n = 1$, we can average each pixel with its four surrounding neighbors using the 3×3 matrix

FIGURE 7.35   Filtering and convolution.

$$\mathbf{H} = \frac{1}{5}\begin{bmatrix} 0 & 1 & 0 \\ 1 & 1 & 1 \\ 0 & 1 & 0 \end{bmatrix}.$$

This filter can be used for antialiasing. We can use more points and weight the center more heavily with

$$\mathbf{H} = \frac{1}{16}\begin{bmatrix} 1 & 2 & 1 \\ 2 & 4 & 2 \\ 1 & 2 & 1 \end{bmatrix}.$$

Note that we must define a border around $\mathbf{A}$ if we want $\mathbf{B}$ to have the same dimensions. Other operations are possible with small matrices. For example, we can use the matrix

$$\mathbf{H} = \begin{bmatrix} 0 & -1 & 0 \\ -1 & 4 & -1 \\ 0 & -1 & 0 \end{bmatrix}$$

to detect changes in value or edges in the image. If the matrix $\mathbf{H}$ is $k \times k$, we can implement a filter by accumulating k^2 images in the framebuffer, each time adding in a shifted version of $\mathbf{A}$.

We can implement some imaging operations using the fragment shader. Consider the shader

```
varying  vec4 color;
varying  vec2 texCoord;

uniform sampler2D texture;

void main()
{
  float d = 0.01;

  vec4 left   = texture2D(texture, texCoord - vec2(d, 0));
  vec4 right  = texture2D(texture, texCoord + vec2(d, 0));
  vec4 bottom = texture2D(texture, texCoord - vec2(0, d));
  vec4 top    = texture2D(texture, texCoord + vec2(0, d));

  gl_FragColor = color * abs(right - left + top - bottom);
  gl_FragColor.a = 1.0;
}
```

which we can apply to our texture-mapped cube with the checkerboard texture. This fragment shader performs a simple convolution differentiation by looking at the differences in color values between texture values surrounding the specified texture coordinates.

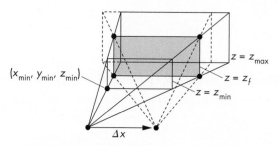

FIGURE 7.36   Depth-of-field jitter.

7.10.8 Other Multipass Methods

We can also use blending for filtering in time and depth. For example, if we jitter an object and render it multiple times, leaving the positions of the other objects unchanged, we get dimmer copies of the jittered object in the final image. If the object is moved along a path, rather than randomly jittered, we see the trail of the object. This **motion-blur** effect is similar to the result of taking a photograph of a moving object using a long exposure time. We can adjust the object's α value so as to render the final position of the object with greater opacity or to create the impression of speed differences.

We can use filtering in depth to create focusing effects. A real camera cannot produce an image with all objects in focus. Objects within a certain distance from the camera, the camera's **depth of field**, are in focus; objects outside it are out of focus and appear blurred. Computer graphics produces images with an infinite depth of field because we do not have to worry about the limitations of real lenses. Occasionally, however, we want to create an image that looks as though it were produced by a real camera, or to defocus part of a scene so as to emphasize the objects within a desired depth of field. This time, the trick is to move the viewer in a manner that leaves a particular plane fixed, as shown in Figure 7.36. Suppose that we wish to keep the plane at $z = z_f$ in focus and to leave the near ($z = z_{min}$) and far ($z = z_{max}$) clipping distances unchanged. If we use `Frustum`, we specify the near clipping rectangle (x_{min}, x_{max}, y_{min}, y_{max}). If we move the viewer from the origin in the x direction by Δx, we must change min to

$$x'_{min} = x_{min} + \frac{\Delta x}{z_f}(z_f - z_{near}).$$

Similar equations hold for x_{max}, y_{min}, and y_{max}. As we increase Δx and Δy, we create a narrower depth of field.

7.11   GPGPU

We have seen some interesting possibilities that arise from our ability to manipulate data using fragment shaders. Although our example arose from our desire to render geometry with interesting effects, our example of the fragment shader taking an approximate derivative of a texture image suggests how we can use the fragment shader to perform image-processing operations.

Consider the following. Suppose our geometry comprises only a single square with diagonal corners at $(-1, -1, 0)$ and $(1, 1, 0)$, specified as two triangles. Using the default orthogonal projection and an identity matrix for the model view, the rectangle fills the window on the display so all we see are the colors we assign to the fragments. If we use a texture to determine the color, then the display shows the texture map. Thus, if the texture map is an image we create with code, an image from the Web, or data from an experiment, we have a simple image display program. Here are the core parts:

```
// Set up square and texture coordinates

var pointsArray = [ ];
var texCoordsArray = [ ];
var texture = new Uint8Array(texSize*texSize);

pointsArray.push(vec2(-1, -1));
pointsArray.push(vec2(-1, 1));
pointsArray.push(vec2(1, 1));
pointsArray.push(vec2(1, -1));
texCoordsArray.push(vec2(0, 0));
texCoordsArray.push(vec2(0, 1));
texCoordsArray.push(vec2(1, 1));
texCoordsArray.push(vec2(1, 0));

// Within the texture configuration

gl.texImage2D(gl.TEXTURE_2D, 0, gl.LUMINANCE, texSize, texSize, 0,
gl.LUMINANCE, gl.UNSIGNED_BYTE, data);

// Render once

gl.clear(gl.COLOR_BUFFER_BIT);
gl.drawArrays(gl.TRIANGLE_FAN, 0, 4);
```

Note that if we have a gray-scale image with only a single color component, we can use unsigned bytes for the data. When we send the image to the GPU, each texel is converted to an RGBA color with component values in the range $(0, 1)$. The vertex shader only needs to send the positions and texture coordinates to the rasterizer,

```
attribute vec2 vPosition;
attribute  vec2 vTexCoord;
varying vec2  fTexCoord;

void main()
{
  fTexCoord = vTexCoord;
  gl_Position = vPosition;
}
```

and the simplest fragment shader outputs the texture map:

```
varying vec2 fTexCoord;
uniform sampler2D texture;

void main()
{
  gl_FragColor = texture2D(texture, fTexCoord);
}
```

We can make the display more interesting by using the fragment shader to alter the grayscale or to replace the shades of gray with colors. For example, consider the following fragment shader:

```
varying vec2 fTexCoord;
uniform sampler2D texture;

void main()
{
  vec4 color = texture2D(texture, fTexCoord);
  if (color.g < 0.5) {
    color.g *= 2.0;
  }
  else {
    color.g = 1.0 - color.g;
  }
  color.b = 1.0 - color.b;

  gl_FragColor = color;
}
```

It leaves the red component unaltered. It inverts the blue component, changing high values to low values and vice versa. The lower half of the green range is increased to cover the full range whereas the upper half of the green range is inverted. Consider what happens if the texture is from a luminance image where each texel has equal red, green, and blue values. Black $(0, 0, 0)$ becomes $(0, 0, 1)$ and appears as blue; white $(1, 1, 1)$ becomes $(1, 0, 0)$ and appears as blue; and a mid gray $(0.5, 0.5, 0.5)$ becomes $(0.5, 1.0, 0.5)$, a shade of green. Some other possibilities are explored in the exercises at the end of the chapter.

We can also use techniques such as convolution to alter the image through the fragment shader. For example, Figure 7.37 shows the result of using the shader

```
varying vec2 texCoord;
uniform sampler2D texture;

void main()
{
  float d = 1.0/256.0;
```

(a)   (b)

FIGURE 7.37 (a) Honolulu image. (b) Honolulu image after convolution.

```
    vec4 left   = texture2D(texture, texCoord - vec2(d, 0));
    vec4 right  = texture2D(texture, texCoord + vec2(d, 0));
    vec4 bottom = texture2D(texture, texCoord - vec2(0, d));
    vec4 top    = texture2D(texture, texCoord + vec2(0, d));

    gl_FragColor = 10.0 * (abs(right - left) + abs(top - bottom));
    gl_FragColor.a = 1.0;
}
```

on the Hawaii image. For each fragment, the shader computes the sum of the absolute values of the differences in values in both the x and y directions by looking at the fragments above, below, right, and left of the given fragment and thus performs an edge detection. Note how the image in panel (b) enhances the detail in panel (a).

We can look at this fragment shader from a somewhat different perspective. The texture map is a two-dimensional array or matrix of numbers. The fragment shader operates on each element of that matrix and produces other numbers—the fragment colors. Hence, we can look at this model of using a texture map on a single rectangle as a way to have the fragment shader act as a programmable matrix processor. There are some major advantages of using the GPU this way. In particular, the GPU can perform operations of this type at extremely high rates due not only to the speed of the fragment shader but also to the inclusion of multiple shader units on a GPU and the inherent parallelism of the basic computational unit being a four-element color. The field of general-purpose computing on a GPU (GPGPU) has led to many new algorithms for computing that have nothing to do with computer graphics, and there are even high-performance computers composed of multiple GPUs rather than CPUs.

However, there are some problems with the development we have presented so far. Although we can compute a color or value for each fragment in the matrix or rectangle, our only access to these values is through the framebuffer, either as the colors we see displayed or by the slow operation of reading framebuffer colors back to the CPU. In addition, because we have no way yet to modify the texture, we cannot do much that is dynamic without loading in a new texture from the the CPU, another slow operation. Even more limiting is that virtually all framebuffers—the ones we allocate through the local window system—store color components as unsigned bytes, so we lack the resolution to do serious numerical computing.

WebGL provides a solution to these problems through **off-screen buffers**—extra buffers that are under the control of the graphics system but are not visible on the display. We will be able to render into such buffers and use the result of the rendering to create new textures for subsequent renderings. We explore this topic in the next sections.

7.12 FRAMEBUFFER OBJECTS

The framebuffer we have been using so far comprises a color buffer, a depth buffer, and other buffers such as a stencil buffer. It is provided by and under the control of the local window system. As we have argued, we would like to have additional buffers available, even if they cannot be displayed and are off-screen buffers. WebGL provides this facility through **framebuffer objects** (FBOs), which are handled entirely by the graphics system. Because FBOs exist within the graphics memory, not only can we have multiple off-screen buffers but transfers among these buffers do not incur the slow transfers between the CPU and GPU or the overhead of the local window system. We create and bind framebuffer objects much as we did with texture objects and vertex array objects. However, with FBOs we attach the resources we need for rendering to them.

To use off-screen buffers, we start by creating and binding a framebuffer object just as we would the normal framebuffer:

```
var framebuffer = gl.createFramebuffer();
gl.bindFramebuffer(gl.FRAMEBUFFER, framebuffer);
```

At this point, this framebuffer is the one into which our geometry will be rendered, and because it is an off-screen buffer, anything rendered into this buffer will not be visible on the display. However, our FBO is empty. We still must attach to it the resources we need to render into it. For a general three-dimensional scene, we need a color buffer to render into and a depth buffer for hidden-surface removal. A buffer attachment to an FBO is called a **renderbuffer**, and each renderbuffer can provide the necessary storage for the type of buffer needed.

However, if we want to render a texture that we can use in a later rendering, we can render directly into a texture and do not need a renderbuffer attachment for a color buffer. The **render-to-texture** process is the one we will employ in our examples. For a three-dimensional scene, we still need a depth buffer. We can create and bind the necessary buffers by creating a renderbuffer,

```
renderbuffer = gl.createRenderbuffer();
gl.bindRenderbuffer(gl.RENDERBUFFER, renderbuffer);
```

and then adding the attachment

```
gl.renderbufferStorage(gl.DEPTH_COMPONENT16, width, height);
```

which specifies the depth and resolution of the buffer so that the necessary amount of storage can be allocated. Because we want to render to texture—that is, render into a buffer that we can use as a texture image—we first must specify the required memory by setting up a texture object with the usual procedure, with one difference. Consider the following typical initialization:

```
texture1 = gl.createTexture();
gl.activeTexture(gl.TEXTURE0);
gl.bindTexture(gl.TEXTURE_2D, texture1);
gl.pixelStorei(gl.UNPACK_FLIP_Y_WEBGL, true);
gl.texImage2D(gl.TEXTURE_2D, 0, gl.RGBA, 512, 512, 0,
                gl.RGBA, gl.UNSIGNED_BYTE, null);
gl.generateMipmap(gl.TEXTURE_2D);
gl.texParameteri(gl.TEXTURE_2D, gl.TEXTURE_MIN_FILTER,
                gl.NEAREST_MIPMAP_LINEAR);
gl.texParameteri(gl.TEXTURE_2D, gl.TEXTURE_MAG_FILTER,
                gl.NEAREST);
```

The only difference between this example and our previous ones is that we specify a null image in `gl.texImage2D` because we have yet to create the texture image. Nevertheless, the information is sufficient to allocate the required texture memory. Finally, we attach this texture object to our FBO:

```
gl.framebufferTexture2D(gl.FRAMEBUFFER, gl.COLOR_ATTACHMENT0,
                        gl.TEXTURE_2D, texture1, 0);
```

The parameter `gl.COLOR_ATTACHMENT0` identifies the attachment as a color buffer. The final parameter is the mipmap level.

We can now do a normal rendering by setting up our geometry, vertex arrays, and other resources. However, because there is a fair amount of overhead in setting up the FBO, we can check if we have done all the required steps by

```
var status = gl.checkFramebufferStatus(gl.FRAMEBUFFER);
if (status !== gl.FRAMEBUFFER_COMPLETE) {
  alert('Framebuffer Not Complete');
}
```

Once we have rendered to the off-screen buffer, we can return to the window system framebuffer by unbinding all the resources we bound to the FBO with another set of binds:

```
gl.bindFramebuffer(gl.FRAMEBUFFER, null);
gl.bindRenderbuffer(gl.RENDERBUFFER, null);
```

If we do not want to use the texture we rendered into, we can unbind that texture:

```
gl.bindTexture(gl.TEXTURE_2D, null);
```

However, since we plan to use the texture we just created for a normal render, we can bind it to the default framebuffer

```
gl.bindTexture(gl.TEXTURE_2D, texture1);
```

Here is a simple but complete example. In it we render a low-resolution triangle to texture, then use the resulting image as a texture map for a rectangle. The triangle is rendered red on a gray background.

```
var canvas;
var gl;

// Quad texture coordinates

var texCoord = [
  vec2(0, 0),
  vec2(0, 1),
  vec2(1, 1),
  vec2(1, 1),
  vec2(1, 0),
  vec2(0, 0)
];

// Quad vertices

var vertices = [
  vec2(-0.5, -0.5),
  vec2(-0.5,  0.5),
  vec2(0.5, 0.5),
  vec2(0.5, 0.5),
  vec2(0.5,  -0.5),
  vec2(-0.5, -0.5)
];

// Triangle vertices

var pointsArray = [
  vec2(-0.5, -0.5),
  vec2(0, 0.5),
  vec2(0.5, -0.5)
];

var program1, program2;
var texture1;

var framebuffer, renderbuffer;
```

```
window.onload = function init() {
  canvas = document.getElementById("gl-canvas");

  gl = WebGLUtils.setupWebGL(canvas);
  if (!gl) { alert("WebGL isn't available"); }

  // Create an empty texture

  texture1 = gl.createTexture();
  gl.activeTexture(gl.TEXTURE0);
  gl.bindTexture(gl.TEXTURE_2D, texture1);
  gl.pixelStorei(gl.UNPACK_FLIP_Y_WEBGL, true);
  gl.texImage2D(gl.TEXTURE_2D, 0, gl.RGBA, 64, 64, 0, gl.RGBA,
                gl.UNSIGNED_BYTE, null);
  gl.generateMipmap(gl.TEXTURE_2D);
  gl.texParameteri(gl.TEXTURE_2D, gl.TEXTURE_MIN_FILTER,
                   gl.NEAREST_MIPMAP_LINEAR);
  gl.texParameteri(gl.TEXTURE_2D, gl.TEXTURE_MAG_FILTER, gl.NEAREST);
  gl.bindTexture(gl.TEXTURE_2D, null);

  // Allocate a framebuffer object

  framebuffer = gl.createFramebuffer();
  gl.bindFramebuffer(gl.FRAMEBUFFER, framebuffer);
  renderbuffer = gl.createRenderbuffer();
  gl.bindRenderbuffer(gl.RENDERBUFFER, renderbuffer);

  // Attach color buffer

  gl.framebufferTexture2D(gl.FRAMEBUFFER, gl.COLOR_ATTACHMENT0,
  gl.TEXTURE_2D, texture1, 0);

  // Check for completeness

  var status = gl.checkFramebufferStatus(gl.FRAMEBUFFER);
  if (status != gl.FRAMEBUFFER_COMPLETE)
    alert('Frame Buffer Not Complete');

  //  Load shaders and initialize attribute buffers

  program1 = initShaders(gl, "vertex-shader1", "fragment-shader1");
  program2 = initShaders(gl, "vertex-shader2", "fragment-shader2");

  gl.useProgram(program1);

  // Create and initialize a buffer object with triangle vertices

  var buffer1 = gl.createBuffer();
  gl.bindBuffer(gl.ARRAY_BUFFER, buffer1);
  gl.bufferData(gl.ARRAY_BUFFER, flatten(pointsArray), gl.STATIC_DRAW);
```

```
// Initialize the vertex position attribute from the vertex shader

var vPosition = gl.getAttribLocation(program1, "vPosition");
gl.vertexAttribPointer(vPosition, 2, gl.FLOAT, false, 0, 0);
gl.enableVertexAttribArray(vPosition);

// Render one triangle

gl.viewport(0, 0, 64, 64);
gl.clearColor(0.5, 0.5, 0.5, 1.0);
gl.clear(gl.COLOR_BUFFER_BIT);
gl.drawArrays(gl.TRIANGLES, 0, 3);

// Bind to window system framebuffer, unbind the texture

gl.bindFramebuffer(gl.FRAMEBUFFER, null);
gl.bindRenderbuffer(gl.RENDERBUFFER, null);

gl.disableVertexAttribArray(vPosition);
gl.useProgram(program2);

gl.activeTexture(gl.TEXTURE0);
gl.bindTexture(gl.TEXTURE_2D, texture1);

// Send data to GPU for normal render

var buffer2 = gl.createBuffer();
gl.bindBuffer(gl.ARRAY_BUFFER, buffer2);
gl.bufferData(gl.ARRAY_BUFFER, new flatten(vertices),
              gl.STATIC_DRAW);

var vPosition = gl.getAttribLocation(program2, "vPosition");
gl.vertexAttribPointer(vPosition, 2, gl.FLOAT, false, 0, 0);
gl.enableVertexAttribArray(vPosition);

var buffer3 = gl.createBuffer();
gl.bindBuffer(gl.ARRAY_BUFFER, buffer3);
gl.bufferData(gl.ARRAY_BUFFER, flatten(texCoord), gl.STATIC_DRAW);

var vTexCoord = gl.getAttribLocation(program2, "vTexCoord");
gl.vertexAttribPointer(vTexCoord, 2, gl.FLOAT, false, 0, 0);
gl.enableVertexAttribArray(vTexCoord);

gl.uniform1i(gl.getUniformLocation(program2, "texture"), 0);
gl.clearColor(1.0, 1.0, 1.0, 1.0);
gl.viewport(0, 0, 512, 512);

render();
}
```

```
function render()
{
  gl.clearColor(0.0, 0.0, 1.0, 1.0);
  gl.clear(gl.COLOR_BUFFER_BIT);

  // render quad with texture
  gl.drawArrays(gl.TRIANGLES, 0, 6);
}
```

The shaders are

```
// Vertex shader 1

attribute  vec4 vPosition;

void main()
{
  gl_Position = vPosition;
}

// Vertex shader 2

attribute vec4 vPosition;
attribute vec2 vTexCoord;

varying vec2 fTexCoord;

void main()
{
  fTexCoord = vTexCoord;
  gl_Position = vPosition;
}

// Fragment shader 1

precision mediump float;

void main()
{
  gl_FragColor = vec4(1.0, 0.0, 0.0, 1.0);
}

// Fragment shader 2

precision mediump float;

varying  vec2 fTexCoord;

uniform sampler2D texture;
```

FIGURE 7.38   Image produced by rendering to texture.

```
void main()
{
  gl_FragColor = texture2D(texture, fTexCoord);
}
```

The resulting image is shown in Figure 7.38.

We can use this technique in a number of ways. Suppose that we want to do an environmental map on an object in a totally computer-generated scene. We can create six texture maps with six renders to texture, each with the camera at the center of the object but each time pointed in a different direction. As a final step, we use a cube map texture with these texture images to render the entire scene to the framebuffer.

Next we will examine two applications that we can implement with FBOs—applications that are not possible to do efficiently (or at all) with just the standard framebuffer. The first example involves adding dynamic behavior in which each rendering depends on the results from a previous rendering. The second example uses FBOs to implement picking.

7.13   BUFFER PING-PONGING

In Chapter 3, we introduced double buffering as a way to guarantee a smooth display by always rendering into a buffer (the back buffer) that is not visible and then, once the rendering is done, swapping this buffer with the buffer that is being displayed (the front buffer). What we could not do well was access the front buffer so we could use its contents in determining what to render. To do so would have involved reading the front buffer back to the CPU and then sending its data back to the GPU. However, this strategy was not possible even if we were willing to read data back from the framebuffer, because in WebGL we cannot write discrete information directly to the framebuffer.

With FBOs we can accomplish this kind of data transfer by rendering to texture to create a new texture map and then using the new texture map to determine the next texture map through another render to texture. We will see that we can accomplish this technique by switching (**ping-ponging**) between a pair of FBOs.

We can illustrate this technique with a simple example that, while it may seem contrived, will be the basis of some procedural modeling methods we will discuss in Chapter 10. In this example, we will diffuse the results of an initial rendering over time. Visually, we will see a display akin to what we might see as a colored drop of water is placed in a glass of clear water and its color slowly distributes over the surface.

Figure 7.39 shows the Sierpinski gasket we developed in Chapter 2. Figure 7.40 shows its colors diffused by the method we will develop. We start the process by creating a texture image from rendering a scene to texture. Because this step is only needed to establish our initial conditions, the program object we use is not needed in subsequent renderings. For the next step, we render a single rectangle (two triangles) to a new texture, applying the texture we created in the first rendering to determine the fragment colors. The following fragment shader averages texels in a small neighborhood to diffuse the values of the first texture by averaging the texture color at four of the fragment's neighbors as it is applied to the rectangle:

```
uniform sampler2D texture;
uniform float d;
uniform float s;

varying vec2 texCoord;
```

FIGURE 7.39 Sierpinski gasket.

FIGURE 7.40   Sierpinski gasket diffused.

```
void main()
{
  vec4 left   = texture2D(texture, texCoord - vec2(d, 0));
  vec4 right  = texture2D(texture, texCoord + vec2(d, 0));
  vec4 bottom = texture2D(texture, texCoord - vec2(0, d));
  vec4 top    = texture2D(texture, texCoord + vec2(0, d));

  gl_FragColor = (left + right + top + bottom)/s;
}
```

The constant d is based on the distance to the neighbors and is determined by the resolution of the texture image. The second constant s controls the amount of smoothing. For example, if s is set to 4, we are averaging with no change in the average color across the image. A larger value of s reduces the brightness of the resulting image.

At this point we have rendered to texture the original texture map, producing a diffused version of it. What we want to do next is repeat the process by using the image we just created as a texture map and rendering again with our diffusion shader. We can accomplish this process using a pair of texture maps and a pair of off-screen buffers and ping-ponging between them, much as we discussed in Chapter 3 when we introduced front and back buffers.

The process goes as follows, starting with the image we want to diffuse as the initial texture map. Creating this initial image and the various parameters and buffers we need is fairly standard and will be part of the initialization. The interesting part is the rendering loop. In the initialization, we define a boolean variable

```
var flag = true;
```

that we use to indicate which set of buffers we are using. We start the render function by creating a framebuffer texture using one of the two texture objects we created in the initialization, which will be the one we render into:

```
if (flag) {
  gl.bindTexture(gl.TEXTURE_2D, texture1);
  gl.framebufferTexture2D(gl.FRAMEBUFFER, gl.COLOR_ATTACHMENT0,
                          gl.TEXTURE_2D, texture2, 0);
}
else {
  gl.bindTexture(gl.TEXTURE_2D, texture2);
  gl.framebufferTexture2D(gl.FRAMEBUFFER, gl.COLOR_ATTACHMENT0,
                          gl.TEXTURE_2D, texture1, 0);
}
```

Next we render our rectangle using the texture map

```
gl.clear(gl.COLOR_BUFFER_BIT);
gl.drawArrays(gl.TRIANGLES, 0, 6);
```

We want to see the result at each step, so we need to do a normal rendering to the standard framebuffer. We unbind the FBO and swap the textures, so we are using the image we just created as the new texture map for this rendering,

```
gl.bindFramebuffer(gl.FRAMEBUFFER, null);
```

```
gl.bindTexture(gl.TEXTURE_2D, flag ? texture2 : texture1);
```

and render

```
gl.clear(gl.COLOR_BUFFER_BIT);
gl.drawArrays(gl.TRIANGLES, 0, 6);
```

Now we can swap the textures and repeat the process:

```
flag = !flag;
requestAnimFrame(render);
```

For clarity, we have omitted some of the bookkeeping such as switching among the program objects. A complete program is on the book's website.

7.14 PICKING

We introduced picking—the process of selecting objects on the display with a pointing device—in Chapter 3 but lacked the tools to implement it. Using off-screen rendering, we can implement a fairly straightforward process that works in most circumstances. Consider the following simple example. Suppose that we have a display composed of just two objects, say, a blue triangle and a red square, on a white background. We could read the color in the framebuffer at the location of our mouse and then use this color to determine if the mouse is pointing to the square, the triangle, or just the background. The problem is that we almost never have such a simple display with only a handful of shades.

If the objects were three-dimensional and lit, then their surfaces would show many shades. If, in addition, we used texture mapping, each object could show hundreds of different colors, as could the background. Consequently, although the idea has merit, we cannot implement it so simply.

Suppose that we have an off-screen buffer into which we can render. This time, we render the scene without lighting and texture and assign a unique solid color to each object and the background. We can then read the color in the off-screen buffer corresponding to the mouse location. Because each object has been rendered in a different color, we can use a table to determine which object corresponds to the color we read. Once the picking is done, we go back to normal rendering in the standard framebuffer.

The following simple example illustrates this process using the color cube we first rendered in Chapter 4. Initially, we colored each face in one of the solid colors (red, green, blue, cyan, magenta, yellow). Subsequently, we saw many ways to color the faces based on these colors. For example, by assigning these colors to each of the vertices and using the default color interpolation, the colors we displayed on each face were a blend of the vertex colors. Later, we learned to put texture images on the surfaces. We even used reflection maps to determine the displayed color. Now, suppose that we want to identify a particular face of the cube on the display when it is rendered by one of these methods. We cannot determine the face from the displayed color both because there are so many shades and because a particular shade can appear on the display of multiple facets. In addition, the shade of any point on the cube can change with the orientation and position of the code and the lights. Consequently, there may not exist an inverse mapping between displayed colors and faces of the cube.

Using off-screen rendering solves this problem. We can set up a framebuffer object with a texture attachment into which we render. If we enable culling, we do not need to do hidden-surface removal and so do not need a renderbuffer object. The render to texture can be initiated through an event listener. When we click the mouse within the viewport, it binds the framebuffer object and renders the cube with each face as a solid color. We then read the color of the pixel corresponding to the mouse location and check its color to determine the face. Finally, we do a normal rendering. Let's look at the code in a little more detail. First, within the initialization, we set up our FBO:

```
gl.enable(gl.CULL_FACE);

var texture = gl.createTexture();
gl.bindTexture(gl.TEXTURE_2D, texture);
gl.pixelStorei(gl.UNPACK_FLIP_Y_WEBGL, true);
gl.texImage2D(gl.TEXTURE_2D, 0, gl.RGBA, 512, 512, 0, gl.RGBA,
gl.UNSIGNED_BYTE, null);
gl.generateMipmap(gl.TEXTURE_2D);
```

```
// Allocate a framebuffer object

framebuffer = gl.createFramebuffer();
gl.bindFramebuffer(gl.FRAMEBUFFER, framebuffer);

// Attach color buffer

gl.framebufferTexture2D(gl.FRAMEBUFFER, gl.COLOR_ATTACHMENT0,
                        gl.TEXTURE_2D, texture, 0);

// Check for completeness

var status = gl.checkFramebufferStatus(gl.FRAMEBUFFER);
if (status !== gl.FRAMEBUFFER_COMPLETE) {
  alert('Framebuffer Not Complete');
}

gl.bindFramebuffer(gl.FRAMEBUFFER, null);
```

Next, consider the colors. We set the base colors as in our previous examples,

```
var vertexColors = [
  vec4(0.0, 0.0, 0.0, 1.0),  // black
  vec4(1.0, 0.0, 0.0, 1.0),  // red
  vec4(1.0, 1.0, 0.0, 1.0),  // yellow
  vec4(0.0, 1.0, 0.0, 1.0),  // green
  vec4(0.0, 0.0, 1.0, 1.0),  // blue
  vec4(1.0, 0.0, 1.0, 1.0),  // magenta
  vec4(1.0, 1.0, 1.0, 1.0),  // white
  vec4(0.0, 1.0, 1.0, 1.0)   // cyan
];
```

and set up vertex arrays for them and the vertex positions.

In this example, we can use a single vertex shader and a fragment shader if we use a uniform variable to tell the fragment shader whether it is to perform a normal rendering or render the faces in one of the base colors. A normal render would be indicated by a 0,

```
gl.uniform1i(gl.getUniformLocation(program, "i"), 0);
gl.drawArrays(gl.TRIANGLES, 0, 36);
```

using two triangles for each face, whereas a rendering to texture would use the uniform variable i to indicate which color to use:

```
for (var i = 0; i < 6; ++i) {
  gl.uniform1i(gl.getUniformLocation(program, "i"), i+1);
  gl.drawArrays(gl.TRIANGLES, 6*i, 6);
}
```

The vertex shader is the rotation shader from previous examples that passes through the color to the fragment shader:

```
attribute  vec4 vPosition;
attribute  vec4 vColor;
varying vec4 color;

uniform vec3 theta;

void main()
{
  vec3 angles = radians(theta);
  vec3 c = cos(angles);
  vec3 s = sin(angles);

  mat4 rx = mat4(1.0,   0.0,   0.0, 0.0,
                 0.0,   c.x,   s.x, 0.0,
                 0.0,  -s.x,   c.x, 0.0,
                 0.0,   0.0,   0.0, 1.0);

  mat4 ry = mat4(c.y, 0.0, -s.y, 0.0,
                 0.0, 1.0,  0.0, 0.0,
                 s.y, 0.0,  c.y, 0.0,
                 0.0, 0.0,  0.0, 1.0);

  mat4 rz = mat4(c.z, -s.z, 0.0, 0.0,
                 s.z,  c.z, 0.0, 0.0,
                 0.0,  0.0, 1.0, 0.0,
                 0.0,  0.0, 0.0, 1.0);

  color = vColor;
  gl_Position = rz * ry * rx * vPosition;
}
```

The fragment shader is

```
uniform int i;
varying vec4 color;

void main()
{
  vec4 c[7];
  c[0] = color;
  c[1] = vec4(1.0, 0.0, 0.0, 1.0);
  c[2] = vec4(0.0, 1.0, 0.0, 1.0);
  c[3] = vec4(0.0, 0.0, 1.0, 1.0);
  c[4] = vec4(1.0, 1.0, 0.0, 1.0);
  c[5] = vec4(0.0, 1.0, 1.0, 1.0);
  c[6] = vec4(1.0, 0.0, 1.0, 1.0);

  // Render normally using the vertex's color
  if (i == 0) { gl_FragColor = c[0];
  // Render into texture with base colors
  else if (i == 1) { gl_FragColor = c[1]; }
```

```
  else if (i == 2) { gl_FragColor = c[2]; }
  else if (i == 3) { gl_FragColor = c[3]; }
  else if (i == 4) { gl_FragColor = c[4]; }
  else if (i == 5) { gl_FragColor = c[5]; }
  else if (i == 6) { gl_FragColor = c[6]; }
}
```

The reason for the odd-looking `if` statement is that WebGL's shading language does not contain all the features of JavaScript or C. Specifically, although the `switch` keyword is reserved, there is no `switch` statement available in shaders, so we compensate with a large `if` with many `else` clauses.

The real work is in the event listener. The event listener is triggered by a mouse click.

```
canvas.addEventListener("mousedown", function() {

  // Render to texture with base colors
  gl.bindFramebuffer(gl.FRAMEBUFFER, framebuffer);
  gl.clear(gl.COLOR_BUFFER_BIT);
  gl.uniform3fv(thetaLoc, Theta);
  for (var i = 0; i < 6; ++i) {
    gl.uniform1i(gl.getUniformLocation(program, "i"), i+1);
    gl.drawArrays(gl.TRIANGLES, 6*i, 6);
  }

  // Get mouse position
  var x = event.clientX;
  var y = canvas.height -event.clientY;

  // Get color at mouse location and output it
  gl.readPixels(x, y, 1, 1, gl.RGBA, gl.UNSIGNED_BYTE, color);

  // Find which color was read and output it
  var colorNames = [
    "background",
    "blue",
    "green",
    "cyan",
    "red",
    "magenta",
    "yellow",
    "white"
  ];

  var nameIndex = 0;

  if (color[0] == 255) nameIndex += (1 << 2);
  if (color[1] == 255) nameIndex += (1 << 1);
  if (color[2] == 255) nameIndex += (1 << 0);
  console.log(colorNames[nameIndex]);
```

```
// Normal render
gl.bindFramebuffer(gl.FRAMEBUFFER, null);
gl.uniform1i(gl.getUniformLocation(program, "i"), 0);
gl.clear(gl.COLOR_BUFFER_BIT);
gl.uniform3fv(thetaLoc, theta);
gl.drawArrays(gl.TRIANGLES, 0, 36);
});
```

One potential issue may arise with some low-precision or older display devices. Displays that cannot display many colors (and thus are subject to producing some jaggedness when colors change across a surface) smooth out this transition by randomizing the low-order bits of the color components through a process called **dithering**. If the display is dithered, the low-order bits for a color are randomized, which breaks up the jaggedness. Then when we use gl.readPixels, it returns slightly different values for pixels that were assigned the same color. For example, the red component for a gray color assigned as an RGB color of (127, 127, 127) may return 126, 127 or 128. When we test the color, we cannot then just check if the component is exactly 127. We can either check only the higher-order bits or disable dithering by

```
gl.disable(gl.DITHER);
```

when we do the read.

Note that if we have multiple objects and want to identify the object rather than a face on a single cube, although the program will be longer, we will go through exactly the same steps. We will do an off-screen rendering with each object rendered in a different solid color. We can then identify objects rather than faces by reading the color and mapping it back to an identifier for the object.

SUMMARY AND NOTES

In the early days of computer graphics, practitioners worked with only two- and three-dimensional geometric objects, whereas those practitioners who were involved with only two-dimensional images were considered to be working in image processing. Advances in hardware have made graphics and image-processing systems practically indistinguishable. For those practitioners involved with synthesizing images—certainly a major part of computer graphics—this merging of fields has brought forth a multitude of new techniques. The idea that a two-dimensional image or texture can be mapped to a three-dimensional surface in no more time than it takes to render the surface with constant shading would have been unthinkable 15 years ago. Now, these techniques are routine.

Techniques such as texture mapping have had an enormous effect on real-time graphics. In fields such as animation, virtual reality, and scientific visualization, we use hardware texture mapping to add detail to images without burdening the geometric pipeline. The use of blending techniques through the alpha channel allows the application programmer to perform tasks such as antialiasing and to create effects such as fog and depth of field that, until recently, were done on different types of architectures after the graphics had been created.

Mapping methods provide some of the best examples of the interactions among graphics hardware, software, and applications. Consider texture mapping. Although it was first described and implemented purely as a software algorithm, once people saw its ability to create scenes with great visual complexity, hardware developers started putting large amounts of texture memory in graphics systems. Once texture mapping was implemented in hardware, it could be done in real time, a development that led to the redesign of many applications, notably computer games.

Recent advances in GPUs provide many new possibilities based on programmable shaders. First, the programmability of the fragment processor makes possible new texture manipulation techniques while preserving interactive speeds. Second, the inclusion of large amounts of memory on the GPU removes one of the major bottlenecks in discrete methods, namely, many of the transfers of image data between processor memory and the GPU. Third, GPU architectures are designed for rapid processing of discrete data by incorporating a high degree of parallelism for fragment processing. Finally, the availability of floating-point framebuffers eliminates many of the precision issues that plagued techniques that manipulated image data.

In this chapter, we have concentrated on techniques that are supported by presently available hardware and APIs. Many of the techniques introduced here are recent. Many more have appeared in the literature and can be implemented only on programmable processors.

SUGGESTED READINGS

Environment mapping was developed by Blinn and Newell [Bli76]. Texture mapping was first used by Catmull; see the review by Heckbert [Hec86]. Hardware support for texture mapping came with the SGI Reality Engine; see Akeley [Ake93]. Perlin and Hoffert [Per89] designed a noise function to generate two- and three-dimensional texture maps. Many texture synthesis techniques are discussed in Ebert et al [Ebe02].

The aliasing problem in computer graphics has been of importance since the advent of raster graphics; see Crow [Cro81]. The first concerns were with rasterization of lines, but later other forms of aliasing arose with animations [Mag85] and ray tracing [Gla89]. The image-processing books [Pra78, Gon08, Cas96] provide an introduction to signal processing and aliasing in two dimensions. The books by Glassner [Gla95] and Watt and Policarpo [Wat98] are aimed at practitioners of computer graphics.

Many of the blending techniques, including use of the alpha channel, were suggested by Porter and Duff [Por84]. The *OpenGL Programming Guide* [Shr13] contains many examples of how buffers can be used. The recent literature includes many new examples of the use of buffers. See the recent issues of the journals *Computer Graphics* and *IEEE Computer Graphics and Applications*.

Technical details on most of the standard image formats can be found in [Mia99, Mur94].

EXERCISES

7.1   How does texture mapping use an image (or texture) to influence the color of a fragment?

7.2   In the movies and television, we get dimmer copies of the jittered object, known as motion-blur effect. What causes the effect? Explain your answer.

7.3   We can attempt to display sampled data by simply plotting the points and letting the human visual system merge the points into shapes. Why is this technique dangerous if the data are close to the Nyquist limit (see Appendix D)?

7.4   Why does the computer flicker in a television, video, or a movie? Give a proper reason.

7.5   Why is linear filtering a better option than point sampling in texture sampling?

7.6   Suppose that we have two translucent surfaces characterized by opacities α_1 and α_2. What is the opacity of the translucent material that we create by using the two in series? Give an expression for the transparency of the combined material.

7.7   Assume that we view translucent surfaces as filters of the light passing through them. Develop a blending model based on the complementary colors CMY.

7.8   In Section 7.10, we used $1 - \alpha$ and α for the destination and source blending factors, respectively. What would be the visual difference if we used 1 for the destination factor and kept α for the source factor?

7.9   Create interactive paintbrushes that add color gradually to an image. Also use blending to add erasers that gradually remove images from the screen.

7.10 Devise a method of using texture mapping for the display of arrays of three-dimensional pixels (voxels).

7.11 Show how we can accomplish swapping back buffer to front buffer type of data transfer by rendering to texture to create a new texture map and then using the new texture map to determine the next texture map through another render to texture.

7.12 Compare simple texture mapping to bump mapping.

7.13 Suppose that a set of objects is texture-mapped with regular patterns such as stripes and checkerboards. What is the difference in aliasing patterns that we would see when we switch from parallel to perspective views?

7.14 Consider a scene composed of simple objects, such as parallelepipeds, that are instanced at different sizes. Suppose you have a single texture map and you are asked to map this texture to all the objects. How would you map the texture so that the pattern would be the same size on each face of each object?

7.15 Write a program using mipmaps in which each mipmap is constructed from a different image. Is there a practical application for such a program?

7.16 Using your own image-processing code for convolution, implement a general 3×3 filtering program for luminance images.

7.17 Take an image from a digital camera, or from some another source, and apply 5×5 smoothing and sharpening filters, repetitively. Pay special attention to the difference between the two images.

7.18 Repeat Exercise 7.17 but first add a small amount of random noise to the image. Describe the differences between the results of the two exercises.

7.19 One of the most effective methods of altering the contrast of an image is to allow the user to design a lookup table interactively. Consider a graph in which a curve is approximated with three connected line segments. Write a program that displays an image, allows the user to specify the line segments interactively, and shows the image after it has been altered by the curve.

7.20 Devise a method to convert the values obtained from a cube map to values for a spherical map.

7.21 Write an interactive program that will return the colors of pixels on the display.

7.22 Suppose that we want to create a cube that has a black-and-white checkerboard pattern texture-mapped to its faces. Can we texture-map the cube so that the colors alternate as we traverse the cube from face to face?

7.23 Which types of color buffer are used to render and used as attachment to a FBO?

7.24 The color gamut in chromaticity coordinates is equivalent to the triangle in RGB space that is defined by the primaries. Write a program that will display this triangle and the edges of the cube in which it lies. Each point on the triangle should have the color determined by its coordinates in RGB space. This triangle is called the **Maxwell triangle**.

7.25 Find the matrix that converts NTSC RGB and use it to redisplay the color gamut of your display in xy chromaticity coordinates.

7.26 What are some examples of multi-pass rendering?

7.27 What is the process of selecting objects on the display with a pointing device?

7.28 Suppose that you are given a function $f(x, z)$. We can display the values over some range of x and z by evaluating the function for evenly spaced values of x and z and then converting these computed values to colors as in Section 7.10. Show how to carry out this process in the fragment shader, thus avoiding any loops and computation in the application.

CHAPTER 8

FROM GEOMETRY
TO PIXELS

We now turn to the next steps in the pipeline: clipping, rasterization, and hidden-surface removal. Although we have yet to consider some major areas of computer graphics that are available to the application programmer, there are several reasons for considering these topics at this point. First, you may be wondering how your programs are processed by the system that you are using: how lines are drawn on the screen, how polygons are filled, and what happens to primitives that lie outside the viewing volumes defined in your program. Second, our contention is that if we are to use a graphics system efficiently, we need to have a deeper understanding of the implementation process: which steps are easy and which tax our hardware and software. Third, our discussion of implementation will open the door to new capabilities that are supported by the latest hardware.[1]

Learning implementation involves studying algorithms. As when we study any algorithm, we must be careful to consider such issues as theoretical versus practical performance, hardware versus software implementations, and the specific characteristics of an application. Although we can test whether a WebGL implementation works correctly in the sense that it produces the correct pixels on the screen, there are many choices for the algorithms employed. We focus on the basic operations that are both necessary to implement a standard API and required whether the rendering is done by a pipeline architecture or by another method, such as ray tracing. Consequently, we present a variety of the basic algorithms for each of the principal tasks in an implementation.

Although in this chapter our primary concern is with the basic algorithms that are used to implement the rendering pipeline employed by WebGL, we will also see algorithms that may be used by other rendering strategies or by layers above WebGL, such as when we work with scene graphs. We will focus on three issues: clipping, rasterization, and hidden-surface removal. Clipping involves eliminating objects that lie outside the viewing volume and thus cannot be visible in the image. Rasterization produces fragments from the remaining objects. These fragments can contribute to

---

1. Because the topics in this chapter are common to both desktop OpenGL and WebGL, we will use OpenGL to refer to both.

the final image. Hidden-surface removal determines which fragments correspond to objects that are visible, namely, those that are in the view volume and are not blocked from view by other objects closer to the camera. We will also touch on some issues concerning the display of fragments on a variety of output devices.

8.1   BASIC IMPLEMENTATION STRATEGIES

Let's begin with a high-level view of the implementation process. In computer graphics, we start with an application program, and we end with an image. We can again consider this process as a black box (Figure 8.1) whose inputs are the vertices and states defined in the program—geometric objects, attributes, camera specifications—and whose output is an array of colored pixels in the framebuffer.

Within the black box, we must perform many tasks, including transformations, clipping, shading, hidden-surface removal, and rasterization of the primitives that can appear on the display. These tasks can be organized in a variety of ways, but regardless of the strategy that we adopt, we must always do two things: We must pass every geometric object through the system, and we must assign a color to every pixel in the color buffer that is displayed.

Suppose that we think of what goes into the black box in terms of a single program that carries out the entire process. This program takes as input a set of vertices specifying geometric objects and produces as output pixels in the framebuffer. Because this program must assign a value to every pixel and must process every geometric primitive (and every light source), we expect this program to contain at least two loops that iterate over these basic variables.

If we wish to write such a program, then we must immediately address the following question: Which variable controls the outer loop? The answer we choose determines the flow of the entire implementation process. There are two fundamental strategies, often called the **image-oriented** and the **object-oriented** approaches.

In the object-oriented approach, the outer loop iterates over the objects. We can think of the program as controlled by a loop of this form:

```
for (each_object) {
  render(object);
}
```

A pipeline renderer fits this description. Vertices are defined by the program and flow through a sequence of modules that transforms them, colors them, and determines whether they are visible. A polygon might flow through the steps illustrated in Figure 8.2. Note that after a polygon passes through geometric processing, the rasterization of this polygon can potentially affect any pixels in the framebuffer. Most

FIGURE 8.1   High-level view of the graphics process.

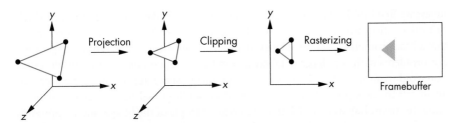

FIGURE 8.2   Object-oriented approach.

implementations that follow this approach are based on construction of a rendering pipeline containing hardware or software modules for each of the tasks. Data (vertices) flow forward through the system.

In the past, the major limitations of the object-oriented approach were the large amount of memory required and the high cost of processing each object independently. Any geometric primitive that emerges from the geometric processing can potentially affect any set of pixels in the framebuffer; thus, the entire color buffer—and various other buffers, such as the depth buffer used for hidden-surface removal—must be of the size of the display and must be available at all times. Before memory became both inexpensive and dense, this requirement was considered to be a serious problem. Now various pipelined geometric processors are available that can process tens of millions of polygons per second. In fact, precisely because we are doing the same operations on every primitive, the hardware to build an object-based system is fast and relatively inexpensive, with many of the functions implemented with special-purpose chips.

Today, the main limitation of object-oriented implementations is that they cannot handle most global calculations. Because each geometric primitive is processed independently—and in an arbitrary order—complex shading effects that involve multiple geometric objects, such as reflections, cannot be handled except by approximate methods. The major exception is hidden-surface removal, where the z-buffer is used to store global information.

Image-oriented approaches loop over pixels, or rows of pixels called **scan lines**, that constitute the framebuffer. In pseudocode, the outer loop of such a program is of the following form:

```
for (each_pixel) {
  assign_a_color(pixel);
}
```

For each pixel, we work backward, trying to determine which geometric primitives can contribute to its color. The advantages of this approach are that we need only limited display memory at any time and that we can hope to generate pixels at the rate and in the order required to refresh the display. Because the results of most calculations do not differ greatly from pixel to pixel (or scan line to scan line), we can use this coherence in our algorithms by developing incremental forms for many of the steps in the implementation. The main disadvantage of this approach is that, unless we first build a data structure from the geometric data, we do not know which primitives affect which pixels. Such a data structure can be complex and may imply that all the geometric data must be available at all times during the rendering process. For problems with very large databases, even having a good data representation may not avoid memory issues. However, because image-space approaches have access to all objects for each pixel, they are well suited to handle global effects, such as shadows and reflections. Ray tracing (Chapter 12) is an example of the image-based approach.

We lean toward the object-based approach, although we look at examples of algorithms suited for both approaches. Note that within these two major categories specified by two loops, each may contain other loops. One example is tile-based rendering that breaks up the framebuffer into small pieces or tiles, each of which is rendered separately. This approach is often used on devices such as smart phones. Another example is the renderer used with Renderman that subdivides objects into very small pieces called microfacets and then determines a color for each one.

8.2   FOUR MAJOR TASKS

We start by reviewing the blocks in the pipeline, focusing on those blocks that we have yet to discuss in detail. There are four major tasks that any graphics system must perform to render a geometric entity, such as a three-dimensional polygon, as that entity passes from definition in a user program to possible display on an output device:

1. Modeling
2. Geometry processing
3. Rasterization
4. Fragment processing

Figure 8.3 shows how these tasks might be organized in a pipeline implementation. Regardless of the approach, all four tasks must be carried out.

8.2.1 Modeling

The usual results of the modeling process are sets of vertices that specify a group of geometric objects supported by the rest of the system. We have seen a few examples that required some modeling by the user, such as the approximation of spheres in Chapter 6. In Chapters 9, 10, and 11, we explore other modeling techniques.

We can look at the modeler as a black box that produces geometric objects and is usually a user program. Yet, there are other tasks that the modeler might perform. Consider, for example, clipping: the process of eliminating parts of objects

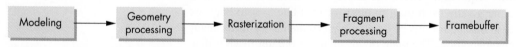

FIGURE 8.3   Implementation tasks.

that cannot appear on the display because they lie outside the viewing volume. A user can generate geometric objects in her program, and she can hope that the rest of the system can process these objects at the rate at which they are produced, or the modeler can attempt to ease the burden on the rest of the system by minimizing the number of objects that it passes on. The latter approach often means that the modeler may do some of the same jobs as the rest of the system, albeit with different algorithms. In the case of clipping, the modeler, knowing more about the specifics of the application, can often use a good heuristic to eliminate many, if not most, primitives before they are sent on through the standard viewing process.

8.2.2 Geometry Processing

Geometry processing works with vertices. The goals of the geometry processor are to determine which geometric objects appear on the display and to assign shades or colors to the vertices of these objects. Four processes are required: projection, primitive assembly, clipping, and shading.

Usually, the first step in geometry processing is to change representations from object coordinates to camera or eye coordinates using the model-view transformation. As we saw in Chapter 5, the conversion to camera coordinates is only the first part of the viewing process. The second step is to transform vertices using the projection transformation to a normalized view volume in which objects that might be visible are contained in a cube centered at the origin. Vertices are now represented in clip coordinates. Not only does this normalization convert both parallel and orthographic projections to a simple orthographic projection in a simple volume but, in addition, we simplify the clipping process, as we shall see in Section 8.7.

Geometric objects are transformed by a sequence of transformations that may reshape and move them (modeling) or may change their representations (viewing). Eventually, only those primitives that fit within a specified volume, the **view volume**, can appear on the display after rasterization. We cannot, however, simply allow all objects to be rasterized, hoping that the hardware will take care of primitives that lie wholly or partially outside the view volume. The implementation must carry out this task before rasterization. One reason is that rasterizing objects that lie outside the view volume is inefficient because such objects cannot be visible. Another reason is that when vertices reach the rasterizer, they can no longer be processed individually and first must be assembled into primitives. Primitives that lie partially in the viewing volume can generate new primitives with new vertices for which we must carry out shading calculations. Before clipping can take place, vertices must be grouped into objects, a process known as **primitive assembly**.

Note that even though an object lies inside the view volume, it will not be visible if it is obscured by other objects. Algorithms for **hidden-surface removal** (or **visible-surface determination**) are based on the three-dimensional spatial relationships among objects. This step is normally carried out as part of fragment processing.

As we saw in Chapter 6, colors can be determined on either a per-vertex or per-fragment basis. If they are assigned on a per-vertex basis, they can be sent from the application as vertex attributes or computed in the vertex shader. If lighting is enabled, vertex colors are computed using a lighting model that can be implemented in the application or in the vertex shader.

After clipping takes place, the remaining vertices are still in four-dimensional homogeneous coordinates. Perspective division converts them to three-dimensional representation in normalized device coordinates.

Collectively, these operations constitute what has been called **front-end processing**. All involve three-dimensional calculations, and all require floating-point arithmetic. All generate similar hardware and software requirements. All are carried out on a vertex-by-vertex basis. We will discuss clipping, the only geometric step that we have yet to consider, in Section 8.3.

8.2.3 Rasterization

Even after geometric processing has taken place, we still need to retain depth information for hidden-surface removal. However, only the x, y values of the vertices are needed to determine which pixels in the framebuffer can be affected by the primitive. For example, after perspective division, a line segment that was specified originally in three dimensions by two vertices becomes a line segment specified by a pair of three-dimensional vertices in normalized device coordinates. To generate a set of fragments that give the locations of the pixels in the framebuffer corresponding to these vertices, we only need their x, y components or, equivalently, the results of the orthogonal projection of these vertices. We determine these fragments through a process called **rasterization** or **scan conversion**. For line segments, rasterization determines which fragments should be used to approximate a line segment between the projected vertices. For polygons, rasterization determines which pixels lie inside the two-dimensional polygon determined by the projected vertices.

The colors that we assign to these fragments can be determined by the vertex attributes or obtained by interpolating the shades at the vertices that are computed, as in Chapter 6. Objects more complex than line segments and polygons are usually approximated by multiple line segments and triangles, and thus most graphics systems do not have special rasterization algorithms for them. We shall see exceptions to this rule for some special curves and surfaces in Chapter 11.

The rasterizer starts with vertices in normalized device coordinates but outputs fragments whose locations are in units of the display—**window coordinates**. As we saw in Chapters 2 and 5, the projection of the clipping volume must appear in the assigned viewport. In WebGL, this final transformation is done after projection and is two-dimensional. The preceding transformations have normalized the view volume such that its sides are of length 2 and line up with the sides of the viewport (Figure 8.4), so this transformation is simply

$$x_v = x_{v\min} + \frac{x + 1.0}{2.0}(x_{v\max} - x_{v\min})$$

$$y_v = y_{v\min} + \frac{y + 1.0}{2.0}(y_{v\max} - y_{v\min})$$

$$z_v = z_{v\min} + \frac{z + 1.0}{2.0}(z_{v\max} - z_{v\min}).$$

Recall that for perspective viewing, these z values have been scaled nonlinearly by perspective normalization. However, they retain their original depth order, so they

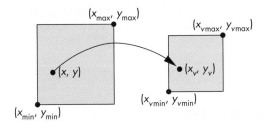

FIGURE 8.4   Viewport transformation.

can be used for hidden-surface removal. We shall use the term **screen coordinates** to refer to the two-dimensional system that is the same as window coordinates but lacks the depth coordinate.

8.2.4 Fragment Processing

In the simplest situations, each fragment is assigned a color by the rasterizer, and this color is placed in the framebuffer at the locations corresponding to the fragment's location. However, there are many other possibilities.

Pixels in texture maps take a separate path and merge with the results of the geometric pipeline at the rasterization stage. Consider what happens when a shaded and texture-mapped polygon is processed. Vertex lighting is computed as part of the geometric processing. The texture values are not needed until after rasterization when the renderer has generated fragments that correspond to locations inside a polygon. At this point, interpolation of per-vertex colors and texture coordinates takes place, and the texture parameters determine how to combine texture colors and fragment colors to determine final colors in the color buffer.

As we have noted, objects that are in the view volume will not be visible if they are blocked by any opaque objects closer to the viewer. The required hidden-surface removal process is typically carried out on a fragment-by-fragment basis.

For the most part, we we will assume that all objects are opaque and thus an object located behind another object is not visible. As we saw in Chapter 7, translucent fragments can be blended into the display, although we must be careful as to how they are ordered.

In most displays, the process of taking the image from the framebuffer and displaying it on a monitor happens automatically and is not of concern to the application program. However, there are numerous problems with the quality of display, such as the jaggedness associated with images on raster displays. In Sections 8.12 and 8.13, we introduce aliasing algorithms for reducing this jaggedness and we discuss problems with color reproduction on displays.

8.3 CLIPPING

We can now turn to clipping, the process of determining which primitives, or parts of primitives, fit within the clipping or view volume defined by the application program. Clipping is done before the perspective division that is necessary if the w component of a clipped vertex is not equal to 1. The portions of all primitives that can possibly be displayed—we have yet to apply hidden-surface removal—lie within the cube

$$w \geq x \geq -w$$

$$w \geq y \geq -w$$

$$w \geq z \geq -w.$$

This coordinate system is called **normalized device coordinates** because it depends on neither the original application units nor the particulars of the display device, although the information to produce the correct image is retained in this coordinate system. Note also that projection has been carried out only partially. We still must do the perspective division and the final orthographic projection.

We shall concentrate on clipping of line segments and polygons because they are the most common primitives to pass down the pipeline. Although the WebGL pipeline does clipping on three-dimensional objects, there are other systems in which the objects are first projected into the x, y plane. Fortunately, many of the most efficient algorithms are almost identical in two and three dimensions, and we will focus on these algorithms.

8.4   LINE-SEGMENT CLIPPING

A **clipper** decides which primitives, or parts of primitives, can possibly appear on the display and be passed on to the rasterizer. Primitives that fit within the specified view volume pass through the clipper, or are **accepted**. Primitives that cannot appear on the display are eliminated, or **rejected** or **culled**. Primitives that are only partially within the view volume must be clipped such that any part lying outside the volume is removed.

Clipping can occur at one or more places in the viewing pipeline. The modeler may clip to limit the primitives that the hardware must handle. The primitives may be clipped after they have been projected from three- to two-dimensional objects. In WebGL, primitives are clipped against a three-dimensional view volume before rasterization. We will develop a sequence of clippers. For both pedagogic and historic reasons, we start with two two-dimensional line-segment clippers. Both extend directly to three dimensions and to clipping of polygons.

8.4.1 Cohen-Sutherland Clipping

The two-dimensional clipping problem for line segments is shown in Figure 8.5. We can assume for now that this problem arises after three-dimensional line segments have been projected onto the projection plane and that the window is part of the projection plane mapped to the viewport on the display. All values are specified as real numbers. We can see that the entire line segment AB appears on the display, whereas none of CD appears. EF and GH have to be shortened before being displayed. Although a line segment is completely determined by its endpoints, GH shows that even if both endpoints lie outside the clipping window, part of the line segment may still appear on the display.

FIGURE 8.5   Two-dimensional clipping.

We could compute the intersections of the lines (of which the segments are parts) with the sides of the window and thus determine the necessary information for clipping. However, we want to avoid intersection calculations, if possible, because each intersection requires a floating-point division. The Cohen-Sutherland algorithm was the first to seek to replace most of the expensive floating-point multiplications and divisions with a combination of floating-point subtractions and bit operations.

The algorithm starts by extending the sides of the window to infinity, thus breaking up space into the nine regions shown in Figure 8.6. Each region can be assigned a unique 4-bit binary number, or **outcode**, $b_0b_1b_2b_3$, as follows. Suppose that (x, y) is a point in the region; then

$$b_0 = \begin{cases} 1 & \text{if } y > y_{max} \\ 0 & \text{otherwise.} \end{cases}$$

Likewise, b_1 is 1 if $y < y_{min}$, and b_2 and b_3 are determined by the relationship between x and the left and right sides of the window. The resulting codes are indicated in Figure 8.6. For each endpoint of a line segment, we first compute the endpoint's outcode, a step that can require eight floating-point subtractions per line segment.

Consider a line segment whose outcodes are given by $o_1 = outcode(x_1, y_1)$ and $o_2 = outcode(x_2, y_2)$. We can now reason on the basis of these outcodes. There are four cases:

1. $(o_1 = o_2 = 0)$. Both endpoints are inside the clipping window, as is true for segment AB in Figure 8.7. The entire line segment is inside, and the segment can be sent on to be rasterized.

2. $(o_1 \neq 0, o_2 = 0$; or vice versa). One endpoint is inside the clipping window; one is outside (see segment CD in Figure 8.7). The line segment must be

1001	1000	1010
0001	0000	0010
0101	0100	0110

$y = y_{max}$

$y = y_{min}$

$x = x_{min} \quad x = x_{max}$

FIGURE 8.6   Breaking up of space and outcodes.

FIGURE 8.7   Cases of outcodes in Cohen-Sutherland algorithm.

shortened. The nonzero outcode indicates which edge or edges of the window are crossed by the segment. One or two intersections must be computed. Note that after one intersection is computed, we can compute the outcode of the point of intersection to determine whether another intersection calculation is required.

3. (o_1 & $o_2 \neq 0$). By taking the bitwise AND of the outcodes, we determine whether or not the two endpoints lie on the same outside edge of the window. If so, the line segment can be discarded (see segment EF in Figure 8.7).

4. (o_1 & $o_2 = 0$). Both endpoints are outside, but they are on the outside of different edges of the window. As we can see from segments GH and IJ in Figure 8.7, we cannot tell from just the outcodes whether the segment can be discarded or must be shortened. The best we can do is to intersect with one of the sides of the window and to check the outcode of the resulting point.

All our checking of outcodes requires only boolean operations. We do intersection calculations only when they are needed, as in the second case, or where the outcodes did not contain enough information, as in the fourth case.

The Cohen-Sutherland algorithm works best when there are many line segments but few are actually displayed. In this case, most of the line segments lie fully outside one or two of the extended sides of the clipping rectangle and can thus be eliminated on the basis of their outcodes. The other advantage is that this algorithm can be extended to three dimensions. The main disadvantage of the algorithm is that it must be used recursively. Consider line segment GH in Figure 8.7. It must be clipped against both the left and top sides of the clipping window. Generally, the simplest way to do so is to use the initial outcodes to determine the first side of the clipping window to clip against. After this first shortening of the original line segment, a new outcode is computed for the new endpoint created by shortening, and the algorithm is reexecuted.

We have not discussed how to compute any required intersections. The form this calculation takes depends on how we choose to represent the line segment, although only a single division should be required in any case. If we use the standard explicit form of a line,

$$y = mx + h,$$

where m is the slope of the line and h is the line's y intercept, then we can compute m and h from the endpoints. However, vertical lines cannot be represented in this form—a critical weakness of the explicit form. If we were interested in only the Cohen-Sutherland algorithm, it would be fairly simple to program all cases directly because the sides of the clipping rectangle are parallel to the axes. However, we are interested in more than just clipping; consequently, other representations of the line and line segment are of importance. In particular, parametric representations are almost always used in computer graphics. We have already seen the parametric form of the line in Chapter 4; the parametric representation of other types of curves is considered in Chapter 11.

8.4.2 Liang-Barsky Clipping

If we use the parametric form for lines, we can approach the clipping of line segments in a different—and ultimately more efficient—manner. Suppose that we have a line segment defined by the two endpoints $\mathbf{p}_1 = [x_1, y_1]^T$ and $\mathbf{p}_2 = [x_2, y_2]^T$. We can use these endpoints to define a unique line that we can express parametrically, either in matrix form,

$$\mathbf{p}(\alpha) = (1 - \alpha)\mathbf{p}_1 + \alpha\mathbf{p}_2,$$

or as two scalar equations,

$$x(\alpha) = (1 - \alpha)x_1 + \alpha x_2$$

$$y(\alpha) = (1 - \alpha)y_1 + \alpha y_2.$$

Note that this form is robust and needs no changes for horizontal or vertical lines. As the parameter α varies from 0 to 1, we move along the segment from $\mathbf{p}_1$ to $\mathbf{p}_2$. Negative values of α yield points on the line on the other side of $\mathbf{p}_1$ from $\mathbf{p}_2$. Similarly, values of $\alpha > 1$ give points on the line past $\mathbf{p}_2$ going off to infinity.

Consider a line segment and the line of which it is part, as shown in Figure 8.8(a). As long as the line is not parallel to a side of the window (if it is, we can handle that situation with ease), there are four points where the line intersects the extended sides of the window. These points correspond to the four values of the parameter: α_1, α_2, α_3, and α_4. One of these values corresponds to the line entering the window; another corresponds to the line leaving the window. Leaving aside, for the moment, how we compute these intersections, we can order them and determine which correspond to intersections that we need for clipping. For the given example,

$$1 > \alpha_4 > \alpha_3 > \alpha_2 > \alpha_1 > 0.$$

Hence, all four intersections are inside the original line segment, with the two in-nermost (α_2 and α_3) determining the clipped line segment. We can distinguish this case from the case in Figure 8.8(b), which also has the four intersections between the endpoints of the line segment, by noting that the order for this case is

$$1 > \alpha_4 > \alpha_2 > \alpha_3 > \alpha_1 > 0.$$

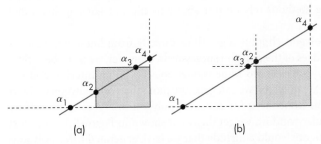

(a)   (b)

FIGURE 8.8   Two cases of a parametric line and a clipping window.

The line intersects both the top and the bottom of the extended window before it intersects either the left or the right; thus, the entire line segment must be rejected. Other cases of the ordering of the points of intersection can be argued in a similar way.

Efficient implementation of this strategy requires that we avoid computing intersections until they are needed. Many lines can be rejected before all four intersections are known. We also want to avoid floating-point divisions where possible. If we use the parametric form to determine the intersection with the top of the window, we find the intersection at the value

$$\alpha = \frac{y_{\max} - y_1}{y_2 - y_1}.$$

Similar equations hold for the other three sides of the window. Rather than computing these intersections, at the cost of a division for each, we instead write the equation as

$$\alpha(y_2 - y_1) = \alpha \Delta y = y_{\max} - y_1 = \Delta y_{\max}.$$

All the tests required by the algorithm can be restated in terms of $\Delta y_{\max}$, Δy, and similar terms for the other sides of the windows. Thus, all decisions about clipping can be made without floating-point division. Only if an intersection is needed (because a segment has to be shortened) is the division done. The efficiency of this approach, compared to that of the Cohen-Sutherland algorithm, is that we avoid multiple shortenings of line segments and the related reexecutions of the clipping algorithm. We forgo discussion of other efficient two-dimensional line-clipping algorithms because, unlike the Cohen-Sutherland and Liang-Barsky algorithms, these algorithms do not extend to three dimensions.

8.5 POLYGON CLIPPING

Polygon clipping arises in a number of ways. Certainly, we want to be able to clip polygons against rectangular windows for display. However, we may at times want windows that are not rectangular. Other parts of an implementation, such as shadow generation and hidden-surface removal, can require clipping of polygons against other polygons. For example, Figure 8.9 shows the shadow of a polygon that we create by clipping a polygon that is closer to the light source against polygons that are farther away. Many antialiasing methods rely on our ability to clip polygons against other polygons.

We can generate polygon-clipping algorithms directly from line-clipping algorithms by clipping the edges of the polygon successively. However, we must be careful to remember that a polygon is a two-dimensional object with an interior, and depending on the form of the polygon, we can generate more than one polygonal object by clipping. Consider the nonconvex (or **concave**) polygon in Figure 8.10(a). If we clip it against a rectangular window, we get the result shown in Figure 8.10(b). Most viewers looking at this figure would conclude that we have generated three polygons by clipping. Unfortunately, implementing a clipper that can increase the number of

FIGURE 8.9 Polygon clipping in shadow generation.

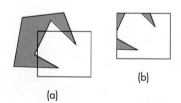

(b)

(a)

FIGURE 8.10 Clipping of a concave polygon. (a) Before clipping. (b) After clipping.

objects can be a problem. We could treat the result of the clipper as a single polygon, as shown in Figure 8.11, with edges that overlap along the sides of the window, but this choice might cause difficulties in other parts of the implementation.

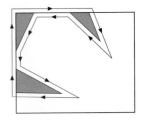

FIGURE 8.11   Creation of a single polygon.

Convex polygons do not present such problems. Clipping a convex polygon against a rectangular window can leave at most a single convex polygon (see Exercise 8.3). A graphics system might then either forbid the use of concave polygons or divide (tessellate) a given polygon into a set of convex polygons, as shown in Figure 8.12. Starting with version 4.1, desktop OpenGL includes tessellation shaders.

For rectangular clipping regions, both the Cohen-Sutherland and the Liang-Barsky algorithms can be applied to polygons on an edge-by-edge basis. There is another approach, developed by Sutherland and Hodgeman, that fits well with the pipeline architectures that we have discussed.

A line-segment clipper can be envisioned as a black box whose input is the pair of vertices from the segment to be tested and clipped, and whose output either is a pair of vertices corresponding to the clipped line segment or is nothing if the input line segment lies outside the window (Figure 8.13).

Rather than considering the clipping window as four line segments, we can consider it as the object created by the intersection of four infinite lines that determine the top, bottom, right, and left sides of the window. We can then subdivide our clipper into a pipeline of simpler clippers, each of which clips against a single line that is

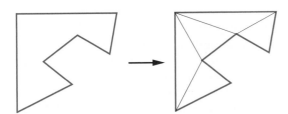

FIGURE 8.12   Tessellation of a concave polygon.

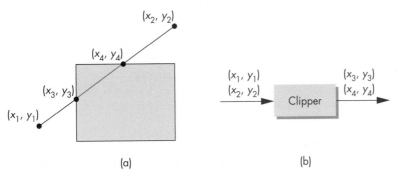

FIGURE 8.13   Two views of clipping. (a) Clipping against a rectangle. (b) Clipper as a black box.

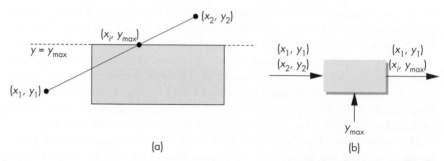

FIGURE 8.14   Clipping against the top of the window. (a) Graphically. (b) Black-box view.

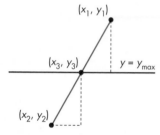

FIGURE 8.15   Intersection with the top of the window.

the extension of an edge of the window. We can use the black-box view on each of the individual clippers.

Suppose that we consider clipping against only the top of the window. We can think of this operation as a black box whose input and output are pairs of vertices, with the value of y_{max} as a parameter known to the clipper (Figure 8.14). Using the similar triangles in Figure 8.15, we see that if there is an intersection, it lies at

$$x_3 = x_1 + (y_{max} - y_1)\frac{x_2 - x_1}{y_2 - y_1}$$

$$y_3 = y_{max}.$$

Thus, the clipper returns one of three pairs: $\{(x_1, y_1), (x_2, y_2)\}$; $\{(x_1, y_1), (x_i, y_{max})\}$; or $\{(x_i, y_{max}), (x_2, y_2)\}$. We can clip against the bottom, right, and left lines independently, using the same equations, with the roles of x and y exchanged as necessary and the values for the sides of the window inserted. The four clippers can now be arranged in the pipeline of Figure 8.16. If we build this configuration in hardware, we have a clipper that is working on four vertices concurrently. Figure 8.17 shows a simple example of the effect of successive clippers on a polygon.

8.6   CLIPPING OF OTHER PRIMITIVES

Our emphasis in Chapters 1 through 5 was on writing programs in which the objects are built from line segments and triangles. We often render the curved objects that we discuss in Chapter 11 by subdividing them into small triangles. In pipeline architectures, we usually find some variant of the clippers that we have presented. Nevertheless, there are situations in which we want either to clip objects before they reach the hardware or to employ algorithms optimized for other primitives.

8.6.1   Bounding Boxes and Volumes

Suppose that we have a many-sided polygon, as shown in Figure 8.18(a). We could apply one of our clipping algorithms, which would clip the polygon by individually clipping all that polygon's edges. However, we can see that the entire polygon lies

FIGURE 8.16   Pipeline clipping. (a) Clipping problem. (b) Pipeline clippers.

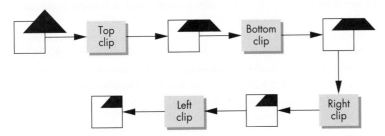

FIGURE 8.17   Example of pipeline clipping.

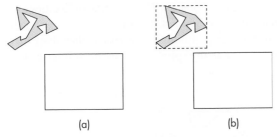

FIGURE 8.18   Using bounding boxes. (a) Polygon and clipping window.
(b) Polygon, bounding box, and clipping window.

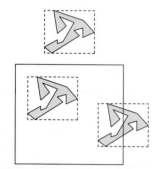

FIGURE 8.19   Clipping with bounding boxes.

outside the clipping window. We can exploit this observation through the use of the axis-aligned bounding box or the extent of the polygon (Figure 8.18(b)): the smallest rectangle, aligned with the window, that contains the polygon. Calculating the bounding box requires merely going through the vertices of the polygon to find the minimum and maximum of both the x and y values.

Once we have the bounding box, we can often avoid detailed clipping. Consider the three cases in Figure 8.19. For the polygon above the window, no clipping is necessary, because the minimum y for the bounding box is above the top of the window. For the polygon inside the window, we can determine that it is inside by comparing the bounding box with the window. Only when we discover that the bounding box straddles the window do we have to carry out detailed clipping, using all the edges of the polygon. The use of extents is such a powerful technique—in both two and three dimensions—that modeling systems often compute a bounding box for each object automatically and store the bounding box with the object.

Axis-aligned bounding boxes work in both two and three dimensions. In three dimensions, they can be used in the application to perform clipping to reduce the burden on the pipeline. Other volumes, such as spheres, can also work well. One of the other applications of bounding volumes is in collision detection (Chapter 10). One of the fundamental operations in animating computer games is to determine if two moving entities have collided. For example, consider two animated characters moving in a sequence of images. We need to know when they collide so that we can alter their paths. This problem has many similarities to the clipping problem because we want to determine when the volume of one intersects the volume of the other. The complexity of the objects and the need to do these calculations very quickly make this problem difficult. A common approach is to place each object in a bounding volume, either an axis-aligned bounding box or a sphere, and to determine if the volumes intersect. If they do, then detailed calculations can be done.

8.6.2 Curves, Surfaces, and Text

The variety of curves and surfaces that we can define mathematically makes it difficult to find general algorithms for processing these objects. The potential difficulties can be seen from the two-dimensional curves in Figure 8.20. For a simple curve, such as a quadric, we can compute intersections, although at a cost higher than that for lines. For more complex curves, such as the spiral, not only must intersection

(a)

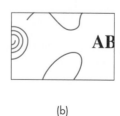

(b)

FIGURE 8.20   Curve clipping.

calculations be computed with numerical techniques, but even determining how many intersections we must compute may be difficult. We can avoid such problems by approximating curves with line segments and surfaces with planar polygons. The use of bounding boxes can also prove helpful, especially in cases such as quadratics, where we can compute intersections exactly but would prefer to make sure that the calculation is necessary before carrying it out.

The handling of text differs from API to API, with many APIs allowing the user to specify how detailed a rendering of text is required. There are two extremes. On one end, text is stored as bit patterns and is rendered directly by the hardware without any geometric processing. Any required clipping is done in the framebuffer. At the other extreme, text is defined like any other geometric object and is then processed through the standard viewing pipeline. WebGL allows both cases by not having a separate text primitive. The user can choose which mode she prefers by defining either bitmapped characters using pixel operations or stroke characters using the standard primitives.

8.6.3 Clipping in the Framebuffer

We might also consider delaying clipping until after objects have been projected and converted into screen coordinates. Clipping can be done in the framebuffer through a technique called **scissoring**. However, it is usually better to clip geometric entities before the vertices reach the framebuffer; thus, clipping within the framebuffer generally is required only for raster objects, such as blocks of pixels.

8.7   CLIPPING IN THREE DIMENSIONS

In three dimensions, we clip against a bounded volume rather than against a bounded region in the plane. The simplest extension of two-dimensional clipping to three dimensions is for the right parallelepiped clipping region (Figure 8.21),

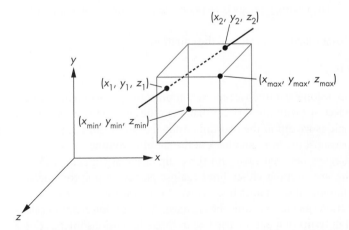

FIGURE 8.21   Three-dimensional clipping against a right parallelepiped.

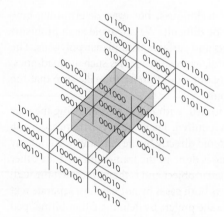

FIGURE 8.22   Cohen-Sutherland regions in three dimensions.

$$x_{min} \leq x \leq x_{max}$$

$$y_{min} \leq y \leq y_{max}$$

$$z_{min} \leq z \leq z_{max}$$

or in clip space:

$$-w \leq x \leq w$$

$$-w \leq y \leq w$$

$$-w \leq z \leq w.$$

Our three clipping algorithms (Cohen-Sutherland, Liang-Barsky, Sutherland-Hodgeman) and the use of extents can be extended to three dimensions. For the Cohen-Sutherland algorithm, we replace the 4-bit outcode with a 6-bit outcode. The additional 2 bits are set if the point lies either in front of or behind the clipping volume (Figure 8.22). The testing strategy is virtually identical for the two- and three-dimensional cases.

For the Liang-Barsky algorithm, we add the equation

$$z(\alpha) = (1 - \alpha)z_1 + \alpha z_2$$

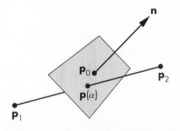

FIGURE 8.23   Plane–line intersection.

to obtain a three-dimensional parametric representation of the line segment. We have to consider six intersections with the surfaces that form the clipping volume, but we can use the same logic as we did in the two-dimensional case. Pipeline clippers add two modules to clip against the front and back of the clipping volume.

The major difference between two- and three-dimensional clippers is that in three dimensions we are clipping either lines against planes or polygons against planes instead of clipping lines against lines as we do in two dimensions. Consequently, our intersection calculations must be changed. A typical intersection calculation can be posed in terms of a parametric line in three dimensions intersecting a plane (Figure 8.23). If we write the line and plane equations in matrix form (where **n**

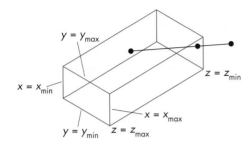

FIGURE 8.24   Clipping for orthographic viewing.

FIGURE 8.25   Clipping for oblique viewing.

is the normal to the plane and $\mathbf{p}_0$ is a point on the plane), we must solve the equations

$$\mathbf{p}(\alpha) = (1 - \alpha)\mathbf{p}_1 + \alpha\mathbf{p}_2$$

$$\mathbf{n} \cdot (\mathbf{p}(\alpha) - \mathbf{p}_0) = 0$$

for the α corresponding to the point of intersection. This value is

$$\alpha = \frac{\mathbf{n} \cdot (\mathbf{p}_0 - \mathbf{p}_1)}{\mathbf{n} \cdot (\mathbf{p}_2 - \mathbf{p}_1)}$$

and computation of an intersection requires six multiplications and a division. However, if we look at the standard viewing volumes, we see that simplifications are possible. For orthographic viewing (Figure 8.24), the view volume is a right parallelepiped, and each intersection calculation reduces to a single division, as it did for two-dimensional clipping.

When we consider an oblique view (Figure 8.25), we see that the clipping volume is no longer a right parallelepiped. Although you might think that we have to compute dot products to clip against the sides of the volume, here is where the normalization process that we introduced in Chapter 5 pays dividends. We showed that an oblique projection is equivalent to a shearing of the data followed by an orthographic projection. Although the shear transformation distorts objects, they are distorted such that they project correctly by an orthographic projection. The shear also distorts the clipping volume from a general parallelepiped to a right parallelepiped. Figure 8.26(a) shows a top view of an oblique volume with a cube inside the volume. Figure 8.26(b)

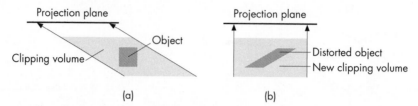

FIGURE 8.26   Distortion of view volume by shear. (a) Top view before shear. (b) Top view after shear.

shows the volume and object after they have been distorted by the shear. As far as projection is concerned, carrying out the oblique transformation directly or replacing it by a shear transformation and an orthographic projection requires the same amount of computation. When we add in clipping, it is clear that the second approach has a definite advantage because we can clip against a right parallelepiped. This example illustrates the importance of considering the incremental nature of the steps in an implementation. Analysis of either projection or clipping in isolation fails to demonstrate the importance of the normalization process.

For perspective projections, the argument for normalization is just as strong. By carrying out the perspective-normalization transformation from Chapter 5, but not the orthographic projection, we again create a rectangular clipping volume and simplify all subsequent intersection calculations.

8.8   RASTERIZATION

We are now ready to take the final step in the journey from the specification of geometric entities in an application program to the formation of fragments: rasterization of primitives. In this chapter, we are concerned with only line segments and polygons, both of which are defined by vertices. We can assume that we have clipped the primitives such that each remaining primitive is inside the view volume.

Fragments are potential pixels. Each fragment has a color attribute and a location in screen coordinates that corresponds to a location in the color buffer. Fragments also carry depth information that can be used for hidden-surface removal. To clarify the discussion, we will ignore hidden-surface removal until Section 8.11, and thus we can work directly in screen coordinates. Because we are not considering hidden-surface removal, translucent fragments, or antialiasing, we can develop rasterization algorithms in terms of the pixels that they color.

We further assume that the color buffer is an $n \times m$ array of pixels, with $(0, 0)$ corresponding to the lower-left corner. Pixels can be set to a given color by a single function inside the graphics implementation of the form

```
var writePixel(ix, iy, value);
```

The argument `value` can be either an index, in color-index mode, or a pointer to an RGBA color. On the one hand, a color buffer is inherently discrete; it does not make sense to talk about pixels located at places other than integer values of ix and iy. On the other hand, screen coordinates, which range over the same values as do ix and iy, are real numbers. For example, we can compute a fragment location such as (63.4, 157.9) in screen coordinates but must realize that the nearest pixel is centered either at (63, 158) or at (63.5, 157.5), depending on whether pixels are considered to be centered at whole or half integer values.

Pixels have attributes that are colors in the color buffer. Pixels can be displayed in multiple shapes and sizes that depend on the characteristics of the display. We address this matter in Section 8.13. For now, we can assume that a pixel is displayed as a square, whose center is at the location associated with the pixel and whose side is equal to the distance between pixels. In WebGL, the centers of pixels are located at values halfway between integers. There are some advantages to this choice (see Exercise 8.19). We also assume that a concurrent process reads the contents of the color buffer and creates the display at the required rate. This assumption, which holds in many systems that have dual-ported memory, allows us to treat the rasterization process independently of the display of the framebuffer contents.

The simplest scan conversion algorithm for line segments has become known as the **DDA algorithm**, after the digital differential analyzer, an early electromechanical device for digital simulation of differential equations. Because a line satisfies the differential equation $dy/dx = m$, where m is the slope, generating a line segment is equivalent to solving a simple differential equation numerically.

Suppose that we have a line segment defined by the endpoints (x_1, y_1) and (x_2, y_2). Because we are working in a color buffer, we assume that these values have been rounded to integer values, so the line segment starts and ends at a known pixel.[2] The slope is given by

$$m = \frac{y_2 - y_1}{x_2 - x_1} = \frac{\Delta y}{\Delta x}.$$

We assume that

$$0 \le m \le 1.$$

FIGURE 8.27 Line segment in window coordinates.

We can handle other values of m using symmetry. Our algorithm is based on writing a pixel for each value of ix in `write_pixel` as x goes from x_1 to x_2. If we are on the line segment, as shown in Figure 8.27, for any change in x equal to Δx, the corresponding changes in y must be

$$\Delta y = m\Delta x.$$

As we move from x_1 to x_2, we increase x by 1 in each iteration; thus, we must increase y by

$$\Delta y = m.$$

FIGURE 8.28 Pixels generated by DDA algorithm.

2. This assumption is not necessary to derive an algorithm. If we use a fixed-point representation for the endpoints and do our calculations using fixed-point arithmetic, then we retain the computational advantages of the algorithm and produce a more accurate rasterization.

FIGURE 8.29   Pixels generated by high- and low-slope lines.

FIGURE 8.30   Pixels generated by revised DDA algorithm.

Although each x is an integer, each y is not, because m is a floating-point number and we must round it to find the appropriate pixel, as shown in Figure 8.28. Our algorithm, in pseudocode, is

```
for (ix = x1; ix <= x2; ++ix) {
    y += m;
    writePixel(x, round(y), line_color);
}
```

where `round` is a function that rounds a real number to an integer. The reason that we limited the maximum slope to 1 can be seen from Figure 8.29. Our algorithm is of this form: For each x, find the best y. For large slopes, the separation between pixels that are colored can be large, generating an unacceptable approximation to the line segment. If, however, for slopes greater than 1, we swap the roles of x and y, the algorithm becomes this: For each y, find the best x. For the same line segments, we get the approximations in Figure 8.30. Note that the use of symmetry removes any potential problems from either vertical or horizontal line segments. You may want to derive the parts of the algorithm for negative slopes.

Because line segments are determined by vertices, we can use interpolation to assign a different color to each pixel that we generate. We can also generate various dash and dot patterns by changing the color that we use as we generate pixels. Neither of these effects has much to do with the basic rasterization algorithm, as the latter's job is only to determine which pixels to color rather than to determine the color that is used.

8.9   BRESENHAM'S ALGORITHM

The DDA algorithm appears efficient. Certainly it can be coded easily, but it requires a floating-point addition for each pixel generated. Bresenham derived a line-rasterization algorithm that, remarkably, avoids all floating-point calculations and has become the standard algorithm used in hardware and software rasterizers.

We assume, as we did with the DDA algorithm, that the line segment lies between the integer points (x_1, y_1) and (x_2, y_2) and that the slope satisfies

$$0 \le m \le 1.$$

This slope condition is crucial for the algorithm, as we can see with the aid of Figure 8.31. Suppose that we are somewhere in the middle of the scan conversion of our line segment and have just placed a pixel at $(i + \frac{1}{2}, j + \frac{1}{2})$. We know that the line of which the segment is part can be represented as

$$y = mx + h.$$

At $x = i + \frac{1}{2}$, this line must pass within one-half the length of the pixel at $(i + \frac{1}{2}, j + \frac{1}{2})$;[3] otherwise, the rounding operation would not have generated this pixel. If

---

3. We are assuming that the pixels' centers are located halfway between integers.

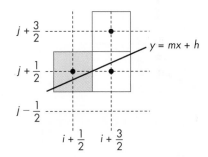

FIGURE 8.31   Conditions for Bresenham's algorithm.

FIGURE 8.32   Decision variable for Bresenham's algorithm.

we move ahead to $x = i + \frac{3}{2}$, the slope condition indicates that we must set the color of one of only two possible pixels: either the pixel at $(i + \frac{3}{2}, j + \frac{1}{2})$ or the pixel at $(i + \frac{3}{2}, j + \frac{3}{2})$. Having reduced our choices to two pixels, we can pose the problem anew in terms of the **decision variable** $d = a - b$, where a and b are the distances between the line and the upper and lower candidate pixels at $x = i + \frac{3}{2}$, as shown in Figure 8.32. If d is positive, the line passes closer to the lower pixel, so we choose the pixel at $(i + \frac{3}{2}, j + \frac{1}{2})$; otherwise, we choose the pixel at $(i + \frac{3}{2}, j + \frac{3}{2})$. Although we could compute d by computing $y = mx + b$, we hesitate to do so because m is a floating-point number.

We obtain the computational advantages of Bresenham's algorithm through two further steps. First, we replace floating-point operations with fixed-point operations. Second, we apply the algorithm incrementally. We start by replacing d with the new decision variable

$$d = (x_2 - x_1)(a - b) = \Delta x(a - b),$$

a change that cannot affect which pixels are drawn, because it is only the sign of the decision variable that matters. If we substitute for a and b, using the equation of the line and noting that

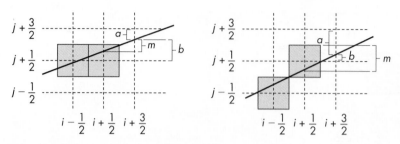

FIGURE 8.33   Incrementing the values of a and b.

$$m = \frac{y_2 - y_1}{x_2 - x_1} = \frac{\Delta y}{\Delta x}$$

$$h = y_2 - mx_2,$$

then we can see that d is an integer. We have eliminated floating-point calculations, but the direct computation of d requires a fair amount of fixed-point arithmetic.

Let us take a slightly different approach. Suppose that d_k is the value of d at $x = k + \frac{1}{2}$. We would like to compute d_{k+1} incrementally from d_k. There are two situations, depending on whether or not we incremented the y location of the pixel at the previous step; these situations are shown in Figure 8.33. By observing that a is the distance between the location of the upper candidate location and the line, we see that a increases by m only if x was increased by the previous decision; otherwise, it decreases by $m - 1$. Likewise, b either decreases by m or increases by $1 - m$ when we increment x. Multiplying by Δx, we find that the possible changes in d are either $-2\Delta y$ or $2(\Delta x - \Delta y)$. We can state this result in the form

$$d_{k+1} = d_k - \begin{cases} 2\Delta y & \text{if } d_k > 0 \\ 2(\Delta y - \Delta x) & \text{otherwise.} \end{cases}$$

The calculation of each successive pixel in the color buffer requires only an addition and a sign test. This algorithm is so efficient that it has been incorporated as a single instruction on graphics chips. See Exercise 8.14 for calculation of the initial value d_0.

8.10   POLYGON RASTERIZATION

One of the major advantages that the first raster systems brought to users was the ability to display filled polygons. At that time, coloring each point in the interior of a polygon with a different shade was not possible in real time, and the phrases *rasterizing polygons* and *polygon scan conversion* came to mean filling a polygon with a single color. Unlike rasterization of lines, where a single algorithm dominates, there are many viable methods for rasterizing polygons. The choice depends heavily on the implementation architecture. We concentrate on methods that fit with our pipeline approach and can also support shading. In Sections 8.10.1 through 8.10.4, we survey a number of other approaches.

8.10.1 Inside–Outside Testing

As we have seen, the only type of polygon supported by WebGL is a triangle. Because triangles are convex and flat, there is never a problem of determining if a point is inside or outside the triangle.

More general polygons arise in practice. For example, Scalable Vector Graphics (SVG) is a two-dimensional vector-style API that is supported by most browsers. Applications can specify a path by a set of vertices that determine a complex polygon that must be rendered in a consistent way.

For nonflat polygons,[4] we can work with their projections (Section 8.10.5), or we can use the first three vertices to determine a plane to use for the interior. For flat nonsimple polygons, we must decide how to determine whether a given point is inside or outside of the polygon. Conceptually, the process of filling the inside of a polygon with a color or pattern is equivalent to deciding which points in the plane of the polygon are interior (inside) points.

The **crossing** or **odd–even test** is the most widely used test for making inside–outside decisions. Suppose that **p** is a point inside a polygon. Any ray emanating from **p** and going off to infinity must cross an odd number of edges. Any ray emanating from a point outside the polygon and entering the polygon crosses an even number of edges before reaching infinity. Hence, a point can be defined as being inside if after drawing a line through it and following this line, starting on the outside, we cross an odd number of edges before reaching it. For the star-shaped polygon in Figure 8.34, we obtain the inside coloring shown. Odd–even testing is easy to implement and integrates well with the standard rendering algorithms. Usually, we replace rays through points with scan lines, and we count the crossing of polygon edges to determine inside and outside.

FIGURE 8.34 Filling with the odd–even test.

However, we might want our fill algorithm to color the star polygon as shown in Figure 8.35, rather than as shown in Figure 8.34. The **winding** test allows us to do that. This test considers the polygon as a knot being wrapped around a point or a line. To implement the test, we consider traversing the edges of the polygon from any starting vertex and going around the edge in a particular direction (which direction does not matter) until we reach the starting point. We illustrate the path by labeling the edges, as shown in Figure 8.35(a). Next we consider an arbitrary point. The **winding number** for this point is the number of times it is encircled by the edges of the polygon. We count clockwise encirclements as positive and counterclockwise encirclements as negative (or vice versa). Thus, points outside the star in Figure 8.35 are not encircled and have a winding number of 0, points that were filled in Figure 8.34 all have a winding number of 1, and points in the center that were not filled by the odd–even test have a winding number of 2. If we change our fill rule to be that a point is inside the polygon if its winding number is not zero, then we fill the inside of the polygon as shown in Figure 8.35(b).

---

4. Strictly speaking, there is no such thing as a nonflat polygon because the interior is not defined unless it is flat. However, from a programming perspective, we can *define* a polygon by simply giving a list of vertices, regardless of whether or not they lie in the same plane.

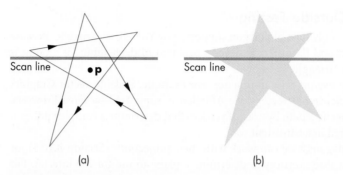

FIGURE 8.35   Fill using the winding number test.

FIGURE 8.36   Removal of a triangle from a polygon.

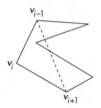

FIGURE 8.37   Vertex inside triangle.

FIGURE 8.38   Splitting into two polygons.

8.10.2 WebGL and Concave Polygons

Because WebGL renders only triangles that are flat and convex, we still have the problem of what to do with more general polygons. One approach is to work with the application to ensure that they only generate triangles. Another is to provide software that can tessellate a given polygon into flat convex polygons, usually triangles. There are many ways to divide a given polygon into triangles. A good tessellation should not produce triangles that are long and thin; it should, if possible, produce sets of triangles that can use supported features, such as triangle strips and triangle fans.

Let's consider one approach to tessellating or triangularizing an arbitrary simple polygon with n vertices. From the construction, it will be clear that we always obtain a triangularization using exactly $n - 2$ triangles. We assume our polygon is specified by an ordered list of vertices $v_0, v_1, \ldots, v_{n-1}$. Thus, there is an edge from v_0 to v_1, from v_1 to v_2, and finally from v_{n-1} to v_0. The first step is to find the leftmost vertex, v_i, a calculation that requires a simple scan of the x components of the vertices. Let v_{i-1} and v_{i+1} be the two neighbors of v_i (where the indices are computed modulo n). These three vertices form the triangle v_{i-1}, v_i, v_{i+1}. If the situation is as in Figure 8.36, then we can proceed recursively by removing v_i from the original list, and we will have a triangle and a polygon with $n - 1$ vertices.

However, because the polygon may not be convex, the line segment from v_{i-1} to v_{i+1} can cross other edges, as shown in Figure 8.37. We can test for this case by checking if any of the other vertices lie to the left of the line segment and inside the triangle determined by v_{i-1}, v_i, v_{i+1}. If we connect v_i to the leftmost of these vertices, we split the original triangle into two polygons (as in Figure 8.38), each of which has at least two vertices fewer than the original triangle. Using the leftmost vertex ensures that the two polygons are simple. Hence, we can proceed recursively with these two triangles, knowing that in the end we will have all triangles.

Note that the worst-case performance of this method occurs when there are no vertices in the triangle formed by v_{i-1}, v_i, v_{i+1}. We require $O(n)$ tests to make sure that this is the case, and if it is we then remove only one vertex from the original polygon. Consequently, the worst-case performance is $O(n^2)$. However, if we know in advance that the polygon is convex, these tests are not needed and the method is $O(n)$. The best performance in general occurs when the splitting results in two polygons with an equal number of vertices. If such a split occurs on each step, the method would be

$O(n \log n)$. The Suggested Readings at the end of the chapter include methods that are guaranteed to be $O(n \log n)$, but they are more complex than the method outlined here. In practice, we rarely work with polygons with so many vertices that we need the more complex methods.

We have thus far only discussed polygonal objects specified by a single continuous edge going from vertex to vertex. More complex cases arise when the object contains holes, as, for example, if we consider rendering the letter "A" with triangles. In this case, the tessellation problem is more complex. The fixed-function OpenGL pipeline supported a software tessellator, but that has been replaced by a tessellation shader, which became available with version 4.1. However, this type of shader is not yet supported by WebGL.

8.10.3 Fill and Sort

A different approach to rasterization of polygons starts with the idea of a polygon processor: a black box whose inputs are the vertices for a set of two-dimensional polygons and whose output is a framebuffer with the correct pixels set. Suppose that we consider filling each polygon with a constant color—a choice we make only to clarify the discussion. First, consider a single polygon. The basic rule for filling a polygon is as follows: *If a point is inside the polygon, color it with the inside (fill) color.* This conceptual algorithm indicates that polygon fill is a sorting problem, where we sort all the pixels in the framebuffer into those that are inside the polygon and those that are not. From this perspective, we obtain different polygon fill algorithms using different ways of sorting the points. We introduce three possibilities in Sections 8.10.4 and 8.11.

- Flood fill
- Scan line fill
- Odd–even fill

8.10.4 Flood Fill

We can display an unfilled polygon by rasterizing its edges into the framebuffer using Bresenham's algorithm. Suppose that we have only two colors: a background color (white) and a foreground, or drawing, color (black). We can use the foreground color to rasterize the edges, resulting in a framebuffer colored as shown in Figure 8.39 for a simple polygon. If we can find an initial point (x, y) inside the polygon—a **seed point**—then we can look at its neighbors recursively, coloring them with the foreground color if they are not edge points. The **flood fill algorithm** can be expressed in pseudocode, assuming that there is a function `read_pixel` that returns the color of a pixel:

FIGURE 8.39 Polygon displayed by edges.

```
function floodFill(x, y)
{
  if (readPixel(x, y) == WHITE)
  {
    writePixel(x, y, BLACK);
    floodFill(x-1, y);
    floodFill(x+1, y);
```

(a)

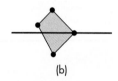

(b)

FIGURE 8.40   Singularities.
(a) Zero or two edge crossings.
(b) One edge crossing.

```
    floodFill(x, y-1);
    floodFill(x, y+1);
  }
}
```

We can obtain a number of variants of flood fill by removing the recursion. One way to do so is to work one scan line at a time.

8.10.5 Singularities

We can extend most polygon fill algorithms to other shapes if we use care (see Exercise 8.17). Polygons have the distinct advantage that the locations of their edges are known exactly. Even polygons can present problems, however, when vertices lie on scan lines. Consider the two cases in Figure 8.40. If we are using an odd–even fill definition, we have to treat these two cases differently. For case (a), we can count the intersection of the scan line with the vertex as either zero or two edge crossings; for case (b), the vertex–scan line intersection must be counted as one edge crossing.

We can fix our algorithm in one of two ways. We can check to see which of the two situations we have and then count the edge crossings appropriately. Or we can prevent the special case of a vertex lying on an edge—a **singularity**—from ever arising. We rule it out by ensuring that no vertex has an integer y value. If we find one that does, we perturb its location slightly. Another method—one that is especially valuable if we are working in the framebuffer—is to consider a virtual framebuffer of twice the resolution of the real framebuffer. In the virtual framebuffer, pixels are located only at even values of y, and all vertices are located only at odd values of y. Placing pixel centers halfway between integers, as OpenGL does, is equivalent to using this approach.

8.11   HIDDEN-SURFACE REMOVAL

Although every fragment generated by rasterization corresponds to a location in a color buffer, we do not want to display the fragment by coloring the corresponding pixel if the fragment is from an object behind another opaque object. Hidden-surface removal (or visible-surface determination) is done to discover what part, if any, of each object in the view volume is visible to the viewer or is obscured from the viewer by other objects. We describe a number of techniques for a scene composed purely of planar polygons. Because most renderers will have subdivided surfaces into polygons at this point, this choice is appropriate. Line segments can be handled by slight modifications (see Exercise 8.7).

8.11.1 Object-Space and Image-Space Approaches

The study of hidden-surface-removal algorithms clearly illustrates the variety of available algorithms, the differences between working with objects and working with images, and the importance of evaluating the incremental effects of successive algorithms in the implementation process.

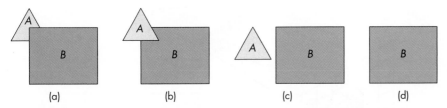

FIGURE 8.41   Two polygons. (a) *B* partially obscures *A*. (b) *A* partially obscures *B*. (c) Both *A* and *B* are visible. (d) *B* totally obscures *A*.

Consider a scene composed of k three-dimensional opaque flat polygons, each of which we can consider to be an individual object. We can derive a generic **object-space approach** by considering the objects pairwise, as seen from the center of projection. Consider two such polygons, A and B. There are four possibilities (Figure 8.41):

1. A completely obscures B from the camera; we display only A.

2. B obscures A; we display only B.

3. A and B both are completely visible; we display both A and B.

4. A and B partially obscure each other; we must calculate the visible parts of each polygon.

For complexity considerations, we can regard the determination of which case we have and any required calculation of the visible part of a polygon as a single operation. We proceed iteratively. We pick one of the k polygons and compare it pairwise with the remaining $k - 1$ polygons. After this procedure, we know which part (if any) of this polygon is visible, and we render the visible part. We are now done with this polygon, so we repeat the process with any of the other $k - 1$ polygons. Each step involves comparing one polygon, pairwise, with the other remaining polygons until we have only two polygons remaining, and we compare these to each other. We can easily determine that the complexity of this calculation is $O(k^2)$. Thus, without deriving any of the details of any particular object-space algorithm, we should suspect that the object-space approach works best for scenes that contain relatively few polygons.

The **image-space approach** follows our viewing and ray-casting model, as shown in Figure 8.42. Consider a ray that leaves the center of projection and passes through a pixel. We can intersect this ray with each of the planes determined by our k polygons, determine for which planes the ray passes through a polygon, and finally, for those rays, find the intersection closest to the center of projection. We color this pixel with the shade of the polygon at the point of intersection. Our fundamental operation is the intersection of rays with polygons. For an $n \times m$ display, we have to carry out this operation nmk times, giving $O(k)$ complexity.[5] Again, without looking at the details of the operations, we were able to get an upper bound. In general, the $O(k)$ bound accounts for the dominance of image-space methods. The $O(k)$ bound is a worst-case bound. In practice, image-space algorithms perform much better (see Exercise 8.9).

---

5. We can use more than one ray for each pixel to increase the accuracy of the rendering.

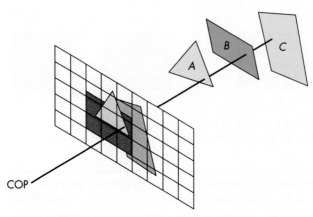

FIGURE 8.42   Image-space hidden-surface removal.

However, because image-space approaches work at the fragment or pixel level, their accuracy is limited by the resolution of the framebuffer.

8.11.2 Sorting and Hidden-Surface Removal

The $O(k^2)$ upper bound for object-oriented hidden-surface removal might remind you of the poorer sorting algorithms, such as bubble sort. Any method that involves brute-force comparison of objects by pairs has $O(k^2)$ complexity. But there is a more direct connection, which we exploited in the object-oriented sorting algorithms in Section 8.11.1. If we could organize objects by their distances from the camera, we should be able to come up with a direct method of rendering them.

But if we follow the analogy, we know that the complexity of good sorting algorithms is $O(k \log k)$. We should expect the same to be true for object-oriented hidden-surface removal, and, in fact, such is the case. As with sorting, there are multiple algorithms that meet these bounds. In addition, there are related problems involving comparison of objects, such as collision detection, that start off looking as if they are $O(k^2)$ when, in fact, they can be reduced to $O(k \log k)$.

FIGURE 8.43   Polygon with spans.

8.11.3 Scan Line Algorithms

The attraction of a **scan line algorithm** is that such a method has the potential to generate pixels as they are displayed. Consider the polygon in Figure 8.43, with one scan line shown. If we use our odd–even rule for defining the inside of the polygon, we can see three groups of pixels, or **spans**, on this scan line that are inside the polygon. Note that each span can be processed independently for lighting or depth calculations, a strategy that has been employed in some hardware that has parallel span processors. For our simple example of constant fill, after we have identified the spans, we can color the interior pixels of each span with the fill color.

The spans are determined by the set of intersections of polygons with scan lines. The vertices contain all the information that we need to determine these intersections, but the method that we use to represent the polygon determines the order in which these intersections are generated. For example, consider the polygon in Figure 8.43, which has been represented by an ordered list of vertices. The most obvious way to generate scan line–edge intersections is to process edges defined by successive vertices. Figure 8.44 shows these intersections, indexed in the order in which this method would generate them. Note that this calculation can be done incrementally (see Exercise 8.18). However, as far as fill is concerned, this order is far from the one we want. If we are to fill one scan line at a time, we would like the intersections sorted, first by scan lines and then by order of x on each scan line, as shown in Figure 8.45. A brute-force approach might be to sort all the intersections into the desired order. However, a large or jagged polygon might intersect so many edges that the n intersections can be large enough that the $O(n \log n)$ complexity of the sort makes the calculation too slow for real-time implementations; consider, for example, a polygon that spans one-half of the scan lines.

A number of methods avoid the general search. One, originally known as the **y–x algorithm**, creates a bucket for each scan line. As edges are processed, the intersections with scan lines are placed in the proper buckets. Within each bucket, an insertion sort orders the x values along each scan line. The data structure is shown in Figure 8.46. Once again, we see that a properly chosen data structure can speed up the algorithm. We can go even further by reconsidering how to represent polygons. If we do so, we arrive at the scan line method that was introduced in Section 8.10.1.

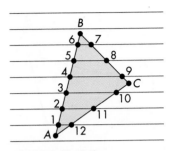

FIGURE 8.44 Polygon generated by vertex list.

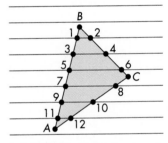

FIGURE 8.45 Desired order of vertices.

8.11.4 Back-Face Removal

In Chapter 6, we noted that in WebGL we can choose to render only front-facing polygons. For situations where we cannot see back faces, such as scenes composed of convex polyhedra, we can reduce the work required for hidden-surface removal by eliminating all back-facing polygons before we apply any other hidden-surface-removal algorithm. The test for **culling** a back-facing polygon can be derived from Figure 8.47. We see the front of a polygon if the normal, which comes out of the front face, is pointed toward the viewer. If θ is the angle between the normal and the viewer, then the polygon is facing forward if and only if

$$-90 \leq \theta \leq 90$$

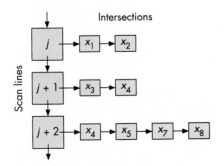

FIGURE 8.46 Data structure for y–x algorithm.

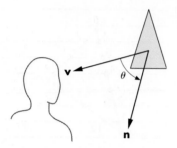

FIGURE 8.47   Back-face test.

or, equivalently,

$$\cos \theta \geq 0.$$

The second condition is much easier to test because, instead of computing the cosine, we can use the dot product:

$$\mathbf{n} \cdot \mathbf{v} \geq 0.$$

We can simplify this test even further if we note that usually it is applied after transformation to normalized device coordinates. In this system, all views are orthographic, with the direction of projection along the z-axis. Hence, in homogeneous coordinates,

$$\mathbf{v} = \begin{bmatrix} 0 \\ 0 \\ 1 \\ 0 \end{bmatrix}.$$

Thus, if the polygon is on the surface

$$ax + by + cz + d = 0$$

in normalized device coordinates, we need only check the sign of c to determine whether we have a front- or back-facing polygon. This test can be implemented easily in either hardware or software; we must simply be careful to ensure that removing back-facing polygons is correct for our application.

There is another interesting approach to determining back faces. The algorithm is based on computing the area of the polygon in screen coordinates. Consider the polygon in Figure 8.48 with n vertices. Its area a is given by

$$a = \frac{1}{2} \sum_i (y_{i+1} + y_i)(x_{i+1} - x_i),$$

where the indices are taken modulo n (see Exercise 8.28). A negative area indicates a back-facing polygon.

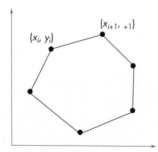

FIGURE 8.48   Computing the area of a polygon.

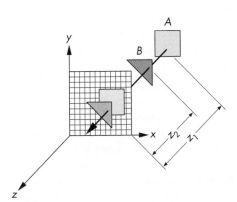

FIGURE 8.49   The z-buffer algorithm.

8.11.5 The z-Buffer Algorithm

The **z-buffer algorithm** is the most widely used hidden-surface-removal algorithm. It has the advantages of being easy to implement in either hardware or software, and of being compatible with pipeline architectures, where it can execute at the speed at which fragments are passing through the pipeline. Although the algorithm works in image space, it loops over the polygons rather than over pixels and can be regarded as part of the scan conversion process that we discussed in Section 8.10.

Suppose that we are in the process of rasterizing one of the two polygons shown in Figure 8.49. We can compute a color for each point of intersection between a ray from the center of projection and a pixel, using interpolated values of the vertex shades computed as in Chapter 6. In addition, we must check whether this point is visible. It will be visible if it is the closest point of intersection along the ray. Hence, if we are rasterizing B, its shade will appear on the screen because the distance z_2 is less than the distance z_1 to polygon A. Conversely, if we are rasterizing A, the pixel that corresponds to the point of intersection will not appear on the display. Because we are proceeding polygon by polygon, however, we do not have the information on all other polygons as we rasterize any given polygon. However, if we keep depth information with each fragment, then we can store and update depth information for each location in the framebuffer as fragments are processed.

Suppose that we have a buffer, the z-buffer, with the same resolution as the framebuffer and with depth consistent with the resolution that we wish to use for distance. For example, if we have a 1024×1280 display and we use standard integers for the depth calculation, we can use a 1024×1280 z-buffer with 32-bit elements. Initially, each element in the depth buffer is initialized to a depth corresponding to the maximum distance away from the center of projection.[6] The color buffer is initialized to the background color. At any time during rasterization and fragment processing,

---

6. If we have already done perspective normalization, we should replace the center of projection with the direction of projection because all rays are parallel. However, this change does not affect the z-buffer algorithm, because we can measure distances from any arbitrary plane, such as the plane $z = 0$, rather than from the COP.

each location in the z-buffer contains the distance along the ray corresponding to the location of the closest intersection point on any polygon found so far.

The calculation proceeds as follows. We rasterize, polygon by polygon, using one of the methods from Section 8.10. For each fragment on the polygon corresponding to the intersection of the polygon with a ray through a pixel, we compute the depth from the center of projection. We compare this depth to the value in the z-buffer corresponding to this fragment. If this depth is greater than the depth in the z-buffer, then we have already processed a polygon with a corresponding fragment closer to the viewer, and this fragment is not visible. If the depth is less than the depth in the z-buffer,[7] then we have found a fragment closer to the viewer. We update the depth in the z-buffer and place the shade computed for this fragment at the corresponding location in the color buffer. Note that for perspective views, the depth we are using in the z-buffer algorithm is the distance that has been altered by the normalization transformation that we discussed in Chapter 4. Although this transformation is nonlinear, it preserves relative distances. However, this nonlinearity can introduce numerical inaccuracies, especially when the distance to the near clipping plane is small.

Unlike other aspects of rendering where the particular implementation algorithms may be unknown to the user, for hidden-surface removal, WebGL uses the z-buffer algorithm. This exception arises because the application program must initialize the z-buffer explicitly every time a new image is to be generated.

The z-buffer algorithm works well with image-oriented approaches to implementation because the amount of incremental work is small. Suppose that we are rasterizing a polygon, scan line by scan line—an option we examined in Section 8.10. The polygon is part of a plane (Figure 8.50) that can be represented as

$$ax + by + cz + d = 0.$$

Suppose that (x_1, y_1, z_1) and (x_2, y_2, z_2) are two points on the polygon (and the plane). If

$$\Delta x = x_2 - x_1$$

$$\Delta y = y_2 - y_1$$

$$\Delta z = z_2 - z_1,$$

then the equation for the plane can be written in differential form as

$$a\Delta x + b\Delta y + c\Delta z = 0.$$

This equation is in window coordinates, so each scan line corresponds to a line of constant y and $\Delta y = 0$ as we move across a scan line. On a scan line, we increase x in unit steps, corresponding to moving one pixel in the framebuffer, and Δx is constant.

---

7. In WebGL, we can use the function `gl.depthFunc` to decide what to do when the distances are equal.

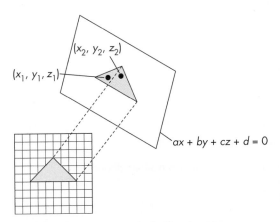

FIGURE 8.50   Incremental z-buffer algorithm.

Thus, as we move from point to point across a scan line,

$$\Delta z = -\frac{a}{c}\Delta x.$$

This value is a constant that needs to be computed only once for each polygon.

   Although the worst-case performance of an image-space algorithm is proportional to the number of primitives, the performance of the z-buffer algorithm is proportional to the number of fragments generated by rasterization, which depends on the area of the rasterized polygons.

8.11.6 Scan Conversion with the z-Buffer

We have already presented most of the essentials of polygon rasterization. In Section 8.10.1, we discussed the odd–even and winding tests for determining whether a point is inside a polygon. In Chapter 6, we learned to shade polygons by interpolation. Here we have only to put together the pieces and to consider efficiency.

   Suppose that we follow the pipeline once more, concentrating on what happens to a single polygon. The vertices and normals pass through the geometric transformations one at a time. The vertices must be assembled into a polygon before the clipping stage. If our polygon is not clipped out, its vertices and normals can be passed on for shading and hidden-surface removal. At this point, although projection normalization has taken place, we still have depth information. If we wish to use an interpolative shading method, we can compute the lighting at each vertex.

   Three tasks remain: computation of the final orthographic projection, hidden-surface removal, and shading. Careful use of the z-buffer algorithm can accomplish all three tasks simultaneously. Consider the dual representations of a polygon illustrated in Figure 8.51. In panel (a), the polygon is represented in three-dimensional normalized device coordinates; in panel (b), it is shown after projection in screen coordinates.

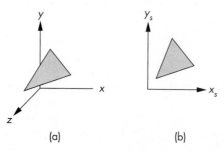

FIGURE 8.51   Dual representations of a polygon. (a) Normalized device coordinates. (b) Screen coordinates.

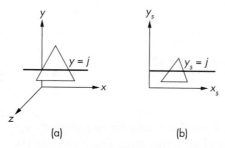

FIGURE 8.52   Dual representations of a scan line. (a) In normalized device coordinates. (b) In screen coordinates.

The strategy is to process each polygon, one scan line at a time. If we work again in terms of these dual representations, we can see that a scan line, projected backward from screen coordinates, corresponds to a line of constant y in normalized device coordinates (Figure 8.52). Suppose that we simultaneously march across this scan line and its back projection. For the scan line in screen coordinates, we move one pixel width with each step. We use the normalized-device-coordinate line to determine depths incrementally and to see whether or not the pixel in screen coordinates corresponds to a visible point on the polygon. Having computed shading for the vertices of the original polygon, we can use interpolation to obtain the correct color for visible pixels. This process requires little extra effort over the individual steps that we have already discussed. It is controlled, and thus limited, by the rate at which we can send polygons through the pipeline. Modifications such as applying bit patterns, called stipple patterns, or texture to polygons require only slight changes.

8.11.7 Depth Sort and the Painter's Algorithm

Although image-space methods are dominant in hardware due to the efficiency and ease of implementation of the z-buffer algorithm, often object-space methods are used within the application to lower the polygon count. **Depth sort** is a direct implementation of the object-space approach to hidden-surface removal. We present the algorithm for a scene composed of planar polygons; extensions to other classes of ob-

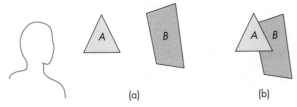

FIGURE 8.53   Painter's algorithm. (a) Two polygons and a viewer are shown.
(b) Polygon *A* partially obscures *B* when viewed.

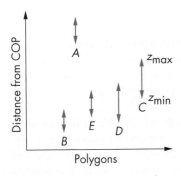

FIGURE 8.54   The *z* extents of sorted polygons.

jects are possible. Depth sort is a variant of an even simpler algorithm known as the
painter's algorithm.

Suppose that we have a collection of polygons that is sorted based on their
distance from the viewer. For the example in Figure 8.53(a), we have two polygons. To
a viewer, they appear as shown in Figure 8.53(b), with the polygon in front partially
obscuring the other. To render the scene correctly, we could find the part of the
rear polygon that is visible and render that part into the framebuffer—a calculation
that requires clipping one polygon against the other. Or we could use an approach
analogous to the way a painter might render the scene. She probably would paint
the rear polygon in its entirety and then the front polygon, painting over that part
of the rear polygon not visible to the viewer in the process. Both polygons would be
rendered completely, with the hidden-surface removal being done as a consequence
of the **back-to-front rendering** of the polygons.[8] The two questions related to this
algorithm are how to do the sort and what to do if polygons overlap. Depth sort
addresses both, although in many applications additional efficiencies can be found
(see, for example, Exercise 8.10).

Suppose we have already computed the extent of each polygon. The next step
of depth sort is to order all the polygons by their maximum *z* distance from the
viewer. This step gives the algorithm the name *depth sort*. Suppose that the order is
as shown in Figure 8.54, which depicts the *z* extents of the polygons after the sort. If

---

8. In ray tracing and scientific visualization, we often use *front-to-back rendering* of polygons.

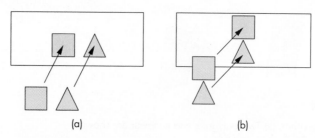

FIGURE 8.55   Test for overlap in x and y extents. (a) Nonoverlapping x extents. (b) Nonoverlapping y extents.

FIGURE 8.56   Polygons with overlapping extents.

FIGURE 8.57   Cyclic overlap.

FIGURE 8.58   Piercing polygons.

the minimum depth—the z value—of a given polygon is greater than the maximum depth of the polygon behind the one of interest, we can paint the polygons back-to-front and we are done. For example, polygon A in Figure 8.54 is behind all the other polygons and can be painted first. However, the others cannot be painted based solely on the z extents.

If the z extents of two polygons overlap, we still may be able to find an order to paint (render) the polygons individually and yield the correct image. The depth-sort algorithm runs a number of increasingly more difficult tests, attempting to find such an ordering. Consider a pair of polygons whose z extents overlap. The simplest test is to check their x and y extents (Figure 8.55). If either of the x or y extents do not overlap,[9] neither polygon can obscure the other and they can be painted in either order. Even if these tests fail, it may still be possible to find an order in which we can paint the polygons individually. Figure 8.56 shows such a case. All the vertices of one polygon lie on the same side of the plane determined by the other. We can process the vertices (see Exercise 8.12) of the two polygons to determine whether this case exists.

Two troublesome situations remain. If three or more polygons overlap cyclically, as shown in Figure 8.57, there is no correct order for painting. The best we can do is to divide at least one of the polygons into two parts and attempt to find an order to paint the new set of polygons. The second problematic case arises if a polygon can pierce another polygon, as shown in Figure 8.58. If we want to continue with depth sort, we must derive the details of the intersection—a calculation equivalent to clipping one polygon against the other. If the intersecting polygons have many vertices, we may want to try another algorithm that requires less computation. A performance analysis of depth sort is difficult because the particulars of the application determine how often the more difficult cases arise. For example, if we are working with polygons that describe the surfaces of solid objects, then no two polygons can intersect. Nevertheless, it should be clear that, because of the initial sort, the complexity must be at least $O(k \log k)$, where k is the number of objects.

---

9. The x and y extent tests apply to only a parallel view. Here is another example of the advantage of working in normalized device coordinates *after* perspective normalization.

8.12 ANTIALIASING

Rasterized line segments and edges of polygons look jagged. Even on a display device that has a resolution as high as 1024×1280, we can notice these defects in the display. This type of error arises whenever we attempt to go from the continuous representation of an object, which has infinite resolution, to a sampled approximation, which has limited resolution. The name **aliasing** has been given to this effect because of the tie with aliasing in digital signal processing.

Aliasing errors are caused by three related problems with the discrete nature of the framebuffer. First, if we have an $n \times m$ framebuffer, the number of pixels is fixed, and we can generate only certain patterns to approximate a line segment. Many different continuous line segments may be approximated by the same pattern of pixels. We can say that all these segments are **aliased** as the same sequence of pixels. Given the sequence of pixels, we cannot tell which line segment generated the sequence. Second, pixel locations are fixed on a uniform grid; regardless of where we would like to place pixels, we cannot place them at other than evenly spaced locations. Third, pixels have a fixed size and shape.

At first glance, it might appear that there is little we can do about such problems. Algorithms such as Bresenham's algorithm are optimal in that they choose the closest set of pixels to approximate lines and polygons. However, if we have a display that supports more than two colors, there are other possibilities. Although mathematical lines are one-dimensional entities that have length but not width, rasterized lines must have a width in order to be visible. Suppose that each pixel is displayed as a square of width 1 unit and can occupy a box of 1-unit height and width on the display. Our basic framebuffer can work only in multiples of one pixel;[10] we can think of an idealized line segment in the framebuffer as being one pixel wide, as shown in Figure 8.59. Of course, we cannot draw this line because it does not consist of our square pixels. We can view Bresenham's algorithm as a method for approximating the ideal one-pixel-wide line with real pixels. If we look at the ideal one-pixel-wide line, we can see that it partially covers many pixel-sized boxes. It is our scan conversion algorithm that forces us, for lines of slope less than 1, to choose exactly one pixel value for each value of x. If, instead, we shade each pixel by the percentage of the ideal line that crosses it, we get the smoother-appearing image shown in Figure 8.60(b). This technique is known as **antialiasing by area averaging**. The calculation is similar to polygon clipping. There are other approaches to antialiasing, as well as antialiasing algorithms that can be applied to other primitives, such as polygons. Color Plate 8 shows aliased and antialiased versions of a small area of the object in Color Plate 1.

A related problem arises because of the simple way that we are using the z-buffer algorithm. As we have specified that algorithm, the color of a given pixel is determined by the shade of a single primitive. Consider the pixel shared by the

FIGURE 8.59   Ideal raster line.

---

10. Some framebuffers permit operations in units of less than one pixel through multisampling methods.

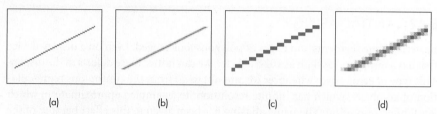

FIGURE 8.60   Aliased versus antialiased line segments. (a) Aliased line segment. (b) Antialiased line segment. (c) Magnified aliased line segment. (d) Magnified antialiased line segment.

FIGURE 8.61   Polygons that share a pixel.

three polygons shown in Figure 8.61. If each polygon has a different color, the color assigned to the pixel is the one associated with the polygon closest to the viewer. We could obtain a much more accurate image if we could assign a color based on an area-weighted average of the colors of the three triangles.

We have discussed only one type of aliasing: **spatial domain aliasing**. When we generate sequences of images, such as for animations, we also must be concerned with **time domain aliasing**. Consider a small object moving in front of the projection plane that has been ruled into pixel-sized units, as shown in Figure 8.62. If our rendering process sends a ray through the center of each pixel and determines what it hits, then sometimes we intersect the object and sometimes, if the projection of the object is small, we miss the object. The viewer will have the unpleasant experience of seeing the object flash on and off the display as the animation progresses.

Both time domain and spatial domain aliasing arise because we do not take sufficient samples for the content of the image. The theory behind sampling and aliasing is discussed in Appendix D. There are several ways to deal with aliasing problems that are now supported by most GPUs and APIs, including WebGL. The two most popular approaches are multisampling and **supersampling**. We introduced multisampling in Section 7.10.6 as a blending technique for antialiasing. Supersampling is conceptually somewhat similar but creates a framebuffer with a resolution 2, 4, or 8 times that of the color buffer we display. We can do so with an off-screen buffer and render into this high-resolution buffer. At the end of the rendering, for each pixel in the color

FIGURE 8.62   Time-domain aliasing.

buffer we use an average of the 4, 16, or 64 corresponding pixels in the off-screen buffer.

Image-based renderers use similar approaches. For example, with a ray tracer we can cast multiple rays per pixel. What is common to all antialiasing techniques is that they require considerably more computation than does rendering without antialiasing, although with hardware support in the GPU, the penalty can be minimal.

8.13 DISPLAY CONSIDERATIONS

In most interactive applications, the application programmer need not worry about how the contents of the framebuffer are displayed. From the application programmer's perspective, as long as she uses double buffering, the process of writing into the framebuffer is decoupled from the process of reading the framebuffer's contents for display. The hardware redisplays the present contents of the framebuffer at a rate sufficient to avoid flicker—usually 60 to 85 Hz—and the application programmer worries only about whether or not her program can fill the framebuffer fast enough. As we saw in Chapter 3, the use of double buffering allows the display to change smoothly, even if we cannot push our primitives through the system as fast as we would like.

Numerous other problems affect the quality of the display and often cause users to be unhappy with the output of their programs. For example, the displays of two monitors may have the same nominal resolution but may display pixels of different sizes (see Exercises 8.22 and 8.23).

Perhaps the greatest source of problems with displays concerns the basic physical properties of displays: the range of colors they can display and how they map software-defined colors to the values of the primaries for the display. The color gamuts of different displays can differ greatly. In addition, because the primaries on various systems are different, even when two different monitors can produce the same visible color, they may require different values of the primaries to be sent to the displays from the graphics system. In addition, the mapping between brightness values defined by the program and what is displayed is nonlinear.

WebGL does not address these issues directly, because colors are specified as RGB values that are independent of any display properties. In addition, because RGB primaries are limited to the range 0.0 to 1.0, it is often difficult to account for the full range of color and brightness detectable by the human visual system. However, if we expand on our discussion of color and the human visual system from Chapter 2, we can gain some additional control over color in WebGL.

8.13.1 Color Systems

Our basic assumption about color, supported by the three-color theory of human vision, is that the three color values that we determine for each pixel correspond to the tristimulus values that we introduced in Chapter 2. Thus, a given color is a point in a color cube, as in Figure 8.63, and can be written symbolically as

$$C = T_1\mathbf{R} + T_2\mathbf{G} + T_3\mathbf{B}.$$

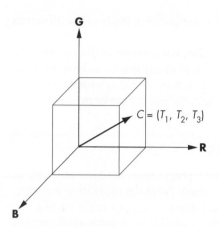

FIGURE 8.63 Color cube.

However, there are significant differences across RGB systems. For example, suppose that we have a yellow color that WebGL has represented with the RGB triplet (0.8, 0.6, 0.0). If we use these values to drive both a CRT and a film image recorder, we will see different colors, even though in both cases the red is 80 percent of maximum, the green is 60 percent of maximum, and there is no blue. The reason is that the film dyes and the CRT phosphors have different color distributions. Consequently, the range of displayable colors (or the color **gamut**) is different for each.

In the graphics community, the emphasis has been on device-independent graphics; consequently, the real differences among display properties are not addressed by most APIs. Fortunately, the colorimetry literature contains the information we need. Standards for many of the common color systems exist. For example, CRTs are based on the National Television Systems Committee (NTSC) RGB system. We can look at differences in color systems as being equivalent to different coordinate systems for representing our tristimulus values. If $\mathbf{C}_1 = [R_1, G_1, B_1]^T$ and $\mathbf{C}_2 = [R_2, G_2, B_2]^T$ are the representations of the same color in two different systems, then there is a 3×3 color conversion matrix $\mathbf{M}$ such that

$$\mathbf{C}_2 = \mathbf{M}\mathbf{C}_1.$$

Whether we determine this matrix from the literature or by experimentation, it allows us to produce similar displays on different output devices.

There are numerous potential problems even with this approach. The color gamuts of the two systems may not be the same. Hence, even after the conversion of tristimulus values, a color may not be producible on one of the systems. Second, the printing and graphic arts industries use a four-color subtractive system (CMYK) that adds black (K) as a fourth primary. Conversion between RGB and CMYK often requires a great deal of human expertise. Third, there are limitations to our linear color theory. The distance between colors in the color cube is not a measure of how far apart the colors are perceptually. For example, humans are particularly sensitive to color shifts in blue. Color systems such as YUV and CIE Lab have been created to address such issues.

Most RGB color systems are based on the primaries in real systems, such as CRT phosphors and film dyes. None can produce all the colors that we can see. Most color standards are based on a theoretical three-primary system called the **XYZ color system**. Here, the Y primary is the luminance of the color. In the XYZ system, all colors can be specified with positive tristimulus values. We use 3×3 matrices to convert from an XYZ color representation to representations in the standard systems. Color specialists often prefer to work with **chromaticity coordinates** rather than tristimulus values. The chromaticity of a color consists of the three fractions of the color in the three primaries. Thus, if we have the tristimulus values T_1, T_2, and T_3, for a particular RGB color, its chromaticity coordinates are

$$t_1 = \frac{T_1}{T_1 + T_2 + T_3}$$

$$t_2 = \frac{T_2}{T_1 + T_2 + T_3}$$

$$t_3 = \frac{T_3}{T_1 + T_2 + T_3}.$$

Adding the three equations, we have

$$t_1 + t_2 + t_3 = 1,$$

and thus we can work in the two-dimensional t_1, t_2 space, finding t_3 only when its value is needed. The information that is missing from chromaticity coordinates, which was contained in the original tristimulus values, is the sum $T_1 + T_2 + T_3$, a value related to the intensity of the color. When working with color systems, this intensity is often not important to issues related to producing colors or matching colors across different systems.

Because each color fraction must be nonnegative, the chromaticity values are limited by

$$1 \geq t_i \geq 0.$$

All producible colors must lie inside the triangle in Figure 8.64. Figure 8.65 shows this triangle for the XYZ system and a curve of the representation for each visible spectral line. For the XYZ system, this curve must lie inside the triangle. Figure 8.65 also shows the range of colors (in x, y chromaticity coordinates) that are producible on a typical color printer or CRT. If we compare the two figures, we see that the colors inside the curve of pure spectral lines but outside the gamut of the physical display cannot be displayed on the physical device.

One defect of our development of color is that RGB color is based on how color is produced and measured rather than on how we perceive color. When we see a given color, we describe it not by three primaries but based on other properties, such as the name we give the color and how bright a shade we see. The hue-lightness-saturation

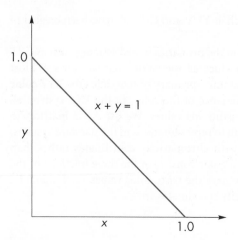

FIGURE 8.64   Triangle of producible colors in chromaticity coordinates.

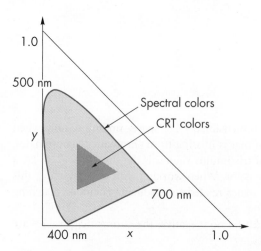

FIGURE 8.65   Visible colors and color gamut of a display.

(HLS) system is used by artists and some display manufacturers. The **hue** is the name we give to a color: red, yellow, gold. The **lightness** is how bright the color appears. **Saturation** is the color attribute that distinguishes a pure shade of a color from a shade of the same hue that has been mixed with white, forming a pastel shade. We can relate these attributes to a typical RGB color, as shown in Figure 8.66(a). Given a color in the color cube, the lightness is a measure of how far the point is from the origin (black). If we note that all the colors on the principal diagonal of the cube, going from black to white, are shades of gray and are totally unsaturated, then the saturation is a measure of how far the given color is from this diagonal. Finally, the hue is a measure of where the color vector is pointing. HLS colors are usually described in terms of a

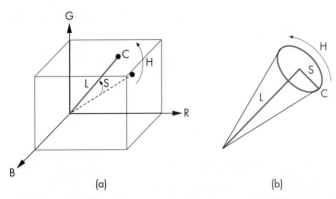

FIGURE 8.66 Hue-lightness-saturation color. (a) Using the RGB color cube. (b) Using a single cone.

color cone, as shown in Figure 8.66(b), or a double cone that also converges at the top. From our perspective, we can look at the HLS system as providing a representation of an RGB color in polar coordinates.

8.13.2 The Color Matrix

RGB colors and RGBA colors can be manipulated as any other vector type. In particular, we can alter their components by multiplying by a matrix we call the **color matrix**. For example, if we use an RGBA color representation, the matrix multiplication converts a color, *rgba*, to a new color, $r'g'b'a'$, by the matrix multiplication

$$
\begin{bmatrix} r' \\ g' \\ b' \\ a' \end{bmatrix} = \mathbf{C} \begin{bmatrix} r \\ g \\ b \\ a \end{bmatrix}.
$$

Thus, if we are dealing with opaque surfaces for which $A = 1$, the matrix

$$
\mathbf{C} = \begin{bmatrix} -1 & 0 & 0 & 1 \\ 0 & -1 & 0 & 1 \\ 0 & 0 & -1 & 1 \\ 0 & 0 & 0 & 1 \end{bmatrix}
$$

converts the additive representation of a color to its subtractive representation.

8.13.3 Gamma Correction

In Chapter 1, we defined brightness as perceived intensity and observed that the human visual system perceives intensity in a logarithmic manner, as depicted in Figure 8.67. One consequence of this property is that if we want the brightness steps to appear to be uniformly spaced, the intensities that we assign to pixels should

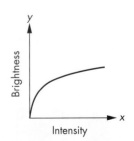

FIGURE 8.67 Logarithmic brightness.

increase exponentially. These steps can be calculated from the measured minimum and maximum intensities that a display can generate.

With CRT displays, compensation for the human's brightness curve was automatic because the intensity I of a CRT is related to the voltage V applied by

$$I \propto V^{\gamma}$$

or

$$\log I = c_0 + \gamma \log V.$$

For CRTs the constant γ is approximately 2.4, so combining this function with the brightness intensity curve yields an approximately linear brightness response.

There is an additional problem with CRTs. It is not possible to have a CRT whose display is totally black when no signal is applied. The minimum displayed intensity is called the **dark field** value and can be problematic, especially when multiple CRTs are used to project images.

Flat-panel displays can adjust their response curves by allowing the user to change the gamma by the use of lookup tables. This is called **gamma correction**. The choice of a proper gamma is complicated not only by the particular display technology but also by factors such as the ambient light under which the display is viewed. In addition, images such as JPEGs are gamma-encoded by applying a gamma to the RGB components, which is then undone by the corresponding gamma correction using the inverse of the encoding gamma. However, the system that produces the image may use a different gamma than the one on which the image is displayed, thus further complicating the process. In addition, when we generate texture images, we may want to gamma-encode them before we apply them to an object, adding another level of complexity to the display process.

One color system that is focused on display devices such as computer displays and printers is the sRGB color space. It is based on a gamma of 2.2 for the display for most of the RGB values, but for lower values it increases the inverse gamma, resulting in brighter images when displayed. sRGB is now supported by most systems, including WebGL, and is becoming standard for the Internet.

8.13.4 Dithering and Halftoning

We have specified a color buffer by its spatial resolution (the number of pixels) and by its precision (the number of colors it can display). If we view these separate numbers as fixed, we say that a high-resolution black-and-white laser printer can display only 1-bit pixels. This argument also seems to imply that any black-and-white medium, such as a book, cannot display images with multiple shades. We know from experience that this is not the case; the trick is to trade spatial resolution for grayscale or color precision. **Halftoning** techniques in the printing industry use photographic means to simulate gray levels by creating patterns of black dots of varying size. The human visual system tends to merge small dots together and sees not the dots but rather an intensity proportional to the ratio of white to black in a small area.

Digital halftones differ because the size and location of displayed pixels are fixed. Consider a 4×4 group of 1-bit pixels, as shown in Figure 8.68. If we look at this pattern from far away, we see not the individual pixels but a gray level based on

FIGURE 8.68   Digital halftone patterns.

the number of black pixels. For our 4×4 example, although there are 2^{16} different patterns of black and white pixels, there are only 17 possible shades, corresponding to 0 to 16 black pixels in the array. There are many algorithms for generating halftone, or **dither**, patterns. The simplest picks 17 patterns (for our example) and uses them to create a display with 17 rather than 2 gray levels, although at the cost of decreasing the spatial resolution by a factor of 4.

The simple algorithm—always using the same array to simulate a shade—can generate beat, or moiré, patterns when displaying anything regular. Such patterns arise whenever we image two regular phenomena, because we see the sum and differences of their frequencies. Such effects are closely related to the aliasing problems we discussed in Chapter 7.

Many dithering techniques are based on simply randomizing the least significant bit of the luminance or of each color component. More sophisticated dither algorithms use randomization to create patterns with the correct average properties but avoid the repetition that can lead to moiré effects (see Exercise 8.26).

Halftoning (or dithering) is often used with color, especially with hard-copy displays, such as ink-jet printers, that can produce only fully on or off colors. Each primary can be dithered to produce more visual colors. WebGL supports such displays and allows the user to enable dithering (`glEnable(gl.DITHER)`). Color dithering allows color monitors to produce smooth color displays, and normally dithering is enabled. Because dithering is so effective, displays could work well with a limited number of bits per color, allowing framebuffers to have a limited amount of memory. Although few displays are dithered, if you are using one then applications that read pixels such as with picking should disable dithering so as to obtain consistent values for a color.

SUMMARY AND NOTES

We have presented an overview of the implementation process, including a sampling of the most important algorithms. Regardless of what the particulars of an implementation are—whether the tasks are done primarily in hardware or in software, whether we are working with a special-purpose graphics workstation or with a simple graphics terminal, and what the API is—the same tasks must be done. These tasks include implementation of geometric transformations, clipping, and rasterization. The relationship among hardware, software, and APIs is an interesting one.

The Geometry Engine that was the basis of many Silicon Graphics workstations is a VLSI chip that performed geometric transformations and clipping through a hardware pipeline. GL, the predecessor of OpenGL, was developed as an API for users of these workstations. Much of the OpenGL literature also follows the pipeline approach. We should keep in mind, however, that WebGL is an API: It says very little about the underlying implementation. In principle, an image defined by a WebGL program could be obtained from a ray tracer. We should carry away two lessons from our emphasis on pipeline architectures. First, this architecture provides an aid to the application programmer in understanding the process of creating images. Second, at present, the pipeline view can lead to efficient hardware and software implementations.

The example of the z-buffer algorithm is illustrative of the relationship between hardware and software. Fifteen years ago, many hidden-surface-removal algorithms were used, of which the z-buffer algorithm was only one. The availability of fast, dense, inexpensive memory has made the z-buffer algorithm the dominant method for hidden-surface removal.

A related example is that of workstation architectures, where special-purpose graphics chips have made remarkable advances in just the past few years. Not only has graphics performance increased at a rate that exceeds Moore's law, but many new features have become available in the graphics processors. The whole approach we have taken in this book is based on these architectures.

So what does the future hold? Certainly, graphics systems will get faster and less expensive. More than any other factor, advances in hardware probably will dictate what future graphics systems look like. At present, hardware development is being driven by the video game industry. For less than $100, we can purchase a graphics card that exceeds the performance of graphics workstations that a few years ago would have cost more than $100,000. The features and performance of these cards are optimized for the needs of the computer game industry. Thus, we do not see uniform speedups in the various graphics functions that we have presented. In addition, new hardware features are appearing far faster than they can be incorporated into standard APIs. However, the speed at which these processors operate has challenged both the graphics and scientific communities to discover new algorithms to solve problems that until now had always been solved using conventional architectures.

On the software side, the low cost and speed of recent hardware has enabled software developers to produce rendering software that allows users to balance rendering time and quality of rendering. Hence, a user can add some ray-traced objects to a scene, the number depending on how long she is willing to wait for the rendering. The future of standard APIs is much less clear. On one hand, users in the scientific community prefer stable APIs so that application code will have a long lifetime. On the other hand, users want to exploit new hardware features that are not supported on all systems. OpenGL has tried to take a middle road. Until OpenGL 3.1, all releases were backward compatible, so applications developed on earlier versions were guaranteed to run on new releases. OpenGL 3.1 and later versions deprecated many core features of earlier versions, including immediate mode rendering and most of the default behavior of the fixed-function pipeline. This major change in philosophy has allowed OpenGL to rapidly incorporate new hardware features. For those who need to run older code, almost all implementations support a compatibility extension with all the deprecated functions.

Numerous advanced architectures under exploration use massive parallelism. How parallelism can be exploited most effectively for computer graphics is still an open issue. Our two approaches to rendering—object-oriented and image-oriented—lead to two entirely different ways to develop a parallel renderer, which we shall explore further in Chapter 12.

We have barely scratched the surface of implementation. The literature is rich with algorithms for every aspect of the implementation process. The references should help you to explore this topic further.

SUGGESTED READINGS

The books by Rogers [Rog85], Foley [Foley90], and Hughes and colleagues [Hug13] contain many more algorithms than we present here. Also see the series *Graphic Gems* [Gra90, Gra91, Gra92, Gra94, Gra95] and *GPU Gems* [Ngu07, Pha05]. Books such as Möller and Haines [Mol02] and Eberly [Ebe01] cover the influence of recent advances in hardware.

The Cohen-Sutherland [Sut63] clipping algorithm goes back to the early years of computer graphics, as does Bresenham's algorithm [Bre63, Bre87], which was originally proposed for pen plotters. See [Lia84] and [Sut74a] for the Liang-Barsky and Sutherland-Hodgeman clippers.

Algorithms for triangulation can be found in references on computational geometry. See, for example, de Berg [deB08], which also discusses Delaunay triangulation, discussed in Chapter 11.

The *z*-buffer algorithm was developed by Catmull [Cat75]. See Sutherland [Sut74b] for a discussion of various approaches to hidden-surface removal.

Our decision to avoid details of the hardware does not imply that the hardware is either simple or uninteresting. The rate at which a modern graphics processor can display graphical entities requires sophisticated and clever hardware designs [Cla82, Ake88, Ake93]. The discussion by Molnar and Fuchs in [Fol90] shows a variety of approaches.

Pratt [Pra78] provides matrices to convert among various color systems. Half-tone and dithering are discussed by Jarvis [Jar76] and by Knuth [Knu87].

EXERCISES

8.1 Consider two line segments represented in parametric form:

$$\mathbf{p}(\alpha) = (1 - \alpha)\mathbf{p}_1 + \alpha\mathbf{p}_2$$

$$\mathbf{q}(\beta) = (1 - \beta)\mathbf{q}_1 + \beta\mathbf{q}_2.$$

Find a procedure for determining whether the segments intersect and, if they do, for finding the point of intersection.

8.2 Suggest a method to determine whether an entire line segment is inside the clipping window.

8.3 Prove that clipping a convex object against another convex object results in at most one convex object.

8.4 In what way can you decide which primitive will appear on the display and be passed on to the rasterizer?

8.5 Because both normals and vertices can be represented in homogeneous coordinates, both can be operated on by the model-view transformation. Show that normals may not be preserved by the transformation.

8.6   Derive the viewport transformation. Express it in terms of the three-dimensional scaling and translation matrices used to represent affine transformations in two dimensions.

8.7   Pre-raster-graphics systems were able to display only lines. Programmers produced three-dimensional images using hidden-line-removal techniques. Many current APIs allow us to produce wireframe images, composed of only lines, in which the hidden lines that define nonvisible surfaces have been removed. How does this problem differ from that of the polygon hidden-surface removal that we have considered? Derive a hidden-line-removal algorithm for objects that consist of the edges of planar polygons.

8.8   Often we display functions of the form $y = f(x, z)$ by displaying a rectangular mesh generated by the set of values $\{f(x_i, z_j)\}$ evaluated at regular intervals in x and z. Hidden-surface removal should be applied because parts of the surface can be obscured from view by other parts. Derive two algorithms, one using hidden-surface removal and the other using hidden-line removal, to display such a mesh.

8.9   Although we argued that the complexity of the image-space approach to hidden-surface removal is proportional to the number of polygons, performance studies have shown almost constant performance. Explain this result.

8.10   Consider a scene composed of only solid, three-dimensional polyhedra. Can you devise an object-space, hidden-surface-removal algorithm for this case? How much does it help if you know that all the polyhedra are convex?

8.11   We can look at object-space approaches to hidden-surface removal as analogous to sorting algorithms. However, we argued that the former's complexity is $O(k^2)$. We know that only the worst-performing sorting algorithms have such poor performance, and most are $O(k \log k)$. Does it follow that object-space, hidden-surface-removal algorithms have similar complexity? Explain your answer.

8.12   Devise a method for testing whether one planar polygon is fully on one side of another planar polygon.

8.13   What are the differences between two-dimensional clippers and three-dimensional clippers? Cohen-Sutherland algorithm uses a 6-bit outcode instead of 4-bit outcode. What is the use of these additional 2 bits? What are the advantages of the z-buffer algorithm?

8.14   Write a program to generate the locations of pixels along a rasterized line segment using Bresenham's algorithm. Check that your program works for all slopes and all possible locations of the endpoints. What is the initial value of the decision variable?

8.15   Bresenham's algorithm can be extended to circles. Convince yourself of this statement by considering a circle centered at the origin. Which parts of the circle must be generated by an algorithm and which parts can be found by symmetry? Can you find a part of the circle such that if we know a point generated by a scan conversion algorithm, we can reduce the number of candidates for the next pixel?

8.16 Show how to use a bounding box to test whether two animated objects will collide when in motion.

8.17 Suppose that you try to extend flood fill to arbitrary closed curves by scan-converting the curve and then applying the same fill algorithm that we used for polygons. What problems can arise if you use this approach?

8.18 Consider the edge of a polygon between vertices at (x_1, y_1) and (x_2, y_2). Derive an efficient algorithm for computing the intersection of all scan lines with this edge. Assume that you are working in window coordinates.

8.19 Vertical and horizontal edges are potentially problematic for polygon fill algorithms. How would you handle these cases for the algorithms that we have presented?

8.20 In two-dimensional graphics, if two polygons overlap, we can ensure that they are rendered in the same order by all implementations by associating a priority attribute with each polygon. Polygons are rendered in reverse-priority order; that is, the highest-priority polygon is rendered last. How should we modify our polygon fill algorithms to take priority into account?

8.21 A polygon-clipping algorithm can be generated directly from line-clipping algorithms by clipping the edges of the polygon successively. What is the problem of implementing such clipping? What are the different polygons that do not show such a problem?

8.22 Although an ideal pixel is a square of 1 unit per side, most CRT systems generate round pixels that can be approximated as circles of uniform intensity. If a completely full unit square has intensity 1.0 and an empty square has intensity 0.0, how does the intensity of a displayed pixel vary with the radius of the circle?

8.23 Consider a bilevel display with round pixels. Do you think it is wiser to use small circles or large circles for foreground-colored pixels? Explain your answer.

8.24 When does a system have minimum displayed intensity called "the dark field value"?

8.25 Suppose that a monochrome display has a minimum intensity output of I_{min} (a CRT display is never completely black) and a maximum output of I_{max}. Given that we perceive intensities in a logarithmic manner, how should we assign k intensity levels such that the steps appear uniform?

8.26 Generate a halftone algorithm based on the following idea. Suppose that gray levels vary from 0.0 to 1.0 and that we have a random-number generator that produces random numbers that are uniformly distributed over this interval. If we pick a gray level g, $g/100$ percent of the random numbers generated will be less than g.

8.27 Images produced on displays that support only a few colors or gray levels tend to show contour effects because the viewer can detect the differences between adjacent shades. One technique for avoiding this visual effect is to add a little noise (jitter) to the pixel values. Why does this technique work? How much noise should you add? Does it make sense to conclude that the degraded image created by the addition of noise is of higher quality than the original image?

8.28 Show that the area of a two-dimensional polygon, specified by the vertices $\{x_1, y_i\}$, is given by $\frac{1}{2} \sum_i (y_{i+1} + y_i)(x_{i+1} - x_i)$. What is the significance of a negative area? *Hint:* Consider the areas of the trapezoids formed by two successive vertices and corresponding values on the x-axis.

CHAPTER 9

MODELING AND HIERARCHY

Models are abstractions of the world—both of the real world in which we live and of virtual worlds that we create with computers. We are familiar with mathematical models that are used in all areas of science and engineering. These models use equations to model the physical phenomena that we wish to study. In computer science, we use abstract data types to model organizations of objects; in computer graphics, we model our worlds with geometric objects. When we build a mathematical model, we must choose carefully which type of mathematics fits the phenomena that we wish to model. Although ordinary differential equations may be appropriate for modeling the dynamic behavior of a system of springs and masses, we would probably use partial differential equations to model turbulent fluid flow. We go through analogous processes in computer graphics, choosing which primitives to use in our models and how to show relationships among them. Often, as is true of choosing a mathematical model, there are multiple approaches, so we seek models that can take advantage of the capabilities of our graphics systems.

In this chapter, we explore multiple approaches to developing and working with models of geometric objects. We consider models that use as building blocks a set of simple geometric objects: either the primitives supported by our graphics systems or a set of user-defined objects built from these primitives. We extend the use of transformations from Chapter 4 to include hierarchical relationships among the objects. The techniques that we develop are appropriate for applications, such as robotics and figure animation, where the dynamic behavior of the objects is characterized by relationships among the parts of the model.

The notion of hierarchy is a powerful one and is an integral part of object-oriented methodologies. We extend our hierarchical models of objects to hierarchical models of whole scenes, including cameras, lights, and material properties. Such models allow us to extend our graphics APIs to more object-oriented systems and also give us insight into using graphics over networks and distributed environments, such as the World Wide Web.

9.1 SYMBOLS AND INSTANCES

Our first concern is how we can store a model that may include many sophisticated objects. There are two immediate issues: how we define an object more complex than the ones we have dealt with until now, and how we represent a collection of these objects. Most APIs take a minimalist approach toward primitives: They contain only a few primitives, leaving it to the application to construct more complex objects from these primitives. Sometimes additional libraries provide objects built on top of the basic primitives. We assume that we have available a collection of basic three-dimensional objects provided by these sources.

We can take a nonhierarchical approach to modeling by regarding these objects as **symbols** and by modeling our world as a collection of symbols. Symbols can include geometric objects, fonts, and application-specific sets of graphical objects. Symbols are usually represented at a convenient size and orientation. For example, a cylinder is usually oriented parallel to one of the axes, as shown in Figure 9.1, often with a unit height, a unit radius, and its bottom centered at the origin.

y

x

z

FIGURE 9.1 Cylinder symbol.

Most APIs make a distinction between the frame in which the symbol is defined, which we have called the model frame, and the object or world frame. This distinction can be helpful when the symbols are purely shapes, such as the symbols that we might use for circuit elements in a CAD application, and have no physical units associated with them. In WebGL, we have to set up the transformation from the frame of the symbol to the object coordinate frame within the application. Thus, the model-view matrix for a given symbol is the concatenation of an instance transformation that brings the symbol into object coordinates and a matrix that brings the symbol into the eye frame.

The instance transformation that we introduced in Chapter 4 allows us to place instances of each symbol in the model, at the desired size, orientation, and location. Thus, the instance transformation

$$\mathbf{M} = \mathbf{TRS}$$

is a concatenation of a translation, a rotation, and a scale (and possibly a shear), as shown in Figure 9.2. Consequently, WebGL programs often contain repetitions of code of the following form:

```
var s = vec3(sx, sy, sz); // scale factors
var d = vec3(dx, dy, dz); // translation vector
var r = vec3(rx, ry, rz); // rotation angles

instanceMatrix = scale(s);
instanceMatrix = mult(instanceMatrix, rotateX(rx));
instanceMatrix = mult(instanceMatrix, rotateY(ry));
instanceMatrix = mult(instanceMatrix, rotateZ(rz));
instanceMatrix = mult(instanceMatrix, translate(instance, d));

modelViewMatrix = mult(modelViewMatrix, instanceMatrix);

cylinder(); // or some other symbol
```

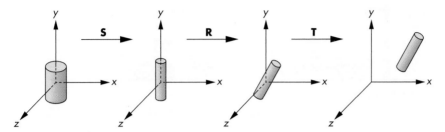

FIGURE 9.2   Instance transformation.

Symbol	Scale	Rotate	Translate
1	s_x, s_y, s_z	$\theta_x, \theta_y, \theta_z$	d_x, d_y, d_z
2			
3			
1			
1			
·			
·			

FIGURE 9.3   Symbol–instance transformation table.

In this example, the instance matrix is computed and alters the current model-view matrix. The resulting model-view matrix can be sent to the vertex shader using `gl.uniformMatrix4fv`. The code for `cylinder` generates vertices and can send them to the vertex shader using `gl.uniform`. Alternately, we can apply the model-view matrix in the application as we generate the vertices. We can also think of such a model in the form of a table, as shown in Figure 9.3. Here each symbol is assumed to have a unique numerical identifier. The table stores this identifier and the parameters necessary to build the instance transformation matrix. The table shows that this modeling technique contains no information about relationships among objects. However, the table contains all the information required to draw the objects and is thus a simple data structure or model for a group of geometric objects. We could search the table for an object, change the instance transformation for an object, and add or delete objects. However, the flatness of the representation limits us.

9.2   HIERARCHICAL MODELS

Suppose that we wish to build a model of an automobile that we can animate. As a first approximation, we can compose the model from five parts—the chassis and the four wheels (Figure 9.4)—each of which we can describe using our standard graphics primitives. Two frames of a simple animation of the model are shown in Figure 9.5. We could write a program to generate this animation by noting that if each wheel

FIGURE 9.4   Automobile model.

FIGURE 9.5   Two frames of animation.

has a radius r, then a 360-degree rotation of a wheel must correspond to the car moving forward (or backward) a distance of $2\pi r$. The program could then contain one function to generate each wheel and another to generate the chassis. All these functions could use the same input, such as the desired speed and direction of the automobile. In pseudocode, our program might look like this:

```
main()
{
  var s; // speed
  var d = new Array(3); // direction
  var t; // time

  // Determine speed and direction at time t

  drawRightFrontWheel(s, d);
  drawLeftFrontWheel(s, d);
  drawRightRearWheel(s, d);
  drawLeftRearWheel(s, d);
  drawChassis(s, d);
}
```

This program is just the kind that we do *not* want to write. It is linear and it shows none of the relationships among the components of the automobile. There are two types of relationships that we would like to exploit. First, we cannot separate the movement of the car from the movement of the wheels. If the car moves forward, the wheels must turn.[1] Second, we would like to use the fact that all the wheels of the automobile are identical; they are merely located in different places, with different orientations.

We can represent the relationships among parts of the models, both abstractly and visually, with graphs. Mathematically, a **graph** consists of a set of **nodes** (or vertices) and a set of **edges**. Edges connect pairs of nodes or possibly connect a node to itself. Edges can have a direction associated with them; the graphs we use here are all **directed graphs**, which are graphs that have their edges leaving one node and entering another.

---

1. It is not clear whether we should say the wheels move the chassis, as in a real car, or the chassis moves the wheels, as when a child pushes a toy car. From a graphics perspective, the latter view is probably more useful.

FIGURE 9.6   Tree structure for an automobile.

The most important type of graph we use is a tree. A (connected) **tree** is a directed graph without closed paths or loops. In addition, each node but one—the **root node**—has one edge entering it. Thus, every node except the root has a **parent node**, the node from which an edge enters, and can have one or more **child nodes**, nodes to which edges are connected. A node without children is called a **leaf** or **terminal node**. Figure 9.6 shows a tree that represents the relationships in our car model. The chassis is the root node, and all four wheels are its children. Although a mathematical graph is a collection of set elements, in practice, both the edges and nodes can contain additional information. For our car example, each node can contain information defining the geometric objects associated with it. The information about the location and orientation of the wheels can be stored either in their nodes or in the edges connecting them with their parent.

In most cars the four wheels are identical, so storing the same information on how to draw each one in four nodes is inefficient. We can use the ideas behind the instance transformation to allow us to use a single prototype wheel in our model. If we do so, we can replace the tree structure by the **directed acyclic graph** (**DAG**) in Figure 9.7. Because a DAG has no loops, if we follow any path of directed edges from a node, the path terminates at another node, and in practice, working with DAGs is no more difficult than with trees. For our car, we can store the information that positions each instance of the single prototype wheel in the chassis node, in the wheel node, or with the edges.

Both forms—trees and DAGs—are **hierarchical** methods of expressing the relationships in the physical model. In each form, various elements of a model can be related to other parts—their parents and their children. We will explore how to express these hierarchies in a graphics program.

FIGURE 9.7   Directed-acyclic-graph (DAG) model of an automobile.

9.3   A ROBOT ARM

Robotics provides many opportunities for developing hierarchical models. Consider the simple robot arm illustrated in Figure 9.8(a). We can model it with three simple objects, or symbols, perhaps using only two parallelepipeds and a cylinder. Each of the symbols can be built up from our basic primitives.

The robot arm consists of the three parts shown in Figure 9.8(b). The mechanism has three degrees of freedom, two of which can be described by **joint angles** between

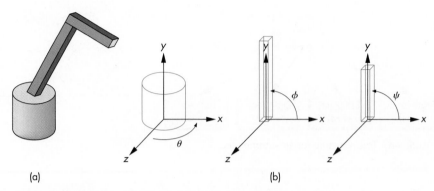

FIGURE 9.8   Robot arm. (a) Total model. (b) Components.

components and the third by the angle the base makes with respect to a fixed point on the ground. In our model, each joint angle determines how to position a component with respect to the component to which it is attached, or, in the case of the base, the joint angle positions it relative to the surrounding environment. Each joint angle is measured in each component's own frame. We can rotate the base about its vertical axis by an angle θ. This angle is measured from the x-axis to some fixed point on the bottom of the base. The lower arm of the robot is attached to the base by a joint that allows the arm to rotate in the plane $z = 0$ in the arm's frame. This rotation is specified by an angle ϕ that is measured from the x-axis to the arm. The upper arm is attached to the lower arm by a similar joint, and it can rotate by an angle ψ, measured like that for the lower arm, in its own frame. As the angles vary, we can think of the frames of the upper and lower arms as moving relative to the base. By controlling the three angles, we can position the tip of the upper arm in three dimensions.

Suppose we wish to write a program to render our simple robot model. Rather than specifying each part of the robot and its motion independently, we take an incremental approach. The base of the robot can rotate about the y-axis in its frame by the angle θ. Thus, we can describe the motion of any point $\mathbf{p}$ on the base by applying a rotation matrix $\mathbf{R}_y(\theta)$ to it.

The lower arm is rotated about the z-axis in its own frame, but this frame must be shifted to the top of the base by a translation matrix $\mathbf{T}(0, h_1, 0)$, where h_1 is the height above the ground to the point where the joint between the base and the lower arm is located. However, if the base has rotated, then we must also rotate the lower arm, using $\mathbf{R}_y(\theta)$. We can accomplish the positioning of the lower arm by applying $\mathbf{R}_y(\theta)\,\mathbf{T}(0, h_1, 0)\,\mathbf{R}_z(\phi)$ to the arm's vertices. We can interpret the matrix $\mathbf{R}_y(\theta)\mathbf{T}(0, h_1, 0)$ as the matrix that positions the lower arm *relative* to the object frame and $\mathbf{R}_z(\phi)$ as the matrix that positions the lower arm *relative* to the base. Equivalently, we can interpret these matrices as positioning the frames of the lower arm and base relative to the object frame, as shown in Figure 9.9.

When we apply similar reasoning to the upper arm, we find that this arm has to be translated by a matrix $\mathbf{T}(0, h_2, 0)$ relative to the lower arm and then rotated by $\mathbf{R}_z(\psi)$. The matrix that controls the upper arm is thus $\mathbf{R}_y(\theta)\,\mathbf{T}(0, h_1, 0)\,\mathbf{R}_z(\phi)\,\mathbf{T}(0,$

FIGURE 9.9   Movement of robot components and frames.

h_2, 0) $\mathbf{R}_z(\psi)$. The form of the display function for a WebGL program to display the robot as a function of the joint angles (using the array `theta[3]` for θ, ϕ, and ψ) shows how we can alter the model-view matrix incrementally to display the various parts of the model efficiently:

```
function render()
{
  gl.clear(gl.COLOR_BUFFER_BIT | gl.DEPTH_BUFFER_BIT);

  modelViewMatrix = rotate(theta[Base], 0, 1, 0);
  base();

  modelViewMatrix = mult(modelViewMatrix,
                     translate(0.0, BASE_HEIGHT, 0.0));
  modelViewMatrix = mult(modelViewMatrix,
                     rotate(theta[LowerArm], 0, 0, 1));
  lowerArm();

  modelViewMatrix  = mult(modelViewMatrix,
                     translate(0.0, LOWER_ARM_HEIGHT, 0.0));
  modelViewMatrix  = mult(modelViewMatrix,
                     rotate(theta[UpperArm], 0, 0, 1));
  upperArm();

  requestAnimFrame(render);
}
```

Note that we have described the positioning of the arm independently of the details of the individual parts. As long as the positions of the joints do not change, we can alter the form of the robot by changing only the functions that draw the three parts. This separation makes it possible to write separate functions to describe the components and to animate the robot. Figure 9.10 shows the relationships among the parts of the robot arm as a tree. The complete program on the website implements the structure and allows you to animate the robot with the mouse through a menu. It uses three parallelepipeds for the base and arms. In each case, the instance transformation must scale the cube to the desired size, and because the cube vertices are centered at the origin, each cube must be raised to have its bottom in the plane $y = 0$. The product of the model-view and instance transformations is sent to the vertex shader followed by the vertices (and colors if desired) for each part of the robot. Because the model-view matrix is different for each part of the robot, we render each part once its data have sent to the GPU. Note that in this example, because we are using cubes for all the parts, we need to send the points to the GPU only once. However, if the parts were using different symbols, then we would need to use `gl.drawArrays` in each drawing function.

Returning to the tree in Figure 9.10, we can look at it as a tree data structure of nodes and edges—as a graph. If we store all the necessary information in the nodes, rather than in the edges, then each node (Figure 9.11) must contain at least three items:

FIGURE 9.10   Tree structure for the robot arm in Figure 9.8.

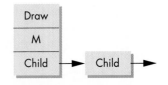

FIGURE 9.11   Node representation.

- A pointer to a function that draws the object represented by the node
- A homogeneous-coordinate matrix that positions, scales, and orients this node (and its children) relative to the node's parent
- Pointers to children of the node

Certainly, we can include other information in a node, such as a set of attributes (color, texture, material properties) that applies to the node. Drawing an object described by such a tree requires performing a tree **traversal**. That is, we must visit every node; at each node, we must compute the matrix that applies to the primitives pointed to by the node and must display these primitives. Our WebGL program shows an incremental approach to this traversal.

This example is a simple one: There is only a single child for each of the parent nodes in the tree. The next example shows how we handle more complex models.

FIGURE 9.12   A humanoid figure.

9.4   TREES AND TRAVERSAL

Figure 9.12 shows a boxlike representation of a humanoid that might be used for a robot model or in a virtual reality application. If we take the torso as the root element, we can represent this figure with the tree shown in Figure 9.13. Once we have positioned the torso, the position and orientation of the other parts of the model are determined by the set of joint angles. We can animate the figure by defining the motion of its joints. In a basic model, the knee and elbow joints might each have only a single degree of freedom, like the robot arm, whereas the joint at the neck might have two or three degrees of freedom.

Let's assume that we have functions, such as `head` and `leftUpperArm`, that draw the individual parts (symbols) in their own frames. We can now build a set of nodes for our tree by defining matrices that position each part relative to its parent, exactly as we did for the robot arm. If we assume that each body part has been defined at the desired size, each of these matrices is the concatenation of a translation matrix with a rotation matrix. We can show these matrices, as we do in Figure 9.14, by using

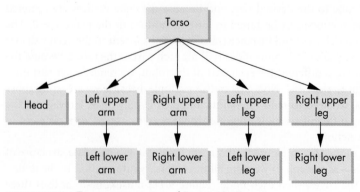

FIGURE 9.13   Tree representation of Figure 10.12.

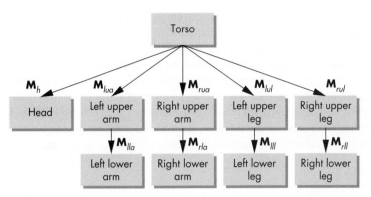

FIGURE 9.14   Tree with matrices.

the matrices to label the edges of the tree. Remember that each matrix represents the incremental change when we go from the parent to the child.

The interesting part of this example is how we perform the traversal of the tree to draw the figure. In principle, we could use any tree traversal algorithm, such as a depth-first or breadth-first search. Although in many applications it is insignificant which traversal algorithm is used, we will see that there are good reasons for always using the same algorithm for traversing our graphs. We will always traverse our trees left to right, depth first. That is, we start with the left branch, follow it to the left as deep as we can go, then go back up to the first right branch, and proceed recursively. This order of traversal is called a **preorder traversal**.

We can write a tree traversal function in one of two ways. We can do the traversal explicitly in the application code, using stacks to store the required matrices and attributes as we move through the tree. We can also do the traversal recursively. In this second approach, the code is simpler because the storage of matrices and attributes is done implicitly. We develop both approaches because both are useful and because their development yields further insights into how we can build graphics systems.

9.4.1 A Stack-Based Traversal

Consider the drawing of the figure by a function `figure`. This function might be called from the display callback or from a mouse callback in an animation that uses the mouse to control the joint angles. The model-view matrix, $\mathbf{M}$, in effect when this function is invoked, determines the position of the figure relative to the rest of the scene (and to the camera). The first node that we encounter results in the torso being drawn with $\mathbf{M}$ applied to all the torso's primitives. We then trace the leftmost branch of the tree to the node for the head. There we invoke the function `head` with the model-view matrix updated to $\mathbf{MM}_h$. Next, we back up to the torso node, then go down the subtree defining the left arm. This part looks just like the code for the robot arm: We draw the left-upper arm with the matrix $\mathbf{MM}_{lua}$ and the left-lower arm with matrix $\mathbf{MM}_{lua}\,\mathbf{M}_{lll}$. Then we move on to the right arm, left leg, and right leg. Each time we switch limbs, we must back up to the root and recover $\mathbf{M}$.

It is probably easiest to think in terms of the current transformation matrix of Chapter 4: the model-view matrix **C** that is applied to the primitives defined at a node.[2] The matrix **C** starts out as **M**, is updated to $\mathbf{MM_h}$ for the head, and later to $\mathbf{MM_{lul}\,M_{lll}}$, and so on. The application program must manipulate **C** before each call to a function defining a part of the figure. Note that as we back up the tree to start the right upper arm, we need **M** again. Rather than re-forming it (or any other matrix we might need to reuse in a more complex model), we can store (push) it on a stack and recover it with a pop. We can use the standard stack methods to push and pop our `mat4` arrays. Thus, we can initialize and push a model-view matrix on the stack by

```
var stack =[ ];
stack.push(modelViewMatrix);
```

and recover it by

```
modelViewMatrix = stack.pop();
```

Our traversal code will have translations and rotations intermixed with pushes and pops of the model-view matrix. Consider the code (without parameter values) for the beginning of the function `figure`:

```
var modelViewMatrix = mat4();
var mvStack = [ ];

function figure()
{
  mvStack.push(modelViewMatrix);
  torso();
  modelviewMatrix = mult(modelViewMatrix, translate);
  modelViewMatrix = mult(modelViewMatrix, rotate);
  head();

  modelViewMatrix = mvStack.pop();
  mvStack.push(modelViewMatrix);
  modelviewMatrix = mult(modelViewMatrix, translate);
  modelViewMatrix = mult(modelViewMatrix, rotate);
  leftUpperArm();

  modelViewMatrix = mvStack.pop();
  mvStack.push(modelViewMatrix);
  modelviewMatrix = mult(modelViewMatrix, translate);
  modelViewMatrix = mult(modelViewMatrix, rotate);
  leftLowerArm();

  modelViewMatrix = mvStack.pop();
  mvStack.push(modelViewMatrix);
  modelview = mult(modelViewMatrix, translate);
  modelViewMatrix = mult(modelViewMatrix, rotate);
  rightUpperArm();
```

---

2. We can ignore the projection matrix for now.

```
modelViewMatrix = stack.pop();
mvStack.push(modelViewMatrix);
    .
    .
    .
```

The first push duplicates the current model-view matrix, putting the copy on the top of the model-view matrix stack. This method of pushing allows us to work immediately with the other transformations that alter the model-view matrix, knowing that we have preserved a copy on the stack. The following calls to `translate` and `rotate` determine $\mathbf{M}_h$ and concatenate it with the initial model-view matrix. We can then generate the primitives for the head. The subsequent pop recovers the original model-view matrix. Note that we must do another push to leave a copy of the original model-view matrix that we can recover when we come back to draw the right leg.

The functions for the individual parts are similar to the previous example. Here is the `torso` function:

```
function torso()
{
  instanceMatrix = mult(modelViewMatrix,
                        translate(0.0, 0.5*torsoHeight, 0.0));
  instanceMatrix = mult(instanceMatrix,
                        scale4(torsoWidth, torsoHeight, torsoWidth));
  gl.uniformMatrix4fv(modelViewMatrixLoc, false, flatten(instance));

  for (var i = 0; i < 6; ++i) {
    gl.drawArrays(gl.TRIANGLE_FAN, 4*i, 4);
  }
}
```

You should be able to complete this example by continuing in a similar manner.

The website contains a complete program that implements this figure with a menu that will allow you to change the various joint angles. The individual parts are implemented using parallelepipeds, and the entire model can be shaded as we discussed in Chapter 6.

We have not considered how attributes such as color and material properties are handled by our traversal of a hierarchical model. Attributes are state variables: Once set, they remain in place until changed again. Hence, we must be careful as we traverse our tree. For example, suppose that within the code for `torso`, we set the color to red; then within the code for `head`, we set the color to blue. If there are no other color changes, the color will still be blue as we traverse the rest of the tree and may remain blue after we leave the code for `figure`. Here is an example in which the particular traversal algorithm can make a difference, because the current state can be affected differently depending on the order in which the nodes are visited.

This situation may be disconcerting, but there is a solution. We can create other stacks that allow us to deal with attributes in a manner similar to our use of the model-view matrix. If we push the attributes on the attribute stack on entrance to the function `figure`, and pop on exit, we have restored the attributes to their original state. Moreover, we can use additional pushes and pops within `figure` to control how attributes are handled in greater detail.

In a more complex model, we can apply these ideas recursively. If, for example, we want to use a more detailed model of the head—one incorporating eyes, ears, a nose, and a mouth—then we could model these parts separately. The head would then itself be modeled hierarchically, and its code would include the pushing and popping of matrices and attributes.

Although we have discussed only trees, if two or more nodes call the same function, we really have a DAG, but DAGs present no additional difficulties.

Color Plates 22 and 27 show hierarchical models of robots and figures used in simulations. These objects were created with high-level interactive software that relies on our ability to traverse hierarchical structures to render the models.

The approach that we used to describe hierarchical objects is workable but has limitations. The code is explicit and relies on the application programmer to push and pop the required matrices and attributes. In reality, we implemented a stack-based representation of a tree. The code was hardwired for the particular example and thus would be difficult to extend or use dynamically. The code also does not make a clear distinction between building a model and rendering it. Although many application programmers write code in this form, we prefer to use it primarily to illustrate the flow of a WebGL program that implements tree hierarchies. We now turn to a more general and powerful approach to working with tree-structured hierarchies.

FIGURE 9.15 (a) Tree. (b) Left-child, right-sibling representation.

9.5 USE OF TREE DATA STRUCTURES

Our second approach is to use a standard tree data structure to represent our hierarchy and then to render it with a traversal algorithm that is independent of the model. We use a **left-child, right-sibling** structure.

Consider the alternate representation of a tree in Figure 9.15. It is arranged such that all the elements at the same level are linked top to bottom. The children of a given node are represented as a second list arranged from the leftmost child to the rightmost. This second list points downward in Figure 9.15. This representation describes the structure of our hierarchical figure, but the structure still lacks the graphical information.

At each node, we must store the information necessary to draw the object: a function that defines the object and the homogeneous-coordinate matrix that positions the object relative to its parent. Consider the following node structure:

```
function createNode(transform, render, sibling, child)
{
  var node = {
    transform: transform,
    render: render,
    sibling: sibling,
    child: child
  };

  return node;
}
```

The array `transform` stores a 4 × 4 homogeneous-coordinate matrix . When we render the node, this matrix must first be composed with the current model-view matrix. Then the function `render`, which includes the graphics primitives, is executed. We also store a member for the sibling node on the right and a member for the leftmost child. For our figure, we must create 10 nodes corresponding to the 10 parts of our model: the torso node, head node, left upper arm node, right upper arm node, left lower arm node, right lower arm node, left upper leg node, right upper leg node, left lower leg node, and right lower leg node.

We can specify the nodes as part of the initialization. We create an empty node structure

```
var figure = [ ];
for (var i = 0; i < numNodes; ++i) {
  figure[i] = createNode(null, null, null, null);
}
```

Each node is assigned an index, and we fill these nodes using a function:

```
function initNodes(id)
{
  var m = mat4();

  switch (id) {
    case torsoId:
      .
      .
      .
```

For example, consider the root of the figure tree—the torso node. It can be oriented by a rotation about the y-axis. We can form the required rotation matrix using our matrix functions, and the function to be executed after forming the matrix is `torso`. The torso node has no siblings, and its leftmost child is the head node, so the torso node is given as follows:

```
case torsoId:
  m = rotate(theta[torsoId], 0, 1, 0);
  figure[torsoId] = createNode(m, torso, null, headId);
  break;
```

If we use a cube as the basis for the torso, the drawing function might look like

```
function torso()
{
  instanceMatrix = mult(modelViewMatrix,
                        translate(0.0, 0.5*torsoHeight, 0.0));
  instanceMatrix = mult(instanceMatrix,
                        scale4(torsoWidth, torsoHeight, torsoWidth));
  gl.uniformMatrix4fv(modelViewMatrixLoc, false,
                      flatten(instanceMatrix));
```

```
for (var i = 0; i < 6; ++i) {
    gl.drawArrays(gl.TRIANGLE_FAN, 4*i, 4);
  }
}
```

The instance transformation first scales the cube to the desired size and then translates it so its bottom lies in the plane $y = 0$.

The torso is the root node of the figure, so its code is a little different from the other nodes. Consider the specification for the left upper arm node,

```
case leftUpperArmId:
  m = translate(-(torsoWidth + upperArmWidth), 0.9*torsoHeight, 0.0);
  m = mult(m, rotate(theta[leftUpperArmId], 1, 0, 0));
  figure[leftUpperArmId] = createNode(null, leftUpperArm,
                                      rightUpperArmId, leftLowerArmId);
  figure[leftUpperArmId].transform = m;
  break;
```

and the **leftUpperArm** function,

```
function leftUpperArm()
{
  instanceMatrix = mult(modelViewMatrix,
                        translate(0.0, 0.5*upperArmHeight, 0.0));
  instanceMatrix = mult(instanceMatrix, scale4(upperArmWidth,
                        upperArmHeight, upperArmWidth));
  gl.uniformMatrix4fv(modelViewMatrixLoc, false, flatten(instance));

  for (var i = 0; i < 6; ++i) {
    gl.drawArrays(gl.TRIANGLE_FAN, 4*i, 4);
  }
}
```

The upper arm must be translated relative to the torso and its own width to put the center of rotation in the correct place. The node for the upper arm has both a sibling (the upper right arm) and a child (the lower left leg). To render the left upper arm, we first compute an instance transformation that gives it the desired size and position so its bottom is also on the plane $y = 0$. This instance matrix is concatenated with the current model-view matrix to position the upper left arm correctly in object coordinates. The other nodes are specified in a similar manner.

Traversing the tree in the same order (preorder traversal) as in Section 9.4 can be accomplished by the recursive code as follows:

```
function traverse(id)
{
  if (id == null) return;

  mvStack.push(modelViewMatrix);
  modelViewMatrix = mult(modelViewMatrix, figure[id].transform);
```

```
figure[id].render();

if (figure[id].child != null) {
  traverse(figure[id].child);
}
modelViewMatrix = mvStack.pop();
if (figure[id].sibling != null) {
  traverse(figure[id].sibling);
}
}
```

To render a non-null node, we first save the graphics state with mvStack.push. We then use the matrix at the node to modify the model-view matrix. We then draw the objects at the node with the function pointed to by f. Finally, we traverse all the children recursively. Note that because we have multiplied the model-view matrix by the local matrix, we are passing this altered matrix to the children. For the siblings, however, we do not want to use this matrix, because each has its own local matrix. Hence, we must return to the original state with mvStack.pop before traversing the children. If we are changing attributes within nodes, either we can push and pop attributes within the rendering functions, or we can push the attributes when we push the model-view matrix.

One of the nice aspects of this traversal method is that it is completely independent of the particular tree; thus, we can use a generic render function such as the following:

```
function render()
{
  gl.clear(gl.COLOR_BUFFER_BIT);
  traverse(torsoId);
  requestAnimFrame(render);
}
```

The complete code is given on the website. In this code, we again animate the figure by controlling individual joint angles with sliders. Thus, the dynamics of the program are in the event handlers, each of which changes an angle, recomputes the appropriate node matrix, and then initiates a rendering. For example, the first slider controls the torso and its code is

```
document.getElementById("slider0").onchange = function() {
  theta[torsoId ] = event.srcElement.value;
  initNodes(torsoId);
};
```

Our model can be changed dynamically. We can change the parameters of the parts. We can also change parts and add other parts to the model. For example, if the figure models a robot, we can can add hands (or grippers) and then have the hands grasp a variety of tools.

Note that as we have coded our examples, there is a fixed traversal order for the graph. If we had applied some other traversal algorithm, we could have produced a different image if we made any state changes within the graph, such as changing transformations or attributes. We can avoid some of these potential problems if we are careful to isolate parts of our code by pushing and popping attributes and matrices in each node (although there is a performance penalty for doing so too often).

9.6   ANIMATION

The models that we developed for our two examples—the robot and the figure—are **articulated**: The models consist of rigid parts connected by joints. We can make such models change their positions in time—animate them—by altering the values of a small set of parameters. Hierarchical models allow us to model the compound motions incorporating the physical relationships among the parts of the model. What we have not discussed is how to alter the parameters over time so as to achieve the desired motion.

Of the many approaches to animation, a few basic techniques are of particular importance when we work with articulated figures. These techniques arise both from traditional hand animation and from robotics.

In the case of our robot model, consider the problem of moving the tip of the upper arm from one position to another. The model has three degrees of freedom—the three angles that we can specify. Although each set of angles has a unique position for the tip, the converse is not true. Given a desired position of the tip of the arm, there may be no set of angles that place the tip as desired, a single set of angles that yields the specified position, or multiple sets of angles that place the tip at the desired position.

Studying **kinematics** involves describing the position of the parts of the model based on only the joint angles. We can use our hierarchical modeling methods either to determine positions numerically or to find explicit equations that give the position of any desired set of points in the model in terms of the joint angles. Thus, if θ is an array of the joint angles and $\mathbf{p}$ is an array whose elements are the vertices in our model, a kinematic model is of the form

$$\mathbf{p} = f(\theta).$$

Likewise, if we specify the rates of change of the joint angles—the joint velocities—then we can obtain velocities of points on the model.

The kinematic model neglects matters such as the effects of inertia and friction. We could derive more complex differential equations that describe the dynamic behavior of the model in terms of applied forces—a topic that is studied in robotics.

Whereas both kinematics and dynamics are ways of describing the forward behavior of the model, in animation, we are more concerned with **inverse kinematics** and **inverse dynamics**: Given a desired state of the model, how can we adjust the joint angles so as to achieve this position? There are two major concerns. First, given an environment including the robot and other objects, we must determine whether there exists a sequence of angles that achieves the desired state. There may be no single-valued function of the form

$$\theta = f^{-1}(\mathbf{p}).$$

For a given $\mathbf{p}$, we cannot tell in general if there is any θ that corresponds to this position or if there are multiple values of θ that satisfy the equation. Even if we can find a sequence of joint angles, we must ensure that as we go through this sequence our model does not hit any obstacles or violate any physical constraints. Even though for a model as simple as our robot we might be able to find equations that give the joint angles in terms of the position, we cannot do so in general because the forward equations do not have unique inverses. The figure model, which has 11 degrees of freedom, should give you an idea of how difficult it is to solve this problem.

A basic approach to overcoming these difficulties comes from traditional hand-animation techniques. In **key-frame animation**, the animator positions the objects at a set of times—the key frames. In hand animation, animators then can fill in the remaining frames, a process called **in-betweening**. In computer graphics, we can automate in-betweening by interpolating the joint angles between the key frames or, equivalently, by using simple approximations to obtain the required dynamic equations between key frames. Using GPUs, much of the work required for in-betweening can now be automated as part of the pipeline, often using the programmability of recent GPUs. We can also use the spline curves that we develop in Chapter 11 to give smooth methods of filling in between key frames. Although we can develop code for the interpolation, both a skillful (human) animator and good interactive methods are crucial if we are to choose the key frames and the positions of objects in these frames.

9.7 GRAPHICAL OBJECTS

Graphics was one of the first examples of the benefits of object-oriented programming (OOP). OpenGL, however, was designed to be close enough to the hardware so that OpenGL applications would render efficiently. Consequently, until recent shader-based versions of OpenGL became the standard, OpenGL and most other APIs lacked any object orientation and were heavily dependent on the state of the graphics system. Consider the simple example of drawing a green triangle. In immediate mode graphics, we would first set the current color, a state variable, to green, and then send three vertices to the graphics system and render them as a triangle. That the three vertices would be interpreted as specifying a triangle and whether the triangle was to be filled or not was also dependent on first setting some state variables.

From a physical perspective, this model seems somewhat strange. Most of us would regard the greenness of the triangle to be a property of the triangle rather than something that is completely independent of it. When we add the notion of material properties, the graphical approach becomes even more dissonant with physical reality. With shader-based WebGL, we can avoid some of these issues. We set up vertex attribute arrays so we can align colors and other attributes with vertices. However, this facility provides only a partial solution. As we saw in the previous section when we built hierarchical models, we could use JavaScript to construct objects including nodes and the individual parts that made up the model. Let's start by reviewing some basic object-oriented concepts.

9.7.1 Methods, Attributes, and Messages

Our programs manipulate data. The data may be in many forms, ranging from numbers to strings to the geometric entities that we build in our applications. In traditional imperative programming, the programmer writes code to manipulate the data, usually through functions. The data are passed to a function through the function's parameters. Data are returned in a similar manner. To manipulate the data sent to it, the function must be aware of how those data are organized. Consider, for example, the cube that we have used in many of our previous examples. We have seen that we can model it in various ways, including with vertex pointers, edge lists, and lists of polygon vertices. The application programmer may care little about which model is used and may prefer to regard the cube as an atomic entity or an *object*. In addition, she may care little about the details of how the cube is rendered to the screen: which shading model or which polygon fill algorithm is used. She can assume that the cube "knows how to render itself" and that conceptually the rendering algorithm is tied to the object itself. In some ways, WebGL supports this view by using the state of the graphics system to control rendering. For example, the color of the cube, its orientation, and the lights that are applied to its surfaces can all be part of the state of the graphics system and may not depend on how the cube is modeled.

However, if we are working with a physical cube, we might find this view a bit strange. The location of a physical cube is tied to the physical object, as are its color, size, and orientation. Although we could use WebGL to tie some properties to a virtual cube—through vertex attribute arrays, pushing and popping various attributes and matrices—the underlying programming model does not support these ideas well. For example, a function that transforms the cube would have to know exactly how the cube is represented and would work as shown in Figure 9.16.

The application programmer would write a function that takes as its inputs a pointer to the cube's data and the parameters of the transformation. It would then manipulate the data for the cube and return control to the application program (perhaps also returning some values).

Object-oriented design and programming look at manipulation of objects in a fundamentally different manner. Even in the early days of object-oriented programming, languages such as Smalltalk recognized that computer graphics provides excellent examples of the power of the object-oriented approach. Recent trends within the software community indicate that we can combine our pipeline orientation with an object orientation to build even more expressive and high-performance graphics systems.

FIGURE 9.16   Imperative programming paradigm.

FIGURE 9.17   Object-oriented paradigm.

Object-oriented programming languages define **objects** as modules with which we build programs. These modules include the data that define the module, such as the vertices for our cube, properties of the module (**attributes**), and the functions (**methods**) that manipulate the module and its attributes. We send **messages** to objects to invoke a method. This model is shown in Figure 9.17.

The advantage to the writer of the application program is that she now does not need to know how the cube is represented; she needs to know only what functionality the cube object supports—what messages she can send to it.

9.7.2 A Cube Object

Suppose that we wish to create a cube object in JavaScript that has a color attribute and a homogeneous-coordinate instance transformation associated with it. We could use a constructor of the form

```
function Cube(vertices, color, transform)
{
  this.vertices = vertices
  this.color = color;
  this.transform = transform;

  // Add code to initialize if arguments missing

  // Add code to send data to GPU
}
```

The implementation part of the structure contains the information on how a cube is actually represented. Typically, an application programmer does not need this information and needs to change only the color or matrix associated with the cube.

Once the constructor has been defined, instances of the cube object can be created as are other basic data types:

```
var aCube = new Cube(myVertices, myColor, myInstance);
```

A default cube can be created by

```
var bCube = new Cube();
```

Attributes that are part of the class definition can be changed for each instance of the cube either through the initialization or through functions that can be added to the prototype. For example, we can have functions

```
Cube.rotateX(theta);
Cube.rotateY(theta);
Cube.rotateZ(theta);
Cube.translate(d);
Cube.scale(s);
Cube.color(c);
```

that allow us to set up the instance transformation and color of a cube.

9.7.3 Objects and Hierarchy

One of the major advantages of object-oriented design is the ability to reuse code and to build more sophisticated objects from a small set of simple objects. As in Section 9.4, we can build a figure object from cubes and have multiple instances of this new object, each with its own color, size, location, and orientation. A class for the humanoid figure could refer to the classes for arms and legs; the class for a car could refer to classes for wheels and a chassis. Thus, we would once more have treelike representations similar to those that we developed in Section 9.5.

Often in object-oriented design, we want the representations to show relationships more complex than the parent–child relationship that characterizes trees. As we have used trees, the structure is such that the highest level of complexity is at the root and the relationship between a parent and child is a "has-a" relationship. Thus, the stick figure has two arms and two legs, whereas the car has four wheels and a chassis.

We can look at hierarchy in a different manner, with the simplest objects being the top of the hierarchy and the relationship between parents and children being an "is-a" relationship. This type of hierarchy is typical of taxonomies. A mammal is an animal. A human is a mammal. We used this relationship in describing projections. A parallel projection is a planar geometric projection; an oblique projection is a parallel projection. Such "is-a" relationships allow us to define multiple complex objects from simpler objects and also allow the more complex object to inherit properties from the simpler object. Thus, if we write the code for a parallel projection, the oblique projection code can use this code and refine only the parts that are necessary to convert the general parallel projection to an oblique one. For geometric objects, we can define base objects with a default set of properties, such as color and material properties. An application programmer could then use these properties or change them in instances of the prototype object. These concepts are supported by languages such as C++ and JavaScript that allow for subclasses and inheritance.

Consider again our figure model. Each of the parts can be described using the cube object with a proper instance transformation. What is lacking is the functionality to specify the interconnection of these parts. Because the model is hierarchical, we can use a new function called add to describe such relationships; for example, for the torso:

```
torso = new Cube();

// Set attributes here
```

```
torso.add(head);
torso.add(leftUpperArm);
torso.add(rightUpperArm);
torso.add(leftUpperLeg)1
torso.add(rightUpperLeg);
```

and for the left upper leg:

```
leftUpperLeg = new Cube();

// Set attributes here

leftUpperLeg.add(leftLowerLeg);
```

Although, at first glance, this approach is similar to the one we used to develop the figure model, the `add` function performs one additional key operation. For each of our base objects, the vertices are in model coordinates, which are independent of the position, orientation or size of the objects in the final model. Each of these objects is typically specified in a convenient size, orientation, and position. A cube is usually centered at the origin in model coordinates, aligned with the axes in this system, and has a side length of 1 unit. When the instance transformation is applied, the rotation is done about the origin in model coordinates. As we have seen, when we animated the figure model, we concatenated local modeling transformations together to get the proper transformation for each part. Our `add` function does this operation for us, using the instance transformations of the parent and each of its children.

9.7.4 Geometric and Nongeometric Objects

Suppose that we now want to build an object-oriented graphics system. What objects should we include? For a basic system, we want to have our basic objects—points, line segments, and triangles—and some higher-level objects, such as cubes, spheres, cylinders, and cones. It is less clear how we should deal with attributes, light sources, and viewers. For example, should a material property be associated with an object such as a cube, or is it a separate object? The answer can be either or both. We could create a cube class in which there is an attribute for each of the ambient, diffuse, and specular material properties that we introduced with the Phong model in Chapter 6. We could also define a material class using code such as the following:

```
function Material(ambient, diffuse, specular, shininess)
{
  this.specular = specular;
  this.shininess = shininess;
  this.diffuse = diffuse;
  this.ambient =  ambient;
}
```

Light sources are geometric objects—they have position and orientation among their features—and we can easily add a light source object:

```
function Light(type, near, position, orientation,
               ambient, diffuse, specular)
{
  this.type = type;
  this.near = near;
  this.position = position;
  this.orientation = orientation;
  this.specular = specular;
  this.diffuse = diffuse;
  this.ambient = ambient;
}
```

We might also define separate types of lights (ambient, diffuse, specular, emissive). We could define a camera object in a similar manner:

```
function Camera(type, position, volume)
{
  this.type = type; // perspective or parallel
  this.position = position; //center or direction of projection
  this.volume =  volume; // clipping volume
}
```

Once we have built up a collection of objects, we can use it to describe a scene. To take advantage of the hierarchical relationships that we have introduced, we develop a new tree structure called a **scene graph**.

9.8 SCENE GRAPHS

Our approach has been to write complete application programs, including the shaders and user interface. We built our objects and the relationships among them in our own code. The last two sections have shown that we can take a higher-level approach based on using a set of predefined objects. To form an image or scene,[3] we can create an API that describes the scene in terms of these entities. A simple scene with just a cube, possibly scaled and rotated and with lighting, could be described by code such as

```
myScene = new Scene();
myCube = new Cube();

// Set cube instance here

myMaterial = new Material();

// Set material properties here
```

---

3. Some scene graph APIs use the term *scene* to refer only to the geometric objects and their properties without a viewer or camera.

```
myCube.add(myMaterial);
myScene.add(myCube);

// Set light properties here

myLight = new Light();
myScene.add(myLight);

myScene.render();
```

Consider our first robot example. The description of the robot might take the form

```
base = new Cylinder();
upperArm = new Cube();
lowerArm = new Cube();
base.add(lowerArm);
lowerArm.add(upperArm);
```

Figure 9.18 shows a scene graph that describes a more complex scene.

The scene graph we have just described is equivalent to a WebGL program in the sense that we can use the tree to generate the program in a totally mechanical fashion. This approach was taken by Open Inventor and later by Open Scene Graph (OSG), both object-oriented APIs that were built on top of OpenGL. Open Inventor and OSG programs build, manipulate, and render a scene graph. Execution of a program causes traversal of the scene graph, which in turn executes graphics functions that are implemented in OpenGL. There are also scene graph APIs for WebGL, such as three.js and scene.js, which are referenced at the end of this chapter.

The notion of scene graphs couples nicely with the object-oriented paradigm introduced in Section 9.7. We can regard all primitives, attributes, and transformations as software objects, and we can define classes to manipulate these entities. From this perspective, we can make use of concepts such as data encapsulation to build up scenes of great complexity with simple programs that use predefined software objects.

FIGURE 9.18   Scene graph.

FIGURE 9.19   Modern
graphics architecture.

We can even support animations through software objects that appear as nodes in the scene graph but cause parameters to change and the scene to be redisplayed.

Graphics software systems are evolving to the configuration shown in Figure 9.19. OpenGL is the rendering engine. It usually sits on top of another layer known as the **hardware abstraction layer** (**HAL**), which is a virtual machine that communicates with the physical hardware. Above OpenGL is an object-oriented layer that supports scene graphs and a storage mechanism. User programs can be written for any of the layers, depending on what facilities are required by the application. Note that this organization is essentially the same whether we are working with desktop OpenGL or WebGL.

9.9   IMPLEMENTING SCENE GRAPHS

A simple scene graph as we described in the previous section has two important advantages but poses a major implementation problem. First, by providing an API at a level above the rendering, application programs need to know little about the details of the graphics system nor do they need to write shaders to visualize a scene. Second, the API need not be coupled to a particular renderer. Thus, we should be able to take our scene description, encode it in some form into a database, and then render the model as a separate operation using a variety of renderers, ranging from real-time renderers such as WebGL to slower renderers such as ray tracers that can provide more realistic visual effects. The challenge is how we can get decent performance from a scene graph API when we do need interactive behavior. If we try to implement something close to the API we have described, the most direct approach would be one that would make heavy use of the CPU rather than the GPU. We can learn what is possible through an examination of Open Scene Graph, which is the basis of the scene graphs available for WebGL.

Open Scene Graph is probably the most popular of the full scene-graph APIs and provides much of the functionality lacking in our example. In addition to supporting a wider variety of nodes, there are two additional concepts that are key to OSG. First, one of the benefits of a higher level of software than OpenGL is that such software can balance the workload between the CPU and the GPU. Consider how we process geometry in OpenGL. An application produces primitives that are specified through sets of vertices. As we have seen, OpenGL's main concern is rendering. All geometric primitives pass down at least part of the pipeline. It is only at the end of vertex processing that primitives that lie outside the view volume are clipped out. If a primitive is blocked from the viewer by another opaque geometric object and cannot appear in the final image, it nevertheless passes through most of the pipeline, and only during hidden-surface removal will it be eliminated. Although present GPUs can process millions of vertices per second, many applications have such complex geometry that even these GPUs cannot render the geometry at a sufficiently high frame rate. OSG uses two strategies, occlusion culling and level-of-detail rendering, to lower the rendering load.

Occlusion culling seeks to eliminate objects that cannot be visible because they are blocked by other objects before they enter the rendering pipeline. In Figure 9.20, we see that the square lies in the view volume and blocks the triangle from view.

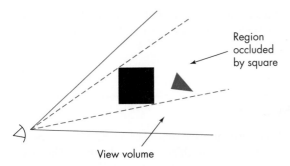

FIGURE 9.20   Occlusion.

Although the z-buffer algorithm would yield a correct rendering, because OpenGL processes each object independently, it cannot discover the occlusion. However, all the geometry is stored in the OSG scene graph, as is the information on the viewer. Hence, OSG can use one of many algorithms to go through the scene graph and cull objects. We will examine an approach to occlusion culling in Section 9.10 that uses binary spatial partitioning.

The second strategy is based on an argument similar to the one that we used to justify mipmaps for texture mapping. If we can tell that a geometric object will render to a small area of the display, we do not need to render all the detail that might be present in its geometry. Once more, the necessary information can be placed in the scene graph. OSG has a level-of-detail node whose children are the models of an object with different levels of geometric complexity. The application program sets up these nodes. During the traversal of the scene graph, OSG determines which level of detail to use.

Level-of-detail rendering is important not only to OSG but also to real-time applications, such as interactive games that are built using proprietary game engines. Game engines are very large, complex software objects that may comprise millions of lines of code. Although a game engine may use OpenGL or DirectX to render the graphics and make extensive use of programmable shaders, a game engine also has to handle the game play and manage complex interactions that might involve multiple players. Game engines use scene graphs to maintain all the needed information, including the geometry and texture maps, and use level of detail extensively in processing their scene graphs. In the next section, we will examine some related issues involving graphics over the Internet.

The second major difference between our simple scene graph and OSG is how the scene graph is processed for each frame. OSG uses three traversals rather than the single traversal in our simple scene graph. The goal of the traversal process is to create a list of the geometry that will be rendered. This list contains the geometry at the best level of detail and only the geometry that has survived occlusion culling. In addition, the geometry has been sorted so that translucent surfaces will be rendered correctly.

The first traversal deals with updates to the scene graph that might be generated by callbacks that handle interaction or changes to the geometry from the application program. The second traversal builds a list of the geometry that has to be rendered.

This traversal uses occlusion culling, translucency, level of detail, and bounding volumes. The final traversal goes through the geometry list and issues the necessary OpenGL calls to render the geometry.

9.10   OTHER TREE STRUCTURES

Tree and DAG structures provide powerful tools to describe scenes; trees are used in a variety of other ways in computer graphics, of which we consider three. The first is the use of expression trees to describe an object hierarchy for solid objects; the other two describe spatial hierarchies that we can use to increase the efficiency of many rendering algorithms.

9.10.1 CSG Trees

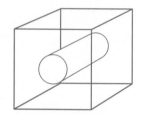

FIGURE 9.21   Wireframe that has two possible interpretations.

The polygonal representation of objects that we have used has many strengths and a few weaknesses. The most serious weakness is that polygons describe only the surfaces that enclose the interior of a three-dimensional object, such as a polyhedron. In CAD applications, this limitation causes difficulties whenever we must employ any volumetric properties of the graphical object, such as its weight or its moment of inertia. In addition, because we display an object by drawing its edges or surfaces, there can be ambiguities in the display. For example, the wireframe shown in Figure 9.21 can be interpreted either as a cube with a hole through it created by removal of a cylinder or as a solid cube composed of two different materials.

Constructive solid geometry (CSG) addresses these difficulties. Assume that we start with a set of atomic solid geometric entities, such as parallelepipeds, cylinders, and spheres. The attributes of these objects can include surface properties, such as color or reflectivity, but also volumetric properties, such as size and density. In describing scenes of such objects, we consider those points in space that constitute each object. Equivalently, each object is a set of points, and we can use set algebra to form new objects from these solid primitives.

CSG modeling uses three set operations: union, intersection, and set difference. The **union** of two sets A and B, written $A \cup B$, consists of all points that are either in A or in B. The **intersection** of A and B, $A \cap B$, is the set of all points that are in both A and B. The **set difference**, $A - B$, is the set of points that are in A but not in B. Figure 9.22 shows two objects and possible objects created by the three set operations.

Objects are described by algebraic expressions. The expression $(A - B) \cap (C \cup D)$ might describe an object such as the one illustrated in Figure 9.23.

Typically, we store and parse algebraic expressions using expression trees, where internal nodes store operations and terminal nodes store operands. For example, the tree in Figure 9.24 is a CSG tree that represents the object $(A - B) \cap (C \cup D)$ in Figure 9.23. We can evaluate or render the CSG tree by a **postorder** traversal; that is, we recursively evaluate the tree to the left of a node and the tree on the right of the node, and finally use these values to evaluate the node itself. Rendering of objects in CSG often is done with a variant of ray tracing; see Exercise 9.10 and Chapter 12.

FIGURE 9.22 Set operations.

FIGURE 9.23 CSG object.

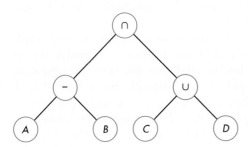

FIGURE 9.24 CSG tree.

9.10.2 BSP Trees

Scene graphs and CSG trees describe hierarchical relationships among the parts of an object. We can also use trees to describe the object space and encapsulate the spatial relationships among groups of objects. These relationships can lead to fast methods of **visibility testing** to determine which objects might be seen by a camera,

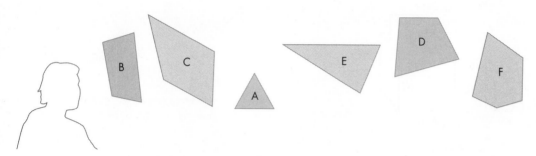

FIGURE 9.25   Collection of polygons and a viewer.

thus avoiding processing all objects with tests such as the z-buffer algorithm. These techniques have become very important in real-time animations for computer games.

One approach to spatial hierarchy starts with the observation that a plane divides or partitions three-dimensional space into two parts (half spaces). Successive planes subdivide space into increasingly smaller partitions. In two dimensions, we can use lines to partition space.

Consider the polygons shown in Figure 9.25, with the viewer located as indicated. Arguing as we did in Chapter 8, there is an order in which to paint these polygons so that the image will be correct. Rather than using a method such as depth sort each time we want to render these polygons, we can store the relative-positioning information in a tree. We start the construction of the tree using the plane of one polygon to separate groups of polygons that are in front of it from those that are behind it. For example, consider a simple world in which all the polygons are parallel and are oriented with their normals parallel to the z-axis. This assumption makes it easier to illustrate the algorithm but does not affect the algorithm as long as the plane of any polygon separates the other polygons into two groups. In this world, the view from the z direction is as shown in Figure 9.26.

Plane A separates the polygons into two groups, one containing B and C, which are in front of A, and the second containing D, E, and F, which are behind A. We use this plane to start a **binary space partition tree** (**BSP tree**) that stores the separating planes and the order in which they are applied. Thus, in the BSP tree in Figure 9.27, A is at the root, B and C are in the left subtree, and D, E, and F are in the right subtree. Proceeding recursively, C is behind the plane of B, so we can complete the left subtree. The plane of D separates E and F, thus completing the right subtree. Note that for a given set of polygons, there are multiple possible BSP trees corresponding to the order in which we choose to make our partitions. In the general case, if a separating plane intersects a polygon, then we can break up the polygon into two polygons, one in front of the plane and one behind it, similar to what we did with overlapping polygons in the depth sort algorithm in Chapter 8.

We can use this tree to paint the polygons by doing a **backward in-order traversal**. That is, we traverse the tree recursively, drawing the right subtree first, followed by the root, and finally by the left subtree. One of the advantages of BSP trees is that we can use the same tree even if the viewer moves, by changing the traversal algorithm. If the viewer moves to the back, as shown in Figure 9.28, then we can paint the

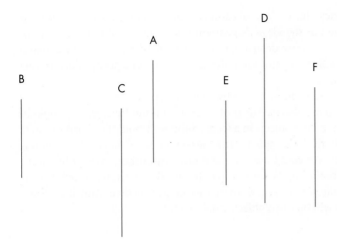

FIGURE 9.26   Top view of polygons.

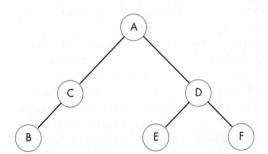

FIGURE 9.27   Binary space partition (BSP) tree.

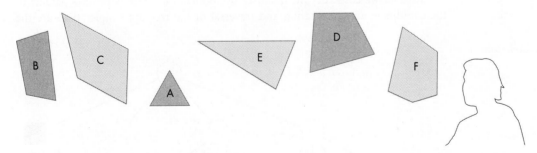

FIGURE 9.28   Movement of the viewer to the back.

polygons using a standard in-order traversal—left subtree, root, right subtree. Also note that we can use the algorithm recursively wherever planes separate sets of polygons or other objects into groups, called **clusters**. Thus, we might group polygons into polyhedral objects, then group these polyhedra into clusters. We can then apply the algorithm within each cluster. In applications such as flight simulators, where the model does not change but the viewer's position does, the use of BSP trees can be efficient for doing visible-surface determination during rendering. The tree contains all the required information to paint the polygons; the viewer's position determines the traversal algorithm.

BSP trees are but one form of hierarchy to divide space. Another is the use of bounding volumes, such as spheres. The root of a tree of bounding spheres would be the sphere that contains all the objects in a scene. Subtrees would then correspond to groups of objects within the larger sphere, and the root nodes would be the bounding spheres for each object. We could use the same idea with other types of bounding volumes, such as the bounding boxes that we discussed in Chapter 8. Spheres are particularly good for interactive games, where we can quickly determine if an object is potentially visible or whether two objects might collide.

9.10.3 Quadtrees and Octrees

One limitation of BSP trees is that the planes that separate polygons can have an arbitrary orientation so that construction of the tree can be costly, involving ordering and often splitting of polygons. Octrees and quadtrees avoid this problem by using separating planes and lines parallel to the coordinate axes.

Consider the two-dimensional picture in Figure 9.29. We assume that this picture is composed of black and white pixels, perhaps formed by the rendering of a three-dimensional scene. If we wish to store the scene, we can save it as a binary array. But notice the great deal of coherence in the picture. Pixels of each color are clustered together. We can draw two lines as in Figure 9.30, dividing the region into quadrants. Noting that one quadrant is all white, we can assign a single color to it. For the other three, we can subdivide again and continue subdividing any quadrant that contains pixels of more than a single color. This information can be stored in a tree called a **quadtree**, in which each level corresponds to a subdivision and each node has four children. Thus, the quadtree for our original simple picture is as shown in Figure 9.31.

Because we construct the quadtree by subdividing space with lines parallel to the coordinate axes, formation and traversal of the tree are simpler than are the

FIGURE 9.29 Two-dimensional space of pixels.

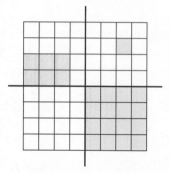

FIGURE 9.30 First subdivision of space.

FIGURE 9.31 Quadtree.

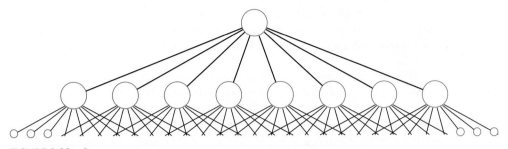

FIGURE 9.32   Octree.

corresponding operations for a BSP tree. One of the most important advantages of quadtrees is that they can reduce the amount of memory needed to store images.

Quadtrees partition two-dimensional space. They can also be used to partition object space in a manner similar to BSP trees and thus can be traversed in an order depending on the position of the viewer so as to render correctly the objects in each region. In three dimensions, quadtrees extend to **octrees**. The partitioning is done by planes parallel to the coordinate axes, and each step of the partitioning subdivides space into eight octants, as shown in Figure 9.32.

Octrees are used for representing volume data sets that consist of volume elements called **voxels**, as shown in Figure 9.33. The arguments that have been made for quadtrees and octrees can also be applied to the spatial partitioning of objects, rather than pixels or voxels. For example, we can use recursive subdivision of two- or three-dimensional space for clipping. After each subdivison, we compare the bounding box of each object with each subdivided rectangle or cube to determine if the object lies in that region of the subdivided space.

FIGURE 9.33   Volume data set.

SUMMARY AND NOTES

The speed at which modern hardware can render geometric objects has opened up the possibilities of a variety of modeling systems. As users of computer graphics, we need a large arsenal of techniques if we are to make full use of our graphics systems. We have introduced hierarchical modeling. Not only are there the many other approaches that we will have investigated in this chapter and the next, but we can combine these techniques to generate new ones. The Suggested Readings will help you to explore modeling methods.

We have presented basic themes that apply to most approaches to modeling. One is the use of hierarchy to incorporate relationships among objects in a scene. We have seen that we can use fundamental data structures, such as trees and DAGs, to represent such relationships; traversing these data structures becomes part of the rendering process. The use of scene graphs in Open Scene Graph, VRML, and Java3D allows the application programmer to build complex animated scenes from a combination of predefined and user-defined software modules. For WebGL, three.js is the most popular scene-graph package.

Tree-structured models are also used to describe complex shaders that involve the interaction of light sources, material properties, atmospheric effects, and a variety of local reflection models. These could be implemented with RenderMan, GLSL, or DirectX.

Object-oriented approaches are standard for complex applications and for applications that are distributed over networks. Unfortunately, there has not been agreement on a single object-oriented API. However, the actual rendering in most high-end systems is done at the OpenGL level, because the closeness of this API to the hardware makes for efficient use of the hardware. Consequently, both application programmers and system developers need to be familiar with multiple levels of APIs.

Chapter 10 presents an entirely different, but complementary, approach to modeling based on procedural methods.

SUGGESTED READINGS

Hierarchical transformations through the use of a matrix stack were described in the graphics literature more than 40 years ago [New73]. The PHIGS API [ANSI88] was the first to incorporate them as part of a standard package. See Watt [Wat92] for an introduction to the use of articulated figures in animation. The paper by Lassiter [Las87] shows the relationship between traditional animation techniques as practiced in the movie industry and animation in computer graphics.

BSP trees were first proposed by Fuchs, Kedem, and Naylor [Fuc80] for use in visibility testing and were later used in many other applications, such as CSG. See [Mol02] for additional applications.

Scene graphs are the heart of Open Inventor [Wer94]. The Open Inventor database format is the basis of VRML [Har96]. Most recent APIs, such as Java3D [Swo00] and DirectX [Kov97], are object oriented. For a discussion of Java and applets, see [Cha98] and [Arn96]. Trees are integral to the RenderMan Shading Language [Ups89], where they are used to construct shaders. Modeling systems, such as Maya, allow the user to specify different shaders and rendering algorithms for different objects. See [Mar07] for an introduction to Open Scene Graph.

Many applications of visibility testing can be found in [Mol02].

The use of scene graphs in game engine design is discussed in [Ebe01]. How the engine looks to a game programmer is described for the Torque engine in [Mau06].

EXERCISES

9.1   For our simple robot model, describe the set of points that can be reached by the tip of the upper arm.

9.2   Find equations for the position of any point on the simple robot in terms of the joint angles. Can you determine the joint angles from the position of the tip of the upper arm? Explain your answer.

9.3   Given two points in space that are reachable by the robot, describe a path between them in terms of the joint angles.

9.4 Write a simple circuit layout program in terms of a symbol–instance transformation table. Your symbols should include the shapes for circuit elements such as resistors, capacitors, and inductors for electrical circuits, or the shapes for various gates (AND, OR, NOT) for logical circuits.

9.5 We can write a description of a binary tree, such as we might use for a search, as a list of nodes with pointers to its children. Write a WebGL program that will take such a description and display the tree graphically.

9.6 Robotics is only one example in which the parts of the scene show compound motion, where the movement of some objects depends on the movement of other objects. Other examples include bicycles (with wheels), airplanes (with propellers), and merry-go-rounds (with horses). Pick an example of compound motion. Write a graphics program to simulate your selection.

9.7 Given two polygons with the same number of vertices, write a program that will generate a sequence of images that converts one polygon into the other.

9.8 Starting with the tree node in Section 9.5, add an attribute to the node and make any required changes to the traversal algorithm.

9.9 Build a simple scene-graph system that includes polygons, materials, a viewer, and light sources.

9.10 How does constructive solid geometry (CSG) address the weakness of polygonal representation of objects?

9.11 Show how Octrees can be used for ordering and often splitting of polygons.

9.12 Write a program that will allow the user to construct simple articulated figures from a small collection of basic shapes. Your program should allow the user to place the joints, and it should animate the resulting figures.

9.13 Is it possible to use a BSP tree to paint polygons by doing a backward in-order traversal?

9.14 Using the scene graph we developed in this chapter, add the ability to store scene graphs in text format and to read them from files.

9.15 Show how to add light property to a scene graph.

9.16 Starting with the robot in Section 9.3, add a hand or "gripper" to the end of the arm.

9.17 Add transformation to a cube object and show it by code fragments.

9.18 BSP trees can be made more efficient if they are used hierarchically with objects grouped in clusters. Visibility checking is then done using the bounding volumes of the clusters. Implement such an algorithm and use it with a scene-graph renderer.

CHAPTER 10

PROCEDURAL METHODS

So far, we have assumed that the geometric objects we wish to create can be described by their surfaces, and that these surfaces can be modeled (or approximated) by convex planar polygons. Our use of polygonal objects was dictated by the ease with which we could describe these objects and our ability to render them on existing systems. The success of computer graphics attests to the importance of such models.

Nevertheless, even as these models were being used in large CAD applications for flight simulators, in computer animations, in interactive video games, and to create special effects in films, both users and developers recognized the limitations of these techniques. Physical objects such as clouds, smoke, and water did not fit this style of modeling. Adding physical constraints and modeling complex behaviors of objects were not part of polygonal modeling. In response to such problems, researchers have developed procedural models, which use algorithmic methods to build representations of the underlying phenomena, generating polygons only as needed during the rendering process.

10.1 ALGORITHMIC MODELS

When we review the history of computer graphics, we see that the desire to create increasingly more realistic graphics has always outstripped advances in hardware. Although we can render hundreds of millions of triangles per second on existing commodity hardware, applications such as flight simulation, virtual reality, and computer games can demand rendering speeds in the billions of triangles per second. Furthermore, as rendering speeds have increased, database sizes also have increased dramatically. A single data set may contain more than 1 billion triangles.

Often, however, applications have such needs because they use existing software and modeling paradigms. Astute researchers and application programmers have suggested that we would not require as many polygons if we could render a model generating only those polygons that are visible and that project to an area at least the size of one pixel. We have seen examples of this idea in previous chapters; for example, when we considered culling polygons before they reached the rendering pipeline. Nevertheless, a more productive approach has been to reexamine the way in which we do our modeling and seek techniques, known as **procedural methods**, that generate geometrical objects in a manner different from what we have seen so far. Procedural methods span a wide range of techniques. What they have in common is that they describe objects in an algorithmic manner and produce polygons only when needed as part of the rendering process.

In many ways, procedural models can be understood by an analogy with methods that we use to represent irrational numbers—such as square roots, sines, and cosines—in a computer. Consider, for example, three ways of representing $\sqrt{2}$. We can say that numerically

$$\sqrt{2} = 1.414\ldots,$$

filling in as many digits as we like; or, more abstractly, we can define $\sqrt{2}$ as the positive number x such that

$$x^2 = 2.$$

However, within the computer, $\sqrt{2}$ might be the result of executing an algorithm. For example, consider Newton's method. Starting with an initial approximation $x_0 = 1$, we compute the recurrence

$$x_{k+1} = \frac{x_k}{2} + \frac{1}{x_k}.$$

Each successive value of x_k is a better approximation to $\sqrt{2}$. From this perspective, $\sqrt{2}$ is defined by an algorithm; equivalently, it is defined through a program. For objects we deal with in computer graphics, we can take a similar approach. For example, a sphere centered at the origin can be defined as the mathematical object that satisfies the equation

$$x^2 + y^2 + z^2 = r^2.$$

It also is the result of the tetrahedron subdivision process that we developed in Chapter 6 and of our program for doing that subdivision. A potential benefit of the second view is that when we render spheres, we can render small spheres (in screen space) with fewer triangles than we would need for large spheres.

A second type of problem with polygonal modeling has been the difficulty of combining computer graphics with physical laws. Although we can build and animate polygonal models of real-world objects, it is far more difficult to make these graphical objects act as solids and not penetrate one another.

We introduce four of many possible approaches to procedural modeling. In the first, we work with particles that obey Newton's laws. We then design systems of particles that are capable of complex behaviors that arise from solving sets of differential equations—a routine numerical task for up to thousands of particles. The positions of the particles yield the locations at which to place our standard geometric objects in a world model.

The second approach—language-based models—enables us to control complexity by replacing polygonal models with models similar to those used for both natural and computer languages. With these models we can approximate many natural objects with a few rules that generate the required graphical entities. Combined with fractal geometry, these models allow us to generate images using only the number of polygons required for display.

The third approach—fractal geometry—is based on the self-similarity that we see in many natural phenomena. Fractal geometry gives us a way of generating models at any desired level of detail.

Finally, we present procedural noise as a method of introducing a controlled amount of randomness into our models. Procedural noise has been used to create texture maps, turbulent behavior in fluid models, realistic motion in animations, and fuzzy objects such as clouds.

10.2 PHYSICALLY BASED MODELS AND PARTICLE SYSTEMS

One of the great strengths—and weaknesses—of modeling in computer graphics is that we can build models based on any principles we choose. The graphical objects that we create may have little connection with physical reality. Historically, the attitude was that if something looked right, that was sufficient for most purposes. Not being constrained by physical models, which are often either not known or too complex to simulate in real time, allows the creation of the special effects that we see in computer games and movies. In fields such as scientific visualization, this flexibility allows mathematicians to "see" shapes that do not exist in the usual three-dimensional space and to display information in new ways. Researchers and engineers can construct prototypes of objects that are not limited by our ability to construct them with present materials and equipment.

However, when we wish to simulate objects in the real world and to see the results of this simulation on our display, we can get into trouble. Often, it is easy to make a model for a group of objects moving through space, but it is far more difficult to keep track of when two objects collide and to have the graphics system react in a physically correct manner. Indeed, it is far easier in computer graphics to let a ball go directly through a wall than to model the ball bouncing off the surface, incorporating the correct elastic rebound.

Recently, researchers have become interested in **physically based modeling**, a style of modeling in which the graphical objects obey physical laws. Such modeling can follow either of two related paths. In one, we model the physics of the underlying process and use the physics to drive the graphics. For example, if we want a solid object to appear to tumble in space and to bounce from various surfaces, we can, at least in principle, use our knowledge of dynamics and continuum mechanics to derive the required equations. This approach is beyond the scope of a first course in computer graphics and we shall not pursue it. The other approach is to use a combination of basic physics and mathematical constraints to control the dynamic behavior of our objects. We follow this approach for a group of particles.

Particle systems are collections of particles, typically point masses, in which the dynamic behavior of the particles can be determined by the solution of sets of coupled differential equations. Particle systems have been used to generate a wide variety of behaviors in a number of fields. In fluid dynamics, people use particle systems to model turbulent behavior. Rather than solving partial differential equations, we can simulate the behavior of the system by following a group of particles in which all the particles are subject to the same forces and constraints. We can also use particles to model solid objects. For example, a deformable solid can be modeled as a three-dimensional array of particles that are held together by springs. When the object is subjected to external forces, the particles move and their positions approximate the shape of the solid object.

Computer graphics practitioners have used particles to model such diverse phenomena as fireworks, the flocking behavior of birds, and wave action. In these applications, the dynamics of the particle system gives the positions of the particles, but at each location we can place a graphical object, rather than a point.

In all these cases, we work with a group of particles, each member of which we can regard as a point mass. We use physical laws to write equations that we can solve numerically to obtain the state of these particles at each time step. As a final step, we can render each particle as a graphical object—perhaps as a colored point for a fireworks application or a cartoon character in an animation.

10.3   NEWTONIAN PARTICLES

We consider a set of particles that is subject to Newton's laws. Although there is no reason that we could not use other physical laws or construct a set of our own (virtual) physical laws, the advantage of starting with Newtonian particles is that we can obtain a wide range of behaviors using simple, well-understood physics. A Newtonian particle must obey Newton's second law, which states that the mass of the particle (m) times that particle's acceleration ($\mathbf{a}$) is equal to the sum of the forces ($\mathbf{f}$) acting on the particle, or symbolically,

$$m\mathbf{a} = \mathbf{f}.$$

Note that both the acceleration and force are vectors, usually in three dimensions. One consequence of Newton's laws is that for an ideal point-mass particle—one whose total mass is concentrated at a single point—its state is completely determined by its position and velocity. Thus, in three-dimensional space, an ideal particle has six degrees of freedom, and a system of n particles has $6n$ state variables—the positions and velocities of all the particles. Within some reference frame, the state of the ith particle is given by two three-element column matrices,[1] a position matrix,

$$\mathbf{p}_i = \begin{bmatrix} x_i \\ y_i \\ z_i \end{bmatrix},$$

---

1. We have chosen to use three-dimensional arrays here, rather than homogeneous-coordinate representations, both to be consistent with the way these equations are usually written in the physics literature and to simplify the resulting differential equations.

and a velocity matrix,

$$\mathbf{v}_i = \begin{bmatrix} \dot{x}_i \\ \dot{y}_i \\ \dot{z}_i \end{bmatrix} = \begin{bmatrix} \frac{dx}{dt} \\ \frac{dy}{dt} \\ \frac{dz}{dt} \end{bmatrix}.$$

Knowing that acceleration is the derivative of velocity and that velocity is the derivative of position, we can write Newton's second law for a particle as the six coupled, first-order differential equations

$$\dot{\mathbf{p}}_i = \mathbf{v}_i$$

$$\dot{\mathbf{v}}_i = \frac{1}{m_i}\mathbf{f}_i(t).$$

Hence, the dynamics of a system of n particles is governed by a set of $6n$ coupled, ordinary differential equations.

In addition to its state, each particle may have a number of attributes, including its mass (m_i), and a set of properties that can alter its behavior and how it is displayed. For example, some attributes govern how we render the particle and determine its color, shape, and surface properties. Note that, although the dynamics of a simple particle system is based on each particle being treated as a point mass, the user can specify how each particle should be rendered. For example, each particle may represent a person in a crowd scene, or a molecule in a chemical-synthesis application, or a piece of cloth in the simulation of a flag blowing in the wind. In each case, the underlying particle system governs the location and the velocity of the center of mass of the particle. Once we have the location of a particle, we can place the desired graphical object at that location.

The set of forces on the particles, $\{\mathbf{f}_i\}$, determines the behavior of the system. These forces are determined by the state of the particle system and can change with time. We can base these forces on simple physical principles, such as spring forces, or on physical constraints that we wish to impose on the system; or we can base them on external forces, such as gravity, that we wish to apply to the system. By designing the forces carefully, we can obtain the desired system behavior.

The dynamic state of the system is obtained by numerical methods that involve stepping through approximations to the set of differential equations. A typical time step is based on computing the forces that apply to the n particles through a user-defined function, using these forces to update the state through a numerical differential equation solver, and finally using the new positions of the particles and their attributes to render whatever graphical objects we wish to place at the particles' locations. Thus, in pseudocode, we have a loop of the form

```
var time, delta;
var state[6n], force[3n];

state = get_initial_state();
```

```
for (time = t0; time < time_final; time += delta) {
  // Compute forces
  force = force_function(state, time);

  // Apply standard differential equation solver
  state = ode(force, state, time, delta);

  // Display result
  render(state, time);
}
```

The main component that we must design in a given application is the function that computes the forces on each particle.

10.3.1 Independent Particles

There are numerous simple ways that particles can interact and determine the forces that act on each particle. If the forces that act on a given particle are independent of other particles, the force on the ith particle can be described by the equation

$$\mathbf{f}_i = \mathbf{f}_i(\mathbf{p}_i, \mathbf{v}_i).$$

A simple case occurs where each particle is subject only to a constant gravitational force

$$\mathbf{f}_i/m_i = \mathbf{g}.$$

If this force points down, then

$$\mathbf{g} = \begin{bmatrix} 0 \\ -g \\ 0 \end{bmatrix},$$

where g is positive, and each particle will trace out a parabolic arc. If we add a term proportional to the velocity, we can have the particle subject to frictional forces, such as drag. If some of the attributes, such as color, change with time and if we give each particle a (random) lifetime, then we can simulate phenomena such as fireworks. More generally, external forces are applied independently to each point. If we allow the particles to drift randomly and render each as a large object, rather than as a point, we can model clouds or flows with independent particles.

10.3.2 Spring Forces

If, in a system of n particles, all particles are independent, then the force calculation is $O(n)$. In the most general case, the computation of the forces on a given particle may involve contributions due to pairwise interactions with all the other particles, an $O(n^2)$ computation. For large particle systems, an $O(n^2)$ computation is too slow to be useful. Often, we can reduce this complexity by having a particle interact with only those particles that are close to it.

Consider the example of using particles to create a surface whose shape varies over time, such as a curtain or a flag blowing in the wind. We can use the location

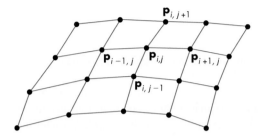

FIGURE 10.1 Mesh of particles.

of each particle as a vertex for a rectangular mesh, as shown in Figure 10.1. The shape of the mesh changes over time, as a result both of external forces that act on each particle, such as gravity or wind, and of forces between particles that hold the mesh together, giving it the appearance of a continuous surface. We can approximate this second type of force by considering the forces between a particle and its closest neighbors. Thus, if $\mathbf{p}_{ij}$ is the location of the particle at row i, column j of the mesh, the force calculation for $\mathbf{p}_{ij}$ needs to consider only the forces between $\mathbf{p}_{i, j}$ and $\mathbf{p}_{i+1, j}$, $\mathbf{p}_{i-1, j}$, $\mathbf{p}_{i, j+1}$, and $\mathbf{p}_{i, j-1}$, which is an $O(n)$ calculation.

One method to model the forces among particles is to consider adjacent particles as connected by a spring. Consider two adjacent particles, located at $\mathbf{p}$ and $\mathbf{q}$, connected by a spring, as shown in Figure 10.2. Let $\mathbf{f}$ denote the force acting on $\mathbf{p}$ from $\mathbf{q}$. A force $-\mathbf{f}$ acts on $\mathbf{q}$ from $\mathbf{p}$. The spring has a resting length s, which is the distance between particles if the system is not subject to external forces and is allowed to come to rest. When the spring is stretched, the force acts in the direction $\mathbf{d} = \mathbf{p} - \mathbf{q}$; that is, it acts along the line between the points. This force obeys **Hooke's law**,

FIGURE 10.2 Particles connected by a spring.

$$\mathbf{f} = -k_s(|\mathbf{d}| - s)\frac{\mathbf{d}}{|\mathbf{d}|},$$

where k_s is the spring constant and s is the length of the spring when it is at rest. This law shows that the farther apart the two particles are stretched, the stronger is the force attracting them back to the resting position. Conversely, when the ends of the spring are pushed together, the force pulls them back such that their positions move to a separation by the resting length s. As we have stated Hooke's law, however, there is no damping (or friction) in the system. A system of masses and springs defined in such a manner will oscillate forever when perturbed. We can include a **drag**, or **damping term**, in Hooke's law. The damping force operates in the same direction as the spring force, but depends on the velocity between the particles. The fraction of the velocity that contributes to damping is proportional to the projection of the velocity vector onto the vector defined by the two points, as shown in Figure 10.3. Mathematically, Hooke's law with the damping term is given by

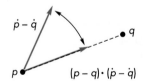

FIGURE 10.3 Computation of the spring damping force.

$$\mathbf{f} = -\left(k_s(|\mathbf{d}| - s) + k_d\frac{\dot{\mathbf{d}} \cdot \mathbf{d}}{|\mathbf{d}|}\right)\frac{\mathbf{d}}{|\mathbf{d}|}.$$

Here, k_d is the damping constant, and

$$\dot{\mathbf{d}} = \dot{\mathbf{p}} - \dot{\mathbf{q}}.$$

A system of masses and springs with damping that is not subjected to external forces will eventually come to rest.

The four images in Color Plate 32 show a mesh that is generated from the locations of a set of particles. Each interior particle is connected to its four neighbors by springs. The particles are also subject to external forces—the wind. At each time step, once the positions of the particles are determined, we can render the mesh using techniques such as texture mapping (Section 7.5) to create the detailed appearance of the surface.

10.3.3 Attractive and Repulsive Forces

Whereas spring forces are used to keep a group of particles together, repulsive forces push particles away from one another and attractive forces pull particles toward one another. We could use repulsive forces to distribute particles over a surface, or if the particles represent locations of objects, to keep objects from hitting one another. We could use attractive forces to build a model of the solar system or to create applications that model satellites revolving about the earth. The equations for attraction and repulsion are essentially the same except for a sign. Physical models of particle behavior may include both attractive and repulsive forces. See Exercise 10.14.

For a pair of particles, located at $\mathbf{p}$ and $\mathbf{q}$, the repulsive force acts in the direction $\mathbf{d} = \mathbf{p} - \mathbf{q}$ and is inversely proportional to the particles' distance from each other. For example, we could use the expression

$$\mathbf{f} = -k_r \frac{\mathbf{d}}{|\mathbf{d}|^3}$$

for an inverse-square-law term. Changing the minus sign to a plus sign and replacing k_r by $(m_a m_b)/g$ gives us the attractive force between two particles of mass m_a and m_b, where g is the gravitational constant.

In the general case, where each particle is subject to forces from all other particles, the computation of attractive and repulsive forces is $O(n^2)$. Unlike meshes of particles connected by springs, where we attempt to keep the particles in the same topological arrangement, particles subject to attractive and repulsive forces usually change their positions relative to one another. Hence, strategies to avoid the $O(n^2)$ force calculation are more complex. One approach is to divide space into three-dimensional cells, each of which can contain multiple particles or even no particles, as shown in Figure 10.4.

For forces that are inversely proportional to distance, we can choose a cell size such that the forces on a particle from particles in other than its own or adjacent cells are negligible. If this partitioning is possible, then the $O(n^2)$ calculation is reduced to $O(n)$. However, there is a cost to partitioning, and particles can move from one cell to another. The difficulty of the first problem depends on the particular application, because we can often obtain an initial particle distribution with little effort, but at other times we might have to do a sort. We can solve the second problem by looking at

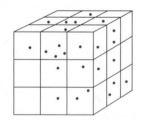

FIGURE 10.4   Division of space into cells.

the particle positions after each time step and redistributing the particles or, perhaps, changing the cells. We can use various data structures to store the particles and cell information.

One other approach that is often used is to replace interactions among particles by interactions between particles and a force field. For example, when we compute the gravitational force on a point mass on the surface of the earth, we use the value of the gravitational field rather than the point-to-point force between the point mass of the particle and a second large point mass at the center of the earth. If we were concerned with only the mass of the earth and our point on the surface, the two approaches would require about the same amount of work. However, if we were to also include the force from the moon, the situation would be more complex. If we used point masses, we would have two point-to-point forces to compute for our mass on the surface, but if we knew the gravitational field, the calculation would be the same as before. Of course, the calculation of the field is more complex when we consider the moon; for particle systems, however, we can often neglect distant particles, so the particle-field method may be more efficient. We can often compute the approximate field on a grid, then use the value at the nearest grid point to give the forces on each particle. After the new state of each particle has been computed, we can update the field. Both of these strategies can often reduce the $O(n^2)$ calculation of forces to $O(n \log n)$.

10.4 SOLVING PARTICLE SYSTEMS

Consider a particle system of n particles. If we restrict ourselves to the simple forces that we just described, the entire particle system can be described by $6n$ ordinary differential equations of the form

$$\dot{\mathbf{u}} = \mathbf{g}(\mathbf{u}, t),$$

where $\mathbf{u}$ is an array of the $6n$ position and velocity components of our n particles, and $\mathbf{g}$ includes any external forces applied to the particles. Thus, if we have two particles $\mathbf{a}$ and $\mathbf{b}$ connected by a spring without damping, we might have

$$\mathbf{u}^T = [\, u_0 \quad u_1 \quad u_2 \quad u_3 \quad u_4 \quad u_5 \quad u_6 \quad u_7 \quad u_8 \quad u_9 \quad u_{10} \quad u_{11} \,]$$
$$= [\, a_x \quad a_y \quad a_z \quad \dot{a}_x \quad \dot{a}_y \quad \dot{a}_z \quad b_x \quad b_y \quad b_z \quad \dot{b}_x \quad \dot{b}_y \quad \dot{b}_z \,].$$

Given the external forces and the state of the particle system $\mathbf{u}$ at any time t, we can evaluate

$$\mathbf{g}^T = \left[u_3 \quad u_4 \quad u_5 \quad -kd_x \quad -kd_y \quad -kd_z \quad u_9 \quad u_{10} \quad u_{11} \quad kd_x \quad kd_y \quad kd_z \right].$$

Here k is the spring constant and $d_x, d_y,$ and d_z are the components of the normalized vector d between $\mathbf{a}$ and $\mathbf{b}$. Thus, we must first compute

$$\mathbf{d} = \frac{1}{\sqrt{(u_0 - u_5)^2 + (u_1 - u_6)^2 + (u_2 - u_7)^2}} \begin{bmatrix} u_0 - u_6 \\ u_1 - u_7 \\ u_2 - u_8 \end{bmatrix}.$$

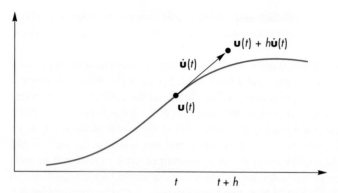

FIGURE 10.5   Approximation of the solution of a differential equation.

Numerical ordinary differential equation solvers rely on our ability to evaluate **g** to approximate **u** at future times. We can develop a family of differential equation solvers based upon Taylor's theorem. The simplest is known as Euler's method. Suppose that we integrate the expression

$$\dot{\mathbf{u}} = \mathbf{g}(\mathbf{u}, t)$$

over a short time h:

$$\int_t^{t+h} \dot{\mathbf{u}} d\tau = \mathbf{u}(t+h) - \mathbf{u}(t) = \int_t^{t+h} \mathbf{g}(\mathbf{u}, \tau) d\tau.$$

If h is small, we can approximate the value of **g** over the interval $[t, t+h]$ by the value of **g** at t; thus,

$$\mathbf{u}(t+h) \approx \mathbf{u}(t) + h\mathbf{g}(\mathbf{u}(t), t).$$

This expression shows that we can use the value of the derivative at t to get us to an approximate value of $\mathbf{u}(t+h)$, as shown in Figure 10.5.

This expression matches the first two terms of the Taylor expansion; we can write it as

$$\mathbf{u}(t+h) = \mathbf{u}(t) + h\dot{\mathbf{u}}(t) + O(h^2) = \mathbf{u}(t) + h\mathbf{g}(\mathbf{u}(t), t) + O(h^2),$$

showing that the error we incur in making the approximation is proportional to the square of the step size.

This method is particularly easy to implement. We evaluate the forces (both external and among particles) at time t, compute **g**, multiply it by h, and add it to the present state. We can apply this method iteratively to compute further values at $t + 2h, t + 3h, \ldots$. The work involved is one calculation of the forces for each time step.

There are two potential problems with Euler's method: accuracy and stability. Both are affected by the step size. The accuracy of Euler's method is proportional to the square of the step size. Consequently, to increase the accuracy we must cut the step size, thus increasing the time it takes to solve the system. A potentially more serious problem concerns stability. As we go from step to step, the per-step errors that we make come from two sources: the approximation error that we made by using the Taylor series approximation and the numerical errors that we make in computing the functions. These errors can either cancel themselves out as we compute further states, or they can accumulate and give us unacceptably large errors that mask the true solution. Such behavior is called **numerical instability**. Fortunately, for the standard types of forces that we have used, if we make the step size small enough, we can guarantee stability. Unfortunately, the required step size for stability may be so small that we cannot solve the equations numerically in a reasonable amount of time. This unstable behavior is most pronounced for spring-mass systems, where the spring constant determines the stiffness of the system and leads to what are called **stiff** sets of differential equations.

There are two general approaches to this problem. One is to seek another type of ordinary differential equation solver, called a stiff equation solver—a topic that is beyond the scope of this book. Another is to find other differential equation solvers similar in philosophy to Euler's method but with a higher per-step accuracy. We derive one such method because it gives us insight into the family of such methods. References to both approaches are given at the end of the chapter.

Suppose that we start as before by integrating the differential equations over a short time interval to obtain

$$\mathbf{u}(t + h) = \mathbf{u}(t) + \int_{t}^{t+h} \mathbf{g}(\mathbf{u}, \tau)d\tau.$$

This time, we approximate the integral by an average value over the interval $[t, t + h]$:

$$\int_{t}^{t+h} \mathbf{g}(\mathbf{u}, \tau)d\tau \approx \frac{h}{2}(\mathbf{g}(\mathbf{u}(t), t) + \mathbf{g}(\mathbf{u}(t + h), t + h)).$$

The problem now is we do not have $\mathbf{g}(\mathbf{u}(t + h), t + h)$; we have only $\mathbf{g}(\mathbf{u}(t), t)$. We can use Euler's method to approximate $\mathbf{g}(\mathbf{u}(t + h), t + h)$; that is, we can use

$$\mathbf{g}(\mathbf{u}(t + h), t + h) \approx \mathbf{g}(\mathbf{u}(t) + h\mathbf{g}(\mathbf{u}(t), t), t + h).$$

This method is known as the **improved Euler method** or the **Runge-Kutta method of order 2**. Note that to go from t to $t + h$, we must evaluate $\mathbf{g}$ twice. However, if we were to use Taylor's theorem to evaluate the per-step error, we would find that it is now $O(h^3)$. Thus, even though we are doing more work per step, we can use larger step sizes, and the method is stable for step sizes larger than those for which Euler's method was stable. In general, we can use increasingly more accurate per-step formulas and derive a set of methods called the Runge-Kutta formulas. The most popular is the fourth-order method that has a per-step error of $O(h^4)$ and requires four function evaluations per step. In practice, we can do even better with this number of function evaluations, achieving errors of $O(h^5)$. More important, good solvers adjust their own step size so as to ensure stability.

10.5   CONSTRAINTS

Simply allowing a group of particles to change state according to a set of differential equations is often insufficient to model real-world behavior such as collisions. Although the impact of an object hitting a wall is subject to Newton's laws, if we were to model the object as a collection of particles, the resulting system would be too complex for most purposes. Instead, we regard conditions such as the one in which two solid objects cannot penetrate each other as constraints that can be stated separately from the laws governing individual particle behavior.

There are two types of constraints that we can impose on particles. **Hard constraints** are those that must be adhered to exactly. For example, a ball must bounce off a wall; it cannot penetrate the wall and emerge from the other side. Nor can we allow the ball just to come close and then go off in another direction. **Soft constraints** are those that we need only come close to satisfying. For example, we might want two particles to be separated by approximately a specified distance, as in a particle mesh.

10.5.1 Collisions

Although, in general, hard constraints can be difficult to impose, there are a few situations that can be dealt with directly for ideal point particles. Consider the problem of collisions. We can separate the problem into two parts: detection and reaction. Suppose that we have a collection of particles and other geometric objects and the particles repel one another. We therefore need to consider only collisions between each particle and the other objects. If there are n particles and m polygons that define the geometric objects, at each time step we can check whether any particle has gone through any of the polygons.

Suppose that one of the particles has penetrated a polygon, as shown in Figure 10.6. We can detect this collision by inserting the position of the particle into the equation of the plane of the polygon. If the time step of our differential equation solver is small, we can assume that the velocity between time steps is constant, and we can use linear interpolation to find the time at which the particle actually hit the polygon.

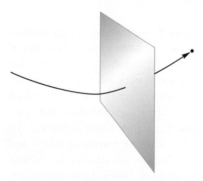

FIGURE 10.6   Particle penetrating a polygon.

What happens to the particle after a collision is similar to what happens when light reflects from a surface. If there is an **elastic collision**, the particle loses none of its energy, so its speed is unchanged. However, its direction after the collision is in the direction of a perfect reflection. Thus, given the normal at the point of collision P_c and the previous position of the particle P_0, we can compute the direction of a perfect reflection, as we did in Chapter 6, using the vector from the particle to the surface and the normal at the surface, as shown in Figure 10.7:

$$\mathbf{r} = (2(\mathbf{p}_0 - \mathbf{p}_c) \cdot \mathbf{n})\, \mathbf{n} - (\mathbf{P}_0 - \mathbf{P}_c).$$

The particle will end up a distance along this reflector equal to the distance it would have penetrated the polygon in the absence of collision detection, as shown in Figure 10.8.

The velocity is changed to be along the direction of reflection, with the same magnitude. Equivalently, the tangential component of the velocity—the part in the plane of the polygon—is unchanged, whereas the direction of the normal component is reversed.

FIGURE 10.7   Particle reflection.

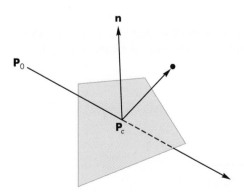

FIGURE 10.8   Position after collision.

A slightly more complex calculation is required for an **inelastic collision** in which the particle loses some of its energy when it collides with another object. The **coefficient of restitution** of a particle is the fraction of the normal velocity retained after the collision. Thus, the angle of reflection is computed as for the elastic collision, and the normal component of the velocity is multiplied by the coefficient of restitution. See Section 10.6.4 for an example.

The major cost of dealing with collisions is the complexity of detection. In applications such as games, approximate detection often is sufficient. In this case, we can replace complex objects consisting of many polygons by simple objects, such as their bounding volumes, for which collision detection is simpler.

Note that the use of particles avoids the complex calculations necessary for objects with finite sizes. In many ways, solving the collision problem is similar to clipping arbitrary objects against one another; the calculation is conceptually simple but is in practice time consuming and messy. In addition, if we have objects with finite size, we have to consider inertial forces, thereby increasing the dimension of the system of equations that we must solve. Consequently, in computer graphics, we are usually willing to accept an approximate solution using ideal point particles, and we obtain an acceptable rendering by placing objects at the location of the particle.

There is another case of hard constraints that often arises and can be handled correctly: contact forces. Suppose that we have a particle that is subject to a force pushing it along a surface, as shown in Figure 10.9. The particle cannot penetrate the surface, and it cannot bounce from the surface because of the force being applied to it. We can argue that the particle is subject to the tangential component of the applied force—that is, the part of the applied force along the surface. We can also apply frictional terms in this direction.

Note that collision detection, as opposed to how we deal with a collision once it has been detected, is often another $O(n^2)$ calculation. Consider, for example, a game such as pool, in which balls are moving around a table, or a simulation of molecules moving within a bounded volume. As any pair of particles can collide, a brute-force approach would be to check all pairs of particles at each time step. Faster approaches involve bounding box methods and hardware support for collision detection.

10.5.2 Soft Constraints

Most hard constraints are difficult to enforce. For example, if we want to ensure that a particle's velocity is less than a maximum velocity or that all the particles have a constant amount of energy, then the resulting mathematics is far more difficult than

FIGURE 10.9   Contact force.

what we have already seen, and such constraints do not always lead to a simple set of ordinary differential equations.

In many situations, we can work with soft constraints: constraints that we only need to come close to satisfying. For example, if we want a particle whose location is **p** to remain near the position $\mathbf{p}_0$, we can consider the **penalty function** $|\mathbf{p} - \mathbf{p}_0|^2$. The smaller this function is, the closer we are to obeying the constraint. This function is one example of an **energy function** whose value represents the amount of some type of energy stored in the system. In physics, such functions can represent quantities, such as the potential or kinetic energy in the system. Physical laws can be written either as differential equations, like those we used for our particles, or in terms of the minimization of expressions involving energy terms. One advantage of the latter form is that we can express constraints or desired behavior of a system directly in terms of potential or energy functions. Conversion of these expressions to force laws is a mechanical process, but its mathematical details are beyond the scope of this book.

10.6 A SIMPLE PARTICLE SYSTEM

Let's build a simple particle system that can be expanded to more complex behaviors. Our particles are all Newtonian, so their state is described by their positions and velocities. In addition, each particle can have its own color index and mass. We start with the following structure:

```
function particle()
{
  var p = { };
  p.color = vec4(0, 0, 0, 1);
  p.position = vec4(0, 0, 0, 1);
  p.velocity = vec4(0, 0, 0, 0);
  p.mass = 1;

  return p;
}
```

In terms of the affine spaces that we introduced in Chapter 4, if we use four-dimensional homogeneous coordinates for our positions, velocities, and forces, particle positions must have a fourth component of 1, whereas both velocities and forces must have a fourth component of 0.

A particle system is an array of particles

```
var particleSystem = [ ];
```

We can initialize the system with the particles in random locations inside a centered cube with side length 2.0 and with random velocities as follows:

```
for (var i = 0; i < numParticles; ++i) {
  particleSystem[i].mass = 1.0;
  particleSystem[i].color = vertexColors[i % numColors];
```

```
for (var j = 0; j < 3; ++j) {
  particleSystem[i].position[j] = 2.0 * Math.random() - 1.0;
  particleSystem[i].velocity[j] = speed * 2.0 * Math.random() - 1.0;
}

particleSystem[i].position[3] = 1.0;
}

for (var i = 0; i < numParticles; ++i) {
  pointsArray.push(particleSystem[i].position);
  colorsArray.push(particleSystem[i].color);
}
```

10.6.1 Displaying the Particles

Given the position of a particle, we can display it using any set of primitives that we like. A simple starting place is to display each particle as a point. Here is a render function that first updates the particle positions and then renders them:

```
function render()
{
  gl.clear(gl.COLOR_BUFFER_BIT);

  update();
  gl.drawArrays(gl.POINTS, numVertices, numParticles);

  requestAnimFrame(render);
}
```

10.6.2 Updating Particle Positions

We use an update function to compute forces and update the particle positions and velocities. Once the forces on each particle are computed, the Euler integration is

```
for (var i = 0; i < numParticles; ++i) {
  particleSystem[i].position = add(particleSystem[i].position,
  scale(speed*dt, particleSystem[i].velocity));
  particleSystem[i].velocity = add(particleSystem[i].velocity,
  scale(speed*dt/ particleSystem[i].mass, forces(i)));
}
```

The positions are updated using the velocity, and the velocity is updated by computing the forces on that particle. We have assumed that the time interval is short enough that we can compute the forces on each particle as we update its state. A more robust strategy would be to compute all the forces on all the particles first and put the results into an array that can be used to update the state.

We shall use the collision function to keep the particles inside a box. It could also be used to deal with collisions between particles.

10.6.3 Collisions

We use the collision function to keep the particles inside the initial axis-aligned box. Our strategy is to increment the position of each particle and then check if the particle has crossed one of the sides of the box. If it has crossed a side, then we can treat the bounce as a reflection. Thus, we need only change the sign of the velocity in the normal direction and to keep the particle on the same side of the box. If coef, the coefficient of restitution, is less than 1.0, the particles will slow down when they hit a side of the box. We do this calculation on a component-by-component basis:

```
function collision(particleId)
{
  coef = (elastic ? 0.9 : 1.0);

  for (var i = 0; i < 3; ++i) {
    particleSystem[particleId].velocity[i] *= -coef;

    if (particleSystem[particleId].position[i] >= 1.0) {
      particleSystem[particleId].position[i] =
        1.0 - coef * (particleSystem[particleId].position[i] - 1.0);
    }
    if (particleSystem[particleId].position[i] <= -1.0) {
      particleSystem[particleId].position[i] =
        -1.0 - coef * (particleSystem[particleId].position[i] + 1.0);
    }
  }
}
```

Once we have updated the particle positions and velocities, we can resend these data to the GPU in the update function:

```
colorsArray = [ ];
pointsArray = [ ];

for (var i = 0; i < numParticles; ++i) {
  pointsArray.push(particleSystem[i].position);
  colorsArray.push(particleSystem[i].color);
}
gl.bindBuffer(gl.ARRAY_BUFFER, cBufferId);
gl.bufferSubData(gl.ARRAY_BUFFER, 0, flatten(colorsArray));
gl.bindBuffer(gl.ARRAY_BUFFER, vBufferId);
gl.bufferSubData(gl.ARRAY_BUFFER, 0, flatten(pointsArray));
```

This strategy may seem a bit troublesome, since it requires a retransfer of all the data to the GPU for each time step. If we ignore interactions between particles such as spring forces, attraction, and repulsion, we can avoid the transfers and do the updating in the vertex shader. See Exercise 10.23. However, when we consider interparticle forces, we cannot do so in a simple manner because the vertex shader works on a vertex-by-vertex basis. Hence, each particle is a single vertex that has no knowledge of the other particles. In Section 10.7, we will carry out a more complex calculation using render to texture in which each particle can see information about other particles in the texture image, which is shared by all vertices. But first let's look at the force calculations.

10.6.4 Forces

If the forces are set to zero, the particles will bounce around the box on random paths continuously. If the coefficient of restitution is less than 1.0, eventually the particles will slow to a halt. The easiest force to add is gravity. For example, if all the particles have the same mass, we can add a gravitational term in the y direction. We can add repulsion in the force function by looking at the distance between pairs of points. Here is a simple force function that has as input the identifier of the particle and uses the input from two buttons to turn gravity and repulsion on and off.

```
function force(ParticleI)
{
  var force = vec4(0, 0, 0, 0);

  if (gravity) {
    force[1] = -0.5;  // simple gravity
  }

  if (repulsion) {
    for (var ParticleK = 0; ParticleK < numParticles; ++ParticleK) {
    // Repulsive force
    if (ParticleK != ParticleI) {
      var t =  normalize(subtract(particleSystem[ParticleI].position,
                      particleSystem[ParticleK].position));
      var d2 = dot(t, t);

      force = add(force, scale(0.01/d2, t));
    }
  }
}

  return (force);
}
```

We can also add attractive forces (see Exercise 10.14) by a similar computation. The exercises at the end of the chapter suggest some other extensions to the system. The website contains the code for the program.

10.6.5 Flocking

Some of the most interesting applications of particle systems are for simulating complex behaviors among the particles. Perhaps a more accurate statement is that we can produce what appears to be complex behavior using some simple rules for how particles interact. A classic example is simulating the flocking behavior of birds. How does a large group of birds maintain a flock without each bird knowing the positions

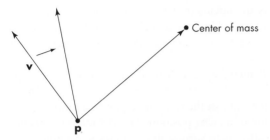

FIGURE 10.10   Changing a particle's direction.

of all the other birds? We can investigate some possibilities by making some minor modifications to our particle system.

One possibility is to alter the direction of each particle so the particle steers toward the center of the system. Thus each time we want to update the system, we first compute the average position:

```
var cm = [ ];

for (var k = 0; k < 3; ++k) {
  cm[k] = 0;

  for (var i = 0; i < numParticles; ++i) {
    cm[k] += particles[i].postition[k];
  }

  cm[k] /= numParticles;
}
```

Then we can compute a new velocity direction, as in Figure 10.10, that lies between the updated velocity vector `particles[i].velocity` and the vector from `particles[i].position` to the average position. See Exercise 10.20.

10.7   AGENT-BASED MODELS

In our examples so far, all the particles were the same because, although they can have different colors and move to different positions with different velocities, they are all subject to the same forces. However, there is nothing that prevents us from modeling different behaviors for different particles or different types of particles. For example, if we want to simulate the interaction of various atomic particles, some would have positive charges, some would have negative charges, and some would have no charge. Thus, the repulsion forces on a particular particle would depend on its charge and that of its neighbors. In a prey-predator simulation, the prey, such as rabbits, would have different behaviors than their predators, such as foxes. In a traffic simulation, we might want each car to have its own destination. In addition, we often want to incorporate local information to alter the behavior of our simulated particles. For example, if our agents are moving over a terrain, the local shape of the surface will affect their behavior. In these kinds of simulations, we usually use the term **agents** rather than particles and refer to the modeling process as **agent-based modeling**(ABM).

It is fairly straightforward to extend our approach to a model in which each agent has its own individual properties. We can also use a texture map to store a terrain. At each iteration, we could then use the value of the texel corresponding to the agent's position as part of the determination of its next position. An even more interesting case is one in which the agents can affect their surroundings. A classic example is the modeling of ant behavior. As ants move, they leave pheromones, chemical traces that provide signals to other ants. In our terms, the agents are changing the environment.

We can use the render-to-texture techniques that we developed in Chapter 7 to build such models. Let's consider the following simplified model that has many of the characteristics of an ant simulation. We have two types of agents that we can display as points in different colors. The agents are assigned initial random positions in a rectangle. If they simply move randomly in two dimensions, at any time we would see a display as in Color Plate 29, which shows 100 agents, 50 of each color.[2] Initially, the texture that we use to model a surface is white, so when we display the agents we see an image of points distributed randomly on a white background. We can get some more complex dynamic behavior starting as follows. Each agent still moves randomly but leaves its color on the surface by rendering the points to a texture. This trace of the agents is diffused to its neighbors on each iteration. Color Plate 30 shows the same 100 agents with their diffused trails. We see areas in which there is one of the two colors, indicating that only one type visited the spot recently or at all. Faded colors indicate that an agent has visited the spot long ago. Areas of gray are places where both types of agents visited the spot at approximately the same time. Areas of white indicate that no agent has visited the spot or the trail has completely faded away. Because we have not used the information in the texture map to control the movement of the agents, this simulation is not very different from our earlier examples of render to texture.

Given that we can read the color at each location of an agent with a sampler, we can use past behavior stored in the texture image to alter the next move so it is not purely random. Let's consider a somewhat artificial example that will give a vivid display that shows the possibilities. Suppose that at each iteration, for each point we check the color at that location in the texture map using `gl.readPixels`. If the color at the location matches the color of the agent and has a high value, we move the agent to a point called an **attractor**. The key part of the code is

```
for (var i = 0; i < numPoints; ++i) {
  vertices[4+i][0] += 0.01 * (2.0*Math.random() - 1.0);
  vertices[4+i][1] += 0.01 * (2.0*Math.random() - 1.0);

  if (vertices[4+i][0] >  1.0) { vertices[4+i][0] -= 2.0; }
  if (vertices[4+i][0] < -1.0) { vertices[4+i][0] += 2.0; }
```

---

2. Agents that move outside the default region reenter on the opposite side.

```
   if (vertices[4+i][1] >  1.0) { vertices[4+i][1] -= 2.0; }
   if (vertices[4+i][1] < -1.0) { vertices[4+i][1] += 2.0; }
}

for (var i = 0; i < numPoints/2; ++i) {
  var x = Math.floor(511 * vertices[4+i][0]);
  var y = Math.floor(511 * vertices[4+i][1]);
  var color = new Uint8Array(4);

  gl.readPixels(x, y, 1, 1, gl.RGBA, gl.UNSIGNED_BYTE, color);

  if (color[0] > 128) { vertices[4+i][0] = 0.5; }
  if (color[0] > 128) { vertices[4+i][1] = 0.5; }
}

for (var i = numPoints/2; i < numPoints; ++i) {
  var x = Math.floor(511 * vertices[4+i][0]);
  var y = Math.floor(511 * vertices[4+i][1]);
  var color = new Uint8Array(4);

  gl.readPixels(x, y, 1, 1, gl.RGBA, gl.UNSIGNED_BYTE, color);

  if (color[1] > 128) { vertices[4+i][0] = -0.5; }
  if (color[1] > 128) { vertices[4+i][1] = -0.5; }
}

gl.bufferSubData(gl.ARRAY_BUFFER, 0, flatten(vertices));
```

The two-dimensional points are stored in the array `vertices`, with the first four vertices used for the rectangle that contains the texture. The first half of the particles are green and the rest are magenta. We move all the particles randomly and then read the color at the new location. For each green particle, if the color at the new location is over half magenta, we move the particle to $(0.5, 0.5)$. For each magenta particle, if the color at the new location is over half green, we move the particle to $(-0.5, -0.5)$. Color Plate 31 shows the tendency of the two types of agents to move toward these attractors. Note that once the agents reach attractors, they start moving randomly again. Also, we can see that some agents have never encountered a high value of their color in the texture so are still moving around randomly near their initial locations. The full programs (`particleDiffusion1` and `particleDiffusion2`) are on the website for the book.

10.8 LANGUAGE-BASED MODELS

Graphs, such as trees and DAGs that we introduced in Chapter 9, offer but one way of representing hierarchical relationships among objects. In this section, we look at language-based models for representing relationships. Not only do these methods provide an alternate way of showing relationships but also they lead to procedural methods for describing objects, such as plants and terrain.

If we look at natural objects, such as plants, we see that, although no two trees are identical, we may have no difficulty telling the difference between two species of trees. Various methods have been proposed that give different realizations each time the program is run, but that have clear rules for defining the structure. We look at the use of tree data structures for generating objects that look like plants.

In computer science, tree data structures are used for describing the parsing of sentences into constituent parts, in both computer and natural languages. For computer programs, doing this parsing is part of compiling the statements in a computer program. For natural languages, we parse sentences to determine whether they are grammatically correct. The tree that results from the parsing of a correct sentence gives the structure or syntax of that sentence. The interpretation of the individual elements in the tree—the words—give the meaning or semantics of the sentence.

If we look at only the syntax of a language, there is a direct correlation between the rules of the language and the form of the trees that represent the sentences. We can extend this idea to hierarchical objects in graphics, relating a set of rules and a tree-structured model. These systems are known as **tree grammars**. A grammar can be defined by a set of symbols and a set of symbol-replacement rules, or **productions**, that specify how to replace a symbol by one or more symbols. Typical rules are written as

$A \rightarrow BC$

$B \rightarrow ABA.$

Given a set of productions, we can generate an infinite number of strings. In general, there is more than one rule that we can apply to a given symbol at any time, and, if we select randomly which rule to apply, we can generate a different string each time the program is executed. Programs can be written that not only generate such strings but also take strings as input and test whether the strings are valid members of the set of strings generated by a given set of rules. Thus, we might have a set of rules for generating a certain type of object, such as a tree or a bush, and a separate program that can identify objects in a scene based on which grammar generates the shape.

The interpretation of the symbols in a string converts the string to a graphical object. There are numerous ways to generate rules and to interpret the resulting strings as graphical objects. One approach starts with the **turtle graphics** (Exercise 2.4) system. In turtle graphics, we have three basic ways of manipulating a graphics cursor, or **turtle**. The turtle can move forward 1 unit, turn right, or turn left. Suppose that the angle by which the turtle can turn is fixed. We can then denote our three operations as F, R, and L. Any string of these operations has a simple graphical interpretation. For example, if the angle is 120 degrees, the string *FRFRFR* generates an equilateral triangle. We use the special symbols [and] to denote pushing and popping the state of the turtle (its position and orientation) onto a stack (an operation equivalent to using parentheses). Consider the production rule

$F \rightarrow FLFRRFLF,$

FIGURE 10.11   The Koch curve rule.

(a)

(b)

FIGURE 10.12   Space-filling curves. (a) Koch curve. (b) Koch snowflake.

with an angle of 60 degrees. The graphical interpretation of this rule is shown in Figure 10.11. If we apply the rule again, in parallel to all instances of F, we get the curve in Figure 10.12(a); if we apply it to a triangle, we get the closed curve in Figure 10.12(b). These curves are known as the **Koch curve** and **Koch snowflake**, respectively. If we scale the geometric interpretation of the curve each time that we execute the algorithm, so as to leave the original vertices in their original locations, we find we are generating a longer curve at each iteration, but this curve always lies inside the circle determined by the original vertices. In the limit, we have a curve that has infinite length, never crosses itself, but fits in a finite circle. It also is continuous but has a discontinuous derivative everywhere.

Another classic example is the **Hilbert curve.** Hilbert curves are formed from four simple primitives we can call A_0, B_0, C_0, and D_0, shown in Figure 10.13. Each is a first-order Hilbert curve. The arrows are there to indicate that we start drawing each in one corner. There are four Hilbert curves of each order N, which we can call A_N, B_N, C_N, and D_N. We form each from the order $N - 1$ curves by combining the four types according to the rules:

$$A_N = B_{N-1} \uparrow A_{N-1} \rightarrow A_{N-1} \downarrow C_{N-1}$$

$$B_N = A_{N-1} \rightarrow B_{N-1} \uparrow B_{N-1} \leftarrow D_{N-1}$$

$$C_N = D_{N-1} \leftarrow C_{N-1} \downarrow C_{N-1} \rightarrow A_{N-1}$$

$$D_N = C_{N-1} \downarrow D_{N-1} \leftarrow D_{N-1} \uparrow B_{N-1}$$

FIGURE 10.13   The zero-order Hilbert patterns.

FIGURE 10.14   Hilbert rule for type A.

FIGURE 10.15   Second-order Hilbert curve.

FIGURE 10.16   The rule $F \rightarrow F[RF]F[LF]F$.

FIGURE 10.17   Second iteration of the rule in Figure 10.16.

The interpretation of theses rules is that the Nth pattern is formed by combining four patterns of order $N - 1$ in specified directions. We can see from Figure 10.14 for the first-order curve A_1 that **links** corresponding to the arrows in the formulas must be added to connect the patterns. Note also that each pattern starts in a different corner. When the curves are drawn, the arrows are left out, and the links are displayed as solid lines, we obtain curves such as in Figure 10.15.

If we scale the lengths of links as we go to higher-order curves, we can verify that, like the Koch curves, the Hilbert curves get longer and longer, never crossing themselves, but always fit in the same box. In the limit, the Hilbert curves fill every point in the box and are known as **space-filling curves**.

The push and pop operators allow us to develop side branches. Consider the rule

$$F \rightarrow F[RF]F[LF]F,$$

where the angle is 27 degrees (Figure 10.16). Note that we start at the bottom and the angle is measured as a right or left deviation from forward.

If we start with a single line segment, the resulting object is that shown in Figure 10.16. We can proceed in a number of ways. One method is to apply the rule again to each F in the sequence, resulting in the object in Figure 10.17. We can also adjust the length corresponding to a forward movement of the turtle so that branches get smaller on successive iterations. The object resembles a bush and will look more like a bush if we iterate a few more times. However, having only one rule and applying it in parallel results in every bush looking the same.

A more interesting strategy is to apply the rule *randomly* to occurrences of F. If we do so, our single rule can generate both of the objects in Figure 10.18. Adding a few more productions and controlling the probability function that determines which rule is to be applied next allows the user to generate a variety of types of trees. With only slight modifications, we can also draw leaves at the ends of the branches.

FIGURE 10.18   Results of random application of the rule from Figure 10.16.

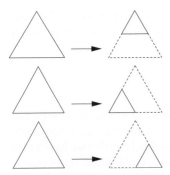

FIGURE 10.19   Three rules for the Sierpinski gasket.

One of the attractions of this strategy is that we have defined a class of objects based on only a handful of rules and a few parameters. Suppose that we wish to create a group of trees. The direct approach is to generate as many objects as needed, representing each one as a collection of geometric objects (lines, polygons, curves). In a complex scene, we might then be overwhelmed with the number of primitives generated. Depending on the viewing conditions, most of these primitives might not appear in the image, because they would be clipped out or would be too far from the viewer to be rendered at a visible size. In contrast, using our procedural method, we describe objects by simple algorithms and generate the geometric objects only when we need them and only to the level of detail that is required.

We can also describe a grammar directly in terms of shapes and affine transformations, creating a **shape grammar**. Consider our old friend the Sierpinski gasket. We can define a subdivision step in terms of three affine transformations, each of which scales the original triangle to one-half the size, and places the small copy in a different position, as in Figure 10.19. We can apply these rules randomly, or apply all three in parallel. In either case, in the limit, we derive the gasket.

We now have three related procedural methods that can generate either models of natural objects or models of interesting mathematical objects. The examples of the Koch curve and the Sierpinski gasket introduce a new aspect to the generation process: a method that can be applied recursively and that, each time it is executed, generates detail similar in shape to the original object. Such phenomena can be explored through fractal geometry.

10.9   RECURSIVE METHODS AND FRACTALS

The language-based procedural models offer but one approach to generating complex objects with simple programs. Another approach, based on **fractal geometry**, uses the self-similarity of many real-world objects. Fractal geometry was developed by Mandelbrot, who was able to create a branch of mathematics that enables us to work with interesting phenomena that the tools of ordinary geometry cannot handle. Workers in computer graphics have used the ideas of fractal geometry not only to create beautiful and complex objects but also to model many real-world entities that are not modeled easily by other methods. Graphical objects generated by fractals have been called **graftals.**

10.9.1 Rulers and Length

There are two pillars to fractal geometry: the dependence of geometry on scale and self-similarity. We can examine both through the exploration of one of the questions that led to fractal geometry: What is the length of a coastline? Say that we have a map of a coastline. Because a typical stretch of coastline is wavy and irregular, we cannot easily measure the length of coastline between two points. We can try to make such a measurement using a map or aerial photograph. We can take a string, lay it over the image of the coastline, and then measure the length of the string using the scale of the map to convert distances. However, if we obtain a second map that shows a closer view of the coastline, we see more detail. The added detail looks much like the view of the first map, but with additional inlets and protrusions visible. If we take our string and measure the length on the second map, taking into account the difference in scale between the two maps, we will measure a greater distance. We can continue this experiment by going to the coast and trying to measure with even greater precision. We find new detail, perhaps even to the level of measuring individual pebbles along the shore. In principle, we could continue this process down to the molecular level, each time seeing a similar picture with more detail and measuring a greater length.

If we want to get any useful information, or at least a measurement on which two people might agree, we must either limit the resolution of the map or, equivalently, pick the minimum unit that we can measure. In computer graphics, if we use perspective views, we have a similar problem, because what detail we see depends on how far we are from the object.

We can approach these problems mathematically by considering our recursion for the Koch snowflake in Section 10.8. Here, each line segment of length 1 was replaced by four line segments of length 1/3 (Figure 10.20). Hence, each time that we replace a segment, we span the distance between the same two endpoints with a curve four-thirds the length of the original. If we consider the limit as we iterate an infinite number of times, the issue of dimension arises. The curve cannot be an ordinary one-dimensional curve because, in the limit, it has infinite length and its first derivative is discontinuous everywhere. It is not a two-dimensional object, however, because it does not fill a two-dimensional region of the plane. We can resolve this problem by defining a fractional dimension.

FIGURE 10.20   Lengthening of the Koch curve.

FIGURE 10.21   Line segment, square, and cube.

FIGURE 10.22   Subdivision of the objects for $h = \frac{1}{3}$.

10.9.2 Fractal Dimension

Consider a line segment of length 1, a unit square, and a unit cube, as shown in Figure 10.21. Under any reasonable definition of *dimension*, the line segment, square, and cube are one-, two-, and three-dimensional objects, respectively. Suppose that we have a ruler, whose resolution is h, where $h = \frac{1}{n}$ is the smallest unit that we can measure. We assume that n is an integer. We can divide each of these objects into similar units in terms of h, as shown in Figure 10.22. We divide the line segment into $k = n$ identical segments, the square into $k = n^2$ small squares, and the cube into $k = n^3$ small cubes. In each case, we can say that we have created new objects by scaling the original object by a factor of h and replicating it k times. Suppose that d is the dimension of any one of these objects. What has remained constant in the subdivision is that the whole is the sum of the parts. Mathematically, for any of the objects, we have the equality

$$\frac{k}{n^d} = kn^{-d} = 1.$$

Solving for d, we can define the **fractal dimension** as

$$d = \frac{\ln k}{\ln n}.$$

In other words, the fractal dimension of an object is determined by how many similar objects we create by subdivision. Consider the Koch curve. We create four similar objects by the subdivision (scaling) of the original by a factor of 3. The corresponding fractal dimension is

$$d = \frac{\ln 4}{\ln 3} = 1.26186.$$

Now consider the Sierpinski gasket. A scaling step is shown in Figure 10.23. Each time that we subdivide a side by a factor of 2, we keep three of the four triangles created, and

FIGURE 10.23   Subdivision of the Sierpinski gasket.

FIGURE 10.24 Solid gasket.

FIGURE 10.25 Subdivision of a cube.

$$d = \frac{\ln 3}{\ln 2} = 1.58496.$$

In both examples, we can view the object created by the subdivision as occupying more space than a curve but less space than a filled area. We can create a solid version of the gasket in a three-dimensional space by starting with a tetrahedron and subdividing each of the faces, as shown in Figure 10.24. We keep the four tetrahedrons at the original vertices, discarding the region in the middle. The object that we create has a fractal dimension of

$$d = \frac{\ln 4}{\ln 2} = 2,$$

even though it does not lie in the plane. Also note that although the volume is reduced by each subdivision, the surface area is increased. Suppose that we start with a cube and divide it into thirds, as shown in Figure 10.25. Next, we remove the center by pushing out the pieces in the middle of each face and the center, thus leaving 20 of the original 27 subcubes. This object has a fractal dimension of

$$d = \frac{\ln 20}{\ln 3} = 2.72683.$$

Although these constructions are interesting and easy to generate graphically at any level of recursion, they are by themselves not useful for modeling the world. However, if we add randomness, we get a powerful modeling technique.

10.9.3 Midpoint Division and Brownian Motion

A fractal curve has dimension $1 \leq d < 2$. Curves with lower fractal dimension appear smoother than curves with higher fractal dimension. A similar statement holds for surfaces that have fractal dimension $2 \leq d < 3$. In computer graphics, there are many situations where we would like to create a curve or surface that appears random, but that has a measurable amount of roughness. For example, the silhouette of a mountain range forms a curve that is rougher (has higher fractal dimension) than the skyline of the desert. Likewise, a surface model of mountain terrain should have a higher fractal dimension than the surface of farmland. We also often want to generate these objects in a resolution-dependent manner. For example, the detail that we generate for a terrain used in speed-critical applications, such as in a flight simulator, should be generated at high resolution for only those areas near the aircraft.

The random movement of particles in fluids is known as **Brownian motion**. Simulating such motion provides an interesting approach to generating natural curves and surfaces. Physicists have modeled Brownian motion by forming polylines in which each successive point on the polyline is displaced by a random distance and in a random direction from its predecessor. True Brownian motion is based on a particular random-number distribution that generates paths that match physical particle paths. In computer graphics, we are more concerned with rapid computation, and with the ability to generate curves with a controllable amount of roughness; thus, we use the term *Brownian motion* in this broader sense.

FIGURE 10.26 Midpoint displacement. (a) Original line segment. (b) Line segment after subdivision.

FIGURE 10.27 Fractal curves with 1, 2, 4, 8, and 16 segments.

Although we could attempt to generate Brownian motion through the direct generation of a polyline, a more efficient method is to use a simple recursive process. Consider the line segment in Figure 10.26(a). We find its midpoint; then we displace the midpoint in the normal direction, by a random distance, as in Figure 10.26(b). We can repeat this process any number of times to produce curves like that in Figure 10.27. The variance of the random-number generator, or the average displacement, should be scaled by a factor, usually of $\frac{1}{2}$, each time, because the line segments are shortened at each stage. We can also allow the midpoint to be displaced in a random direction, rather than only along the normal. If the random numbers are always positive, we can create skylines. If we use a zero-mean Gaussian random-number generator, with variance proportional to $l^{2(2-d)}$, where l is the length of the segment to be subdivided, then d is the fractal dimension of the resulting curve. The value $d = 1.5$ corresponds to true Brownian motion.

10.9.4 Fractal Mountains

The best-known uses of fractals in computer graphics have been to generate mountains and terrain. We can generate a mountain with our tetrahedron subdivision process by adding in a midpoint displacement. Consider one facet of the tetrahedron, as shown in Figure 10.28. First, we find the midpoints of the sides; then we displace

FIGURE 10.28   Midpoint subdivision of a tetrahedron facet.

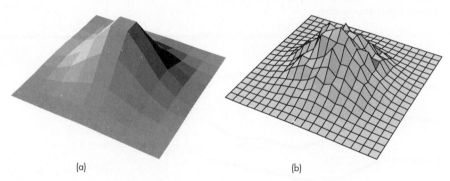

(a)   (b)

FIGURE 10.29   Fractal terrain. (a) Mesh. (b) Subdivided mesh with displaced vertices.

each midpoint, creating four new triangles. Once more, by controlling the variance of the random-number generator, we can control the roughness of the resulting object. Note that we must take great care in how the random numbers are generated if we are to create objects that are topologically correct and do not fold into themselves; see the Suggested Readings at the end of this chapter.

This algorithm can be applied equally well to any mesh. We can start with a flat mesh of rectangles in the x, z plane and subdivide each rectangle into four smaller rectangles, displacing all vertices upward (in the y direction). Figure 10.29 shows one example of this process. Section 10.10 presents another approach that can be used for generating terrain.

10.9.5 The Mandelbrot Set

The famous Mandelbrot set is an interesting example of fractal geometry that can be easily generated with WebGL's texture map functionality. Although the Mandelbrot set is easy to generate, it shows great complexity in the patterns it generates. It also provides a good example of generating images and using color lookup tables. In this discussion, we assume that you have a basic familiarity with complex arithmetic.

We denote a point in the complex plane as

$$\mathbf{z} = x + \mathbf{i}y,$$

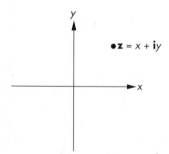

FIGURE 10.30   Complex plane.

where x is the real part and y is the imaginary part of $\mathbf{z}$ (Figure 10.30). If $\mathbf{z}_1 = x_1 + \mathbf{i}y_1$ and $\mathbf{z}_2 = x_2 + \mathbf{i}y_2$ are two complex numbers, complex addition and multiplication

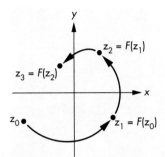

FIGURE 10.31   Paths from complex recurrence.

are defined by

$$\mathbf{z}_1 + \mathbf{z}_2 = x_1 + x_2 + \mathbf{i}(y_1 + y_2)$$

$$\mathbf{z}_1 \mathbf{z}_2 = x_1 x_2 - y_1 y_2 + \mathbf{i}(x_1 y_2 + x_2 y_1).$$

The pure imaginary number $\mathbf{i}$ has the property that $\mathbf{i}^2 = -1$. A complex number $\mathbf{z}$ has magnitude given by

$$|\mathbf{z}|^2 = x^2 + y^2.$$

In the complex plane, a function

$$\mathbf{w} = F(\mathbf{z})$$

maps complex points into complex points. We can use such a function to define a complex recurrence of the form

$$\mathbf{z}_{k+1} = F(\mathbf{z}_k),$$

where $\mathbf{z}_0 = \mathbf{c}$ is a given initial point. If we plot the locations of $\mathbf{z}_k$ for particular starting points, we can see several of the possibilities in Figure 10.31. For a particular function F, some initial values generate sequences that go off to infinity. Others may repeat periodically, and still other sequences converge to points called **attractors**. For example, consider the function

$$\mathbf{z}_{k+1} = \mathbf{z}_k^2,$$

where $\mathbf{z}_0 = \mathbf{c}$. If $\mathbf{c}$ lies outside the unit circle, the sequence $\{\mathbf{z}_k\}$ diverges; if $\mathbf{c}$ is inside the unit circle, $\{\mathbf{z}_k\}$ converges to an attractor at the origin; if $|\mathbf{c}| = 1$, each $\mathbf{z}_k$ is on the unit circle. If we consider the points for which $|\mathbf{c}| = 1$, we can see that, depending on the value of $\mathbf{c}$, we will generate either a finite number of points or all the points on the unit circle.

A more interesting example is the function

$$\mathbf{z}_{k+1} = \mathbf{z}_k^2 + \mathbf{c},$$

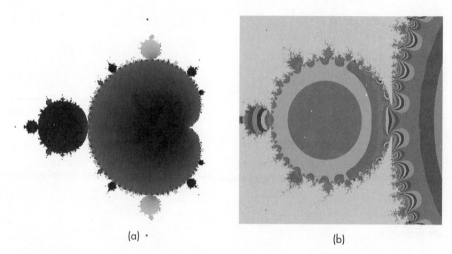

(a) ·   (b)

FIGURE 10.32   Mandelbrot set. (a) Black and white coloring. (b) Detail along edges.

with $\mathbf{z}_0 = 0 + \mathbf{i}0$. The point $\mathbf{c}$ is in the **Mandelbrot set** if and only if the points generated by this recurrence remain finite. Thus, we can break the complex plane into two groups of points: those that belong to the Mandelbrot set and those that do not. Graphically, we can take a rectangular region of the plane and color points black if they are in the set and white if they are not (Figure 10.32(a)). However, it is the regions on the edges of the set that show the most complexity, so we often want to magnify these regions.

The computation of the Mandelbrot set can be time consuming, but there are a few tricks to speed it up. The area centered at $\mathbf{c} = -0.5 + \mathbf{i}0.0$ is of the most interest, although we probably want to be able to change both the size and the center of our window.

We can usually tell after a few iterations whether a point will go off to infinity. For example, if $|\mathbf{z}_k| > 2$, successive values will be larger, and we can stop the iteration. It is more difficult to tell whether a point near the boundary will converge. Consequently, an approximation to the set is usually generated as follows. We fix a maximum number of iterations. If, for a given $\mathbf{c}$, we can determine that the point diverges, we color white the point corresponding to $\mathbf{c}$ in our image. If, after the maximum number of iterations, $|\mathbf{z}_k|$ is less than some threshold, we decide that it is in the set, and we color it black. For other values of $|\mathbf{z}_k|$, we assign a unique color to the point corresponding to $\mathbf{c}$. These colors are usually based on the value of $|\mathbf{z}_k|$ after the last iteration or alternately on how rapidly the points converge or diverge.

The book's website contains a program (`mandelbrot`) that generates an approximation to the set. The user can set the size and center of the rectangle and the number of iterations to be carried out. The magnitudes of the numbers $\mathbf{z}_k$ are clamped to the range 0.0 to 1.0. We generate an $n \times m$ 1-byte array `image` by looping over all pixels up to the maximum number of iterations.

We display the image as a texture mapped onto a square comprising two triangles. Hence, the vertices and texture coordinates can be given using a unit square as

```
var points = [
  vec4(0.0, 0.0, 0.0, 1.0),
  vec4(0.0, 1.0, 0.0, 1.0),
  vec4(1.0, 1.0, 0.0, 1.0),
  vec4(1.0, 0.0, 0.0, 1.0)
];

var texCoord = [
  vec2(0, 0),
  vec2(0, 1),
  vec2(1, 1),
  vec2(1, 0)
];
```

We set up a texture map just as in Chapter 7. We can create a texture image in many ways. The simplest is to construct an $n \times m$ luminance image

```
var texImage = new Uint8Array(4*n*m);
```

from the values generated by the calculation of the set and then display it by first converting it to an RGBA image. This is done by mapping gray levels given by the iteration result v to colors with code such as

```
v = Math.min(v, 1.0);          // clamp if > 1
texImage[4*i*m+4*j]   = 255 * v;
texImage[4*i*m+4*j+1] = 255 * (0.5 * (Math.sin(v*Math.PI/180) + 1.0));
texImage[4*i*m+4*j+2] = 255 * (1.0 - v);
texImage[4*i*m+4*j+3] = 255;
```

We specify an intensity-to-red map that assigns no red to black (0.0), assigns full red to white (1.0), and linearly interpolates between these values for the other intensities. For blue, we go from full blue for zero intensity to no blue for full intensity. We assign the intensity-to-green values sinusoidally. This green assignment enhances the detail in regions where there are slow changes in intensity (Figure 10.32(b)). The render function is

```
function render()
{
  gl.clear(gl.COLOR_BUFFER_BIT);
  gl.drawArrays(gl.TRIANGLE_FAN, 0, 4);
  requestAnimFrame(render);
}
```

This implementation makes little use of the capability of a GPU since all the calculations are done in the CPU and we only use the shaders to display the resulting texture image. In the next section, we will use a fragment shader to do all the computation.

10.9.6 Mandelbrot Fragment Shader

Each point we compute for the Mandelbrot set corresponds to a fragment in the color buffer, and its computation does not involve any surrounding points. Consequently, we can compute these values in a shader by providing the shader with the location of the fragment. The GLSL built-in variable `gl_FragCoord` is available to fragment shaders and provides the location of the fragment in window coordinates. Suppose that we specify a rectangle in our application and then execute a `gl.drawArrays(gl.TRIANGLES, 0, 6)` on the two triangles that make up the rectangle. The rasterizer then generates a fragment for each pixel in the color buffer, regardless of whether or not we have sent any colors to the shaders. Using `gl_FragCoord.x` and `gl_FragCoord.y`, we can generate the colors for each fragment using essentially the same code for the Mandelbrot set that we used in the CPU version. Here is such a shader:

```
precision mediump float;

uniform float cx;
uniform float cy;
uniform float height;
uniform float width;

void main()
{
  const int max = 100;            // number of interations per point
  const float PI = 3.14159;
  float n = 1024.0;               //color buffer width
  float m = 1024.0;               //color buffer height
  float v;

  float x = gl_FragCoord.x * (width / (n - 1.0)) + cx - width / 2.0;
  float y = gl_FragCoord.y * (height / (m - 1.0)) + cy - height / 2.0;

  float ax = 0.0, ay = 0.0;
  float bx, by;

  for (int k = 0; k < max; ++k) {
    // Compute c = c^2 + p
    bx = ax*ax - ay*ay;
    by = 2.0*ax*ay;
    ax = bx + x;
    ay = by + y;
    v = ax*ax + ay*ay;

    if (v > 4.0) { break; }  // assume not in set if mag > 2
  }

  // Assign gray level to point based on its magnitude */

  v = min(v, 1.0);  // clamp if v > 1
```

```
  gl_FragColor.r = v;
  gl_FragColor.g = 0.5* sin(2.0*PI*v) + 1.0;
  gl_FragColor.b = 1.0 - v;
  gl_FragColor.a = 1.0;
}
```

Note that this code is almost identical to the code we developed in the previous section, but there are no loops over the rows and columns since each fragment causes an execution of the shader. We pass in the center and the size of the window as uniform variables. Not only does this version, `mandelbrot2` on the website, free up the CPU, it makes use of two of the most powerful features of the GPU. First, we take advantage of the speed at which the GPU can carry out floating-point operations. Second, we get to make use of the multiple processors on recent GPUs. Thus, rather than compute the color for one pixel at a time as we did with the CPU-based version, now we can use the available processors on the GPU to compute up to hundreds of fragment colors concurrently. The exercises at the end of chapter suggest some ways to make this example interactive.

10.10 PROCEDURAL NOISE

We have used pseudorandom-number generators to generate the Sierpinski gasket and for fractal subdivision. The use of pseudorandom-number generators has many other uses in computer graphics, ranging from generating textures to generating models of natural objects such as clouds and fluids. However, there are both practical and theoretical reasons why the simple random-number generator that we have used is not a good choice for many applications.

Let's start with the idea of **white noise**. White noise is what we get from thermal activity in electrical circuits or what we see on a television screen when we tune to a channel that has no signal. Ideal white noise has the property that if we look at a sequence of samples we can find no correlation among the samples and thus we cannot predict the next sample from the previous samples. Mathematically, white noise has the property that its power spectrum—the average spectrum we would see in the frequency domain—is flat; all frequencies are present with equal strength.

Within the computer we can generate pseudorandom sequences of numbers. These random-number generators, such as the function `random` that we have used, produce uncorrelated sequences, but because the sequences repeat after a long period, they are not truly random, although they work well enough for most applications. However, for many other applications white noise is not what we need. Often we want randomness but do not want successive samples to be totally uncorrelated. For example, suppose that we want to generate some terrain for an interactive game. We can use a polygonal mesh whose heights vary randomly. True white noise would give a very rough surface due to the high-frequency content in the noise. If want a more realistic surface that might model a fairly smooth terrain, we would want adjacent vertices to be close to each other. Equivalently, we would like to remove high frequencies from the noise generator, or at least alter or "color" the spectrum.

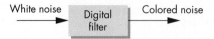

FIGURE 10.33   Generating correlated random numbers.

There is an additional problem with the high frequencies in white noise: aliasing. As we can see from Appendix D, sampling will cause aliasing of frequencies about the Nyquist rate, which can lead to annoying visual artifacts in the image.

There are various possible solutions to these problems. Assume that we want to generate a sequence of random samples that are band-limited and for which we know the frequencies that should be present. We could sample the sum of sinusoidal terms with low frequencies and random amplitudes and phases. This method of **Fourier synthesis** works in principle but requires expensive evaluations of trigonometric functions for each sample. Another class of methods is based on Figure 10.33. If the process is a digital filtering of the white noise, we can design the filter to include the frequencies we want at the desired magnitude and phase. Because this noise has a nonuniform spectrum, it is often called **colored noise**.

If we start with what we would like to see in a method, we can design a procedural approach that is based on Figure 10.33 but is much more computationally feasible. Besides wanting to minimize the computation required, we want repeatability and locality. If we use a random method to form a pattern or a texture, we must be able to repeat it exactly as we regenerate an object. We also want to be able to generate our pattern or texture using only local instead of global data.

Suppose that we generate a pseudorandom sequence on a one-, two- or three-dimensional grid (or lattice) in which the grid points are integers. We can use the values at the grid points to generate points for noninteger values; that is, for points between the cells determined by adjacent grid values. For example, suppose that we want to generate a two-dimensional texture. We start by forming a rectangular array of pseudorandom numbers. We can use this array to generate values for any (s, t) texture coordinates by interpolation. A simple interpolation would be to find the cell corresponding to a given (s, t) pair and use bilinear interpolation on the values at the corners to get an interior value.

This method generates what is known as **value noise**. We can control the smoothness by selecting how large a part of the array we use. For example, suppose that we generate a 256×256 array of pseudorandom numbers and use bilinear interpolation to form a 128×128 texture. We can use a single cell and interpolate the desired 128×128 texture values using only the four values at the corners of the cell. In this case we would get a very smooth texture image. Alternately, we could use a larger part of the array. If we used a 4×4 part of the array, each of the 16 cells would be interpolated to provide 64 values of the texture. Since we would be using 16 of the pseudorandom numbers, this texture would show more variation than our first example. We could use a 128×128 part of the pseudorandom array. In this case, we would not need any interpolation and would have a completely uncorrelated texture.

The problem with this process is that bilinear interpolation over each cell will result in visible artifacts as we go from cell to cell forming our texture. We can get around this problem by using an interpolation formula that uses data from adjacent cells to give a smoother result. The most common methods use cubic polynomials of the type that we will study in Chapter 11. Without going into detail on any particular type, we note that a cubic polynomial has four coefficients and thus we need four data points to specify it. For a two-dimensional process, we need the data at the eight adjacent cells or 16 (4 × 4) data points to determine values within that cell. In three dimensions, we need data at the 26 adjacent cells or 64 data points. Although we would get a smoother result, in two or three dimensions the amount of computation and the required data manipulation make this method problematic.

The solution to this problem is to use **gradient noise**. Suppose that we model noise in three dimensions as a continuous function $n(x, y, x)$. Near a grid point (i, j, k), where i, j, and k are integers, we can approximate $n(x, y, x)$ by the first terms of the Taylor series

$$n(x, y, z) \approx n(i, j, k) + (x - i)\frac{\partial n}{\partial x} + (y - j)\frac{\partial n}{\partial y} + (z - k)\frac{\partial n}{\partial z}.$$

The vector

$$\mathbf{g} = \begin{bmatrix} g_x \\ g_y \\ g_z \end{bmatrix} = \begin{bmatrix} \frac{\partial n}{\partial x} \\ \frac{\partial n}{\partial x} \\ \frac{\partial n}{\partial x} \end{bmatrix}$$

is the gradient at (i, j, k). Note that $x - i$, $y - j$, and $z - k$ are the fractional parts of the position within a cell. To generate gradient noise, we first compute normalized pseudeorandom gradient vectors at each grid point. We can get these vectors by generating a set of uniformly distributed random points on a unit sphere. We fix the values at the grid points to be zero ($n(i, j, k) = 0$). In three dimensions, within each cell, we have eight gradient vectors, one from each corner of the cell, that we can use to approximate $n(x, y, x)$. The standard technique is to use a filtered (smoothed) interpolation of these gradients to generate noise at points inside the cell. Noise generated in this manner is often called **Perlin noise** after its original creator, or just *noise*. This noise function is built into RenderMan and GLSL. The actual implementation of noise uses a hash table so that rather than finding random gradients for the entire grid, only 256 or 512 pseudorandom numbers are needed. Figure 10.34 shows two-dimensional gradient noise at three different frequencies. Each is a 256 × 256 luminance image that starts with the same array of pseudorandom numbers.

Procedural noise has been used in many ways. For example, adding a small amount of noise to the joint positions in our figure model can give a sense of realism to the model. Adding a nonlinearity, such as taking the absolute value in the noise generator, generates sequences that have been used to model turbulence in flows and

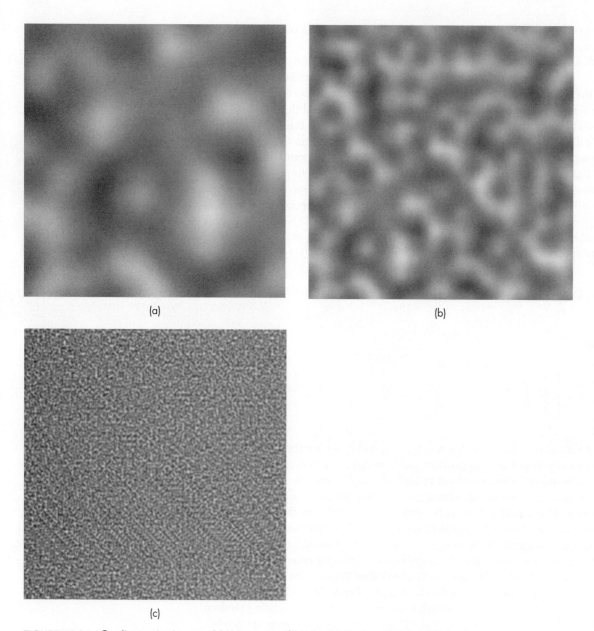

FIGURE 10.34   Gradient noise images. (a) Using noise. (b) Using 50 * noise. (c) Using 100 * noise.

to generate textures. Procedural noise is also used for modeling fuzzy objects such as simulated clouds.

SUMMARY AND NOTES

Procedural methods have advantages in that we can control how many primitives we produce and at which point in the process these primitives are generated. Equally important is that procedural graphics provides an object-oriented approach to building models—an approach that should be of increasing importance in the future.

Combining physics with computer graphics provides a set of techniques that has the promise of generating physically correct animations and of providing new modeling techniques. Recent examples, such as the use of physical modeling for the motion of 1000 balloons in Pixar Animation Studio's *Up*, show how the solution of complex systems of equations can provide the foundations of an animation.

Particle systems are but one example of physically based modeling, but they represent a technique that has wide applicability. One of the most interesting and informative exercises that you can undertake at this point is to build a particle system.

Particle methods are used routinely in commercial animations, both for simulation of physical phenomena, such as fire, clouds, and moving water, and in determining the positions of animated characters. Particle systems have also become a standard approach to simulating physical phenomena; they often replace complex partial differential equation models and are used even if a graphical result is not needed. In interactive games and simulations, each particle can be given complex behavioral rules. This merging of graphics and artificial intelligence is core to agent-based modeling.

Fractals provide another method for generating objects with simple algorithms and programs that produce images that appear to have great complexity. Procedural noise has been at the heart of almost all procedural modeling methods, and its true power is often best demonstrated when it is combined with one or more of the other methods that we have presented.

As we look ahead, we see a further convergence of graphics methods with methods from physics, mathematics, and other sciences. Historically, given the available computing power, we were content to accept visuals that "looked okay" but were not especially close to the correct physics in applications such as simulation and interactive games. Even in applications in which we might spend days rendering a single frame, the true physics was still too complex to simulate well. However, with the continued advances in available computing power and the lowered cost of accessing such power, we expect to see more and more physically correct modeling in all applications of computer graphics.

SUGGESTED READINGS

Particle systems were introduced in computer graphics by Reeves [Ree83]. Since then, they have been used for a variety of phenomena, including flocking of birds [Rey87], fluid flow, fire, modeling of grass, and display of surfaces [Wit94a]. Particles are also used extensively in physics and mathematics and provide an alternative to solving complex systems of partial differential equations that characterize fluid flow and solid mechanics. See, for example, [Gre88]. Our approach follows Witkin [Wit94b]. Many examples of procedural modeling are in [Ebe02]. For a discussion of agent-based modeling using NetLogo, see[Rai11] and http://ccl.northwestern.edu/netlogo/.

There is a wealth of literature on fractals and related methods. The paper by Fournier [Fou82] was the first to show the fractal mountain. For a deeper treatment of fractal mathematics, see the books by Mandelbrot [Man82] and Peitgen [Pei88]. The use of graph grammars has appeared in a number of forms [Pru90, Smi84, Lin68]. Both Hill [Hil07] and Prusinkiewicz [Pru90] present interesting space-filling curves and surfaces. Barnsley's iterated-function systems [Bar93] provide another approach to the use of self-similarity; they have application in such areas as image compression.

Gradient noise is due to Perlin [Per82, Per85, Per02]. Many applications to texture and object generation are in [Ebe02], as is a discussion of value noise.

EXERCISES

10.1 Find the set of ordinary differential equations required for the dynamics of a system of n particles.

10.2 How could you determine the fractal dimension of a coastline? How would you verify that the shape of a coastline is indeed a fractal?

10.3 Start with the tetrahedron subdivision program that we used in Chapter 6 to approximate a sphere. Convert this program into one that will generate a fractal mountain.

10.4 We can write a description of a binary tree, one we might use for a search, as a list of nodes with pointers to its children. Write a data structure to implement such a binary search tree, and a function in C++ that will display the nodes in traversal.

10.5 Write a program for a simple particle system of masses and springs. Render the particle system as a mesh of quadrilaterals. Include a form of interaction that allows a user to put particles in their initial positions.

10.6 Extend Exercise 10.5 by adding external forces to the particle system. Create an image of a flag blowing in the wind.

10.7 Write a program to fractalize a mesh. Try to use real elevation data for the initial positions of the mesh.

10.8 Write a program that, given two polygons with the same number of vertices, will generate a sequence of images that converts one polygon into the other.

10.9 If we use the basic formula that we used for the Mandelbrot set, but this time fix the value of the complex number c and find the set of initial points for which we obtain convergence, we have the Julia set for that c. Write a program to display Julia sets. *Hint:* Use values of c near the edges of the Mandelbrot set.

10.10 Write the mechanism, followed by a particle system, for deciding the position of a graphical object.

10.11 Extend Exercise 10.9 to simulate the explosion of a polyhedron.

10.12 Combine alpha blending (Chapter 7), sphere generation (Chapter 6), and fractals to create clouds.

10.13 Use fractals to generate the surface of a virtual planet. Your output should show continents and oceans.

10.14 In the Lennard-Jones particle system, particles are attracted to one another by a force proportional to the inverse of the distance between them raised to the 12th power, but are repelled by another force proportional to the inverse of the same distance raised to the 24th power. Simulate such a system in a box. To make the simulation easier, you can assume that a particle that leaves the box reenters the box from the opposite side.

10.15 Create a particle system in which the region of interest is subdivided into cubes of the same size. A particle can only interact with particles in its own cube and the cubes adjacent to it.

10.16 In animations, particle systems are used to give the positions of the characters. Once the positions are determined, two-dimensional images of the characters can be texture-mapped onto polygons at these positions. Build such a system for moving characters, subject to both external forces that move them in the desired direction and repulsive forces that keep them from colliding. How can you keep the polygons facing the camera?

10.17 Add an unique identity to each particle in the particle system. Re-implement the particle system using a doubly linked list of particles rather than an array so that the particles can be manipulated more easily.

10.18 Render particles in the example particle system with shaded approximations to spheres.

10.19 Use a spring-mass system to simulate a hair or a blade of grass by connecting four points in a chain.

10.20 Experiment with various flocking algorithms. For example, particles may update their velocities to move in the direction away from the center of mass of all particles. Another approach is to have each particle move toward a particle with certain position.

10.21 Add procedural noise to the figure model so that at rest there is a slight movement of each joint.

10.22 Implement a fractal landscape using procedural noise. Include the capability to move the viewer and to zoom in and out.

10.23 Convert the simple particle system to perform the updating of positions and velocities in the vertex shader. You may ignore particle–particle forces such as repulsion.

10.24 Starting with the Mandelbrot fragment shader, alter the program to estimate the floating-point operation (FLOP) rate of your GPU.

CHAPTER 11

CURVES AND SURFACES

The world around us is full of objects of remarkable shapes. Nevertheless, in computer graphics, we continue to populate our virtual worlds with flat objects. We have a good reason for such persistence. Graphics systems can render flat three-dimensional polygons at high rates, including doing hidden-surface removal, shading, and texture mapping. We could take the approach that we took with our sphere model and define curved objects that are, in (virtual) reality, collections of flat polygons. Alternatively, and as we will do here, we can provide the application programmer with the means to work with curved objects in her program, leaving the eventual rendering of these objects to the implementation.

We introduce three ways to model curves and surfaces, paying most attention to the parametric polynomial forms. We also discuss how curves and surfaces can be rendered on current graphics systems, a process that usually involves subdividing the curved objects into collections of flat primitives. From the application programmer's perspective, this process is transparent because it is part of the implementation. It is important to understand the work involved, however, so that we can appreciate the practical limitations we face in using curves and surfaces.

11.1 REPRESENTATION OF CURVES AND SURFACES

Before proceeding to our development of parametric polynomial curves and surfaces, we pause to summarize our knowledge of the three major types of object representation—explicit, implicit, and parametric—and to consider the advantages and disadvantages of each form. We can illustrate the salient points using only lines, circles, planes, and spheres.

11.1.1 Explicit Representation

The **explicit form** of a curve in two dimensions gives the value of one variable, the **dependent variable**, in terms of the other, the **independent variable**. In x, y space, we might write

$$y = f(x),$$

or if we are fortunate, we might be able to invert the relationship and express x as a function of y:

$$x = g(y).$$

There is no guarantee that either form exists for a given curve. For the line, we usually write the equation

$$y = mx + h,$$

in terms of its slope m and y-intercept h, even though we know that this equation does not hold for vertical lines. This problem is one of many coordinate-system–dependent effects that cause problems for graphics systems and, more generally, for all fields where we work with the design and manipulation of curves and surfaces. Lines and circles exist independently of any representation, and any representation that fails for certain orientations, such as vertical lines, has serious deficiencies.

Circles provide an even more illustrative example. Consider a circle of radius r centered at the origin. A circle has constant **curvature**—a measure of how rapidly a curve is bending at a point. No closed two-dimensional curve can be more symmetric than the circle. However, the best we can do, using an explicit representation, is to write one equation for half of it,

$$y = \sqrt{r^2 - x^2},$$

and a second equation,

$$y = -\sqrt{r^2 - x^2},$$

for the other half. In addition, we must also specify that these equations hold only if

$$0 \le |x| \le r.$$

In three dimensions, the explicit representation of a curve requires two equations. For example, if x is again the independent variable, we have two dependent variables:

$$y = f(x) \qquad z = g(x).$$

A surface requires two independent variables, and a representation might take the form

$$z = f(x, y).$$

As is true in two dimensions, a curve or surface may not have an explicit representation. For example, the equations

$$y = ax + b \qquad z = cx + d$$

describe a line in three dimensions, but these equations cannot represent a line in a plane of constant x. Likewise, a surface represented by an equation of the form

$$z = f(x, y)$$

cannot represent a sphere, because a given x and y can generate zero, one, or two points on the sphere.

11.1.2 Implicit Representations

Most of the curves and surfaces with which we work have implicit representations. In two dimensions, an **implicit curve** can be represented by the equation

$$f(x, y) = 0.$$

Our two examples—the line and the circle centered at the origin—have the respective representations

$$ax + by + c = 0$$

$$x^2 + y^2 - r^2 = 0.$$

The function f, however, is really a testing, or **membership**, function that divides space into those points that belong to the curve and those that do not. It allows us to take an x, y pair and to evaluate f to determine whether this point lies on the curve. In general, however, it gives us no analytic way to find a value y on the curve that corresponds to a given x, or vice versa. The implicit form is less coordinate-system–dependent than is the explicit form, however, in that it does represent all lines and circles.

In three dimensions, the implicit form

$$f(x, y, z) = 0$$

describes a surface. For example, any plane can be written as

$$ax + by + cz + d = 0$$

for constants a, b, c, and d. A sphere of radius r centered at the origin can be described by

$$x^2 + y^2 + z^2 - r^2 = 0.$$

Curves in three dimensions are not as easily represented in implicit form. We can represent a curve as the intersection, if it exists, of the two surfaces:

$$f(x, y, z) = 0 \qquad g(x, y, z) = 0.$$

Thus, if we test a point (x, y, z) and it is on both surfaces, then it must lie on their intersection curve. In general, most of the curves and surfaces that arise in real applications have implicit representations. Their use is limited by the difficulty in obtaining points on them.

Algebraic surfaces are those for which the function $f(x, y, z)$ is the sum of polynomials in the three variables. Of particular importance are the **quadric** surfaces, where each term in f can have degree up to 2.[1] Quadrics are of interest not only because they include useful objects (such as spheres, disks, and cones) but also because when we intersect these objects with lines, at most two intersection points are generated. We will use this characteristic to render quadrics in Section 11.9 and for use in ray tracing in Chapter 12.

11.1.3 Parametric Form

The **parametric form** of a curve expresses the value of each spatial variable for points on the curve in terms of an independent variable, u, the **parameter**. In three dimensions, we have three explicit functions:

$$x = x(u) \qquad y = y(u) \qquad z = z(u).$$

One of the advantages of the parametric form is that it is the same in two and three dimensions. In the former case, we simply drop the equation for z. A useful interpretation of the parametric form is to visualize the locus of points $\mathbf{p}(u) = [x(u) \ y(u) \ z(u)]^T$ being drawn as u varies, as shown in Figure 11.1. We can think of the derivative

$$\frac{d\mathbf{p}(u)}{du} = \begin{bmatrix} \frac{dx(u)}{du} \\ \frac{dy(u)}{du} \\ \frac{dz(u)}{du} \end{bmatrix}$$

FIGURE 11.1   Parametric curve.

as the velocity with which the curve is traced out, and pointing in the direction tangent to the curve.

Parametric surfaces require two parameters. We can describe a surface by three equations of the form

$$x = x(u, v) \qquad y = y(u, v) \qquad z = z(u, v),$$

or we can use the column matrix

$$\mathbf{p}(u, v) = \begin{bmatrix} x(u, v) \\ y(u, v) \\ z(u, v) \end{bmatrix}.$$

As u and v vary over some interval, we generate all the points $\mathbf{p}(u, v)$ on the surface. As we saw with our sphere example in Chapter 6, the vectors given by the column matrices

$$\frac{\partial \mathbf{p}}{\partial u} = \begin{bmatrix} \frac{\partial x(u,v)}{\partial u} \\ \frac{\partial y(u,v)}{\partial u} \\ \frac{\partial z(u,v)}{\partial u} \end{bmatrix} \quad \text{and} \quad \frac{\partial \mathbf{p}}{\partial v} = \begin{bmatrix} \frac{\partial x(u,v)}{\partial v} \\ \frac{\partial y(u,v)}{\partial v} \\ \frac{\partial z(u,v)}{\partial v} \end{bmatrix}$$

---

1. Degree is measured as the sum of the powers of the individual terms, so x, yz, or z^2 can be in a quadric, but xy^2 cannot.

determine the tangent plane at each point on the surface. In addition, as long as these vectors are not parallel, their cross product gives the normal (Figure 11.2) at each point; that is,

$$\mathbf{n} = \partial\mathbf{p}/\partial u \times \partial\mathbf{p}/\partial v.$$

The parametric form of curves and surfaces is the most flexible and robust for computer graphics. We could still argue that we have not fully removed all dependencies on a particular coordinate system or frame, because we are still using the x, y, and z for a particular representation. It is possible to develop a system solely on the basis of $\mathbf{p}(u)$ for curves and $\mathbf{p}(u, v)$ for surfaces. For example, the **Frenet frame** is often used for describing curves in three-dimensional space, and it is defined starting with the tangent and the normal at each point on the curve. As in our discussion of bump mapping in Chapter 7, we can compute a binormal for the third direction. However, this frame changes for each point on the curve. For our purposes, the parametric form for x, y, z within a particular frame is sufficiently robust.

FIGURE 11.2 Tangent plane and normal at a point on a parametric surface.

11.1.4 Parametric Polynomial Curves

Parametric forms are not unique. A given curve or surface can be represented in many ways, but we will find that parametric forms in which the functions are polynomials in u for curves and polynomials in u and v for surfaces are of most use in computer graphics. Many of the reasons will be summarized in Section 11.2.

Consider a curve of the form[2]

$$\mathbf{p}(u) = \begin{bmatrix} x(u) \\ y(u) \\ z(u) \end{bmatrix}.$$

A polynomial parametric curve of degree[3] n is of the form

$$\mathbf{p}(u) = \sum_{k=0}^{n} u^k \mathbf{c}_k,$$

where each $\mathbf{c}_k$ has independent x, y, and z components; that is,

$$\mathbf{c}_k = \begin{bmatrix} c_{xk} \\ c_{yk} \\ c_{zk} \end{bmatrix}.$$

The $n + 1$ column matrices $\{\mathbf{c}_k\}$ are the coefficients of $\mathbf{p}$; they give us $3(n + 1)$ degrees of freedom in how we choose the coefficients of a particular $\mathbf{p}$. There is no coupling, however, among the x, y, and z components, so we can work with three independent

---

2. At this point there is no need to work in homogeneous coordinates; in Section 11.8 we will work in them to derive NURBS curves.

3. The OpenGL literature often uses the term *order* to mean one greater than the degree.

equations, each of the form

$$p(u) = \sum_{k=0}^{n} u^k c_k,$$

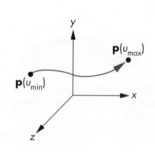

FIGURE 11.3   Curve segment.

where p is any one of x, y, or z. There are $n + 1$ degrees of freedom in $p(u)$. We can define our curves for any range interval of u,

$$u_{\min} \le u \le u_{\max};$$

however, with no loss of generality (see Exercise 11.3), we can assume that $0 \le u \le 1$. As the value of u varies over its range, we define a **curve segment**, as shown in Figure 11.3.

11.1.5 Parametric Polynomial Surfaces

We can define a parametric polynomial surface as

$$\mathbf{p}(u, v) = \begin{bmatrix} x(u, v) \\ y(u, v) \\ z(u, v) \end{bmatrix} = \sum_{i=0}^{n} \sum_{j=0}^{m} \mathbf{c}_{ij} u^i v^j.$$

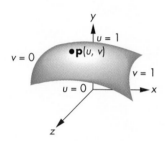

FIGURE 11.4   Surface patch.

We must specify $3(n + 1)(m + 1)$ coefficients to determine a particular surface $\mathbf{p}(u, v)$. We will always take $n = m$ and let u and v vary over the rectangle $0 \le u, v \le 1$, defining a **surface patch**, as shown in Figure 11.4. Note that any surface patch can be viewed as the limit of a collection of curves that we generate by holding either u or v constant and varying the other. Our strategy will be to define parametric polynomial curves and to use the curves to generate surfaces with similar characteristics.

11.2   DESIGN CRITERIA

The way curves and surfaces are used in computer graphics and computer-aided design is often different from the way they are used in other fields and from the way you may have seen them used previously. There are many considerations that determine why we prefer to use parametric polynomials of low degree, including

- Local control of shape
- Smoothness and continuity
- Ability to evaluate derivatives
- Stability
- Ease of rendering

FIGURE 11.5   Model airplane.

We can understand these criteria with the aid of a simple example. Suppose that we want to build a model airplane, using flexible strips of wood for the structure. We can build the body of the model by constructing a set of cross sections and then connecting them with longer pieces, as shown in Figure 11.5. To design our cross sections, we might start with a picture of a real airplane or sketch a desired curve.

One such cross section might be like that shown in Figure 11.6. We could try to get a single global description of this cross section, but that description probably would not be what we want. Each strip of wood can be bent to only a certain shape before breaking and can bend in only a smooth way. Hence, we can regard the curve in Figure 11.6 as only an approximation to what we actually build, which might be more like Figure 11.7. In practice, we probably will make our cross section out of a number of wood strips, each of which will become a curve segment for the cross section. Thus, not only will each segment have to be smooth, but we also want a degree of smoothness where the segments meet at **join points**.

FIGURE 11.6   Cross-section curve.

Note that although we might be able to ensure that a curve segment is smooth, we have to be particularly careful at the join points. Figure 11.8 shows an example in which, although the two curve segments are smooth, the derivative is discontinuous at the join point. The usual definition of **smoothness** is given in terms of the derivatives along the curve. A curve with discontinuities is of little interest to us. Generally, a curve with a continuous first derivative is smoother than a curve whose first derivative has discontinuities (and so on for the higher derivatives). These notions become more precise in Section 11.3. For now, it should be clear that for a polynomial curve

FIGURE 11.7   Approximation of cross-section curve.

$$\mathbf{p}(u) = \sum_{k=0}^{n} \mathbf{c}_k u^k,$$

all derivatives exist and can be computed analytically. Consequently, the only places where we can encounter continuity difficulties are at the join points.

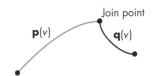

FIGURE 11.8   Derivative discontinuity at join point.

We would like to design each segment individually, rather than designing all the segments by a single global calculation. One reason for this preference is that we would like to work interactively with the shape, carefully molding it to meet our specifications. When we make a change, this change will affect the shape in only the area where we are working. This sort of local control is but one aspect of a more general stability principle: *Small changes in the values of input parameters should cause only small changes in output variables.* Another statement of this principle is: *Small changes in independent variables should cause only small changes in dependent variables.*

Working with our piece of wood, we might be able to bend it to approximate the desired shape by comparing it to the entire curve. More likely, we would consider data at a small number of **control**, or **data**, **points** and would use only those data to design our shape. Figure 11.9 shows a possible curve segment and a collection of control points. Note that the curve passes through, or **interpolates**, some of the control points but only comes close to others. As we will see throughout this chapter, in computer graphics and CAD we are usually satisfied if the curve passes close to the control-point data, as long as it is smooth in the sense that it does not change direction very often in the region of interest. Thus, although curves such as polynomials have continuous derivatives, a high-degree polynomial with many inflection points where its derivative changes sign is not considered smooth.

FIGURE 11.9   Curve segment and control points.

This example shows many of the reasons for working with polynomial parametric curves. In fact, the spline curves that we discuss in Sections 11.7 and 11.8 derive their name from a flexible wood or metal device that shipbuilders used to design the shape of hulls. Each spline was held in place by pegs or weights, and the bending properties of the material gave the curve segment a polynomial shape.

Returning to computer graphics, remember that we need methods for rendering curves (and surfaces). A good mathematical representation may be of limited value if we cannot display the resulting curves and surfaces easily. We would like to display whatever curves and surfaces we choose with techniques similar to those used for flat objects, including color, shading, and texture mapping.

11.3   PARAMETRIC CUBIC POLYNOMIAL CURVES

Once we have decided to use parametric polynomial curves, we must choose the degree of the curve. On one hand, if we choose a high degree, we will have many parameters that we can set to form the desired shape, but evaluation of points on the curve will be costly. In addition, as the degree of a polynomial curve becomes higher, there is more danger that the curve will contain more bends and be less suitable for modeling a smooth curve or surface. On the other hand, if we pick too low a degree, we may not have enough parameters with which to work. However, if we design each curve segment over a short interval, we can achieve many of our purposes with low-degree curves. Although there may be only a few degrees of freedom, these few may be sufficient to allow us to produce the desired shape in a small region. For this reason, most designers, at least initially, work with cubic polynomial curves.

We can write a cubic parametric polynomial using a row and column matrix as

$$\mathbf{p}(u) = \mathbf{c}_0 + \mathbf{c}_1 u + \mathbf{c}_2 u^2 + \mathbf{c}_3 u^3 = \sum_{k=0}^{3} \mathbf{c}_k u^k = \mathbf{u}^T \mathbf{c},$$

where

$$\mathbf{c} = \begin{bmatrix} \mathbf{c}_0 \\ \mathbf{c}_1 \\ \mathbf{c}_2 \\ \mathbf{c}_3 \end{bmatrix} \qquad \mathbf{u} = \begin{bmatrix} 1 \\ u \\ u^2 \\ u^3 \end{bmatrix} \qquad \mathbf{c}_k = \begin{bmatrix} c_{kx} \\ c_{ky} \\ c_{kz} \end{bmatrix}.$$

Thus, $\mathbf{c}$ is a column matrix containing the coefficients of the polynomial; it is what we wish to determine from the control-point data. We will derive a number of types of cubic curves. The types will differ in how they use the control-point data. We seek to find 12 equations in 12 unknowns for each type, but because x, y, and z are independent, we can group these equations into three independent sets of four equations in four unknowns. When we discuss NURBS in Section 11.8.4, we will be working in homogeneous coordinates, so we will have to use the w-coordinate and thus will have four sets of four equations in four unknowns.

The design of a particular type of cubic will be based on data given at some values of the parameter u. These data might take the form of interpolating conditions in which the polynomial must agree with the data at some points. The data may also require the polynomial to interpolate some derivatives at certain values of the parameter. We might also have smoothness conditions that enforce various continuity conditions at the join points that are shared by two curve segments. Finally, we may have conditions that are not as strict, requiring only that the curve pass close to several known data points. Each type of condition will define a different type of curve, and depending on how we use some given data, the same data can define more than a single curve.

11.4 INTERPOLATION

Our first example of a cubic parametric polynomial is the cubic **interpolating polynomial**. Although we rarely use interpolating polynomials in computer graphics, the derivation of this familiar polynomial illustrates the steps we must follow for our other types, and the analysis of the interpolating polynomial illustrates many of the important features by which we evaluate a particular curve or surface.

Suppose that we have four control points in three dimensions: $\mathbf{p}_0$, $\mathbf{p}_1$, $\mathbf{p}_2$, and $\mathbf{p}_3$. Each is of the form

$$\mathbf{p}_k = \begin{bmatrix} x_k \\ y_k \\ z_k \end{bmatrix}.$$

We seek the coefficients $\mathbf{c}$ such that the polynomial $\mathbf{p}(u) = \mathbf{u}^T \mathbf{c}$ passes through, or interpolates, the four control points. The derivation should be easy. We have four three-dimensional interpolating points; hence, we have 12 conditions and 12 unknowns. First, however, we have to decide at which values of the parameter u the interpolation takes place. Lacking any other information, we can take these values to be the equally spaced values $u = 0, \frac{1}{3}, \frac{2}{3}, 1$. Remember that we have decided to let u always vary over the interval $[0, 1]$. The four conditions are thus

$$\mathbf{p}_0 = \mathbf{p}(0) = \mathbf{c}_0,$$

$$\mathbf{p}_1 = \mathbf{p}\left(\frac{1}{3}\right) = \mathbf{c}_0 + \frac{1}{3}\mathbf{c}_1 + \left(\frac{1}{3}\right)^2 \mathbf{c}_2 + \left(\frac{1}{3}\right)^3 \mathbf{c}_3,$$

$$\mathbf{p}_2 = \mathbf{p}\left(\frac{2}{3}\right) = \mathbf{c}_0 + \frac{2}{3}\mathbf{c}_1 + \left(\frac{2}{3}\right)^2 \mathbf{c}_2 + \left(\frac{2}{3}\right)^3 \mathbf{c}_3,$$

$$\mathbf{p}_3 = \mathbf{p}(1) = \mathbf{c}_0 + \mathbf{c}_1 + \mathbf{c}_2 + \mathbf{c}_3.$$

We can write these equations in matrix form as

$$\mathbf{p} = \mathbf{A}\mathbf{c},$$

where

$$\mathbf{p} = \begin{bmatrix} \mathbf{p}_0 \\ \mathbf{p}_1 \\ \mathbf{p}_2 \\ \mathbf{p}_3 \end{bmatrix}$$

and

$$
\mathbf{A} =
\begin{bmatrix}
1 & 0 & 0 & 0 \\
1 & \frac{1}{3} & \left(\frac{1}{3}\right)^2 & \left(\frac{1}{3}\right)^3 \\
1 & \frac{2}{3} & \left(\frac{2}{3}\right)^2 & \left(\frac{2}{3}\right)^3 \\
1 & 1 & 1 & 1
\end{bmatrix}.
$$

The matrix form here has to be interpreted carefully. If we interpret $\mathbf{p}$ and $\mathbf{c}$ as column matrices of 12 elements, the rules of matrix multiplication are violated. Instead, we view $\mathbf{p}$ and $\mathbf{c}$ each as a four-element column matrix whose elements are three-element row matrices. Hence, multiplication of an element of $\mathbf{A}$, a scalar, by an element of $\mathbf{c}$, a three-element column matrix, yields a three-element column matrix, which is the same type as an element of $\mathbf{p}$.[4] We can show that $\mathbf{A}$ is nonsingular, and we can invert it to obtain the **interpolating geometry matrix**

$$
\mathbf{M}_I = \mathbf{A}^{-1} =
\begin{bmatrix}
1 & 0 & 0 & 0 \\
-5.5 & 9 & -4.5 & 1 \\
9 & -22.5 & 18 & -4.5 \\
-4.5 & 13.5 & -13.5 & 4.5
\end{bmatrix}
$$

and the desired coefficients

$$
\mathbf{c} = \mathbf{M}_I \mathbf{p}.
$$

Suppose that we have a sequence of control points $\mathbf{p}_0, \mathbf{p}_1, \ldots, \mathbf{p}_m$. Rather than deriving a single interpolating curve of degree m for all the points—a calculation we could do by following a derivation similar to the one for cubic polynomials—we can derive a set of cubic interpolating curves, each specified by a group of four control points, and each valid over a short interval in u. We can achieve continuity at the join points by using the control point that determines the right side of one segment as the first point for the next segment (Figure 11.10). Thus, we use $\mathbf{p}_0, \mathbf{p}_1, \mathbf{p}_2, \mathbf{p}_3$ to find the first segment, we use $\mathbf{p}_3, \mathbf{p}_4, \mathbf{p}_5, \mathbf{p}_6$ for the second, and so on. Note that if each segment is derived for the parameter u varying over the interval $(0, 1)$, then the matrix $\mathbf{M}_I$ is the same for each segment. Although we have achieved continuity for the sequence of segments, derivatives at the join points will not be continuous.

11.4.1 Blending Functions

We can obtain additional insights into the smoothness of the interpolating polynomial curves by rewriting our equations in a slightly different form. We can substitute

---

4. We could use row matrices for the elements of $\mathbf{p}$ and $\mathbf{c}$: In that case, ordinary matrix multiplications would work because we would have a 4×4 matrix multiplying a 4×3 matrix. However, this method would fail for surfaces. The real difficulty is that we should be using *tensors* to carry out the mathematics—a topic beyond the scope of this book.

FIGURE 11.10   Joining of interpolating segments.

the interpolating coefficients into our polynomial; we obtain

$$\mathbf{p}(u) = \mathbf{u}^T \mathbf{c} = \mathbf{u}^T \mathbf{M}_I \mathbf{p},$$

which we can write as

$$\mathbf{p}(u) = \mathbf{b}(u)^T \mathbf{p},$$

where

$$\mathbf{b}(u) = \mathbf{M}_I^T \mathbf{u}$$

is a column matrix of the four **blending polynomials**

$$\mathbf{b}(u) = \begin{bmatrix} b_0(u) \\ b_1(u) \\ b_2(u) \\ b_3(u) \end{bmatrix}.$$

Each blending polynomial is a cubic. If we express $\mathbf{p}(u)$ in terms of these blending polynomials as

$$\mathbf{p}(u) = b_0(u)\mathbf{p}_0 + b_1(u)\mathbf{p}_1 + b_2(u)\mathbf{p}_2 + b_3(u)\mathbf{p}_3 = \sum_{i=0}^{3} b_i(u)\mathbf{p}_i,$$

then we can see that the polynomials blend together the individual contributions of each control point and enable us to see the effect of a given control point on the entire curve. These blending functions for the cubic interpolating polynomial are shown in Figure 11.11 and are given by the equations

$$b_0(u) = -\frac{9}{2}\left(u - \frac{1}{3}\right)\left(u - \frac{2}{3}\right)(u - 1)$$

$$b_1(u) = \frac{27}{2}u\left(u - \frac{2}{3}\right)(u - 1)$$

$$b_2(u) = -\frac{27}{2}u\left(u - \frac{1}{3}\right)(u - 1)$$

$$b_3(u) = \frac{9}{2}u\left(u - \frac{1}{3}\right)\left(u - \frac{2}{3}\right).$$

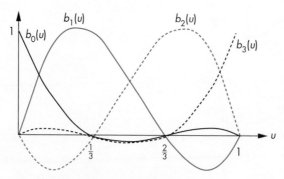

FIGURE 11.11   Blending polynomials for interpolation.

Because all the zeros of the blending functions lie in the closed interval $[0, 1]$, the blending functions must vary substantially over this interval and are not particularly smooth. This lack of smoothness is a consequence of the interpolating requirement that the curve must pass through the control points, rather than just come close to them. This characteristic is even more pronounced for interpolating polynomials of higher degree. This problem and the lack of derivative continuity at the join points account for limited use of the interpolating polynomial in computer graphics. However, the same derivation and analysis process will allow us to find smoother types of cubic curves.

11.4.2 The Cubic Interpolating Patch

There is a natural extension of the interpolating curve to an interpolating patch. A **bicubic surface patch** can be written in the form

$$\mathbf{p}(u, v) = \sum_{i=0}^{3} \sum_{j=0}^{3} u^i v^j \mathbf{c}_{ij},$$

where $\mathbf{c}_{ij}$ is a three-element column matrix of the x, y, and z coefficients for the ijth term in the polynomial. If we define a 4×4 matrix whose elements are three-element column matrices,

$$\mathbf{C} = [\, \mathbf{c}_{ij} \,],$$

then we can write the surface patch as

$$\mathbf{p}(u, v) = \mathbf{u}^T \mathbf{C} \mathbf{v},$$

where

$$\mathbf{v} = \begin{bmatrix} 1 \\ v \\ v^2 \\ v^3 \end{bmatrix}.$$

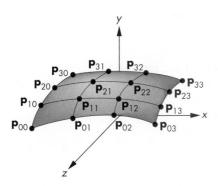

FIGURE 11.12   Interpolating surface patch.

A particular bicubic polynomial patch is defined by the 48 elements of $\mathbf{C}$; that is, 16 three-element vectors.

     Suppose that we have 16 three-dimensional control points $\mathbf{p}_{ij}$, $i = 0, \ldots, 3$, $j = 0, \ldots, 3$. We can use these points to specify an interpolating surface patch, as shown in Figure 11.12. If we assume that these data are used for interpolation at the equally spaced values of both u and v of 0, $\frac{1}{3}$, $\frac{2}{3}$, and 1, then we get three sets of 16 equations in 16 unknowns. For example, for $u = v = 0$, we get the three independent equations

$$
\mathbf{p}_{00} = [\, 1 \quad 0 \quad 0 \quad 0 \,]\,\mathbf{C}
\begin{bmatrix}
1 \\
0 \\
0 \\
0
\end{bmatrix}
= \mathbf{c}_{00}.
$$

Rather than writing down and solving all these equations, we can proceed in a more direct fashion. If we consider $v = 0$, we get a curve in u that must interpolate $\mathbf{p}_{00}$, $\mathbf{p}_{10}$, $\mathbf{p}_{20}$, and $\mathbf{p}_{30}$. Using our results on interpolating curves, we write this curve as

$$
\mathbf{p}(u, 0) = \mathbf{u}^T \mathbf{M}_I
\begin{bmatrix}
\mathbf{p}_{00} \\
\mathbf{p}_{10} \\
\mathbf{p}_{20} \\
\mathbf{p}_{30}
\end{bmatrix}
= \mathbf{u}^T \mathbf{C}
\begin{bmatrix}
1 \\
0 \\
0 \\
0
\end{bmatrix}.
$$

Likewise, the values of $v = \frac{1}{3}$, $\frac{2}{3}$, 1 define three other interpolating curves, each of which has a similar form. Putting these curves together, we can write all 16 equations as

$$
\mathbf{u}^T \mathbf{M}_I \mathbf{P} = \mathbf{u}^T \mathbf{C} \mathbf{A}^T,
$$

where $\mathbf{A}$ is the inverse of $\mathbf{M}_I$. We can solve this equation for the desired coefficient matrix

$$
\mathbf{C} = \mathbf{M}_I \mathbf{P} \mathbf{M}_I^T,
$$

and substituting into the equation for the surface, we have

$$\mathbf{p}(u, v) = \mathbf{u}^T \mathbf{M}_I \mathbf{P} \mathbf{M}_I^T \mathbf{v}.$$

We can interpret this result in several ways. First, the interpolating surface can be derived from our understanding of interpolating curves—a technique that will enable us to extend other types of curves to surfaces. Second, we can extend our use of blending polynomials to surfaces. By noting that $\mathbf{M}_I^T \mathbf{u}$ describes the interpolating blending functions, we can rewrite our surface patch as

$$\mathbf{p}(u, v) = \sum_{i=0}^{3} \sum_{j=0}^{3} b_i(u) b_j(v) \mathbf{p}_{ij}.$$

Each term $b_i(u)b_j(v)$ describes a **blending patch**. We form a surface by blending together 16 simple patches, each weighted by the data at a control point. The basic properties of the blending patches are determined by the same blending polynomials that arose for interpolating curves; thus, most of the characteristics of surfaces are similar to those of curves. In particular, the blending patches are not particularly smooth, because the zeros of the functions $b_i(u)b_j(v)$ lie inside the unit square in u, v space. Surfaces formed from curves using this technique are known as **tensor-product surfaces**. Bicubic tensor-product surfaces are a subset of all surface patches that contain up to cubic terms in both parameters. They are an example of **separable surfaces**, which can be written as

$$\mathbf{p}(u, v) = \mathbf{f}(\mathbf{u})\mathbf{g}(v),$$

where $\mathbf{f}$ and $\mathbf{g}$ are suitably chosen row and column matrices, respectively. The advantage of such surfaces is that they allow us to work with functions in u and v independently.

11.5 HERMITE CURVES AND SURFACES

We can use the techniques that we developed for interpolating curves and surfaces to generate various other types of curves and surfaces. Each type is distinguished from the others by the way we use the data at control points.

11.5.1 The Hermite Form

Suppose that we start with only the control points $\mathbf{p}_0$ and $\mathbf{p}_3$,[5] and again, we insist that our curve interpolate these points at the parameter values $u = 0$ and $u = 1$, respectively. Using our previous notation, we have the two conditions

$$\mathbf{p}(0) = \mathbf{p}_0 = \mathbf{c}_0$$

$$\mathbf{p}(1) = \mathbf{p}_3 = \mathbf{c}_0 + \mathbf{c}_1 + \mathbf{c}_2 + \mathbf{c}_3.$$

---

5. We use this numbering to be consistent with our interpolation notation, as well as with the numbering that we use for Bézier curves in Section 11.6.

We can get two other conditions if we assume that we know the derivatives of the function at $u = 0$ and $u = 1$. The derivative of the polynomial is simply the parametric quadratic polynomial

$$\mathbf{p}'(u) = \begin{bmatrix} \frac{dx}{du} \\ \frac{dy}{du} \\ \frac{dz}{du} \end{bmatrix} = \mathbf{c}_1 + 2u\mathbf{c}_2 + 3u^2\mathbf{c}_3.$$

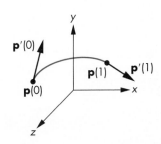

FIGURE 11.13   Definition of the Hermite cubic.

If we denote the given values of the two derivatives as $\mathbf{p}'_0$ and $\mathbf{p}'_3$, then our two additional conditions (Figure 11.13) are

$$\mathbf{p}'_0 = \mathbf{p}'(0) = \mathbf{c}_1$$

$$\mathbf{p}'_3 = \mathbf{p}'(1) = \mathbf{c}_1 + 2\mathbf{c}_2 + 3\mathbf{c}_3.$$

We can write these equations in matrix form as

$$\begin{bmatrix} \mathbf{p}_0 \\ \mathbf{p}_3 \\ \mathbf{p}'_0 \\ \mathbf{p}'_3 \end{bmatrix} = \begin{bmatrix} 1 & 0 & 0 & 0 \\ 1 & 1 & 1 & 1 \\ 0 & 1 & 0 & 0 \\ 0 & 1 & 2 & 3 \end{bmatrix} \mathbf{c}.$$

Letting $\mathbf{q}$ denote the data matrix

$$\mathbf{q} = \begin{bmatrix} \mathbf{p}_0 \\ \mathbf{p}_3 \\ \mathbf{p}'_0 \\ \mathbf{p}'_3 \end{bmatrix},$$

we can solve the equations to find

$$\mathbf{c} = \mathbf{M}_H \mathbf{q},$$

where $\mathbf{M}_H$ is the **Hermite geometry** matrix

$$\mathbf{M}_H = \begin{bmatrix} 1 & 0 & 0 & 0 \\ 0 & 0 & 1 & 0 \\ -3 & 3 & -2 & -1 \\ 2 & -2 & 1 & 1 \end{bmatrix}.$$

The resulting polynomial is given by

$$\mathbf{p}(u) = \mathbf{u}^T \mathbf{M}_H \mathbf{q}.$$

FIGURE 11.14   Hermite form at join point.

We use this method as shown in Figure 11.14, where both the interpolated value and the derivative are shared by the curve segments on the two sides of a join point, and thus both the resulting function and the first derivative are continuous over all segments.

We can get a more accurate idea of the increased smoothness of the Hermite form by rewriting the polynomial in the form

$$\mathbf{p}(u) = \mathbf{b}(u)^T \mathbf{q},$$

where the new blending functions are given by

$$\mathbf{b}(u) = \mathbf{M}_H^T \mathbf{u} = \begin{bmatrix} 2u^3 - 3u^2 + 1 \\ -2u^3 + 3u^2 \\ u^3 - 2u^2 + u \\ u^3 - u^2 \end{bmatrix}.$$

These four polynomials have none of their zeros inside the interval $(0, 1)$ and are much smoother than the interpolating polynomial blending functions (see Exercise 11.21).

We can go on and define a bicubic Hermite surface patch through these blending functions,

$$\mathbf{p}(u, v) = \sum_{i=0}^{3} \sum_{j=0}^{3} b_i(u) b_j(v) \mathbf{q}_{ij},$$

where $\mathbf{Q} = [\mathbf{q}_{ij}]$ is the extension of $\mathbf{q}$ to surface data. At this point, however, this equation is just a formal expression. It is not clear what the relationship is between the elements of $\mathbf{Q}$ and the derivatives of $\mathbf{p}(u, v)$. Four of the elements of $\mathbf{Q}$ are chosen to interpolate the corners of the patch, whereas the others are chosen to match certain derivatives at the corners of the patch. In most interactive applications, however, the user enters point data rather than derivative data; consequently, unless we have analytic formulations for the data, usually we do not have these derivatives. However, the approach we took with the Hermite curves and surfaces will lead to the Bézier forms that we introduce in Section 11.6.

FIGURE 11.15   Continuity at the join point.

11.5.2 Geometric and Parametric Continuity

Before we discuss the Bézier and spline forms, we examine a few issues concerning continuity and derivatives. Consider the join point in Figure 11.15. Suppose that the polynomial on the left is $\mathbf{p}(u)$ and the one on the right is $\mathbf{q}(u)$. We enforce various continuity conditions by matching the polynomials and their derivatives at $u = 1$ for $\mathbf{p}(u)$, with the corresponding values for $\mathbf{q}(u)$ at $u = 0$. If we want the function to be continuous, we must have

$$\mathbf{p}(1) = \begin{bmatrix} p_x(1) \\ p_y(1) \\ p_z(1) \end{bmatrix} = \mathbf{q}(0) = \begin{bmatrix} q_x(0) \\ q_y(0) \\ q_z(0) \end{bmatrix}.$$

All three parametric components must be equal at the join point; we call this property C^0 **parametric continuity.**

When we consider derivatives, we can require, as we did with the Hermite curve, that

$$\mathbf{p}'(1) = \begin{bmatrix} p'_x(1) \\ p'_y(1) \\ p'_z(1) \end{bmatrix} = \mathbf{q}'(0) = \begin{bmatrix} q'_x(0) \\ q'_y(0) \\ q'_z(0) \end{bmatrix}.$$

If we match all three parametric equations and the first derivative, we have C^1 parametric continuity.

If we look at the geometry, however, we can take a different approach to continuity. In three dimensions, the derivative at a point on a curve defines the tangent line at that point. Suppose that instead of requiring matching of the derivatives for the two segments at the join point, we require only that their derivatives be proportional:

$$\mathbf{p}'(1) = \alpha \mathbf{q}'(0),$$

for some positive number α. If the tangents of the two curves are proportional, then they point in the same direction, but they may have different magnitudes. We call this type of continuity G^1 **geometric continuity**.[6] If the two tangent vectors only need to be proportional, then we have only two conditions to enforce, rather than three, leaving one extra degree of freedom that we can potentially use to satisfy some other criterion. We can extend this idea to higher derivatives and can talk about both C^n and G^n continuity.

Although two curves that have only G^1 continuity at the join points have a continuous tangent at the join points, the value of the constant of proportionality—or equivalently, the relative magnitudes of the tangents on the two sides of the join point—does matter. Curves with the same tangent direction but different magnitudes differ, as shown in Figure 11.16. The curves $\mathbf{p}(u)$ and $\mathbf{q}(u)$ share the same endpoints, and the tangents at the endpoints point in the same direction, but the curves are different. This result is exploited in many painting programs, where the user can interactively change the magnitude, leaving the tangent direction unchanged. However, in other applications, such as animation, where a sequence of curve segments describes the path of an object, G^1 continuity may be insufficient (see Exercise 11.10).

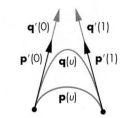

FIGURE 11.16 Change of magnitude in G^1 continuity.

11.6 BÉZIER CURVES AND SURFACES

Comparing the Hermite form to the interpolating form is problematic; we are comparing forms with some similarities but with significant differences. Both are cubic polynomial curves, but the forms do not use the same data; thus, they cannot be compared on equal terms. We can use the same control-point data that we used to derive the interpolating curves to approximate the derivatives in the Hermite curves. The resulting Bézier curves are excellent approximations to the Hermite curves and are comparable to the interpolating curves because they have been obtained using the same data. In addition, because these curves do not need derivative information, they are well suited for use in graphics and CAD.

6. G^0 continuity is the same as C^0 continuity.

11.6.1 Bézier Curves

Consider again the four control points: $\mathbf{p}_0$, $\mathbf{p}_1$, $\mathbf{p}_2$, and $\mathbf{p}_3$. Suppose that we still insist on interpolating known values at the endpoints with a cubic polynomial $\mathbf{p}(u)$:

$$\mathbf{p}_0 = \mathbf{p}(0)$$

$$\mathbf{p}_3 = \mathbf{p}(1).$$

Bézier proposed that rather than using the other two control points, $\mathbf{p}_2$ and $\mathbf{p}_3$, for interpolation, we use them to approximate the tangents at $u = 0$ and $u = 1$. Because the control points are equally spaced in parameter space, we can use the linear approximations

$$\mathbf{p}'(0) \approx \frac{\mathbf{p}_1 - \mathbf{p}_0}{\frac{1}{3}} = 3(\mathbf{p}_1 - \mathbf{p}_0)$$

$$\mathbf{p}'(1) \approx \frac{\mathbf{p}_3 - \mathbf{p}_2}{\frac{1}{3}} = 3(\mathbf{p}_3 - \mathbf{p}_2),$$

FIGURE 11.17 Approximating tangents.

as shown in Figure 11.17. Applying these approximations to the derivatives of our parametric polynomial, $\mathbf{p}(u) = \mathbf{u}^T\mathbf{c}$, at the two endpoints, we have the two conditions

$$3\mathbf{p}_1 - 3\mathbf{p}_0 = \mathbf{c}_1$$

$$3\mathbf{p}_3 - 3\mathbf{p}_2 = \mathbf{c}_1 + 2\mathbf{c}_2 + 3\mathbf{c}_3$$

to add to our interpolation conditions

$$\mathbf{p}_0 = \mathbf{c}_0$$

$$\mathbf{p}_3 = \mathbf{c}_0 + \mathbf{c}_1 + \mathbf{c}_2 + \mathbf{c}_3.$$

At this point, we again have three sets of four equations in four unknowns that we can solve, as before, to find

$$\mathbf{c} = \mathbf{M}_B\mathbf{p},$$

where $\mathbf{M}_B$ is the **Bézier geometry matrix**

$$\mathbf{M}_B = \begin{bmatrix} 1 & 0 & 0 & 0 \\ -3 & 3 & 0 & 0 \\ 3 & -6 & 3 & 0 \\ -1 & 3 & -3 & 1 \end{bmatrix}.$$

The cubic Bézier polynomial is thus

$$\mathbf{p}(u) = \mathbf{u}^T\mathbf{M}_B\mathbf{p}.$$

We use this formula exactly as we did for the interpolating polynomial. If we have a set of control points $\mathbf{p}_0, \ldots, \mathbf{p}_n$, we use $\mathbf{p}_0$, $\mathbf{p}_1$, $\mathbf{p}_2$, and $\mathbf{p}_3$ for the first curve; $\mathbf{p}_3$, $\mathbf{p}_4$, $\mathbf{p}_5$, and $\mathbf{p}_6$ for the second; and so on. It should be clear that we have C^0 continuity,

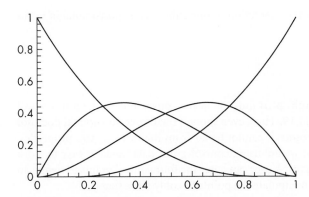

FIGURE 11.18 Blending polynomials for the Bézier cubic.

but we have given up the C^1 continuity of the Hermite polynomial because we use different approximations on the left and right of a join point.

We can see important advantages to the Bézier curve by examining the blending functions in Figure 11.18. We write the curve as

$$\mathbf{p}(u) = \mathbf{b}(u)^T \mathbf{p},$$

where

$$\mathbf{b}(u) = \mathbf{M}_B^T \mathbf{u} = \begin{bmatrix} (1-u)^3 \\ 3u(1-u)^2 \\ 3u^2(1-u) \\ u^3 \end{bmatrix}.$$

These four polynomials are one case of the **Bernstein polynomials**,

$$b_{kd}(u) = \frac{d!}{k!(d-k)!} u^k (1-u)^{d-k},$$

which can be shown to have remarkable properties. First, all the zeros of the polynomials are either at $u = 0$ or at $u = 1$. Consequently, for each blending polynomial,

$$b_{id}(u) > 0 \quad \text{for } 1 > u > 0.$$

Without any zeros in the interval, each blending polynomial must be smooth, with at most one point where the derivative is zero in the interval $1 > u > 0$. We can also show that, in this interval (see Exercise 11.5),

$$1 > b_{id}(u)$$

and

$$\sum_{i=0}^{d} b_{id}(u) = 1.$$

FIGURE 11.19   Convex hull and the Bézier polynomial.

Under these conditions, the representation of our cubic Bézier polynomial in terms of its blending polynomials,

$$\mathbf{p}(u) = \sum_{i=0}^{3} b_i(u)\mathbf{p}_i,$$

is a convex sum. Consequently, $\mathbf{p}(u)$ must lie in the convex hull of the four control points, as shown in Figure 11.19. Thus, even though the Bézier polynomial does not interpolate all the control points, it cannot be far from them. These two properties, combined with the fact that we are using control-point data, make it easy to work interactively with Bézier curves. A user can enter the four control points to define an initial curve, and then can manipulate the points to control the shape.

11.6.2 Bézier Surface Patches

We can generate the **Bézier surface patches** through the blending functions. If $\mathbf{P}$ is a 4×4 array of control points,

$$\mathbf{P} = \left[\mathbf{p}_{ij} \right],$$

then the corresponding Bézier patch is

$$\mathbf{p}(u, v) = \sum_{i=0}^{3} \sum_{j=0}^{3} b_i(u) b_j(v) \mathbf{p}_{ij} = \mathbf{u}^T \mathbf{M}_B \mathbf{P} \mathbf{M}_B^T \mathbf{v}.$$

The patch is fully contained in the convex hull of the control points (Figure 11.20) and interpolates $\mathbf{p}_{00}$, $\mathbf{p}_{03}$, $\mathbf{p}_{30}$, and $\mathbf{p}_{33}$. We can interpret the other conditions as approximations to various derivatives at the corners of the patch.

Consider the corner for $u = v = 0$. We can evaluate $\mathbf{p}(u)$ and the first partial derivatives to find

$$\mathbf{p}(0, 0) = \mathbf{p}_{00}$$

$$\frac{\partial \mathbf{p}}{\partial u}(0, 0) = 3(\mathbf{p}_{10} - \mathbf{p}_{00})$$

$$\frac{\partial \mathbf{p}}{\partial v}(0, 0) = 3(\mathbf{p}_{01} - \mathbf{p}_{00})$$

$$\frac{\partial^2 \mathbf{p}}{\partial u \partial v}(0, 0) = 9(\mathbf{p}_{00} - \mathbf{p}_{01} + \mathbf{p}_{10} - \mathbf{p}_{11}).$$

FIGURE 11.20   Bézier patch.

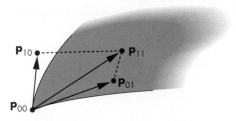

FIGURE 11.21   Twist at corner of Bézier patch.

The first three conditions are clearly extensions of our results for the Bézier curve. The fourth can be seen as a measure of the tendency of the patch to divert from being flat, or to **twist**, at the corner. If we consider the quadrilateral specified by these points (Figure 11.21), the points will lie in the same plane only if the twist is zero. Color Plates 25 and 26 use Bézier patches to create a smooth surface from elevation data.

11.7   CUBIC B-SPLINES

In practice, the cubic Bézier curves and surface patches are widely used. They have one fundamental limitation: At the join points (or patch edges, for surfaces), we have only C^0 continuity. If, for example, we were to use these curves to design our model-airplane cross sections, as shown in Section 11.2, and then were to attempt to build those cross sections, we might be unhappy with the way that the pieces meet at the join points.

It might seem that we have reached the limit of what we can do with cubic parametric polynomials, and that if we need more flexibility, we have to either go to high-degree polynomials or shorten the interval and use more polynomial segments. Both of these tactics are possibilities, but there is another: We can use the same control-point data but not require the polynomial to interpolate any of these points. If we can come close to the control points and get more smoothness at the join points, we may be content with the result.

11.7.1   The Cubic B-Spline Curve

In this section, we illustrate a particular example of a B-spline curve and show how we can obtain C^2 continuity at the join points with a cubic. In Section 11.8, we give a short introduction to a more general approach to splines—an approach that is general enough to include the Bézier curves as a special case. Consider four control points in the middle of a sequence of control points: $\{\mathbf{p}_{i-2}, \mathbf{p}_{i-1}, \mathbf{p}_i, \mathbf{p}_{i+1}\}$. Our previous approach was to use these four points to define a cubic curve such that, as the parameter u varied from 0 to 1, the curve spanned the distance from $\mathbf{p}_{i-2}$ to $\mathbf{p}_{i+1}$, interpolating $\mathbf{p}_{i-2}$ and $\mathbf{p}_{i+1}$. Instead, suppose that as u goes from 0 to 1, we span only the distance between the middle two control points, as shown in Figure 11.22. Likewise, we use $\{\mathbf{p}_{i-3}, \mathbf{p}_{i-2}, \mathbf{p}_{i-1}, \mathbf{p}_i\}$ between $\mathbf{p}_{i-2}$ and $\mathbf{p}_{i-1}$, and $\{\mathbf{p}_{i-1}, \mathbf{p}_i, \mathbf{p}_{i+1}, \mathbf{p}_{i+2}\}$ between $\mathbf{p}_i$ and $\mathbf{p}_{i+1}$. Suppose that $\mathbf{p}(u)$ is the curve we use between $\mathbf{p}_{i-1}$ and $\mathbf{p}_i$, and $\mathbf{q}(u)$ is the curve to its left, used between $\mathbf{p}_{i-2}$ and $\mathbf{p}_{i-1}$. We can match conditions at $\mathbf{p}(0)$ with

FIGURE 11.22   Four points that define a curve between the middle two points.

conditions at $\mathbf{q}(1)$. Using our standard formulation, we are looking for a matrix $\mathbf{M}$, such that the desired cubic polynomial is

$$\mathbf{p}(u) = \mathbf{u}^T \mathbf{M} \mathbf{p},$$

where $\mathbf{p}$ is the matrix of control points

$$\mathbf{p} = \begin{bmatrix} \mathbf{p}_{i-2} \\ \mathbf{p}_{i-1} \\ \mathbf{p}_i \\ \mathbf{p}_{i+1} \end{bmatrix}.$$

We can use the same matrix to write $\mathbf{q}(u)$ as

$$\mathbf{q}(u) = \mathbf{u}^T \mathbf{M} \mathbf{q},$$

where

$$\mathbf{q} = \begin{bmatrix} \mathbf{p}_{i-3} \\ \mathbf{p}_{i-2} \\ \mathbf{p}_{i-1} \\ \mathbf{p}_i \end{bmatrix}.$$

In principle, we could write a set of conditions on $\mathbf{p}(0)$ that would match conditions for $\mathbf{q}(1)$, and we could write equivalent conditions matching various derivatives of $\mathbf{p}(1)$ with conditions for another polynomial that starts there. For example, the condition

$$\mathbf{p}(0) = \mathbf{q}(1)$$

requires continuity at the join point, without requiring interpolation of any data. Enforcing this condition gives one equation for the coefficients of $\mathbf{M}$. There are clearly many sets of conditions that we can use; each set can define a different matrix.

We can take a shortcut to deriving the most popular matrix, by noting that we must use symmetric approximations at the join point. Hence, any evaluation of conditions on $\mathbf{q}(1)$ cannot use $\mathbf{p}_{i-3}$, because this control point does not appear in the equation for $\mathbf{p}(u)$. Likewise, we cannot use $\mathbf{p}_{i+1}$ in any condition on $\mathbf{p}(0)$. Two conditions that satisfy this symmetry condition are

$$\mathbf{p}(0) = \mathbf{q}(1) = \frac{1}{6}(\mathbf{p}_{i-2} + 4\mathbf{p}_{i-1} + \mathbf{p}_i),$$

$$\mathbf{p}'(0) = \mathbf{q}'(1) = \frac{1}{2}(\mathbf{p}_i - \mathbf{p}_{i-2}).$$

If we write $\mathbf{p}(u)$ in terms of the coefficient array $\mathbf{c}$,

$$\mathbf{p}(u) = \mathbf{u}^T \mathbf{c},$$

these conditions are

$$\mathbf{c}_0 = \frac{1}{6}(\mathbf{p}_{i-2} + 4\mathbf{p}_{i-1} + \mathbf{p}_i)$$

$$\mathbf{c}_1 = \frac{1}{2}(\mathbf{p}_i - \mathbf{p}_{i-2}).$$

We can apply the symmetric conditions at $\mathbf{p}(1)$:

$$\mathbf{p}(1) = \mathbf{c}_0 + \mathbf{c}_1 + \mathbf{c}_2 + \mathbf{c}_3 = \frac{1}{6}(\mathbf{p}_{i-1} + 4\mathbf{p}_i + \mathbf{p}_{i+1})$$

$$\mathbf{p}'(1) = \mathbf{c}_1 + 2\mathbf{c}_2 + 3\mathbf{c}_3 = \frac{1}{2}(\mathbf{p}_{i+1} - \mathbf{p}_{i-1})$$

We now have four equations for the coefficients of $\mathbf{c}$, which we can solve for a matrix $\mathbf{M}_S$, the **B-spline geometry matrix**,

$$\mathbf{M}_S = \frac{1}{6}\begin{bmatrix} 1 & 4 & 1 & 0 \\ -3 & 0 & 3 & 0 \\ 3 & -6 & 3 & 0 \\ -1 & 3 & -3 & 1 \end{bmatrix}.$$

This particular matrix yields a polynomial that has several important properties. We can see these properties by again examining the blending polynomials:

$$\mathbf{b}(u) = \mathbf{M}_S^T \mathbf{u} = \frac{1}{6}\begin{bmatrix} (1-u)^3 \\ 4 - 6u^2 + 3u^3 \\ 1 + 3u + 3u^2 - 3u^3 \\ u^3 \end{bmatrix}.$$

These polynomials are shown in Figure 11.23. We can show, as we did for the Bézier polynomials, that

$$\sum_{i=0}^{3} b_i(u) = 1,$$

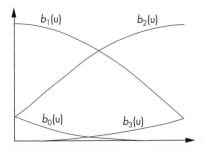

FIGURE 11.23   Spline blending functions.

FIGURE 11.24 Convex hull for spline curve.

and, in the interval $1 > u > 0$,

$$1 > b_i(u) > 0.$$

Thus, the curve must lie in the convex hull of the control points, as shown in Figure 11.24. Note that the curve is used for only part of the range of the convex hull. We defined the curve to have C^1 continuity; in fact, it has C^2 continuity,[7] as we can verify by computing $\mathbf{p}''(u)$ at $u = 0$ and $u = 1$ and seeing that the values are the same for the curves on the right and left. It is for this reason that spline curves are so important. From a physical point of view, metal will bend such that the second derivative is continuous. From a visual perspective, a curve made of cubic segments with C^2 continuity will be seen as smooth, even at the join points.

Although we have used the same control-point data as we used for the Bézier cubic to derive a smoother cubic curve, we must be aware that we are doing three times the work that we would do for Bézier or interpolating cubics. The reason is that we are using the curve between only control point $i - 1$ and control point i. A Bézier curve using the same data would be used from control point $i - 2$ to control point $i + 1$. Hence, each time we add a control point, a new spline curve must be computed, whereas for Bézier curves, we add the control points three at a time.

11.7.2 B-Splines and Basis

Instead of looking at the curve from the perspective of a single interval, we can gain additional insights by looking at the curve from the perspective of a single control point. Each control point contributes to the spline in four adjacent intervals. This property guarantees the locality of the spline; that is, if we change a single control point, we can affect the resulting curve in only four adjacent intervals. Consider the control point $\mathbf{p}_i$. In the interval between $u = 0$ and $u = 1$, it is multiplied by the blending polynomial $b_2(u)$. It also contributes to the interval on the left through $\mathbf{q}(u)$. In this interval, its contribution is $b_1(u + 1)$—we must shift the value of u by 1 to the left for this interval.

The total contribution of a single control point can be written as $B_i(u)\mathbf{p_i}$, where B_i is the function

$$B_i(u) = \begin{cases} 0 & u < i - 2 \\ b_0(u + 2) & i - 2 \leq u < i - 1 \\ b_1(u + 1) & i - 1 \leq u < i \\ b_2(u) & i \leq u < i + 1 \\ b_3(u - 1) & i + 1 \leq u < i + 2 \\ 0 & u \geq i + 2. \end{cases}$$

---

7. If we are concerned with only G^2, rather than with C^2, continuity, we can use the extra degrees of freedom to give additional flexibility in the design of the curves; see Barsky [Bar83].

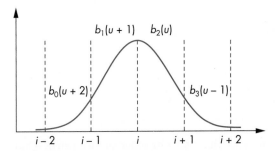

FIGURE 11.25   Spline basis function.

FIGURE 11.26   Approximating function over interval.

This function is pictured in Figure 11.25. Given a set of control points $\mathbf{p}_0, \ldots, \mathbf{p}_m$, we can write the entire spline with the single expression[8]

$$\mathbf{p}(u) = \sum_{i=1}^{m-1} B_i(u)\mathbf{p}_i.$$

This expression shows that for the set of functions $B(u - i)$, each member is a shifted version of a single function, and the set forms a basis for all our cubic B-spline curves. Given a set of control points, we form a piecewise polynomial curve $\mathbf{p}(u)$ over the whole interval as a linear combination of basis functions. Figure 11.26 shows the function and the contributions from the individual basis functions. The general theory of splines that we develop in Section 11.8 expands this view by allowing higher-degree polynomials in the intervals and by allowing different polynomials in different intervals.

11.7.3 Spline Surfaces

B-spline surfaces can be defined in a similar way. If we start with the B-spline blending functions, the surface patch is given by

$$\mathbf{p}(u, v) = \sum_{i=0}^{3} \sum_{j=0}^{3} b_i(u)b_j(v)\mathbf{p}_{ij}.$$

---

8. We determine the proper conditions for the beginning and end of the spline in Section 11.8.

FIGURE 11.27   Spline surface patch.

This expression is of the same form as are those for our other surface patches, but as we can see from Figure 11.27, we use the patch over only the central area, and we must do nine times the work that we would do with the Bézier patch. However, because of inheritance of the convex hull property and the additional continuity at the edges from the B-spline curves, the B-spline patch is considerably smoother than a Bézier patch constructed from the same data.

11.8   GENERAL B-SPLINES

Suppose that we have a set of control points $\mathbf{p}_0, \ldots, \mathbf{p}_m$. The general approximation problem is to find a function $\mathbf{p}(u) = [x(u)\ \ y(u)\ \ z(u)]^T$, defined over an interval $u_{max} \geq u \geq u_{min}$ that is smooth and close, in some sense, to the control points. Suppose we have a set of values $\{u_k\}$, called **knots**, such that

$$u_{min} = u_0 \leq u_1 \leq \cdots \leq u_n = u_{max}.$$

We call the sequence $u_0, u_1, \ldots, u_n$ the **knot array**.[9] In splines, the function $\mathbf{p}(u)$ is a polynomial of degree d between the knots,

$$\mathbf{p}(u) = \sum_{j=0}^{d} \mathbf{c}_{jk} u^j \quad u_k < u < u_{k+1}.$$

Thus, to specify a spline of degree d, we must specify the $n(d + 1)$ three-dimensional coefficients $\mathbf{c}_{jk}$. We get the required conditions by applying various continuity requirements at the knots and interpolation requirements at control points.

For example, if $d = 3$, then we have a cubic polynomial in each interval, and, for a given n, we must specify $4n$ conditions. There are $n - 1$ internal knots. If we want C^2 continuity at the knots, we have $3n - 3$ conditions. If, in addition, we want to interpolate the $n + 1$ control points, we have a total of $4n - 2$ conditions. We can pick the other two conditions in various ways, such as by fixing the slope at the ends of the curve. However, this particular spline is global; we must solve a set of $4n$ equations in $4n$ unknowns, and each coefficient will depend on all the control points. Thus, although such a spline provides a smooth curve that interpolates the control points, it is not well suited to computer graphics and CAD.

---

9. Most researchers call this sequence the *knot vector*, but that terminology violates our decision to use *vector* for only directed line segments.

FIGURE 11.28   First three basis functions.

11.8.1 Recursively Defined B-Splines

The approach taken in B-splines is to define the spline in terms of a set of basis, or blending, functions, each of which is nonzero over only the regions spanned by a few knots. Thus, we write the function $\mathbf{p}(u)$ as an expansion

$$\mathbf{p}(u) = \sum_{i=0}^{m} B_{id}(u)\mathbf{p}_i,$$

where each function $B_{id}(u)$ is a polynomial of degree d, except at the knots, and is zero outside the interval $(u_{i_{\min}}, u_{i_{\max}})$. The name *B-splines* comes from the term *basis splines*, in recognition that the set of functions $\{B_{id}(u)\}$ forms a basis for the given knot sequence and degree. Although there are numerous ways to define basis splines, of particular importance is the set of splines defined by the **Cox-deBoor recursion:**[10]

$$B_{k0} = \begin{cases} 1 & u_k \leq u \leq u_{k+1} \\ 0 & \text{otherwise} \end{cases}$$

$$B_{kd} = \frac{u - u_k}{u_{k+d} - u_k} B_{k,d-1}(u) + \frac{u_{k+d} - u}{u_{k+d+1} - u_{k+1}} B_{k+1,\,d-1}(u).$$

Each of the first set of functions, B_{k0}, is constant over one interval and is zero everywhere else; each of the second, B_{k1}, is linear over each of two intervals and is zero elsewhere; each of the third, B_{k2}, is quadratic over each of three intervals; and so on (Figure 11.28). In general, B_{kd} is nonzero over the $d + 1$ intervals between u_k and u_{k+d+1}, and it is a polynomial of degree d in each of these intervals. At the knots, there is C^{d-1} continuity. The convex hull property holds because

$$\sum_{i=0}^{m} B_{i,d}(u) = 1$$

and

$$1 \geq B_{id}(u) \geq 0,$$

in the interval $u_{\max} \geq u \geq u_{\min}$.

---

10. This formula is also known as the *deCasteljau recursion*.

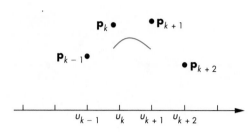

FIGURE 11.29   Uniform B-spline.

However, because each B_{id} is nonzero in only $d+1$ intervals, each control point can affect only $d+1$ intervals, and each point on the resulting curve is within the convex hull defined by these $d+1$ control points.

Note that careful examination of the Cox-deBoor formula shows that each step of the recursion is a linear interpolation of functions produced in the previous step. Linear interpolation of polynomials of degree k produces polynomials of degree $k+1$.

A set of spline basis functions is defined by the desired degree and the knot array. Note that we need what appears to be $d-1$ "extra" knot values to specify our spline because the recursion requires u_0 through u_{n+d} to specify splines from u_0 to u_{n+1}. These additional values are determined by conditions at the beginning and end of the whole spline.

Note that we have made no statement about the knot values other than that $u_k \leq u_{k+1}$. If we define any 0/0 term that arises in evaluating the recursion as equal to 1, then we can have repeated, or multiple, knots. If the knots are equally spaced, we have a **uniform spline**. However, we can achieve more flexibility by allowing not only nonuniform knot spacing but also repeated ($u_k = u_{k+1}$) knots. Let's examine a few of the possibilities.

11.8.2 Uniform Splines

Consider the uniform knot sequence $\{0, 1, 2, \ldots, n\}$. The cubic B-spline we discussed in Section 11.7 could be derived from the Cox-deBoor formula with equally spaced knots. We use the numbering that we used there (which is shifted from the Cox-deBoor indexing); between knots k and $k+1$, we use the control points $\mathbf{p}_{k-1}$, $\mathbf{p}_k$, $\mathbf{p}_{k+1}$, and $\mathbf{p}_{k+2}$. Thus, we have a curve defined for only the interval $u=1$ to $u=n-1$. For the data shown in Figure 11.29, we define a curve that does not span the knots. In certain situations, such as that depicted in Figure 11.30, we can use the periodic nature of the control-point data to define the spline over the entire knot sequence. These **uniform periodic B-splines** have the property that each spline basis function is a shifted version of a single function.

FIGURE 11.30   Periodic uniform B-spline.

11.8.3 Nonuniform B-Splines

Repeated knots have the effect of pulling the spline closer to the control point associated with the knot. If a knot at the end has multiplicity $d+1$, the B-spline of degree

d must interpolate the point. Hence, one solution to the problem of the spline not having sufficient data to span the desired interval is to repeat knots at the ends, forcing interpolation at the endpoints, and using uniform knots everywhere else. Such splines are called **open splines**.

The knot sequence $\{0, 0, 0, 0, 1, 2, \ldots, n-1, n, n, n, n\}$ is often used for cubic B-splines. The sequence $\{0, 0, 0, 0, 1, 1, 1, 1\}$ is of particular interest, because, in this case, the cubic B-spline becomes the cubic Bézier curve. In the general case, we can repeat internal knots and we can have any desired spacing of knots.

11.8.4 NURBS

In our previous development of B-splines, we have assumed that $\mathbf{p}(u)$ is the array $[x(u) \ y(u) \ z(u)]^T$. In two dimensions, however, we could have replaced it with simply $[x(u) \ y(u)]^T$, and all our equations would be unchanged. Indeed, the equations remain unchanged if we go to four-dimensional B-splines. Consider a control point in three dimensions:

$$\mathbf{p}_i = [x_i \quad y_i \quad z_i].$$

The weighted homogeneous-coordinate representation of this point is

$$\mathbf{q}_i = w_i \begin{bmatrix} x_i \\ y_i \\ z_i \\ 1 \end{bmatrix}.$$

The idea is to use the weights w_i to increase or decrease the importance of a particular control point. We can use these weighted points to form a four-dimensional B-spline. The first three components of the resulting spline are simply the B-spline representation of the weighted points,

$$\mathbf{q}(u) = \begin{bmatrix} x(u) \\ y(u) \\ z(u) \end{bmatrix} = \sum_{i=0}^{n} B_{i,d}(u) w_i \mathbf{p}_i.$$

The w component is the scalar B-spline polynomial derived from the set of weights:

$$w(u) = \sum_{i=0}^{n} B_{i,d}(u) w_i.$$

In homogeneous coordinates, this representation has a w component that may not be equal to 1; thus, we must do a perspective division to derive the three-dimensional points:

$$\mathbf{p}(u) = \frac{1}{w(u)} \mathbf{q}(u) = \frac{\sum_{i=0}^{n} B_{i,d}(u) w_i \mathbf{p}_i}{\sum_{i=0}^{n} B_{i,d}(u) w_i}.$$

Each component of $\mathbf{p}(u)$ is now a rational function in u, and because we have not restricted the knots in any way, we have derived a **nonuniform rational B-spline (NURBS)** curve.

NURBS curves retain all the properties of our three-dimensional B-splines, such as the convex hull and continuity properties. They have two other properties that make them of particular interest in computer graphics and CAD.

If we apply an affine transformation to a B-spline curve or surface, we get the same function as the B-spline derived from the transformed control points. Because perspective transformations are not affine, most splines will not be handled correctly in perspective viewing. However, the perspective division embedded in the construction of NURBS curves ensures that NURBS curves are handled correctly in perspective views.

Quadric surfaces are usually specified by algebraic implicit forms. If we are using nonrational splines, we can only approximate these surfaces. However, quadrics can be shown to be a special case of quadratic NURBS curves; thus, we can use a single modeling method, NURBS curves, for the most widely used curves and surfaces (see Exercises 11.14 and 11.15). Color Plate 5 shows the mesh generated by a NURBS modeling of the surfaces that make up the object in Color Plate 1. In WebGL, we ultimately render this mesh with triangles.

11.8.5 Catmull-Rom Splines

If we relax the requirement that our curves and surfaces must lie within the convex hull of the data, we can use our data to form other types of splines. One of the most popular is the Catmull-Rom spline.

Consider again the four control points, $\mathbf{p}_0$, $\mathbf{p}_1$, $\mathbf{p}_2$, and $\mathbf{p}_3$, that we used in our derivation of the Bézier curve. Suppose that rather than deriving a cubic polynomial that interpolates $\mathbf{p}_0$ and $\mathbf{p}_1$, we interpolate the middle points $\mathbf{p}_1$ and $\mathbf{p}_2$:

$$\mathbf{p}(0) = \mathbf{p}_1$$

$$\mathbf{p}(1) = \mathbf{p}_2.$$

Thus, like the B-spline, our polynomial will be defined over a shorter interval, and each time that we add a new control point, we find a new curve.

FIGURE 11.31 Constructing the Catmull-Rom spline.

We use the points $\mathbf{p}_0$ and $\mathbf{p}_3$ to specify tangents at $\mathbf{p}_1$ and $\mathbf{p}_2$ (Figure 11.31):

$$\mathbf{p}'(0) \approx \frac{\mathbf{p}_2 - \mathbf{p}_0}{2}$$

$$\mathbf{p}'(1) \approx \frac{\mathbf{p}_3 - \mathbf{p}_1}{2}.$$

We now have four conditions on the curve

$$\mathbf{p}(u) = \mathbf{c}_0 + \mathbf{c}_1 u + \mathbf{c}_2 u^2 + \mathbf{c}_3 u^3,$$

which yield the equations

$$\mathbf{p}_1 = \mathbf{c}_0$$

$$\mathbf{p}_2 = \mathbf{c}_0 + \mathbf{c}_1 + \mathbf{c}_2 + \mathbf{c}_3$$

$$\frac{\mathbf{p}_2 - \mathbf{p}_0}{2} = \mathbf{c}_1$$

$$\frac{\mathbf{p}_3 - \mathbf{p}_1}{2} = \mathbf{c}_1 + 2\mathbf{c}_2 + 3\mathbf{c}_3.$$

Note that because, as u goes from 0 to 1, we only go from $\mathbf{p}_1$ to $\mathbf{p}_2$, so $\mathbf{p}_0$ and $\mathbf{p}_2$ are separated by two units in parameter space, as are $\mathbf{p}_1$ and $\mathbf{p}_3$. In addition, these four conditions ensure that the resulting curves are continuous and have continuous first derivatives at the control points, even though we do not have the convex hull property.

Solving the four equations yields

$$\mathbf{p}(u) = \mathbf{u}^T \mathbf{M}_R \mathbf{p},$$

where $\mathbf{M}_R$ is the Catmull-Rom geometry matrix

$$\mathbf{M}_R = \frac{1}{2} \begin{bmatrix} 0 & 2 & 0 & 0 \\ -1 & -0 & 1 & 0 \\ 2 & -5 & 4 & -1 \\ -1 & 3 & -3 & -1 \end{bmatrix}.$$

11.9 RENDERING CURVES AND SURFACES

Once we have specified a scene with curves and surfaces, we must find a way to render it. There are several approaches, depending on the type of representation. For explicit and parametric curves and surfaces, we can evaluate the curve or surface at a sufficient number of points so that we can approximate it with our standard flat objects. We focus on this approach for parametric polynomial curves and surfaces.

For implicit surfaces, we can compute points on the object that are the intersection of rays from the center of projection through pixels with the object. We can then use these points to specify curve sections or meshes that can be rendered directly. However, except for quadrics (Section 11.11), the intersection calculation requires the solution of nonlinear equations of too high a degree to be practical for real-time computation.

Consider the cubic parametric Bézier polynomial

$$\mathbf{b}(u) = (1-u)^3 \mathbf{p}_0 + (1-u)^2 u \mathbf{p}_1 + (1-u)u^2 \mathbf{p}_0 + u^3 \mathbf{p}_3.$$

If we want to evaluate it at N equally spaced values of u and put the results into an array points as in our previous examples, the code for a two-dimensional example can be as simple as

```
function bezier(u)
{
   var b = [ ];
   var a = 1 - u;
   b.push(u*u*u);
   b.push(3*a*u*u);
   b.push(3*a*a*u);
   b.push(a*a*a);

   return b;
}

var d = 1.0/(N - 1.0);

for (var i = 0; i < N; ++i) {
  var u = i*d;
  for (var j = 0; j < 2; ++j) {
    pointsArray[i][j] = dot(bezier(u), p[i][j]);
  }
}
```

where the control-point data are in the array p of vec2s.

11.9.1 Polynomial Evaluation Methods

Suppose that we have a representation over our standard interval

$$\mathbf{p}(u) = \sum_{i=0}^{n} \mathbf{c}_i u^i, \quad 0 \le u \le 1.$$

We can evaluate $\mathbf{p}(u)$ at some set of values $\{u_k\}$, and we can use a polyline (or gl.LINE_STRIP) to approximate the curve. Rather than evaluate each term u^k independently, we can group the terms as

$$\mathbf{p}(u) = \mathbf{c}_0 + u(\mathbf{c}_1 + u(\mathbf{c}_2 + u(\cdots + \mathbf{c}_n u))).$$

This grouping shows that we need only n multiplications to evaluate each $p(u_k)$; this algorithm is known as **Horner's method**. For our typical cubic $\mathbf{p}(u)$, the grouping becomes

$$\mathbf{p}(u) = \mathbf{c}_0 + u(\mathbf{c}_1 + u(\mathbf{c}_2 + u\mathbf{c}_3)).$$

If the points $\{u_i\}$ are spaced uniformly, we can use the method of **forward differences** to evaluate $\mathbf{p}(u_k)$ using $O(n)$ additions and no multiplications. The forward differences are defined iteratively by the formulas

$$\Delta^{(0)}\mathbf{p}(u_k) = \mathbf{p}(u_k)$$

$$\Delta^{(1)}\mathbf{p}(u_k) = \mathbf{p}(u_{k+1}) - \mathbf{p}(u_k)$$

$$\Delta^{(m+1)}\mathbf{p}(u_k) = \Delta^{(m)}\mathbf{p}(u_{k+1}) - \Delta^{(m)}\mathbf{p}(u_k).$$

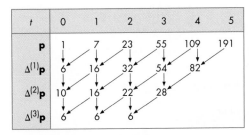

t	0	1	2	3	4	5
p	1	7	23	55	109	191
$\Delta^{(1)}$**p**	6	16	32	54	82	
$\Delta^{(2)}$**p**	10	16	22	28		
$\Delta^{(3)}$**p**	6	6	6			

FIGURE 11.32   Construction of a forward-difference table.

t	0	1	2	3	4	5
p	1	7	23	55 → 109 → 191		
$\Delta^{(1)}$**p**	6	16	32 → 54 → 82			
$\Delta^{(2)}$**p**	10	16 → 22 → 28				
$\Delta^{(3)}$**p**	6 → 6 → 6					

FIGURE 11.33   Use of a forward-difference table.

If $u_{k+1} - u_k = h$ is constant, we can show that if $\mathbf{p}(u)$ is a polynomial of degree n, then $\Delta^{(n)}\mathbf{p}(u_k)$ is constant for all k. This result suggests the strategy illustrated in Figure 11.32 for the scalar cubic polynomial

$$p(u) = 1 + 3u + 2u^2 + u^3.$$

We need the first $n + 1$ values of $p(u_k)$ to find $\Delta^{(n)}p(u_0)$. But once we have $\Delta^{(n)}p(u_0)$, we can copy this value across the table and work upward, as shown in Figure 11.33, to compute successive values of $p(u_k)$, using the rearranged recurrence

$$\Delta^{(m-1)}(p_{k+1}) = \Delta^{(m)}p(u_k) + \Delta^{(m-1)}p(u_k).$$

This method is efficient, but it is not without its faults: It applies only to a uniform grid, and it is prone to accumulation of numerical errors.

11.9.2 Recursive Subdivision of Bézier Polynomials

The most elegant rendering method performs recursive subdivision of the Bézier curve. The method is based on the use of the convex hull and never requires explicit evaluation of the polynomial. Suppose that we have a cubic Bézier polynomial (the method also applies to higher-degree Bézier curves). We know that the curve must lie within the convex hull of the control points. We can break the curve into two separate polynomials, $\mathbf{l}(u)$ and $\mathbf{r}(u)$, each valid over one-half of the original interval. Because the original polynomial is a cubic, each of these polynomials also is a cubic. Note that because each is to be used over one-half of the original interval, we must rescale

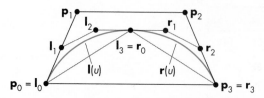

FIGURE 11.34   Convex hulls and control points.

the parameter u for $\mathbf{l}$ and $\mathbf{r}$ so that as u varies over the range $(0, 1)$, $\mathbf{l}(u)$ traces the left half of $\mathbf{p}(u)$ and $\mathbf{r}(u)$ traces the right half of $\mathbf{p}$. Each of our new polynomials has four control points that both specify the polynomial and form its convex hull. We denote these two sets of points by $\{\mathbf{l}_0, \mathbf{l}_1, \mathbf{l}_2, \mathbf{l}_3\}$ and $\{\mathbf{r}_0, \mathbf{r}_1, \mathbf{r}_2, \mathbf{r}_3\}$; the original control points for $\mathbf{p}(u)$ are $\{\mathbf{p}_0, \mathbf{p}_1, \mathbf{p}_2, \mathbf{p}_3\}$. These points and the two convex hulls are shown in Figure 11.34. Note that the convex hulls for $\mathbf{l}$ and $\mathbf{r}$ must lie inside the convex hull for p, a result known as the **variation-diminishing property** of the Bézier curve.

Consider the left polynomial. We can test the convex hull for flatness by measuring the deviation of $\mathbf{l}_1$ and $\mathbf{l}_2$ from the line segment connecting $\mathbf{l}_0$ and $\mathbf{l}_3$. If they are close, we can draw the line segment instead of the curve. If they are not close, we can divide $\mathbf{l}$ into two halves and test the two new convex hulls for flatness. Thus, we have a recursion that never requires us to evaluate points on a polynomial, but we have yet to discuss how to find $\{\mathbf{l}_0, \mathbf{l}_1, \mathbf{l}_2, \mathbf{l}_3\}$ and $\{\mathbf{r}_0, \mathbf{r}_1, \mathbf{r}_2, \mathbf{r}_3\}$. We will find the hull for $\mathbf{l}(u)$; the calculation for $\mathbf{r}(u)$ is symmetric. We can start with

$$\mathbf{p}(u) = \mathbf{u}^T \mathbf{M}_B \begin{bmatrix} \mathbf{p}_0 \\ \mathbf{p}_1 \\ \mathbf{p}_2 \\ \mathbf{p}_3 \end{bmatrix},$$

where

$$\mathbf{M}_B = \begin{bmatrix} 1 & 0 & 0 & 0 \\ -3 & 3 & 0 & 0 \\ 3 & -6 & 3 & 0 \\ -1 & 3 & -3 & -1 \end{bmatrix}.$$

The polynomial $\mathbf{l}(u)$ must interpolate $\mathbf{p}(0)$ and $\mathbf{p}\left(\frac{1}{2}\right)$; hence,

$$\mathbf{l}(0) = \mathbf{l}_0 = \mathbf{p}_0,$$

$$\mathbf{l}(1) = \mathbf{l}_3 = \mathbf{p}\left(\frac{1}{2}\right) = \frac{1}{8}(\mathbf{p}_0 + 3\mathbf{p}_1 + 3\mathbf{p}_2 + \mathbf{p}_3).$$

At $u = 0$, the slope of $\mathbf{l}$ must match the slope of $\mathbf{p}$, but, because the parameter for $\mathbf{i}$ covers only the range $(0, \frac{1}{2})$, while u varies over $(0, 1)$, implicitly we have made the substitution $\bar{u} = 2u$. Consequently, derivatives for $\mathbf{l}$ and $\mathbf{p}$ are related by $d\bar{u} = 2du$, and

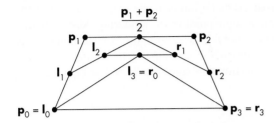

FIGURE 11.35   Construction of subdivision curves.

$$l'(0) = 3(l_1 - l_0) = p'(0) = \frac{3}{2}(p_1 - p_0).$$

Likewise, at the midpoint,

$$l'(1) = 3(l_3 - l_2) = p'\left(\frac{1}{2}\right) = \frac{3}{8}(-p_0 - p_1 + p_2 + p_3).$$

These four equations can be solved algebraically. Alternatively, this solution can be expressed geometrically, with the aid of Figure 11.35. Here, we construct both the left and right sets of control points concurrently. First, we note that the interpolation condition requires that

$$l_0 = p_0$$

$$r_3 = p_3.$$

We can verify by substitution in the four equations that the slopes on the left and right yield

$$l_1 = \frac{1}{2}(p_0 + p_1)$$

$$r_2 = \frac{1}{2}(p_2 + p_3).$$

The interior points are given by

$$l_2 = \frac{1}{2}\left(l_1 + \frac{1}{2}(p_1 + p_2)\right)$$

$$r_1 = \frac{1}{2}\left(r_2 + \frac{1}{2}(p_1 + p_2)\right).$$

Finally, the shared middle point is given by

$$l_3 = r_0 = \frac{1}{2}(l_2 + r_1).$$

The advantage of this formulation is that we can determine both sets of control points using only shifts (for the divisions by 2) and additions. However, one of the advantages of the subdivision approach is that it can be made adaptive, and only one of the sides may require subdivision at some point in the rendering. Also, note that because the rendering of the curve need not take place until the rasterization stage of the pipeline and can be done in screen or window coordinates, the limited resolution of the display places a limit on how many times the convex hull needs to be subdivided (Exercise 11.24).

11.9.3 Rendering Other Polynomial Curves by Subdivision

Just as any polynomial is a Bézier polynomial, it is also an interpolating polynomial, a B-spline polynomial, and any other type of polynomial for a properly selected set of control points. The efficiency of the Bézier subdivision algorithm is such that we are usually better off converting another curve form to Bézier form and then using the subdivision algorithm.[11] A conversion algorithm can be obtained directly from our curve formulations. Consider a cubic Bézier curve. We can write it in terms of the Bézier matrix $\mathbf{M}_B$ as

$$\mathbf{p}(u) = \mathbf{u}^T \mathbf{M}_B \mathbf{p},$$

where $\mathbf{p}$ is the **geometry matrix** of control points. The same polynomial can be written as

$$\mathbf{p}(u) = \mathbf{u}^T \mathbf{M} \mathbf{q},$$

where $\mathbf{M}$ is the matrix for some other type of polynomial and $\mathbf{q}$ is the matrix of control points for this type. We assume that both polynomials are specified over the same interval. The polynomials will be identical if we choose

$$\mathbf{q} = \mathbf{M}^{-1} \mathbf{M}_B \mathbf{p}.$$

For the conversion from interpolation to Bézier, the controlling matrix is

$$\mathbf{M}_B^{-1} \mathbf{M}_I = \begin{bmatrix} 1 & 0 & 0 & 0 \\ -\frac{5}{6} & 3 & -\frac{3}{2} & \frac{1}{3} \\ \frac{1}{3} & -\frac{3}{2} & 3 & -\frac{5}{6} \\ 0 & 0 & 0 & 1 \end{bmatrix}.$$

For the conversion between cubic B-splines and cubic Bézier curves, it is

$$\mathbf{M}_B^{-1} \mathbf{M}_S = \frac{1}{6} \begin{bmatrix} 1 & 4 & 1 & 0 \\ 0 & 4 & 2 & 0 \\ 0 & 2 & 4 & 0 \\ 0 & 1 & 4 & 1 \end{bmatrix}.$$

---

11. Even systems that do not render using subdivision are often optimized for rendering Bézier curves by other methods. Hence, we still might want to convert any type of polynomial curve or surface to a Bézier curve or surface.

FIGURE 11.36 Cubic polynomials generated as Bézier curves by conversion of control points. (a) Bézier polynomial. (b) Interpolating polynomial. (c) B-spline polynomial.

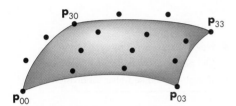

FIGURE 11.37 Cubic Bézier surface.

Figure 11.36 shows four control points and the cubic Bézier polynomial, interpolating polynomial, and spline polynomial. The interpolating and spline forms were generated as Bézier curves, from the new control points derived from the matrices $\mathbf{M}_B^{-1}\mathbf{M}_I$ and $\mathbf{M}_B^{-1}\mathbf{M}_S$. All three curves were generated using recursive subdivision of Bézier curves. Note that for the spline case, the resulting curve is generated between only the second and third of the original control points.

11.9.4 Subdivision of Bézier Surfaces

We can extend our subdivision algorithm to Bézier surfaces. Consider the cubic surface in Figure 11.37, with the 16 control points shown. Each four points in a row or column determine a Bézier curve that can be subdivided. However, our subdivision algorithm should split the patch into four patches, and we have no control points along the center of the patch. We can proceed in two steps.

First, we apply our curve subdivision technique to the four curves determined by the 16 control points in the v direction. Thus, for each of $u = 0, \frac{1}{3}, \frac{2}{3}, 1$, we create two groups of four control points, with the middle point shared by each group. There are then seven different points along each original curve; these points are indicated in Figure 11.38 by circles. We see that there are three types of points: original control points that are kept after the subdivision (gray), original control points that are discarded after the subdivision (white), and new points created by the subdivision (black). We now subdivide in the u direction using these points. Consider the rows of constant v, where v is one of $0, \frac{1}{3}, \frac{2}{3}, 1$. There are seven groups of four points (Figure 11.38). Each group defines a Bézier curve for a constant v. We can subdivide in the u direction, each time creating two groups of four points, again with the middle point shared. These points are indicated in Figure 11.39. If we divide

FIGURE 11.38   First subdivision of surface.

FIGURE 11.39   Points after second subdivision.

FIGURE 11.40   Subdivided quadrant.

these points into four groups of 16, with points on the edges shared (Figure 11.40), each quadrant contains 16 points that are the control points for a subdivided Bézier surface.

Compared to the calculation for curves, the test for whether the new convex hull is flat enough to stop a subdivision process is more difficult. Many renderers use a fixed number of subdivisions, often letting the user pick the number. If a high-quality rendering is desired, we can let the subdivision continue until the projected size of the convex hull is less than the size of one pixel.

11.10   THE UTAH TEAPOT

We conclude our discussion of parametric surfaces with an example of recursive subdivision of a set of cubic Bézier patches. The object that we show has become known as the **Utah teapot**. The data for the teapot were created at the University of Utah by Mike Newell for testing of various rendering algorithms. These data have been used in the graphics community for more than 40 years. The teapot data consist of the control points for 32 bicubic Bézier patches. They are given in terms of 306 vertices. The first 12 patches define the body of the teapot; the next four define the handle; the next four define the spout; the following eight define the lid; and the final four define the bottom. For historical reasons, the up direction for the teapot is z rather than y. The examples on the website switch the z and y values to reorient the teapot in a more familiar manner. These data are widely available.

For purposes of illustration, let's assume that we want to subdivide each patch n times and, after these subdivisions, we will render the final vertices using either line segments or polygons passing through the four corners of each patch. Thus, our final drawing can be accomplished using the following function (for line segments), which puts the four corner points (which must interpolate the surface) into the `points` array that will be rendered as two triangles, either with lines or filled:

```
function drawPatch(p)
{
    points.push(p[0][0]);
    points.push(p[0][3]);
    points.push(p[3][3]);
    points.push(p[0][0]);
    points.push(p[3][3]);
    points.push(p[3][0]);
}
```

Note that we are assuming the 4×4 array specifying the patch is either a `mat4` or an array of four-element arrays where each element is a `vec4`. We build our patch subdivider from the curve subdivider for a cubic curve specified by the four points in `c`, producing the left control points in `l` and the right control points in `r` for the two curves produced by the subdivision:

```
function divideCurve(c, r, l)
{
    // Divides c into left (l) and right (r) curve data

    var mid = mix(c[1], c[2], 0.5);

    l[0] = vec4(c[0]);
    l[1] = mix(c[0], c[1], 0.5);
    l[2] = mix(l[1], mid, 0.5);

    r[3] = vec4(c[3]);
    r[2] = mix(c[2], c[3], 0.5);
    r[1] = mix(mid, r[2], 0.5);

    r[0] = mix(l[2], r[1], 0.5);
    l[3] = vec4(r[0]);
}
```

The patch subdivider is easier to write—but is slightly less efficient—if we assume that we have a matrix transpose function `transpose`. This code is then

```
function dividePatch(p, count)
{
  if (count > 0) {
    var a = mat4();
    var b = mat4();
    var t = mat4();
    var q = mat4();
    var r = mat4();
    var s = mat4();

    // Subdivide curves in u direction, transpose results, divide
    // in u direction again (equivalent to subdivision in v)

    for (var k = 0; k < 4; ++k) {
      var pp = p[k];
      var aa = vec4();
      var bb = vec4();

      divideCurve(pp, aa, bb);

      a[k] = vec4(aa);
      b[k] = vec4(bb);
    }

    a = transpose(a);
    b = transpose(b);

    for (var k = 0; k < 4; ++k) {
      var pp = vec4(a[k]);
      var aa = vec4();
      var bb = vec4();

      divideCurve(pp, aa, bb);

      q[k] = vec4(aa);
      r[k] = vec4(bb);
    }

    for (var k = 0; k < 4; ++k) {
      var pp = vec4(b[k]);
      var aa = vec4();
      var bb = vec4();

      divideCurve(pp, aa, bb);

      s[k] = vec4(aa);
      t[k] = vec4(bb);
    }

    // Recursive division of four resulting patches
```

FIGURE 11.41 Rendered teapots.

```
    dividePatch(q, count - 1);
    dividePatch(r, count - 1);
    dividePatch(s, count - 1);
    dividePatch(t, count - 1);
  }
  else {
    drawPatch(p);
  }
}
```

Complete teapot-rendering programs using both wire frame and shaded polygons are given on the website, as is a program for rendering the teapot using direct evaluation of the parametric polynomials. The website contains the teapot data.

Figure 11.41 shows the teapot as a wireframe and with shading. Note that the various patches have different curvatures and sizes; thus, carrying out all subdivisions to the same depth can create many unnecessarily small polygons.

11.11 ALGEBRAIC SURFACES

Although quadrics can be generated as a special case of NURBS curves, this class of algebraic objects is of such importance that it merits independent discussion. Quadrics are the most important case of the algebraic surfaces that we introduced in Section 11.1.

11.11.1 Quadrics

Quadric surfaces are described by implicit algebraic equations in which each term is a polynomial of the form $x^i y^j z^k$, with $i + j + k \leq 2$. Any quadric can be written in the form

$$q(x, y, z) = a_{11}x^2 + 2a_{12}xy + a_{22}y^2 + a_{33}z^2 + 2a_{23}yz + 2a_{13}xz$$
$$+ b_1 x + b_2 y + b_3 z + c = 0.$$

This class of surfaces includes ellipsoids, paraboloids, and hyperboloids. We can write the general equation in matrix form in terms of the three-dimensional column matrix $\mathbf{p} = [x \ y \ z]^T$ as the **quadratic form**

$$\mathbf{p}^T \mathbf{A} \mathbf{p} + \mathbf{b}^T \mathbf{p} + c = 0,$$

where

$$\mathbf{A} = \begin{bmatrix} a_{11} & a_{12} & a_{13} \\ a_{12} & a_{22} & a_{23} \\ a_{13} & a_{23} & a_{33} \end{bmatrix} \qquad \mathbf{b} = \begin{bmatrix} b_1 \\ b_2 \\ b_3 \end{bmatrix}.$$

The 10 independent coefficients in $\mathbf{A}$, $\mathbf{b}$, and c determine a given quadric. However, for the purpose of classification, we can apply a sequence of rotations and translations that reduces a quadric to a standard form without changing the type of surface. In three dimensions, we can write such a transformation as

$$\mathbf{p}' = \mathbf{Mp} + \mathbf{d}.$$

This substitution creates another quadratic form with $\mathbf{A}$ replaced by the matrix $\mathbf{M}^T\mathbf{A}\mathbf{M}$. The matrix $\mathbf{M}$ can always be chosen to be a rotation matrix such that $\mathbf{D} = \mathbf{M}^T\mathbf{A}\mathbf{M}$ is a diagonal matrix. The diagonal elements of $\mathbf{D}$ can be used to determine the type of quadric. If, for example, the equation is that of an ellipsoid, the resulting quadratic form can be put in the form

$$a'_{11}x'^2 + a'_{22}y'^2 + a_{33}z'^2 - c' = 0,$$

where all the coefficients are positive. Note that because we can convert to a standard form by an affine transformation, quadrics are preserved by affine transformations and thus fit well with our other standard primitives.

11.11.2 Rendering of Surfaces by Ray Casting

Quadrics are easy to render because we can find the intersection of a quadric with a ray by solving a scalar quadratic equation. We represent the ray from $\mathbf{p}_0$ in the direction $\mathbf{d}$ parametrically as

$$\mathbf{p} = \mathbf{p}_0 + \alpha\mathbf{d}.$$

Substituting into the equation for the quadric, we obtain the scalar equation for α:

$$\alpha^2\mathbf{d}^T\mathbf{A}\mathbf{d} + \alpha\mathbf{d}^T(\mathbf{b} + 2\mathbf{A}\mathbf{p}_0) + \mathbf{p}_0^T\mathbf{A}\mathbf{p}_0 + \mathbf{b}^T\mathbf{d} + c = 0.$$

As for any quadratic equation, we may find zero, one, or two real solutions. We can use this result to render a quadric into the framebuffer or as part of a ray-tracing calculation. In addition, we can apply our standard shading model at every point on a quadric because we can compute the normal by taking the derivatives

$$\mathbf{n} = \begin{bmatrix} \frac{\partial q}{\partial x} \\ \frac{\partial q}{\partial y} \\ \frac{\partial q}{\partial z} \end{bmatrix} = 2\mathbf{A}\mathbf{p} - \mathbf{b}.$$

This method of rendering can be extended to any algebraic surface. Suppose that we have an algebraic surface

$$q(\mathbf{p}) = q(x, y, z) = 0.$$

As part of the rendering pipeline, we cast a ray from the center of projection through each pixel. Each of these rays can be written in the parametric form

$$\mathbf{p}(\alpha) = \mathbf{p}_0 + \alpha \mathbf{d}.$$

Substituting this expression into q yields an implicit polynomial equation in α:

$$q(\mathbf{p}(\alpha)) = 0.$$

We can find the points of intersection by numerical methods, or for quadrics, by the quadratic formula. If we have terms up to $x^i y^j z^k$, we can have $i + j + k$ points of intersection, and the surface may require considerable time to render.

11.12 SUBDIVISION CURVES AND SURFACES

Let's reexamine our subdivision formula from Section 11.9.2 from a slightly different perspective. We start with four points—$\mathbf{p}_0$, $\mathbf{p}_1$, $\mathbf{p}_2$, $\mathbf{p}_3$—and end up with seven points. We can call these new points $\mathbf{s}_0, \ldots, \mathbf{s}_6$. We can view each of these sets of points as defining a piecewise linear curve, as illustrated in Figure 11.42.

We can use our subdivision formulas to relate the two sets of points:

$$\mathbf{s}_0 = \mathbf{p}_0$$

$$\mathbf{s}_1 = \tfrac{1}{2}(\mathbf{p}_0 + \mathbf{p}_1)$$

$$\mathbf{s}_2 = \tfrac{1}{4}(\mathbf{p}_0 + 2\mathbf{p}_1 + \mathbf{p}_2)$$

$$\mathbf{s}_3 = \tfrac{1}{8}(\mathbf{p}_0 + 3\mathbf{p}_1 + 3\mathbf{p}_2 + \mathbf{p}_3)$$

$$\mathbf{s}_4 = \tfrac{1}{4}(\mathbf{p}_1 + 2\mathbf{p}_2 + \mathbf{p}_3)$$

$$\mathbf{s}_5 = \tfrac{1}{2}(\mathbf{p}_2 + \mathbf{p}_3)$$

$$\mathbf{s}_6 = \mathbf{p}_3.$$

The second curve is said to be a **refinement** of the first. As we saw in Section 11.9.2, we can continue the process iteratively and in the limit converge to the B-spline. However, in practice, we want to carry out only enough iterations so that the resulting piecewise linear curve connecting the new points looks smooth. How many iterations

FIGURE 11.42 (a) Piecewise linear curve determined by four points. (b) Piecewise linear curve after one subdivision step.

we need to carry out depends on the size of the projected convex hull, which can be determined from the camera specifications. Thus, we have a method that allows us to render curves at different levels of detail.

These ideas and their benefits are not limited to B-splines. Over the past few years, a variety of methods for generating these **subdivision curves** have appeared. Some interpolate points—such as p_0 and p_3—while others do not interpolate any of the original points. But in all cases, the refined curves converge to a smooth curve.

11.12.1 Mesh Subdivision

The next issue we examine is how we can apply these ideas to surfaces. A theory of **subdivision surfaces** has emerged that deals with both the theoretical and practical aspects of these ideas. Rather than generating a general subdivision scheme, we will focus on meshes of triangles and meshes of quadrilaterals. In practice, many modeling programs produce one of these types of meshes or a mesh consisting of only triangles and quadrilaterals. If we start with a more general mesh, we can use tessellation to replace the original mesh with one consisting of only triangles or quadrilaterals.

We can form a quadrilateral mesh from an arbitrary mesh using the Catmull-Clark method. We divide each edge in half, creating a new vertex at the midpoint. We create an additional vertex at the **centroid** of each polygon; that is, the point that is the average of the vertices that form the polygon. We then form a quadrilateral mesh by connecting each original vertex to the new vertices on either side of it and connecting the two new vertices to the centroid. Figure 11.43 shows the subdivision for some simple polygons. Note that in each case the subdivision creates a quadrilateral mesh.

Once we have created the quadrilateral mesh, it is clear that successive subdivisions create a finer quadrilateral mesh. However, we have yet to do anything to create a smoother surface. In particular, we want to ensure as much continuity as possible at the vertices.

Consider the following procedure. First, we compute the average position of each polygon, its centroid. Then, we replace each vertex by the average of the centroids of all the polygons that contain the vertex. At this point, we have a smoother surface but one for which, at vertices not of valence 4, we can see sharp changes in smoothness.

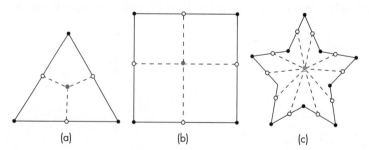

(a)   (b)   (c)

FIGURE 11.43   Polygon subdivision. (a) Triangle. (b) Rectangle. (c) Star-shaped polygon.

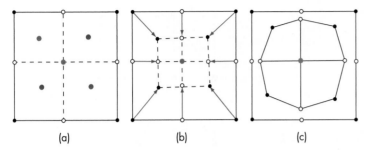

FIGURE 11.44   Catmull-Clark subdivision.

The Catmull-Clark scheme produces a smoother surface with one additional step. For each vertex not of valence 4, we replace it by

$$\mathbf{p} = \mathbf{p}_0 + \frac{4}{k}\mathbf{p}_1,$$

where $\mathbf{p}_0$ is the vertex position before the averaging step, $\mathbf{p}_1$ is its position after the averaging step, and k is the valence of the vertex. The **valence** of a vertex is the number of polygons that share the vertex. This method tends to move edge vertices at corners more than other outer vertices. Figure 11.44 shows the sequence for a single rectangle. In Figure 11.44(a), the original vertices are black and the vertices at the midpoints of the edges are white. The centroid of the original polygon is the gray vertex at the center, and the centroids of the subdivided polygons are shown as colored vertices. Figure 11.44(b) shows the movement of the vertices by averaging, and Figure 11.44(c) shows the final Catmull-Clark subdivision after the correction factor has been applied.

This scheme does not work as well for meshes that start with all triangles, because the interior vertices have high valences that do not change with refinement. For triangular meshes, there is a simple method called *Loop subdivision* that we can describe as a variant of the general scheme. We start by doing a standard subdivision of each triangle by connecting the bisectors of the sides to create four triangles. We proceed as before but use a weighted centroid of the vertices, with a weight of 1/4 for the vertex that is being moved and 3/8 for the other two vertices that form the triangle. We can get a smoother surface by taking a weighted average of the vertex positions before and after the averaging step, as we did for the Catmull-Clark scheme. Loop's method uses a weight of $\frac{5}{3} - \frac{8}{3}(\frac{3}{8} + \frac{1}{4}\cos(\frac{2\pi}{k}))^2$. Figure 11.45 shows a simple triangle mesh and the resulting mesh after the subdivision step.

The figures in Color Plate 28 were developed using subdivision surfaces. Figure 11.46 shows a sequence of meshes generated by a subdivision surface algorithm and the rendered surface from the highest-resolution mesh. Note that the original mesh contains polygons with different numbers of sides and vertices with different valences. Also, note that as the mesh is subdivided, each subdivision step yields a smoother surface.

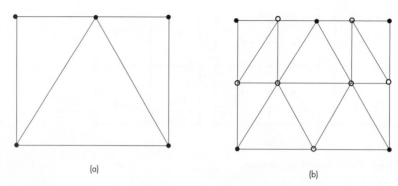

(a)

(b)

FIGURE 11.45   Loop subdivision. (a) Triangular mesh. (b) Triangles after one subdivision.

FIGURE 11.46   Successive subdivisions of polygonal mesh and rendered surface. (Images courtesy of Caltech Multi-Res Modeling Group)

We have not covered some tricky issues, such as the data structures needed to ensure that when we insert vertices we get consistent results for shared edges. The references in the Suggested Readings should help you get started.

11.13 MESH GENERATION FROM DATA

In all our examples, we have assumed that the positions for our data were given either at the nodes of a rectangular grid or possibly at the nodes of a general graph. In many circumstances, we are given a set of locations that we know are from a surface, but otherwise the locations are unstructured. Thus, we have a list of locations but no notion of which points are close to each other.

11.13.1 Height Fields Revisited

One example of how such data arise is topography, where we might take measurements of the heights of random points on the ground from an airplane or satellite, such as the height fields we considered in Chapter 5, where they were based on these measurements being taken over a regular grid in which $y = 0$ represents the ground. Consequently, the height data were of the form y_{ij}, all of which could be stored in a matrix. Here, the data are obtained at random unstructured locations, so the starting point is a set of values $\{x_i, y_i, z_i\}$. The topography example has some structure in that we know all the points lie on a single surface and that no two points can have the same x_i and z_i. Figure 11.47 shows a set of points, all of which are above the plane $y = 0$. These points can be projected onto the plane $y = 0$, as in Figure 11.48. We seek an algorithm that connects these points into a triangular mesh, as shown in Figure 11.49. The mesh in the plane can then be projected back up to connect the original data with triangles. These three-dimensional triangles can be rendered to give an approximation to the surface that yielded the data. Figure 11.50 shows this mesh.

In the next section, we examine how we can obtain a triangular mesh from a set of points in the plane.

11.13.2 Delaunay Triangulation

Given a set of points in a plane, there are many ways to form a triangular mesh that uses all the points as vertices. Even four vertices that specify a convex quadrilateral

FIGURE 11.47   Height data.

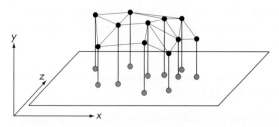

FIGURE 11.48   Height data projected onto the plane $y = 0$.

FIGURE 11.49   Triangular mesh.

FIGURE 11.50   Three-dimensional mesh.

(a)   (b)

FIGURE 11.51   Two splits of a quadrilateral.

can form a two-triangle mesh in two ways, depending on which way we draw a diagonal. For a mesh of n vertices, there will be $n - 2$ triangles in the mesh but many ways to triangulate the mesh. From the graphics perspective, not all the meshes from a given set of vertices are equivalent. Consider the two ways we can triangulate the four points in Figure 11.51. Because we always want a mesh in which no edges cross, the four edges colored in black must be in the mesh. Note that they form the convex hull of the four points. Hence, we only have a choice as to the diagonal. In Figure 11.51(a), the diagonal creates two long, thin triangles whereas the diagonal in Figure 11.51(b) creates two more robust triangles. We prefer the second case because long, thin triangles tend to render badly, showing artifacts from the interpolation of vertex attributes.

In general, the closer a triangle is to an equilateral triangle, the better it is for rendering. In more mathematical terms, the best triangles have the largest minimum interior angle. If we compare two triangular meshes derived from the same set of points, we can say the better mesh is the one with the largest minimum interior angle of all the triangles in the mesh. Although it may appear that determining such a mesh for a large number of triangles is difficult, we can approach the problem in a manner that will yield the largest minimum angle.

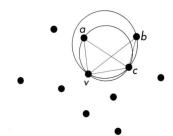

FIGURE 11.52   Circles determined by possible triangulations.

Consider some vertices in the plane that will be part of a mesh (Figure 11.52). Focusing on vertex v, it appears that one of the triangles a, v, c or v, c, b should be part of the mesh. Recall that three points in the plane determine a unique circle that interpolates them. Note that the circle formed by a, v, c does not include another point, whereas the circle formed by v, c, b does. Moreover, the triangle formed by a, v, c has a larger minimum angle than the triangle formed by v, c, b. Because these two triangles share an edge, we can only use one of them in our mesh.

These observations suggest a strategy known as **Delaunay triangulation**. Given a set of n points in the plane, the Delaunay triangulation has the following properties, any one of which is sufficient to define the triangulation:

1. For any triangle in Delaunay triangulation, the circle passing through its three vertices has no other vertices in its interior.

2. For any edge in the Delaunay triangulation, there is a circle passing through the endpoints (vertices) of this edge that includes no other vertex in its interior.

3. If we consider the set of angles of all the triangles in a triangulation, the Delaunay triangulation has the greatest minimum angle.

Proofs of these properties are in the Suggested Readings at the end of the chapter. The third property ensures that the triangulation is a good one for computer graphics. The first two properties follow from how we construct the triangulation.

We start by adding three vertices such that all the points in the set of vertices lie inside the triangle formed by these three vertices, as in Figure 11.53. These extra vertices and the edges connecting them to other vertices can be removed at the end. We next pick a vertex v from our data set at random and connect it to the three added vertices, thus creating three triangles, as shown in Figure 11.54. Note there is no way a circle determined by any three of the four vertices can include the other, so we need not do any testing yet.

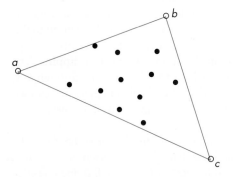

FIGURE 11.53   Starting a Delaunay triangulation.

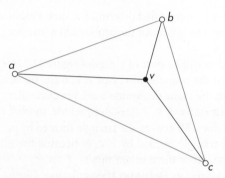

FIGURE 11.54   Triangulation after adding first data point.

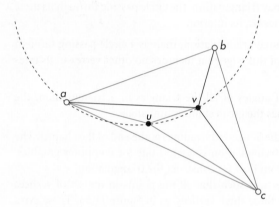

FIGURE 11.55   Adding a vertex requiring flipping.

We next pick a vertex u randomly from the remaining vertices. From Figure 11.55, we see that this vertex lies inside the triangle formed by a, v, and c and that the three triangles it forms do not present a problem. However, the edge between a and v is a diagonal for the quadrilateral formed by a, u, v, and b, and the circle that interpolates a, u, and v has b in its interior. Hence, if we use this edge, we will violate the criteria for a Delaunay triangulation. There is a simple solution to this problem. We can choose the other diagonal of the quadrilateral and replace the edge between a and v with an edge between u and b, an operation called **flipping**. The resulting partial mesh is shown in Figure 11.56. Now the circle passing through u, v, and b does not include any other vertices, nor do any of the other circles determined by any of the triangles. Thus, we have a Delaunay triangulation of a subset of the points.

We continue the process by adding another randomly chosen vertex from the original set of vertices, flipping as necessary. Note that it is not sufficient in general to flip only one edge corresponding to a just-added vertex. The act of flipping one edge

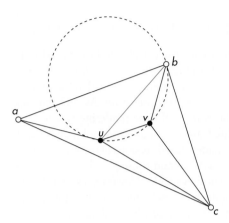

FIGURE 11.56   Mesh after flipping.

can require the flipping of other edges, so the process is best described recursively. Because each flip gives an improvement, the process terminates for each added vertex, and once we have added all the vertices, we can remove the three vertices we added to get started and all the edges connected to them. On average, the triangulation has a $O(n \log n)$ complexity.

There are some potential problems with our approach that arise because we create the mesh in a plane and project it back up to the data points. A triangle that has almost equal angles in the plane may not have such nice angles when the corresponding original vertices are connected to form a triangle in three dimensions. A potential solution would be to apply a similar strategy directly to the three-dimensional data rather than projecting them onto a plane. For each set of four points, we can determine a unique sphere that they interpolate. Thus, we can define a three-dimensional Delaunay triangulation as one in which no other data point lies in the sphere, and we use the four points to specify a tetrahedron. Unfortunately, determining such a spatial division requires far more work than Delaunay triangulation in the plane.

11.13.3 Point Clouds

Delaunay triangulation relied on the assumption that our data were $2\frac{1}{2}$-dimensional; that is, we knew they came from a single surface and could be recovered from their projections onto a plane. In many situations, we have data that are completely unstructured, and often these data sets are very large. For example, laser scans can output tens of millions of points in a short time. Such data sets are known as **point clouds**. Often, such data are displayed directly using point primitives. Because we can shade points in WebGL as we would a surface, a high density of shaded points can show three-dimensional structure, especially if the camera can be moved interactively.

11.14   GRAPHICS API SUPPORT FOR CURVES AND SURFACES

Traditionally, curves and surfaces were constructed exclusively on the CPU, with the resulting generated primitives transmitted to the rendering system for processing. However, as we have seen, curves and surfaces can generate a considerable number of primitives depending upon the requested levels of tessellation. As such, the use of dynamically tessellated curves and surfaces for real-time rendering was limited. Recently, graphics APIs supporting all of the features of modern graphics hardware, such as OpenGL or Direct3D, now support shader-based versions of tessellated curves and surfaces. Given the design goals of OpenGL ES, and subsequently WebGL, support for accelerated rendering is not currently available. However, we will briefly describe the advanced shading stages available in OpenGL and Direct3D for rendering curves and surfaces to stimulate your investigation of advanced topics.

11.14.1 Tessellation Shading

In OpenGL and Direct3D's geometry processing pipelines, tessellation shading immediately follows vertex shading, if it is enabled. In both of these APIs, the tessellation shading stage is executed by running two shaders, with additional operations occurring between the two shaders. We will use principally OpenGL's nomenclature for describing the operations.

As compared to the geometric primitives available in WebGL, tessellation introduced a new primitive, the **patch**. A patch is merely a logical collection of any number vertices, which are initially processed by the current vertex shader. An example of a patch would be the 16 vertices of a Bézier surface. Once the input patch vertices are processed, they are passed to the first of the two shaders used by tessellation, the **tessellation control shader** (called the **hull shader** in Direct3D). The tessellation control shader is responsible for two operations: specifying how much the patch is to be tessellated and potentially modifying the patch's vertices (i.e., creating additional vertices or reducing the number of vertices). An example of having the number of input patch vertices different from the output might be generating geometry for a fixed-sized, screen-aligned quadrilateral called a **sprite**, specified by its position. In this case, the input patch for each sprite would be a single vertex. The tessellation control shader would create three additional vertices to fully specify the geometry of the sprite.

After the tessellation control shader has completed processing of all the vertices in its patch, the graphics pipeline determines how finely to tessellate the patch based on the guidance of the tessellation control shader. Effectively, the tessellation control shader specifies how many primitives to create around the patch's boundary, as well as how many primitives to create in its interior. The process used for doing this generates a set of parametric (x, y) coordinates that lie within the unit square. These coordinates, known as **tessellation coordinates**, are fed individually into the next shading stage, the **tessellation evaluation shader**.

The tessellation evaluation shader is responsible for transforming each tessellation coordinate, along with the data of the output patch, into a final vertex that is subsequently either processed by more vertex shading or passed into the rasterizer for fragment generation. Consider the processing we did for the Bézier surface: in that case, we used a coordinate pair (u, v) as input into the Bézier blending functions. Using a tessellation evaluation shader, the (u, v) coordinates would determine the tessellation coordinates generated by the graphics pipeline, and the tessellation evaluation shader would contain the code for evaluating the blending functions to produce the final vertex corresponding to that tessellation parameter.

The benefit of using tessellation is that it allows geometric primitives to be generated inside the GPU, without intervention by any other part of the system. This provides a more optimized solution for models that can be described using parametric surfaces, by reducing the work that the CPU needs to do to compute the geometry and by optimizing the data transfer to the GPU.

11.14.2 Geometry Shading

Both OpenGL and Direct3D support a final geometry processing phase called **geometry shading**. As with tessellation shading, geometry shaders are not available in either OpenGL ES or WebGL. However, we once again provide a cursory description of them for completeness.

Geometry shaders perform only a single shader pass per primitive and are conceptually simpler than the pair of tessellation shaders. A geometry shader accepts as input a geometric primitive (e.g., a point or triangle), described by its vertices, and allows for the output of an arbitrary number (up to a specified maximum) of generated geometric primitives. The geometry shader has access to all of the vertices, and can generate new primitives by emitting new vertices as well as by specifying the end of a primitive, all under the control of the geometry shader.

Similar to tessellation shading, geometry shading benefits by being executed exclusively on the GPU, thus allowing for performance optimization and reduced application memory and bandwidth requirements.

SUMMARY AND NOTES

Once again, we have only scratched the surface of a deep and important topic. Also once again, our focus has been on what we can do with a graphics system using a standard API such as WebGL. The earlier fixed-function OpenGL pipeline supported Bézier surfaces through functions called **evaluators** that computed the values of the Bernstein polynomials of any degree. However, as we have seen, computing these values in our code and in shaders is not difficult.

From this perspective, there are huge advantages to using parametric Bézier curves and surfaces. The parametric form is robust and is easy to use interactively because the required data are points that can be entered and manipulated interactively. The subdivision algorithm for Bézier curves and surfaces gives us the ability to render the resulting objects to any desired degree of accuracy.

We have seen that although Bézier surfaces are easy to render, splines can provide additional smoothness and control. The texts in the Suggested Readings discuss many variants of splines that are used in the CAD community.

Quadric surfaces are used extensively with ray tracers, because solving for the points of intersection between a ray and a quadric requires the solution of only a scalar quadratic equation. Deciding whether the point of intersection between a ray and the plane determined by a flat polygon is inside the polygon can be more difficult than solving the intersection problem for quadric surfaces. Hence, many ray tracers allow only infinite planes, quadrics, and, perhaps, convex polygons.

Subdivision surfaces have become increasingly more important for two reasons. First, because commodity hardware can render polygons at such high rates, we can often achieve the desired smoothness using a large number of polygons that can be rendered faster than a smaller number of surface patches. However, future hardware may change this advantage if rendering of curved surfaces is built into the rasterizer. Second, because we can render a subdivision surface at any desired level of detail, we can often use subdivision very effectively by not rendering a highly subdivided surface when it projects to a small area on the screen.

SUGGESTED READINGS

The book by Farin [Far88] provides an excellent introduction to curves and surfaces. It also has an interesting preface in which Bézier discusses the almost simultaneous discovery by him and deCasteljau of the surfaces that bear Bézier's name. Unfortunately, deCasteljau's work was described in unpublished technical reports, so deCasteljau did not receive the credit he deserved until recently. Books such as those by Rogers [Rog90], Foley [Fol90], Bartels [Bar87], and Watt [Wat00] discuss many other forms of splines. See Rogers [Rog00] for an introduction to NURBS. The Catmull-Rom splines were proposed in [Cat75].

The book by Faux [Fau80] discusses the coordinate-free approach to curves and surfaces and the Frenet frame.

Although the book edited by Glassner [Gla89] primarily explores ray tracing, the section by Haines has considerable material on working with quadrics and other algebraic surfaces.

There has been much recent activity on subdivision curves and surfaces. For some of the seminal work in the area, see [Che95], [Deb96], [Gor96], [Lev96], [Sei96], and [Tor96]. Our development follows [War04]. Catmull-Clark subdivision was proposed in [Cat78]. See also [War03] and [Sta03]. Delaunay triangulation is covered in most books on computational geometry; see [deB08].

EXERCISES

11.1 Consider an algebraic surface $p(u, v) = u^T C v$. What types of geometric figures does it describe?

11.2 Consider the explicit equation $y = mx + h$. What types of geometric figures does it describe?

11.3 Suppose that you have a polynomial $p(u) = \sum_{k=0}^{n} c_k u^k$. Find a polynomial $q(v) = \sum_{k=0}^{n} d_k v^k$ such that, for each point of p in the interval (a, b), there is a point v in the range $0 \leq v \leq 1$ such that $p(u) = q(v)$.

11.4 Show that as long as the four control points for the cubic interpolating curve are defined at unique values of the parameter u, the interpolating geometry matrix always exists.

11.5 What are the advantages of the parametric form of curves?

11.6 State the significance of the variation-diminishing property of the Bézier curve.

11.7 Find the criteria for the smoothness of a curve.

11.8 Suppose that we render Bézier patches by adaptive subdivision so that each patch can be subdivided a different number of times. Do we maintain continuity along the edges of the patches? Explain your answer.

11.9 Write a WebGL program that will take as input a set of control points and produce the interpolating, B-spline, and Bézier curves for these data.

11.10 Suppose that you use a set of spline curves to describe a path in time that an object will take as part of an animation. How might you notice the difference between G^1 and C^1 continuity in this situation?

11.11 Write a program to generate a cubic Bézier polynomial from an arbitrary number of points entered interactively. The user should be able to manipulate the control points interactively.

11.12 What is the significance of the convex hull of the control points of the Bézier curve?

11.13 How do derivatives help in curve formation?

11.14 Derive the open rational quadratic B-spline with the knots $\{0, 0, 0, 0, 1, 1, 1, 1\}$ and the weights $w_0 = w_2 = 1$ and $w_1 = w$.

11.15 Using the result of Exercise 11.14, show that if $w = \frac{r}{1-r}$, for $0 \leq r \leq 1$, then you get all the conic sections. *Hint*: Consider $r < \frac{1}{2}$ and $r > \frac{1}{2}$.

11.16 What is the significance of the Hermite geometry matrix?

11.17 What are tensor product surfaces? What is the difference between bicubic tensor product surfaces and tensor product surfaces?

11.18 For a 1024×1280 display screen, what is the maximum number of subdivisions that are needed to render a cubic polynomial surface?

11.19 Suppose you have three points P_0, P_1, and P_2. First, connect successive points with parametric line segments where u ranges from 0 to 1 for each. Next, linearly interpolate between successive pairs of line segments by connecting points for the same value of u with a line segment and then using the same value of u to obtain a value along this new line segment. How can you describe the curve created by this process?

11.20 Extend Exercise 11.19 by considering four points. Linearly interpolate, first between the three curves constructed in that exercise and, second, between the two curves thus created. Describe the final curve determined by the four points.

11.21   What happens in the cubic Bézier curve if the values of the first and the last control points are the same?

11.22   What is the significance of the nonuniform rational B-spline (NURBS) curve? What will happen when we apply affine transformation to a B-spline curve or surface?

11.23   Suppose that we divide a Bézier surface patch, first along the u direction. Then in v, we only subdivide one of the two patches we have created. Show how this process can create a gap in the resulting surface. Find a simple solution to this difficulty.

11.24   Write a program to carry out subdivision of triangular or quadrilateral meshes. When the subdivision is working correctly, add the averaging step to form a smoother surface.

11.25   What is the significance of the rendering method that performs recursive subdivision of the Bézier curve.

11.26   Find the variation-diminishing property of the Bézier curve.

CHAPTER 12

ADVANCED RENDERING

In this final chapter, we consider a variety of alternative approaches to the standard pipeline rendering strategy we have used for interactive applications. We have multiple motivations for introducing these other approaches. We want to be able to incorporate effects, such as global illumination, that usually are not possible to render in real time. We also want to produce high-quality images whose resolution is beyond that of standard computer displays. For example, a single frame of a digital movie may contain over 10 million pixels and take hours to render. In addition, the best rendering technique for a standard computer may not be the best technique for a device such as a smart phone.

Unlike previous chapters, in this one we will consider a number of topics that may at first appear unrelated. Most of these topics are advanced, thus inviting further study, and may become increasingly more important as the power of GPUs continues to grow.

12.1 GOING BEYOND PIPELINE RENDERING

Almost everything we have done so far has led us to believe that given a scene description containing geometric objects, cameras, light sources, and attributes, we could render the scene in close to real time using available hardware and software. This view dictated that we would use a pipeline renderer of the type described by the WebGL architecture and supported by GPUs. Although we have developed a reasonably large bag of tricks that enable us to handle most applications and get around many of the consequences of using the local lighting model supported by such renderers, there are still limitations on what we can do. For example, there are many global illumination situations that we cannot approximate well with a pipeline renderer. We would also like to generate images with higher resolution than is supported by a standard GPU. We might also want to generate images that contain fewer aliasing artifacts. In many situations, we are willing either to render at slower speeds or to use multiple computers to achieve these goals. In this chapter, we introduce a variety of techniques, all of which are of current interest to both researchers and practitioners.

First, we examine other rendering strategies that are based on the physics of image formation. Our original discussion of image formation was based on following rays of light. That approach was built on a very simple physical model and led to the ray-tracing paradigm for rendering. We start by exploring this model in greater detail than in previous chapters and show how to get started writing your own ray tracer.

We can take approaches to rendering, other than ray tracing, that are also based on physics. We will examine an approach based on energy conservation and consider an integral equation, the **rendering equation**, that describes a closed environment with light sources and reflective surfaces. Although this equation is not solvable in general, we can develop a rendering approach called **radiosity** that satisfies the rendering equation when all surfaces are perfectly diffuse reflectors.

We will also look at two approaches that are somewhere between physically correct renderers and real-time renderers. One is the approach taken in RenderMan. The other is an approach to rendering that starts with images. Although these methods are different from each other, both have become important in the animation industry.

We then turn to the problems of working with large data sets and high-resolution displays. These problems are related because large data sets contain detail that requires displays with a resolution beyond what we can get with standard commodity devices such as LCD panels. We will consider solutions that employ parallelism, making use of commodity components, both processors and graphics cards.

Finally, we introduce image-based rendering, in which we start with multiple two-dimensional images of a three-dimensional scene and try to use these images to obtain an image from another viewpoint.

12.2   RAY TRACING

In many ways, ray tracing is a logical extension to rendering with a local lighting model. It is based on our previous observation that of the light rays leaving a source, the only ones that contribute to our image are those that enter the lens of our synthetic camera, passing through the center of projection. Figure 12.1 shows several of the possible interactions with a single point source and perfectly specular surfaces. Rays can enter the lens of the camera directly from the source, from interactions with a surface visible to the camera, after multiple reflections from surfaces, or after transmission through one or more surfaces.

Most of the rays that leave a source do not enter the lens and do not contribute to our image. Hence, attempting to follow all rays from a light source is a time-wasting endeavor. However, if we reverse the direction of the rays and consider only those rays that start at the center of projection, we know that these **cast rays** must contribute to the image. Consequently, we start our ray tracer as shown in Figure 12.2. Here we have included the image plane and we have ruled it into pixel-sized areas. Knowing that we must assign a color to every pixel, we must cast at least one ray through each pixel. Each cast ray intersects either a surface or a light source, or goes off to infinity without striking anything. Pixels corresponding to this latter case can be assigned a background color. Rays that strike surfaces—for now, we can assume that all surfaces are opaque—require us to calculate a shade for the point of intersection. If we were simply to compute the shade at the point of intersection, using the modified Phong

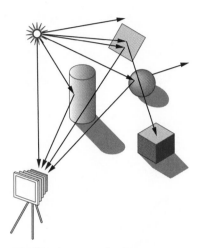

FIGURE 12.1 Rays leaving source.

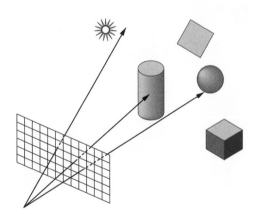

FIGURE 12.2 Ray-casting model.

model, we would produce the same image as our local renderer. However, we can do much more.

Note that the process that we have described so far requires all the same steps as we use in our pipeline renderer: object modeling, projection, and visible-surface determination. However, the order in which the calculations are carried out is different. The pipeline renderer works on a vertex-by-vertex basis; the ray tracer works on a pixel-by-pixel basis.

In ray tracing, rather than immediately applying our reflection model, we first check whether the point of intersection between the cast ray and the surface is illuminated. We compute **shadow**, or **feeler**, **rays** from the point on the surface to each source. If a shadow ray intersects a surface before it meets the source, the light is blocked from reaching the point under consideration and this point is in shadow, at

FIGURE 12.3   Shadow rays.

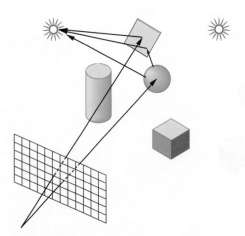

FIGURE 12.4   Ray tracing with a mirror.

least from this source. No lighting calculation needs to be done for sources that are blocked from a point on the surface. If all surfaces are opaque and we do not consider light scattered from surface to surface, we have an image that has shadows added to what we have already done without ray tracing. The price we pay is the cost of doing a type of hidden-surface calculation for each point of intersection between a cast ray and a surface. Figure 12.3 shows the shadow rays (solid lines) for two cast rays (dashed lines) that hit the cube and sphere. A shadow ray from the cube intersects the cylinder. Hence, the point of intersection on the cube from the cast ray is illuminated by only one of the two sources.

Suppose that some of our surfaces are highly reflective, like those shown in Figure 12.4. We can follow the shadow ray as it bounces from surface to surface, until it either goes off to infinity or intersects a source. Figure 12.4 shows just two of the

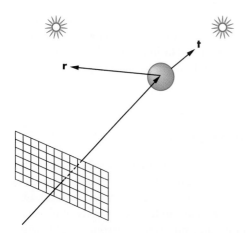

FIGURE 12.5   Ray tracing with reflection and transmission.

paths. The left cast ray intersects the mirror and the shadow ray to the light source on the left is not blocked, so if the mirror is in front of the second source, the point of intersection is illuminated by only one source. The cast ray on the right intersects the sphere, and in this case a shadow can reflect from the mirror to the source on the left; in addition, the point of intersection is illuminated directly by the source on the left. Such calculations are usually done recursively and take into account any absorption of light at surfaces.

Ray tracing is particularly good at handling surfaces that both reflect light and transmit light through refraction. Using our basic paradigm, we follow a cast ray to a surface (Figure 12.5) with the property that if a ray from a source strikes a point, then the light from the source is partially absorbed and some of this light contributes to the diffuse reflection term. The rest of the incoming light is divided between a transmitted ray and a reflected ray. From the perspective of the cast ray, if a light source is visible at the intersection point, then we need to perform three tasks. First, we must compute the contribution from the light source at the point, using our standard reflection model. Second, we must cast a ray in the direction of a perfect reflection. Third, we must cast a ray in the direction of the transmitted ray. These two cast rays are treated just like the original cast ray; that is, they may intersect other surfaces, they can end at a source, or they can go off to infinity. At each surface that these rays intersect, additional rays may be generated by reflection and transmission of light. Figure 12.6 shows a single cast ray and the path it can follow through a simple environment. Figure 12.7 shows the **ray tree** generated. This tree shows which rays must be traced; it is constructed dynamically by the ray-tracing process.

Although our ray tracer uses the Blinn-Phong model to include a diffuse term at the point of intersection between a ray and a surface, the light that is scattered diffusely at this point is ignored. If we were to attempt to follow such light, we would have so many rays to deal with that the ray tracer might never complete execution. Thus, ray tracers are best suited for highly reflective environments. Color Plate 15 was rendered with a public-domain ray tracer. Although the scene contains only a few

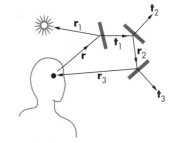

FIGURE 12.6   Simple ray-traced environments.

FIGURE 12.7   Ray tree corresponding to Figure 12.6.

objects, the reflective and transparent surfaces could not have been rendered realistically without the ray tracer. Also, note the complexity of the shadows in the scene, another effect created automatically by ray tracing. The image also demonstrates that ray tracers can incorporate texture mapping with no more difficulty than with our pipeline renderer.

12.3   BUILDING A SIMPLE RAY TRACER

The easiest way to describe a ray tracer is recursively, through a single function that traces a ray and calls itself for the reflected and transmitted rays. Most of the work in ray tracing goes into the calculation of intersections between rays and surfaces. One reason it is difficult to implement a ray tracer that can handle a variety of objects is that as we add more complex objects, computing intersections becomes problematic. Consequently, most basic ray tracers support only flat and quadric surfaces.

We have seen the basic considerations that determine the ray-tracing process. Building a simple recursive ray tracer that can handle simple objects—quadrics and polyhedra—is quite easy. In this section, we will examine the basic structure and the functions that are required. Details can be found in the Suggested Readings at the end of the chapter.

We need two basic functions. The recursive function `trace` follows a ray, specified by a point and a direction, and returns the shade of the first surface that it intersects. It uses the function `intersect` to find the location of the closest surface that the specified ray intersects.

12.3.1 Recursive Ray Tracing

Let's consider the procedure `trace` in pseudocode. We give it a starting point p and a direction d, and it returns a color. In order to stop the ray tracer from recursing forever, we can specify a maximum number of steps, `max`, that it can take. We will assume, for simplicity, that we have only a single light source whose properties, as well as the description of the objects and their surface properties, are all available globally. If there are additional light sources, we can add their contributions in a manner similar to the way in which we deal with the single source.

```
function trace(p, d, step)
{
  color local, reflected, transmitted;
  point q;
  normal n;

  if (step > max) {
    return(backgroundColor);
  }

  q = intersect(p, d, status);
```

```
  if (status == light_source) {
    return(lightSourceColor);
  }
  if (status == no_intersection) {
    return(backgroundColor);
  }

  n = normal(q);
  r = reflect(q, n);
  t = transmit(q, n);

  local = phong(q, n, r);
  reflected = trace(q, r, step+1);
  transmitted = trace(q, t, step+1);

  return(local + reflected + transmitted);
}
```

Note that the calculation of reflected and transmitted colors must take into account how much energy is absorbed at the surface before reflection and transmission. If we have exceeded the maximum number of steps, we return a specified background color. Otherwise, we use `intersect` to find the intersection of the given ray with the closest object. This function must have the entire database of objects available to it, and it must be able to find the intersections of rays with all types of objects supported. Consequently, most of the time spent in the ray tracer, and the complexity of the code, is hidden in `intersect`. We examine some of the intersection issues in Section 12.3.2.

If the ray does not intersect any object, we can return a status variable from `intersect` and return the background color from `trace`. Likewise, if the ray intersects the light source, we return the color of the source. If an intersection is returned, there are three components to the color at this point: a local color that can be computed using the modified Phong (or any other) model, a reflected color, and, if the surface is translucent, a transmitted color. Before computing these colors, we must compute the normal at the point of intersection, as well as the direction of reflected and transmitted rays, as in Chapter 6. The complexity of computing the normal depends on the class of objects supported by the ray tracer, and this calculation can be part of the function `trace`.

The computation of the local color requires a check to see if the light source is visible from the point of closest intersection. Thus, we cast a feeler or shadow ray from this point toward the light source and check whether it intersects any objects. We note that this process can also be recursive because the shadow ray might hit a reflective surface, such as a mirror, or a translucent surface, such as a piece of glass. In addition, if the shadow ray hits a surface that itself is illuminated, some of this light should contribute to the color at q. Generally, we ignore these possible contributions because they will slow the calculation significantly. Practical ray tracing requires that we make some compromises and is never quite correct physically.

Next, we have two recursive steps that compute the contributions from the reflected and transmitted rays starting at q using `trace`. It is these recursions that make this code a ray tracer rather than a simple ray-casting rendering in which we find the first intersection and apply a lighting model at that point. Finally, we add the three colors to obtain the color at p.

12.3.2 Calculating Intersections

Most of the time spent in a typical ray tracer is in the calculation of intersections in the function `intersect`. Hence, we must be very careful in limiting the objects to those for which we can find intersections easily. The general intersection problem can be expressed cleanly if we use an implicit representation of our objects. Thus, if an object is defined by the surface(s)

$$f(x, y, z) = f(\mathbf{p}) = 0,$$

and a ray from a point $\mathbf{p}_0$ in the direction $\mathbf{d}$ is represented by the parametric form

$$\mathbf{p}(t) = \mathbf{p}_0 + t\mathbf{d},$$

then the intersections are given for the values of t such that

$$f(\mathbf{p}_0 + t\mathbf{d}) = 0,$$

which is a scalar equation in t. If f is an algebraic surface, then f is a sum of polynomial terms of the form $x^i y^j z^k$ and $f(\mathbf{p}_0 + t\mathbf{d})$ is a polynomial in t. Finding the intersections reduces to finding all the roots of a polynomial. Unfortunately, there are only a few cases that do not require numerical methods.

One is quadrics. In Chapter 11, we saw that all quadrics could be written in the quadratic form

$$\mathbf{p}^T \mathbf{A}\mathbf{p} + \mathbf{b}^T\mathbf{p} + c = 0.$$

Substituting in the equation for a ray leaves us with a scalar quadratic equation to solve for the values of t that yield zero, one, or two intersections. Because the solution of the quadratic equation requires only the taking of a single square root, ray tracers can handle quadrics without difficulty. In addition, we can eliminate those rays that miss a quadric object and those that are tangent to it before taking the square root, further simplifying the calculation.

Consider, for example, a sphere centered at $\mathbf{p}_c$ with radius r, which can be written as

$$(\mathbf{p} - \mathbf{p}_c) \cdot (\mathbf{p} - \mathbf{p}_c) - r^2 = 0.$$

Substituting in the equation of the ray

$$\mathbf{p}(t) = \mathbf{p}_0 + t\mathbf{d},$$

we get the quadratic equation

$$\mathbf{d} \cdot \mathbf{d}t^2 + 2(\mathbf{p}_0 - \mathbf{p}_c) \cdot \mathbf{d}t + (\mathbf{p}_0 - \mathbf{p}_c) \cdot (\mathbf{p}_0 - \mathbf{p}_c) - r^2 = 0.$$

Planes are also simple. We can take the equation for the ray and substitute it into the equation of a plane

$$\mathbf{p} \cdot \mathbf{n} + c = 0,$$

which yields a scalar equation that requires only a single division to solve. Thus, for the ray

$$\mathbf{p} = \mathbf{p}_0 + t\mathbf{d},$$

we find

$$t = -\frac{\mathbf{p}_0 \cdot \mathbf{n} + c}{\mathbf{n} \cdot \mathbf{d}}.$$

However, planes by themselves have limited applicability in modeling scenes. We are usually interested in either the intersection of multiple planes that form convex objects (polyhedra) or a piece of a plane that defines a flat polygon. For polygons, we must decide whether the point of intersection lies inside or outside the polygon. The difficulty of such a test depends on whether the polygon is convex and, if not convex, whether it is simple. These issues are similar to the rendering issues that we discussed for polygons in Chapter 8. For convex polygons, there are very simple tests that are similar to the tests for ray intersections with polyhedra that we consider next.

Although we can define polyhedra by their faces, we can also define them as the convex objects that are formed by the intersection of planes. Thus, a parallelepiped is defined by six planes and a tetrahedron by four. For ray tracing, the advantage of this definition is that we can use the simple ray–plane intersection equation to derive a ray–polyhedron intersection test.

We develop the test as follows. Let's assume that all the planes defining our polyhedron have normals that are outward facing. Consider the ray in Figure 12.8 that intersects the polyhedron. It can enter and leave the polygon only once. It must enter through a plane that is facing the ray and leave through a plane that faces in the direction of the ray. However, this ray must also intersect all the planes that form the polyhedron (except those parallel to the ray).

Consider the intersections of the ray with all the front-facing planes—that is, those whose normals point toward the starting point of the ray. The entry point must be the intersection farthest along the ray. Likewise, the exit point is the nearest intersection point of all the planes facing away from the origin of the ray, and the entry point must be closer to the initial point than the exit point. If we consider a ray that misses the same polyhedron, as shown in Figure 12.9, we see that the farthest intersection with a front-facing plane is farther from the initial point than the closest intersection with a back-facing plane. Hence, our test is to find these possible entry and exit points by computing the ray–plane intersection points, in any order, and updating the possible entry and exit points as we find the intersections. The test can be halted if we ever find a possible exit point closer than the present entry point or a possible entry point farther than the present exit point.

Consider the two-dimensional example illustrated in Figure 12.10 that tests for a ray–convex polygon intersection in a plane. Here lines replace planes, but the logic

FIGURE 12.8 Ray intersecting a polyhedron with outward-facing normals shown.

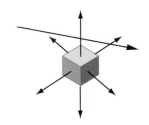

FIGURE 12.9 Ray missing a polyhedron with outward-facing normals shown.

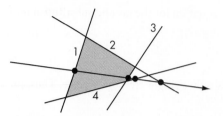

FIGURE 12.10   Ray intersecting a convex polygon.

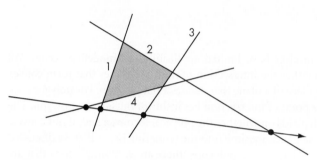

FIGURE 12.11   Ray missing a convex polygon.

is the same. Suppose that we do the intersections with the lines in the order 1, 2, 3, 4. Starting with line 1, we find that this line faces the initial point by looking at the sign of the dot product of the normal with the direction of the ray. The intersection with line 1 then yields a possible entry point. Line 2 faces away from the initial point and yields a possible exit point that is farther away than our present estimate of the entry point. Line 3 yields an even closer exit point but still one that is farther than the entry point. Line 4 yields a farther exit point that can be discarded. At this point, we have tested all the lines and conclude the ray passes through the polygon.

Figure 12.11 has the same lines and the same convex polygon but shows a ray that misses the polygon. The intersection with line 1 still yields a possible entry point. The intersections with lines 2 and 3 still yield possible exit points that are farther than the entry point. But the intersection with line 4 yields an exit point closer than the entry point, which indicates that the ray must miss the polygon.

12.3.3 Ray-Tracing Variations

Most ray tracers employ multiple methods for determining when to stop the recursive process. One method that is fairly simple to implement is to neglect all rays that go past some distance, assuming that such rays go off to infinity. We can implement this test by assuming that all objects lie inside a large sphere centered at the origin. Thus, if we treat this sphere as an object colored with a specified background color, whenever the intersection calculation determines that this sphere is the closest object, we terminate the recursion for the ray and return the background color.

Another simple termination strategy is to look at the fraction of energy remaining in a ray. When a ray passes through a translucent material or reflects from a shiny surface, we can estimate the fraction of the incoming energy that is in these outgoing rays and how much has been absorbed at the surface. If we add an energy parameter to the ray tracer,

```
function trace(p, d, steps, energy)
```

then we need only add a line of code to check if there is sufficient energy remaining to continue tracing a ray.

There are many improvements we can make to speed up a ray tracer or make it more accurate. For example, it is fairly simple to replace the recursion in the ray tracer with iteration. Much of the work in finding intersections often can be avoided by the use of bounding boxes or bounding spheres, because the intersection with these objects can be done very quickly. Often, bounding volumes can be used to group objects effectively, as can the BSP trees that we introduced in Chapter 9.

Because ray tracing is a sampling method, it is subject to aliasing errors. As we saw in Chapter 8, aliasing errors occur when we do not have enough samples. However, in our basic ray tracer, the amount of work is proportional to the number of rays. Many ray tracers use a stochastic sampling method in which the decision as to where to cast the next ray is based upon the results of rays cast thus far. Thus, if rays do not intersect any objects in a particular region, few additional rays will be cast toward it, while the opposite holds for rays that are cast in a direction where they intersect many objects. This strategy is also used in RenderMan (Section 12.7). Although we could argue that stochastic sampling only works in a probabilistic sense—as there may well be small objects in areas that are not well sampled—it has the advantage that images produced by stochastic sampling tend not to show the moiré patterns characteristic of images produced using uniform sampling.

Ray tracing is an inherently parallel process, as every ray can be cast independently of every other ray. However, the difficulty is that every ray can potentially intersect any object. Hence, every tracing of a ray needs access to all objects. In addition, when we follow reflected and transmitted rays, we tend to lose any locality that might have helped us avoid a lot of data movement. Consequently, parallel ray tracers are best suited for shared-memory parallel architectures. With the availability of multicore processors with 64-bit addressing, commodity computers can support sufficient memory to make ray tracing a viable alternative in many applications.

12.4 THE RENDERING EQUATION

Most of the laws of physics can be expressed as conservation laws, such as the conservation of momentum and the conservation of energy. Because light is a form of energy, an energy-based approach can provide an alternative to ray tracing. Consider the closed environment shown in Figure 12.12. We see some surfaces that define the closed environment, some objects, and a light source inside. Physically, all these surfaces, including the surface of the light source, can be modeled in the same way. Although each one may have different parameters, each obeys the same physical laws.

FIGURE 12.12 Closed environment with four objects and a light source.

FIGURE 12.13   A simple surface.

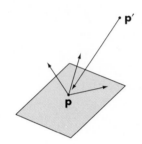

FIGURE 12.14   Light from $\mathbf{p}'$ arriving at $\mathbf{p}$.

Any surface can absorb some light and reflect some light. Any surface can be an emitter of light. From the ray-tracing perspective, we can say that the shades that we see are the result of an infinite number of rays bouncing around the environment, starting with sources and not ending until all the energy has been absorbed. However, when we look at the scene, we see the steady state; that is, we see each surface having its own shades. We do not see how the rays have bounced around; we see only the end result. The energy approach allows us to solve for this steady state directly, thus avoiding tracing many rays through many reflections.

Let's consider just one surface, as shown in Figure 12.13. We see rays of light entering from many directions and other rays emerging, also possibly in all directions. The light leaving the surface can have two components. If the surface is a light source, then some fraction of the light leaving the surface is from emission. The rest of the light is the reflection of incoming light from other surfaces. Hence, the incoming light also consists of emissions and reflections from other surfaces.

We can simplify the analysis by considering two arbitrary points $\mathbf{p}$ and $\mathbf{p}'$, as shown in Figure 12.14. If we look at the light arriving at and leaving $\mathbf{p}$, the energy must balance. Thus, the emission of energy, if there is a source at $\mathbf{p}$, and the reflected light energy must equal the incoming light energy from all possible points $\mathbf{p}'$. Let $i(\mathbf{p}, \mathbf{p}')$ be the intensity of light leaving the point $\mathbf{p}'$ and arriving at the point $\mathbf{p}$.[1] The rendering equation

$$i(\mathbf{p}, \mathbf{p}') = v(\mathbf{p}, \mathbf{p}') \left(\epsilon(\mathbf{p}, \mathbf{p}') + \int \rho(\mathbf{p}, \mathbf{p}', \mathbf{p}'') i(\mathbf{p}', \mathbf{p}'') d\mathbf{p}'' \right)$$

expresses this balance. The intensity leaving $\mathbf{p}'$ consists of two parts. If $\mathbf{p}'$ is an emitter of light (a source), there is a term $\epsilon(\mathbf{p}, \mathbf{p}')$ in the direction of $\mathbf{p}$. The second term is the contribution from reflections from every possible point ($\mathbf{p}''$) that is reflected at $\mathbf{p}'$ in the direction of $\mathbf{p}$. The function $\rho(\mathbf{p}, \mathbf{p}', \mathbf{p}'')$ is called the **bidirectional reflection distribution function**, or **BRDF**, and characterizes the material properties at $\mathbf{p}'$. The Lambertian model for diffuse surfaces and the Phong model for specular reflection are both simple examples of BRDFs. $v(\mathbf{p}, \mathbf{p}')$ has two possible values. If there is an opaque surface between $\mathbf{p}$ and $\mathbf{p}'$, then the surface occludes $\mathbf{p}'$ from $\mathbf{p}$ and no light from $\mathbf{p}'$ reaches $\mathbf{p}$. In this case, $v(\mathbf{p}, \mathbf{p}') = 0$. Otherwise, we must account for the effect of the distance between $\mathbf{p}$ and $\mathbf{p}'$ and

$$v(\mathbf{p}, \mathbf{p}') = \frac{1}{r^2},$$

where r is the distance between the two points.

Although the form of the rendering equation is wonderfully simple, solving it in general is not an easy task. The main difficulty is the dimensionality. For a material whose properties are the same at each point, the BRDF is a four-dimensional function

---

1. We are being careful to avoid introducing the units and terminology of radiometry. We see the intensity of light. Energy is the integral of intensity over time, but if the light sources are unchanging, then we are in the steady state and this distinction does not matter. Most references work with the energy or intensity per unit area (the **energy flux**) rather than energy or intensity.

because we can characterize the incoming and outgoing directions by two angles each, such as by elevation and azimuth. If the properties change over the surface, we have a six-dimensional function because we need two additional variables to fix a position on a two-dimensional surface. In addition, we have not included an additional variable for the wavelength of light, which would be necessary to work with color.

There have been some efforts to solve a general form of the rendering equation by numerical methods. Most of these have been Monte Carlo methods that are somewhat akin to stochastic sampling. Recently, **photon mapping** has become a viable approach. Photon mapping follows individual photons, the carriers of light energy, from where they are produced at the light sources to where they are finally absorbed by surfaces in the scene. Photons typically go through multiple reflections and transmissions from creation to final absorption. The potential advantage of this approach is that it can handle complex lighting of the sort that characterizes real-world scenes.

Although we argued when we discussed ray tracing that, because such a small percentage of light emitted from sources reaches the viewer, tracing rays from a source is inefficient, photon mapping uses many clever strategies to make the process computationally feasible. In particular, photon mapping uses a conservation of energy approach combined with Monte Carlo methods. For example, consider what happens when light strikes a diffuse surface. As we have seen, the reflected light is diffused in all directions. In photon mapping, when a photon strikes a diffuse surface, a photon can be reflected or absorbed. Whether the photon is absorbed or the specified angle of reflection, if it is reflected, is determined stochastically in a manner that yields the correct results on average. Thus, what happens to two photons that strike a surface at the same place and with the same angle of incidence can be very different. The more photons that are generated from sources, the greater the accuracy—but at the cost of tracing more photons.

There are special circumstances that simplify the rendering equation. For example, for perfectly specular surfaces, the reflection function is nonzero only when the angle of incidence equals the angle of reflection and the vectors lie in the same plane. Under these circumstances, ray tracing can be looked at as a method for solving the rendering equation.

The other special case that leads to a viable rendering method occurs when all surfaces are perfectly diffuse. In this case, the amount of light reflected is the same in all directions. Thus, the intensity function depends only on $\mathbf{p}$. We examine this case in the next section.

12.5 RADIOSITY

One way to simplify the rendering equation is to consider an environment in which all the surfaces are perfectly diffuse reflectors. Because a perfectly diffuse surface looks the same to all viewers, the corresponding BRDF is far simpler than the general cases considered by the rendering equation.

Note, however, that although a perfectly diffuse surface reflects light equally in all directions, even if the surface is flat, it can show variations in shading that are

FIGURE 12.15 Simple scene with diffuse surfaces.

not shown when we render using the modified Phong lighting model. Suppose that we have a simple scene, such as that shown in Figure 12.15, in which all the surfaces are perfectly diffuse. If we render this scene with a distant light source, each polygon surface is rendered as a single color. If this were a real scene, however, some of the diffuse reflections from the red wall would fall on the white wall, causing red light to be added to the white light reflected from those parts of the white wall that are near the red wall. Diffuse light reflected from the white wall would have a similar effect on the red wall. Our simple shading model has not considered these **diffuse–diffuse interactions**.

An ideal global renderer would capture these interactions. The radiosity method can approximate them very well using an energy approach that was originally used for solving problems in heat transfer.

The basic radiosity method breaks up the scene into small flat polygons, or **patches**, each of which can be assumed to be perfectly diffuse and renders in a constant shade. First we must find these shades. Once we have found them, we will have assigned a color to each patch that is independent of the viewer. Effectively, we have assigned colors to a set of polygon patches in a three-dimensional environment. We can now place the viewer wherever we wish and render the scene in a conventional manner, using a pipeline renderer.

12.5.1 The Radiosity Equation

Let's assume our scene consists of n patches numbered from 1 to n. The **radiosity** of patch i, b_i, is the light intensity (energy/unit time) per unit area leaving the patch. Typically, the radiosity would be measured in units such as *watts/meter*^{2}. Because we are measuring intensity at a fixed wavelength, we can think of a radiosity function $b_i(\lambda)$ that determines the color of patch i. Suppose that patch i has area a_i. Because we have assumed that each patch is a perfectly diffuse surface, the total intensity leaving patch i is $b_i a_i$. Following reasoning similar to that which we used to derive the rendering equation, the emitted intensity consists of an emissive component, also assumed to be constant across the patch, and a reflective component due to the intensities of all other patches whose light strikes patch i, and we obtain the equation

$$b_i a_i = e_i a_i + \rho_i \sum_{j=0}^{n} f_{ji} b_j a_j.$$

The term f_{ij} is called the **form factor** between patch i and patch j. It represents the fraction of the energy leaving patch j that reaches patch i. The form factor depends on how the two patches are oriented relative to each other, how far they are from each other, and whether any other patches occlude the light from patch j and prevent it from reaching patch i. We will discuss the calculation of these factors in the next subsection. The reflectivity of patch i is ρ_i.

There is a simple relationship between the factors f_{ij} and f_{ji} known as the **reciprocity equation**,

$$f_{ij} a_i = f_{ji} a_j.$$

Substituting into the equation for the patch intensities, we find

$$b_i a_i = e_i a_i + \rho_i \sum_{j=0}^{n} f_{ij} b_j a_i.$$

We can now divide by a_i, obtaining an equation for the patch radiosity:

$$b_i = e_i + \rho_i \sum_{j=0}^{n} f_{ij} b_j.$$

This result is called the **radiosity equation**.

Assuming that we have computed the form factors, we have a set of n linear equations in the n unknown radiosities. Comparing this equation to the rendering equation, we can see that if the patches were made smaller and smaller, in the limit we would have an infinite number of patches. The sum would become an integral, and the resulting radiosity equation would be a special case of the rendering equation in which all surfaces are perfectly diffuse reflectors.

We can put these equations in matrix form by defining a column matrix of radiosities

$$\mathbf{b} = [b_i],$$

a column matrix of the patch emissions

$$\mathbf{e} = [e_i],$$

a diagonal matrix from the reflection coefficients

$$\mathbf{R} = [r_{ij}], \qquad a_{ij} = \begin{cases} \rho_i & \text{if } i = j \\ 0 & \text{otherwise,} \end{cases}$$

and a matrix of the form factors

$$\mathbf{F} = [f_{ij}].$$

Now the set of equations for the radiosities becomes

$$\mathbf{b} = \mathbf{e} + \mathbf{RFb}.$$

We can write the formal solution as

$$\mathbf{b} = [\mathbf{I} - \mathbf{RF}]^{-1}\mathbf{e}.$$

12.5.2 Solving the Radiosity Equation

Although it can be shown that the radiosity equation must have a solution, the real difficulties are practical. A typical scene will have thousands of patches, so that solving the equations by a direct method, such as Gaussian elimination, usually is not possible. Most methods rely on the fact that the matrix $\mathbf{F}$ is sparse. Most of its elements are effectively zero because most patches are sufficiently far from one another so that almost none of the light that a patch emits or reflects reaches most other patches.

Solutions of sets of equations involving sparse matrices are based on iterative methods that require the multiplication of these sparse matrices, an efficient operation. Suppose that we use the equation for the patches to create the iterative equation

$$\mathbf{b}^{k+1} = \mathbf{e} + \mathbf{RFb}^k.$$

Each iteration of this equation requires the matrix multiplication $\mathbf{RFb}^k$, which, assuming $\mathbf{F}$ is sparse, requires $O(n)$ operations, rather than the $O(n^2)$ operations for the general case. In terms of the individual radiosities, we have

$$b_i^{k+1} = e_i + \sum_{j=1}^{n} \rho_i f_{ij} b_j^k.$$

This method, which is known as Jacobi's method, will converge for this problem regardless of the initial starting point $\mathbf{b}^0$.

In general, patches are not self-reflecting, so that $f_{ij} = 0$. If we apply updates as soon as they are available, we obtain the Gauss-Seidel method:

$$b_i^{k+1} = e_i + \sum_{j=1}^{i-1} \rho_i f_{ij} b_j^{k+1} + \sum_{j=i+1}^{n} \rho_i f_{ij} b_j^k.$$

There is another possible iteration that provides additional physical insight. Consider the scalar formula

$$\frac{1}{1-x} = \sum_{i=0}^{\infty} x^i,$$

which holds if $|x| < 1$. The matrix form of this equation for $\mathbf{RF}$ is[2]

$$[\mathbf{I} - \mathbf{RF}]^{-1} = \sum_{i=0}^{\infty} (\mathbf{RF})^i.$$

Thus, we can write $\mathbf{b}$ as

$$\mathbf{b} = \sum_{i=0}^{\infty} (\mathbf{RF})^i \mathbf{e}$$

$$= \mathbf{e} + (\mathbf{RF})\mathbf{e} + (\mathbf{RF})^2\mathbf{e} + (\mathbf{RF})^3\mathbf{e} + \cdots.$$

We can use this expression, terminating it at some point, to approximate $\mathbf{b}$. Each term has an interesting physical interpretation. The first term, $\mathbf{e}$, is the direct light emitted from each patch so that an approximate solution with just this term will show only the sources. The second term, $(\mathbf{RF})\mathbf{e}$, adds in the light that is the result

---

2. The formula converges if the magnitudes of all the eigenvalues of $\mathbf{BF}$ are less than unity, a condition that must be true for the radiosity equation.

of exactly one reflection of the sources onto other patches. The next term adds on the contribution from double reflections, and so on for the other terms.

12.5.3 Computing Form Factors

At this point, we have ways of solving for the patch radiosities that are reasonably efficient, but we have yet to discuss the calculation of the form factors. We start with a general derivation of an equation for the form factor between two patches, and then we will look at how we might find approximate form factors using the tools that we have available.

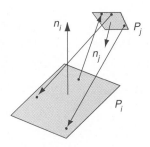

FIGURE 12.16   Two patches.

Consider two perfectly diffuse flat patches, P_i and P_j, as shown in Figure 12.16, which we have drawn without any other patches that might cause occlusion. Each patch has a normal that gives its orientation. Although each patch emits light equally in all directions, the amount of light leaving two different points on P_j that reaches any point on P_i is different because of the different distances between two points on P_j and a point on P_i. Thus, to collect all the light from P_j that falls on P_i, we must integrate over all points on P_j. The same reasoning applies to two points on P_i that receive light from a point on P_j; they will receive a different amount of light, and thus to determine the light falling on P_i, we must also integrate over all points on P_i.

We can derive the required integral based on our understanding of diffuse shading from Chapter 6. Consider a small area on each patch, da_i and da_j. Each can be considered to be an ideal diffuse reflector (Figure 12.17). They are a distance r apart, where r is the distance between two points, $\mathbf{p}_i$ and $\mathbf{p}_j$, at the center of the two small areas. The light leaving da_j goes in the direction $\mathbf{d} = \mathbf{p}_i - \mathbf{p}_j$. However, the intensity of this light is reduced or foreshortened by $\cos \phi_j$, where ϕ_j is the angle between the normal for patch j and the vector $\mathbf{d}$. Likewise, the light arriving at da_i is foreshortened by $\cos \phi_i$, where ϕ_i is the angle between the normal for patch i and the vector $\mathbf{d}$. To obtain the desired form factor, f_{ij}, we must also account for the distance between the patches and the possibility of occlusion. We can do both by first defining the term

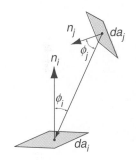

FIGURE 12.17   Foreshortening between two small patches.

$$o_{ij} = \begin{cases} 1 & \text{if } \mathbf{p}_j \text{ is visible from } \mathbf{p}_i \\ 0 & \text{otherwise.} \end{cases}$$

Then, by averaging over the total area of the patch, we obtain the form factor equation

$$f_{ij} = \frac{1}{a_i} \int_{a_i} \int_{a_j} o_{ij} \frac{\cos \phi_i \cos \phi_j}{\pi r^2} da_i da_j.$$

Although the form of this integral is simple, there are only a few special cases for which it can be solved analytically. For real scenes, we need numerical methods. Because there are n^2 form factors, most methods are a compromise between accuracy and time.

We will sketch two approaches. The first method starts with the notion of two-step mappings that we used in our discussion of texture mapping in Chapter 7. Consider two patches again, this time with a hemisphere separating them, as shown in Figure 12.18. Suppose that we want to compute the light from P_i that reaches P_j

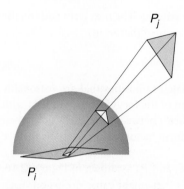

FIGURE 12.18 Projecting a patch on a hemisphere.

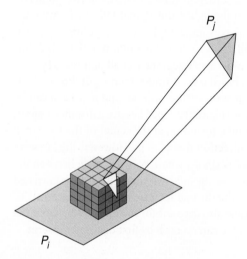

FIGURE 12.19 Projecting a patch on a hemicube and onto another patch.

at a point $\mathbf{p}_i$. We center the hemisphere at this point and orient the patch so that the normal is pointing up. We can now project P_j onto the hemisphere and observe that we can use the projected patch for our computation of the form factor, rather than the original patch. If we convert to polar coordinates, the form factor equation becomes simpler for the projected patch. However, for each small area of P_i, we have to move the hemisphere and add the contribution from each area.

A simpler approach for most graphics applications is to use a hemicube rather than a hemisphere, as shown in Figure 12.19. The hemicube is centered like the hemisphere, but its surface is divided into small squares called pixels. The light that strikes patch i is independent of the type of intermediate surface that we use. The advantage of the hemicube is that its surfaces are either parallel to or orthogonal to P_i. Consequently, it is straightforward to project P_j onto the hemicube and to compute the contribution of each pixel on the hemicube to the light that reaches point $\mathbf{p}_i$. Thus, if the surface of the hemicube is divided into m pixels, numbered 1 to m, then we can compute the contribution of those pixels that are projections of P_j and are visible from $\mathbf{p}_i$ and add them to form the **delta form factor** Δf_{ij}, which is the contribution of P_j to the small area da_i at the center of the hemicube. We then get the desired form factor by adding the contributions of all the delta form factors. The contributions from each pixel can be computed analytically once we know whether P_j projects on it, a calculation that is similar to the ray-tracing calculation required to determine whether an object is visible from a light source. The details are included in the Suggested Readings at the end of the chapter.

Another approach to computing form factors exploits our ability to use a graphics system to compute simple renderings very rapidly. Suppose that we want to compute f_{ij}. If we illuminate P_i with a known amount of light only from P_j, we will have an experimental measurement of the desired form factor. We can approximate this measurement by placing point light sources on P_j and then rendering the scene with whatever renderer we have available. Because of the possibility that another patch obscures P_i from P_j, we must use a renderer that can handle shadows.

12.5.4 Carrying Out Radiosity

In practice, radiosity rendering has three major steps. First, we divide the scene into a mesh of patches, as shown in Figure 12.20. This step requires some skill, because

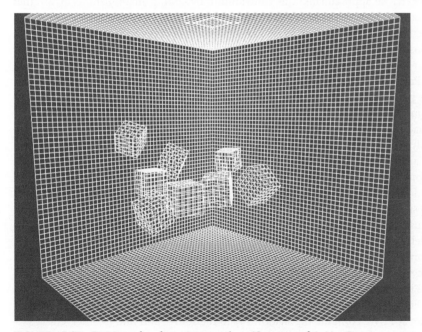

FIGURE 12.20 Division of surfaces into patches. (Courtesy of A. Van Pernis, K. Rasche, and R. Geist, Clemson University)

more patches require the calculation of more form factors. However, it is the division of surfaces into patches that allows radiosity to yield images with subtle diffuse–diffuse interactions. The creation of the initial mesh often can be done interactively, allowing the placement of more patches in regions such as corners between surfaces where we expect to see diffuse–diffuse interactions. Another approach is based on the observation that the radiosity of a large surface is equal to the area-weighted sum of the radiosities of any subdivision of it. Hence, we can start with a fairly rough mesh and refine it later (**progressive radiosity**). Once we have a mesh, we can compute the form factors, the most computationally intense part of the process.

With the mesh and the computed form factors, we can solve the radiosity equation. We form the emission array **e** using the values for the light sources in the scene and assign colors to the surfaces, forming **R**. Now we can solve the radiosity equation to determine **b**. The components of **b** act as the new colors of the patches. We can now place the viewer in the scene and render with a conventional renderer.

12.6   GLOBAL ILLUMINATION AND PATH TRACING

If we observe the shading on an object in a real scene, it consists of three components: any emission from the object, light that is reflected from a source that strikes the object directly and is reflected in the direction of the eye, and light that reflects from other surfaces in the scene. This last term is called **indirect illumination** and is particularly difficult for both pipeline renderers and ray tracers. With pipeline renderers, we approximated this contribution by adding an ambient term, a rather poor approximation to the lighting in a real scene. With a basic ray tracer, we ignored reflections from diffuse surfaces by following only the reflected and transmitted rays. Radiosity provided only a partial solution since it required all surfaces to be diffuse rather than allowing for arbitrary BRDFs.

Path tracing avoids these problems by using Monte Carlo methods to approximate the BRDF at every surface. Suppose that we cast a ray from the eye and find its first intersection with the closest surface, and at this point of intersection the surface is opaque and Lambertian. Rather than sending out feeler rays to sources, we randomly select one or more directions along which we continue our path(s). We do a similar probabilistic generation of path directions at each surface we intersect, not stopping until we either hit a source or determine that the ray is heading to infinity. Along each path, we must keep track of the accumulated losses to absorption at each surface. Note that when we do pure path tracing, we cannot use point sources because the probability that a path will intersect one is almost nil. Sources should be modeled as distributed emissive surfaces, which leads to much more realistic illumination than with ray tracing or pipeline rendering. Variants of path tracing add in some direct illumination terms as would be computed by other methods.

Figures 12.21 and 12.22 show the difference between ray tracing and path tracing. Figure 12.21 shows a single ray from the eye that intersects an opaque diffuse sphere at P. We compute the shadow ray to the source and find no intervening surfaces. Now we can compute a diffuse contribution at P from the source and the reflectivity at P. Finally, we follow the reflected ray s, which goes off to infinity and makes

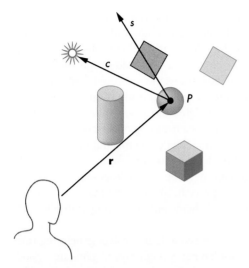

FIGURE 12.21   Ray tracing one ray.

FIGURE 12.22   Path tracing one ray.

no contribution to the image. In Figure 12.22, the same ray from the eye intersects the sphere at P, but now we sample the BRDF three times to obtain the rays a, b, and c. In path tracing, we do not cast a ray to the source and do not compute a diffuse contribution at P from the source, although we do have to keep track of the fact that the ray from the eye was reflected from the sphere. Ray a intersects the gray polygon at Q. We sample the BRDF at Q and generate some new rays in multiple directions, which we follow. We do the same thing at R where ray c intersects the blue polygon. Ray b

does not intersect any surfaces and either terminates at a source or goes off to infinity. If it terminates at a source, we can apply the source color and go back down the path that got us to the source to compute the color contribution to the image. If the path goes off to infinity, we have a number of choices. We could simply discard this path. We could apply a background color in the same way as we would apply the color of a source. A more interesting choice is to use a **global illumination model**. Recall from Figure 12.18 that we can project incoming light onto a hemisphere and use that hemisphere for lighting calculations. The basic idea behind global or environmental light is to form such a hemisphere either by modeling or by making measurements of a real environment. Thus, if we wanted the lighting to come from a sky filled with clouds, we could measure incoming light at all angles on a partially cloudy day or generate a similar distribution with the types of procedural modeling that we discussed in Chapter 10. In either case, we could use this hemispheric lighting with our path tracer.

Because path tracing is a Monte Carlo technique that involves generating rays probabilistically, we are caught between not having enough rays to generate a good image and taking too long to compute enough paths for an acceptable image. If we use too few samples, the resulting images can be extremely noisy. Some implementations of path tracing compensate for this situation by progressively updating the image. A first noisy image is generated quickly and if none of the components of the scene change, the image is continually refined by incorporating more paths. There are also techniques for combining path tracing with direct illumination using ray tracing. References to these techniques are in the Suggested Readings at the end of the chapter.

12.7 RENDERMAN

There are other approaches to rendering that have arisen from the needs of the animation industry. Although interaction is required in the design of an animation, real-time rendering is not required when the final images are produced. Of greater importance is producing images free of rendering artifacts, such as the jaggedness and moiré patterns that arise from aliasing. However, rendering the large number of frames required for a feature-length film cannot be done with ray tracers or radiosity renderers, even though animations are produced using large numbers of computers—**render farms**—whose sole task is to render scenes at the required resolution. In addition, neither ray tracers nor radiosity renderers alone produce images that have the desired artistic qualities.

The RenderMan interface is based on the use of the modeling–rendering paradigm that we introduced in Chapter 1. The design of a scene is done interactively, using simple renderers that might display only lines. When the design is complete, the objects, lights, material properties, cameras, motion descriptions, and textures can be described in a file that can be sent to a high-quality renderer or to a render farm.

In principle, this off-line renderer could be any type of renderer. However, given the special needs of the animation industry, Pixar developed both the interface (RenderMan) and a renderer called Reyes that was designed to produce the types of images needed for commercial motion pictures. Like a ray tracer, Reyes was designed to work one pixel at a time. Unlike a ray tracer, it was not designed to incorporate global illumination effects. By working one pixel at a time, Reyes collects all the light from all objects at a resolution that avoids aliasing problems. Reyes divides (**dices**) objects—both polygonal and curved—into **micropolygons**, which are small quadrilaterals that project to a size of about half of a pixel. Because each micropolygon projects to such a small area, it can be flat-shaded, thereby simplifying its rendering. The smooth shading of surfaces is accomplished by coloring the micropolygons carefully during the dicing process.

Reyes incorporates many other interesting techniques. It uses random or stochastic sampling rather than point sampling to reduce visible aliasing effects. Generally, it works on small regions of the frame at one time to allow efficient use of textures. Note that even with its careful design, a single scene with many objects and complex lighting effects can take hours to render.

There are many renderers of this type available, some either public domain or shareware. Some renderers are capable of incorporating different rendering styles within one product. Thus, we might use ray tracing on a subset of the objects that have shiny surfaces. Likewise, we might want to use radiosity on some other subset of the surfaces. In general, these renderers support a large variety of effects and allow the user to balance rendering time against sophistication and image quality.

12.8 PARALLEL RENDERING

In many applications, particularly in the scientific visualization of large geometric data sets, we create images from data sets that might contain hundreds of gigabytes of data and generate hundreds of millions of polygons. This situation presents two immediate challenges. First, if we are to display this many polygons, how can we do so when commodity displays and projectors have a resolution of about 2 million pixels? Even the best displays support only about 5 million pixels. Second, if we have multiple frames to display, either from new data or because of transformations of the original data set, we need to be able to render this large amount of geometry faster than can be achieved even with the best GPUs.

A popular solution to the display resolution problem is to build a **power wall**, a large projection surface that is illuminated by an array of projectors (Figure 12.23), each with the resolution of 1280×1024, or 1920×1080 for HD projectors. Generally, the light output from the projectors is tapered at the edges, and the displays are overlapped slightly to create a seamless image. We can also create high-resolution displays from arrays of standard-size LCD panels, although at the cost of seeing small separations between panels, which can give the appearance of a window with multiple panes.

One approach to both these problems is to use clusters of standard computers connected with a high-speed network. Each computer might have a commodity graphics card. Note that such configurations are one aspect of a major revolution in high-performance computing. Formerly, supercomputers were composed of expensive, fast processors that usually incorporated a high degree of parallelism in their

FIGURE 12.23 Power wall using six projectors.

designs. These processors were custom designed and required special interfaces, peripheral systems, and environments that made them extremely expensive and thus affordable only by a few government laboratories and large corporations. Over the last decade, commodity processors have become extremely fast and inexpensive. In addition, the trend is toward incorporating multiple processors in the same CPU or GPU, thus creating the potential for various types of parallelism ranging from using a single CPU with multiple graphics cards, to using many multicore CPUs, or to using GPUs with hundreds of programmable processors.

Consequently, there are multiple ways we can distribute among the various processors the work that must be done to render a scene. The simplest approach is to execute the same application program on each processor but have each use a different window that corresponds to where the processor's display is located in the output array. Given the speed of modern CPUs and GPUs and the large amount of memory available to them, this is often a viable approach. However, for very large data sets, this approach often will not work because the front end of the system cannot process the geometry fast enough.

We will examine three other possibilities. In this taxonomy, the key difference is where in the rendering process we assign, or sort, primitives to the correct areas of the display. Where we place this step leads to the designations **sort first**, **sort middle**, and **sort last**.

Suppose that we start with a large number of processors of two types: geometry processors and raster processors. This distinction corresponds to the two phases

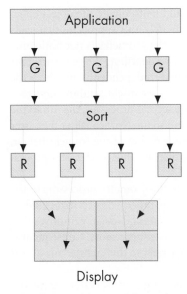

FIGURE 12.24   Sort-middle rendering.

of the rendering pipeline that we discussed in Chapter 8. The geometry processors can handle front-end floating-point calculations, including transformations, clipping, and shading. The raster processors manipulate bits and handle operations such as rasterization. Note that the present general-purpose processors and graphics processors can each do either of these tasks. Consequently, we can apply the following strategies to either the CPUs or the GPUs. We can achieve parallelism among distinct nodes, within a processor chip through multiple cores, or within the GPU. The use of the sorting paradigm will help us organize the architectural possibilities.

12.8.1 Sort-Middle Rendering

Consider a group of geometry processors (each labeled with a G) and raster processors (each labeled with an R) connected as shown in Figure 12.24. Suppose that we have an application that generates a large number of geometric primitives. It can use multiple geometry processors in two obvious ways. It can run on a single processor and send different parts of the geometry generated by the application to different geometry processors. Alternatively, we can run the application on multiple processors, each of which generates only part of the geometry. At this point, we need not worry about how the geometry gets to the geometry processors (as the best way is often application dependent) but about how to best employ the geometry processors that are available.

Assume that we can send any primitive to any of the geometry processors, each of which acts independently. When we use multiple processors in parallel, a major concern is **load balancing**; that is, having each of the processors do about the same amount of work so that none are sitting idle for a significant amount of time, thus wasting resources. One obvious approach would be to divide the object coordinate space equally among the processors. Unfortunately, this approach often leads to poor load balancing because in many applications the geometry is not uniformly distributed in object space. An alternative approach is to distribute the geometry uniformly among the processors as objects are generated, independently of where the geometric objects are located. Thus, with n processors, we might send the first geometric entity to the first processor, the second to the second processor, the nth to the nth processor, the $(n + 1)$-st to the first processor, and so on. Now consider the raster processors. We can assign each of these to a different region of the framebuffer or, equivalently, assign each to a different region of the display. Thus, each raster processor renders a fixed part of screen space.

Now the problem is how to assign the outputs of the geometry processors to the raster processors. Note that each geometry processor can process objects that could go anywhere on the display. Thus, we must sort their outputs and assign primitives that emerge from the geometry processors to the correct raster processors. Consequently, some sorting must be done before the raster stage. We refer to this architecture as *sort middle*.

This configuration was popular with high-end graphics workstations before programmable GPUs became available and special hardware was needed for each task. High-end graphics workstations used fast internal buses to convey information through the sorting step. Recent GPUs contain multiple geometry processors and multiple fragment processors (or processors that can be used as either type) and so can be looked at as sort-middle processors. However, the type of sort-middle approaches of the past, using specialized hardware, are no longer used.

12.8.2 Sort-Last Rendering

With sort-middle rendering, the number of geometry processors and the number of raster processors could be different. Now suppose that each geometry processor is connected to its own raster processor, as shown in Figure 12.25. This configuration would be what we would have with a collection of standard PCs, each with its own graphics card. On a GPU with multiple integrated vertex and fragment processors, we can consider each processor as a separate computer. Once again, let's not worry about how each processor gets the application data and instead focus on how this configuration can process the geometry generated by the application.

Just as with sort middle, we can load-balance the geometry processors by sending primitives to them in an order that ignores where on the display they might lie once they are rasterized. However, precisely because of this way of assigning geometry and lacking a sort in the middle, each raster processor must have a framebuffer that is the full size of the display. Because each geometry/raster pair contains a full pipeline, each pair produces a correct hidden-surface-removed image *for part of the geometry*. Figure 12.26 shows three images that are each correct for part of the geometry. The fourth image is the result of combining the first three to form a correct image containing all the geometry.

We can combine the partial images with a compositing step, as displayed in Figure 12.26. For the compositing calculations, we need not only the images in the color

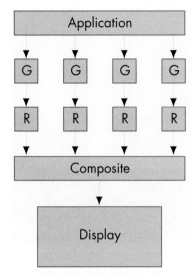

FIGURE 12.25 Sort-last rendering.

buffers of the geometry processors but also the depth information, because we must know for each pixel which of the raster processors contains the pixel corresponding to the closest point to the viewer.[3] Fortunately, if we are using our standard WebGL pipeline, the necessary information is in the z buffer. For each pixel, we need only compare the depths in each of the z buffers and write the color in the framebuffer of the processor with the closest depth. The difficulty is determining how to do this comparison efficiently when the information is stored on many processors.

Conceptually, the simplest approach, sometimes called **binary-tree compositing**, is to have pairs of processors combine their information. Consider the example shown in Figure 12.27, where we have four geometry/raster pipelines, numbered 0–3. Processors 0 and 1 can combine their information to form a correct image for the geometry they have seen, while processors 2 and 3 do the same thing concurrently with their information. Let's assume that we form these new images on processors 1 and 3. Thus, processors 0 and 2 have to send *both* their color buffers *and* their z buffers to their neighbors (processors 1 and 3, respectively). We then repeat the process between processors 1 and 3, with the final image being formed in the framebuffer of processor 3. Note that the code is very simple. The geometry/raster pairs each do an ordinary rendering. The compositing step requires only reading pixels and some simple comparisons. However, in each successive step of the compositing process, only half the processors that were used in the previous step are still needed. In the end, the final image is prepared on a single processor.

There is another approach to the compositing step known as **binary-swap compositing** that avoids the idle processor problem. In this technique, each processor is

---

3. For simplicity, we are assuming that all the geometric objects are opaque.

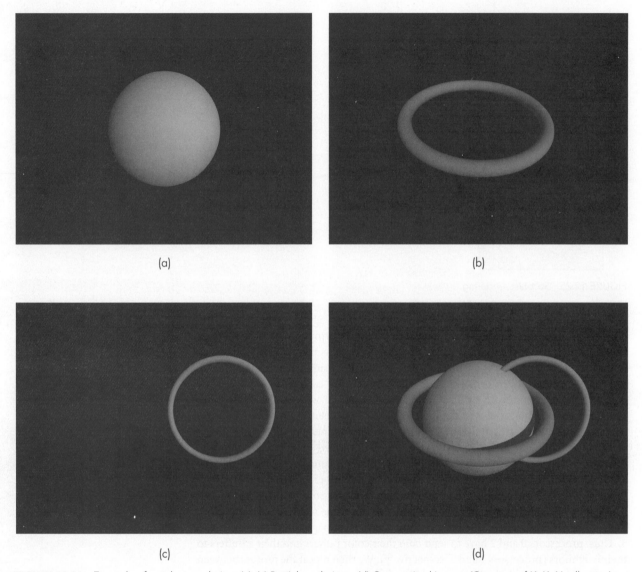

(a)

(b)

(c)

(d)

FIGURE 12.26   Example of sort-last rendering. (a)–(c) Partial renderings. (d) Composited image. (Courtesy of K. K. Neelkantan)

responsible for one part of the final image. Hence, for compositing to be correct, each processor must see all the data. If we have n processors involved in the compositing, we can arrange them in a round-robin fashion, as shown in Figure 12.28. The compositing takes n steps (rather than the $\log n$ steps required by tree compositing). On the first step, processor 0 sends portion 0 of its framebuffer to processor 1 and receives portion n from processor n. The other processors do a similar send and receive of the

FIGURE 12.27   Binary-tree compositing.

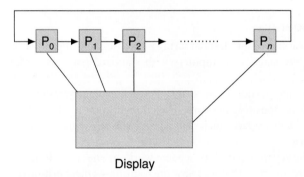

Display

FIGURE 12.28   Binary-swap compositing.

portion of the color and depth buffers of their neighbors. At this point, each processor can update one area of the display that will be correct for the data from a pair of processors. For processor 0, this will be region n. On the second round, processor 0 will receive from processor n the data from region $n - 1$, which is correct for the data from processors n and $n - 1$. Processor 0 will also send the data from region n, as will the other processors for part of their framebuffers. All the processors will now have a region that is correct for the data from three processors. Inductively, it should be clear that after $n - 1$ steps, each processor has $1/n$ of the final image. Although we have taken more steps, far less data has been transferred than with tree compositing, and we have used all processors in each step.

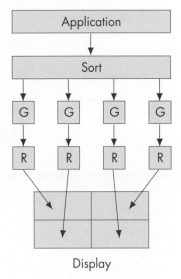

FIGURE 12.29   Sort-first rendering.

12.8.3 Sort-First Rendering

One of the most appealing features of sort-last rendering is that we can pair geometric and raster processors and use standard computers with standard graphics cards. Suppose that we could decide first where each primitive lies on the final display. Then we could assign a separate portion of the display to each geometry/raster pair and avoid the necessity of a compositing network. The configuration might look as illustrated in Figure 12.29. Here we have included a processor at the front end to assign primitives to processors.

The front-end sort is the key to making this scheme work. In one sense, it might seem impossible, since we are implying that we know the solution—where primitives appear in the display—before we have solved the problem for which we need the geometric pipeline. But things are not hopeless. Many problems are structured so that we can know this information in advance. We also can get the information back from the pipeline to find the mapping from object coordinates to screen coordinates. In addition, we need not always be correct. A primitive can be sent to multiple geometry processors if it straddles more than one region of the display. Even if we send a primitive to the wrong processor, that processor may be able to send it on to the correct processor. Because each geometry processor performs a clipping step, we are assured that the resulting image will be correct.

Sort-first rendering does not address the load-balancing issue, because if there are regions of the screen with very few primitives, the corresponding processors will not be very heavily loaded. However, sort-first rendering has one important advantage over sort-last rendering: It is ideally suited for generating high-resolution displays. For example, a 4×5 array of HD (1920×1980) displays contains over 40 million pixels.

12.9 HARDWARE GPU IMPLEMENTATIONS

As with many technologies, GPU development has undergone several iterations of design evolution. Initially, when graphics systems were first implemented in hardware (before they were called GPUs), virtually the entire graphics pipeline was implemented using hardware specialized for the task, and the APIs that passed data to the graphics system were very simple. Initially, these graphics hardware systems were very large due to a number of factors: silicon hardware manufacturing capabilities (i.e., fabrication of integrated circuits), printed circuit board layout, and thermal conditions, to name a few. As generations of graphics systems evolved, along with the technology to produce them, systems became smaller, faster, and more capable. Similarly, as CPU technology evolved, various graphics tasks that previously required dedicated hardware could be computed on the CPU, and the more graphics-intensive activities (e.g., texture mapping and rasterization) were reserved for processing on the graphics subsystem.

At the time of this writing, GPUs are in roughly their fifth evolutionary cycle: from simple framebuffers to image generators, graphics workstations, modern personal computers, and most recently, mobile graphics systems. This is an imprecise classification scheme, as each generation subsumes the best features of the previous and each cycle takes a long time to close.

Modern GPUs—those of a programmable nature—were initially deployed in personal computers and then evolved into mobile and embedded devices. Of those architectures, there are basically two distinct flavors: **immediate-mode renderers**, which are graphics systems that immediately process a graphics primitive when its draw call is made; and **tile-based renderers** (sometimes called **deferred renderers**), which do some processing on graphics primitives when their draw call is made but then finish processing the primitives at a later time.

Immediate-mode rendering GPUs, such as those developed by AMD and NVIDIA, are fully programmable, massively parallel computation machines. Their general operation is to effectively process geometry (e.g., using vertex shaders), emitting transformed graphics primitives as fast as possible, and then rasterizing and shading their generated fragments using vast arrays (usually containing several hundred programmable processors), in a sort-last rendering configuration. While there are many computational components at work on these types of graphics cards, the primary computing resource is an almost general-purpose programmable processor. Since these processors allow any type of shader (e.g., vertex, fragment, or others, depending on the executing graphics API), they are often referred to as unified shader engines.

These types of architectures are extremely fast, capable of processing hundreds of millions of triangles and shading many billions of fragments per second. They can achieve these massive rates because of dedicated, high-bandwidth data buses, considerable power supplies, and large, localized memory usually contained within an add-on graphics card in the system. However, for the latest graphics systems—mobile smart phones and tablets—these resources are not as plentiful, and different rendering paradigms are employed to work within the constraints of the environment.

While some mobile graphics systems employ immediate-mode rendering techniques, most mobile graphics systems are tile based. Similar to parallel rendering described in Section 12.8, the framebuffer is partitioned into tiles, which are merely small rectangular regions, and the geometry is binned (i.e., sorted) by transforming the incoming geometric primitives and taking note of which tiles the geometric primitive intersects. Once all the primitives for a frame have been issued, transformed, and binned, then each tile can be rasterized. This is a form of sort-first rendering and is used for a number of reasons. Foremost, it permits the GPU to have a small framebuffer memory—generally sized to match the resolution of a tile—which reduces the size of the processor and allows the framebuffer to be internal to the mobile device's application processor. The final image is then constructed by combining all of the rendered tiles. This integration of the framebuffer into the main processor also helps to reduce the amount of data moved around in memory, which is a very power-consuming operation, particularly when the device is powered by a battery.

The rasterization of the primitives in tiles can also occur by different methods. The simplest tile-based systems work like miniature immediate-mode renderers, rasterizing the primitives recorded for the tile and shading and depth-testing all of the generated fragments. This approach generally keeps the GPU design simpler but may also waste processing by shading fragments that are occluded. A second approach used in tile-based rendering is deferred shading. This technique recognizes that transformation and placement of fragments is a different operation from determining their color. Therefore, the system can determine which fragment will ultimately be visible for a pixel, and then compute only the color of that fragment, ignoring the color shading for all other fragments that would have occupied that pixel. These systems, while potentially saving energy by reducing computation in some cases, are also more complex to implement and need special cases for alpha-blending primitives.

One other interesting point of tile-based rendering is that it is an example of embarrassingly parallel computation. Each tile is self-contained—it contains all of the information required to shade all of its pixels—and so each tile can be processed independently. As such, many modern embedded devices contain multiple GPUs, which work in parallel, processing different tiles to generate the final image. The by-product of this design is that a system can effectively scale to any pixel-filling rate required by employing more cores in the processor. Of course, this comes at a cost of using more silicon area in the application processor, and more system power, but it allows a scalability that is not possible in immediate-mode renderers without additional algorithmic modification.

12.10   IMPLICIT FUNCTIONS AND CONTOUR MAPS

Suppose that we have an implicit function in two dimensions:

$$f(x, y) = c.$$

For each value of c, $f(x, y)$ can describe no, one, or multiple curves. If a solution exists, each curve describes a **contour** of f; that is, a curve of constant c. The most familiar form of contour plots or **topo maps** are maps where each (x, y) is a point on the surface and c is the altitude. Although the function f may be simple, there is no general method for finding a value of x for a given y and c, or a y from x and c. We can, however, sample f over a grid for one or more values of c to obtain good approximations to the contour curves for these values of c, using a method called **marching squares**, which we will extend to volume rendering in the following section.

12.10.1 Marching Squares

Suppose that we sample the function $f(x, y)$ at evenly spaced points on a rectangular array (or lattice or grid) in x and y, thus creating a set of samples $\{f_{ij} = f(x_i, y_j)\}$ for

$$x_i = x_0 + i\Delta x, \quad i = 0, 1, \dots, N - 1$$

$$y_j = y_0 + j\Delta y, \quad j = 0, 1, \dots, M - 1,$$

where Δx and Δy are the spacing between samples in the x and y directions, respectively. Other than for simplifying the development, the equal spacing is not necessary. Equivalently, we might have obtained a set of $N \times M$ samples by making measurements of some physical quantity on a regular grid, or the samples might have come directly from a device such as a laser range finder or a satellite.

Suppose that we would like to find an approximation to the implicit curve

$$f(x, y) = c$$

for a particular value of c, our contour value. For a given value of c, there may be no contour curve, a single contour curve, or multiple contour curves. If we are working with sampled data, then we can only approximate a contour curve. Our strategy for constructing an approximate contour curve is to construct a curve of connected line segments—a **piecewise linear curve**. We start with the rectangular **cell** determined by the four grid points (x_i, y_j), (x_{i+1}, y_j), (x_{i+1}, y_{j+1}), (x_i, y_{j+1}), as shown in Figure 12.30. Our algorithm finds the line segments on a cell-by-cell basis, using only the values of z at the corners of a cell to determine whether the desired contour passes through the cell.

In general, the sampled values that we have at the corners of the cell are not equal to the contour value. However, the contour curve might still pass through the cell. Consider the simple case where only one of the values at the corners—say, f_{ij}—is greater than c and the values at the other vertices of the cell are less than c:

$$f_{ij} > c$$

$$f_{i+1, j} < c$$

$$f_{i+1, j+1} < c$$

$$f_{i, j+1} < c.$$

We can show this situation either as in Figure 12.31(a), where we have indicated the values relative to c, or as in Figure 12.31(b), where we have colored black the

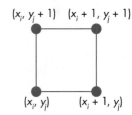

$(x_i, y_j + 1) \quad (x_i + 1, y_j + 1)$

$(x_i, y_j) \quad (x_i + 1, y_j)$

FIGURE 12.30   Rectangular cell.

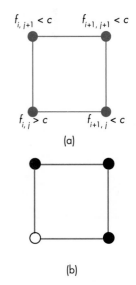

$f_{i, j+1} < c \qquad f_{i+1, j+1} < c$

$f_{i, j} > c \qquad f_{i+1, j} < c$

(a)

(b)

FIGURE 12.31   Labeling the vertices of a cube. (a) Thresholding of the vertices. (b) Coloring of the vertices.

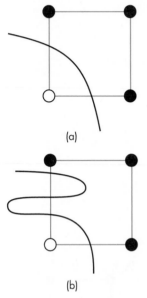

(a)

(b)

FIGURE 12.32 Contour crossing a cell edge. (a) Once. (b) Multiple times.

vertices for which the value is less than c and have colored white the vertex whose value is greater than c. Looking at this situation, we can see that if the function f that generated the data is reasonably well behaved, then the contour curve must cross the two edges that have one white vertex and one black vertex. Equivalently, if the function $f(x, y) - c$ is greater than 0 at one vertex and less than 0 at an adjacent vertex, it must be equal to 0 somewhere in between. This situation is shown in Figure 12.32(a).

Figure 12.32(a) shows only one way that the contour might cross the edge. The contour also might cross three times, as shown in Figure 12.32(b), or any odd number of times. Each of these interpretations is consistent with the sampled data. We will always use the interpretation that a single crossing of an edge by a contour is more likely for smooth functions than are multiple crossings. This choice is an example of the **principle of Occam's razor**, which states that *if there are multiple possible explanations of a phenomenon that are consistent with the data, choose the simplest one*.

Returning to our example cell, if we can estimate where the contour intersects the two edges, then we can join the points of intersection with a line segment. We can even draw this line segment immediately because the computation for other cells is independent of what we do with this cell. But where do we place the intersections? There are two simple strategies. We could simply place the intersection halfway between the black and the white vertices. However, if a is only slightly greater than c and b is much less than c, then we expect the intersection of the contour with the edge of a cell to be closer to (x_i, y_j) than to (x_{i+1}, y_j). A more sophisticated strategy uses interpolation. Consider two vertices that share an edge of a cell and have values on opposite sides of c; for example,

$$f(x_i, y_i) = a \quad a > c$$

$$f(x_{i+1}, y_j) = b \quad b < c.$$

If the two vertices are separated by an x spacing Δx, then we can interpolate the point of intersection using a line segment, as shown in Figure 12.33.

This line segment intersects the x-axis at

$$x = x_i + \frac{(a - c)\Delta x}{a - b}.$$

We use this point for one endpoint of our line segment approximation to the contour in this cell, and we do a similar calculation for the intersection on the other edge that has a black and a white vertex.

$f_{i,i} = a$ $f_{i+1,i} = b$

FIGURE 12.33 Interpolation of the intersection of a cell edge.

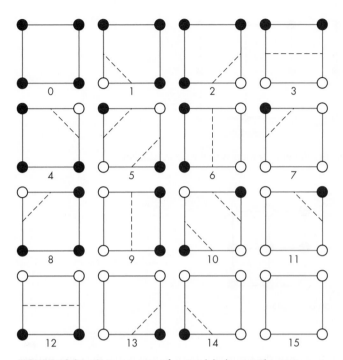

FIGURE 12.34   Sixteen cases of vertex labelings with contours.

Our discussion so far has been in terms of a particular cell for which one vertex is colored white and the others are colored black. There are 16 ($= 2^4$) ways that we can color the vertices of a cell using only black and white. All could arise in our contour problem. These cases are shown in Figure 12.34, as is a simple way of drawing line segments consistent with the data. If we study these cases, numbered 0–15 from left to right, we see that there are two types of symmetry. One is rotational. All cases that can be converted to the same cube by rotation, such as cases 1 and 2, have a single line segment cutting off one of the vertices. There is also symmetry between cases that we can convert to each other by switching all black vertices to white vertices and vice versa, such as cases 0 and 15. Once we take symmetry into account, only four cases are truly unique. These cases are shown in Figure 12.35. Hence, we need code that can draw line segments for only four cases, and we can map all other cases into these four.

FIGURE 12.35   Four unique cases of vertex labelings.

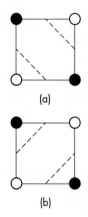

(a)

(b)

FIGURE 12.36 Ambiguous interpretation.

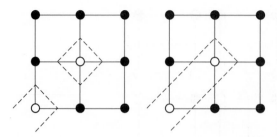

FIGURE 12.37   Example of different contours with the same labeling.

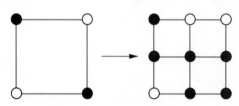

FIGURE 12.38   Subdivision of a square.

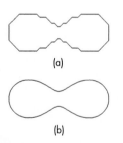

(a)

(b)

FIGURE 12.39 An Oval of Cassini. (a) Using the midpoint. (b) Using interpolation.

The first case is trivial because the simplest interpretation is that the contour does not pass through the cell, and we draw no line segments. The second case is the one that we just discussed; it generates one line segment. The third case is also simple: We can draw a single line segment that goes from one edge to the opposite edge.

The final case is more difficult and more interesting because it contains an ambiguity. We have the two equally simple interpretations shown in Figure 12.36; we must decide which one to use. If we have no other information, we have no reason to prefer one over the other, and we can pick one at random. Alternatively, we could always use only one of the possibilities. But as Figure 12.37 shows, we get different results depending on which interpretation we choose. Another possibility is to subdivide the cell into four smaller cells, as shown in Figure 12.38, generating a new data point in the center. We can obtain the value at this point either from the function, if we know it analytically, or by averaging the values at the corners of the original cell. Hopefully, none of these smaller cells is an ambiguous case. If any is ambiguous, we can further subdivide it.

Figure 12.39 shows two curves corresponding to a single contour value for the Ovals of Cassini function

$$f(x, y) = (x^2 + y^2 + a^2)^2 - 4a^2x^2 - b^4,$$

with $a = 0.49$ and $b = 0.5$. We constructed the curve in part (a) always using the midpoint for the point of intersection of the curve with an edge of a cell. We constructed the curve in part (b) using interpolation to obtain the point of intersection. The function was sampled on a 50×50 grid. Figure 12.40 is derived from terrain data in an area around Honolulu, Hawaii. We display multiple contours at equally spaced

FIGURE 12.40   Contour plot of Honolulu data.

contour values. The area without a curve is the ocean whereas the left part of the display shows the Diamond Head crater. The data is available on the book's website and consists of an array of altitudes above sea level. These are the same data we used in previous chapters to display a mesh and an image.

There are other ways to construct contour curves. One is to start with a cell that is known to have a piece of the contour and then follow this contour to adjacent cells as necessary to complete the contour. However, the marching squares method has the advantage that all cells can be dealt with independently—we march through the data—and the extension to three dimensions for volumetric data is straightforward.

12.10.2 Marching Triangles

We can also display contours using triangles instead of squares by dividing each square into two triangles along a diagonal and then considering each triangle independently. Because each triangle has only three vertices, there are only eight colorings and when we eliminate symmetries there are only two distinct cases: one with all the vertices colored the same and one with a single vertex in one color and the other two in the second color. The approach appears not have to any ambiguities because we eliminated the ambiguity by choosing one of the two possible diagonals for each square. However, if we had chosen the other diagonal we would obtain a slightly different curve, which is equivalent to how we dealt with the ambiguity problem for marching squares. We also note that compared with marching squares, where we deal with four vertices at a time, here, by processing two triangles for each square, we work with six vertices at a time.

12.11   VOLUME RENDERING

Our development of computer graphics has focused on the display of surfaces. Hence, even though we can render an object so we see its three-dimensionality, we do so by modeling it as a set of two-dimensional surfaces within a three-dimensional space and then rendering these surfaces. This approach does not work well if we have a set of data in which each value represents a value at a point within a three-dimensional region.

Consider a function f that is defined over some region of three-dimensional space. Thus, at every point within this region, we have a scalar value $f(x, y, z)$ and we say that f defines a **scalar field**. For example, at each point f might be the density inside an object, or the absorption of X-rays in the human body as measured by a computed-tomography (CT) scan, or the translucency of a slab of glass. Visualization of scalar fields is more difficult than the problems we have considered so far, for two reasons. First, three-dimensional problems have more data with which we must work. Consequently, operations that are routine for two-dimensional data, such as reading files and performing transformations, present practical difficulties. Second, when we had a problem with two independent variables, we were able to use the third dimension to visualize scalars. When we have three independent variables, we lack the extra dimension to use for display. Nevertheless, if we are careful, we can extend our previously developed methods to visualize three-dimensional scalar fields.

The field of **volume rendering** deals with these problems. Most of the methods for visualizing such volumetric data sets are extensions of the methods we have developed, and we will survey a few approaches in the next few sections. Further detail can be found in the Suggested Readings at the end of the chapter.

12.11.1 Volumetric Data Sets

We start with a discrete set of data that might have been obtained from a set of measurements of some physical process, such as a medical data set from a CT scan. Alternately, we might obtain data by evaluating (or sampling) a function $f(x, y, z)$ at a set of points $\{x_i, y_i, z_i\}$, creating a **volumetric data set**.

Assume that our samples are taken at equally spaced points in x, y, and z, as shown in Figure 12.41—a simplifying but not necessary assumption. Thus,

$$x_i = x_0 + i\Delta x$$

$$y_i = y_0 + j\Delta y$$

$$z_i = z_0 + k\Delta z,$$

and we can define

$$f_{ijk} = f(x_i, y_j, z_k).$$

Each f_{ijk} can be thought of as the average value of the scalar field within a right parallelepiped of sides Δx, Δy, Δz centered at (x_i, y_j, z_k). We call this parallelepiped a volume element, or **voxel**.

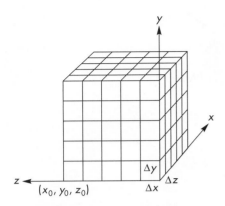

FIGURE 12.41   A volumetric data set.

The three-dimensional array of voxel values that corresponds to equally spaced samples is called a **structured data set**, because we do not need to store the information about where each sample is located in space. The terms *structured data set* and *set of voxels* are often used synonymously.

Scattered data require us to store this information in addition to the scalar values, and such data sets are called **unstructured**. Visualization of unstructured data sets is more complex but can be done with the same techniques that we use for structured data sets; consequently, we will not pursue this topic.

Even more so than for two-dimensional data, there are multiple ways to display these data sets. However, there are two basic approaches: direct volume rendering and isosurfaces. **Direct volume rendering** makes use of every voxel in producing an image; isosurface methods use only a subset of the voxels. For a function $f(x, y, z)$, an **isosurface** is the surface defined by the implicit equation

$$f(x, y, z) = c.$$

The value of the constant c is the **isosurface value.** For the discrete problem where we start with a set of voxels, isosurface methods seek to find approximate isosurfaces.

12.11.2 Visualization of Implicit Functions

Isosurface visualization is the natural extension of contours to three dimensions and thus has a connection to visualization of implicit functions. Consider the implicit function in three dimensions

$$g(x, y, z) = 0,$$

where g is known analytically. If any points satisfy this equation, then this function describes one or more surfaces. Simple examples include spheres, planes, more general quadrics, and the torus of radius r and cross section a:

$$(x^2 + y^2 + z^2 - r^2 - a^2)^2 - 4a^2(r^2 - z^2) = 0.$$

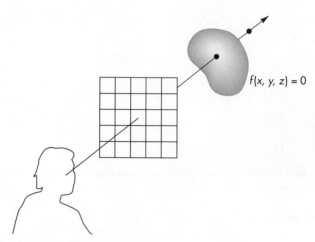

FIGURE 12.42   Ray casting of an implicit function.

As we discussed in Chapter 11, g is a membership function that allows us to test whether a particular point lies on the surface, but there is no general method for finding points on the surface. Thus, given a particular g, we need visualization methods to "see" the surface.

One way to attack this problem involves using a simple form of ray tracing sometimes referred to as **ray casting**. Figure 12.42 shows a function, a viewer, and a projection plane. Any projector can be written in the form of a parametric function:

$$\mathbf{p}(t) = \mathbf{p}_0 + t\mathbf{d}.$$

It also can be written in terms of the individual components:

$$x(t) = x_0 + td_x$$
$$y(t) = y_0 + td_y$$
$$z(t) = z_0 + td_z.$$

Substituting into the implicit equation, we obtain the *scalar* equation in t,

$$f(x_0 + td_x, y_0 + td_y, z_0 + td_z) = u(t) = 0.$$

The solutions of this equation correspond to the points where the projector (ray) enters or leaves the isosurface. If f is a simple function, such as a quadric or a torus, then $u(t)$ may be solvable directly, as we saw in our discussion of ray tracing in Section 12.3.

Once we have the intersections, we can apply a simple shading model to the surface. The required normal at the surface is given by the partial derivatives at the point of intersection:

$$\mathbf{n} = \begin{bmatrix} \frac{\partial f(x,y,z)}{\partial x} \\ \frac{\partial f(x,y,z)}{\partial y} \\ \frac{\partial f(x,y,z)}{\partial z} \end{bmatrix}.$$

Usually, we do not bother with global illumination considerations and thus do not compute either shadow rays (to determine whether the point of intersection is illuminated) or any reflected and traced rays. For scenes composed of simple objects, such as quadrics, ray casting not only is a display technique but also performs visible surface determination and often is used with CSG models. For functions more complex than quadrics, the amount of work required by the intersection calculations is prohibitive and we must consider alternate methods. First, we generalize the problem from one of viewing surfaces to one of viewing volumes.

Suppose that instead of the surface described by $g(x, y, z) = 0$, we consider a scalar field $f(x, y, z)$, which is specified at every point in some region of three-dimensional space. If we are interested in a single value c of f, then the visualization problem is that of displaying the isosurface:

$$g(x, y, z) = f(x, y, z) - c = 0.$$

Sometimes, displaying a single isosurface for a particular value of c is sufficient. For example, if we are working with CT data, we might pick c to correspond to the X-ray density of the tissues that we want to visualize. In other situations, we might display multiple isosurfaces.

Finding isosurfaces usually involves working with a discretized version of the problem, replacing the continuous function g by a set of samples taken over some grid. Our prime isosurface visualization method is called marching cubes, and is the three-dimensional version of marching squares.

12.12 ISOSURFACES AND MARCHING CUBES

Assume that we have a data set $\{f_{ijk}\}$, where each voxel value is a sample of the scalar field $f(x, y, z)$, and when the samples are taken on a regular grid, the discrete data form a set of voxels. We seek an approximate isosurface using the sampled data to define a polygonal mesh. For any value of c, there may be no surface, one surface, or many surfaces that satisfy the equation for a given value of c. Given how well we can display three-dimensional triangles, we describe a method, called **marching cubes**, that approximates a surface by generating a set of three-dimensional triangles, each of which is an approximation to a piece of the isosurface.

We have assumed that our voxel values $\{f_{ijk}\}$ are on a regular three-dimensional grid that passes through the centers of the voxels. If they are not, we can use an interpolation scheme to obtain values on such a grid. Eight adjacent grid points specify a three-dimensional cell, as shown in Figure 12.43. Vertex (i, j, k) of the cell is assigned the data value f_{ijk}. We can now look for parts of isosurfaces that pass through each of these cells, based on only the values at the vertices.

For a given isosurface value c, we can color the vertices of each cell black or white, depending on whether the value at the vertex is greater than or less than c. There are

FIGURE 12.43 Voxel cell.

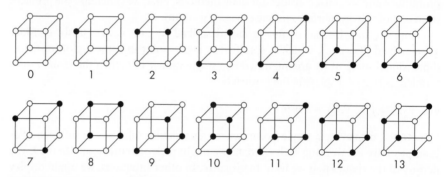

FIGURE 12.44 Vertex colorings.

256 ($= 2^8$) possible vertex colorings, but, once we account for symmetries, there are only the 14 unique cases shown in Figure 12.44.[4] Using the simplest interpretation of the data, we can generate the points of intersection between the surface and the edges of the cubes by linear interpolation between the values at the vertices. Finally, we can use the triangular polygons to tessellate these intersections, forming pieces of a triangular mesh passing through the cell. These tessellations are shown in Figure 12.45. Note that not all these tessellations are unique.

Like the cells from our contour plots, each three-dimensional cell can be processed individually. In terms of the sampled data, each interior voxel value contributes to eight cells. We can go through the data, row by row, then plane by plane. As we do so, the location of the cell that we generate marches through the data set, giving the algorithm its name.

As each cell is processed, any triangles that it generates are sent off to be displayed through our graphics pipeline, where they can be lit, shaded, rotated, texture-mapped, and rasterized. Because the algorithm is so easy to parallelize and, like the contour plot, can be table-driven, marching cubes is a popular way of displaying three-dimensional data.

---

4. The original paper by Lorensen and Cline [Lor87] and many of the subsequent papers refer to 15 cases, but 2 of those cases are symmetric.

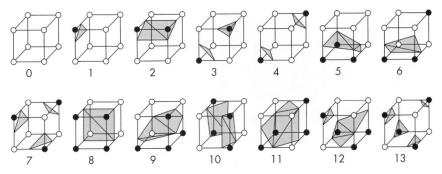

FIGURE 12.45   Tessellations for marching cubes.

FIGURE 12.46   Ambiguity problem for marching cubes. (a) Cell. (b) One interpretation of the cell. (c) A second interpretation.

Marching cubes is both a data reduction algorithm and a modeling algorithm. Both simulations and imaging systems can generate data sets containing from 10^7 to 10^9 voxels. With data sets this large, simple operations (such as reading in the data, rescaling the values, or rotating the data set) are time-consuming, memory-intensive tasks. In many of these applications, however, after executing the algorithm, we might have only 10^3 to 10^4 three-dimensional triangles—a number of geometric objects handled easily by a graphics system. We can rotate, color, and shade the surfaces in real time to interpret the data. In general, few voxels contribute to a particular isosurface; consequently, the information in the unused voxels is not in the image.

There is an ambiguity problem in marching cubes. The problem can arise whenever we have different colors assigned to the diagonally opposite vertices of a side of a cell. Consider the cell coloring in Figure 12.46(a). Figures 12.46(b) and 12.46(c) show two ways to assign triangles to these data. If we compare two isosurfaces generated with the two different interpretations, areas where these cases arise will have completely different shapes and topologies. The wrong selection of an interpretation for a particular cell can leave a hole in an otherwise smooth surface. Researchers have attempted to deal with this problem; no approach works all the time. As we saw with contour plots, an always-correct solution requires more information than is present in the data.

FIGURE 12.47   Slicing a cube to form tetrahedra.

FIGURE 12.48   Tetrahedron created by slicing a cube.

12.13   MARCHING TETRAHEDRA

Just as we were able to extend marching squares to marching triangles, we can extend marching cubes to marching tetrahedra by subdividing each cube into six tetrahedra. Starting with a cube determined by six vertices as in marching cubes, we cut the cube in half three times by slicing it with three planes. Each plane passes through two diagonally opposite edges as shown in Figure 12.47, thus creating six tetrahedra, one for each original vertex. In addition, all the vertices of each tetrahedron are the vertices of the cube.

Consider one tetrahedron as shown in Figure 12.48. There are 16 possible vertex colorings, but only the three in Figure 12.49 are unique; all the others can be obtained by symmetry and the only possible triangulations are shown in Figure 12.50.

FIGURE 12.49   Tetrahedron colorings.

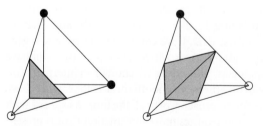

FIGURE 12.50   Tetrahedral triangulations.

Although the process appears simpler because we have only three cases to consider, instead of working with a single cube we must consider six tetrahedra. Note that although there is no ambiguity once we have sliced the cube, there are multiple ways to do the slicing, each of which can lead to a different set of triangles. Although marching cubes is still the most frequently used method for obtaining isosurfaces, tetrahedral methods are important for meshing sparse data sets.

12.14 MESH SIMPLIFICATION

We have looked at marching cubes as a method of generating small triangular pieces of an isosurface. Equivalently, we can view the output of the algorithm as one or more triangular meshes. These meshes are highly irregular even though they are composed of only triangles.

One of the disadvantages of marching cubes is that the algorithm can generate many more triangles than are really needed to display the isosurface. One reason for this phenomenon is that the number of triangles primarily depends on the resolution of the data set, rather than on the smoothness of the isosurface. Thus, we can often create a new mesh with far fewer triangles such that the rendered surfaces are visually indistinguishable. There are multiple approaches to this **mesh simplification** problem.

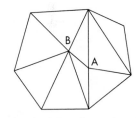

FIGURE 12.51   Original mesh.

One popular approach, called **triangle decimation**, seeks to simplify the mesh by removing some edges and vertices. Consider the mesh in Figure 12.51. If we move vertex A to coincide with vertex B, we eliminate two triangles and obtain the simplified mesh in Figure 12.52. Decisions as to which triangles are to be removed can be made using criteria such as the local smoothness or the shape of the triangles. The latter criterion is important because long, thin triangles do not render well.

Other approaches are based on resampling the surface generated by the original mesh, thus creating a new set of points that lie on the surface. These points are unstructured, lacking the connectivity in the original mesh. Thus, we are free to connect them in some optimal way. Probably the most popular technique is the Delaunay triangulation procedure from Chapter 11.

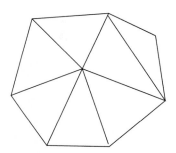

FIGURE 12.52   Mesh after simplification.

Another approach to resampling is to place points on the original mesh or select a subset of the vertices and then use a particle system to control the final placement of the points (particles). Repulsive forces among the particles cause the particles to move to positions that lead to a good mesh.

12.15 DIRECT VOLUME RENDERING

The weakness of isosurface rendering is that not all voxels contribute to the final image. Consequently, we could miss the most important part of the data by selecting the wrong isovalue. **Direct volume rendering** constructs images in which all voxels can make a contribution to the image. Usually these techniques are either extensions of the compositing methods we introduced in Chapter 7 or applications of ray tracing. Because the voxels typically are located on a rectangular grid, once the location of

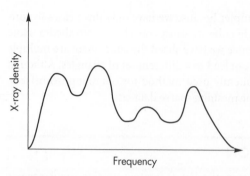

FIGURE 12.53   Histogram of CT data.

the viewer is known, there is an ordering by which we can do either front-to-back or back-to-front rendering.

Early methods for direct volume rendering treated each voxel as a small cube that was either transparent or completely opaque. If the image was rendered in a front-to-back manner, rays were traced until the first opaque voxel was encountered on each ray; then the corresponding pixel in the image was colored black. If no opaque voxel was found along the ray, the corresponding pixel in the image was colored white. If the data set was rendered back to front, a painter's algorithm was used to paint only the opaque voxels. Both techniques produced images with serious aliasing artifacts due to treating each voxel as a cube that was projected to the screen. They also failed to display the information in all the voxels. With the use of color and opacity, we can avoid or mitigate these problems.

12.15.1 Assignment of Color and Opacity

We start by assigning a color and transparency to each voxel. For example, if the data are from a CT scan of a person's head, we might assign colors based on the X-ray density. Soft tissues (low densities) might be red, fatty tissues (medium densities) might be blue, hard tissues (high densities) might be white, and empty space might be black. Often, these color assignments can be based on looking at the distribution of voxel values—the **histogram** of the data. Figure 12.53 shows a histogram with four peaks. We can assign a color to each peak, and, if we use indexed color, we can assign red, green, and blue to the color indices through tables determined from curves such as those shown in Figure 12.54. If these data came from a CT scan, the skull might account for the low peak on the left and be assigned white, whereas empty space might correspond to the rightmost peak in the histogram and be colored black.

Opacities are assigned on the basis of which voxels we wish to emphasize in the image. If we want to show the brain but not the skull, we can assign zero opacity to the values corresponding to the skull. The assignment of colors and opacities is a pattern recognition problem that we will not pursue. Often, a user interface allows the user to control these values interactively. Here, we are interested in how to construct a two-dimensional image after these assignments have been made.

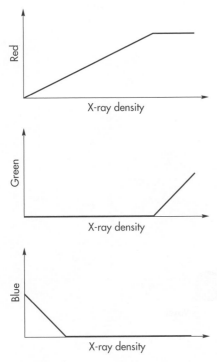

FIGURE 12.54 Color curves for computed-tomography data.

12.15.2 Splatting

Once colors and opacities are assigned, we can assign a geometric shape to each voxel and apply the compositing techniques from Chapter 7. One method is to apply back-to-front painting. Consider the group of voxels in Figure 12.55. Here, the term *front* is defined relative to the viewer. For three-dimensional data sets, once we have positioned the viewer relative to the data set, *front* defines the order in which we process the array of voxels. As we saw in Chapter 9, octrees can provide an efficient mechanism for storing voxel data sets. Positioning the viewer determines an order for traversing the octree.

One particularly simple way to generate an image is known as **splatting**. Each voxel is assigned a simple shape, and this shape is projected onto the image plane. Figure 12.56 shows a spherical voxel and the associated splat, or **footprint**. Note that if we are using a parallel projection and each voxel is assigned the same shape, the splats differ in only color and opacity. Thus, we do not need to carry out a projection for each voxel, but rather can save the footprint as a bitmap that can be rendered into the framebuffer.

The shape to assign each voxel is a sampling issue of the type we considered in Chapter 8 and Appendix D. If the process that generated the data were ideal, each splat would be the projection of a three-dimensional sinc function. The use of hexagonal or elliptical splats is based on approximating a voxel with a parallelepiped

FIGURE 12.55   Volume of voxels.

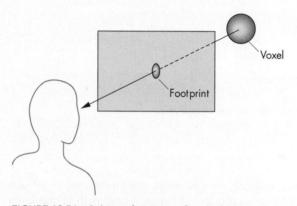

FIGURE 12.56   Splat, or footprint, of a voxel.

or ellipsoid rather than using the reconstruction part of the sampling theorem. A better approximation is to use a Gaussian splat, which is the projection of a three-dimensional Gaussian approximation to the sinc function (see Appendix D).

The key issue in creating a splatted image is how each splat is composited into the image. The data, being on a grid, are already sorted with respect to their distance from the viewer or the projection plane. We can go through the data back to front, adding the contributions of each voxel through its splat. We start with a background image and blend in successive splats.

12.15.3 Volume Ray Tracing

An alternative direct-volume-rendering technique is front-to-back rendering by ray tracing (Figure 12.57). Using the same compositing formulas that we used for splatting along a ray, we determine when an opaque voxel is reached and we stop trac-

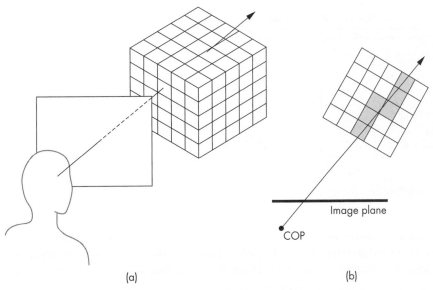

FIGURE 12.57 Volume ray casting. (a) Three-dimensional view. (b) Top view.

ing this ray immediately. The difficulty with this approach is that a given ray passes through many slices of the data, and thus we need to keep all the data available.

It should be clear that the issues that govern the choice between a back-to-front and a front-to-back renderer are similar to the issues that arise when we choose between an image-oriented renderer and an object-oriented renderer. We have merely added opacity to the process. Consequently, a volume ray tracer can produce images that have a three-dimensional appearance and can make use of all the data. However, the ray-traced image must be recomputed from scratch each time that the viewing conditions change or that we make a transformation on the data.

The approach used most often in volume ray tracing is usually called **ray casting**, because we generally display only the shading at the intersection of the ray with the voxels and do not bother with shadow rays. Recently, researchers have explored various strategies to use GPUs for much of the calculation.

12.15.4 Texture Mapping of Volumes

The hardware and software support for texture mapping is the basis for another approach to direct volume rendering using three-dimensional textures, which are supported in desktop OpenGL. Suppose that we have sufficient texture memory to hold our entire data set. We can now define a set of planes parallel to the viewer. We can map texture coordinates to world coordinates such that these planes cut through the texture memory, forming a set of parallel polygons, as shown in Figure 12.58. We now texture-map the voxels to these polygons for display. Because we need only a few hundred polygons to be compatible with the number of data points that we have in most problems, we place little burden on our rendering hardware. Unlike all the other

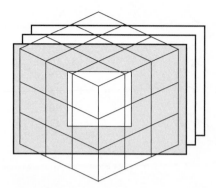

FIGURE 12.58   Slicing of three-dimensional texture memory with polygons.

volume-rendering methods, this one is fast enough that we can move the viewer in real time and do interactive visualization. There is, however, an aliasing problem with this technique that depends on the angle the polygons make with the texture array.

12.16   IMAGE-BASED RENDERING

Recently there has been a great deal of interest in starting with a set of two-dimensional images and either extracting three-dimensional information or forming new images from them. This problem has appeared in many forms over the years. Some of the most important examples in the past have included the following:

- Using aerial photographs to obtain terrain information
- Using a sequence of two-dimensional X-rays to obtain a three-dimensional image in computerized axial tomography (CT)
- Obtaining geometric models from cameras in robotics
- Warping one image into another (morphing)

Recent applications have focused on creating new images from a sequence of stored images that have been carefully collected. For example, suppose that we take a sequence of photographs of an object—a person, a building, or a CAD model—and want to see the object from a different viewpoint. If we had a three-dimensional model, we would simply move the viewer or the object and construct the new image. But what can we do if we have only two-dimensional information? These problems all fit under the broad heading of **image-based rendering**. Techniques involve elements of computer graphics, image processing, and computer vision.

12.16.1 A Simple Example

We can get some idea of the issues involved by considering the problem shown in Figure 12.59. On the left is a perspective camera located at a point $\mathbf{p}_1$, and on the right is a second camera located at $\mathbf{p}_2$. Consider a point $\mathbf{q}$ that is imaged by both cameras. Assuming that we know everything about these cameras—their locations, orientations, fields of view—can we determine $\mathbf{q}$ from the two images produced by

FIGURE 12.59   Two cameras imaging the same point.

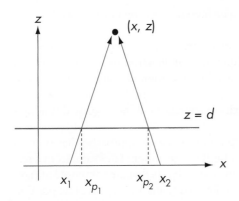

FIGURE 12.60   Top view of the two cameras.

the cameras? Figure 12.60 has a top view of a simplified version of the problem with the two cameras both located on the x-axis and with their image planes parallel at $z = d$. Using our standard equations for projections, we have the two relationships

$$\frac{x_1 - x_{p1}}{d} = \frac{x_1 - x}{z}$$

$$\frac{x_2 - x_{p2}}{d} = \frac{x_2 - x}{z}.$$

These are two linear equations in the unknowns x and z that we can solve, yielding

$$z = \frac{d\Delta x}{\Delta x - \Delta x_p}$$

$$x = \frac{x_{p1}\Delta x - x_1 \Delta x_p}{\Delta x - \Delta x_p},$$

where $\Delta x = x_2 - x_1$ and $\Delta x_p = x_{p2} - x_{p1}$.

Thus, we have determined $\mathbf{q}$ from the two images. This result does not depend on where the cameras are located; moving them only makes the equations a little more complex. Once we have $\mathbf{q}$, we can obtain an image from any viewpoint.

On closer examination, we can see some practical problems. First, there are numerical problems. Any small errors in the measurement of the camera position can cause large errors in the estimate of $\mathbf{q}$. Such numerical issues have plagued many of the traditional applications, such as terrain measurement. One way around such problems is to use more than two measurements and then to determine a best estimate of the desired position.

There are other potentially serious problems. For example, how do we obtain the points $\mathbf{p}_1$ and $\mathbf{p}_2$? Given the images from the two cameras, we need a method of identifying corresponding points. This problem is one of the fundamental problems in computer vision and one for which there are no perfect solutions. Note that if there

FIGURE 12.61   Imaging with occlusion.

is occlusion, the same point may not even be present in the two images, as shown in Figure 12.61.

Many early techniques were purely image based, using statistical methods to find corresponding points. Other techniques were interactive, requiring the user to identify corresponding points. Recently, within the computer graphics community, there have been some novel approaches to the problem. We will mention a few of the more noteworthy ones. The details of each are referenced in the Suggested Readings at the end of the chapter.

One way around the difficulties in pure image-based approaches has been to use geometric models, rather than points, for the registration. For example, in a real environment, we might know that there are many objects that are composed of right parallelepipeds. This extra information can be used to derive very accurate position information.

One use of image-based techniques has been to generate new images for a single viewer from a sequence of images. Variations of this general problem have been used in the movie industry, in providing new images in virtual reality applications, such as Apple's QuickTime VR, and for viewing objects remotely.

Others have looked at the mathematical relationship between two-dimensional images and the light distribution in a three-dimensional environment. Each two-dimensional image is a sample of a four-dimensional light field. In a manner akin to how three-dimensional images are constructed from two-dimensional projections in computerized axial tomography, two-dimensional projections from multiple cameras can be used to reconstruct the three-dimensional world. Two of these techniques are known as the **lumigraph** and **light-field rendering**. Because all the information about a scene is contained in the light field, there is growing interest in measuring the light field, something that, given the large amount of data involved, was not possible until recently. One of the interesting applications of measuring the light field is in re-lighting a scene. In such applications, the lighting that was in the scene is removed and it is relit using the light field generated by sources at other locations.

SUMMARY AND NOTES

This chapter has illustrated that there are many approaches to rendering. The physical basis for rendering with global illumination is contained in the rendering equation. Unfortunately, it contains too many variables to be solvable, even by numerical methods, for the general case. Radiosity and ray tracing can handle some global effects, although they make opposite assumptions on the types of surfaces that are in the scene. Monte Carlo methods such as path tracing and photon mapping can handle arbitrary BDRFs but require a tremendous amount of computation to avoid producing noisy images. As GPUs become more and more powerful, they can handle much of the computation required by alternate rendering methods. Consequently, we may see less of a distinction than presently exists between pipeline approaches and all other rendering methods for real-time applications.

Although the speed and cost of computers make it possible to ray-trace scenes and carry out radiosity calculations that were not possible a few years ago, these techniques alone are not the solution to all problems in computer graphics. If we look at what has been happening in the film, television, and game industries, it appears that we can create photorealistic imagery using a wealth of modeling methods and a variety of commercial and shareware renderers. However, there is a growing acceptance of the view that photorealism is not the ultimate goal. Hence, we see increasing interest in such areas as combining realistic rendering and computer modeling with traditional hand animation. The wide range of image-based methods fits in well with many of these applications.

Most of what we see on the consumer end of graphics is driven by computer games. It appears that no matter how fast and inexpensive processors are, the demands of consumers for more sophisticated computer games will continue to force developers to come up with faster processors with new capabilities. As high-definition television (HDTV) becomes more the standard, we are seeing a greater variety of high-resolution displays available at reasonable prices. Recently, there has been a heightened interest in games on smart phones. As we have seen with WebGL, we can run three-dimensional applications on such devices, but with them we have the added necessity of low power consumption.

On the scientific side, the replacement of traditional supercomputers by clusters of commodity computers will continue to have a large effect on scientific visualization. The enormous data sets generated by applications run on these clusters will drive application development on the graphics side. Not only will these applications need imagery generated for high-resolution displays, but the difficulties of storing these data sets will drive efforts to visualize these data as fast as they can be generated.

Of particular interest is the realization by the scientific community that GPUs are in fact mini-supercomputers that perform floating-point operations at high rates. A single GPU, such as NVIDIA's Tesla, can have thousands of processors. The Titan supercomputer at Oak Ridge National Laboratories has over 18,000 GPUs and can achieve up to 27 petaFLOPS, where the GPUs are doing the most of the computation. On the software side, APIs such as CUDA and OpenCL are designed to support computation rather than graphics on GPUs.

What is less clear is the future of computer architectures and how they will affect computer graphics. Commodity computers, such as the Apple MacPro, have multiple buses that support multiple graphics cards and multiple processors, each with multiple cores. Game boxes are starting to use alternate components, such as the IBM cell processor that drives the Sony PlayStation 3. At the high end, a number of exascale (1 exaFLOP $= 10^{18}$ FLOPS) supercomputers are under development. Such computers will likely contain a variety of GPU, CPU, and other computing components. How we can best use these components is an open issue. What can be said with a great degree of certainty is that there is still much to be done in computer graphics.

SUGGESTED READINGS

Ray tracing was introduced by Appel [App68] and popularized by Whitted [Whi80]. Many of the early papers on ray tracing are included in a volume by Joy and colleagues [Joy88]. The book by Glassner [Gla89] is particularly helpful if you plan to write your own ray tracer. Many of the tests for intersections are described in Haines's chapter in [Gla89] and in the *Graphics Gems* series [Gra90, Gra91, Gra92, Gra94, Gra95]. See also [Suf07] and [Shi03]. There are many excellent ray tracers available (see, for example, [War94]). See [Shi09] and [Suf07] for an introduction to path tracing and its relation to ray tracing.

The rendering equation is due to Kajiya [Kaj86]. Radiosity is based on a method first used in heat transfer [Sie81]. It was first applied in computer graphics by Goral and colleagues [Gor84]. Since its introduction, researchers have done a great deal of work on increasing its efficiency [Coh85, Coh88, Coh93] and incorporating specular terms [Sil89]. The method of using point light sources to find form factors appeared in [Kel97]. Photon mapping has been popularized by Jensen [Jen01].

The RenderMan interface is described in [Ups89]. The Reyes rendering architecture was first presented in [Coo87]. Maya [Wat02] allows multiple types of renderers.

For an introduction to NVIDIA's Compute Unified Device Architecture, see [San10] and [Coo12]. The OpenCL API [Mun12] is one of the Khronos standards that includes OpenGL and WebGL.

The sorting classification of parallel rendering was suggested by Molnar and colleagues [Mol94]. See [Eld00] for a slightly different classification that incorporates shaders. Also see [Mol02] for a discussion that includes the effects of bus speeds. The advantages of sort-middle architectures were used in SGI's high-end workstations such as the InfiniteReality graphics [Mon97]. The sort-last architecture was developed as part of the PixelFlow architecture [Mol92]. Binary-swap compositing was suggested by [Ma94]. Software for sort-last renderings using clusters of commodity computers is discussed in [Hum01]. Power walls are described in [Her00, Che00].

The marching squares method is a special case of the marching cubes method popularized by Lorenson and Kline [Lor87]. The method has been rediscovered many times. The ambiguity problem is discussed in [Van94]. Early attempts to visualize volumes were reported by Herman [Her79] and by Fuchs [Fuc77]. Ray-tracing volumes were introduced by Levoy [Lev88]. Splatting is due to Westover [Wes90]. Particles can also be used for visualization [Wit94a, Cro97]. Many other visualization strategies are discussed in [Gal95, Nie97]. One approach to building visualization applications is to use an object-oriented toolkit [Sch06].

Image-based rendering by warping frames was part of Microsoft's Talisman hardware [Tor96]. Apple's QuickTime VR [Che95] was based on creating new views from a single viewpoint from a 360-degree panorama. Debevec and colleagues [Deb96] showed that by using a model-based approach, new images from multiple viewpoints could be constructed from a small number of images. Other warping methods were proposed in [Sei96]. Work on the lumigraph [Gor96] and light fields [Lev96] established the mathematical foundations for image-based techniques. Applications to image-based lighting are in [Rei05].

EXERCISES

12.1   Devise a test for whether a point is inside a convex polygon based on the idea that the polygon can be described by a set of intersecting lines in a single plane.

12.2   Extend your algorithm from Exercise 12.1 to polyhedra that are formed by the intersection of planes.

12.3   Derive an implicit equation for a torus whose center is at the origin. You can derive the equation by noting that a plane that cuts through the torus reveals two circles of the same radius.

12.4   Using the result from Exercise 12.3, show that you can ray-trace a torus using the quadratic equation to find the required intersections.

12.5   Consider a ray passing through a sphere. Find the point on this ray closest to the center of the sphere. *Hint:* Consider a line from the center of the sphere that is normal to the ray. How can you use this result for intersection testing?

12.6   We can get increased accuracy from a ray tracer by using more rays. Suppose that for each pixel, we cast a ray through the center of the pixel and through its four corners. How much more work does this approach require as compared to the one-ray-per-pixel ray tracer?

12.7   In the sort-middle approach to parallel rendering, what type of information must be conveyed between the geometry processors and raster processors?

12.8   What changes would you have to make to our parallel rendering strategies if we were to allow translucent objects?

12.9   One way to classify parallel computers is by whether their memory is shared among the processors or distributed so that each processer has its own memory that is not accessible to other processors. How does this distinction affect the various rendering strategies that we have discussed?

12.10   Generalize the simple example of imaging the same point from two viewers to the general case in which the two viewers can be located at arbitrary locations in three dimensions.

12.11   Build a simple ray tracer that can handle only planes and spheres. There are many interesting data sets available on the Internet with which to test your code.

12.12   Why is the approach used most often in volume ray tracing often called ray casting? Build a simple ray caster. There are many interesting data sets available on the Internet with which to test your code.

12.13   Suppose that you have an algebraic function in which the highest term is $x^i y^j z^k$. What is the degree of the polynomial that we need to solve for the intersection of a ray with the surface defined by this function?

12.14   Consider again an algebraic function in which the highest term is $x^i y^j z^k$. If $i = j = k$, how many terms are in the polynomial that is created when we intersect the surface with a parametric ray?

12.15   For one or more WebGL implementations, find how many triangles per second can be rendered. Determine what part of the rendering time is spent in hidden-surface removal, shading, texture mapping, and rasterization. If you are using a commodity graphics card, how does the performance that you measure compare with the specifications for the card?

12.16   Determine the pixel performance of your graphics card. Determine how many pixels per second can be read or written. Do the reading and writing of pixels occur at different rates? Is there a difference in writing texture maps?

12.17   Build a sort-last renderer using WebGL for the rendering on each processor. You can do performance tests using applications that generate triangles or triangular meshes.

12.18   Explain why, as we add more processors, the performance of sort-first rendering will eventually get worse.

12.19   Write a WebGL program to carry out marching squares.

INITIALIZING SHADERS

We omitted in the text the details of initializing the shaders. This process involves a set of WebGL functions that, while necessary for initialization, do not convey any core computer graphics concepts, so we have left them for this separate appendix. The initialization process requires reading in the shader source, compiling the shaders, and linking together the shaders into a program object, all of which use some WebGL functions that are largely unchanged over different applications.

There are at least three ways to input shaders in WebGL. The first is to have the shader source as a string in the application. For example, simple pass-through vertex and fragment shaders could be specified by the strings

```
var vshader = "attribute vec4 position;\
               void main() { gl_Position = position; }";
var fshader = "void main() { gl_FragColor =\
                             vec4(1.0, 0.0, 0.0, 1.0); }";
```

and then compiled. However, this method is unwieldy for all but the most trivial shaders, so we will not consider it further. Although we could put all our code in a single HTML file, we prefer to use multiple files, including a base HTML file to bring in the necessary initialization files and an application file. For the shaders, we have chosen to put them in the base HTML file primarily because this option should work with all recent browsers. Our first shader initialization method will describe the initialization for this configuration in detail.

The third option is similar to how shaders are input for more complex applications, where we have much longer shaders or want an application that can use multiple shaders. Here we want to have the shaders in separate files, each of which contains only code in GLSL.

A.1 SHADERS IN THE HTML FILE

Let's start with our example of the Sierpinski gasket from Chapter 2. The shaders were in the HTML file within `<script>` tags as

```
<script id="vertex-shader" type="x-shader/x-vertex">
attribute vec4 vPosition;

void main()
{
  gl_Position = vPosition;
}
</script>

<script id="fragment-shader" type="x-shader/x-fragment">
void main()
{
  gl_FragColor = vec4(1.0, 0.0, 0.0, 1.0);
}
</script>
```

There are two types of information in the `<script>` tags. The `id` gives us a reference to the shader that can be used in the application file and the `type` identifies the type of content to HTML. We can now look at the `initShaders` function that is invoked from the application by

```
initShaders(gl, vertexShaderId, fragmentShaderId);
```

where `gl` is the WebGL context and the `vertexShaderId` and `fragmentShaderId` arguments are the identifiers in the HTML file.

The first step is to get the vertex shader identifier from the HTML file:

```
var vertElem = document.getElementById(vertexShaderId);
```

Ignoring error checking for now, we can then create a shader object for a vertex shader, add the shader source code from the HTML file to this object and compile the code:

```
var vertShdr = gl.createShader(gl.VERTEX_SHADER);
gl.shaderSource(vertShdr, vertElem.text);
gl.compileShader(vertShdr);
```

We go through the same steps for the fragment shader using the parameter `gl.FRAGMENT_SHADER` to create a fragment shader object. The shaders are attached to a program object

```
var program = gl.createProgram();
gl.attachShader(program, vertShdr);
gl.attachShader(program, fragShdr);
```

which can then be linked and, if successful, have the program identifier returned to the application:

```
gl.linkProgram(program);
return program;
```

The complete code with error checking is given here:

```
function initShaders(gl, vertexShaderId, fragmentShaderId)
{
  var vertShdr;
  var fragShdr;

  var vertElem = document.getElementById(vertexShaderId);
  if (!vertElem) {
    alert("Unable to load vertex shader " + vertexShaderId);
    return -1;
  }
  else {
    vertShdr = gl.createShader(gl.VERTEX_SHADER);
    gl.shaderSource(vertShdr, vertElem.text);
    gl.compileShader(vertShdr);

    if (!gl.getShaderParameter(vertShdr, gl.COMPILE_STATUS)) {
      var msg = "Vertex shader failed to compile.  The error log is:"
        + "<pre>" + gl.getShaderInfoLog(vertShdr) + "</pre>";
      alert(msg);
      return -1;
    }
  }

  var fragElem = document.getElementById(fragmentShaderId);
  if (!fragElem) {
    alert("Unable to load vertex shader " + fragmentShaderId);
    return -1;
  }
  else {
    fragShdr = gl.createShader(gl.FRAGMENT_SHADER);
    gl.shaderSource(fragShdr, fragElem.text);
    gl.compileShader(fragShdr);

    if (!gl.getShaderParameter(fragShdr, gl.COMPILE_STATUS)) {
      var msg = "Fragment shader failed to compile.  The error log is:"
        + "<pre>" + gl.getShaderInfoLog(fragShdr) + "</pre>";
      alert(msg);
      return -1;
    }
  }

  var program = gl.createProgram();
  gl.attachShader(program, vertShdr);
  gl.attachShader(program, fragShdr);
  gl.linkProgram(program);

  if (!gl.getProgramParameter(program, gl.LINK_STATUS)) {
```

```
    var msg = "Shader program failed to link.  The error log is:"
      + "<pre>" + gl.getProgramInfoLog(program) + "</pre>";
    alert(msg);
    return -1;
  }

  return program;
}
```

A.2 READING SHADERS FROM SOURCE FILES

We usually prefer to keep our shaders in a separate directory as pure GLSL files (e.g., fshader.glsl and vshader.glsl) rather than in the HTML file and then have the application read them in directly from this directory. For example,

```
var program = initShaders(gl, "shaders/vshader.glsl",
                              "shaders/fshader.glsl");
```

Consider then the alternate code for initShaders:

```
function loadFileAJAX(name)
{
  var xhr = new XMLHttpRequest();
  var okStatus = (document.location.protocol === "file:" ? 0 : 200);
  xhr.open('GET', name, false);
  xhr.send(null);
  return xhr.status == (okStatus ? xhr.responseText : null);
}

function initShaders(gl, vShaderName, fShaderName)
{
  function getShader(gl, shaderName, type)
  {
    var shader = gl.createShader(type);
    var shaderScript = loadFileAJAX(shaderName);

    if (!shaderScript) {
      alert("Could not find shader source: " + shaderName);
    }

    gl.shaderSource(shader, shaderScript);
    gl.compileShader(shader);

    if (!gl.getShaderParameter(shader, gl.COMPILE_STATUS)) {
      alert(gl.getShaderInfoLog(shader));
      return -1;
    }
```

```
    return shader;
}

var vertexShader = getShader(gl, vShaderName, gl.VERTEX_SHADER);
var fragmentShader = getShader(gl, fShaderName, gl.FRAGMENT_SHADER);
var program = gl.createProgram();

if (vertexShader < 0 || fragmentShader < 0 ) {
  alert("Could not initialize shaders");
  return -1;
}

gl.attachShader(program, vertexShader);
gl.attachShader(program, fragmentShader);
gl.linkProgram(program);

if (!gl.getProgramParameter(program, gl.LINK_STATUS)) {
  alert("Could not initialize shaders");
  return -1;
}

return program;
}
```

Except for the load file function, this version is almost identical to our first version. It uses one standard method of reading in an external file. The details are unimportant here and there are many other ways to perform the read file operation. The problem is that many browsers will refuse to carry out the operation, which is known as a *cross-origin request* and is considered a security hole. Some browsers will allow this form from a remote site and use only the remote files, which is safe, but will not run the code locally. This variant is on the website for some of the examples in the text so you can try them with your browser.

SPACES

Computer graphics is concerned with the representation and manipulation of sets of geometric elements, such as points and line segments. The necessary mathematics is found in the study of various types of abstract spaces. In this appendix, we review the rules governing three such spaces: the (linear) vector space, the affine space, and the Euclidean space. The **(linear) vector space** contains only two types of objects: scalars, such as real numbers, and vectors. The **affine space** adds a third element: the point. **Euclidean spaces** add the concept of distance.

The vectors of interest in computer graphics are directed line segments and the n-tuples of numbers that are used to represent them. In Appendix C, we discuss matrix algebra as a tool for manipulating n-tuples. In this appendix, we are concerned with the underlying concepts and rules. It is probably helpful to think of these entities (scalars, vectors, points) as abstract data types, and the axioms as defining the valid operations on them.

B.1   SCALARS

Ordinary real numbers and the operations on them are one example of a **scalar field**. Let S denote a set of elements called **scalars**, $\alpha, \beta, \ldots$. Scalars have two fundamental operations defined between pairs. These operations are often called addition and multiplication, and are symbolized by the operators $+$ and $\cdot$,[1] respectively. Hence, for $\forall \alpha, \beta \in S, \alpha + \beta \in S$, and $\alpha \cdot \beta \in S$. These operations are associative, commutative, and distributive; $\forall \alpha, \beta, \gamma \in S$:

$$\alpha + \beta = \beta + \alpha$$

$$\alpha \cdot \beta = \beta \cdot \alpha$$

$$\alpha + (\beta + \gamma) = (\alpha + \beta) + \gamma$$

$$\alpha \cdot (\beta \cdot \gamma) = (\alpha \cdot \beta) \cdot \gamma$$

---

1. Often, if there is no ambiguity, we can write $\alpha\beta$ instead of $\alpha \cdot \beta$.

$$\alpha \cdot (\beta + \gamma) = (\alpha \cdot \beta) + (\alpha \cdot \gamma).$$

There are two special scalars—the additive identity (0) and the multiplicative identity (1)—such that $\forall \alpha \in S$:

$$\alpha + 0 = 0 + \alpha = \alpha,$$

$$\alpha \cdot 1 = 1 \cdot \alpha = \alpha.$$

Each element α has an additive inverse, denoted $-\alpha$, and a multiplicative inverse, denoted $\alpha^{-1} \in S$, such that

$$\alpha + (-\alpha) = 0,$$

$$\alpha \cdot \alpha^{-1} = 1.$$

The real numbers using ordinary addition and multiplication form a scalar field, as do the complex numbers (under complex addition and multiplication) and rational functions (ratios of two polynomials).

B.2   VECTOR SPACES

A vector space, in addition to scalars, contains a second type of entity: **vectors**. Vectors have two operations defined: vector–vector addition and scalar–vector multiplication. Let u, v, w denote vectors in a vector space V. Vector addition is defined to be closed ($u + v \in V$, $\forall u, v \in V$), commutative ($u + v = v + u$), and associative ($u + (v + w) = (u + v) + w$). There is a special vector $\mathbf{0}$ (the **zero vector**) defined such that $\forall u \in V$:

$$u + \mathbf{0} = u.$$

Every vector u has an additive inverse denoted by $-u$ such that

$$u + (-u) = \mathbf{0}.$$

Scalar–vector multiplication is defined such that, for any scalar α and any vector u, αu is a vector in V. The scalar–vector operation is distributive. Hence,

$$\alpha(u + v) = \alpha u + \alpha v$$

$$(\alpha + \beta)u = \alpha u + \beta u.$$

The two examples of vector spaces that we use are geometric vectors (directed line segments) and the n-tuples of real numbers. Consider a set of directed line segments that we can picture as shown in Figure B.1. If our scalars are real numbers, then scalar–vector multiplication changes the length of a vector, but not that vector's direction (Figure B.2).

Vector–vector addition can be defined by the **head-to-tail axiom**, which we can visualize easily for the example of directed line segments. We form the vector $u + v$

FIGURE B.1   Directed line segments.

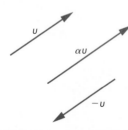

FIGURE B.2   Scalar–vector multiplication.

by connecting the head of u to the tail of v, as shown in Figure B.3. You should be able to verify that all the rules of a vector field are satisfied.

The second example of a vector space is n-tuples of scalars—usually, real or complex numbers. Hence, a vector can be written as

$$v = (v_1, v_2, \ldots, v_n).$$

Scalar–vector multiplication and vector–vector addition are given by

$$u + v = (u_1, u_2, \ldots, u_n) + (v_1, v_2, \ldots, v_n)$$

$$= (u_1 + v_1, u_2 + v_2, \ldots, u_n + v_n)$$

$$\alpha v = (\alpha v_1, \alpha v_2, \ldots, \alpha v_n).$$

FIGURE B.3 Head-to-tail axiom for vectors.

This space is denoted $\mathbf{R}^n$ and is the vector space in which we can manipulate vectors using matrix algebra (Appendix C).

In a vector space, the concepts of linear independence and basis are crucial. A **linear combination** of n vectors $u_1, u_2, \ldots, u_n$ is a vector of the form

$$u = \alpha_1 u_1 + \alpha_2 u_2 + \cdots + \alpha_n u_n.$$

If the only set of scalars such that

$$\alpha_1 u_1 + \alpha_2 u_2 \cdots + \alpha_n u_n = 0$$

is

$$\alpha_1 = \alpha_2 = \cdots = \alpha_n = 0,$$

then the vectors are said to be **linearly independent**. The greatest number of linearly independent vectors that we can find in a space gives the **dimension** of the space. If a vector space has dimension n, any set of n linearly independent vectors forms a **basis**. If $v_1, v_2, \ldots, v_n$ is a basis for V, any vector v can be expressed uniquely in terms of the basis vectors as

$$v = \beta_1 v_1 + \beta_2 v_2 + \cdots + \beta_n v_n.$$

The scalars $\{\beta_i\}$ give the **representation** of v with respect to the basis $v_1, v_2, \ldots, v_n$. If $v'_1, v'_2, \ldots, v'_n$ is some other basis (the number of vectors in a basis is constant), then there is a representation of v with respect to this basis; that is,

$$v = \beta'_1 v'_1 + \beta'_2 v'_2 + \cdots + \beta'_n v'_n.$$

There exists an $n \times n$ matrix $\mathbf{M}$ such that

$$\begin{bmatrix} \beta'_1 \\ \beta'_2 \\ \vdots \\ \beta'_N \end{bmatrix} = \mathbf{M} \begin{bmatrix} \beta_1 \\ \beta_2 \\ \vdots \\ \beta_N \end{bmatrix}.$$

We derive **M** in Appendix C. This matrix gives a way of changing representations through a simple linear transformation involving only scalar operations for carrying out matrix multiplication. More generally, once we have a basis for a vector space, we can work only with representations. If the scalars are real numbers, then we can work with n-tuples of reals and use matrix algebra, instead of doing operations in the original abstract vector space.

FIGURE B.4   Identical vectors.

B.3   AFFINE SPACES

A vector space lacks any geometric concepts, such as location and distance. If we use the example of directed line segments as the natural vector space for our geometric problems, we get into difficulties because these vectors, just like the physicist's vectors, have magnitude and direction but no position. The vectors shown in Figure B.4 are identical.

If we think of this problem in terms of coordinate systems, we can express a vector in terms of a set of basis vectors that define a **coordinate system**. Figure B.5(a) shows three basis vectors emerging from a particular reference point, the **origin**. The location of the vectors in Figure B.5(b) is equally valid, however, because vectors have no position. In addition, we have no way to express this special point, because our vector space has only vectors and scalars as its members.

We can resolve this difficulty by introducing an affine space that adds a third type of entity—points—to a vector space. The points $(P, Q, R, \ldots)$ form a set. There is a single new operation, **point–point subtraction**, that yields a vector. Hence, if P and Q are any two points, the subtraction

$$v = P - Q$$

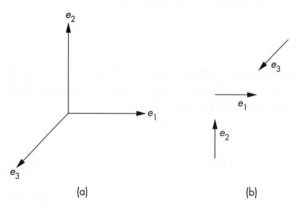

(a)   (b)

FIGURE B.5   Coordinate system. (a) Basis vectors located at the origin. (b) Arbitrary placement of basis vectors.

always yields a vector in V. Conversely, for every v and every P, we can find a Q such that the preceding relation holds. We can thus write

$$Q = v + P,$$

defining a vector–point addition. A consequence of the head-to-tail axiom is that for any three points P, Q, R,

$$(P - Q) + (Q - R) = (P - R).$$

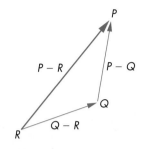

FIGURE B.6   Head-to-tail axiom for points.

If we visualize the vector $P - Q$ as the line segment from the point Q to the point P, using an arrow to denote direction, the head-to-tail axiom can be drawn as shown in Figure B.6.

Various properties follow from affine geometry. Perhaps the most important is that if we use a frame, rather than a coordinate system, we can specify both points and vectors in an affine space. A **frame** consists of a point P_0 and a set of vectors $v_1, v_2, \ldots, v_n$ that defines a basis for the vector space. Given a frame, an arbitrary vector can be written uniquely as

$$v = \alpha_1 v_1 + \alpha_2 v_2 + \cdots + \alpha_n v_n,$$

and an arbitrary point can be written uniquely as

$$P = P_0 + \beta_1 v_1 + \beta_2 v_2 + \cdots + \beta_n v_n.$$

The two sets of scalars, $\{\alpha_1, \ldots, \alpha_n\}$ and $\{\beta_1, \ldots, \beta_n\}$, give the representations of the vector and point, respectively, with each representation consisting of n scalars. We can regard the point P_0 as the origin of the frame; all points are defined from this reference point.

If the origin never changes, we can worry about only those changes of frames corresponding to changes in coordinate systems. In computer graphics, however, we usually have to deal with making changes in frames and with representing objects in different frames. For example, we usually define our objects within a physical frame. The viewer, or camera, can be expressed in terms of this frame, but, as part of the image creation process, it is to our advantage to express object positions with respect to the camera frame—a frame whose origin usually is located at the center of projection.

B.4   EUCLIDEAN SPACES

Although affine spaces contain the necessary elements for building geometric models, there is no concept of how far apart two points are, or of what the length of a vector is. Euclidean spaces have such a concept. Strictly speaking, a Euclidean space contains only vectors and scalars.

Suppose that E is a Euclidean space. It is a vector space containing scalars $(\alpha, \beta, \gamma, \ldots)$ and vectors $(u, v, w, \ldots)$. We assume that the scalars are the ordinary real numbers. We add a new operation—the **inner (dot) product**—that combines two vectors to form a real. The inner product must satisfy the properties that, for any three vectors u, v, w and scalars α, β,

$$u \cdot v = v \cdot u$$

$$(\alpha u + \beta v) \cdot w = \alpha u \cdot w + \beta v \cdot w$$

$$v \cdot v > 0 \text{ if } v \neq 0$$

$$\mathbf{0} \cdot \mathbf{0} = 0.$$

If

$$u \cdot v = 0,$$

then u and v are **orthogonal**. The magnitude (length) of a vector is usually measured as

$$|v| = \sqrt{v \cdot v}.$$

Once we add affine concepts, such as points, to the Euclidean space, we naturally get a measure of distance between points, because, for any two points P and Q, $P - Q$ is a vector, and hence

$$|P - Q| = \sqrt{(P - Q) \cdot (P - Q)}.$$

We can use the inner product to define a measure of the angle between two vectors:

$$u \cdot v = |u||v| \cos \theta.$$

It is easy to show that $\cos \theta$, as defined by this formula, is 0 when the vectors are orthogonal, lies between -1 and $+1$, and has magnitude 1 if the vectors are parallel ($u = \alpha v$).

B.5   PROJECTIONS

We can derive several of the important geometric concepts from the use of orthogonality. The concept of **projection** arises from the problem of finding the shortest distance from a point to a line or plane. It is equivalent to the following problem. Given two vectors, we can take one of them and divide it into two parts, one parallel and one orthogonal to the other vector, as shown in Figure B.7 for directed line segments. Suppose that v is the first vector and w is the second. Then w can be written as

$$w = \alpha v + u.$$

The parallel part is αv, but for u to be orthogonal to v we must have

$$u \cdot v = 0.$$

Because u and v are defined to be orthogonal,

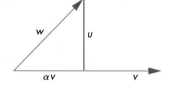

FIGURE B.7   Projection of one vector onto another.

$$w \cdot v = \alpha v \cdot v + u \cdot v = \alpha v \cdot v,$$

allowing us to find

$$\alpha = \frac{w \cdot v}{v \cdot v}.$$

The vector αv is the projection of w onto v, and

$$u = w - \frac{w \cdot v}{v \cdot v} v.$$

We can extend this result to construct a set of orthogonal vectors from an arbitrary set of linearly independent vectors.

B.6   GRAM-SCHMIDT ORTHOGONALIZATION

Given a set of basis vectors $a_1, a_2, \ldots, a_n$ in a space of dimension n, it is relatively straightforward to create another basis $b_1, b_2, \ldots, b_n$ that is **orthonormal**; that is, a basis in which each vector has unit length and is orthogonal to every other vector in the basis, or mathematically:

$$b_i \cdot b_j = \begin{cases} 1 & \text{if } i = j \\ 0 & \text{otherwise.} \end{cases}$$

Hence, there is no real loss of generality in using orthogonal (Cartesian) coordinate systems.

We proceed iteratively. We look for a vector of the form

$$b_2 = a_2 + \alpha b_1,$$

which we can make orthogonal to b_1 by choosing α properly. Taking the dot product, we must have

$$b_2 \cdot b_1 = 0 = a_2 \cdot b_1 + \alpha b_1 \cdot b_1.$$

Solving, we have

$$\alpha = -\frac{a_2 \cdot b_1}{b_1 \cdot b_1}$$

and

$$b_2 = a_2 - \frac{a_2 \cdot b_1}{b_1 \cdot b_1} b_1.$$

We have constructed the orthogonal vector by removing the part parallel to b_1, that is, the projection of a_2 onto b_1.

The general iterative step is to find a vector

$$b_k = a_k + \sum_{i=1}^{k-1} \alpha_i b_i$$

that is orthogonal to $b_1, \ldots, b_{k-1}$. There are $k - 1$ orthogonality conditions that allow us to find

$$\alpha_i = -\frac{a_k \cdot b_i}{b_i \cdot b_i}.$$

We can normalize each vector, either at the end of the process, by replacing b_i by $b_i/|b_i|$ or, more efficiently, by normalizing each b_i as soon as possible.

SUGGESTED READINGS

There are many excellent books on linear algebra and vector spaces. For practitioners of computer graphics, the preferred approach is to start with vector-space ideas and to see linear algebra as a tool for working with general vector spaces. Unfortunately, most of the linear algebra textbooks are concerned only with the Euclidean spaces of n-tuples, $\mathbf{R}^n$. See Bowyer and Woodwark [Bow83] and Banchoff and Werner [Ban83].

Affine spaces can be approached in a number of ways. See Foley [Fol90] for a more geometric development.

EXERCISES

B.1 Prove that the complex numbers form a scalar field. What are the additive and multiplicative identity elements?

B.2 Prove that the rational functions form a scalar field.

B.3 Prove that the rational functions with real coefficients form a vector space.

B.4 Prove that the number of elements in a basis is unique.

B.5 Consider a set of n real functions $\{f_i(x)\}$, $i = 1, \ldots, n$. Show how to form a vector space of functions with these elements. Define *basis* and *dimension* for this space.

B.6 Show that the set of polynomials of degree up to n form an n-dimensional vector space.

B.7 The most important Euclidean space is the space of n-tuples, $a_1, \ldots, a_n$: $\mathbf{R}^n$. Define the operations of vector–vector addition and scalar–vector multiplication in this space. What is the dot product in $\mathbf{R}^n$?

B.8 Suppose that you are given three vectors in $\mathbf{R}^3$. How can you determine whether they form a basis?

B.9 Consider the three vectors in $\mathbf{R}^3$: $(1, 0, 0)$, $(1, 1, 0)$, and $(1, 1, 1)$. Show that they are linearly independent. Derive an orthonormal basis from these vectors, starting with $(1, 0, 0)$.

APPENDIX C

MATRICES

In computer graphics, the major use of matrices is in the representation of changes in coordinate systems and frames. In the studies of vector analysis and linear algebra, the use of the term *vector* is somewhat different. Unfortunately, computer graphics relies on both these fields, and the interpretation of *vector* has caused confusion. To remedy this situation, we use the terms *row matrix* and *column matrix*, rather than the linear algebra terms of *row vector* and *column vector*. We reserve the term *vector* to denote directed line segments, and occasionally, as in Appendix B, to denote the abstract-data-type vector that is an element of a vector space.

This appendix reviews the major results that you will need to manipulate matrices in computer graphics. We almost always use matrices that are 4×4. Hence, the parts of linear algebra that deal with manipulations of general matrices, such as the inversion of an arbitrary square matrix, are of limited interest. Most implementations, instead, implement inversion of 4×4 matrices directly in the hardware or software.

C.1 DEFINITIONS

A **matrix** is an $n \times m$ array of scalars, arranged conceptually as n rows and m columns. Often, n and m are referred to as the row and column **dimensions** of the matrix, and, if $m = n$, we say that the matrix is a **square matrix** of dimension n. We use real numbers for scalars almost exclusively, although most results hold for complex numbers as well. The elements of a matrix $\mathbf{A}$ are the members of the set of scalars, $\{a_{ij}\}$, $i = 1, \ldots, n, j = 1, \ldots, m$. We write $\mathbf{A}$ in terms of its elements as

$$\mathbf{A} = [\, a_{ij} \,].$$

The **transpose** of an $n \times m$ matrix $\mathbf{A}$ is the $m \times n$ matrix that we obtain by interchanging the rows and columns of $\mathbf{A}$. We denote this matrix as $\mathbf{A}^T$, and it is given as

$$\mathbf{A}^T = [\, a_{ji} \,].$$

The special cases of matrices with one column ($n \times 1$ matrix) and one row ($1 \times m$ matrix) are called **column matrices** and **row matrices**. We denote column matrices with lowercase letters:

$$\mathbf{b} = [\,b_i\,].$$

The transpose of a row matrix is a column matrix; we write it as $\mathbf{b}^T$.

C.2   MATRIX OPERATIONS

There are three basic matrix operations: scalar–matrix multiplication, matrix–matrix addition, and matrix–matrix multiplication. You can assume that the scalars are real numbers, although all these operations are defined in the same way when the elements of the matrices and the scalar multipliers are of the same type.

Scalar–matrix multiplication is defined for any size matrix $\mathbf{A}$; it is simply the element-by-element multiplication of the elements of the matrix by a scalar α. The operation is written as

$$\alpha\mathbf{A} = [\,\alpha a_{ij}\,].$$

We define **matrix–matrix addition**, the sum of two matrices, by adding the corresponding elements of the two matrices. The sum makes sense only if the two matrices have the same dimensions. The sum of two matrices of the same dimensions is given by the matrix

$$\mathbf{C} = \mathbf{A} + \mathbf{B} = [\,a_{ij} + b_{ij}\,].$$

For **matrix–matrix multiplication**, the product of an $n \times l$ matrix $\mathbf{A}$ by an $l \times m$ matrix $\mathbf{B}$ is the $n \times m$ matrix

$$\mathbf{C} = \mathbf{AB} = [\,c_{ij}\,],$$

where

$$c_{ij} = \sum_{k=1}^{l} a_{ik}b_{kj}.$$

The matrix–matrix product is thus defined only if the number of columns of $\mathbf{A}$ is the same as the number of rows of $\mathbf{B}$. We say that $\mathbf{A}$ premultiplies $\mathbf{B}$, or that $\mathbf{B}$ postmultiplies $\mathbf{A}$.

Scalar–matrix multiplication obeys a number of simple rules that hold for any matrix $\mathbf{A}$, and for scalars α and β, such as

$$\alpha(\beta\mathbf{A}) = (\alpha\beta)\mathbf{A}$$

$$\alpha\beta\mathbf{A} = \beta\alpha\mathbf{A},$$

all of which follow from the fact that our matrix operations reduce to scalar multiplications on the scalar elements of a matrix. For matrix–matrix addition, we have the **commutative** property. For any $n \times m$ matrices $\mathbf{A}$ and $\mathbf{B}$:

$$\mathbf{A} + \mathbf{B} = \mathbf{B} + \mathbf{A}.$$

We also have the **associative** property, which states that for any three $n \times m$ matrices $\mathbf{A}$, $\mathbf{B}$, and $\mathbf{C}$:

$$\mathbf{A} + (\mathbf{B} + \mathbf{C}) = (\mathbf{A} + \mathbf{B}) + \mathbf{C}.$$

Matrix–matrix multiplication, although associative,

$$\mathbf{A}(\mathbf{BC}) = (\mathbf{AB})\mathbf{C},$$

is almost never commutative. Not only is it almost always the case that $\mathbf{AB} \neq \mathbf{BA}$ but also one product may not even be defined when the other is. In graphics applications, where matrices represent transformations such as translation and rotation, these results express that the order in which you carry out a sequence of transformations is important. A rotation followed by a translation is not the same as a translation followed by a rotation. However, if we do a rotation followed by a translation followed by a scaling, we get the same result if we first combine the scaling and translation, preserving the order, and then apply the rotation to the combined transformation.

The identity matrix $\mathbf{I}$ is a square matrix with 1s on the diagonal and 0s elsewhere:

$$\mathbf{I} = [\, a_{ij} \,], \qquad a_{ij} = \begin{cases} 1 & \text{if } i = j \\ 0 & \text{otherwise.} \end{cases}$$

Assuming that the dimensions make sense,

$$\mathbf{AI} = \mathbf{A}$$
$$\mathbf{IB} = \mathbf{B}.$$

C.3 ROW AND COLUMN MATRICES

The $1 \times n$ and $n \times 1$ row and column matrices are of particular interest to us. We can represent either a vector or a point in three-dimensional space,[1] with respect to some frame, as the column matrix

$$\mathbf{p} = \begin{bmatrix} x \\ y \\ z \end{bmatrix}.$$

We use lowercase letters for column matrices. The transpose of $\mathbf{p}$ is the row matrix

$$\mathbf{p}^T = [\, x \quad y \quad z \,].$$

Because the product of an $n \times l$ and an $l \times m$ matrix is an $n \times m$ matrix, the product of a square matrix of dimension n and a column matrix of dimension n is a new column matrix of dimension n. Our standard mode of representing transformations of points is to use a column matrix of two, three, or four dimensions to represent

---

1. The homogeneous-coordinate representation introduced in Chapter 4 distinguishes between the representation of a point and the representation of a vector.

a point (or vector), and a square matrix to represent a transformation of the point (or vector). Thus, the expression

$$\mathbf{p}' = \mathbf{A}\mathbf{p}$$

yields the representation of a transformed point (or vector), and expressions such as

$$\mathbf{p}' = \mathbf{A}\mathbf{B}\mathbf{C}\mathbf{p}$$

describe sequences, or **concatenations**, of transformations. Note that because the matrix–matrix product is associative, we do not need parentheses in this expression.

Many computer graphics books prefer to use row matrices to represent points. If we do so, using the fact that the transpose of a product can be written as

$$(\mathbf{AB})^T = \mathbf{B}^T \mathbf{A}^T,$$

then the concatenation of the three transformations can be written in row form as

$$\mathbf{p}'^T = \mathbf{p}^T \mathbf{C}^T \mathbf{B}^T \mathbf{A}^T.$$

The professed advantage of this form is that, in English, we read the transformations in the order in which they are performed; first **C**, then **B**, then **A**. Almost all the scientific, mathematics, and engineering literature, however, uses column matrices rather than row matrices. Consequently, we prefer the column form. Although the choice is conceptually simple, in practice you have to be careful regarding which one your API is using, since not only is the order of transformations reversed but also the transformation matrices themselves must be transposed.

C.4 RANK

In computer graphics, the primary use of matrices is as representations of points and of transformations. If a square matrix represents the transformation of a point or vector, we are often interested in whether or not the transformation is reversible, or **invertible**. Thus, if

$$\mathbf{q} = \mathbf{A}\mathbf{p},$$

we want to know whether we can find a square matrix **B** such that

$$\mathbf{p} = \mathbf{B}\mathbf{q}.$$

Substituting for **q**,

$$\mathbf{p} = \mathbf{B}\mathbf{q} = \mathbf{B}\mathbf{A}\mathbf{p} = \mathbf{I}\mathbf{p} = \mathbf{p}$$

and

$$\mathbf{B}\mathbf{A} = \mathbf{I}.$$

If such a **B** exists, it is the **inverse** of **A**, and **A** is said to be **nonsingular**. A noninvertible matrix is **singular**. The inverse of **A** is written as $\mathbf{A}^{-1}$.

The fundamental result about inverses is as follows: *The inverse of a square matrix exists if and only if the determinant of the matrix is nonzero.* Although the determinant of **A** is a scalar, denoted by $|\mathbf{A}|$, its computation, for anything but low-dimensional matrices, requires almost as much work as does computation of the inverse. These calculations are $O(n^3)$ for an n-dimensional matrix. For the two-, three-, and four-dimensional matrices of interest in computer graphics, we can compute determinants by Cramer's rule and inverses using determinants, or we can use geometric reasoning. For example, the inverse of a translation is a translation back to the original location, and thus the inverse of a translation matrix must be a translation matrix. We pursued this course in Chapter 4.

For general nonsquare matrices, the concept of rank is important. We can regard a square matrix as a row matrix whose elements are column matrices or, equivalently, as a column matrix whose elements are row matrices. In terms of the vector-space concepts of Appendix B, the rows of an $n \times m$ matrix are elements of the Euclidean space $\mathbf{R}^m$, whereas the columns are elements of $\mathbf{R}^n$. We can determine how many rows (or columns) are **linearly independent**. The row (column) **rank** is the maximum number of linearly independent rows (columns), and thus *for an $n \times n$ matrix, the row rank and the column rank are the same and the matrix is nonsingular if and only if the rank is n*. Thus, a matrix is invertible if and only if its rows (and columns) are linearly independent.

C.5 CHANGE OF REPRESENTATION

We can use matrices to represent changes in bases for any set of vectors satisfying the rules of Appendix B. Suppose that we have a vector space of dimension n. Let $\{u_1, u_2, \ldots, u_n\}$ and $\{v_1, v_2, \ldots, v_n\}$ be two bases for the vector space. Hence, a given vector v can be expressed as either

$$v = \alpha_1 u_1 + \alpha_2 u_2 + \cdots + \alpha_n u_n$$

or

$$v = \beta_1 v_1 + \beta_2 v_2 + \cdots + \beta_n v_n.$$

Thus, $(\alpha_1, \alpha_2, \ldots, \alpha_n)$ and $(\beta_1, \beta_2, \ldots, \beta_n)$ are two different representations of v, and each can be expressed, equivalently, as a vector in the Euclidean space $\mathbf{R}^n$ or as a column matrix of dimension n. When we are working with representations rather than with the vectors, we have to be careful to make sure that our notation reflects the difference. We write the representations of v as either

$$\mathbf{v} = [\, \alpha_1 \quad \alpha_2 \quad \ldots \quad \alpha_n \,]^T$$

or

$$\mathbf{v}' = [\, \beta_1 \quad \beta_2 \quad \ldots \quad \beta_n \,]^T,$$

depending on which basis we use.

We can now address the problem of how we convert from the representation $\mathbf{v}$ to the representation $\mathbf{v}'$. The basis vectors $\{v_1, v_2, \ldots, v_n\}$ can be expressed as vectors in the basis $\{u_1, u_2, \ldots, u_n\}$. Thus, there exists a set of scalars γ_{ij} such that

$$u_i = \gamma_{i1}v_1 + \gamma_{i2}v_2 + \cdots + \gamma_{in}v_n, \quad i = 1, \ldots, n.$$

We can write the expression in matrix form for all u_i as

$$\begin{bmatrix} u_1 \\ u_2 \\ \vdots \\ u_n \end{bmatrix} = \mathbf{A} \begin{bmatrix} v_1 \\ v_2 \\ \vdots \\ v_n \end{bmatrix},$$

where $\mathbf{A}$ is the $n \times n$ matrix

$$\mathbf{A} = [\,\gamma_{ij}\,].$$

We can use column matrices to express both $\mathbf{v}$ and $\mathbf{v}'$ in terms of the vectors' representations as

$$\mathbf{v} = \mathbf{a}^T \begin{bmatrix} u_1 \\ u_2 \\ \vdots \\ u_n \end{bmatrix},$$

where

$$\mathbf{a} = [\,\alpha_i\,].$$

We can define $\mathbf{b}$ as

$$\mathbf{b} = [\,\beta_i\,],$$

and we can write $\mathbf{v}'$ as

$$\mathbf{v}' = \mathbf{b}^T \begin{bmatrix} v_1 \\ v_2 \\ \vdots \\ v_n \end{bmatrix}.$$

The matrix $\mathbf{A}$ relates the two bases, so we find by direct substitution that

$$\mathbf{b}^T = \mathbf{a}^T \mathbf{A}.$$

The matrix $\mathbf{A}$ is the **matrix representation** of the change between the two bases. It allows us to convert directly between the two representations. Equivalently, we can work with matrices of scalars rather than with abstract vectors. For geometric problems, although our vectors may be directed line segments, we can represent them by sets of scalars, and we can represent changes of bases or transformations by direct manipulation of these scalars.

C.6   THE CROSS PRODUCT

Given two nonparallel vectors, u and v, in a three-dimensional space, the cross product gives a third vector, w, that is orthogonal to both. Regardless of the representation, we must have

$$w \cdot u = w \cdot v = 0.$$

We can assign one component of w arbitrarily, because it is the direction of w, rather than the length, that is of importance, leaving us with three conditions for the three components of w. Within a particular coordinate system, if u has components $\alpha_1, \alpha_2, \alpha_3$ and v has components $\beta_1, \beta_2, \beta_3$, then, in this system, the **cross product** is defined as

$$\mathbf{w} = \mathbf{u} \times \mathbf{v} = \begin{bmatrix} \alpha_2\beta_3 - \alpha_3\beta_2 \\ \alpha_3\beta_1 - \alpha_1\beta_3 \\ \alpha_1\beta_2 - \alpha_2\beta_1 \end{bmatrix}.$$

Note that vector w is defined by u and v; we use their representation only when we wish to compute w in a particular coordinate system. The cross product gives a consistent orientation for $u \times v$. For example, consider the x-, y-, and z-axes as three vectors that determine the three coordinate directions of a right-handed coordinate system.[2] If we use the usual x- and y-axes, the cross product $x \times y$ points in the direction of the positive z-axis.

C.7   EIGENVALUES AND EIGENVECTORS

Square matrices are operators that transform column matrices into other column matrices of the same dimension. Because column matrices can represent points and vectors, we are interested in questions such as, when does a transformation leave a point or vector unchanged? For example, every rotation matrix leaves a particular point—the fixed point—unchanged. Let's consider a slightly more general problem. When does the matrix equation

$$\mathbf{Mu} = \lambda\mathbf{u}$$

have a nontrivial solution for some scalar λ, that is, a solution with $\mathbf{u}$ not being a matrix of zeros? If such a solution exists, then $\mathbf{M}$ transforms certain vectors $\mathbf{u}$—its **eigenvectors**—into scalar multiples of themselves. The values of λ for which this relationship holds are called the **eigenvalues** of the matrix. Eigenvalues and eigenvectors are also called **characteristic values** and **characteristic vectors**, respectively. These

---

2. A right-handed coordinate system has positive directions determined by the thumb, index finger, and middle finger of the right hand used for the x-, y-, and z-axes, respectively. Equivalently, on a piece of paper, if positive x points left to right and positive y points bottom to top, then positive z points out of the page.

values characterize many properties of the matrix that are invariant under such operations as changes in representation.

We can find the eigenvalues by solving the equivalent matrix equation

$$\mathbf{Mu} - \lambda\mathbf{u} = \mathbf{Mu} - \lambda\mathbf{Iu} = (\mathbf{M} - \lambda\mathbf{I})\mathbf{u} = \mathbf{0}.$$

This equation can have a nontrivial solution if and only if the determinant[3]

$$|\mathbf{M} - \lambda\mathbf{I}| = 0.$$

If $\mathbf{M}$ is $n \times n$, then the determinant yields a polynomial of degree n in λ. Thus, there are n roots, some of which may be repeated or complex. For each distinct eigenvalue, we can then find a corresponding eigenvector. Note that every multiple of an eigenvector is itself an eigenvector, so that we can choose an eigenvector with unit magnitude. Eigenvectors corresponding to distinct eigenvalues are linearly independent. Thus, if all the eigenvalues are distinct, then any set of eigenvectors corresponding to the distinct eigenvalues form a basis for an n-dimensional vector space.

If there are repeated eigenvalues, the situation can be more complex. However, we need not worry about these cases for the matrices we will use in graphics. Thus, if $\mathbf{R}$ is a 3×3 rotation matrix and $\mathbf{p} = [\,x \quad y \quad z\,]^T$ is the fixed point, then

$$\mathbf{Rp} = \mathbf{p}.$$

Thus, every rotation matrix must have an eigenvalue of 1. This result is the same whether we work in three dimensions or use the four-dimensional homogeneous-coordinate representation in Chapter 4.

Suppose that $\mathbf{T}$ is a nonsingular matrix. Consider the matrix

$$\mathbf{Q} = \mathbf{T}^{-1}\mathbf{MT}.$$

Its eigenvalues and eigenvectors are solutions of the equation

$$\mathbf{Qv} = \mathbf{T}^{-1}\mathbf{MTv} = \lambda\mathbf{v}.$$

But if we multiply by $\mathbf{T}$, this equation becomes

$$\mathbf{MTv} = \lambda\mathbf{Tv}.$$

Thus, the eigenvalues of $\mathbf{Q}$ are the same as those of $\mathbf{M}$, and the eigenvectors are the transformations of the eigenvectors of $\mathbf{M}$. The matrices $\mathbf{M}$ and $\mathbf{Q}$ are said to be **similar**. Many of the transformations that arise in computer graphics involve similar matrices. One interpretation of this result is that changes of coordinate systems leave fundamental properties, such as the eigenvalues, unchanged. If we can find a similarity transformation that converts $\mathbf{M}$ to a diagonal matrix $\mathbf{Q}$, then the diagonal elements of $\mathbf{Q}$ are the eigenvalues of both matrices.

---

3. The general statement, known as the Fredholm alternative, states that the n linear equations in n unknowns $\mathbf{Ax} = \mathbf{b}$ have a unique solution if and only if $|\mathbf{A}| \neq 0$. If $|\mathbf{A}| = 0$, there are multiple nontrivial solutions.

Eigenvalues and eigenvectors have a geometric interpretation. Consider an ellipsoid, centered at the origin, with its axes aligned with the coordinate axes. It can be written as

$$\lambda_1 x^2 + \lambda_2 y^2 + \lambda_3 z^2 = 1$$

for positive values of λ_1, λ_2, and λ_3, or in matrix form,

$$\begin{bmatrix} x & y & z \end{bmatrix} \begin{bmatrix} \lambda_1 & 0 & 0 \\ 0 & \lambda_2 & 0 \\ 0 & 0 & \lambda_3 \end{bmatrix} \begin{bmatrix} x \\ y \\ z \end{bmatrix} = 1.$$

Thus, λ_1, λ_2, and λ_3 are both the eigenvalues of the diagonal matrix and the inverses of the lengths of the major and minor axes of the ellipsoid. If we apply a change of coordinate system through a rotation matrix, we create a new ellipsoid that is no longer aligned with the coordinate axes. However, we have not changed the lengths of the axes of the ellipse, a property that is invariant under coordinate system changes.

C.8   VECTOR AND MATRIX OBJECTS

Although we have avoided using the term *vector* for matrices of one row or one column, much of the literature prefers to use *vector* for such matrices. More problematic for this book has been that GLSL uses *vector* this way. Consequently, we created separate vector and matrix JavaScript objects to use with our examples. These objects are defined in the file `MV.js` that is used in all the examples.

`MV.js` defines separate `vec2`, `vec3`, and `vec4` types for one-, two-, and three-dimensional vectors. It includes arithmetic functions for these types and the usual constructors to create them and work with multiple types in a single application. The objects are for general vectors of these dimensions and are not specialized for homogeneous coordinates. We also include the standard functions for normalization, cross products, dot products, and length.

`MV.js` supports two-, three-, and four-dimensional square matrices (`mat2`, `mat3`, and `mat4`) and the standard arithmetic functions to support their manipulation and operations between vectors and matrices. We also included many of the functions that were in earlier versions of OpenGL and have been deprecated. These include most of the transformation and viewing functions. In most cases, we used the same names as did OpenGL, for example, `rotate`, `scale`, `translate`, `ortho`, `frustum`, `lookAt`.

SUGGESTED READINGS

Some of the standard references on linear algebra and matrices include Strang [Str93] and Banchoff and Werner [Ban83]. See also Rogers and Adams [Rog90] and the *Graphics Gems* series [Gra90, Gra91, Gra92, Gra94, Gra95].

The issue of row versus column matrices is an old one. Early computer graphics books [New73] used row matrices. The trend now is to use column matrices [Fol90], although a few books still use row representations [Wat00]. Within the API, it may not be clear which is being used, because the elements of a square matrix can be represented as a simple array of n^2 elements. Certain APIs, such as OpenGL, allow only postmultiplication of an internal matrix by a user-defined matrix; others, such as PHIGS, support both pre- and postmultiplication.

EXERCISES

C.1   In $\mathbf{R}^3$, consider the two bases $\{(1, 0, 0), (1, 1, 0), (1, 1, 1)\}$ and $\{(1, 0, 0), (0, 1, 0), (0, 0, 1)\}$. Find the two matrices that convert representations between the two bases. Show that they are inverses of each other.

C.2   Consider the vector space of polynomials of degree up to 2. Show that the sets of polynomials $\{1, x, x^2\}$ and $\{1, 1 + x, 1 + x + x^2\}$ are bases. Give the representation of the polynomial $1 + 2x + 3x^2$ in each basis. Find the matrix that converts between representations in the two bases.

C.3   Suppose that $\mathbf{i}$, $\mathbf{j}$, and $\mathbf{k}$ represent the unit vectors in the x, y, and z directions, respectively, in $\mathbf{R}^3$. Show that the cross product $u \times v$ is given by the matrix

$$u \times v = \begin{vmatrix} \mathbf{i} & \mathbf{j} & \mathbf{k} \\ u_1 & u_2 & u_3 \\ v_1 & v_2 & v_3 \end{vmatrix}.$$

C.4   Show that, in $\mathbf{R}^3$,

$$|u \times v| = |u||v|| \sin \theta|,$$

where θ is the angle between u and v.

C.5   Find the eigenvalues and eigenvectors of the two-dimensional rotation matrix

$$\mathbf{R} = \begin{bmatrix} \cos \theta & -\sin \theta \\ \sin \theta & \cos \theta \end{bmatrix}.$$

C.6   Find the eigenvalues and eigenvectors of the three-dimensional rotation matrix

$$\mathbf{R} = \begin{bmatrix} \cos \theta & -\sin \theta & 0 \\ \sin \theta & \cos \theta & 0 \\ 0 & 0 & 1 \end{bmatrix}.$$

SAMPLING AND ALIASING

We have seen a variety of applications in which the conversion from a continuous representation of an entity to a discrete approximation of that entity leads to visible errors in the display. We have used the term *aliasing* to characterize these errors. When we work with buffers, we are always working with digital images, and, if we are not careful, these errors can be extreme. In this section, we examine the nature of digital images and gather facts that will help us to understand where aliasing errors arise and how the effects of these errors can be mitigated.

We start with a continuous two-dimensional image $f(x, y)$. We can regard the value of f as either a gray level in a monochromatic image or the value of one of the primaries in a color image. In the computer, we work with a digital image that is an array of nm pixels arranged as n rows of m pixels. Each pixel has k bits. There are two processes involved in going from a continuous image to a discrete image. First, we must **sample** the continuous image at nm points on some grid to obtain a set of values $\{f_{ij}\}$. Each of these samples of the continuous image is the value of f measured over a small area in the continuous image. Then, we must convert each of these samples into a k-bit pixel by a process known as **quantization.**

D.1 SAMPLING THEORY

Suppose that we have a rectangular grid of locations where we wish to obtain our samples of f, as in Figure D.1. If we assume that the grid is equally spaced, then an ideal sampler would produce a value

$$f_{ij} = f(x_0 + ih_x, y_0 + jh_y),$$

where h_x and h_y are the distances between the grid points in the x and y directions, respectively. Leaving aside for now the fact that no real sampler can make such a precise measurement, there are two important questions. First, what errors have we made in this idealized sampling process? That is, how much of the information in the original image is included in the sampled image? Second, can we go back from the digital image to a continuous image without incurring additional errors? This latter step is called **reconstruction** and describes display processes such as are required in displaying the contents of a framebuffer on a monitor.

FIGURE D.1   Sampling grid.

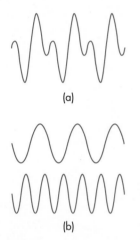

(a)

(b)

FIGURE D.2   One-dimensional decomposition. (a) Function. (b) Components.

The mathematical analysis of these issues uses Fourier analysis, a branch of applied mathematics particularly well suited for explaining problems of digital signal processing. The essence of Fourier theory is that a function, of either space or time, can be decomposed into a set of sinusoids, at possibly an infinite number of frequencies. This concept is most familiar with sound, where we routinely think of a particular sound in terms of its frequency components, or **spectrum**. For a two-dimensional image, we can think of it as being composed of sinusoidal patterns in two spatial frequencies that, when added together, produce the image. Figure D.2(a) shows a one-dimensional function; Figure D.2(b) shows the two sinusoids that form it. Figure D.3 shows two-dimensional periodic functions. Thus, every two-dimensional spatial function $f(x, y)$ has two equivalent representations. One is its spatial form $f(x, y)$; the other is a representation in terms of its spectrum—the frequency domain representation $g(\xi, \eta)$. The value of g is the contribution to f at the two-dimensional spatial frequency (ξ, η). By using these alternate representations of functions, we find that many phenomena, including sampling, can be explained much more easily in the frequency domain.

We can explain the consequences of sampling, without being overwhelmed by the mathematics, if we accept, without proof, the fundamental theorem known as the Nyquist sampling theorem. There are two parts to the theorem: The first allows us to discuss sampling errors, whereas the second governs reconstruction. We examine the second in Section D.2.

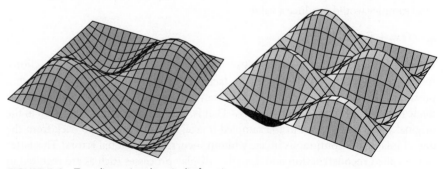

FIGURE D.3   Two-dimensional periodic functions.

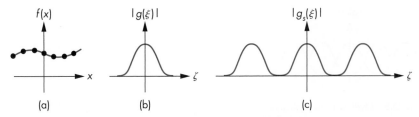

FIGURE D.4   Band-limited function. (a) Function and its samples in the spatial domain. (b) Spectrum of the function. (c) Spectrum of the samples.

Nyquist sampling theorem (part 1): The ideal samples of a continuous function contain all the information in the original function if and only if the continuous function is sampled at a frequency greater than twice the highest frequency in the function.

Thus, if we are to have any chance of not losing information, we must restrict ourselves to functions that are zero in the frequency domain except in a window of width less than the sampling frequency, centered at the origin. The lowest frequency that cannot be in the data so as to avoid aliasing—one-half of the sampling frequency—is called the **Nyquist frequency**. Functions whose spectra are zero outside of some window are known as **band-limited** functions. For a two-dimensional image, the sampling frequencies are determined by the spacing of a two-dimensional grid with x and y spacing of $1/h_x$ and $1/h_y$, respectively. The theorem assumes an ideal sampling process that gathers an infinite number of samples, each of which is the exact value at the grid point. In practice, we can take only a finite number of samples—the number matching the resolution of our buffer. Consequently, we cannot produce a truly band-limited function. Although this result is a mathematical consequence of Fourier theory, we can observe that there will always be some ambiguity inherent in a finite collection of sampled points, simply because we do not know the function outside the region from which we obtained the samples.[1]

The consequences of violating the Nyquist criteria are aliasing errors. We can see where the name *aliasing* comes from by considering an ideal sampling process. Both the original function and its set of samples have frequency domain representations. The spectral components of the sampled function are replicas of the spectrum of the original function, with their centers separated by the sampling frequency. Consider the one-dimensional function in Figure D.4(a), with the samples indicated. Figure D.4(b) shows its spectrum; in Figure D.4(c), we have the spectrum of the sampled function, showing the replications of the spectrum in Figure D.4(b).[2] Because

---

1. This statement assumes no knowledge of the underlying function f, other than a set of its samples. If we have additional information, such as knowledge that the function is periodic, knowledge of the function over a finite interval can be sufficient to determine the entire function.

2. We show the magnitude of the spectrum because the Fourier transform produces complex numbers for the frequency domain components.

FIGURE D.5   Overlapping replicas.

FIGURE D.6   Aliasing.

we have sampled at a rate higher than the Nyquist frequency, there is a separation between the replicas.

Now consider the case in Figure D.5. Here we have violated the Nyquist criterion, and the replicas overlap. Consider the central part of the plot, which is magnified in Figure D.6 and shows only the central replica, centered at the origin, and the replica to its right, centered at ξ_s. The frequency ξ_0 is above the Nyquist frequency $\xi_s/2$. There is, however, a replica of ξ_0, generated by the sampling process from the replica on the right, at $\xi_s - \xi_0$, a frequency less than the Nyquist frequency. The energy at this frequency can be heard, if we are dealing with digital sound, or seen, if we are considering two-dimensional images. We say that the frequency ξ_0 has an **alias** at $\xi_s - \xi_0$. Note that once aliasing has occurred, we cannot distinguish between information that was at a frequency in the original data and information that was placed at this frequency by the sampling process.

We can demonstrate aliasing and ambiguity without using Fourier analysis by looking at a single sinusoid, as shown in Figure D.7. If we sample this sinusoid at twice its frequency, we can recover it from two samples. However, these same two samples are samples of a sinusoid of twice this frequency, and they can also be samples of sinusoids of other multiples of the basic frequency. All these frequencies are aliases of the same original frequency. If we know that the data are band limited, however, then the samples can describe only the original sinusoid.

If we were to do an analysis of the frequency content of real-world images, we would find that the spectral components of most images are concentrated in the lower frequencies. Consequently, although it is impossible to construct a finite-sized image that is band limited, the aliasing errors often are minimal because there is little content in frequencies above the Nyquist frequency, and little content is aliased into frequencies below the Nyquist frequency. The exceptions to this statement arise when there is regular (periodic) information in the continuous image. In the frequency representation, regularity places most of the information at a few frequencies. If any

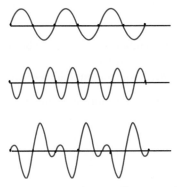

FIGURE D.7 Aliasing of a sinusoid.

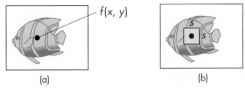

FIGURE D.8 Scanning of an image.
(a) Point sampling. (b) Area averaging.

of these frequencies is above the Nyquist limit, the aliasing effect is noticeable as beat or moiré patterns. Examples that you might have noticed include the patterns that appear on video displays when people in the images wear striped shirts or plaid ties, and wavy patterns that arise both in printed (halftoned) figures derived from computer displays and in digital images of farmland with plowed fields.

Often, we can minimize aliasing by prefiltering before we scan an image or by controlling the area of the data that the scanner uses to measure a sample. Figure D.8 shows two possible ways to scan an image. In Figure D.8(a), we see an ideal scanner. It measures the value of a continuous image at a point, so the samples are given by

$$f_{ij} = f(x_i, y_i).$$

In Figure D.8(b), we have a more realistic scanner that obtains samples by taking a weighted average over a small interval to produce samples of the form

$$f_{ij} = \int_{x_i - s/2}^{x_i + s/2} \int_{y_i - s/2}^{y_i + s/2} f(x, y) w(x, y) \, dy \, dx.$$

By selecting the size of the window s and the weighting function w, we can attenuate high-frequency components in the image and thus we can reduce aliasing. Fortunately, real scanners must take measurements over a finite region, called the **sampling aperture**; thus, some antialiasing takes place even if the user has no understanding of the aliasing problem.

D.2   RECONSTRUCTION

Suppose that we have an (infinite) set of samples, the members of which have been sampled at a rate greater than the Nyquist frequency. The reconstruction of a continuous function from the samples is based on part 2 of the Nyquist sampling theorem.

Nyquist sampling theorem (part 2): We can reconstruct a continuous function $f(x)$ from its samples $\{f_i\}$ by the formula

$$f(x) = \sum_{i=-\infty}^{\infty} f_i \, \mathrm{sinc}(x - x_i).$$

The function $\mathrm{sinc}(x)$ (see Figure D.9) is defined as

$$\mathrm{sinc}(x) = \frac{\sin \pi x}{\pi x}.$$

The two-dimensional version of the reconstruction formula for a function $f(x, y)$ with ideal samples $\{f_{ij}\}$ is

$$f(x, y) = \sum_{i=-\infty}^{\infty} \sum_{j=-\infty}^{\infty} f_{ij} \mathrm{sinc}(x - x_i) \, \mathrm{sinc}(y - y_j).$$

These formulas follow from the fact that we can recover an unaliased function in the frequency domain by using a filter that is zero except in the interval $(-\xi_s/2, \xi_s/2)$—a low-pass filter—to obtain a single replica from the infinite number of replicas generated by the sampling process shown in Figure D.4. The reconstruction of a one-dimensional function is shown in Figure D.10. In two dimensions, the reconstruction involves the use of a two-dimensional sinc, as shown in Figure D.11. Unfortunately, the sinc function cannot be produced in a physical display, because of its negative side lobes. Consider the display problem for a CRT display. We start with a digital image that is a set of samples. For each sample, we can place a spot of light

FIGURE D.9   Sinc function.

FIGURE D.10   One-dimensional reconstruction.

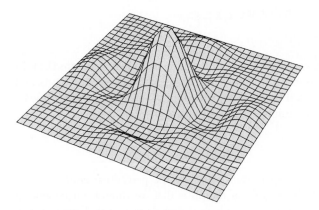

FIGURE D.11   Two-dimensional sinc function.

centered at a grid point on the display surface, as shown in Figure D.12. The value of the sample controls the intensity of the spot, or modulates the beam. We can control the shape of the spot by using techniques such as focusing the beam. The reconstruction formula tells us that the beam should have the shape of a two-dimensional sinc, but because the beam puts out energy, the spot must be nonnegative at all points. Consequently, the display process must produce errors. We can evaluate a real display by considering how well its spot approximates the desired sinc. Figure D.13 shows the sinc and several one-dimensional approximations. The Gaussian-shaped spot corresponds to the shape of many CRT spots, whereas the rectangular spot might correspond to an LCD display with square pixels. Note that we can make either approximation wider or narrower. If we analyze the spot profiles in the frequency domain, we find that the wider spots are more accurate at low frequencies but are less accurate at higher frequencies. In practice, the spot size that we choose is a compromise. Visible differences across monitors often can be traced to different spot profiles.

FIGURE D.12   Display of a point on a CRT.

FIGURE D.13   Display spots. (a) Ideal spot. (b) Rectangular approximation.
(c) Piecewise linear approximation. (d) Gaussian approximation.

D.3   QUANTIZATION

The mathematical analysis of sampling explains a number of important effects. However, we have not included the effect of each sample being quantized into k discrete levels. Given a scalar function g with values in the range

$$g_{min} \le g \le g_{max},$$

a **quantizer** is a function q such that, if $g_i \le g \le g_{i+1}$,

$$q(g) = q_i.$$

Thus, for each value of g, we assign it one of k values, as shown in Figure D.14. In general, designing a quantizer involves choosing the $\{q_i\}$, the quantization levels, and the $\{g_i\}$, the threshold values. If we know the probability distribution for g, $p(g)$, we can solve for the values that minimize the mean square error:

$$e = \int (g - q(g))^2 p(g)\, dg.$$

However, we often design quantizers based on the perceptual issues that we discussed in Chapter 1. A simple rule of thumb is that we should not be able to detect one-level changes, but should be able to detect all two-level changes. Given the threshold for the visual system to detect a change in luminance, we usually need at least 7 or 8 bits (or 128 to 256 levels). We should also consider the logarithmic intensity-brightness response of humans. To do so, we usually distribute the levels exponentially, to give approximately equal perceptual errors as we go from one level to the next.

FIGURE D.14   Quantizer.

REFERENCES

Ado85   Adobe Systems Incorporated, *PostScript Language Reference Manual*, Addison-Wesley, Reading, MA, 1985.

Ake88   Akeley, K., and T. Jermoluk, "High Performance Polygon Rendering," *Computer Graphics*, 22(4), 239–246, 1988.

Ake93   Akeley, K., "Reality Engine Graphics," *Computer Graphics*, 109–116, 1993.

Ang90   Angel, E., *Computer Graphics*, Addison-Wesley, Reading, MA, 1990.

Ang08   Angel, E., *OpenGL: A Primer,* Third Edition, Addison-Wesley, Reading, MA, 2008.

Ang12   Angel, E., and D. Shreiner, *Interactive Computer Graphics*, Sixth Edition, Addison-Wesley, Boston, MA, 2012.

ANSI85 American National Standards Institute (ANSI), *American National Standard for Information Processing Systems—Computer Graphics—Graphical Kernel System (GKS) Functional Description,* ANSI, X3.124-1985, ANSI, New York, 1985.

ANSI88 American National Standards Institute (ANSI), *American National Standard for Information Processing Systems—Programmer's Hierarchical Interactive Graphics System (PHIGS),* ANSI, X3.144-1988, ANSI, New York, 1988.

App68   Appel, A., "Some Techniques for Shading Machine Renderings of Solids," *Spring Joint Computer Conference,* 37–45, 1968.

Arn96   Arnold, K., and J. Gosling, *The Java Programming Language,* Addison-Wesley, Reading, MA, 1996.

Bai12   Bailey, M., and S. Cunningham, *Graphics Shaders*, Second Edition, CRC Press, Boca Ration, FL, 2012.

Ban83   Banchoff, T., and J. Werner, *Linear Algebra Through Geometry,* Springer-Verlag, New York, 1983.

Bar83   Barsky, B.A., and C. Beatty, "Local Control of Bias and Tension in Beta-Splines," *ACM Transactions on Graphics,* 2(2), 109–134, 1983.

Bar87   Bartels, R.H., C. Beatty, and B.A. Barsky, *An Introduction to Splines for Use in Computer Graphics and Geometric Modeling*, Morgan Kaufmann, Los Altos, CA, 1987.

Bar93   Barnsley, M., *Fractals Everywhere,* Second Edition, Academic Press, San Diego, CA, 1993.

Bli76   Blinn, J.F., and M.E. Newell, "Texture and Reflection in Computer Generated Images," *CACM,* 19(10), 542–547, 1976.

Bli77   Blinn, J.F., "Models of Light Reflection for Computer-Synthesized Pictures," *Computer Graphics,* 11(2), 192–198, 1977.

Bli88   Blinn, J.F., "Me and My (Fake) Shadow," *IEEE Computer Graphics and Applications,* 9(1), 82–86, January 1988.

Bow83   Bowyer, A., and J. Woodwark, *A Programmer's Geometry*, Butterworth, London, 1983.

Bre65   Bresenham, J.E., "Algorithm for Computer Control of a Digital Plotter," *IBM Systems Journal*, 25–30, January 1965.

Bre87   Bresenham, J.E., "Ambiguities in Incremental Line Rastering," *IEEE Computer Graphics and Applications*, 31–43, May 1987.

Can12   Cantor, D., and B. Jones, *WebGL Beginner's Guide,* PACKT, Birmingham, UK, 2012.

Car78   Carlbom, I., and J. Paciorek, "Planar Geometric Projection and Viewing Transformations," *Computing Surveys*, 10(4), 465–502, 1978.

Cas96   Castleman, K.C., *Digital Image Processing,* Prentice-Hall, Englewood Cliffs, NJ, 1996.

Cat78a   Catmull, E., "A Hidden-Surface Algorithm with Antialiasing," *Computer Graphics*, 12(3), 6–11, 1978.

Cat78b   Catmull, E., and J. Clark, "Recursively Generated B-Spline Surfaces on Arbitrary Topological Meshes," *Proceedings of Computer-Aided Design, 10*, 350–355, 1978.

Cha98   Chan, P., and R. Lee, *The Java Class Libraries: Java.Applet, Java.Awt, Java.Beans* (Vol. 2), Addison-Wesley, Reading, MA, 1998.

Che95   Chen, S.E., "QuickTime VR: An Image-Based Approach to Virtual Environment Navigation," *Computer Graphics*, 29–38, 1995.

Che00   Chen, K.L. et al., "Building and Using a Scalable Display Wall System," *IEEE Computer Graphics and Applications*, 20(4), 29–37, 2000.

Cla82   Clark, J.E., "The Geometry Engine: A VLSI Geometry System for Graphics," *Computer Graphics*, 16, 127–133, 1982.

Coh85   Cohen, M.F., and D.P. Greenberg, "The Hemi-Cube: A Radiosity Solution for Complex Environments," *Computer Graphics,* 19(3), 31–40, 1985.

Coh88   Cohen, M.F., S.E. Chen, J.R. Wallace, and D.P. Greenberg, "A Progressive Refinement Approach to Fast Radiosity Image Generation," *Computer Graphics*, 22(4), 75–84, 1988.

Coh93   Cohen, M.F., and J.R. Wallace, *Radiosity and Realistic Image Synthesis*, Academic Press Professional, Boston, MA, 1993.

Col01   Colella, V.S., E. Klopfer, and M. Resnick, *Adventures in Modeling: Exploring Complex, Dynamic Systems with StarLogo*, Teachers College Press, Columbia University, NY, 2001.

Coo82   Cook, R.L., and K.E. Torrance, "A Reflectance Model for Computer Graphics," *ACM Transactions on Graphics*, 1(1), 7–24, 1982.

Coo87   Cook, R.L., L. Carpenter, and E. Catmull, "The Reyes Image Rendering Architecture," *Computer Graphics*, 21(4), 95–102, July 1987.

Coo12   Cook, S., *CUDA Programming: A Developer's Guide to Parallel Computing with GPUs (Applications of GPU Computing Series)*, Morgan Kaufmann, San Francisco, 2012.

Coz12   Cozzi, P., and C. Ricchio (Eds.), *OpenGL Insights*, CRC Press, Boca Raton, FL, 2012.

Cro81   Crow, F.C., "A Comparison of Antialiasing Techniques," *IEEE Computer Graphics and Applications*, 1(1), 40–48, 1981.

Cro97   Crossno, P.J., and E. Angel, "Isosurface Extraction Using Particle Systems," *IEEE Visualization*, 1997.

Cro08   Crockford, D., *JavaScript: The Good Parts*, O'Reilly, Sebastopol, CA, 2008.

Deb96   Debevec, P.E., C.J. Taylor, and J. Malik, "Modeling and Rendering Architecture from Photographs: A Hybrid Geometry- and Image-Based Approach," *Computer Graphics*, 11–20, 1996.

deB08   de Berg, M., O. Cheong, M. van Kreveld, and M. Overmars, *Computational Geometry, Third Edition*, Springer-Verlag, Berlin Heidelberg, 2008.

DeR88   DeRose, T.D., "A Coordinate-Free Approach to Geometric Programming," SIGGRAPH Course Notes, *SIGGRAPH*, 1988.

DeR89   DeRose, T.D., "A Coordinate-Free Approach to Geometric Programming," in *Theory and Practice of Geometric Modeling*, W. Strasser and H.P. Seidel (Eds.), Springer-Verlag, Berlin, 1989.

Dre88   Drebin, R.A., L. Carpenter, and P. Hanrahan, "Volume Rendering," *Computer Graphics*, 22(4), 65–74, 1988.

Duc11   Duckett, J., *HTML & CSS*, Wiley, Indianapolis, IN, 2011.

Ebe01   Eberly, D.H., *3D Game Engine Design*, Morgan Kaufmann, San Francisco, 2001.

Ebe02   Ebert, D., F.K. Musgrave, D. Peachey, K. Perlin, and S. Worley, *Texturing and Modeling, A Procedural Approach*, Third Edition, Morgan Kaufmann, San Francisco, 2002.

Eld00   Eldridge, M., I. Homan, and P. Hanrahan, "Pomegranate, A Fully Scalable, Graphics Architecture," *Computer Graphics*, 11(6), 290–296, 2000.

End84   Enderle, G., K. Kansy, and G. Pfaff, *Computer Graphics Programming: GKS—The Graphics Standard*, Springer-Verlag, Berlin, 1984.

Far88   Farin, G., *Curves and Surfaces for Computer Aided Geometric Design*, Academic Press, New York, 1988.

Fau80   Faux, I.D., and M.J. Pratt, *Computational Geometry for Design and Manufacturing*, Halsted, Chichester, England, 1980.

Fer03   Fernando, R., and M.J. Kilgard, *The Cg Tutorial: The Definitive Guide to Programmable Real-Time Graphics*, Addison-Wesley, Reading, MA, 2003.

Fer04   Fernando, R., *GPU Gems: Programming Techniques, Tips, and Tricks for Real-Time Graphics*, Addison-Wesley, Reading, MA, 2004.

Fla11   Flanagan, D., *JavaScript, The Definitive Guide*, Sixth Edition, O'Reilly, Sebastopol, CA, 2011.

Fol90   Foley, J.D., A. van Dam, S.K. Feiner, and J.F. Hughes, *Computer Graphics*, Second Edition, Addison-Wesley, Reading, MA, 1990 (C Version 1996).

Fol94   Foley, J.D., A. van Dam, S.K. Feiner, J.F. Hughes, and R. Phillips, *Introduction to Computer Graphics,* Addison-Wesley, Reading, MA, 1994.

Fos97   Fosner, R., *OpenGL Programming for Windows 95 and Windows NT,* Addison-Wesley, Reading, MA, 1997.

Fou82   Fournier, A., D. Fussell, and L. Carpenter, "Computer Rendering of Stochastic Models," *CACM*, 25(6), 371–384, 1982.

Fuc77   Fuchs, H., J. Duran, and B. Johnson, "A System for Automatic Acquisition of Three-Dimensional Data," *Proceedings of the 1977 NCC*, AFIPS Press, 49–53, Montvale, NJ, 1977.

Fuc80   Fuchs, H., Z.M. Kedem, and B.F. Naylor, "On Visible Surface Generation by a Priori Tree Structures," *SIGGRAPH 80*, 124–133, 1980.

Gal95   Gallagar, R.S., *Computer Visualization: Graphics Techniques for Scientific and Engineering Analysis*, CRC Press, Boca Raton, FL, 1995.

Gla89   Glassner, A.S. (Ed.), *An Introduction to Ray Tracing,* Academic Press, New York, 1989.

Gla95   Glassner, A.S., *Principles of Digital Image Synthesis,* Morgan Kaufmann, San Francisco, 1995.

Gon08   Gonzalez, R., and R.E. Woods, *Digital Image Processing*, Third Edition, Addison-Wesley, Reading, MA, 2008.

Gor84   Goral, C.M., K.E. Torrance, D.P. Greenberg, and B. Battaile, "Modeling the Interaction of Light Between Diffuse Surfaces," *Computer Graphics (SIGGRAPH 84)*, 18(3), 213–222, 1984.

Gor96   Gortler, S.J., R. Grzeszczuk, R. Szeliski, and M.F. Cohen, "The Lumigraph," *Computer Graphics*, 43–54, 1996.

Gou71   Gouraud, H., "Computer Display of Curved Surfaces," *IEEE Trans. Computers,* C-20, 623–628, 1971.

Gra90   *Graphics Gems I*, Glassner, A.S. (Ed.), Academic Press, San Diego, CA, 1990.

Gra91   *Graphics Gems II*, Arvo, J. (Ed.), Academic Press, San Diego, CA, 1991.

Gra92   *Graphics Gems III*, Kirk, D. (Ed.), Academic Press, San Diego, CA, 1992.

Gra94   *Graphics Gems IV*, Heckbert, P. (Ed.), Academic Press, San Diego, CA, 1994.

Gra95   *Graphics Gems V*, Paeth, A. (Ed.), Academic Press, San Diego, CA, 1995.

Gra03   Gray, K., *The Microsoft DirectX 9 Programmable Graphics Pipeline*, Microsoft Press, 2003.

Gre88   Greengard, L.F., *The Rapid Evolution of Potential Fields in Particle Systems,* MIT Press, Cambridge, MA, 1988.

Hal89   Hall, R., *Illumination and Color in Computer Generated Imagery,* Springer-Verlag, New York, 1989.

Har96   Hartman, J., and J. Wernecke, *The VRML 2.0 Handbook*, Addison-Wesley, Reading, MA, 1996.

Hea11   Hearn, D., M.P. Baker, and W.R. Carithers, *Computer Graphics*, Fourth Edition, Prentice-Hall, Englewood Cliffs, NJ, 2011.

Hec84   Heckbert, P.S., and P. Hanrahan, "Beam Tracing Polygonal Objects," *Computer Graphics,* 18(3), 119–127, 1984.

Hec86   Heckbert, P.S., "Survey of Texture Mapping," *IEEE Computer Graphics and Applications,* 6(11), 56–67, 1986.

Her79   Herman, G.T., and H.K. Liu, "Three-Dimensional Display of Human Organs from Computed Tomograms," *Computer Graphics and Image Processing,* 9, 1–21, 1979.

Her00   Hereld, M., I.R. Judson, and R.L. Stevens, "Tutorial: Introduction to Building Projection-Based Tiled Display Systems," *IEEE Computer Graphics and Applications*, 20(4), 22–26, 2000.

Hes99   Hestenes, D., *New Foundations for Classical Mechanics (Fundamental Theories of Physics)*, Second Edition, Kluwer Academic Publishers, Dordrecht, the Netherlands, 1999.

Hil07   Hill, Jr., F.S., and S.M. Kelley, *Computer Graphics*, Third Edition, Prentice Hall, Upper Saddle River, NJ, 2007.

Hop83   Hopgood, F.R.A., D.A. Duce, J.A. Gallop, and D.C. Sutcliffe, *Introduction to the Graphical Kernel System: GKS*, Academic Press, London, 1983.

Hop91   Hopgood, F.R.A., and D.A. Duce, *A Primer for PHIGS*, John Wiley & Sons, Chichester, England, 1991.

Hug13   Hughes, J.F., A. van Dam, M. McGuire, D. Sklar, J.D. Foley, S.K. Feiner, K. Akeley, *Computer Graphics: Principles and Practice*, Third Edition, Addison-Wesley, Boston, MA, 2013.

Hum01   Humphreys, G., M. Eldridge, I. Buck, G. Stoll, M. Everett, and P. Hanrahan, "WireGL: A Scalable Graphics System for Clusters," *SIGGRAPH 2001*, 129–140, 2001.

ISO88   International Standards Organization, *International Standard Information Processing Systems—Computer Graphics—Graphical Kernel System for Three Dimensions (GKS-3D)*, ISO Document Number 8805:1988(E), American National Standards Institute, New York, 1988.

Jar76   Jarvis, J.F., C.N. Judice, and W.H. Ninke, "A Survey of Techniques for the Image Display of Continuous Tone Pictures on Bilevel Displays," *Computer Graphics and Image Processing,* 5(1), 13–40, 1976.

Jen01   Jensen, H.W., "Realistic Image Synthesis Using Photon Mapping," A K Peters, Wellesley, MA, 2001.

Joy88   Joy, K.I., C.W. Grant, N.L. Max, and L. Hatfield, *Computer Graphics: Image Synthesis*, Computer Society Press, Washington, DC, 1988.

Kaj86   Kajiya, J.T., "The Rendering Equation," *Computer Graphics*, 20(4), 143–150, 1986.

Kel97   Keller, H., "Instant Radiosity," *SIGGRAPH 97*, 49–56, 1997.

Kil94a   Kilgard, M.J., "OpenGL and X, Part 3: Integrated OpenGL with Motif," *The X Journal*, SIGS Publications, July/August 1994.

Kil94b   Kilgard, M.J., "An OpenGL Toolkit," *The X Journal*, SIGS Publications, November/December 1994.

Kil96   Kilgard, M.J., *OpenGL Programming for the X Windows System*, Addison-Wesley, Reading, MA, 1996.

Knu87   Knuth, D.E., "Digital Halftones by Dot Diffusion," *ACM Transactions on Graphics*, 6(40), 245–273, 1987.

Kov97   Kovatch, P.J., *The Awesome Power of Direct3D/DirectX*, Manning Publications Company, Greenwich, CT, 1997.

Kue08   Kuehhne, R.P., and J.D. Sullivan, *OpenGL Programming on Mac OS X*, Addison-Wesley, Boston, MA, 2008.

Kui99   Kuipers, J.B., *Quaternions and Rotation Sequences*, Princeton University Press, Princeton, NJ, 1999.

Las87   Lasseter, J., "Principles of Traditional Animation Applied to 3D Computer Animation," *Computer Graphics*, 21(4), 33–44, 1987.

Lev88   Levoy, M., "Display of Surface from Volume Data," *IEEE Computer Graphics and Applications*, 8(3), 29–37, 1988.

Lev96   Levoy, M., and P. Hanrahan, "Light Field Rendering," *Computer Graphics*, 31–42, 1996.

Lia84   Liang, Y., and B. Barsky, "A New Concept and Method for Line Clipping," *ACM Transactions on Graphics*, 3(1), 1–22, 1984.

Lin68   Lindenmayer, A., "Mathematical Models for Cellular Interactions in Biology," *Journal of Theoretical Biology*, 18, 280–315, 1968.

Lin01   Linholm, E., M.J. Kilgard, and H. Morelton, "A User-Programmable Vertex Engine," *SIGGRAPH 2001*, 149–158, 2001.

Lor87   Lorensen, W.E., and H.E. Cline, "Marching Cubes: A High Resolution 3D Surface Construction Algorithm," *Computer Graphics*, 21(4), 163–169, 1987.

Ma94   Ma, K.L., J. Painter, C. Hansen, and M. Krogh, "Parallel Volume Rendering Using Binary-Swap Compositing," *IEEE Computer Graphics and Applications*, 14(4), 59–68, 1994.

Mag85   Magnenat-Thalmann, N., and D. Thalmann, *Computer Animation: Theory and Practice*, Springer-Verlag, Tokyo, 1985.

Man82   Mandelbrot, B., *The Fractal Geometry of Nature,* Freeman Press, New York, 1982.

Mat95   The MathWorks, *Student Edition of MatLab Version 4 Users Guide,* Prentice-Hall, Englewood Cliffs, NJ, 1995.

Mat13   Matsuda, K., and R. Leas, *WebGL Programming Guide: Interactive 3D Programming with WebGL (OpenGL),* Addison-Wesley, Boston, MA, 2013.

Mau06   Maurina, E., *The Game Programmer's Guide to Torque,* A K Peters, Wellesley, MA, 2006.

Max51   Maxwell, E.A., *General Homogeneous Coordinates in Space of Three Dimensions,* Cambridge University Press, Cambridge, England, 1951.

McF11   McFarland, D.S., *JavaScript and jQuery,* Second Edition, O'Reilly, Sebastopol, CA, 2011.

Mia99   Miamo, J., *Compressed Image File Formats,* ACM Press, New York, 1999.

Mol92   Molnar, S., J. Eyles, and J. Poulton, "PixelFlow: High-Speed Rendering Using Image Composition," *Computer Graphics,* 26(2), 231–240, 1992.

Mol94   Molnar, S., M. Cox, D. Ellsworth, and H. Fuchs, "A Sorting Classification of Parallel Rendering," *IEEE Computer Graphics and Applications,* 26(2), 231–240, 1994.

Mol02   Möller, T., and E. Haines, *Real-Time Rendering,* Second Edition, A K Peters, Wellesley, MA, 2002.

Mon97   Montrym, J., D. Baum, D. Dignam, and C. Migdal, "InfiniteReality: A Real-Time Graphics System," *SIGGRAPH 97,* 293–392, 1997.

Mun09   Munshi, A., Ginsberg, D., and D. Shreiner, *OpenGL ES 2.0 Programming Guide,* Addison-Wesley, Upper Saddle River, NJ, 2009.

Mun12   Munshi, A., B.R. Gaster, T.G. Matson, J. Fung, and D. Ginsberg, *OpenCL Programming Guide,* Addison-Wesley, Upper Saddle River, NJ, 2012.

Mur94   Murray, J.D., and W. Van Ryper, *Encyclopedia of Graphics File Formats,* O'Reilly, Sebastopol, CA, 1994.

New73   Newman, W.M., and R.F. Sproull, *Principles of Interactive Computer Graphics,* McGraw-Hill, New York, 1973.

Ngu07   Nguyen, H. (Ed.), *GPU Gems 3,* Addison-Wesley Professional, Boston, MA, 2007.

Nie97   Nielson, G.M., H. Hagen, and H. Muller, *Scientific Visualization: Overviews, Methodologies, and Techniques,* IEEE Computer Society, Piscataway, NJ, 1997.

Ope05   OpenGL Architecture Review Board, *OpenGL Reference Manual,* Fourth Edition, Addison-Wesley, Reading, MA, 2005.

OSF89   Open Software Foundation, *OSF/Motif Style Guide,* Prentice-Hall, Englewood Cliffs, NJ, 1989.

Ost94   Osterhaut, J., *Tcl and the Tk Toolkit,* Addison-Wesley, Reading, MA, 1994.

Pap81   Papert, S., *LOGO: A Language for Learning*, Creative Computer Press, Middletown, NJ, 1981.

Par12   Parisi, T., *WebGL: Up and Running*, O'Reilly, Sebastopol, CA, 2012.

Pav95   Pavlidis, T., *Interactive Computer Graphics in X*, PWS Publishing, Boston, MA, 1995.

Pei88   Peitgen, H.O., and S. Saupe (Eds.), *The Science of Fractal Images*, Springer-Verlag, New York, 1988.

Per85   Perlin, K., "An Image Synthesizer," *Computer Graphics*, 19(3), 287–297, 1985.

Per89   Perlin, K., and E. Hoffert, "Hypertexture," *Computer Graphics*, 23(3), 253–262, 1989.

Per02   Perlin, K., "Improved Noise," *Computer Graphics*, 35(3), 2002.

Pha05   Pharr, M., and R. Fernando (Eds.), *GPU Gems 2: Programming Techniques for High-Performance Graphics and General-Purpose Computation*, Addison-Wesley Professional, Boston, MA, 2005.

PHI89   PHIGS+ Committee, "PHIGS+ Functional Description, Revision 3.0," *Computer Graphics*, 22(3), 125–218, July 1989.

Pho75   Phong, B.T., "Illumination for Computer Generated Scenes," *Communications of the ACM*, 18(6), 311–317, 1975.

Por84   Porter, T., and T. Duff, "Compositing Digital Images," *Computer Graphics*, 18(3), 253–259, 1984.

Pra78   Pratt, W.K., *Digital Image Processing*, Wiley, New York, 1978.

Pru90   Prusinkiewicz, P., and A. Lindenmayer, *The Algorithmic Beauty of Plants*, Springer-Verlag, Berlin, 1990.

Rai11   Railsback, S.F., and V. Grimm, *Agent-Based and Individual-Based Modeling: A Practical Introduction*, Princeton University Press, Princeton, NJ, 2011.

Ree83   Reeves, W.T., "Particle Systems—A Technique for Modeling a Class of Fuzzy Objects," *Computer Graphics*, 17(3), 359–376, 1983.

Rei05   Reinhard, E., G. Ward, S. Pattanaik, and P. Debevec, *High Dynamic Range Imaging: Acquisition, Display, and Image-Based Lighting*, Morgan Kaufmann, San Francisco, 2005.

Rey87   Reynolds, C.W., "Flocks, Herds, and Schools: A Distributed Behavioral Model," *Computer Graphics*, 21(4), 25–34, 1987.

Rie81   Riesenfeld, R.F., "Homogeneous Coordinates and Projective Planes in Computer Graphics," *IEEE Computer Graphics and Applications*, 1(1), 50–56, 1981.

Rob63   Roberts, L.G., "Homogenous Matrix Representation and Manipulation of N-Dimensional Constructs," MS-1505, MIT Lincoln Laboratory, Lexington, MA, 1963.

Rog98   Rogers, D.F., *Procedural Elements for Computer Graphics*, Second Edition, McGraw-Hill, New York, 1998.

Rog90   Rogers, D.F., and J.A. Adams, *Mathematical Elements for Computer Graphics*, McGraw-Hill, New York, 1990.

Rog00   Rogers, D.F., *An Introduction to NURBS: With Historical Perspective*, Morgan Kaufmann, San Francisco, CA, 2000.

Ros09   Rost, R.J., B. Licea-Kane, D. Ginsberg, and J.M. Kessenich, *OpenGL Shading Language*, Third Edition, Addison-Wesley, Reading, MA, 2009.

San10   Sanders, J., and E. Kandrot, *CUDA by Example: An Introduction to General-Purpose GPU Programming*, Addison-Wesley, Saddle River, NJ, 2010.

Sch88   Schiefler, R.W., J. Gettys, and R. Newman, *X Window System*, Digital Press, Woburn, MA, 1988.

Sch06   Schroeder, W., K. Martin, and B. Lorensen, *The Visualization Toolkit: An Object-Oriented Approach to 3D Graphics*, Fourth Edition, Kitware, Clifton Park, NY, 2006.

Seg92   Segal, M., and K. Akeley, *The OpenGL Graphics System: A Specification*, Version 1.0, Silicon Graphics, Mountain View, CA, 1992.

Sei96   Seitz, S.M., and C.R. Dyer, "View Morphing," *SIGGRAPH 96*, 21–30, 1996.

Shi03   Shirley, P., R.K. Morley, and K. Morley, *Realistic Ray Tracing*, Second Edition, A K Peters, Wellesley, MA, 2003.

Shi09   Shirley, P., M. Ashikhmin, and S. Martin, *Fundamentals of Computer Graphics*, Third Edition, A K Peters, Wellesley, MA, 2009.

Sho85   Shoemake, K., "Animating Rotation with Quaternion Curves," *Computer Graphics*, 19(3), 245–254, 1985.

Shr13   Shreiner, D., *OpenGL Programming Guide: The Official Guide to Learning OpenGL, Version 4.3*, Eighth Edition, Addison-Wesley, Reading, MA, 2013.

Sie81   Siegel, R., and J. Howell, *Thermal Radiation Heat Transfer*, Hemisphere, Washington, DC, 1981.

Sil89   Sillion, F.X., and C. Puech, "A General Two-Pass Method Integrating Specular and Diffuse Reflection," *Computer Graphics*, 22(3), 335–344, 1989.

Smi84   Smith, A.R., "Plants, Fractals and Formal Languages," *Computer Graphics*, 18(3),·1–10, 1984.

Sta03   Stam, J., and C. Loop, "Quad/Triangle Subdivision," *Computer Graphics Forum*, 22, 1–7, 2003.

Str93   Strang, G., *Introduction to Linear Alegbra*, Wellesley-Cambridge Press, Wellesley, MA, 1993.

Suf07   Suffern, K., *Ray Tracing from the Ground Up*, A K Peters, Wellesley, MA, 2007.

Sut63   Sutherland, I.E., *Sketchpad, A Man–Machine Graphical Communication System*, SJCC, 329, Spartan Books, Baltimore, MD, 1963.

Sut74a   Sutherland, I.E., and G.W. Hodgeman, "Reentrant Polygon Clipping," *Communications of the ACM*, 17, 32–42, 1974.

Sut74b   Sutherland, I.E., R.F. Sproull, and R.A. Schumacker, "A Characterization of Ten Hidden-Surface Algorithms," *Computer Surveys*, 6(1), 1–55, 1974.

Swo00   Swoizral, H., K. Rushforth, and M. Deering, *The Java 3D API Specification,* Second Edition, Addison-Wesley, Reading, MA, 2000.

Tor67   Torrance, K.E., and E.M. Sparrow, "Theory for Off–Specular Reflection from Roughened Surfaces," *Journal of the Optical Society of America,* 57(9), 1105–1114, 1967.

Tor96   Torborg, J., and J.T. Kajiya, "Talisman: Commodity Realtime 3D Graphics for the PC," *SIGGRAPH 96*, 353–363, 1996.

Tuf83   Tufte, E.R., *The Visual Display of Quantitative Information*, Graphics Press, Cheshire, CT, 1983.

Tuf90   Tufte, E.R., *Envisioning Information*, Graphics Press, Cheshire, CT, 1990.

Tuf97   Tufte, E.R., *Visual Explanations*, Graphics Press, Cheshire, CT, 1997.

Ups89   Upstill, S., *The RenderMan Companion: A Programmer's Guide to Realistic Computer Graphics,* Addison-Wesley, Reading, MA, 1989.

Van94   Van Gelder, A., and J. Wilhelms, "Topological Considerations in Isosurface Generation," *ACM Transactions on Graphics,* 13(4), 337–375, 1994.

War94   Ward, G., "The RADIANCE Lighting Simulation and Rendering System," *SIGGRAPH 94*, 459–472, July 1994.

War03   Warren, J., and H. Weimer, *Subdivision Methods for Geometric Design,* Morgan Kaufmann, San Francisco, 2003.

War04   Warren, J., and S. Schaefer, "A Factored Approach to Subdivision Surfaces," *IEEE Computer Graphics and Applications*, 24(3), 74–81, 2004.

Wat92   Watt, A., and M. Watt, *Advanced Animation and Rendering Techniques,* Addison-Wesley, Wokingham, England, 1992.

Wat98   Watt, A., and F. Policarpo, *The Computer Image*, Addison-Wesley, Wokingham, England, 1998.

Wat00   Watt, A., *3D Computer Graphics*, Third Edition, Addison-Wesley, Wokingham, England, 2000.

Wat02   Watkins, A., *The Maya 4 Handbook*, Charles River Media, Hingham, MA, 2002.

Wer94   Wernecke, J., *The Inventor Mentor*, Addison-Wesley, Reading, MA, 1994.

Wes90   Westover, L., "Footprint Evaluation for Volume Rendering," *Computer Graphics*, 24(4), 367–376, 1990.

Whi80   Whitted, T., "An Improved Illumination Model for Shaded Display," *Communications of the ACM*, 23(6), 343–348, 1980.

Wil78   Williams, L., "Casting Curved Shadows on Curved Surfaces," *SIGGRAPH 78*, 27–27, 1978.

Wit94a   Witkin, A.P., and P.S. Heckbert, "Using Particles to Sample and Control Implicit Surfaces," *Computer Graphics,* 28(3), 269–277, 1994.

Wit94b   Witkin, A. (Ed.), "An Introduction to Physically Based Modeling," Course Notes, *SIGGRAPH 94,* 1994.

Wol91   Wolfram, S., *Mathematica*, Addison-Wesley, Reading, MA, 1991.

Wri11   Wright, R.S., Jr., H. Haemel, G. Sellers, and B. Lipchak, *OpenGL Superbible*, Fifth Edition, Addison-Wesley, Boston, MA, 2011.

Wys82   Wyszecki, G., and W.S. Stiles, *Color Science*, Wiley, New York, 1982.

WEBGL INDEX

SUBJECT INDEX

Color Plate 1 Image of sun object created using NURBS surfaces and rendered with bump mapping.

(Printed with permission from Ed Angel, University of New Mexico.)

Color Plate 2 Wire-frame representation of sun object surfaces.

(Printed with permission from Ed Angel, University of New Mexico.)

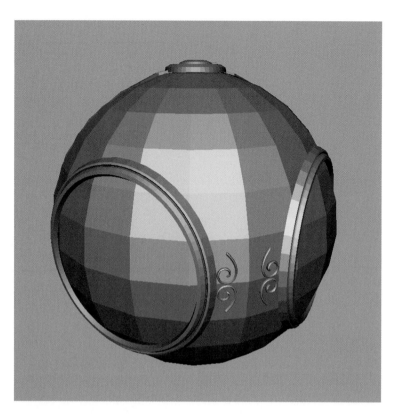

Color Plate 3 Flat-shaded polygonal rendering of sun object.

(Printed with permission from Ed Angel, University of New Mexico.)

Color Plate 4 Smooth-shaded polygonal rendering of sun object.

(Printed with permission from Ed Angel, University of New Mexico.)

Color Plate 5 Wire-frame of NURBS representation of sun object showing the high number of polygons used in rendering the NURBS surfaces.

(Printed with permission from Ed Angel, University of New Mexico.)

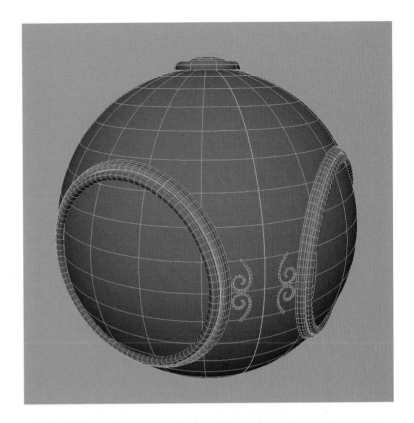

Color Plate 6 Rendering of sun object showing bump map.

(Printed with permission from Ed Angel, University of New Mexico.)

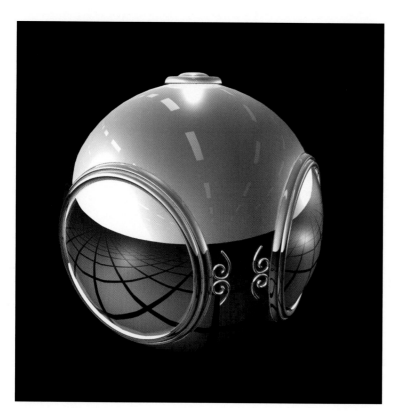

Color Plate 7 Rendering of sun object with an environment map.

(Printed with permission from Ed Angel, University of New Mexico.)

Color Plate 8 Rendering of a small part of the sun object with an environment map.

(Printed with permission from Ed Angel, University of New Mexico.)

(a) Without antialiasing

(b) With antialiasing

Color Plate 9 Axonometric view from outside of temple.

(Printed with permission from Richard Nordhaus, Architect, Albuquerque, NM.)

Color Plate 10 Perspective view of interior of temple.

(Printed with permission from Richard Nordhaus, Architect, Albuquerque, NM.)

Color Plate 11 Cartoon-shaded teapot.

(Printed with permission from Ed Angel,
University of New Mexico.)

Color Plate 12 Reflection map from a color
cube on teapot.

(Printed with permission from Ed Angel,
University of New Mexico.)

Color Plate 13 Interface for animation using Maya.

(Printed with permission from Hue Walker, ARTS Lab, University of New Mexico.)

Color Plate 14 Three-dimensional gasket after five recursion steps.

(Printed with permission from Ed Angel, University of New Mexico.)

Color Plate 15 Rendering using ray tracer.

(Printed with permission from Patrick McCormick.)

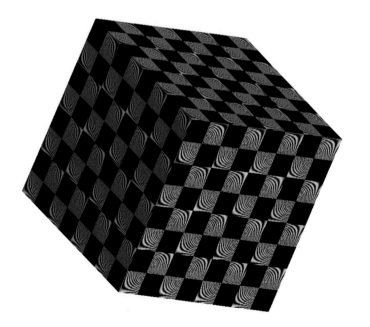

Color Plate 16 Texture mapped cube using two texture units.

(Printed with permission from Ed Angel, University of New Mexico.)

Color Plate 17 Array of Utah teapots with different material properties.

(Printed with permission from SGI.)

Color Plate 18 Phong-Blinn shaded teapots.

(Printed with permission from Ed Angel, University of New Mexico.)

(a) Using per-vertex lighting

(b) Using per-fragment lighting

(c) Area near highlight

(d) Area near highlight

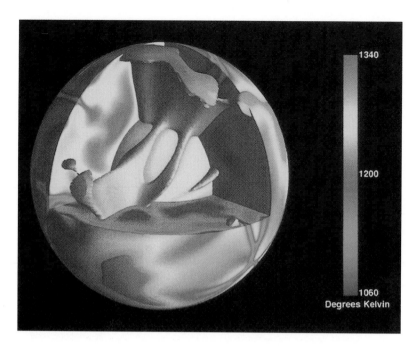

Color Plate 19 Fluid dynamics of the mantle of the Earth. Pseudocolor mapping of temperatures and isotemperature surface.

(Printed with permission from James Painter, Los Alamos National Laboratory.)

Color Plate 20 Volume rendering of CT data.

(Printed with permission from J. Kniss, G. Kindlmann, C. Hansen, Scientific Computing and Imaging Institute, University of Utah.)

Color Plate 21 RGB color cube.

(Printed with permission from University
of New Mexico.)

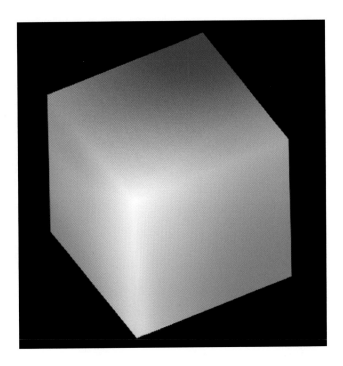

Color Plate 22 Avatar representing a patient
who is being diagnosed and treated by a
remotely located health professional (inset).

(Printed with permission from Tom Caudell,
Dept. of Electrical & Computer Engineering,
University of New Mexico.)

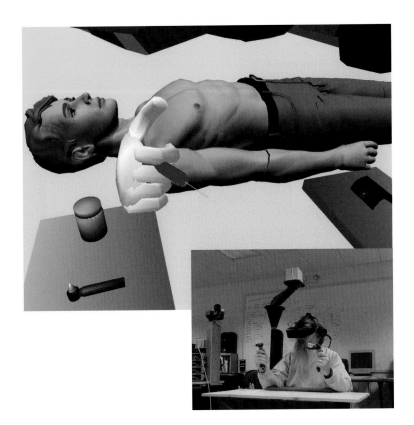

Color Plate 23

(Printed with permission from ARTS Lab, University of New Mexico.)

(a) Cube Environment.

(b) Five virtual cameras at center of cube.

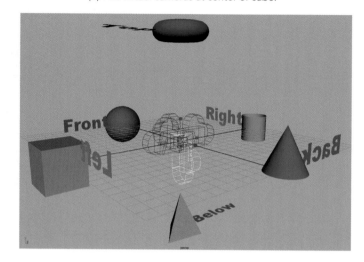

Color Plate 24

(Printed with permission from ARTS Lab, University of New Mexico.)

(a) Five textures maps displayed as an unfolded box.

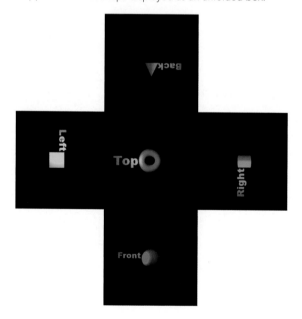

(b) Cube textures mapped to hemisphere.

Color Plate 25 Elevation data for Honolulu, Hawaii, displayed using a quadmesh to define control points for a Bezier surface.

(Printed with permission from Ed Angel, University of New Mexico.)

Color Plate 26 Wire frame of the quadmesh showing lower resolution in flat areas.

(Printed with permission from Ed Angel, University of New Mexico.)

Color Plate 27 Rendering of hierarchical robot figure.

(Printed with permission from Ed Angel, University of New Mexico.)

Color Plate 28 Sphere computed by recursive subdivision of tetrahedrons; triangle colors assigned randomly.

(Printed with permission from Ed Angel, University of New Mexico.)

Color Plate 29 One frame of 100 agents moving randomly.

Color Plate 30 Diffusion of 100 agents.

Color Plate 31 Diffusion of 100 agents showing movement towards attractors.

Color Plate 32 Particle system.

(Reprinted by permission from Lexus, a division of Toyota Motor Sales, U.S.A., Inc.)

(a) Mesh of particles

b) Model of Lexus with surface

(c) Wind blowing mesh off Lexus

d) Mesh blown away from Lexus